MW00855661

FORMATIONS OF
UNITED STATES
COLONIALISM

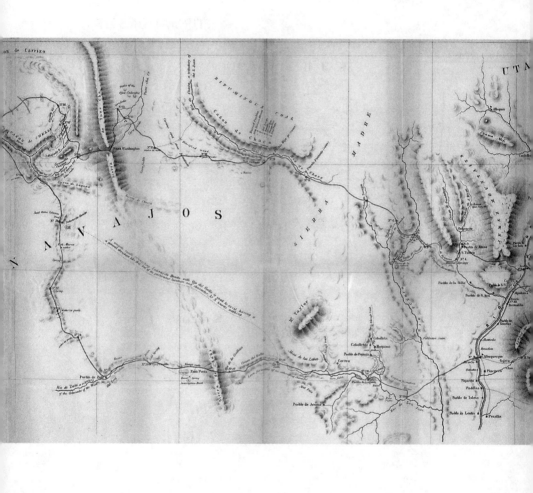

FORMATIONS
OF UNITED STATES
COLONIALISM

ALYOSHA GOLDSTEIN, editor

Duke University Press
Durham and London
2014

© 2014 Duke University Press
All rights reserved
Printed in the United States of America on acid-free paper ∞
Typeset in Scala and Meta type by BW&A Books, Inc.
Library of Congress Cataloging-in-Publication Data
Formations of United States colonialism / Alyosha Goldstein, editor.
pages cm
Includes bibliographical references and index.
ISBN 978-0-8223-5796-4 (hardcover : alk. paper)
ISBN 978-0-8223-5810-7 (pbk. : alk. paper)
ISBN 978-0-8223-7596-8 (e-book)
1. United States—Territories and possessions—History.
2. Colonization—History.
3. Colonies—History. I. Goldstein, Alyosha.
JV527.F67 2014
325'.373—dc23
2014026095

Cover art: Merritt Johnson, *Blowing Out the Border (Sonoran Desert)* (detail),
courtesy of the artist.
Title page art: *Map of the Route pursued in 1849 by the US Troops . . . , in an expedition against the Navajo Indians.* Drawn by Edward Kern. Photo Courtesy
of the Newberry Library, Chicago.

CONTENTS

Toward a Genealogy of the U.S. Colonial Present

The United States of America has never been a uniform or unequivocal geopolitical entity. This is not merely a consequence of prevailing forms of federalism, demographic heterogeneity, or regional particularity. This is not simply a matter of an unavoidable gap between empirical description and the ideal form of the nation-state. Rather, the United States encompasses a historically variable and uneven constellation of state and local governments, indigenous nations, unincorporated territories, free associated commonwealths, protectorates, federally administered public lands, military bases, export processing zones, *colonias*, and anomalies such as the District of Columbia that do not comprehensively delineate an inside and outside of the nation-state. The heterogeneity of this condition is not exceptional to the United States. But even with a burgeoning scholarship scrutinizing U.S. empire and calls for a postnationalist American studies, a critical analytic lens that takes into account the significance of colonialism for the various ways in which the geopolitical configuration of the United States has changed over time remains largely absent.

Rather than simply advocating a comparative approach that centers colonialism, this collection cumulatively argues that analyzing U.S. colonialism demands understanding U.S. empire and the imperial nation-state as itself a comparative project and mode of power. Always already shaped by fluctuating interimperial rivalries and counterclaims against the peoples it subsumes, U.S. colonialism has been neither monolithic nor static. The United States nevertheless remains reliant on the ever-expanding dispossession and disavowal of indigenous peoples, global circuits of expropriated labor, economies of racialization, and its expansive network of military bases—that is, on people and places remade as things in the service of the accumulation of wealth and the exercise of geopolitical power. By refusing to designate one particular form of U.S. colonial rule—or one decisive historical moment, such as 1898, 1848, 1831, or 1787—as categorically expressing and definitive of U.S. colonialism, however contingently produced, this volume contests the disciplinary periodization common within comparative studies that would ascribe an origin, culmination, and subsequent decline or end to U.S. colonialism. As Walter Benjamin argues, "Overcoming the concept of 'progress' and overcoming the concept of 'period of decline' are two sides of one and the same thing."[1] The essays collected here do not subscribe to a mode of comparison whose objective is to establish a norm of colonial power and practice by which different historical cases can be comparatively juxtaposed and evaluated. Instead this book argues that it is precisely the complex reciprocities, seemingly opaque disjunctures, and tense entanglements evident in the diversity of U.S. colonial pasts and presents that reveal the epistemological antagonisms and affinities that offer new insights for anticolonial struggle and new possibilities for critical inquiry.

Bridging the study of North American settler colonialism and U.S. overseas occupation provides a means with which to address both the incongruities and fault lines of the U.S. nation-state and the determined construction of national singularity, coherence, and continuity. Debates about globalization over the course of the last four decades have grappled with an increasing sense of the diminished sovereignty of nation-states, while historical studies of nationalism and nations have similarly highlighted the ways in which the political, economic, and cultural forms of society are porous and contingent. Nevertheless, as contemporary conflicts over immigration reveal with particular intensity, popular investments in the modular nation form and claims to a discrete and territorially delimited political community have definite material force. Likewise, escalating state and municipal fiscal crisis has been paralleled by the proliferation of the U.S. military-surveillance complex throughout the world. The nation-state need not actually be unitary or cohesive in order to decisively enact juridical power "domestically" and exercise coercion "at home and abroad." In this sense, the United States serves here as a volatile assemblage and shifting empirical configuration that cannot adequately contain or circumscribe scholarly inquiry, but that has nevertheless insinuated and asserted its authority in ways that resist being undone by mere exposure or repudiation.

The overlapping, sedimented, and variable conditions and practices of colonization are in this regard fundamental for understanding the complexity and specificity of the United States historically and in the present. To forgo a linear and nationally bounded reading of U.S. history from east to west is to allow the palimpsest of Spanish, British, French, and Dutch colonization, and the *longue durée* of indigenous peoples, to emerge intermittently from beneath the veneer of naturalized borders and periodizations. Progressive chronological narratives of national history rely on such seemingly discrete social and political categories as colonizer, native, and coerced or intentional migrant all blending over time into one people—unified as they are transformed by liberal pluralist equivalence—even as these distinctions in effect are neither transient nor absolute. Likewise, rather than instantiating a decisive narrative of domination and resistance, dynamics of power under colonial rule have always been complicated by discrepant alliances, the aspirations of elites, and social antagonisms that precede and exceed the colonial situation.[2] Yet, colonialism persists as a never fully repressed or entirely manifest structure, especially as settlers aspire to extinguish indigenous peoples and variously affirm and naturalize their own status as native to America. United States colonialism is a continuously failing—or at least a perpetually incomplete—project that labors to find a workable means of resolution to sustain its logic of possession and inevitability by disavowing the ongoing contestation with which it is confronted and violent displacement that it demands. As Audra Simpson argues, "It is in these complicated relationships to the past, to territory, and to governance that Indigeneity is quite simply a key to critical analysis, not as a model of an alternative theoretical project or method . . . but simply as a case that, when considered robustly, fundamentally interrupts what is received, what is ordered, what is supposed to be settled."[3] Jodi Byrd points out, however, that scholarship on U.S. imperialism often readily acknowledges and perhaps even underscores "the annihilation of indigenous nations, cultures, and languages" only to unequivocally "relegate American Indians to the site of already-doneness that begins to linger as unwelcome guest to the future."[4] It is precisely this temporal closure, necropolitical teleology, and complicit blindness to the sustained political, social, cultural, and legal contention by indigenous peoples in the United States that so often continues to diminish and hinder the capacity for scholars, activists, and legislators to productively examine the consequences and interconnections of U.S. colonialism as they have varied across time and place, but never in fact been fully concluded or resolved.

The chapters in this book thus consider the multifaceted claims, exclusions, and disavowals of the United States as it has been constituted with respect to colonialism. The distinct contribution of the collection is to place U.S. overseas empire and settler colonialism into the same analytic frame—not only as a means of comparison, but as sometimes mutually constitutive and sometimes conspicuously disjointed formations. Collectively the essays argue that addressing the multiple histories and present-day formations of colonialism in North America, the Caribbean, and the Pacific are essential for coming to terms with how and why the United States is what it is today. In this sense, this volume revisits the historian Albert Bushnell Hart's early twentieth-century contention that the United States has comprised "nearly every variety of colonies known to history," and, more than this, that this multiplicity must be reckoned with as a significant feature of the present.[5] Contributors build on the insights of recent critical indigenous and ethnic studies, postcolonial theory, critical geography, ethnography, social history, and social, cultural and legal analysis to insist on the enduring significance of colonialism as a vital analytic framework for understanding the imbricated and enmeshed histories and current political conjuncture of the United States. Rather than approaching U.S. colonialism as either a fleeting aberration or a passing stage in the nation's historical development, this collection considers how the social, economic, and political conditions of possibility in and in relation to the United States have been overdetermined by past and persistent formations of colonialism. At the same time, however, the volume's focus on colonialism is not a claim for the absolute primacy or determination-in-the-final-instance of colonialism or an effort to diminish the significance of other axes of antagonism and dispossession. It is intended instead to critically complement and engage projects of non-normative comparative critique attuned to these inconstant and multiple conditions.[6]

This book underlines the complicities, adaptations, and antagonisms that interconnect global, national, regional, and local relations of power. Indeed, the exigencies of our present moment provide an especially auspicious occasion through which to reconsider colonial formations within and with regard to the United States. From this vantage point we can generatively think through a series of questions. How might the diversity of colonial pasts, settler claims, territorial annexations, and overseas occupations be understood in relation to one another? How have specific normative forms of jurisprudence, racialization, violence, militarism, politics, property, and propriety served to at once facilitate and delimit the conditions of colonial dispossession? How and why do these formations matter now? Addressing these questions, this volume examines the specific iterations and consequences of U.S. colonialism as a dynamic historical assemblage with significance for understanding current conditions of social and political possibility.

Michel Foucault's theorization of *genealogy* is particularly useful for addressing U.S. colonialism because of the ways in which it "rejects the metahistorical deployment of ideal significations and indefinite teleologies," turning instead to the analytic of *descent* as "an unstable assemblage of faults, fissures, and heterogeneous layers that threaten the fragile inheritor from within or from underneath."[7] The claims and vectors of descent— entwined as they are with the composition and transaction of property and the calculus of race, resemblance, and self—are crucial for understanding colonialism with regard to the United States. Genealogical accounts can gesture toward the outer limits of knowing and familiarity where there is no certain beginning or end. There is also no overarching causality, only lineal associations, amalgamated intimacies, the speculative horizons of kinship, and insinuated exclusions, inclusions, and indifferences. As a method, genealogy both elucidates the proprietary claims to descent and the lineages of settler nation building and potentially destabilizes claims to an immanent and unilinear history. In the colonial context, as Mark Rifkin argues, genealogy as a corollary to specific indigenous kinship principles that are modes of governance upsets the liberal division between public and private and unsettles the heteronormative colonial imposition of conjugal domesticity over and against kinship as an indigenous political relation.[8] Yet as a biological and biopolitical truth claim, genealogy can serve as precisely the evidentiary logic for parsing inclusion and exclusion that it can call into question as a method.

Within colonial systems of acknowledgement and accountability, such regimes of historical truth claims are problematic not only for the ways in which they demand their own universal priority, but also for the impossible framework of recognition and origin they require of indigenous peoples. As Joanne Barker argues, Native peoples are placed in the untenable position of having to prove an origin, sustained authentic difference, and ontological coherence that precedes and survives colonization while at the same time conforming to these superimposed systems of recognition as a prerequisite to securing their legal status and rights as defined within the system of colonial rule. Barker insists that it is not enough to unsettle the colonial systems of historical knowledge that predominate; it is also necessary to understand the promise and appeal of these systems even for those who are subordinated and dispossessed by their logics. She points out that from this perspective the desire for the truth claims of origin likewise follow from the profound brutalizations, dislocations, and dismemberments perpetrated by colonization and genocide.[9] Genealogy is methodologically useful in this regard insofar as it indexes the predicaments of history's normative binds. But, as Jean O'Brien argues, genealogy as descent can also be the means by which settlers appropriate indigeneity as their "birthright" and render "native" as "non-Indian."[10]

For the contributors to this collection the historical force and convolutions of colonial normalization thus remain paramount. These essays work against the ways in which colonialism is too often used as a generally applicable metaphor or analogy for all forms of domination.[11] This facile ascription does violence to the actual conditions it allegorizes and conflates. As already briefly discussed, conventional forms of comparison entail a similar problematic analytic gloss. According to Johannes Fabian, "There would be no *raison d'être* for the comparative method if it was not classification of entities or traits which first have to be separate and distinct before their similarities can be used to establish taxonomies and developmental sequences."[12] Rey Chow notes how "this hierarchal formulation of comparison, which may be named 'Europe and Its Others,' remains a common norm of comparative literary studies in North America today." Comparison in this sense reaffirms the self-referentiality of Euro-American epistemology and authorizes an "asymmetrical distribution of cultural capital and intellectual labor."[13] There is also the danger, as has been noted in early criticism of Edward Said's *Orientalism*—criticism to which Said subsequently responded[14]—and certain variants of "whiteness studies," of making the study of colonialism ultimately about the colonizers or the colonial imaginary. Moreover, the institutional division of knowledge into discrete academic disciplines is itself a legacy and effect of the ways in which the U.S. state and polity both justified empire and sought to profit from and order a haphazard system of racial governance while occluding the ongoing the violent material dispossessions that underwrite its conditions of possibility. Nevertheless, Chow points out, comparison can be productively rethought in ways attuned to incommensurability and disparity, that weigh the reciprocities, co-constitutions, and uneven dynamics of power; and it is precisely a project of this kind to which this volume aims to contribute.

In order to provide a provisional point of departure for considering the salience of colonialism in the U.S. context, in what follows I briefly discuss the terms *colonialism, imperialism,* and *empire.* I explore what seem to me to be among the most salient elements and significant conjunctures for addressing the "colonial present"—by which I mean the ways in which the current moment is shaped by the fraught historical accumulation and shifting disposition of colonial processes, relations, and practices.[15] The following section considers the colonial geographies of authority and historical trajectories of colonization as they have aspired to various forms of confiscation, occupation, removal, and extraction. Addressing the constitution of sovereign power as it asserts control over specific places and populations, I sketch the configuration of U.S. nation building as a project that has always been in some sense colonial. I then consider some of the key juridical, political, and conceptual mechanisms that underwrote this project and how and why these changed over time. Here I am especially interested in the idea of national founding, and the accounts of temporality with respect to colonialism that serve to foreclose the past or justify inequality and dispossession as a consequence of the dialectical division of what Elizabeth Povinelli calls the "governance of the prior."[16] In conclusion, I outline the organizing editorial logic of the volume and the chapters that follow as an attempt to stage the resonant dynamism of U.S. imperial constellation and formation.

COLONIALISM, IMPERIALISM, EMPIRE

To insist on the significance of colonialism raises the question of an etymology and working definition of the term. However, as Raymond Williams writes of imperialism, *colonialism*, "like any word which refers to fundamental social and political conflict, cannot be reduced, semantically, to single proper meaning. Its important historical and contemporary variations of meaning point to real processes which have to be studied in their own terms."[17] Rather than rehearse the debates on terminology in the voluminous literatures on colonialism, imperialism, and empire, my intention in this section is to examine, in at least a preliminary manner, the ways in which ideas about what colonialism is and what it is not have been central to social and political conflict within and in relation to the United States, as well as how these dynamics have changed over time.[18] Vicente Rafael argues in his contribution to this volume that linguistic diversity has historically accompanied the insistence that the United States "has always been, was meant to be, and must forever remain a monolingual nation." Rafael points out that American endeavors to "improve and perfect" English, to "Americanize" and thus translate English into a national language, were also efforts to distinguish the United States from the ostensible decadence and despotism of British colonial rule. Language thus registers what Nicholas Thomas underscores as "differences between competing models of colonization."[19]

What specific historical processes, assertions, and distinctions are evident in the etymology of *colonialism*? *Colony, colonial,* and *colonization* all precede *colonialism,* which in the sense of a "system of colonial rule" does not appear until the 1880s, in association with the European frenzy to establish interimperial peace while imposing territorial divisions for the systematic plunder of Africa and elsewhere. *Colony* has its roots in the Latin word *colōnia,* which during the Roman empire referenced violence and displacement by indicating the settlement of Roman citizens in recently conquered territory. Yet *colōnia* is also associated with *colōnus,* which can mean colonist, but also simply inhabitant, peasant, or farmer. David Kazanjian observes that the meaning of the term *colonial,* as referring to "a person from a colony," does not appear until the late eighteenth century, and that in the context of the American Revolution and since, the American "colonist" became categorically detached from the expropriative process of conquest and colonization and situated in opposition to British rule.[20] Ann Laura Stoler and Carole McGranahan draw attention to what they call the "social etymology of *colonie*"—that is, "the enduring social relationships of power that remain buried and suspended in political terms"—as its inflections shifted across the nineteenth century variously designating "imperial expansion and modes of confinement, resettlement of delinquents, pauper programs, and the recruitment of empire's pioneers."[21] Social etymology in this sense might also highlight the ways in which the British valorized a Lockean pursuit of "colonization by plantation" in contrast to Spanish New World colonization, which they disparaged as crudely extracting wealth rather than improving the land through cultivation.[22]

What would later be described as modern European colonialism emerged during the sixteenth century as developments in oceanic navigation and transportation provided the basis for increasingly extensive networks of conquest, control, and commerce across the world. Modern colonialism entails techniques and institutions that maintain foreign control over a people or peoples and territory through varying degrees of imperial occupation and settlement, depriving those subjugated of autonomy and self-determination, and justifying this imposition in terms of the (religious, moral, cultural, or racial) superiority of the foreign power. The colonial administration of populations operates in tandem with the juridical, political, military-strategic, economic, and cultural production and control of property, territory, and resources.[23] Slavery, peonage, and labor migration under shifting regimes of racial capitalism have each been essential to the making of the U.S. imperial nation-state.[24] Likewise, colonial expansion inaugurates new histories of violence that saturate all aspects of life and cycles of brutality that exceed conquest.[25] As Achille Mbembe observes, "the colony is a place where an experience of violence and upheaval is lived, where violence is built into structures and institutions . . . [and] insinuates itself into the economy, domestic life, language, consciousness."[26] In this sense, U.S. militarism and militarization both establish the conditions of the nation-state and claim justification for their further imperial expansion as the defense and redeployment of those conditions and calculated disposal of national sacrifice zones.[27]

To underscore the ways in which colonialism is constitutive for the United States is to attend to how and why colonialism marks its founding, historical development, and uneven heterogeneity. An exclusive focus on imperialism and empire with regard to the United States risks losing sight of how territorial seizure, the legal justifications for occupation, the unofficially sanctioned or tolerated illegalities that further underwrote expansion and occupation, and differential modes of governance—including liberal democracy and citizenship—remain the very conditions of possibility for its more indirect forms of rule and the sprawling networks of military encampments and global economies. Settler colonialism is thus an especially significant historical condition for the United States. Patrick Wolfe defines settler colonialism as a "logic of elimination" wherein settlers strive to replace indigenous peoples by force and assimilation and assume priority as native to the land rather than aim mainly to extract value to be accrued by a distant colonial metropole.[28] Yet, settler colonialism in what is now the United States changes over time, shifting in disposition variously from accommodation to annihilation to inclusion of indigenous peoples, while never being reducible to the encounter between "settler" and "native" positionalities. Although the descriptor "settler colonialism" useful for highlighting how the presumption of irrevocability and permanence renders autochthonous certain people settling from elsewhere under the auspices of colonial rule, it can also serve to obscure the forms of heterogeneity and incommensurability that trouble simple binary oppositions.[29] U.S. settler colonialism is likewise necessarily part of a broader interrelated historically mutable collection of practices, institutions, and conditions. As Jodi Byrd points out, the "settler colony's national construction of itself as an ever more perfect multicultural, multiracial democracy" depends on relegating colonialism and slavery to the past while adamantly denying their continued significance—as the ongoing exploitation of land and resources and the racialized justification for dehumanization and expendability—as the material foundation for U.S. global empire.[30] Thus to emphasize colonialism is to acknowledge that continental conquest and the diverse forms of unincorporation, inclusion, and partial sovereignty perpetuated by the United States remain incomplete, unsettling, unresolved, and ongoing.

Imperialism in the broadest sense is the deliberate extension of a nation's power and influence over other peoples or places by military, political, or economic means. Imperialism is the practice of establishing, maintaining, and expanding an empire. As such, imperialism is the overarching category of which colonialism is but one particular strategy linked to specific forms of territorial occupation. The word *imperialism*, like *colonialism*, does not appear until the mid- to late nineteenth century. It is derived from the much older term *imperial*, which comes from the Latin *imperium*, meaning to command, and *imperō* ("command, order"), with the root *parō* ("prepare, arrange; intend"). In his influential 1902 treatise *Imperialism: A Study*, John Hobson argued that a specifically modern form of imperialism was the result of the emergence of monopoly capitalism and the oligopolistic organization of power on which it relied.[31] While Hobson considered this concentration of power antithetical to free market doctrine and a deviation deserving reform, V. I. Lenin drew on Hobson, as well as Rudolf Hilferding's analysis of finance capital, to argue that imperialism was the culmination of the insatiable global trajectory of capitalist development and crisis.[32] In their widely cited 1953 essay "The Imperialism of Free Trade," John Gallagher and Ronald Robinson contend that since the nineteenth century the foreign policy of free trade has increasingly served as a lower-cost and more diplomatically palatable way to achieve imperial control. First Great Britain, and then other European countries and the United States, began to move away from formal modes of imperialism, such as the administration of colonial empires and commercial monopoly, emphasizing instead that former colonies and other non-Euro-American countries open their markets, resources, and labor to the presumably equitable forces of comparative advantage and the ostensibly self-regulating equalizer of global trade.[33] William Roger Louis and Ronald Robinson subsequently made a similar argument about the role of decolonization as a less expensive means of hegemony and profit by the former colonial powers following the Second World War.[34] Scholars such as David Harvey and Giovanni Arrighi describe the "new imperialism" of the twenty-first century as characterized by ever escalating U.S. unilateralism and militarism, as well as an intensified economic pursuit of "accumulation by dispossession."[35] But rather than emphasize only the informal or liberal character of U.S. empire, as many commentators do, it is essential to understand this multivalent informality as fully articulated with both the historically accumulated traces and persistent reconfiguration of colonialism in the more delimited and formal sense—whether in agencies such as the Bureau of Indian Affairs or the Bureau of Land Management, or the interstitial political status of "free associated state."

The "absence of empire in the study of American culture" that Amy Kaplan identified more than twenty years ago is clearly no longer the case.[36] Indeed, as many observers have pointed out, debates and discussions on U.S. empire have become ubiquitous throughout scholarly and popular forums in the years since the United States declared its so-called global War on Terror in 2001. Yet, for all the recent talk and analysis of empire—perhaps because such considerations were in part prompted by exigencies of contemporary war and militarism targeting the Middle East and Islam—the particular historical conditions of colonialism, and their complex persistence and ongoing reconfiguration in North America, the Caribbean, and the Pacific, have rarely been placed at the center of current mainstream debates.[37] Even such an important recent effort to underscore the centrality of colonial empire for the United States as Alfred McCoy and Francisco Scarano's collection *Colonial Crucible: Empire in the Making of the Modern American State* does not substantially include continental colonization and conquest within its frame of inquiry.[38] Interestingly, a century earlier, at the very moment when many observers perceived the United States to be a colonial power—reluctant or not—in regard to Puerto Rico, the Philippines, Guam, and Hawai'i, debate between proimperialist and anti-imperialist advocates explicitly foregrounded the historical specificities of U.S. continental colonialism as a condition through which to address overseas expansion in the wake of the 1898 Treaty of Paris.

In a 1899 *Atlantic Monthly* article in support of U.S. colonial rule, the legal scholar and future president of Harvard University Abbott Lawrence Lowell contended that such territorial acquisitions were both indispensable for future national prosperity and in keeping with U.S. continental expansion historically. He argued, "Until admitted as states . . . [territories have] not differed in any essential particular from that of the North American colonies of England before the outbreak of the Revolution," and thus "there has never been a time, since the adoption of the first ordinance for the government of the Northwest Territory in 1784, when the United States has not had colonies."[39] Likewise, in 1903, Albert Bushnell Hart insisted that American Indian reservations were among "three very distinct types of legally-defined territorial governments [administered by Congress]. . . . In any other country such governments would be called 'colonial.'"[40] Indeed, in another essay Hart similarly asserts: "Notwithstanding that the Revolution was a protest against a colonial regime, the model for the original American Territorial system, which has so far been little altered, was the previous colonial administration of Great Britain." He concludes: "What light does this experience of the last century and a quarter throw upon the future of American colonization? It shows, in the first place, that the idea of national colonies is as old as the republic, and that during the last fifty years the nation has grown accustomed to outlying dependencies."[41] As the historian Walter L. Williams has since demonstrated in his 1980 *Journal of American History* essay, this perspective on the continuities between U.S. continental conquest and overseas colonialism was common among both proimperialist scholars and legislators during the late nineteenth and early twentieth centuries.[42] In the context and aftermath of the Vietnam War, the U.S. Third World Left emphasized the rapacious global interdependencies of U.S. expansion, and this emphasis was taken up by scholars such as Richard Slotkin, Michael Rogin, Richard Drinnon, and Patricia Limerick.[43]

Whereas both journalistic and scholarly reference to U.S. empire has today become commonplace, similar discussion of U.S. colonialism as a contemporary formation remains relatively infrequent outside of Native American studies and leftist or anarchist critique. To a certain extent this has to do with specific developments in U.S. foreign policy discourse between the First World War and the mid-twentieth century. From President Woodrow Wilson's championing national self-determination among his "Fourteen Points" in 1918 to U.S. Cold War rhetoric addressed to the nonaligned world, longstanding claims that the American Revolution was the first anticolonial uprising in modern history were promoted with increasing fervor. In 1954, Secretary of State John Foster Dulles, for instance, declared, "We ourselves are the first colony in modern times to have won independence. We have a natural sympathy with those everywhere who would follow our example." Furthermore, Dulles contended that, contrary to Soviet charges, "when the fortunes of war gave the United States responsibilities in relation to non-self-governing peoples, such as Cuba and the Philippines, we quickly went about the business of developing full self-government in total freedom. Puerto Rico is already self-governing, within our political system, and President Eisenhower has said he would seek its complete independence if it would prefer to go its separate way."[44] It is significant that Dulles saw no need to speak to the circumstances of American Indians—although certain policy makers did seek to characterize the federal government's contemporaneous efforts to terminate its treaty responsibilities to Indian tribes in Cold War terms by associating collective tribal landownership with communism.[45] For him, as for many diplomatic historians and international relations scholars today, colonialism was strictly an overseas affair carried out by Europeans.

Indeed, Dulles's statement paralleled U.S. lobbying to insert the "blue water" doctrine (also known as the "salt water" thesis) as a categorical limit on United Nations policy for decolonization. On December 16, 1952, the UN General Assembly adopted Resolution 637 (VII), which stated that member states of the United Nations "should respect the maintenance of the right to self-determination" and "shall uphold the principle of self-determination for all peoples and nations."[46] The United States and several other UN member states sought to amend the resolution so that to be eligible to request recognition as a "non-self-governing territory" under Chapter XI of the UN Charter—a prerequisite for initiating the decolonization process—a people must be separated from the colonizing country by "blue water" or, at least, have geographically distinct boundaries from the colonizing country. This amendment was included as part of the UN General Assembly Resolution 1541 (XV) on December 15, 1960, the day after the GA adopted the Declaration on the Granting of Independence to Colonial Countries and Peoples. To disqualify the claims of territorially contiguous peoples for independence, justifying their enclosure and placing them beyond the definitional parameters of colonialism, was an enormous victory for settler colonial states that underscores the elasticity and potential instrumentality of territorial taxonomy.[47] In 2007, the UN Declaration on the Rights of Indigenous Peoples undermined the assertion of settler colonial prerogative in this regard, especially as efforts to implement the declaration in U.S. law and policy have accelerated since the United States begrudgingly became one of the last UN member states to endorse the international instrument in 2010.[48]

TERRITORY, JURISDICTION, TEMPORALITY

In her study of local histories of New England, Jean O'Brien argues that these nineteenth-century texts contrive two principal metaphors—"firsting" and "lasting"—as a way to craft "an origin myth that assigns primacy to non-Indians who 'settled' the region in a benign process involving righteous relations with Indians and just property transactions that led to an inevitable and . . . lamentable Indian extinction."[49] The trope of "firsting" (in which, as mentioned above, settlers displace indigenous peoples in order to become "native") sought to convey that "Indian peoples and their cultures represented an 'inauthentic' and prefatory history."[50] Although Native peoples persist—continue to be "lasting"—despite the retroactive confirmation of their death and disappearance in non-Indian narrative—with ubiquitous stories of the "last" and final Indian—these local histories of "first" settlers and their families clear the ground for another inaugural effacement not discussed by O'Brien. This first, touted as new beginning and epochal shift, was the constituent power of settler sovereignty to declare independence and found a new nation.[51] Thus, Thomas Paine concludes "Common Sense" (1776) with the pronouncement that by embracing "the legal voice of the people in Congress . . . we have every opportunity and every encouragement before us, to form the noblest, purest constitution on the face of the earth. We have it in our power to begin the world over again."[52] The contradictions of a people who found and inaugurate themselves has been extensively analyzed, but it is precisely this originary founding that allegedly makes history, place, and politics anew, and renders the past extraneous and foreign.[53] Yet for all the mystical splendor of founding, the new nation continued to confront and contend with the "lasting" of indigenous peoples, in both senses suggested by O'Brien, especially as conflicts over territorial claims, jurisdiction, alliance, and the questions of expansion and incorporation became increasingly manifest.

The interval between the late eighteenth-century juridical design for territorial integration into the Union and the early twentieth-century invention of the category "unincorporated territory" separates two logics of U.S. colonialism.[54] Each of these logics, along with the idea that the American Revolution definitively instituted a postcolonial United States, has also been central to claims that the United States is fundamentally *not* a colonial power. The first rationale contends that the territorial system provided for eventual statehood and citizenship, and therefore continental colonization— made natural, virtuous, and ineluctable in the rhetoric of "expansion"— merely extended the promise of freedom and democracy. A territory, in the legal sense, is a geographical area recognized as being under the jurisdiction but not fully part of a country and subject to distinct laws and governance. William Connolly evocatively points out, "'Territory,' the *Oxford English Dictionary* says, is presumed by most moderns to derive from *terra*. *Terra* means land, earth, nourishment, sustenance; it conveys the sense of a sustaining medium, solid, fading off into indefiniteness. But the form of the word, the OED says, suggests that it derives from *terrere*, meaning to frighten, to terrorize. And *territorium* is 'a place from which people are warned.' Perhaps these two contending derivations continue to occupy territory today. To occupy territory is to receive sustenance and to exercise violence. Territory is land occupied by violence."[55] The Northwest Ordinance of 1787 first delineated the process for the transition of territories to states and the admission of newly created states into the Union, as well as stipulating that new states would be equal to the original thirteen states.[56] As Anders Stephanson notes, Thomas Jefferson's "Empire of and for Liberty" portrayed the United States as "a perpetually growing space for the demonstration of the higher historical purposes of humankind as such, all in the name of self-determination and autonomy. It is a timeless, physically indeterminate space of movement and colonization."[57] The territorial system displaced the geography of conquest and dispossession into a temporal liminality of transformation and deferral—removing indigenous peoples when possible and postponing the question of slavery.[58]

The series of Supreme Court decisions known collectively as the *Insular Cases* (1901–22) devised "unincorporated territory" as a political status in response to island nations seized in the Spanish-American War whose capture was sanctioned by the 1898 Treaty of Paris. The first unincorporated territories were Puerto Rico (1898–1952, and a U.S. Commonwealth or "free associated state" since 1952), Cuba (1898–1902), Guam (1898), and the Philippines (1898–1946), with later additions including American Samoa (1899), the Panama Canal Zone (1904–79), and the U.S. Virgin Islands (1917). The long-term U.S. military occupations of Nicaragua (1912–33), Haiti (1915–34), and the Dominican Republic (1916–24) did not rely on distinguishing political status in this way but instead convey the strategic distinctions mobilized on behalf of U.S. power. In 1947, the UN transferred to the United States the Trust Territory of the Pacific Islands, which included what is now the Marshall Islands, Federated States of Micronesia, Northern Mariana Islands, and Palau; a number of these islands later transitioned from trust territory to unincorporated status. The Northern Mariana Islands became a U.S. Commonwealth in 1978, as did the Marshall Islands, Palau, and the Federated States of Micronesia in 1986. Palau gained independence under international law in 1994. The Panama Canal Zone was also governed as an unincorporated territory from 1904 until 1979, when Panama assumed joint control. Panama assumed full authority over the canal zone at the end of 1999.[59]

Christina Duffy Burnett argues that the salient feature of the *Insular Cases* was that, with the bloody toll of unification by the Civil War partially in mind, the decisions fashioned "a doctrine of territorial deannexation," a new territorial category for U.S. constitutional law that created "a domestic territory that could be governed temporarily, and then later, if necessary, be relinquished."[60] Whereas the promise of statehood supposedly rendered colonization a provisional condition en route to inclusion and equality, "unincorporation" had the effect of positioning the U.S. island colonies as an anomaly, a deviation from the preceding continental development of the nation that could be remedied by returning to or aligning with earlier national precedents and values. United States policy makers cast this allegedly temporary relation as a tutelary project aimed at preparing otherwise incompetent, effectively infantile populations for self-government. In this sense, although claiming to initiate opposite trajectories—one toward inclusion, the other toward independence—the doctrines of territorial incorporation and unincorporation each professed to affirm the benevolent intent of U.S. dominion while justifying particular strategies for territorial acquisition and control.

Both forms of territorial status, nonetheless, were conceived as endeavors to defuse and contain challenges to federal authority involving various configurations of contestation by settlers, land speculators, states, and indigenous and other colonized peoples. Three important aspects of territorial status and the juridical construction of territory more broadly should be emphasized in this regard. First, categories of territory were created without regard to already operative indigenous conceptions of place, belonging, or autonomy, and as a deliberate means of legal justification for asserting to every extent possible federal authority over land and indigenous or subject peoples. The federal government's capacity to do this varied significantly over time. Taking into account, for the moment, only the late eighteenth century: between 1783 and 1786, U.S. officials argued that a majority of Indian peoples had forfeited any rights to their land by siding with the British; however, the Northwest Ordinance signaled a general retreat from this position and an effort to ameliorate sustained indigenous resistance to the imposition of U.S. rule; the Trade and Intercourse Acts of the 1790s sought to restrain the states and assert federal authority over commerce, land transactions, and political relations with indigenous peoples.[61] Yet, even if ignored by U.S. legislation and treaty, indigenous perspectives on place and space persisted and changed over time in relation to normative colonial categories. Considering the ongoing depiction of indigenous peoples as "transitory, dying communities, despite the reality of vitality and strength of Native people who refuse to give ground to the forces of settler-colonialism," Mishuana Goeman argues for the importance of conceiving of "space as not bounded by geo-politics, but storied and continuous," and sustaining "symbolic relationships and obligations rather than inherent rights bounded through nation-state models of borders and citizenship."[62]

Second, the initial U.S. territorial system was largely a continuation of the distribution and delimitation of governance established during the British colonial period. Julian Go observes that "the territorial governments [of the United States] were directly modeled after Britain's own colonies."[63] After independence from England, not only were territorial boundaries of the new states inherited from the colonial period, but the doctrine of state succession maintained that the acts of the preceding colonial governments—except for the "unconstitutional" infringements that precipitated the Revolution itself—remained in force. According to Peter Onuf, this both eased the anxieties of the new nation's propertied classes and "implied that the new states, like their colonial predecessors, were part of a larger community and should be subordinate to a higher authority. American experience in the [British] Empire remained paradigmatic after independence, and state succession theory provided the link."[64] Article IV of the U.S. Constitution (the Territorial Clause) asserts that "Congress shall have Power to dispose of and make all needful Rules and Regulations respecting the Territory or other Property belonging to the United States" without any provision for representation in the national government.[65] The consolidated power of Congress operated much as a de facto colonial government, something that separatists and other critics of federal authority at the time were quick to suggest. The terms of the Northwest Ordinance compounded this dynamic. Every new state would undergo a time when, as James Monroe wrote, "it would 'in effect' be under 'a colonial government similar to that which prevail'd in these States previous to the revolution.'"[66] Continental conquest would recapitulate the conditions of colonialism, even if subsequent slogans such as "manifest destiny" insisted on the inexorability of expansion and if the conceit of national founding asserted originary virtue and naturalized settler habitation. Beginning with the infamous "domestic dependent nation" status for American Indians concocted by Chief Justice John Marshall in *Cherokee Nation v. Georgia* (1831), and especially after the Indian Appropriations Act of 1871 unilaterally ended U.S. treaty making with indigenous nations, the doctrine of plenary power combined authority over territories and tribes under congressional rule.[67]

Third, the shifting inflections of territorial status index federal strategies for control—intended to secure consolidation or differentiation depending on the exigencies of the moment—and the negotiation of this control at distinct historical conjunctures. Sanford Levinson and Bartholomew Sparrow argue that the Louisiana Purchase of 1803 revealed the inadequate provisions and deliberate silences of the Constitution with regard to U.S. expansion, thus forcing into relief fundamental contradictions in the U.S. political system, including "the continued existence of U.S. territories in a nation of states; the discrepant definitions of and rights accruing to 'citizens' of the territories and those of the states; and the problematic constitutional status of the territories in a United States to be governed of, by, and for the people."[68] The 1803 transaction prompted heated debates as to whether republican government could be sustained in the context of expansion, and how the racially diverse and non-English-speaking inhabitants of the Territory of New Orleans—many of whom were Catholic and an increasing number of whom were refugees from Santo Domingo in the aftermath of the Haitian Revolution—were, from the U.S. standpoint, fit for self-government.[69] While Thomas Jefferson sought to allay criticism by placing the new territory under a military governor, this was the first time that the United States explicitly incorporated "aliens" included within the United States involuntarily.[70] The purchase, nevertheless, also allowed Jefferson to devise plans for removing eastern Indian tribes to lands west of the Mississippi River. The War of 1812 interrupted any full-scale implementation of land exchange as a means of displacement, but unremitting pressure by non-Indian settlers, speculators, and states contributed to the ratification of the Indian Removal Act of 1830 and the often genocidal relocation of tribes westward.[71] This was context for Chief Justice John Marshall's invocation of the doctrine of discovery and invention of the "domestic dependent nations" status for American Indian peoples. These were the circumstances that established "Indian Territory" in 1834 and the reservation system subsequently authorized by the Indian Appropriations Act of 1851.[72] The Louisiana Purchase also linked the questions of slavery and expansion, a correlation that became fully articulated with the Missouri Crisis of 1819–20, Wilmot Proviso of 1846, Compromise of 1850, Kansas-Nebraska Act of 1854, and the 1857 *Dred Scott v. Sandford* ruling.[73]

Treaties were a necessary accompaniment to territorial acquisition as a means of securing title and possession, and for aligning the foreign and domestic. Gary Lawson and Guy Seidman note that "The requirement for statehood was . . . necessary to render the acquisition of Louisiana constitutional as a matter of domestic law, but a treaty provision was necessary to convert that domestic requirement into a norm binding as a matter of international law. The extension of domestic legal requirements into international law is one of the central functions of treaties."[74] With regard to indigenous peoples, after the Seven Years War effectively ended French and Spanish competition for North American territory, British and subsequent U.S. treaty making with Native Americans proceeded in the following way: accommodation and compromise (1763–68); a gradual shift from accommodation to a system for transferring land from (1768–75); acknowledgement of indigenous land rights and acquisition by purchase (1786–95); the consolidation of a treaty system characterized by U.S. preponderance that culminated in 1871 with the prospective refusal to officially recognize indigenous peoples as "an independent nation, tribe, or power with whom the United States may contract by treaty" (1796–1871).[75] Robert Nichols thus argues that "social contract theory has developed in a dialectical relationship to the political practice of excluding indigenous peoples from the international realm."[76] In *United States v. Kagama* (1886) the Supreme Court affirmed the 1871 act, holding that Congress had plenary power over all tribes within its borders and asserting with racialized condescension, "The power of the general government over these remnants of a race once powerful . . . is necessary to their protection as well as to the safety of those among whom they dwell."[77]

Yet, if in the history of colonization, treaties have often served imperial powers as mechanisms calculated to affirm indigenous consent to contract, dispossession, and displacement, they have also provided evidence that indigenous sovereign capacity to make treaties under international law was acknowledged and detailed the agreements often subsequently disavowed or neglected by the United States. Scott Richard Lyons writes about the "x-mark" as the indigenous signature on treaties, which he describes as a "coerced sign of consent made under conditions that are not of one's making. It signifies [of the signer] power and a lack of power, agency and a lack of agency. It is a decision one makes when something has already been decided for you, but it is still a decision."[78] Moreover, Lyons characterizes the "x-mark" as indicating indigenous peoples' assent to adapt and transform themselves—to assume the modern political form of nations—in response to colonial incursion. Treaties sustain the double movement of what Kevin Bruyneel calls "colonial time"—a temporal location that situates "tribal sovereignty as a political expression that is out of (another) time, and therefore a threat to contemporary American political life and political space"—as at once indexing tribal acquiescence in the past and asserting tribal sovereignty in the present.[79]

Unintended consequences also follow from the *Insular Cases*, particularly as the cases offered alternate political and economic forms of affiliation in the context of decolonization as sanctioned under UN protocols since the mid-twentieth century.[80] Christina Duffy Burnett and Burke Marshall argue that the "unincorporated territory" status "born of colonialism has been appropriated by colonial subjects," with the many of those who live in such places now rejecting "both statehood and independence, the options denied the inhabitants of the territories by the *Insular Cases* at the turn of the last century." Burnett and Marshall observe that, without endorsing colonialism, "the idea of a relationship to the United States that is somewhere 'in between' that of statehood and independence—somehow both 'foreign' and 'domestic' (or neither)—has not only survived but enjoys substantial support."[81] This would seem to have been precisely the point, when in a 1998 referendum on the island's political status, Puerto Ricans overwhelmingly selected "none of the above," rather than vote for independence, statehood, or their current form of free associated state. "In supporting *ninguna de las anteriores* [none of the above]," Frances Negrón-Muntaner proposes that Puerto Ricans were rejecting "the way the status question itself was posed, the very idea that the U.S. Congress, Constitution, and/or local political parties could conceive of a single solution to address the complexity of Puerto Rican (trans) locations."[82] This repudiation likewise suggests the limit of democracy as the ever-heralded justification and decisive promise of inclusion in settler states more broadly.

Much as the proponents of U.S. continental conquest touted equality and citizenship as the irreproachable telos of territorial expansion, champions of American exceptionalism often insist that liberal democracy is based on the consent of the governed and, as such, the United States is constitutionally opposed to the tyrannies of colonial rule.[83] Modern constitutional democracy was, from this perspective, an altruistic gift generously extended to indigenous peoples and others subjected to U.S. colonial rule on a supposedly interim basis.[84] Indeed, as James Tully argues, "The right of the self-proclaimed civilized imperial powers to extend colonial and international modern constitutional regimes around the world correlated with a 'sacred duty to civilize' the indigenous peoples under their rule."[85] Yet, as Jacques Derrida observes, "the question of calculation, of numerical calculation, of equality according to number" are in certain respects constitutive of "the question of democracy."[86] If "domestically" the settler colonial logic of elimination tacitly underwrites the numerical presumptions of U.S. democracy, internationally and in the wake of decolonization, Derrida contends that the "lack of an established majority for the United States and its allies (for what are called 'Western democracies') [at the United Nations] has no doubt become, with the end of the Cold War, the setting and stage for this rhetoric of rogue states."[87] Although anxiously projected abroad as a counter to a diminished confidence in numbers, the rogue state attribution nonetheless continually threatens to unsettle legitimacy "at home." Audra Simpson argues in this sense: "The cornerstones of democratic governance—consent, citizenship, rule by representation—are revealed to be precarious at best when the experiences of Indigenous peoples are brought to bear on democracy's own promises and tenets."[88] She maintains that sovereignty as asserted by "Indigeneities that move through reservations and urban locales, persistent and insistent 'survivals' (descendants of treaty signatories, descendants of the historically recognized, as well as the unrecognized, in collective or individual form) . . . are nightmarish for the settler state, as they call up both the impermanence of state boundaries and the precarious claims to sovereignty enjoyed by liberal democracies such as the United States."[89] The sense in which the conceit that majoritarian consent mandates historical and political closure thus remains at most an elusive claim that scholarship such as the work included in this book serves to trouble.

OVERVIEW OF THE BOOK

This book's title deliberately invokes the notion of *formation* as it has been used by Ann Laura Stoler and Carole McGranahan, who argue that "imperial formations are polities of dislocation, processes of dispersion, appropriation, and displacement," while also emphasizing "the active and contingent process of their making and unmaking."[90] This introduction is not intended to suggest a single perspective or set of terms shared among all the essays that follow. Readers will find numerous connections and frictions throughout the volume that signal possibilities for further debate and discussion. Valuable analytic tensions and disagreements remain prominent across the thirteen studies that follow in their different assessments of the utility of specific conceptions of colonialism, imperialism, empire, and postcolonialism, even as the essays complement and contribute to the collective endeavor of theorizing formations of U.S. colonialism. It is not the purpose of this volume to be comprehensive or exhaustive in ostensibly identifying or accounting for the primary elements of U.S. colonialism. Rather the collection's aim is to encourage readers to approach the U.S. colonial present genealogically, and to consider the relationships between and across the essays included in a manner similar to the formations they study, as making up what Walter Benjamin calls a *constellation*—a spatial and temporal ensemble akin to montage that, when considered as such, can generatively destabilize and defamiliarize conventional practices of reading and perception that underwrite the comparative project of U.S. empire.[91]

The three sections of this book are intended to provide initial thematic points of entry that can be read sequentially or multidirectionally. The first section, "Histories in Contention," is organized around the requisites of historicity itself and seeks to call attention to and denaturalize the agonistic colonial conditions of possibility for historical claims, evidence, archives, legibility, and discrepant epistemologies. This section underscores the ways in which the past is disputed and deployed with regard to particular claims to sovereignty and belonging. Critical accounts of colonialism have often drawn attention to the politics of temporality and periodization as they have been enunciated through the self-aggrandizing Euro-American terms of civilization, universal history, rule of law, and modernity. Joanne Barker, Berenika Byszewski, Manu Vimalassery, and J. Kēhaulani Kauanui each address specific aspects of how this invented epistemological machinery and the legitimating logics of U.S. colonialism confer and retract the capacity for claiming land and securing historical legibility. Barker examines the ways in which the Delaware Tribe of Indians (the Lenape) have contended with the mutually constitutive logics of imperialism, scientific empiricism, and federal recognition policy. She studies the claims and controversies surrounding the Wallam Olum—an ostensible tribal history that momentarily appeared to bear the inordinate weight of U.S. recognition criteria and substantiate Delaware historical continuity and cultural distinction. In her account of Chaco Canyon, Byszewski considers tensions between the instantiation of territorial and discursive boundaries through maps and the practice of cartography. Her chapter examines the ways in which the mapping expedition led by Lieutenant James H. Simpson after the Mexican Cession of 1848 imaginatively and militarily charted claims to antiquity, and initiated a sustained displacement of the history, politics, and succession of indigenous removal on which the making of Chaco has been predicated. Focusing on the speculative work of rumor documented in official historical accounts, Vimalassery explores what he terms the "archive of counter-sovereignty"— the authorized histories of the Central Pacific Railroad Company, congressional record, and archaeological evidence—for how these sources imagine the encounter between Paiute communities and Chinese migrant labors in the Great Basin and the Sierra Nevada Mountains during the mid- to late nineteenth century. He asks why these particular archives of settler colonialism, labor importation, and industrial expansion take the forms of rumor and conjecture when addressing interactions between Paiutes and Chinese migrants, and what this tells us about the projects these documents. Finally, Kauanui analyzes the ways in which the congressional Apology Resolution of 1993 for the U.S. overthrow of the Hawaiian Kingdom a century earlier figured in the legal case *Office of Hawaiian Affairs, et al. v. State of Hawai'i.* Her chapter considers what colonial juridical regimes, sanctioned forms of historical acknowledgement, and compensatory politics of regretful public sentiment do in the ongoing colonial dynamics of occupation in Hawai'i.

The second section of the book, "Colonial Entanglements" (a phrase borrowed from Jean Dennison), endeavors to problematize the terms and trajectories of colonial "encounter" by emphasizing the entwining of diverse colonial pasts, anticipated futures, and uneven racializations. In this section, Barbara Krauthamer, Augusto Espiritu, Lorena Oropeza, Fa'anofo Lisaclaire Uperesa, and Dean Itsuji Saranillio examine episodes of material interaction, association, and exchange under circumstances of underlying coercion, expropriation, and limited mobility. These essays develop nuanced and provocative inquiries into the multiple conditions and circuits of colonial collision and parse the variously overlapping and incongruent imperial histories that serve as the coordinates of identification and disidentification. Krauthamer focuses on the relationships between missionaries, slaves, and American Indians in the early nineteenth-century U.S. South to examine the complex and often competing goals and consequences of the federal government's colonial agenda. She argues that while there is a substantial literature on the alliances and conflicts between missionaries and southern Indians in their combined opposition to federal efforts to dispossess indigenous peoples, insufficient attention has been devoted to the complicated question of slavery and the role of enslaved people in this context. She thus looks to enslaved people as significant political actors in order to critically analyze the multiplicity of racisms and attendant power struggles in the early nineteenth-century U.S. South. Espiritu, in a decidedly different context, considers the multiple trajectories of and attachments to Hispanism cast through and against the vectors of U.S. empire. Focusing on the influential figures Pedro Albizu Campos, Claro Mayo Recto, and Ramón Grau San Martín, his chapter provides a comparative analysis of the racialized, gendered, and nationalist discourses of prominent political leaders and intellectuals from Cuba, Puerto Rico, and the Philippines. In her chapter on Reies López Tijerina and the Alianza Federal de Mercedes (the Federal Alliance of Land Grants), Oropeza studies the ways in which Tijerina sought to build alliances with American Indians within New Mexico and across the United States in order to challenge U.S. colonialism and the politics of property in the Southwest. She contends that understanding Tijerina's strident anticolonial critique requires addressing the complex and contradictory terms of the "Indo-Hispano" racial politics he articulated. Uperesa examines how and why the sport of football has provided material possibilities and aspirational identification for American Samoans in the context of U.S. political and economic preponderance. She considers the ways in which such possibilities are embedded in developmentalist and ra- cial logics, as well as how these work in tandem with spectacles of mobility and prosperity to channel Samoans and American Samoa into the geopolit- ical circuits of U.S. empire. In his chapter on the ideological and material construction of the Kēpaniwai Heritage Gardens on Maui, Saranillio looks at the staging of liberal multiculturalism as a means of disavowing and displacing colonial violence. He argues for the persistence of Kanaka Maoli epistemologies and ways of life as a crucial recourse for contesting the imperial environmentalities, tourist economies, and military occupations that remake the past for the speculative future of colonial expropriation.

The third section of the volume, "Politics of Transposition," explores normative efforts to translate and render commensurate forms of knowl- edge and ways of being forced into proximity by colonial formations. Julian Aguon, Lanny Thompson, Jennifer Nez Denetdale, and Vicente Rafael each consider the fraught grid of intelligibility that U.S. colonialism and the tech- nologies of empire aim to stabilize and through which presumably proper subjects are to be interpellated. The essays in this section underscore how subjugated knowledges, unruly genealogies, and epistemological incom- mensurabilities disrupt and destabilize the imperial ordering of peoples, places, and pasts. Aguon considers competing legal justifications for colonial occupation and the constitutive relation between colonialism and milita- rism. Emphasizing law's inability to accommodate Chamorro conceptions of the world, he situates escalating U.S. militarization of Guam since 2005 in relation to how international law separately frames the rights of colonized and indigenous peoples on the one hand, and the claims of states on the other. Thompson studies the techniques of power that discipline, divide, and document colonial subjects, spaces, and populations in Puerto Rico during the early twentieth century through the instruments of military cartography. Emphasizing the spatial politics of colonial governmentality, he examines the ways in which the military gaze projected imperial sover- eignty and configured the geography and dispersed institutional apparatus of subjection. Denetdale uses debates over Lynda Lovejoy's candidacy for president of the Navajo Nation in 2010 as a lens through which to scrutinize how competing definitions of "tradition" serve and challenge the normative gender, sexual, and racial politics of tribal nation formation. She examines competing articulations of tradition, and the forms of affiliation and exclusion that these invocations aim to justify, in order to critically elaborate on the erasures and gaps in Diné history and the normative constructs of modern Navajo government. Rafael's chapter concludes the volume by situating the historical dynamics of U.S. colonial formation in relation to the conditions of permanent war undergirding U.S. empire in the twenty-first century. He studies the deployment and precarious utility of technologies of translation in the U.S. "War on Terror" and the occupation of Iraq, demonstrating how the early U.S. nationalist project of a unifying and equalizing idiom of American English and its opposition to linguistic heterogeneity and untranslatability informs today's imperial ventures.

The thematic arrangement of the chapters that follow is intended to suggest initial conjunctures that are generative for an analysis of U.S. colonialism. Yet these groupings are not meant to be definitive. One significant aspect of the volume is precisely the wide-ranging and multiple points of contact and conversation broached by the authors. Alternate or complementary configurations readily present themselves and convey dynamic possibilities for further critical analytic reciprocity and comparison. For instance, Aguon, Thompson, and Byszewski address the specific ways in which cartography serves as a complicit and vested form of knowledge production and spatial governmentality fully encumbered and in the service of competing claims to space, territory, and control. Political economy and the colonially overdetermined relations of production are central to the essays of Vimalassery and Uperesa. Conflicting regimes of racialization are a primary concern for Barker, Krauthamer, Saranillio, and Espiritu. The imperial logic and deployment of law is a key analytic lens for Aguon, Kauanui, and Barker, while the interplay of translation and incommensurability are crucial for both Rafael and Barker. The specific inflections of tradition are a focus for Saranillio, Barker, and Denetdale. Oropeza, Denetdale, and Uperesa each take constructions of gender and sexuality as indispensable to their inquiry. The very heterogeneity and historical mutability of U.S. colonialism and the diverse instantiations of U.S. empire require creative and capacious critical approaches that destabilize the self-evident coherence and singularity of the United States even as they acknowledge its forceful and frequently violent, if also often liberal and incorporative, assertion of prerogative and exclusivity.

NOTES

Many thanks to Julian Go for his vital role in the beginnings of this book, to Courtney Berger for her unwavering support for this project and all-around editorial brilliance, the anonymous readers for their indispensable insights, and to Erin Hanas, Susan Albury, Kathleen Kageff, and Heather Hensley at Duke University Press for their invaluable labor in the making of this book. Thanks also to Merritt Johnson for permission to use her amazing artwork for the book's cover. The American Studies Department at the University of New Mexico generously contributed funding toward the costs of image rights and the index. I am grateful in more ways than can be adequately expressed in words for the intellectual collaboration of Rebecca Schreiber and for the joy that Alia Schreiber-Goldstein brings to my life.

1. Benjamin, *The Arcades Project*, 460.
2. See, for example, Go, *American Empire and the Politics of Meaning*.
3. A. Simpson, "Settlement's Secret," 209.
4. Byrd, *The Transit of Empire*, 20.
5. Hart, "Brother Jonathan's Colonies," 319. This historical formation is not only a matter of the inequalities, exclusions, and injustices of colonial rule. Rather, these dynamics also work in tandem with the constitution of liberal freedoms and state formation. See especially Reddy, *Freedom with Violence*. Denise Ferreira de Silva makes a related argument, but with a focus on how the colonial conditions of possibility and raciality emerge in the ontological context of "globality," a spatial disposition that "fuses particular bodily traits, social configurations, and global regions, in which human difference is reproduced as irreducible and unsublatable" (xix). See Silva, *Toward a Global Idea of Race*.
6. See, for instance, the generative Hong and Ferguson, *Strange Affinities*.
7. Foucault, "Nietzsche, Genealogy, History," 140, 146.
8. Rifkin, *When Did Indians Become Straight?*
9. Barker, *Native Acts*, 223, 221.
10. O'Brien, *Firsting and Lasting*, 51-52.
11. For critiques of this tendency toward analogy and metaphor, see Cooper, *Colonialism in Question*; Teaiwa, "On Analogies." For an excellent critical analysis of the formulation of "internal colonialism," see Byrd, *The Transit of Empire*, 124-46.
12. Fabian, *Time and the Other*, 26-27.
13. Chow, *The Age of the World Target*, 77. Also, see Stoler, "Tense and Tender Ties"; Felski and Friedman, *Comparison*.
14. Said, *Culture and Imperialism*.
15. I adapt the term *colonial present* from Gregory, *The Colonial Present*.
16. Povinelli, *Economies of Abandonment*.
17. R. Williams, *Keywords*, 160. Interestingly, Williams's entry on "imperialism" is symptomatic of precisely the sort of ambivalence toward where and how to situate the United States with regard to colonialism. This is evident in his example of "American imperialism" as indicative of the contemporary ambiguity of "imperialism" more broadly, as well as how it might pertain to the undifferentiated terms *neoimperialism* and *neocolonialism*.
18. Useful introductions include Loomba, *Colonialism/Postcolonialism*; Osterhammel, *Colonialism*; Cooper, *Colonialism in Question*; Calhoun, Cooper, and Moore, *Lessons of Empire*; Veracini, *Settler Colonialism*.

19. Thomas, *Colonialism's Culture*, 9. For scholarship that similarly critically reappraised the turn to colonial discourse analysis, cultural studies of colonialism, subaltern studies, and postcolonial theory during the late 1980s and early 1990s, also see Dirks, *Colonialism and Culture*; Cooper and Stoler, *Tensions of Empire*; McClintock, Mufti, and Shohat, *Dangerous Liaisons*.

20. Kazanjian, "Colonial," 52.

21. Stoler and McGranahan, "Refiguring Imperial Terrains," 4, 36.

22. Greeson, *Our South*, 22.

23. Foucault's insistence on a historical shift from territory to population as the basis of governmentality is not substantiated in the colonial context. Instead, governance of territory and population remain mutually constitutive. See Foucault, *Security, Territory, Population*. Mark Rifkin makes a similar critique of Giorgio Agamben's rethinking of Foucault's conception of biopolitics for the ways in which Agamben misses the significance of the geopolitical for colonialism (Rifkin, "Indigenizing Agamben").

24. E. Lee, *At America's Gates*; Ngai, *Impossible Subjects*; Jung, *Coolies and Cane*; Shah, *Stranger Intimacy*; W. Johnson, *River of Dark Dreams*. On the idea of an "imperial nation-state," see Wilder, *The French Imperial Nation-State*.

25. Blackhawk, *Violence over the Land*; Deer et al., *Sharing Our Stories of Survival*; Hämäläinen and Truett, "On Borderlands."

26. Mbembe, *On the Postcolony*, 174, 175.

27. Lutz, *The Bases of Empire*; Shigematsu and Camacho, *Militarized Currents*; V. Gonzalez, *Securing Paradise*; Khalili, *Time in the Shadows*.

28. Wolfe, "Settler Colonialism and the Elimination of the Native"; Goldstein, "Where the Nation Takes Place"; Morgensen, *Spaces between Us*; A. Simpson, "Settlement's Secret"; Nichols, "Indigeneity and the Settler Contract Today."

29. On the limits of settler colonialism as an analytic, see especially Saldaña-Portillo, *"'How Many Mexicans Is a Horse Worth?'"* Guidotti-Hernández, *Unspeakable Violence*; Jackson, *Creole Indigeneity*.

30. Byrd, *Transit of Empire*, 122–23. Also see Melamed, *Represent and Destroy*.

31. Hobson, *Imperialism*, 1902.

32. Lenin, "Imperialism, the Highest Stage of Capitalism," 1916; Hilferding, *Finance Capital*, 1910.

33. Gallagher and Robinson, "The Imperialism of Free Trade."

34. Louis and Robinson, "The Imperialism of Decolonization."

35. Harvey, *The New Imperialism*; Arrighi, *Adam Smith in Beijing*.

36. Kaplan, "'Left Alone with America.'"

37. An important exception to this tendency is Moon-Kie Jung's argument that the United States has been since its inception an "empire-state" shaped by the historically adaptable perspectives and practices of white supremacy (Jung, "Constituting the U.S. Empire-State and White Supremacy"). Jung derives the category "empire-state" from Cooper, *Colonialism in Question*, 153–203.

38. McCoy and Scarano, *Colonial Crucible*.

39. Lowell, "The Colonial Expansion of the United States," 145.

40. Hart, *Actual Government as Applied under American Conditions*, 368. For a less overtly proimperialist stance that nevertheless reaches similar conclusions, also see Snow, *The Administration of Dependencies*.

41. Hart, "Brother Jonathan's Colonies."

42. Walter Williams, "United States Indian Policy and the Debate over Philippine Annexation." However, as Lanny Thompson notes, policy directives associating the colonial administration of American Indians and the Philippines were not necessarily put into practice by local bureaucrats such as David Barrows, head of the Philippine Commissions' Bureau of Non-Christian Tribes (Thompson, *Imperial Archipelago*, 212–13).

43. Slotkin, *Regeneration Through Violence*; Rogin, *Fathers and Children*; Drinnon, *Facing West*; Limerick, *Legacy of Conquest*.

44. Dulles, "International Unity," 936. Also see J. Pratt, *America's Colonial Experiment*.

45. Cobb, *Native Activism in Cold War America*, 12–13.

46. Rauschning, Wiesbrock, and Lailach, *Key Resolutions of the United Nations General Assembly*, 113.

47. Thornberry, *Indigenous Peoples and Human Rights*, 874–75. Also see Anaya, *International Human Rights and Indigenous Peoples*. Jeff Corntassel notes, "As early as 1949, states began drafting a *Special Report of the United Nations Commission for Indonesia* in order to establish a clear distinction between 'internal' and 'external' self-determination. According to this logic, one could differentiate between 'historical subjugation of an alien population living in a different part of the globe and the historical subjugation of an alien population living on a piece of land abutting that of its oppressors'" (Corntassel, "Toward Sustainable Self-Determination," 127).

48. Pulitano, *Indigenous Rights in the Age of the U.N. Declaration*. Also see Xanthaki, *Indigenous Rights and United Nations Standards*; Goldstein, *Poverty in Common*, 233–43.

49. O'Brien, *Firsting and Lasting*, xv.

50. O'Brien, *Firsting and Lasting*, 52–53.

51. The new nation may be aspirational, but it is equally defensive and exclusive. In constituting the "we" in whose name it is proclaimed, the Declaration of Independence specifies among the tyrannies wrought by King George III against the colonists that he "endeavoured to bring on the Inhabitants of our Frontiers, the merciless Indian Savages, whose known Rule of Warfare, is an undistinguished Destruction, of all Ages, Sexes and Conditions" ("In Congress, July 4, 1776," 169).

52. Paine, "Common Sense," 45.

53. Frank, *Constituent Moments*; Parker, *Common Law, History, and Democracy in America*, 67–116; Honig, "Declarations of Independence." Also see Espejo, *The Time of Popular Sovereignty*.

54. On the logic of "territory" more broadly, see Elden, *The Birth of Territory*.

55. Connolly, "Tocqueville, Territory and Violence," 144.

56. See especially Onuf, *Statehood and Union*.

57. Stephanson, "A Most Interesting Empire," 255.

58. On the territorial system, see Farrand, *The Legislation of Congress for the Government of the Organized Territories of the United States*; Pomeroy, *The Territories and the United States*; Eblen, *The First and Second United States Empires*; Onuf, *The Origins of the Federal Republic*; Lawson and Seidman, *The Constitution of Empire*.

59. On the United States and the trustee system, see Pungong, "The United States and the International Trusteeship System." For more on the Panama Canal, see McGuinness, *Path of Empire* and Greene, *The Canal Builders*.

60. Burnett, "*Untied* States: American Expansion and Territorial Deannexation," 797. Also see Ramos, *American Colonialism in Puerto Rico.*

61. Jones, *License for Empire*; Rockwell, *Indian Affairs and the Administrative State in the Nineteenth Century*; Witgen, *An Infinity of Nations.*

62. Goeman, *Mark My Words*, 87, 117, 118. Glen Coulthard likewise argues that it is a "place-based imaginary that serves as the ethical foundation from which many Indigenous people and communities continue to resist and critique the dual imperatives of state sovereignty and capitalist accumulation that constitute our colonial present" (Coulthard, "Place against Empire," 82).

63. Go, *Patterns of Empire*, 47.

64. Onuf, *The Origins of the Federal Republic*, 22. Also see Hsueh, *Hybrid Constitutions*; Yirush, *Settlers, Liberty, and Empire*; Horsman, *Expansion and American Indian Policy*; R. Williams, "'The People of the States Where They Are Found Are Often Their Deadliest Enemies.'"

65. U.S. Constitution, Article IV, § 3, clause 2.

66. As quoted in Onuf, *The Origins of the Federal Republic*, 44.

67. Wilkins and Lomawaima, *Uneven Ground*, 98–116. Kevin Bruyneel contends that, after the end of the Civil War, 1871 represents "the moment when the renewed American nation and state expressly made its colonial impression by imposing boundaries to restrict and subsume the spatial, historical, and political life of indigenous nations and tribes" (Bruyneel, *The Third Space of Sovereignty*, 66).

68. Levinson and Sparrow, Introduction, 13.

69. G. Hall, *Africans in Colonial Louisiana*; Dawdy, *Building the Devil's Empire.*

70. Levinson and Sparrow, Introduction, 5–8.

71. Prucha, *The Great Father*; Rosen, *American Indians and State Law*; Rifkin, *Manifesting America.*

72. Ronda, "'We Have a Country'"; Trennert, *Alternative to Extinction*; Sutton, "Sovereign States and the Changing Definition of the Indian Reservation."

73. Mason, *Slavery and Politics in the Early American Republic*; W. Johnson, *River of Dark Dreams.*

74. Lawson and Seidman, "The First 'Incorporation' Debate," 34–35.

75. Also see Deloria and Wilkins, *Tribes, Treaties, and Constitutional Tribulations.*

76. Nichols, "Realizing the Social Contract," 44.

77. United States v. Kagama 118 U.S. 375 (1886).

78. S. Lyons, *X-Marks*, 2–3.

79. Bruyneel, *The Third Space of Sovereignty*, 171. On the temporal logics of settler colonialism, also see Povinelli, *Economies of Abandonment.*

80. Burnett and Marshall, "Between the Foreign and the Domestic." On decolonization more broadly, also see Kelly and Kaplan, "Legal Fictions after Empire"; C. Lee, *Making a World after Empire.*

81. Burnett and Marshall, "Between the Foreign and the Domestic," 2.

82. Negrón-Muntaner, Introduction, 5. For scholarship that underscores the coercive and counterinsurgent practices of U.S. colonial rule, see also Malavet, *America's Colony*; Bosque-Pérez and Colón Morera, *Puerto Rico under Colonial Rule.*

83. Fletcher, "Tribal Consent."

84. On related logics of the liberal "gift," see Nguyen, *The Gift of Freedom.*

85. Tully, "The Imperialism of Modern Constitutional Democracy," 331. For a useful comparison, see Chatterjee, *The Politics of the Governed.*

86. Derrida, *Rogues*, 29–30.
87. Derrida, *Rogues*, 98.
88. A. Simpson, "Settlement's Secret," 209.
89. A. Simpson, "Settlement's Secret," 211.
90. Stoler and McGranahan, "Refiguring Imperial Terrains," 8.
91. Benjamin, *The Arcades Project*, 456–88.

PART I   HISTORIES IN CONTENTION

The Specters of Recognition

There is a story I know. It's about the earth and how it floats in space on the back of a turtle. I've heard this story many times, and each time some- one tells the story, it changes. Sometimes the change is simply in the voice of the storyteller. Sometimes the change is in the details. Sometimes in the order of events. Other times it's the dialogue or the response of the audience. But in all the telling of all the tellers, the world never leaves the turtle's back. And the turtle never swims away. . . . The truth about stories is that that's all we are.
— Thomas King, *The Truth about Stories: A Native Narrative*

The questions addressed here include: How have Native peoples been writ- ten into and out of the categories of U.S. modernity's human, and to what le- gal, economic, and social ends? What work have the qualifications of Natives as (in)human done within imperial formations? How have Native peoples (dis)articulated themselves as the modern human?

In *We Have Never Been Modern*, Bruno Latour argues that modernity narrates "the passage of time" by designating the emergence of "a new re- gime, an acceleration, a rupture, a revolution in time."[1] This designation discriminates a teleological progress to civilization from "an archaic and stable past" that is considered "lost" and "vanquished."[2] Latour is concerned with how the ruptures between past (where nature is thought to reside) and present (where society has erupted) deny the hybridity of nature and society. He argues that knowledge and experience are produced within this hybridity and is concerned about the consequences of a denaturalized notion of "human society."

For here I want to remain with Latour's definition of modernity as a tele-ology of social formation and focus on the epistemological and ontological assumptions that that narrative makes about what constitutes the human. I do so because modernity's human—inflected through notions of society in opposition to nature—is the precondition on which all international and constitutional rights to self-determination are based.[3] The question of what counts as human matters, then, not as an esoteric problem of epistemology or ontology—the truth, as it were, of knowing and being—but as a concern over the human's role in arbitrating Native legal rights, economic condi-tions, and social politics within the contexts of the global and the republic. How Natives have been written into and out of the legal categories of the human, and what kinds of humans they are righted to be or not to be, has everything to do with the mitigation of their property in the human and in history and, consequently, with their rights to the self-determination of their governments, territories, cultures, and bodies. Because, after all, "the truth about stories is that that's all we are."[4]

In order to consider these issues, the chapter examines the coproductive relationship of imperialism, scientific empiricism, and federal recognition within the discourses and ideologies of modernity's human. It analyzes the politics of the evidence-as-knowledge demanded of Natives in order to prove historical "continuity" and cultural "distinction" as an "Indian tribe" to secure their recognition.[5] It frames these demands within the struggles of the Delaware Tribe of Indians (Lenape) for recognition, and the specific controversies over the scientific veracity of the Wallam Olum, as a way of thinking through the imperial conditions in which Native humanity and human rights are made contingent on the empire's interests. It concludes by considering the work of modernity in disguising as a thing of the past that which is still very much present: the empire.

BRIEF CONTEXT

For readers unfamiliar with the struggles of the Delaware Tribe for recogni-tion, some context is necessary to frame the analysis that follows.[6] In 1866, the tribe signed its last of twenty treaties with the United States "consenting" to relocate (yet again) from their treatied lands in Kansas to Indian Territory. In 1867, the Delaware ratified an agreement with the Cherokee Nation nego-tiated by the United States that provided for their relocation into Cherokee territory.[7] In 1894 and 1904, the Delaware and Cherokee went before the U.S. Supreme Court over the terms of that agreement, which interpreted the agreement through the provisions of a Cherokee treaty of 1866 to mean that the Delaware had been "incorporated" as "native Cherokee" into the Cherokee Nation (ignoring the provisions of the Delaware treaty ratified the same year).[8]

Despite the rulings, the Bureau of Indian Affairs (BIA) continued direct relations with the Delaware. In *Business Committee of the Delaware Tribe v. Weeks et al.* of 1977, the Court reversed the 1894 and 1904 decisions based on those relations to rule for Delaware "independence" from the Cherokee.[9] But in 1979, the BIA issued a letter to the Delaware, at the political behest of the Cherokee, informing them that their recognition was terminated. In 1996, the Delaware successfully appealed to the BIA and were reinstated. In 1998, the Cherokee appealed.[10] In *Cherokee v. Delaware, et al.* of 2004, the U.S. Court of Appeals for the Tenth Circuit ruled that the BIA had overstepped its authority in reinstating the Delaware. It asserted that the BIA ignored Court precedent regarding Delaware status. It found that the Delaware had not been "independent" since 1867, having relinquished autonomy to the Cherokee by agreement. The decision had the consequence of terminating the Delaware for the second time. In 2006, the Delaware appealed to the U.S. Supreme Court, which declined to hear the case. The BIA instructed the Delaware that they would have to reach an agreement with the Cherokee on the terms of their jurisdiction and territorial rights in Oklahoma in order for them to be reinstated. The controversial agreement that resulted was approved by both tribes and ratified by the Department of the Interior in May 2009.[11] In August 2009, the Delaware appeared on the list of federally recognized tribes issued by the BIA.[12]

In the thick cloud of conflicts with the Cherokee, the Delaware Tribal Council hired David McCutchen, a student at the University of California, Santa Barbara, and the California Institute of Arts, to assist them with research in the preparation of the kind of documentation that the tribe anticipated it would need to satisfy federal criteria for acknowledgement (these criteria were established in 1978, as analyzed below). In 1980, the Council passed a resolution that endorsed McCutchen's findings related to the Wallam Olum. The Wallam Olum is an epic tale purportedly translated into English in 1836. It claimed to record in pictographs and songs Lenape creation, a great flood, a long migration, settlement in the northeastern United States, and existence up to the moment before contact with colonists in the early 1600s.[13] McCutchen's findings were published in 1993 as *The Red Record: The Wallam Olum: The Oldest Native North American History.*[14] Almost immediately, David M. Oestreicher, then a graduate student in anthropology at Rutgers University, began publishing the results of his dissertation on the fraudulence of the Wallam Olum.[15] Following the filing of his dissertation in 1995, the Delaware Council withdrew its endorsement of McCutchen's book and asserted that the Wallam Olum was not an authentic Lenape story.[16] The withdrawal solicited criticisms of the Delaware for having been duped into endorsing a history that was not of its own making.

PART I: IMPERIAL LOGICS

In order to argue that modernity's human articulates a particular kind of relationship between imperialism, scientific empiricism, and federal recognition that undermines Native self-determination—such as experienced by the Delaware Tribe—I need to put into sharp relief the history of the Lenape Wallam Olum and the history of modernity's human. This association reveals the discursive and ideological logics of modernity's human as an empirical truth about what constitutes human society and social development that undergirds the interests of the empire. The logics are so powerful that they transform fraud into evidence and represents genocide as an inevitability of natural evolution.

Translators and Translations

The "original translation" of the Wallam Olum from Lenape into English was self-published by Constantine Samuel Rafinesque in 1836.[17] It was reworked by Ephraim George Squier in 1849 and Daniel Garrison Brinton in 1885.[18] All three were from the New England region and worked through regional historical societies and universities to present and publish their findings. While subscribing to very different perspectives about human origins and migration histories, they maintain together a teleological narrative of an American society achieved through progress. This narrative, as Jean M. O'Brien argues so powerfully in *Firsting and Lasting: Writing Indians Out of Existence in New England*, was necessary to the imperial logics of the genocide and dispossession of Native peoples.[19] Centrally, it maintained that Native extinction had occurred naturally as a result of Native inferiority and not as a consequence of imperialist practices.

Rafinesque's self-published book, *The American Nations; Or, Outlines of Their General History, Ancient and Modern*, offers a hemispheric comparison of the linguistic and cultural similarities of Native groups. In it he assumes the veracity of a Biblical monogenetic history—arguing that Natives migrated to the Americas following a great flood that had raised land masses between China and Alaska making such a migration possible—to explain the relationships among and between the descendants of Moses in the Americas. To support this argument, he includes what he claims is a translation of the Lenape Wallam Olum—an epic tale of Lenape origins in eastern China, a great migration across the Bering Strait into North America, and a long journey across the continent into the northeastern territories of what was to become the United States. In accordance with Mosaic genealogies, it included a chronicle of Lenape male chiefs and concluded dramatically at the moment just before contact with the colonists. Much like Mel Gibson's *Apocalypto* (2006), this denouement fits well within the teleological narratives of both Christian theology and social evolution to figure an ultimately doomed people standing at the precipice of their own tragic extinction, foreshadowed by the ominous arrival of a civilized society.

Some scholars argue that Rafinesque's assertions were unpopular in 1836.[20] This is owing, they maintain, to his claim that Natives had a civilization akin to that of Europeans and one whose demise could be directly linked to European colonization. But despite these alleged controversies, which only further the Wallam Olum's veracity, the translation was repeatedly questioned and questionable.

Rafinesque claimed that his translation was based on a set of birch-bark tablets with pictographic engravings painted in red and a set of transcriptions of accompanied songs. He said that he had acquired the tablets from a botanist named "Dr. Ward of Indiana" and the transcription of the songs from "John Burns" sometime between 1820 and 1822. Despite the fact that neither individual could ever be corroborated to have existed, Rafinesque insisted that Ward had been working in Indiana when he encountered a small Lenape village overrun by an epidemic illness. The village included an elderly man named Olumpees, a record keeper who was deathly ill (also uncorroborated). Ward was able to help Olumpees, and in payment was given the tablets, the only possession the man had to offer.[21] Rafinesque said that Ward turned the tablets over to him because he knew they were valuable and could not understand them. At the same time Rafinesque received the transcriptions of the songs from Burns. Rafinesque said it took him until 1833 to complete his study. His proficiency in Lenape was based entirely on dictionaries produced by missionaries.[22] Sometime between 1833 and his death in 1840, Rafinesque claimed that the original tablets and transcriptions were lost so that all that survived were his translations.

Squier reworked Rafinesque's Wallam Olum for a presentation before the New-York Historical Society and an article for the *American Review* in 1849.[23]

Squier's version reflected his own polygenetic view about human origins and migrations *within* the Americas. As debates within the society ensued over its implications, Henry Rowe Schoolcraft—a geologist and ethnologist respected for his work as a federal agent, legislator, and superintendent of Indian affairs in the Northern Department in Michigan and married to Jane Johnston, an Ojibwa—responded. In personal correspondence to Squier, Schoolcraft asserted that the Wallam Olum was not an authentic Lenape story.[24]

Brinton, a professor of ethnology and archeology at the Academy of Natural Science in Philadelphia and of linguistics and archeology at the University of Pennsylvania, reworked Rafinesque's Wallam Olum to argue for the distinctiveness of the language and cultures of Natives. At the same time, he advanced especially racist ideas about what that distinctiveness meant. Brinton believed that "all races were 'not equally endowed'" and that those lesser races were "disqualified" from the "atmosphere of modern enlightenment."[25] He asserted that the "lesser races" had "an inborn tendency, constitutionally recreant to the codes of civilization" and that they were "therefore technically criminal."[26] He concluded that these "lesser races" did not share in the "*a priori* notions of the rights of man."[27] But because they embodied an earlier stage of social evolution that was on the verge of extinction, they were worthy of study.

Brinton's self-published *The Lenape and Their Legends, with the Complete Text and Symbols of the Walam Olum, A New Translation, and an Inquiry into the Authenticity* begins, "For a long time this record the Walam Olum . . . was supposed to have been lost. Having obtained the original text about a year ago, I printed a few copies and sent them to several educated native Delawares with a request for aid in its translation and opinion on its authenticity."[28] Those to whom he sent Rafinesque's text included "Reverend Albert Anthony, Reverend John Kilbuck, Mr. Horatio Hale, Reverend E. de Schweinitz, Dr. J. Hammond Trumbull, Prof. A. M. Elliott, and General John Mason Brown."[29] He claims that all of these men confirmed the manuscript was "an authentic memorial, the original text" of the Lenape Wallam Olum.[30] "It is a genuine native production, which was repeated orally to someone indifferently conversant with the Delaware language, who wrote it down to the best of his ability. In its present form it can, as a whole, lay no claim either to antiquity, or to purity of linguistic form. Yet, as an authentic modern version, slightly colored by European teachings, of the ancient tribal traditions, it is well worth preservation" and continued study.[31] Brinton provides an overview of Lenape history and then a new translation of the Wallam Olum that conforms to his own racist understandings of social evolution.[32]

The purported translations of the Wallam Olum by Rafinesque, Squier, and Brinton served debates over the history of Native origins, migrations, social development, and culture well into the 1990s.[33] These debates reached a kind of crescendo with McCutchen's illustrated publication in 1993. But in 1995, Oestreicher offered extant evidence of its fabrication. "The so-called Delaware Indian pictographs are not Delaware at all but are in fact hybrid combinations of Egyptian, Chinese, Ojibwa, and even several Mayan symbols newly published at the time. As for the accompanying 'Delaware' text, it was fabricated by Rafinesque from the very sources he claimed to have used as translation aids. . . . As for his claim to have completed the translation by 1833, Rafinesque was simply attempting to predate some of the published sources from which the forgery was crafted."[34] The recurrent reproduction of the Wallam Olum contributes to the way it served racist ideologies and practices in not only justifying but necessitating U.S. imperialism. It offered a history of "the Americas" and the emergence of the United States as an imperial power that negated U.S. genocide and dispossession for an affirmation of Christian theological and social evolutionary perspectives anticipating Native extinction.[35] This modernist tale was the productive force through which the United States rearticulated its genocide and dispossession of Native peoples as tragic but expected, examples of what the United States had left behind in the dust of its own progressive advancement to a fully evolved democratic state. As observed by Latour, this modern state was divorced in all possible ways from the embodied *nature* of the Indian.

Theories and Theorists

The reproduction Rafinesque's Wallam Olum operated within modernity's human. This human was not uniform but universal. It was articulated through imperialism and racism to figure a human to whom the empire's constitutional rights, economic opportunities, and social empowerments could be sutured and legally protected over time—a human that was essentially Caucasian, Christian, capitalist, and civil. So, it is not about the repetition of a deluded story of U.S. advancement to democracy and civilization (though it is that). It is about the juridic, economic, and social assertion of an exclusionary claim—which is *always already* an inclusionary one—on that which is human, a claim central to the production of the democratic state. This is because within imperial narrations, the "finishing" and improvement of civil society is measured by the degree to which that society has "achieved" democracy. The human that is *righted* within that state is the human that is *writed* as the self-determining agent of democracy and history.

The discourses and ideologies of modernity's human were institutionalized in federal military and economic policy primarily through the disciplines of empirical archaeology and anthropology. In *Archaeological Theory and the Politics of Cultural Heritage*, Laurajane Smith shows how, even as these disciplines were established through ignorance and misrepresentation of Native cultural histories and identities, they served to propel U.S. imperial forces by providing the rationale for them: Natives were inferior—if human at all—and so inevitably if tragically "lost" and "vanquished" to the progress of civilization.[36] The role of the anthropologist and archaeologist in this was to study the terms of Native difference for the sake of understanding America's past—as an earlier stage of human development—while being authorized as the experts and advisors on the course of U.S. policies dealing with the "Indian problem." (Even Rafinesque, Squier, and Brinton attempt to make their respective theories relevant to state policy.)

Smith demonstrates how U.S. imperial interests easily appropriated and readily authorized the empirical truths and applicability of empirical anthropology and archaeology. At the same time, she shows how imperialism informed the theories and methods of this anthropology and archaeology.[37] The theories found resonance through social evolutionism, which assumed a unilineal trajectory in the value and consequence of cultural exchange and interracial mixing over time, situating societies along a host of progressive binarisms—from prehistory to history, illiterate to literate, savage to civil, full to mixed, integral to contaminated, et cetera—on their way to either ruin, incorporation, or civilization.

In *Toward a Global Idea of Race*, Denise Ferreira da Silva analyzes the constellation of racial politics informing scientific empiricism.[38] She examines the role of "natural history" in producing and reflecting popular notions of racial difference, beginning with the writings of George Cuvier and Charles Darwin. Cuvier argued that "certain hereditary peculiarities of conformation are observable, which constitute what we termed races. Three of these in particular appear eminently distinct: the 'Caucasian,' or white, the 'Mongolian,' or yellow, and the Ethiopian, or black."[39] He described the "Caucasian" as "distinguished by the beauty of the oval which forms the head; and it is this one which has given rise to the most civilized nations—to those which have generally held the rest in subjection: it varies in complexion and in the color of the hair."[40] He characterized the "Mongolian" and

"Ethiopian" as possessing far less desirable physical attributes and mental capacities and so far less civilized societies.[41]

Concurrently, Darwin introduced the idea of "natural selection" to explain the biological and intellectual variations he perceived between different groups as part of an evolutionary pattern of regulation and specialization.[42] He applied this pattern to differences between groups to argue that "progress . . . has been much more general than retrogression; that man has risen, though by slow and interrupted steps, from a lowly condition to the highest standard as yet attained by him in knowledge, morality and religion."[43] This adaptability provided some groups with advantage over others,[44] as indicated in the differences between groups who had achieved greater degrees of progress through their "high intellectual and moral faculties."[45] Darwin predicted that "the civilized races of man will almost certainly exterminate, and replace, the savage races throughout the world. At the same time, the anthropomorphous apes . . . will no doubt be exterminated. The break between man and his nearest allies will then be wider, for it will intervene between man in a more civilized state, as we may hope, even than the Caucasian, and some ape as low as a baboon, instead of, as now, between the negro or Australian and the gorilla."[46]

Silva shows that Cuvier and Darwin contributed to the presumed universality of social evolutionary schematics as scientifically, biologically, and mentally based, observable, and measurable. Not only did they fuse biology and culture, but they championed a modernist human as the full embodied agent of its own history and ontology—fully realized by reason as a sovereign, self-determined thing, grounded in objectively observable realities and experiences, physically measurable and differentiated. [47]

Lewis Henry Morgan is one of several anthropologists in the United States credited with rendering theories of biological evolution into those of social evolution.[48] Although several of his contemporaries were critical of the unilineality of his paradigms,[49] Karl Marx, Friedrich Engels, Francis Galton, and Sigmund Freud, among others, found Morgan's work important and useful.[50] This reception was owing in part to the way Morgan anchored social evolutionary stages through those of historical materialism. His assertions about the progressive links between property and kinship proved germane to Marx's hypothesis that capitalism usurped communal clan-based forms of labor and Engels's arguments that the capitalist state was an impermanent polity that had replaced egalitarian clan systems.[51] Similarly, Morgan's mapping of "human mental capacity" in relation to property and kinship were found relevant to Galton's equations between genetic heritability, intelligence, and civilization and Freud's theorizations of the phases of psychosexual development. These theoretical cross-pollinations are instructive for understanding scientific empiricism as a discourse and ideology that holds incredibly diverse thinkers together through their commitments to and belief in the objectivity, rationality, and methodological rigor of knowledge. These commitments and beliefs informed the government and popular reception of their theories. For here, I will focus on Morgan's understandings of the human and the multiple social norms that that human advanced in the service of U.S. imperial interests.

Morgan's *Ancient Society: Or Researches in the Lines of Human Progress from Savagery through Barbarism to Civilization* begins:

> Mankind are now known to have existed in Europe in the glacial period, and even back of its commencement, with every probability of their origination in a prior geological age. They have survived many races of animals with which they were contemporaneous, and passed through a process of development, in the several branches of the human family, as remarkable in its courses as in its progress. . . . It can now be asserted upon convincing evidence that savagery preceded barbarism in all the tribes of mankind, as barbarism is known to have preceded civilization. The history of the human race is one in source, one in experience, and one in progress.[52]

Morgan assumes the universality of human supremacy over animals and the environment, and of some human groups over others, based on their unilineal progress through three stages of development: *savagery, barbarism, civilization*. There is much to disentangle, even as Latour has already defined its import. I begin with Morgan's substitutions of "mankind," "human family," and the "human race."

The *Oxford Dictionary of English Etymology* identifies the historical uses of these terms: *mankind* for "human species"; *man* for "human being; adult male"; *human* "pert. to man . . . rel. to *homō* man"; *family* for "group of relatives, kindred; household"; *race* for "set or class of persons, animals, plants; group of persons, etc. having a common ancestry or character."[53] I do not mean to suggest an equivalence between Morgan's substitutions of these terms and their definitional history. But I do want to emphasize the normative gendering and racialization of difference at the ideological root of these substitutions so as not to dismiss them so readily to convention. This normativity is operationalized through Morgan's evolutionary schematics for the family, intelligence, and racial difference and are important in understanding how scientific empiricism became institutionalized as/in federal military and economic policy.

First, the gendered generalization of "mankind" for all of humanity—as a related "family" and "race" "of men" against all others defined as not human, prehuman, not human enough, or animal—is key to Morgan's privileging of men and male-centered practices and heterosexual relations within the "ethnical periods" or "stages of human progress" that he delineates. Morgan assigns women and women-centered practices like matrilineality and matrilocality to the lower stages of savagery and barbarism; he assigns men and men-centered social practices like patrilineality and patrilocality and heterosexual marriage to civilization. These assignments are imbricated within his gendered and sexed staging of the human family.

Within savagery and barbarism, Morgan identifies two types of families within each, both of which he says are bound to blood lineality and sexual relations without a civilized form of property or territory. Within savagery he identifies the *consanguine family* as founded on "the intermarriage among brothers and sisters in a group" and the *punaluan* family as founded on "the intermarriage of several brothers to each other's wives in a group; and of several sisters to each other's husbands in a group."[54] Within barbarism, he defines the *syndyasmian family* as founded on the "joining" or "pairing" of a "male with a female under the form of marriage, but without an exclusive cohabitation" and with the option of divorce or separation for both husband and wife, and the *patriarchal family*, which is "founded upon the marriage of one man to several wives" such as "the special family of the Hebrew pastoral tribes, the chiefs and principal men of which practiced polygamy."[55] Morgan's sexual promiscuity, moral license, and natural affinity within savagery and barbarism gives way to his morally superior and responsible form of the contracted monogamous marriage in civilization. In civilization, Morgan defines the *monogamian family* as "founded upon the marriage of one man with one woman, with an exclusive cohabitation. . . . It is pre-eminently the family of civilized society, and was therefore essentially modern."[56] This superior form of family is articulated through heterosexual marriage, the "idea of property," and a "passion for territory."[57]

Second, Morgan's gendered, sexed, and propertied classificatory schematics of the family are coproduced by his racialization of social difference based on human intellect or "mental capacity." Morgan argues that societies within savagery and barbarism do not exhibit the intelligence or moral character (which he conflates) that would produce proper heterosexual family arrangements. He argues that individuals in savagery choose sexual partners from those who live closest to them and without making any commitments to them or the children they bear, while in barbarism they choose to couple and even marry people outside of their family but in a move that protects the privileges of sexual promiscuity and male polygamy. This is owing to their lack of intelligence and capacity for reason, capitulating to baser impulses for sexual pleasure. In civilization, however, Morgan maintains that humans have attained the full development of their "mental capacity" as they have learned (advanced) to reason and morality and so form heterosexual marriage commitments in relation to proper forms of government, property, and territory.

Third, Morgan assigns all of the "Aryan races" and "Semitic" societies to civilization and all of the "non-Aryan" and "non-Semitic" societies to savagery and barbarism. In addition to family and intelligence, his differentiations of groups is based on his evaluation of the "evidence" of their "inventions and discoveries" in relation to subsistence, government (social and civic institutions), language, religion, architecture, and property.[58] He argues that civilization is characterized by "the establishment of political society" (as opposed to council systems found in savagery and barbarism), literate/written language (as opposed to gestures, signing, and monosyllabic speech found in savagery and barbarism), patrilineal monogamy (as opposed to earlier stages of incest, polygamy, and matrilineality), monotheism (as opposed to polytheism found in savagery and barbarism), single-family dwellings (from the hut and communal homes of savagery and barbarism), and the idea and passion for property and territory, which he maintains is the foundational bases and distinction of civilization from savagery and barbarism.[59]

What these three modalities of progress demonstrate is a particularly sexist, homophobic, and racist correlation of savagery and barbarism with women, nonheterosexual relations, and a lack of intelligence; and the correlation of civilization with men, heterosexual marriage, intelligence, government, property, and territory. These correlations do not mean to disguise the social norms that they advance, nor the judgments that they make about those that do not conform. But what they do intend is to disguise the legal, economic, and social consequences of those norms—to negate or minimize or ignore imperialism for civilization, racism for empiricism, patriarchal sexism for ontological truth. All the while they maintain the idea that what is human can be empirically observed, classified, and measured. All the while they claim that some humans are not, or not enough, human to warrant the recognition, rights, and entitlements of the empire.

Morgan's arguments were readily appropriated within the New England region in which he lived and worked. Claiming the authority of ethnographic observation, Morgan represented himself as offering a means to understand what had become the contradiction "of the day" between the newly founded nation's claims to democracy and the increasing genocide of Native people. Rather than question the nation's claims and actions, following the course of Rafinesque, Squier, and Brinton, Morgan took on the full garb of the empirical scientist to explain them away. Morgan even went so far as to "play the Indian"—to culturally and socially emulate the Native—by establishing the Grand Order of the Iroquois in 1841 for the New York elite.[60] The Grand Order was a literary-historical society focused on the Haudenosaunee Confederacy, a prominent juridic, economic, and cultural association of six Native nations indigenous to New England that included the Seneca, Cayuga, Mohawk, Oneida, Onondaga, and Tuscarora. Men who wanted to join the Grand Order—women were not permitted—had to go through a secret rite of initiation that they called an *"inindianation."* Members learned Haudenosaunee words and phrases, assumed Haudenosaunee names, dressed in Haudenosaunee costume, performed Haudenosaunee rituals, and organized themselves into councils. This "play" empowered them, and Morgan in particular as the Grand Chief, with a virtually unchallenged authority to know and to represent Native culture and its meaning to the United States.[61] Morgan and his Grand Order brothers—and others like them throughout New England and the nation—found an anxiously receptive audience for their expertise on Native people. They gave the region and the nation an especially forgiving explanation for Native "disappearance." As Smith argues, in this context, it is no great surprise that *this* was the science institutionalized in federal military and economic policy.

PART II: IMPERIAL HAUNTS

To haunt does not mean to be present, and it is necessary to introduce haunting into the very construction of a concept. Of every concept, beginning with the concepts of being and time. That is what we would be calling here a hauntology. Ontology opposes it only in a movement of exorcism. Ontology is a conjuration.

—Jacques Derrida, *Specters of Marx*, 161

The imperial logics of modernity's human haunts recognition as recognition functions as the pivot of federal policies regulating the status and rights of

Native peoples. As Derrida suggests in *Specters of Marx*, this haunting is not about presence but the conjuring of an ontology promised. In that promise, federal policies affirm social norms—sexist, homophobic, and racist—that directly attend to the empire's interests, figuring Native peoples as "lost" to the savagery of their nature and failed social organizations, survivors administered as immature "wards" benefiting from federal "guardianship." Nowhere are these logics made more explicit than within the "mandatory criteria" of the "Procedures for Establishing That an American Indian Group Exists as an Indian Tribe" (herein Procedures).[62]

In Continuity and Distinction

In January 1975, the American Indian Policy Review Commission (AIPRC) was established by Senate Joint Resolution 133 to study federal policy, law, and administration concerning "American Indians."[63] In May 1977, the AIPRC issued its final report, offering extensive and rather scathing criticisms of the BIA's administration of Native legal status and rights.

In regards to recognition, the AIPRC criticized the profound effects of termination initiated by House Concurrent Resolution 108 in 1953 as well as the BIA's gross lack of coherent procedures for unrecognized tribes to gain recognition status. On the latter issue, it recommended that the BIA develop procedures for recognition with "valid and consistent" guidelines and criteria applied fairly to all petitioning tribes.[64] It also recommended that adequate funds be provided to unrecognized tribes so that they could prepare the exhaustive documentary evidence required to effectively "argue their cases for recognition."[65] Within months of the report, the BIA published the Procedures, invited public comment, responded, reissued the Procedures, and made final revisions. The Procedures became effective in March 1978. The BIA established the Office of Federal Acknowledgement (OFA), later known as the Branch of Acknowledgement and Research (BAR), to implement the Procedures. The Procedures were revised in 1994, 1997, and 2000 resulting from criticisms of BAR's effectiveness and the financial burdens it placed on petitioning tribes from tribal officials, attorneys, and scholars at regular hearings before the Senate Committee on Indian Affairs.[66] Even with these revisions, criticisms have continued to plague the BAR such as those contained within General Accounting Office (GAO) audits of 2001, 2002, and 2005.[67]

The Procedures detail the process that must be followed for a tribe to be recognized, beginning with a tribe's letter of intent and submission of documentary evidence that it has satisfied the seven "mandatory criteria" for acknowledgement, followed by the evaluation, public comment, and appeal stages. Those groups who can petition for acknowledgement exclude terminated tribes (who must appeal to Congress for reinstatement) and "splinter groups, political factions, communities or groups of any character that have been formed in recent times."[68] The seven "mandatory criteria" that tribes must prove they satisfy to be recognized are summarized by the BIA as follows (emphases added):

> (a) The petitioner has been identified as an American Indian entity *on a substantially continuous* basis since 1900. (b) A predominant portion of the petitioning group comprises a distinct community and has existed as a community *from historical times until the present*. (c) The petitioner has maintained political influence or authority over its members as an autonomous entity *from historical times until the present*. (d) The group must provide a copy of its present governing documents and membership criteria. (e) The petitioner's membership consists of individuals *who descend from a historical Indian tribe or tribes*, which combined and functioned as a single autonomous political entity. (f) The membership of the petitioning group is composed principally of persons who are not members of any acknowledged North American Indian tribe. (g) Neither the petitioner nor its members are the subject of congressional legislation that has expressly terminated or forbidden recognition.[69]

The Procedures explain, "A criterion shall be considered met if the available evidence establishes a reasonable likelihood of the validity of the facts relating to that criterion."[70] This evidence must originate with external sources but "may include one or a combination of the following, as well as other evidence of identification by *other than the petitioner itself or its members*."[71] The externalization of evidence points petitioning tribes to the objective, empirical documents of federal authorities, state and county governments, parishes, churches, "anthropologists, historians, and/or other scholars," newspapers and books, recognized tribes, and Native organizations. All of these various sources are posed, of course, against the "special interests," political biases, and economic ambitions of petitioning tribes.

As I argue in *Native Acts: Law, Recognition, and Cultural Authenticity*, the "mandatory criteria" assume that a tribe petitioning for recognition possesses the qualities that the Procedures identify as characterizing an *existing* "Indian tribe." The "Indian tribe" is not perceived as configured as such within the law or through the processes of petitioning or being recognized.

This implies that the "Indian tribe" and criteria reflect the truths—objectively observable—of what it means to be a tribe existing within the United States. This assumption of truthful (factual) existence depoliticizes not only the law and its regulations but the role of BIA officials; BAR staff; "anthropologists, historians, and/or other scholars"; and Native peoples in recognition (not that these categories of stakeholders are mutually exclusive). Recognition thereby negates the politics of the knowledge and interpretative practices it demands and rearticulates.

The Procedures direct petitioning tribes to read the "mandatory criteria" alongside their definitions to understand the evidence that is expected to prove their tribal existence. For instance, the second criterion and its relevant definition read as follows (emphases in the original): "[Criterion 2] A predominant portion of the petitioning group comprises a distinct *community* and has existed as a *community* from *historical* times until the present."[72] "[Definitions] *Community* means any group of people which can demonstrate that consistent interactions and significant social relationships exist within its membership and that its members are differentiated from and identified as distinct from nonmembers. . . . *Historically, historical* or *history* means dating from first sustained contact with non-Indians."[73] Petitioning tribes must be able to date—by external documentation and expertise—their community distinction "from first sustained contact with non-Indians" to the present. In order to do this, "some combination" of the following must be established: (1) significant rates of marriage occurred within the group or "as may be culturally required" with other "Indian populations"; (2) significant "social relationships" among members; (3) "informal social interaction" among members; (4) "significant" degrees of "shared or cooperative labor or other economic activity" among members; (5) "strong patterns of discrimination or other social distinctions by nonmembers"; (6) "shared sacred or secular ritual activity" involving most of the members; (7) shared "cultural patterns" among a "significant portion" of members that are "different from those of non-Indian populations" with whom the group interacts and as "more than a symbolic identification of the group as Indian" including "language, kinship organization, or religious beliefs and practices"; (8) "the persistence of"; a named, collective Indian identity *continuously* over a period of more than 50 years"; (9) The tribe's "historical *political influence* . . . demonstrating [a] historical community." The second criterion then explains that the criterion will be considered met "at a given point in time" if the evidence submitted demonstrates any one of the following: (1) "more than 50 percent of the members reside in a geographical area exclusively or almost exclusively composed of members of the group," and the balance of the group maintain "consistent interaction with some members of the community"; (2) "at least 50 percent of the marriages in the group are between members of the group"; (3) "at least 50 percent of the group members maintain distinct cultural patterns such as . . . language, kinship organization, or religious beliefs and practices"; (4) "there are distinct community social institutions encompassing most of the members," such as "kinship organizations, formal or informal economic cooperation, or religious organizations."[74] The relevant definitions for the enumeration of "distinction" include:

> *Continuously* or *continuous* means extending from first sustained contact with non-Indians throughout the group's history to the present substantially without interruption. . . . . *Sustained contact* means the period of earliest sustained non-Indian settlement and/or governmental presence in the local area in which the historical tribe or tribes from which the petitioner descends was located historically. . . . *Political influence or authority* means a tribal council, leadership, internal process or other mechanism which the group has used as a means of influencing or controlling the behavior of its members in significant respects, and/or making decisions for the group which substantially affect its members, and/or representing the group in dealing with outsiders in matters of consequence. This process is to be understood in the context of the *history*, culture and social organization of the group.[75]

What the second criterion demonstrates is an imperial logics—a *logos* of the irrelevance of imperialism within history and historical experience, for while there are some allowances for modest gaps and unevenness *in the historical record*, the criterion assumes tribal existence in a "continuity" "from first sustained contact" and "without interruption" to the present. What it means to *exist* as an "Indian tribe," then, is to have made all of the myriad forces of U.S. imperialism irrelevant not only to one's governance, territorial cohesiveness, cultural autonomy, and social interactions but *within the historical record*. Native peoples are situated within an authentic, transportable past that transcends the discursive-material social relations and conditions of domination articulated for them within U.S. imperialism. Historic and current Native struggles over governance, territories, resources, and cultural practices are rendered mute *by the petitioning tribe* in order for them to document that they exist as a tribe in "continuity" and "distinction."

The representational work of recognition instanced by the Procedures is so deeply embedded in modernity's scientific empiricism as an *operationalization* of imperial formation as to be impossible to extrapolate.[76] Imperialism does not need to be present because it is constitutive of the tribe that recognition constructs, located firmly within an ontology and teleology that denies imperialism's relevance. The tribe so constructed does not seek a revolution or reform of imperial social formations but an inhabitance of them. It conjures up the truths of imperialism by documenting an existence void of imperial consequence. Dehumanized, dehistoricized, deculturated—the tribe's *existence* is then recognized.

Following the death of Chief Charles Journeycake in 1895, the Delaware Tribe "began directing its business under the leadership of a business committee. Though it was composed mostly of men from historically leading families, the committee members were approved by the U.S. government. Together, the business committee and the tribe's general council made decisions affecting the Delaware Tribe."[77] In 1977, the Indian Claims Commission (ICC) settled a claim against the United States filed by the Delaware Tribe for violations of its 1854 treaty. The Delaware claimed that the United States had failed to secure a fair price for the lands that they had ceded in Missouri upon their removal to Kansas. The ICC agreed and awarded the tribe $1,199,763.20 in compensation. The funds were to be distributed to the tribe's members who had relocated to Kansas (the Delaware Tribe) and those who relocated to Texas, both from Missouri. The descendants of the "Kansas Delaware"—those who remained in Kansas when the tribe was relocated to Indian Territory—filed a suit for being excluded from the settlement. The District Court ruled in their favor, finding a violation of due process. The Delaware Tribe appealed to the U.S. Supreme Court, which heard the case as *Delaware Tribal Business Committee v. Weeks et al.* in 1977. The Supreme Court reversed the lower court decision because it found that the "Kansas Delaware" had severed their ties to the tribe in 1867 by remaining in Kansas and so had relinquished any rights to share in the collective assets or lands of the tribe.

From the perspective of the Delaware Tribe, what was most important about this decision was that it affirmed their legal status as a federally recognized tribe with the implication that they were independent of the Cherokee Nation.[78] The Court concluded that because the ICC had accepted and rendered a decision on the Delaware Tribe claim, it acknowledged the Delaware as an "Indian tribe." Because Congress managed Delaware lands in Kansas and appropriated funds on behalf of the Delaware Tribe, it too had acknowledged and exercised its "constitutional power" over the Delaware as an "Indian tribe." This finding reversed the Supreme Court rulings in 1894 and 1904. For the Delaware, it was an affirmation that they had never given up their sovereign status.[79] The Cherokee National Council understood the implications of the *Weeks* decision and lobbied directly to the BIA. The result was issued on May 24, 1979, when the BIA sent a memorandum to the Delaware Tribe informing them that all direct relations with the BIA would cease, that they were under the "jurisdictional service authority"[80] of the Cherokee Nation, and that the Cherokee Nation would administer all relations of individual Delaware with the BIA as they would their other citizens. The Delaware Tribe was instructed that they could register as "Cherokee" and participate in Cherokee governance with equal status and rights as "native Cherokee." It would take until 1996 for the Delaware Tribe to successfully appeal the BIA's 1979 decision and be reinstated as a recognized tribe.[81]

In the meantime, the BIA dissuaded the Delaware from petitioning for recognition through BAR because they were not terminated by congressional statute. Without clear guidance from the BIA—really until Ada Deer, the first Native woman to be appointed assistant secretary for Indian Affairs in 1993—the Procedures and its guidelines were all the Delaware had to work with in terms of appealing the BIA's decision. So, they used their limited trust funds to amass documentation on the tribe's history, culture, and politics. This included hiring researchers. When McCutchen presented the Delaware Tribal Council with the Wallam Olum, the council quickly passed a resolution that endorsed it as an authoritative history meeting the criteria for external documentary evidence of the tribe's historical "continuity" and "distinction." When Oestreicher presented the tribe with evidence of the Wallam Olum's fraudulence, the tribe withdrew its endorsement of McCutchen's work and claims about the Wallam Olum.

In Spectrality

> Spectrality does not involve the conviction that ghosts exist or that the past (and maybe even the future they offer to prophesy) is still very much alive and at work, within the living present: all it says, if it can be thought to speak, is that the living present is scarcely as self-sufficient as it claims to be; that we would do well not to count on its density and solidity, which might under exceptional circumstances betray us.
> —Fredric Jameson, "Marx's Purloined Letter," 38

So much of recognition relies on the logics and *logos* of imperialism; on being written out of human history so as to be righted out of the empire's spoils; on being sent to imperial records as evidence of one's existence so as to negate one's cultural histories. In this, as Jameson suggests, the spectrality of recognition is not the ghost—the (false) presence of the past or a prophesy (reading) of the future—that requires, in its kind, an exorcism to purge or an offering to divine. It is, rather, symptomatic of the ontologies and teleologies of modernity. It is entangled in modernity's work at producing and maintaining imperial formations while claiming to embody the best of the modern: democracy, civilization, humanity. It is the spectrality of imperialism.

As Tom Lewis writes in "The Politics of 'Hauntology' in Derrida's *Specters of Marx*," the state of the *specter* is not merely a condition defined by what is not there (as if to represent the real by disembodied negation). It is "the ghostly embodiment of a fear and panic provoked by intimations of an impossible state of being."[82] In recognition's terms, it is the permanence of imperial domination, exploitation, and violence. It is the negation of Native humanity—grief, loss, pain, passion, joy—and the foreclosure of a Native future. And it is all of these things while promising to recognize Natives as equals, as *righted* to self-determination. Is it any wonder that that promise of recognition results in something like the Delaware Tribe's endorsement of the Wallam Olum? Or in its quick retraction of it when it is exposed as a fraud?

A CONCLUSION THAT ISN'T ONE

(In case you are reading this during the wrong season, I tell you that I am sitting on a pile of skunk hides as I write. Perhaps you should join me as you read.)

The Old Man lived in a lodge in the middle of the people's village. He had a beautiful wife and daughter. For reasons no one quite understood he became jealous and brooding. No one could cheer him up or figure out what was wrong, though everyone tried to talk him through it.

One day, a man of the village suggested that, perhaps, the Old Man wanted the rather large tree in front of his lodge pulled up and moved away. So the people, desperate to help, figured it was as good a reason as any and pulled up the tree. But in doing so, they created a large hole where the ground fell through.

The Old Man called his wife and daughter to come out of the lodge and look through the hole. "Come on, Old Woman, let's see what everybody is looking at!" He walked over to the hole with them, and leaned far over to see inside. He stood by and exclaimed, "I have never seen anything like that!" He nudged his wife and daughter to look inside. "I am afraid," said the Old Woman. He nudged her again and said, "You really must take a look. Don't be afraid. I am standing right here." So the Old Woman picked up her daughter and held her tight. She walked over to the hole and leaned far over to look through it. The Old Man grabbed at them and pushed them through the hole. The Old Woman grabbed at a nearby blanket and clump of huckleberries by the roots and soil as they fell through the hole and began to fly down through the clouds to the earth below.

They were flying through the clouds when the Fire Serpent met up with them. "I am sorry that the Old Man tried to kill you. It is me that he is jealous of." He gave her an ear of corn and a beaver. The other spirits watched and decided to hold council. "Who will look out for the Old Woman and her daughter?" After a long discussion, the good one—the Turtle—spoke up and said that she would do it. When the Old Woman and her daughter reached the earth, the Turtle raised her back so that they would have a place to land.

Later, the Old Woman and her daughter wept as she spread the dirt and berries around. The dirt kept getting bigger and bigger until the earth was formed. Then the Old Woman planted the corn and eventually the corn, trees, and grass grew tall. Then the Sun and the Moon and the Stars showed up to keep them company and the Old Woman felt for the first time in a long time that she could stop weeping for herself and her daughter for they were no longer alone.[83]

NOTES

1. Latour, *We Have Never Been Modern*, 10.
2. Latour, *We Have Never Been Modern*, 10.
3. For this chapter I use "self-determination" as used within the Declaration on the Rights of Indigenous Peoples, implying both individual and collective rights to the determination of governance, territorial integrity, and cultural autonomy.
4. King, *The Truth about Stories*.
5. Not all Native nations located in U.S. states or territories seek to be recognized as "Indian tribes" for complex reasons owing in part to U.S. assertions of plenary power over those that are. See Kauanui, "Precarious Positions" and *Hawaiian Blood*.
6. Barker, *Native Acts*. See especially chap. 2, "In Cherokee v. Delaware v. Cherokee," 41–80.
7. It is important to note that neither the Cherokee nor the Delaware are indigenous to those territories that became the state of Oklahoma in 1907 and over which their legal conflicts for governance and territorial rights have been fought.

8. Cherokee Nation v. Journeycake et al. (155 U.S. 196) 1894; Delaware Indians v. Cherokee Nation (193 U.S. 127) 1904.

9. Business Committee of the Delaware Tribe v. Weeks et al. (430 U.S. 73) 1977.

10. Cherokee Nation of Oklahoma v. Delaware Tribe of Indians et al. (389 F.3d 1074, 1077) 2004.

11. Peckham, "Sovereignty Now or Sovereignty Later."

12. The list is published regularly in the Federal Register under the terms of the Federally Recognized Indian Tribe List Act (108 Stat. 4791) of 1994.

13. Rementer, "The Arrival of the Whites."

14. McCutchen, *The Red Record.*

15. Oestreicher, "Unmasking the Walam Olum"; "The Anatomy of the Walam Olum"; "The Tale of a Hoax."

16. See the collection of oral histories by Swann, *Algonquian Spirit,* and Brown and Kohn, *Long Journey Home.*

17. Rafinesque, *The American Nations.*

18. Squier, "Historical and Mythological Traditions of the Algonquians"; Brinton, *The Lenape and Their Legends.*

19. O'Brien, *Firsting and Lasting.*

20. Newman, "The Walam Olum."

21. Why a Delaware record keeper would turn over the tribe's historical record to a non-Delaware person was also never unexplained. Cultural protocol would demand the tablets be given to—at the very least—another clan member if not direct family member.

22. As Jim Rementer writes in "The Arrival of the Whites," "the early Europeans who came to America often concluded that the native languages were less developed than those of the Europeans. . . . What [they] did not realize was that the 'language' [they] had learned was simply a pidgin tongue that had come into use as a trade language between the Lenape and the Dutch, the Swedes, and the English. The words in the pidgin were nearly all Lenape words, the grammar was extremely simplified" (50–51). This recorded language would not have been conducive to communicating complex Lenape histories and cultural perspectives and was the language most frequently recorded in dictionaries produced by missionaries and colonial settlers.

23. Squier's retranslation was reprinted in Beach's edition, *The Indian Miscellany.*

24. Oestreicher "The Tale of a Hoax"; Newman, "The Walam Olum."

25. Quoted in Lofgren, *A Legal-Historical Interpretation of the Plessy Case,* 104–5.

26. Quoted in Lofgren, *A Legal-Historical Interpretation of the Plessy Case,* 104–5.

27. Quoted in Lofgren, *A Legal-Historical Interpretation of the Plessy Case,* 104–5.

28. Brinton, *The Lenape and Their Legends,* 1.

29. Anthony was a Delaware and Anglican missionary in New York; John Kilbuck was a Delaware and Moravian missionary in Alaska; Horatio Hale was a linguist; de Schweinitz was a Moravian bishop; Trumbull was a philologist who worked on translating the Bible into Native languages; Elliott was a literature and language specialist who founded the Modern Language Association; Brown's field is unknown (Brinton, *The Lenape and Their Legends,* 1–2).

30. Brinton, *The Lenape and Their Legends,* 2.

31. Brinton, *The Lenape and Their Legends,* 75.

32. Oestreicher, "Unmasking the Walam Olum"; Newman, "The Walam Olum."

33. Such as represented by Harrington, *Dickon among the Lenape*; Lilly, Voegelin, Weer et al., *Walam Olum, or Red Score*; Weslager, *The Delaware Indians*.
34. Oestreicher, "The Tale of a Hoax," 4, 22.
35. See Dumont's exceptional argument about the theological origins of western science in *The Promise of Poststructuralist Sociology*.
36. Latour, *We Have Never Been Modern*, 10. See Paige Raibmon's powerful description of the "colonial cosmologies" that informed nineteenth-century anthropology and archaeology in *Authentic Indians*.
37. L. Smith, *Archaeological Theory and the Politics of Cultural Heritage*.
38. D. Silva, *Toward a Global Idea of Race*.
39. Cuvier, *The Animal Kingdom Arranged According to Its Organization*, 37.
40. Cuvier, *The Animal Kingdom Arranged According to Its Organization*, 37.
41. Cuvier, *The Animal Kingdom Arranged According to Its Organization*, 37–38; see D. Silva, *Toward a Global Idea of Race*, 106. In *Lectures on the Philosophy of History* (published posthumously in 1837 and 1900), Georg Wilhelm Friedrich Hegel proposed similarly that human consciousness was measurable in social development, such as indicated by concepts of justice and morality, maintaining that slavery, while unjust, would serve as a "phase of education" that would raise the lower races, particularly "the Negro" (see D. Silva, *Toward a Global Idea of Race*, 119–20).
42. Darwin, *On the Origin of Species*.
43. Darwin, *The Descent of Man*, 161.
44. Silva, *Toward a Global Idea of Race*, 109.
45. Darwin, *The Descent of Man*, 156.
46. Darwin, *The Descent of Man*, 172–73; D. Silva, *Toward a Global Idea of Race*, 110.
47. D. Silva, *Toward a Global Idea of Race*, 109–11.
48. Physical evolutionists included Jean-Baptist Lamarck, Alfred Russel Wallace, and Charles Darwin. Other social evolutionists included Edward B. Taylor and Herbert Spencer. See Sujit Sivasundaram's "Race, Empire, and Biology before Darwinism" for the origins of the coproduction of race and science in naturalist theories of evolution. See Rupke's "Darwin's Choice" for a review of other perspectives countering creationism in the latter part of the nineteenth century.
49. Morgan's critics included Franz Boas, whose work represented an uneven move within American anthropology from evolutionism to cultural relativism even while retaining biological determinist arguments about the "primitive mind" and its societies (D. Silva, *Toward a Global Idea of Race*, 131–34, 139–40).
50. In fact Morgan's *Systems of Consanguinity and Affinity of the Human Family* (1868) and *Ancient Society* (1877) are cited as foundational texts within Marxism; both are posted in full on the Marxist Internet Archive. Accessed April 29, 2014. http://www.marxists.org/reference/archive/morgan-lewis/ancient-society.
51. K. Anderson, *Marx on the Margins*, 199.
52. Morgan, *Ancient Society*, 5.
53. According to John O'Meara's *Delaware-English/English-Delaware Dictionary*, "man" (*lúnuw*), "family" (*nxoohóowuw*), and "woman" (*oxkwéew*) have correspondence between the languages, but there are no Delaware words for mankind, human, or race (527, 460, 654).
54. Morgan, *Ancient Society*, 31.
55. Morgan, *Ancient Society*, 31.

56. Morgan, *Ancient Society*, 31.

57. Morgan, *Ancient Society*, 31.

58. Morgan, *Ancient Society*, 5–7, 13.

59. Morgan, *Ancient Society*, 12–13.

60. Bieder, "The Grand Order of the Iroquois."

61. R. Green, "The Tribe Called Wannabee."

62. Procedures for Establishing That an American Indian Group Exists as an Indian Tribe (25 C.F.R. 83) 1978.

63. The AIPRC was established the same year as the Indian Self-Determination and Education Assistance Act (25 U.S.C. 450), which reversed termination policy initiated by House Concurrent Resolution 108 (67 Stat. B122) 1953. It was addressed to American Indian tribes and not Alaska Natives, whose status and rights had been addressed by the Alaska Native Claims Settlement Act (85 Stat. 688) 1971.

64. *American Indian Policy Review Commission Final Report to Congress*, vols. 2 and 3, issued May 17, 1977, 479. Education Resources Information Center. Accessed April 2010. http://www.eric.ed.gov.

65. *American Indian Policy Review Commission*, 479; Quinn, "Federal Acknowledgement of American Indian Tribes"; Miller, *Forgotten Tribes*.

66. The Senate Committee on Indian Affairs become a permanent committee of the U.S. Senate in 1984 and was renamed the Committee on Indian Affairs in 1993.

67. General Accounting Office audits have been called for frequently by antigaming constituencies and elected officials and focus on misinformed concerns that tribes seek recognition status merely to open up lucrative gaming operations, including "Indian Issues: Improvements Needed in Tribal Recognition Process," Report GAO-02-49, November 2, 2001. Accessed April 29, 2014. http://www.gao.gov/assets/600/590102.pdf.

68. Procedures, Part 83.3 Scope.

69. Procedures, Part 83.3 Scope.

70. Procedures, Part 83.6d General Provisions.

71. Procedures, Part 83.6d General Provisions; emphasis added.

72. Procedures, Part 83.7b.

73. Procedures, Part 83.2 Definitions.

74. Procedures, Part 83.7b; emphasis added.

75. Procedures, Part 87.2.

76. Foucault, *Power/Knowledge*.

77. Brown and Kohn, *Long Journey Home*, xxvi.

78. Delaware Tribal Business Committee v. Weeks et al. 1977.

79. Brown and Kohn, *Long Journey Home*; Barker, *Native Acts*.

80. Ahnawake Carroll, "Cherokee Nation Tribal Profile," *Tribal Law Journal* 3, no. 1 (2002/2003). Accessed April 29, 2014. http://tlj.unm.edu/tribal-law-journal/articles/volume_3/carroll/index.php.

81. Brown and Kohn, *Long Journey Home*; Barker, *Native Acts*.

82. Lewis, "The Politics of 'Hauntology' in Derrida's Spectres of Marx," 140.

83. See Bierhorst, "The Delaware Creation Story."

Colonizing Chaco Canyon

Mapping Antiquity in the Territorial Southwest

On August 14, 1849, Lieutenant James H. Simpson of the U.S. Topographical Corps of Engineers was ordered to accompany a punitive expedition into the Navajo borderlands, to "make such a survey of the country as the movements of the troops would permit."[1] This was the first official U.S. mapping of this part of the Southwest after the Mexican Cession and has been recognized by historians as the first sustained window into the region and its people (figure 2.1).[2] Simpson's interest in ancient ruins led him to take side excursions when feasible, twice detaching from the expedition altogether to focus on the objects of antiquity. Most captivating for Simpson was Chaco Canyon, where immense stone ruins of a distant age seemed to be none other than the mythical lost city of the Aztecs. Commenting on more than just the ruins, Simpson remarked that "they discover in the materials of which they are composed, as well as in the grandeur of their design and superiority of their workmanship, a condition of architectural excellence beyond the power of the Indians or New Mexicans of the present day to exhibit."[3]

Chaco Canyon—a complex of monumental stone structures abandoned around eight hundred years ago—is perhaps the most extensively mapped archaeological site in the United States, and also a site valued as a metaphorical "blank spot" on the map, capable of perpetual discovery. It has been variously mapped and imagined as a commodity, a collapsed empire, a cradle of southwestern archaeology, a national park and world heritage site, and an archaeo-astronomical complex. It is also an ancestral center place for two dozen Native American Pueblos and tribes, and the historical homeland of a displaced Navajo community. As such, it remains an important site in which to investigate the ways mapping contributes to the production of contested meanings of the past. At the time the United States claimed the region from Mexico, Navajos were living in dispersed settlements in and around the canyon. Navajos and Pueblo communities continue to have complicated and competing claims to the sacred and historical spaces of Chaco. Although the ruins have remained in indigenous geographies, ceremonialism, and mythical lore over the centuries, the 1849 "discovery" of the ruins reconfigured its meaning in ways that continue to be contested today. These conflicting cartographies of Chaco can be seen as a battle over ownership of the past, a past made manifest as both knowledge and territory.

The ruins are currently within thirty-four thousand acres of Chaco Culture National Historical Park, which manages multiple meanings of place as part of its mission. Maintaining the ruins to evoke the moment of "discovery" serves as the aesthetic of the dominant Chaco imaginary. The park's master plan states, "the primary objective should be to maintain the area, as much as possible, in the condition which existed when first seen by the early explorers. Other signs of man's activities . . . should be hidden."[4] In addition to hiding signs of modernity, however, this management objective elides the history, politics, and cycles of Native removal that went into the making of Chaco. This commitment to a timeless antiquity initiated the forced removal of Navajo families from the park boundaries in the 1930s and 1940s, under the logic of protecting the ruins, and also serves to silence competing claims to a Chacoan present by two dozen culturally affiliated Native communities. In this sense, the colonial mapping of antiquity not only initiates the moment of Chaco's "discovery," when the ruins were forced to stand still, but also continues to make possible, and foreclose, particular claims in the present.

Simpson's cartographic survey picked up where other imperial projects had left off, engaging in the conversation of antiquity and Native races through the new techniques and demands of U.S. military mapping.[5] The particular technologies and field practices of the "cartographic gaze" structured the discovery and interpretation of Chaco, making national history manifest through the creation of "facts on the ground."[6] The survey party's journey of discovery was captured and performed through the traverse map, and the mapping effort helped to fix certain meanings of Chaco that served to silence alternate attachments to place. In Simpson's mapping of the Southwest, notions of antiquity were embedded in the logic of the map, and ideas of nation and civilization were worked through the interpretation of ruins. In this chapter, I trace the particular ways this knowledge was produced through the discovery and mapping of Chaco. My analysis of the map and journal from the Navajo expedition aims to show how both colonial cartographies and representations of ruins were foundational to the ongoing project of settler colonialism and Native American dispossession.

At the time of Simpson's survey, a cartographic imperative accompanied ideas of Manifest Destiny into the uncharted terrain of the Southwest. In this context, mapping functioned as a process, tool, and text of territorialization, helping to incorporate unfamiliar landscapes and peoples into the changing contours of the nation. As historical geographer Brian Harley suggested about the power of cartographic abstraction, "Maps as an impersonal type of knowledge tend to desocialize the territory they represent." Through their implicit claims of representing an objective reality, colonial cartographies obscure the violence of colonial power relations that contribute to the production and deployment of cartographic knowledge.[7] In addition to being historical objects of inquiry, maps reveal the practices, epistemologies, and discourses in which they operate and that they help construct. Rather than increasingly accurate representations of an objective reality, maps are better viewed as constructions of reality that are constituted of, and in turn constitute, a historically specific and contingent constellation of ideas and power relations.[8] Put another way, maps are products of decisions about what to depict and what to leave out; thus, they serve particular social and political interests.[9]

Similar to the ways cartography accompanied westward expansion, the fascination with ruins, and the mapping of territorial and discursive boundaries around antiquity, became a worthy project of Manifest Destiny. In the case of Chaco, just as the map worked to construct a particular vision of material and social landscapes, the interpretation of ruins materialized certain ideas about civilization and drew distinctions between history and prehistory, relegating the latter to observational field science as the best way to understand the distant past. In her study of archaeological practice and settler-colonial state formation in Israel, anthropologist Nadia Abu El-Haj conceives of archaeology as a "historical field science" that attaches history to "facts on the ground" in ways that are then used to legitimate national claims to territory.[10] In a similar way, the U.S. mapping of Chaco created new facts on the ground that linked prehistory to the national story. Discovering, naming, and documenting ruins defined them as resources and areas of scientific and historical interest. The incompleteness of the documentation

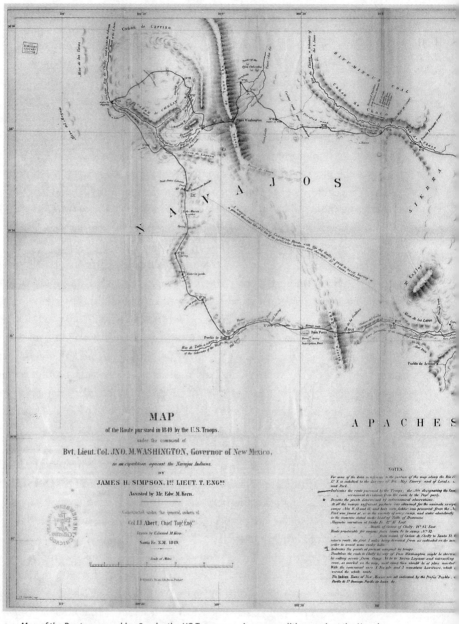

2.1. *Map of the Route pursued in 1849 by the US Troops . . . , in an expedition against the Navajos Indians*, Philadelphia: Duval, 1849, drawn by Edward Kern. Photo Courtesy of the Newberry Library, Chicago. Call # Ayer Map 4F G4321.E1 1849 S5.

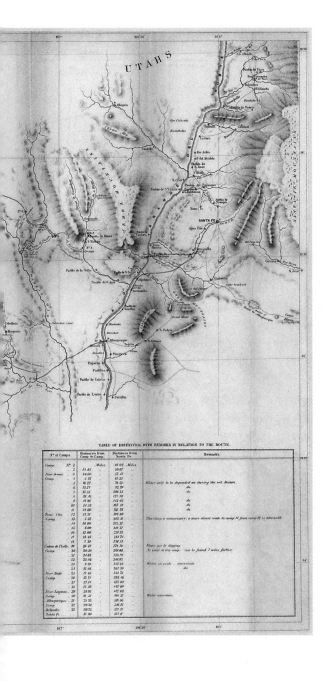

UTAHS

TABLE OF DISTANCES, WITH REMARKS IN RELATION TO THE ROUTE.

N° of Camps.		Distances from Camp to Camp.	Distances from Santa Fe.	Remarks.
Camp	N° 1	. Miles	16.02 Miles	
	2	14.45	30.47	
Near Jemez	3	24.60	57.47	
Camp	4	6.18	63.25	
	5	16.27	79.42	Water only to be depended on during the wet Season.
	6	13.17	92.59	do
	7	12.55	106.54	do
	8	24.45	127.78	do
	9	14.86	142.65	do
	10	24.53	167.18	do
	11	14.60	181.78	
Tune Cha	12	12.51	194.89	
Camp	13	4.32	203.31	This Camp is unnecessary, a more direct route to camp 14 from camp 12 is attainable.
	14	10.00	213.37	
	15	6.00	218.31	
	16	12.00	230.31	
	17	13.43	243.74	
	18	7.39	254.13	
Cañon de Chelly	19	26.43	278.56	Water got by digging
Camp	20	20.30	298.80	No water at this camp can be found 5 miles farther.
	21	24.83	323.91	
	22	23.02	346.93	Water in pools uncertain
	23	8.29	345.22	do
	24	12.06	367.30	
Near Zuñi	25	17.45	384.75	
Camp	26	13.71	398.46	
	27	27.10	425.60	
	28	13.38	437.60	
Near Laguna	29	28.95	472.62	
Camp	30	18.31	490.52	Water uncertain
Albuquerque	31	28.55	519.56	
Camp	32	20.38	540.56	
Bel.Spades	33	30.73	571.21	
Santa Fe		15.80	587.0	

marked them as valuable places to which to return and apply the rigors of historical field science. This construction fashioned territorial claims to particular sites on the ground and contributed to the idea of the Southwest as a living laboratory of prehistory. It also served to separate indigenous histories from the material traces of antiquity.

The military mapping of Chaco combined colonial cartography and the discourse of ruins in ways that created the conditions for, and reinforced the logic of, settler colonialism. Historian Patrick Wolf describes settler colonialism as a particular colonial formation wherein control of territory and reproduction of settler society structures an enduring ideology of "destroying to replace."[11] According to Wolfe, this logic of the elimination of the Native includes programs of assimilation, private property and individualism, and "statistical extermination" through the blood quantum regime. Thus, the logic of settler colonialism extends to all aspects of the settler colonial project that seek to replace the colonized, not merely the areas that are subject to actual settlement. I utilize and extend Wolfe's framework of "the elimination of the Native" to consider the ways in which the logic of settler colonialism is embedded in the colonization of antiquity as a national and scientific space. Antiquity in this sense is taken to mean both the ancient past, or "prehistory" (a term that refers to the time before written records, but also serves to reinforce writing as indicative of a more evolved form of history), and the objects and artifacts in which that prehistory is manifest. In the example of Chaco, the logic of elimination can be seen operating at the territorial level, through the spatial delineation of Native landscapes and artifacts that are subjected to increasing forms of government control, as well as the epistemological level, through scientific claims to the knowledge of the past. Both types of elimination require continual representational removal at various sites, such as cartographic practices and the preservation of ruins.

As a technology of colonialism, cartographic practice materialized ideas of Chaco in the national landscape and constructed it as a space in which to pour multiple desires and impulses of the colonial cultural imagination. While Simpson was constantly aiming to humanize natural landscapes and naturalize social ones, ruins appear to stand in for both without needing much translation. Colonial cartography shaped the ways the past was imagined, for example, by placing monumental architecture at the height of civilization, and nomadism as its regression. Representational erasure through the map also worked to erase the violence of physical and discursive removal from antiquity. Through the Navajo expedition, the interpretation of southwestern landscapes and peoples was worked through discourses of exploration, science, art, and civilization in ways that remade the region into a laboratory of anthropology, and ruins into monuments of a colonial prehistory.

The dominant meaning of the ruins was constituted out of the logic of the map. Geographer Nicholas Blomley describes cartography as a technology of dispossession that both depoliticizes the world into "a series of a priori objects," and also "conceals the process through which it works as an ordering device."[12] Dominant narratives of Chaco also reveal the ways in which the performance of national heritage is part of an ongoing territorialization of indigenous spaces and histories. Mapped as both center and periphery to the national story, Chaco Canyon could be rediscovered and revisited in the footsteps of the first explorers. Preservation practices were thus rationalized, while obscuring their political content as part of a logic of elimination that mapped Native knowledge outside the scientific discourses of antiquity. A critical cartography approach reveals how meanings of Chaco were constituted out of the survey and mapping effort. Through the survey, representations of the ruins were affixed to the map through the *process* of government-sponsored field-based practice, the *tool* of technological science, and the *text* of representational discourse. This multidimensionality of cartographic production allows access to different, albeit interrelated, registers of the settler colonial project, where ruins become a place to form attachments that reproduce the logic of elimination.

In order to understand the ways in which colonial mapping of antiquity served to establish and reinforce the logic of settler colonialism, I begin by examining the role of the traverse map in the interpretation of the Chaco ruins. Then I consider how cartographic practices also mapped the social landscape through the construction of national and nomadic spaces. I follow with a discussion that highlights the tensions between the cartographic process and its product, as well its potential incommensurability with indigenous geographies, both of which work to unsettle the implied stability of the map. I conclude by way of the present and consider how cartographies of antiquity become the arena for both constituting dominant meanings of Chaco, and contesting the ongoing colonization of Native spaces and histories.

MAKING RUINS THROUGH THE TRAVERSE MAP

Although Simpson frames this fascination with southwestern antiquity as a side excursion to the main task of documenting the movements of the military expedition, it fits squarely with his larger task of making natural and human landscapes legible to a new audience. Unlike Simpson's wagon road maps, the Navajo Expedition Journal found a broad readership in its day, including various military, government, and public interests. Shortly after the completion of the expedition, the mapmakers scrambled to complete the report and send it to Washington, following a new Senate resolution from June 8, 1850, which called for "copies of the journals of all reconnaissances returned to the Topographical Bureau by officers of the United States making such surveys within the last year . . . together with copies of the maps and sketches belonging to said reconnaissances."[13] Congress printed three thousand copies of the journal in 1850. At the time, it was common for such military reports to be consumed alongside travel literature by East Coast publics. Reprinted by Lippincott, Grambo and Company in 1852 for a popular audience, the journal was specifically addressed to scientists, armchair explorers, and "lovers of nature."[14] However, the ethnographic flavor of the journal, complete with seventy-five chromolithograph prints of landscapes and Indians, also served to obscure the goal of the expedition as a punitive incursion against the Navajo for not abiding by partial treaties.

In the aftermath of victory in the U.S.-Mexico War, the 1849 U.S. expedition against the Navajo aimed to assert its newfound sovereignty over the region, amassing about four hundred men, including Pueblo and Mexican mounted militias. The map and associated journal produced during the expedition are not silent about the reasons for entering Navajo country: the map charts a bold red line through new terrain, identifies potential resources, and claims the landscape. The expedition circled the Navajo stronghold of Cañon de Chelly—referred to as the *ultima thule* of the expedition—with the goal of signing a comprehensive treaty with the tribe.[15] Along the way, one of the troops killed Navajo Chief Narbona, viewed by the United States as the head chief of the Navajos. One of the stipulations of the new treaty claimed the right of the United States to have their "boundaries fixed and marked, so as to prevent any misunderstanding on this point between them and their neighbors."[16] Thus the map, like the treaty, can be seen as laying the groundwork for future boundary making.[17]

The map from the Navajo expedition is partial and incomplete, leaving large spaces on the map blank. This representation emerges from the techniques of traverse mapping and is similar to other soldier-engineer surveys of the Southwest under the direction of the U.S. Corps of Topographical Engineers.[18] These linear, west-trending surveys sliced up the "empty spaces" of the Southwest, gathering military intelligence and creating snapshots of the people and places now part of the expanding national landscape. The partial view traced by the traverse survey implied the need of future surveys to add to the growing body of knowledge of the Southwest. Unlike other U.S. traverse maps that marked east-west passages, however, the map from the Navajo expedition illuminated the movement of troops to and from Santa Fe in a large circle. This representation created a virtual boundary that defined the reach of U.S. knowledge and also delineated the unruly extent of their new seminomadic enemy.

Simpson's map, more so than those from other western expeditions, resisted the inclusion of data from other sources. Thus, all that appeared on the map was the extent of the cartographer's vision, as aided by an array of scientific instruments. While this partial view revealed the limits of geographical knowledge, it also underscored the increased truth and accuracy of the observational approach. Simpson is explicit about the importance of firsthand knowledge and is careful to point out when he was not the primary observer or was presenting uncertain data. For example, he labels an uncertain wagon route as being "said to exist, having a general direction like this, but of its particular location and character US knows nothing."[19] On the map, he distinguishes between camps plotted by astronomical observation, and those for which he was unable to secure measurements. This distinguishing of secondhand knowledge works to increase the validity of truth claims of his observational knowledge and narrative.

The mapping effort began a story of Chaco based on the quest for observable truths—a lost city whose treasure was knowledge and not gold.[20] Marking ruins alongside other material resources, the cartographic process brought scientific logic to the romance of ruins. The measurements, descriptions, and drawings of the survey materialized the myth of a lost city in the abandoned stone buildings and their representation. Nineteen color plates of the Chaco ruins were included in the journal, including five ground plans, four landscape scenes, two room interiors, sketches of pottery sherds and petroglyphs, and one artistic reconstruction of Hungo Pavi that revived the ruin, peopling it with a lost race. In addition to fixing places and names to the map, the techniques of traverse mapping captured the primacy of observational knowledge and the journey of discovery in ways that developed particular colonial claims to the past.

Pueblo Pintado, located approximately fifteen miles east of the main entrance to the canyon, was the first major ruin the survey party encountered (figure 2.2). Simpson describes seeing the "conspicuous ruin" from afar, shortly after crossing the Continental Divide and upon reaching the Rio Chaco. He reveals in his journal the process of naming the ruin by choosing

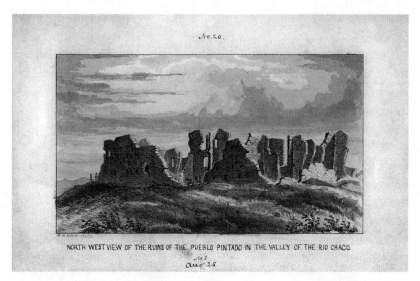

NORTH WEST VIEW OF THE RUINS OF THE PUEBLO PINTADO IN THE VALLEY OF THE RIO CHACO.

2.2. "Northwest View of the Ruins of the Pueblo Pintado in the Valley of the Rio Chaco," drawn by Richard Kern, and included as a plate in the Navajo Expedition Journal. ANSP Library and Archives Collection Number 146.020. © Academy of Natural Sciences.

from among the names offered by various Indians and Mexicans in their charge: "[The ruin was] called, according to some of the Pueblo Indians with us, *Pueblo de Montezuma*; according to the Mexicans, *Pueblo Colorado*. Hosta [a Jemez Pueblo chief] calls it *Pueblo de Ratones*; Sandoval, the friendly Navajo chief with us, *Pueblo Grande*; and Carravahal, our Mexican guide, who probably knows more about it than anyone else, *Pueblo Pintado*."[21]

Exactly why Carravahal was afforded more authority than the other guides is not clear. What is known, however, is that Simpson chose Carravahal to accompany him on the extended excursion through Chaco Canyon the following day, and that he provided names for all of the major ruins—effectively filtering out the added complexity of multiple place-names. Affixing Carravahal's names to the ruins through the map constructs a perceived stability of place-names, silencing alternate attachments to places and stories about the past. Thus, even to this day, the map continues to work in a process of territorialization, reaffirming one history over the rest.

Simpson remarked on nearly two dozen ruins along the expedition, ten of which made up the complex he associated with Chaco Canyon. After setting up camp at a water hole roughly one mile from Pueblo Pintado, Simpson and the two artist-cartographers under his charge, Edward and Richard Kern, were anxious to explore and document the ruin, remarking that "it more than answered their expectations."[22] They proceeded to record it in great detail—measuring and characterizing the fifty-five rooms, noting the thickness of walls, the number of stories, the size and position of openings, and the construction of the wooden roofs, courtyards, and kivas. The Kerns sketched pottery sherds, Indian "hieroglyphics," and landscape scenes. An emphasis on order reflected an aesthetic of science and art where beauty was often found in symmetry and repetition, while at the same time retaining elements of the Romantic sublime. The watercolor of Pintado captures the sublime: windswept grasses and moody skies frame the towering ruin in a jumble of light and shadow, while two small explorers are dwarfed at the base of one of the walls. On the other hand, the masonry is presented as familiar brickwork in the mode of a neoclassical architectural drawing, and the ground plans emphasize regularity of room shapes and sizes.

The cartographers returned to Pueblo Pintado the next morning, stating that "we would gladly, had time permitted, have remained longer to dig among the rubbish of the past; but the troops having already got some miles in advance of us, we were reluctantly obliged to quit."[23] Upon learning that Chaco Canyon contained numerous large ruins like Pueblo Pintado, Simpson obtained permission to detach from the troops entirely the following day to explore and document the stone city, while Edward Kern remained with the regiment to record the official route.

The traverse map embodied not only the accumulation of observational knowledge, but also the journey of the exploration, and movement over new terrain. Notes on available fodder, campsites, alternate routes, and productive lands were linked to spots on the map through the journal and assumed a repeatability of the route by future military engagements, potential settlers, and armchair travelers. The table included on the map emphasized this movement by listing the progression of camps with distances from each other and from Santa Fe, including remarks about the availability of water. It is in this context of journey and repeatability that Simpson relates the discovery of Chaco. The small exploratory party's movement through the canyon is clearly captured on the map. Their detachment from the main column of troops is depicted as a dashed line that makes its way through the canyon, ruin by ruin. The major ruins are individually marked and numbered on the map in the order they were discovered, guiding the reader of the map to visually follow the campaign westward. This detail, and the fact that the camps are similarly numbered in progression, suggests a deliberate presentation of movement through the ruins, attaching the ruins to their process of discovery and fixing them in the moment of encounter. In addition, this

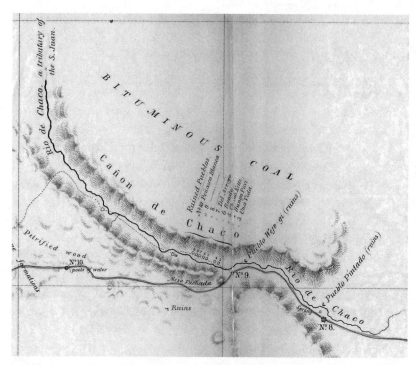

2.3. Detail of *Map of the Route pursued in 1849*, showing the Chaco Canyon ruins. Photo Courtesy of the Newberry Library, Chicago. Call # Ayer Map 4F G4321.E1 1849 S5.

approach marks Chaco as a region, as opposed to a mere point on a map, defined by named topographic features including Cañon de Chaco, Rio de Chaco, and Mesa Fechada (Fajada Butte) (figure 2.3).

Perhaps the most interesting aspect of Simpson's first impression of the ruins is his aesthetic response to the masonry, which then gets translated into a marker of civilization. Simpson's descriptions of Pueblo Pintado clearly mark the site as an important resource in the burgeoning science of man: "it discovers in the masonry a combination of science and art which can only be referred to a higher stage of civilization and refinement than is discoverable in the works of Mexicans or Pueblos of the present day. Indeed, so beautifully diminutive and true are the details of the structure as to cause it, at a little distance, to have all the appearance of a magnificent piece of mosaic work."[24]

Simpson's identification of the marriage of science and art in the stone-work links his cultural aesthetics with this past civilization and contrasts it with that of the Pueblos and Mexicans, who mainly used adobe building technology. His observation that sandstone is a material entirely unknown in the architecture of New Mexico reveals the limits of his knowledge; but, more importantly, it shows how the definition of the region is constructed as the extent of this limited knowledge. Simpson's claim that the material culture of the ruin "can only be referred to a higher stage of civilization and refinement" derives from the inherent truth claims associated with his powers of observation.

Notably missing from Simpson's first impression of Pintado is mention of the Navajos in the conversation of civilization. Later in the journal, after Simpson sees what he calls the "huts" of the Navajos along the expedition, he compares the stability and workmanship of the Chaco ruins with Navajo hogans.[25] He discusses the possibility—first raised by Santa Fe trader Josiah Gregg in the *Commerce of the Prairies*—that the Navajos were part of the civilization of Chaco. This suggestion aimed to resolve the Navajo's semi-sedentary settlement patterns and "primitive" architecture with their exquisite blanket-making technology, which seemed to Simpson to derive from a higher stage of civilization. Simpson develops a few scenarios of how the Navajos could have "regressed" to their current stage, including moral punishment, coming from earlier "stock," or readapting to an increasingly dry climate. Writing before Darwin's *Origin of the Species* and the subsequent turn in ethnology to describe civilization as a trajectory from barbarism to savagery to civilization, Simpson exhibits the seemingly contradictory tendencies of assuming this type of teleological rhetoric of civilization and aiming to explain it away.

Simpson is most interested in discerning the origins of the "lost race" that once inhabited the ruins. In the journal, Simpson engages in a lengthy rumination on the possible origins and associations of Chaco, citing an array of well-known and obscure cartographers, historians, and explorers.[26] Relying heavily on Alexander von Humboldt's approximate location of Aztlan,[27] as well as comparisons to other descriptions of ruins such as Casas Grandes, Simpson deduces that Chaco is most likely Montezuma's lost city of the Aztecs prior to their journey south. While Simpson's embrace of the Montezuma myth was common in the Romantic milieu of his time, his ability to materialize the fabled lost city in a physical place is what begins the newly imagined space of Chaco.

In addition to fixing the myth within the space of the ruin, the mapping effort fixed the ruin within a new geography of antiquity. Placing his discussion of Chaco in the context of North American historians and cartographers, Simpson delineated the discourse of antiquities of his time. This linked the spatial knowledge of territory with the temporal dimension of history. Thus, it is not Simpson's assertion that the site was most likely of Aztec origin that is most important here, but the fact that he draws boundaries around the ways the knowledge of history is produced and legitimized. In this way, competing narratives around Chaco's origins are acceptable, but only within the domain of the prescribed discourse, which excludes other ways of knowing the past. So, when fellow cartographer James W. Abert suggested that ancestors of Pueblo people built the ruins, it still served to enact a separation from indigenous claims to place because the discussion took place in the realm of historical discourse and scientific observation—or prescribed notions of time and space. Thus, Simpson's observations at Chaco sketched the contours of the ways in which southwestern antiquity was to be framed and debated.

Through his privileging of cartographic knowledge and monumental architecture, Simpson also linked his own expedition with past colonial conquests that rose and fell in the Southwest, namely Coronado's search for the Northern Mystery, and what he believed to be the Aztec's prehistoric control of the region.[28] Through the cultural and political work of the surveys, the United States claimed its place in this progressive lineage of conquest, following the Aztec empire and Spanish colonialism. This discourse effectively mapped Chaco as outside of local historical and physical realms. It also exposed the potential incommensurabilities between colonial and indigenous geographies and ways of knowing space and history. In the journal, Simpson provided a glimpse into another way of knowing Chaco, linked to migration stories and movement around a center:

> Sandoval, a very intelligent Navajo chief, also says they were built by Montezuma; but further states that the Navajos and all the other Indians were once but one people, and lived in the vicinity of the Silver mountain; that this mountain is about one hundred miles north of the Chaco ruins; that the Pueblo Indians separated from them, (the Navajos,) and built towns on the Rio Grande and its tributaries; but that "their house continues to be the hut made of bushes." Nothing more satisfactory than this have I been able to get from either Indians or Mexicans.[29]

Migration stories like this one cease to appear in later records of Chaco. Simpson's inclusion of the migration story is in effect its capture: the Cartesian grid of Simpson's reasoning corrals the story, labels it unsatisfactory, and resigns the true origin of Chaco to the realm of mystery, to be probed by other, that is, scientific and literary-historical, means. Simpson's focus on the origin of a lost race made him unable to see how his story performed an erasure of Sandoval's. He effectively forecloses the ability of such unsatisfactory or ambiguous tales to challenge his logic of antiquity. It is this effect of cartographic logic that makes it impossible to know Sandoval through the journal or the map. What it does reveal are the fissures in the totalizing grid of the colonial logic, where alternate conceptions of space and time do not fit neatly within its structure.

This totalizing logic propelled the mission of the mapping effort. Although the map did not claim a comprehensive view of landscape, the accompanying journal integrated many forms of knowledge that suggested an exhaustive reconnaissance of the route. In the time prior to specialist surveys, Simpson also functioned as the expedition's geologist, hydrologist, botanist, and ethnographer, while the Kern brothers created illustrations of landscapes and Indians, and made collections for East Coast patrons. In her analysis of Napoleon's *Description de l'Egypt*, produced after the French survey of their territorial conquests in Egypt, Anna Godlewska emphasizes that maps, images, and texts worked together ideologically to reconstruct an "eternal and immutable" ancient Egypt that replaced Egypt itself.[30] In Simpson's mapping, similar representational practices carved out a prehistory of the Southwest that was framed by a settler-colonial rationality. Along the way, Simpson marked resources important to this logic: settlements, minerals, water holes, and *ruins*. This constellation of notable resources pinned settler-colonial desires to the map, where they became "facts on the ground," waiting for eventual revisiting. In this context, ruins became a particularly potent resource, an arena in which to create and re-create attachments to nation and region.

NATIONAL AND NOMADIC LANDSCAPES

By carving out a particular view of the little known Navajoland, the map and journal helped create and define notions of the nation and the Southwest. These entities were created through historical processes that inhere in social landscapes as opposed to merely physiographic ones. However, as discursive constructs attached to geographical regions, distinctions exist between the ways in which these communities were spatialized and constituted. The Southwest at this time was imagined as a peripheral appendage to the body of the nation, stitched to the national body through traverse surveys and wagon roads that linked the area to predominantly East Coast audiences. The small population of U.S. newcomers in Santa Fe at the time of the 1849 expedition was predominantly military and overwhelmingly male. This made the process of imagining the Southwest through print media a distinctly outsider affair, at least until more significant numbers of people started settling in the region after the coming of the railroad in 1880. The same area that lies "southwest" of U.S. centers of power was previously conceived of as the "northern mystery" or "northern frontier" by Spanish/Mexican geographies, and concurrently as the "center" to many indigenous groups, who possessed varying spatial and temporal boundaries of belonging within and beyond this constructed region. Through the work and authority of the military surveys, Navajoland was refashioned from an imperial borderland to a part of the national landscape of the Southwest, and the Navajo people as a nation within a nation. These conflicting geographies underscore the blurred boundaries of discursive constructions of nation, empire, and region, as well as the concept of mapping itself.

In the Southwest, compounded colonialisms created a complexity and ambiguity around notions of difference that the new regime aimed to sort out.[31] Affixing places to the map was one thing, but making legible the diverse social landscape was often another. The practice of canvassing the landscape coupled with the prioritization of vision eventually led to the elaboration of surveillance technologies that extended from physical to social environments. It was amid the nomadic landscapes of the Navajoland that the material manifestations of ruins asserted themselves in the cartographic imagination as important and timeless islands of interest. In Simpson's glimpse of Navajoland, Romantic representations of a burgeoning national iconography aimed to discursively discipline the perceived wildness of unknown peoples and landscapes. For example, the journal's illustrations reshape sandstone outcrops into the Washington capital, the face of William Penn, Egyptian pyramids, and Greek temples, which made manifest the impulse for a national history through overt symbolism and neoclassical architecture. This type of nationalistic imagery proliferated in the first half of the nineteenth century in painting and literature, as America's natural wonders were molded into icons of antiquity and cultural heritage that was deemed lacking in the young nation.[32] In this context, the nomadism of the Navajo posed a unique threat to the settler nation.

A poignant example of remaking nature through nationalist architecture is Simpson's description of the never-before-seen Navajo stronghold of Cañon de Chelly, fabled to contain an impenetrable fort. The Navajo expedition claimed to be the first outside group to penetrate the canyon and report that the fortification was a natural maze of towering sandstone walls. Simpson described the red sandstone cliffs as "magnificent in their proportions . . . [with the] precision of horizontal joints as can be seen in the custom-house of New York."[33] The building to which Simpson referred was a grand neoclassical structure completed in 1842 by Town and Davis, an architectural firm known for their development of the Greek Revival as the new "national style."[34] This comparison served to nationalize the natural landscape. It also had the effect of imagining the feared Navajo stronghold as a port of entry to a neighboring nation, bringing the imposing canyon down to human size, and obscuring the context of the expedition as an act of domination. Indeed the word "nation" was used liberally throughout the journal in reference to the Navajos. The extent of the U.S. nation, on the other hand, was conjured through national imagery of patriotic places and persons, and specific references to the United States as a political entity.

Representations of Navajos in the map and the journal are a main tension between the two documents: Navajo presence is effectively erased from the map, while in the journal Navajos became one of its main subjects. In the map, Simpson constructed his version of a nomadic landscape. He did not define the Navajo region with boundaries but included a sweeping label for Navajos, Utes, and Apaches that surrounded the settled regions of the Rio Grande. Mexican towns and Native American Pueblos were depicted with a symbol for more permanent settlements. In contrast, no Navajo settlements were called out on the map, despite Simpson's mention of passing Navajo camps and hogans along the route. Cornfields, on the other hand, were frequently depicted—most likely because they provided fodder and food for the troops at multiple camps. From these agricultural plots, one can infer Navajo homesites in these areas, even as discussions of Navajo village life were omitted (figure 2.4). Instead of settlements, Simpson highlighted a number of Navajo trails on the map, some of which made up portions of the official route, and others that trailed off into the blank spots of the map. The inability to observe Navajos en route, to fix them socially and physically, served to separate them from the landscape and anticipated the decades of wars and scorched-earth policy that culminated in the Long Walk of 1864.[35] This positioning also enabled the separation of the Navajos from antiquity, creating a space for ideas of Chaco as separate from the people who live in the area.

While a settled Navajo presence was erased from the map, the journal attempted, unsuccessfully, to settle on a description of Navajo as a people. On the frontispiece of the reprinted journal is an illustration of a Navajo warrior

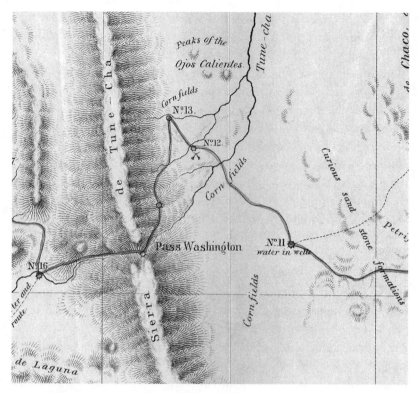

2.4. Detail of *Map of the Route pursued in 1849*, showing cornfields and the site of Chief Narbona's death (the only symbol without accompanying identification on the map). Photo Courtesy of the Newberry Library, Chicago. Call # Ayer Map 4F G4321.E1 1849 S5.

whose label "Navajo Costume" set the stage for depictions of Indians in the grand pageant of the frontier. Portraits of Navajos were only of "important men," such as Chief Narbona, Chief Martinez, and Chief of the San Juan Navajos, mirroring the U.S. policy of consulting only with headmen (figure 2.5). The depictions and drawings of Navajos naturalized them as almost white. Often Simpson described Navajos as having Anglo features, or looking white except for a slightly darker complexion. At Cañon de Chelly, one Navajo was likened in appearance to George Washington, while Navajo Chief Martinez was described as a having the look and air of a Jacobin.

The social and racial ambiguity around representations of Navajos belies the inability of the tools and text of the mapping effort to adequately fix them in the colonial gaze. This was particularly true in ongoing attempts to distinguish between friendly and hostile Navajos during the expedition. While dependent on Navajo guides for knowledge of the landscape and translation,

2.5. *Frontispiece:* "Navajo Costume." ANSP Library and Archives Collection Number 146.052. © Academy of Natural Sciences.

NAVAJO COSTUME.

the regiment was also always on alert for potential Navajo ambush. There was a constant sense of unseen Navajos circling the conspicuous movement of the expedition. Once the military began destroying Navajo cornfields, this threat became more palpable and resulted in instances where soldiers accidently fired on their own troops. Yet Navajos were also depicted as picturesque figures in the landscape in multiple drawings, and individuals were described as intelligent and friendly. This tension is best expressed within the same figure of their sometimes trusted, sometimes sinister, Navajo guide, Antonio Cebolla Sandoval. Described as "a very intelligent Navajo chief" and trusted guide, he was also repeatedly suspected of plotting ambush. Simpson's inability to observe Navajos en route led to his statement that "these people evidently gave signs of being tricky and unreliable, and probably never will be chastened into perfect subjection *until troops are stationed immediately among them.*"[36] This conclusion anticipates future projects of "pacification."

But the journal also provides glimpses of how Navajos were able to navigate the rapidly changing political and social environments after the U.S.-Mexico War. On one level, this can be seen through individual and eclectic patterns of dress that incorporated Spanish conquistador feathered helmets and lances, as well as traditional dress and elements of U.S. military uniforms. On a more overtly political level, what Simpson interpreted as sneaky and unreliable actions on the part of some Navajos also could be read as intentional maneuvering. For example, Sandoval was the main translator for the expedition and in part responsible for determining the course of the reconnaissance. A rich headman and accomplished interlocutor between the Navajo and Spanish, he was adept at moving through different cultural worlds. While he worked for Navajo-Spanish peace prior to U.S. involvement, he also conducted many raids against his own people and was an often-distrusted figure to his fellow Navajos.[37] In another example, knowing that the United States had put itself in the role of protector and peacekeeper in the volatile Southwest, Navajos spread rumors of Ute attacks at Zuni Pueblo in order to get the troops to leave Cañon de Chelly in haste.

Perhaps the most lasting memory of the expedition for Navajos was the killing of Chief Narbona in what was recounted as an accidental skirmish over a horse. Unlike the more complicated figure of Sandoval, Narbona is remembered for his lifelong work toward a lasting peace. Richard Kern described him as "the head chief of the Nation, and a wise man and great warrior. His frame was immense—I should think his height near 6 feet 6 inches. He was near 90 years old when killed."[38] In the journal, Simpson called him alternately "one of their greatest warriors" and the "scourge of the Mexicans."[39] Although the journal recounted the killing of Chief Narbona, it left out the detail that he was also scalped. After the incident, Richard Kern lamented not collecting Narbona's skull to send to his friend and patron, the renowned craniologist Dr. Samuel George Morton, to help him develop his theories on Native American races. "I very much regret," Kern wrote to Morton the following year, "that I had not procured Narbona's cranium, as I think he had the finest head I ever saw on an Indian."[40]

As historian William Goetzmann remarked of this time period in *Exploration and Empire*, "it was a rare week which passed without Dr. Morton's receiving at least one skull from a party of Western explorers."[41] Later on the Navajo expedition, Kern was able to make up for his omission of collecting Narbona's head when he came across another dead Navajo man. Simpson did not reveal Kern's collection of the skull in the journal, but he noted in passing that they came across a dead Navajo man on the way to Zuni Pueblo, and that the Zunis had killed a "Navajo prisoner . . . by direction of a California émigré."[42] In his letter to Morton, Kern added that the Zunis killed him as punishment for stealing from the Anglos. In this very visceral sense, cartographic surveys of the West helped build the scientific foundations of racial categorization and racist ideology. Navajo bodies became another specimen for collection and analysis in East Coast institutions, underscoring the violence of drawing the contours of difference.

UNSETTLING COLONIAL CARTOGRAPHIES

The map and journal from the Navajo expedition reveal the technologies and ideologies that enabled the settler-colonial expansion of the United States, and the physical and discursive delineation of the Southwest as a U.S. region. Couched in the language and logic of the map, this "window" into the area was carved out of colonial interactions with Native knowledges and spatialities. But the map and journal are saturated with the conflicting presence and absence of Native realities in a way that hints at the potential incommensurabilities between colonial and Native relationships to space and place, while at the same time obscuring alternate geographies from view. Given the totalizing quality of the map, or what Mary Louise Pratt calls a "planetary consciousness" that sets the limits of the known and unknown worlds, is it possible to unsettle colonial cartographies in a way that decolonizes spatial knowledges?[43]

As historian Matthew Edney has pointed out, cartographic technologies aimed to decrease the "gap" between material reality and its representation through increased accuracy.[44] But while the technologies of mapping claimed to enlighten the blank spaces of the globe, their grasp on reality was constantly threatened by the contingencies of mapping practice. Factors such as the weather, instrument failure, and alternative place-names always threatened the perceived stability of the map. At the most basic visual level, the dominating and teleological progress of the line on the map representing troop movement attempts to order the underlying instability of the expedition. In particular, the map obscures how the movements and survival of the U.S. military were utterly dependent on Native American and Mexican guides, translators, scouts, and militia. Often, the troops did not follow a single line; Pueblo and Mexican militias were incorporated en route; many people deserted; scouts were continuously moving forward and back, and scoping alternate routes; and one regiment was deployed to Abiquiu, where Utes were said to be concentrating in large numbers.[45] Also, the constant threat of Navajo ambush caused guards to mistakenly fire on their own troops multiple times. In this way, the map works to "smooth out" the day-to-day struggles of the expedition, including movement over the landscape and the multiple encounters and knowledges that both enabled and constrained its course.[46]

In a similar way, the map aims to constrain and rename Native realities by attempting to fix Native spaces in a physical and metaphorical sense. The map and journal reveal tensions between colonial and Native conceptions of space that suggest Native geographies may be incommensurable with the concept of mapping itself. However, many scholars have used the concept of indigenous mapping in order to challenge the epistemologies of the colonial map. Mishuana Goeman uses the concept of mapping both spatially and metaphorically to show how Native women are remapping settler geographies through poetry and prose that "move toward geographies that do not limit, contain, or fix the various scales of space from the body to nation in ways that limits definitions of self and community staked out as property."[47] Goeman forwards Native spatialities that chart "intricate mobilities" and other transects of indigeneity that cut across the fixed quality of colonial spatiality.[48] Similarly, Jodi Byrd argues that foregrounding the originary indigeneity of the New World serves as a potent critique of the ways U.S. colonialism continues to replicate itself through the "elisions, erasures, enjambments, and repetitions of Indianness."[49] According to Byrd, Native histories and epistemologies are the place from which to critique the foundations of an expanding U.S. empire, and provide the ability to recognize the "stakes in decolonial restorative justice tied to land, life, and grievability."[50]

In the realm of colonial cartography, some scholars have considered the hidden indigenous knowledge inherent in colonial maps, which may provide a starting point from which to destabilize the colonial grip on realities linked to land and life.[51] In these contexts, Edney and others have argued that indigenous knowledge gets incorporated and "smoothed out" in maps, while indigenous presence and the representational and real violence of removal gets erased from the record.[52] In her analysis of Prussian naturalist Alexander von Humboldt's scientific mapping of the Americas, Pratt suggests that Humboldt's abstracted geographies of the New World replaced indigenous people with a primordial Nature. She shows how the discourse of Nature remapped the Americas, producing a particular identity of the New World. Despite indigenous erasure, Pratt argues that mapping the "contact zone" produced "transculturated images" infused with indigenous presence.[53] Drawing on Pratt's work, geographer John Pickles forwards the "hetereoglossic" nature of all mapping, where the spaces of transcultural mappings are "derived from and saturated with local knowledges and imagery, reflecting the heteroglossic not monolithic structure of colonial space."[54] He emphasizes the ways maps work to produce realities from the uneven terrain of colonial relations. This approach highlights how colonial realities are produced through historically contingent interactions with Native histories, cultures, and places, which are captured and distorted in the map.

While contact zones and heteroglossic spaces can certainly be inferred from reading colonial maps, this approach tends to elide the violence of mapping and alternate ways of conceiving of time and space. While it is useful for reading colonial maps in ways that reveal the cracks in the façade of planetary consciousness, it also has the potential of subsuming Native geographies within the dominant framework of Western map production. Native peoples of the Southwest engaged in various ways of relating to space and place that reveal potential incommensurabilities with the conceptual form of the colonial map. For example, Native spatiality charted through migration stories, ceremonialism, and pilgrimage rarely emerges through colonial cartographic practices.[55] While knowledge of the terrain, historical routes, and place-names may be translated through the heteroglossic spaces of the map, the overlapping dimensions of alternate geographies seem to exist beyond the logic of the colonial map. As Goeman argues, it is not simply that Native intricate mobilities do not fit within the colonial paradigm, it's that they "operate as transects through spatial relations."[56]

Goeman's metaphorical approach to mapping, highlighting affective and poetic transects, remains attentive to decolonizing dominant constructions of space that constrain material realities. Such an approach to mapping has the potential of destabilizing the concept of mapping as a colonial epistemology. Many scholars emphasize how cognitive geographies enact a spatial ordering that can be described as mapping. These include place memories, ceremonialism, and everyday experiences that create lived spatial patterns that diverge from the concept of the map as product. Although coming from very different academic traditions, some recent considerations of Native spatiality within the area circumscribed by Simpson's map enact alternate geographies that use the concept of mapping as metaphor to varying degrees.

Writing about the differences between government housing and Native spaces on the reservation, Santa Clara architect Rina Swetzell depicts Pueblo cosmology in spatial form as an earth bowl and sky basket that is repeated at the scale of the pueblo, the interior holy sites, and the sacred mountains.[57] Represented by the *sipapu* at the center of the plaza, the center place remains the same at all scales balancing the flow of life in all directions, and is thus fundamentally resistant to notions of boundary making. Interpreting the Navajo Iikááh ceremony at Chaco Canyon, a group of scholars described the practice as a form of "Chaco sacred semantics" that map physical and sacred geographies at Casa Rinconada, or the great kiva.[58] The ceremony is conducted through the ritual of sand painting on the floor of the kiva, created at a particular moment in time that unites celestial alignments with the architecture of the great kiva and stories of creation. Additionally, Navajo weaving can serve multiple purposes as an epistemological space, including ceremony, recording history, and charting landscapes.[59] Weavings from the Long Walk period, for example, often relate the mythical journey of the Monster Twins with the period of exile by charting journeys through physical landscapes in symbolic form. Finally, anthropologists Klara Kelley and Harris Francis present traditional Navajo wayfinding as a verbal map and decode the story of the Traveling Rock route by comparing it to dominant modes of map production.[60] Kelley and Francis explain how the ceremonial story functions as a trail, while certain songs are attached to particular features on the ground, and both are contained within a larger cosmic geography that includes directionality and scale. The authors point out that by representing strings of guideposts, as opposed to a fixed trail, the verbal map is able to withstand the inevitable meandering of a physical trail that is produced by "the vagaries of human history."[61] Except for the last example, these types of spatialized stories do not directly engage with colonial forms of mapping; but, nonetheless, they have the potential of unsettling cartographic logic by charting different relationships to space and place within the metaphorical language of mapping.

In contrast, the relatively recent phenomenon of indigenous countermapping explicitly aims to reframe Native spatialities in the context of dominant map production to be used in legal cases for land and resource rights. In the Southwest, *The Navajo Atlas* and *A Zuni Atlas* were compiled to assert relationships to geographical environments and forward claims to land, resources, and histories.[62] Although these collaborative projects reframe the objectives and content of the atlas, they also work within the terms of dominant map production. In their study of indigenous land rights cases, geographers Joel Wainwright and Joe Bryan have argued that in the context of lawsuits, countermaps "do not reverse colonial social relations as much as they rework them," and that they often reinforce state power by seeking claims in ways legible by the state, such as concepts of private property and bounded territories.[63] In the United States, these forms of countermapping also became operational in the context of Cultural Resource Management, specifically claims to traditional cultural properties, by providing legitimacy for consultation on significant places beyond the boundaries of the reservation.

More often than not, Native connections to place conflict with the ways Western mapping collects and organizes geographical data through physically discernable units and jurisdictional boundaries. At Chaco Canyon, for example, two dozen tribes claim cultural affiliation to the ruins that are managed mainly for their prehistoric significance. In a recent ethnographic study to determine the position of a boundary fence to protect the famous Sundagger petroglygh on Fajada Butte from tourist traffic, members of various tribes identified over a dozen components of Fajada Butte that gave it meaning—including mineral deposits, an old hogan, a prayer shrine, specific plants, and an occupied eagle's nest. The report stressed that "no one suggested that the meaning of Fajada Butte was somehow attached to its being a place used by *ancient* Chacoans."[64] The Native connections to antiquity revealed during this study are not timeless and static conceptions relegated to an eternal prehistory, but changing relationships to the land and peoples of the region. In contrast, the park's claiming of Fajada Butte as a form of ancient science, and the management of its protection, map artificial boundaries around alternate conceptions of place.

In this sense, Western mapping emerges as a regime of knowledge production that orders time in addition to space. Controlling the meaning of space within time, and vice versa, cartographic practices and products work in an ongoing territorialization of alternate geographies and histories and become a technological means through which settler-colonial logic replicates itself. While the variety of Native geographies considered here is potentially foreclosed by the concept of the map itself, they have been variously asserted in ways that can both challenge and uphold the logic of the map. Nonetheless, alternate ways of relating to space and place, not necessarily able to fit with the boundaries or terms of mapping, are being articulated in ways that begin to unsettle the concept of the map itself.

CONTESTED CARTOGRAPHIES OF ANTIQUITY

At Chaco Canyon, Simpson began an origin story of the nation, residing in the antiquity of a civilized past and its discovery. Since the initial mapping, Chaco has been a productive and ever-expanding site for varied ideas of antiquity, civilization, and science, and deemed worthy of increasing forms of national protection and control. Conflicts over the ownership of Chaco Canyon played a key role in the passage of the 1906 American Antiquities Act, and it became one of the country's first national monuments in 1907 (five years before New Mexico became a state). Currently located at the powerful nexus of science, state institutions, and government preservation, Chaco can be read as an evolving site of intellectual and physical conquest, and a monument to a persistent colonialism. Alternate attachments to place were eclipsed by the new geography of antiquity that circumscribed boundaries around the knowledge of the past and its protection.

The military mapping of Chaco fixed the site not only in prehistory, but also in the moment of its "discovery." The map, text, and images of the journal constructed a particular vision of Chaco that remains an important guidepost for the way the national park manages the meaning and material space of the ruins. Thus, the maintenance of the ruins to reflect "the condition which existed when first seen by the early explorers" has become a preservation imperative that requires a full-time Stabilization Crew to continuously rebuild and reconstruct the deteriorating ruins.[65] This labor attempts to freeze time within the landscape of the ruins, conjuring an un-peopled and eternal past to be discovered anew by the visitor, and operates in constant tension with the inherent destructive nature of archaeological practice and the inevitable passage of time. Beyond the ongoing fixing of a colonial moment of discovery, the work of the Stabilization Crew can also be viewed as part of present colonial relations of power between park management and local Navajos, who have worked on the crew to rebuild the ruins for generations (some of the workers are part of families who were removed from the park boundaries in the 1930s and 1940s). The ways in which local Navajos have been employed to contribute to their own dispossession from the landscapes and narratives of the park are subjects for future research. However, this example illustrates how these relationships operate within a logic of antiquity that continues to serve the imperative of Native removal.

Seemingly mundane mappings and disinterested attachments to antiquity constitute an ongoing logic of settler colonialism and thus become important sites in which to challenge the perceived stability of Chaco's meaning, and assert alternate geographies. One example of this is occurring within the ongoing controversy over paving the main access road to the park. San Juan County's proposal to improve the road has precipitated new transformations in the real and imagined landscapes of Chaco, the contours and consequences of which are still unclear. To opponents of the road, the main threat of improvements is an uncontrollable increase in visitation, which would change the "Chaco experience" of solitude and remoteness that many people feel is a prerequisite for imagining the Chacoan past. Similar to stabilizing the ruins, the imperatives of the "Chaco experience" work to relive the moment of "discovery," in this case at the landscape level. This view extends notions of protecting the remoteness of the ruins beyond park boundaries into surrounding Navajo spaces through night sky initiatives, wilderness area proposals, and resistance to road paving and other forms of development.

Through the road conflict, mapping and spatial discourse emerge as persistent sites where various attachments to Chaco are rearticulated and reimagined. In a significant challenge to the narrative of the "Chaco experience," the local community, who call themselves the Diné of Chaco Canyon, used the confluence of the road controversy and the park's centennial to speak out collectively for the first time about their removal from, and their ongoing relationship with, the park. "Today when people say Chaco Canyon, they think of the park, not the community," explains Ramona Begay; "we want these road improvements like any American citizen would."[66] In the summer of 2007, the community staged a commemoration in order to remember a different history.[67] Many of the same people who work on the Stabilization Crew spoke out in support of the road improvement project, effectively destabilizing the same narratives that their labor at the park works to uphold. The event's location north of the park boundary on Navajo land was significant, asserting ownership and presence in space. "Celebrate & Honor the Navajo People," the flyer for the event, stated, "History brings strength."[68] The road map pictured on the flyer ended just before the park boundary, deliberately excluding the iconographic image of park's thirty-four thousand acres from the map. Replacing the dominant icon of the park with its absence, both through the map and the histories being told, this event performed a provocative remapping of the region.

As the history of Simpson's mapping effort suggests, the erasure of historical and sacred attachments to Chaco is not an unfortunate by-product of scientific interpretations of antiquity, but an essential component of the process of defining what Chaco is, by what it is not. In other words, the erasure of various histories from the landscapes of Chaco is instrumental to the creation and maintenance of dominant ideas of place. These silences emerge most obviously through an analysis of the ways cartographic practices construct the meanings of space and time through a particular colonial rationality. Current struggles over the meanings of Chaco, such as the road conflict, are the most recent reworkings of colonial relationships of power that began with the "discovery" of the ruins. As physical markers of a vanished past, ruins become frozen in both a particular prehistory, and at the moment of their "discovery," thus continuing to assert themselves as monuments to a persistent colonialism. Highlighting the tensions between the map and the practice of mapping, and between cartographic logic and other knowledges, not only challenges the ontological status of the map (and ruins) but brings us closer to an understanding of the co-construction of space and time through colonial relations of power. And, perhaps most importantly, it repoliticizes the Southwestern landscape—a landscape long steeped in the romance of ruins—as a socially created space, and an ongoing site of struggle over meaning and material realities.

NOTES

1. J. Simpson, *Journal of a Military Reconnaissance*, 2. Simpson's journal first appeared in the *Reports of the Secretary of War* (Washington, DC, Senate Ex. Doc. 64, 31st Congress, 1st Session, 1850) and was reprinted in 1852 by Lippincott, Grambo and Company. The map, included in both printings, is drawn by Edward Kern, and is entitled *Map of the Route pursued in 1849 by the US Troops, under the command of Bvt. Lieut. Col. Jno. M. Washington, Governor of New Mexico, in an expedition against the Navajos Indians* (Philadelphia: P. S. Duval's Steam Press, 1850).
2. See, for example, Goetzmann, *Exploration and Empire*, and Wheat, *Mapping the Trans-Mississippi West*.
3. J. Simpson, *Journal of a Military Reconnaissance*, 45.
4. *Chaco Canyon National Monument, New Mexico Master Plan*, National Park Service, 1968.
5. For the history of cartography in the Southwest, see Reinhartz and Saxon, *Mapping and Empire*.
6. Geographer John Pickles refers to the "cartographic gaze" as "the particular constellation of ways of seeing with its particular practices and institutions of mapping that emerged in the modern era. . . . It assumes what Adorno called a 'peephole' metaphysics, an observer epistemology, and a Cartesian commitment to vision as the privileged source of 'direct' information about the world." Pickles, *A History of Spaces*, 80. Anthropologist Nadia Abu El-Haj develops the concept of "facts on the ground" as political products of the practices of archaeology in *Facts on the Ground*.
7. Harley, "Maps, Knowledge, and Power," 81.
8. See, for example, Jacob, "Toward a Cultural History of Cartography," for discussion of the "translucent" map versus the "opaque map."
9. Wood, *The Power of Maps*.
10. Abu El-Haj, *Facts on the Ground*, 1–21.
11. Wolfe, "Settler Colonialism and the Elimination of the Native."
12. Blomley, "Law, Property, and the Geography of Violence," 127.
13. J. Simpson, *Reports of the Secretary of War*.
14. J. Simpson, *Journal of a Military Reconnaissance*, 67.

15. The term *ultima thule* was often employed in medieval geographies to denote any distant place located beyond the "borders of the known world."

16. J. Simpson, *Journal of a Military Reconnaissance*, 55.

17. Although the United States had mounted three expeditions against the Navajo since the start of the U.S.-Mexico War in 1846, these were small campaigns designed to gain loyalty and submission of the tribe through partial treaties prior to official claims of sovereignty over Navajo lands. In general, the U.S. government misinterpreted the failure of the treaties—signed with a few Navajo headmen so that regional raiding and warfare would be curbed—as evidence of insincerity that required increased military force, rather than recognizing that Navajo social organization consisted of autonomous bands and not a centralized authority that could be coerced into controlling the whole population. McNitt, *The Navaho Expedition*, xxi–xxxi.

18. See Emory's map *Military Reconnaissance of the Arkansas Rio Del Norte and Rio Gila* for a similar traverse map, and Abert's map in Abert and Peck, *Map of the Territory of New Mexico*, for a contrasting example that fills in the spaces around the survey.

19. J. Simpson, *Map of the Route pursued in 1849*, drawn by Edward Kern.

20. Gold was the main impetus for Spanish imperial expansion to the north. The first description of traveling through Chaco Canyon is from Vizcarra's 1823 Mexican expedition against the Navajo, but the ruins were not documented or mapped, nor were they represented as objects of fascination. Brugge, *A History of the Chaco Navajos*, 12–14.

21. J. Simpson, *Journal of a Military Reconnaissance*, 33.

22. J. Simpson, *Journal of a Military Reconnaissance*, 67.

23. J. Simpson, *Journal of a Military Reconnaissance*, 36.

24. J. Simpson, *Journal of a Military Reconnaissance*, 34.

25. J. Simpson, *Journal of a Military Reconnaissance*, 78–79.

26. J. Simpson, *Journal of a Military Reconnaissance*, 44–47.

27. J. Simpson, *Journal of a Military Reconnaissance*, 44.

28. In 1869, Simpson wrote a Smithsonian Report identifying the disputed location of Coronado's Seven Cities of Cibola. Simpson positioned Coronado's route within the framework of the best available cartographic knowledge at that time. Unlike his own map from the Navajo Expedition, his Coronado map highlights the Cartesian grid that now firmly defines the space of the Southwest. He includes the location of the "Gran Chaco ruins" and the Chaco River north of Coronado's route. J. Simpson, *Coronado's March in Search of the Seven Cities of Cibola*.

29. J. Simpson, *Journal of a Military Reconnaissance*, 44.

30. Godlewska, "Map, Text, and Image."

31. *Compounded colonialisms* is a term used by Ann Stoler in "Tense and Tender Ties," 862.

32. Yablon, *Untimely Ruins*, 45.

33. J. Simpson, *Journal of a Military Reconnaissance*, 76.

34. *Great Buildings* website, "U.S. Custom House." Accessed September 25, 2011. http://www.greatbuildings.com/buildings/U.S._Custom_House.html.

35. The Navajo Long Walk of 1864 refers to the capture and forced relocation of the majority of Navajos via an eighteen-day march to Fort Sumner (Bosque Redondo) on the Pecos River. People were interred there in desperate conditions for four years prior to the eventual return to their homeland.

36. J. Simpson, *Journal of a Military Reconnaissance*, 44, 56.
37. Hoffman, *Navajo Biographies*.
38. Richard Kern, Santa Fe, N.M., to Samuel George Morton, Philadelphia, Pa., 1850, July 3–4, letter, from the Newberry Library, The Edward E.   Ayer Manuscript Collection, 1–8.
39. J. Simpson, *Journal of a Military Reconnaissance*, 60, 56.
40. Richard Kern to Samuel George Morton.
41. Goetzmann, *Exploration and Empire*, 325.
42. J. Simpson, *Journal of a Military Reconnaissance*, 94.
43. Pratt, *Imperial Eyes*, 15–36.
44. See Edney, "The Ideologies and Practices of Mapping and Imperialism," showing how the Great Trigonometric Survey of India was a technological fix aimed to close the gap between representation and reality, and bring practice and knowledge closer to the "cartographic ideal" of a single, complete archive.
45. J. Simpson, *Journal of a Military Reconnaissance*, 10.
46. Edney develops the concept of maps "smoothing out" the complexity of mapping practice and its representation in *Mapping an Empire*.
47. Goeman, *Mark My Words*, 11.
48. Goeman, *Mark My Words*, 7.
49. Byrd, *Transit of Empire*, xiii.
50. Byrd, *Transit of Empire*, xiii.
51. See, for example, Edney, *Mapping an Empire*; Pickles, *A History of Spaces*; and Pratt, *Imperial Eyes*.
52. Edney, *Mapping an Empire*; for representational violence of colonial cartographies, see Blackhawk, *Violence over the Land*.
53. Pratt, "Alexander von Humboldt and the Reinvention of America," in *Imperial Eyes*, 109–40.
54. Pickles, *A History of Spaces*, 119.
55. See, for example, Kelley and Francis, *Navajo Sacred Places*; Basso, *Wisdom Sits in Places*; Ortiz, *The Tewa World*.
56. Goeman, *Mark My Words*, 7.
57. Swentzell, "Pueblo Space, Form and Mythology."
58. Williams, Blackhorse, Stein, and Friedman, "Iikááh."
59. Willink and Zolbrod, *Weaving a World*.
60. Kelley and Francis. "Traditional Navajo Maps and Wayfinding."
61. Kelley and Francis. "Traditional Navajo Maps and Wayfinding," 99.
62. Goodman, *The Navajo Atlas*; Ferguson, *A Zuni Atlas*.
63. Wainwright and Bryan, "Cartography, Territory, Property," 153.
64. Stoffle et al., *American Indians and Fajada Butte*, 39.
65. *Chaco Culture National Historical Park Management Plan*, National Park Service, 1968.
66. Ramona Begay, comments recorded at a public meeting for the San Juan County Road 7950 Improvements Project, in Aztec, New Mexico, October 18, 2007. Records located at Parametrix, Albuquerque, NM.
67. Natasha Kaye Johnson, "Tears Shed for Chaco: Former Canyon Residents Recall Legacy of Forced Removal," *Gallup Independent*, August 31, 2007.
68. Flyer from the commemoration event obtained from Ramona Begay, 2007.

MANU VIMALASSERY

The Prose of Counter-Sovereignty

In August 1867, as Central Pacific Railroad construction moved into Paiute territory a month after Chinese workers went on strike, Central Pacific employment of Chinese labor dropped precipitously, never to reach the same giddy heights as those required during the slog through the Sierra Nevada summit wall. According to Charles Crocker, director of construction for the Central Pacific, Chinese workers heeded fantastical stories spread by Paiutes. He wrote to his associate, "The most tremendous yarns have been circulated among them and we have lost about 1000 through fear of moving out on the desert. They have been told there are Snakes fifty feet long that swallow Chinamen whole and Indians 25 feet high that eat men and women and five of them will eat a Chinaman for breakfast and hundreds of other equally as ridiculous stories."[1] It was their irrational fear, stoked by the stories told by Native people, Crocker suggested, that limited the employment of Chinese workers for the railroad. The ultimate controlling factor for employment rates was, in this telling, neither the needs of Capital nor the demands of Labor, but rather the imperial interaction: the encounter of Paiutes with the agents of colonialism in the form of railroad workers and managers. To explain the unfolding of negotiations over production between Central Pacific directors and Chinese workers, Crocker resorted to a third party, the people whose territory the railroad was built over and through. There is an anxiety that shows its face here, about the ongoing, unfinished nature of a colonial process that must face the simple fact of Paiute survival and continuity, and about the incomplete sanctity and integrity of the capital that materializes out of settler colonialism, which grounds its claim in an assertion of counter-sovereignty.

The invocation of "counter-sovereignty" in this chapter is distinct from Lisa Ford's location of settler claims and enactments of sovereignty that emerged from what she calls "the legal obliteration of indigenous customary law," which she locates in settler states' criminal jurisdiction over violence between indigenous people.[2] Ford focuses on the interrelationship of sovereignty, jurisdiction, and territory, in the production of "nation statehood," with an emphasis on questions of state legitimacy.[3] Contemporaneous southeastern Indian nation claims raise questions of the full explanatory power of U.S. and Georgian criminal jurisdiction for the developing settler states' legal and practical evisceration of southeastern Indian sovereignties. It was not only the customary law of these indigenous communities that was legally obliterated, but also their claims to "nation statehood" deserving of recognition on a basis of parity.

The invocation of "counter-sovereignty" in this essay proceeds, first, from a sense that settler invocations of sovereignty require acknowledgment of indigenous sovereignties, however muted or displaced, in order to maintain any semblance of stability or coherence. This can be seen in the land grants that fueled Central Pacific Railroad production. Underlying any continuity and singularity to these claims of exclusive ownership, in market terms, of Central Pacific lands, was recognition of the prior Paiute, and other indigenous, claims on that same land. Barring any such recognition, however displaced or muted, Central Pacific claims to land would themselves be vulnerable to the same relations of conquest, whether through market terms or through force, that established and sustained a colonial order over Paiute territory. Counter-sovereignty, as visible in Central Pacific land grants and elsewhere, is a project of balancing the chaotic violence of the colonial episteme on one side of the ledger: that of the (implicitly recognized) indigenous sovereign, in order to secure political and economic space for the settler sovereign.

Settler sovereignty, as invoked in this essay, is always necessarily a reactive (if not always reactionary) claim: it is accurately considered a claim of counter-sovereignty. Colonial perception of indigenous sovereignty takes form through fact and empiricism, capital and value. While prior sovereignties of Paiutes haunted Central Pacific colonialism, the railroad also relied on a racialized, imported labor force. Chinese workers were integral to the Central Pacific's construction process as racialized workers, and decidedly not as enfranchised members of Nevada settler society. The possibility of Chinese (and other racialized) claims to full participation in counter-sovereignty threatened a racial capitalist economy that rooted itself in colonialism. Chinese labor (disciplined by Chinese merchant capital) and other racialized labor sustained and expanded the production of capital in the colonial political economy, and doing so, this labor sustained and expanded colonialism over Paiute lives and territory. The possibility of Chinese workers as an alien, excluded pool of labor that fueled racial capitalism, engaging on their own accord with Paiutes, the recognition of whose sovereignty provided coherence and stability to settler claims of capital in land, threatened the political economy of counter-sovereignty. Claiming a status of fact for that counter-sovereignty, such possibilities of alien and native interactions were cast as rumors.

Was Central Pacific Railroad capital, which derived from federal land grants and the surplus produced by railroad laborers, vulnerable to being slowed by a rumor? The location of Crocker's story was, itself, set in place at a crossroads of federal Indian and railroad policy. The secretary of the interior and the secretary of the treasury communicated over the path of the railroad, and of land grants, "fixing a point at the Western base of the Sierra Nevada Mountains, through which the main line of the Pacific Rail Road shall pass."[4]

For a historian working in the Central Pacific Railroad archives, Crocker's story raises questions, rather than answering them, and begins a line of inquiry, rather than providing an exotic sidebar. This, after all, may be the only mention of Chinese and Paiute interactions in the archive of Central Pacific Railroad production. To find more, we must turn elsewhere. Lalla Scott, for example, documented a story of a Chinese railroad work gang who shared food with a group of Paiutes living near their work camps during one segment of railroad construction near Humboldt Lake, in Nevada Territory.[5] Interactions between Chinese and Paiutes are recorded as rumors in the archives of Nevada settlement and colonization. The interactions between these two groups opens possibilities of a history in which settler claims to legitimacy and authority are seen as properly peripheral, coercive, and reliant, ultimately, on violence.

Following the strategies of railroad capitalists, attempts to write a history of Chinese and Paiute interactions in the nineteenth century rely on speculation as a method. While capitalists speculate on ways to maximize future profits, this speculation looks to the past to mine objects, rumors, and tangles of contracts in order to map a field of possible histories of interactions between Chinese migrants and Paiutes. Casting shadows back onto the behemoth of expanding (racial) Capital, these histories underscore the speculative enterprise of a history of U.S. expansion under the banner of abstract universal Capital, moving from a Newtonian universe of colonial justification to a quantum field of historical and political probability. The history of counter-sovereignty is part of the rumor community of settler sovereignty, constantly repeated in the present, a testament of faith in colonialism.[6] Speculation, grounded only in the power to end the prospect of life and its reproduction: this is the limit of history.

Historians often seek access to the voice of the colonized, the voice of the people, through rumors. Dim echoes sounding through the caverns of colonial archives, these rumors appear at a remove from their community of meaning and interpretation. This remove, a gulf between a living, supple rumor and its cold reduction into fact is one of those chasms productively shaping the historiography of colonialism, reaching across the social and subjective constraints of the colonial historian's institutional location.[7] To dismiss rumors as problematic sources misses the point that rumors indelibly shape the historiography of colonialism.

In the analysis of rumors, questions of their origins and causes are often irrelevant. Rumors veer away from the metaphysics of colonial knowledge and justification, with their neatly ordered sequences that flatter colonizers' or elites' pretensions to power. Instead they focus historians' attention on the social reproduction of meaning, the repetition and transformation of "local knowledge," and on the social effects of those processes.[8] The community of a living rumor—its constituents and audience—outlines its boundaries as it echoes through times. To speak, hear, and repeat such messages is to participate in a rumor's community: the rumor of the colonized is an inclusive, democratic form of communication.

A rumor does more, though, than create a community of shared knowledge. It also breathes life into a community of interpretation, a particular vantage point on a colonial situation.[9] Implicit within rumor is a distrust of colonizers and local elites. Instead, the community of interpretation called into motion by rumor grounds itself within shared experiences, interpreted through a common repertoire, maintained and nurtured as a basis for navigating the collisions, collusions, and traumas of colonialism. In this way, rumors can provide historians access to an anticolonial politics, whose organizing terms and forms emerge from the daily life of the colonized.[10]

Rumors as they appear in colonial archives often chronicle more than a critique of colonial power; they also outline a field of possible responses. Here, again, the boundaries of a rumor's community become significant.[11]

Shared knowledge and planned response must be guarded and policed, lest they fall into the hands of those who collude with the agents of colonial coercion. Hence, the repeated appearances of rumors in the archives of colonialism, in which colonial bureaucrats and corporate and military authorities see their work as rooting out rumors and preempting assaults on their power and reason. Rumors appear in the colonial archive laden with fear and anxiety, with the awareness that the antiseptic face of colonial authority is only sustained through a constant escalation of violence, an overtly aggressive and nervous stance.[12]

Rumors in settler colonial situations are distinct from the sweeping outline rendered above. Rumor is usually taken to provide access to the voices of the colonized, the people, or the masses; in settler colonial situations, rumors may have played an important function in delineating and substantiating the claims and contours of a settler identity, speaking to the historian of settler nationalism with a sort of ancestral voice.[13] This clarifies distinctions between the operations and renewal of power in generic colonial situations, compared to settler colonial ones. Considering North American colonialism as a historical precursor to the forms of modern imperialism that developed elsewhere in the world, this may also suggest a strange resonance between some forms of anticolonial resistance and settler colonial identities.

In nineteenth-century Nevada Territory, rumors played just such a role. These were communities that took their founding impulse in rumors of precious metals, information shared through informal networks alongside government reports and mass media. Until the development and expansion of a continental telegraph network, information about Indians, in particular, passed through newspaper exchanges that reprinted articles without attribution, often contradictory, and couched in speculation and rumor.[14] Terry Knopf described functional interpretations of rumors, "Rumors . . . explain what is not clear, provide details, answer questions, aid in decision-making and, above all, relieve collective tension."[15] These rumors were, at the same time, important circuits for the reproduction of paranoid fantasies of racial supplantation, whether by Native peoples, Asiatic aliens, or others.[16] Rumor was the flame that warmed the melting pot.[17]

To claim membership in the nascent community of late nineteenth-century Nevada was to claim participation as audience and coauthor of the constitutive rumors of the community. Across language, cultures, and histories of migration and settlement, rumors forged a community of interpretation among those who came to call themselves "Nevadans" and "Americans." The rumors that spread within this community, preserved in its archives, record the perspectives shared in the community, and its interpretation of a common situation. We might follow Tamotsu Shibutani's analysis of rumor as a collective transaction, one involving a division of labor that works to settle on a shared interpretation of events, "a collective formation that arises in the collaboration of many."[18] This community of interpretation has an afterlife in the historiography of settler colonialism that covers rumor's ideological birthmarks in the costume of dispassionate fact.[19] Gary Fine and Patricia Turner remind us, "What people believe is true reflects how they perceive themselves, their associates, and the conditions under which they live."[20]

With no particular point of origin, circulating through official and informal means, elaborated on and improvised through repetition and reinterpretation, the rumors that grounded Nevadan settlers in place lent themselves to a sort of democratic possibility, a mutual claim to ownership that could simultaneously allow for and preserve hierarchy and social difference within the community, while delineating boundaries and borders for who was included. Ralph Rosnow and Gary Fine argued that rumors are most often fueled by "a desire for meaning, a quest for clarification and closure."[21]

To participate in the political trappings of Nevadan society—to vote, to claim rights in property or in court—is, then, to participate in the rumor of counter-sovereignty, the absurd claim that has to be continually repeated in order to enfold itself in a shroud of legitimacy, beyond the threat of violence that lingers in the silence that follows its utterance. Rumor manifests here as a form of collective problem solving, the problems being the prior occupancy and ongoing existence of indigenous communities, and the social reproduction of imported racialized laborers.[22] In Paiute histories, this threat was often realized in catastrophic violence inflicted by whites on Paiute communities, and settlers' rumors of counter-sovereignty played a part in this.[23] This repetition, moreover, is about much more than an interpretation or a story. It is the foundation of a set of policies, of a way of acting, couched in invasion and occupation.[24] Rumor thrives in situations of war and politics, those constitutive elements of counter-sovereignty.[25] What Knopf described, of rumor's function in another context, is applicable here: "rumors are not only a refinement and crystallization of hostile beliefs, but a realization of them as well—a confirmation by 'reality'—reality as perceived by the group of people involved."[26]

The function of rumor in this settler colonial historiography is distinct from other colonial situations. Here, a critical historiography of settler colonialism would necessarily participate in rumor control rather than rumor interpretation, rumor control that is grounded in the authority, not of the empirical fact of the colonial expert, but of Paiutes and other Great Basin peoples. This critical historiography would refuse its function as part of the communication channels and institutional channels of the rumor community.[27] It would turn away from the standards of evidence that shape the rumor community.[28]

An anticolonial approach to U.S. history calls for rumor control as one of its contributions. Rumors of counter-sovereignty, themselves, emerge at the very intersection of colonialism and historiography.[29] Like all rumors, they are couched in nonnormative evidence. Claims of counter-sovereignty made through the repetition and dispersion of rumors, and their dissimulation as empirical fact, deviates from the experiential memories of Paiutes who controlled their territory.[30] Rumors raise questions of the competence and trustworthiness of sources, questions central to empiricist approaches to telling history, which often mask the violence patchily recorded and enacted in archives of counter-sovereignty.[31] Hence, in the folklore of the settler community, we see moments of origin in contact, fantasies of Native disappearance, and paranoia about invasion and displacement from the south or the west, from those who cannot share entirely in the authorship or reception of the rumor of counter-sovereignty.

Rumor takes its place, in the Nevada/U.S. colonial order, as part of a speculative counterpoint, trumpeting its melody amid the euphonic pap of settler colonial society. This was a community, after all, that had its founding basis in economic speculation, in the feverish futurity of gold rush. Colonists arrived in the region and scanned riverbeds and ledges, imagining likely sites to tap a vein, strike a lode. Theirs was an extractive social order. The landscape, and the people on it, were insignificant or irrelevant to their dreams and plans. Stories circulated about what kind of place was more likely to produce gold or silver, or about poor miners who struck it rich, fueling their shared community, directing and shaping desires, cohering into collective speculations on the possibilities contained in the land. In the speculative milieu of Nevada mining society, rumors were an example of talk that had actual value.[32]

Speculation also arose through relations and management of risk among the colonists' community, and the Paiutes it sought to displace. In the months following the announcement of the Comstock Lode in 1859, the white population in the vicinity swelled from two hundred to six thousand.[33] Because of the nature of the gold and silver deposits in the region, mining relied on mechanization, which lent itself to concentration of production in mining corporations, and reliance on financial investments from California and New York.[34] The risks that the colonists faced were spread unevenly across their community, and these risks were often discharged onto Paiutes and other Native communities in the area, where they took material form as impoverishment, hunger, and violence.

Paying so little heed to Paiutes' productive work that nurtured the necessities for life, the settler community of rumor turned ravenously on the landscape, pulling out stands of trees, diverting streams, hunting and fishing the waters and land clean of fish and game animals.[35] The community of rumor radically reshaped the landscape of Paiute life in the region. Those trees were vital sources of piñons, those streams and hills sources of meat and fish.[36] Risks arising from industrial development were socialized outward, displaced onto Native peoples, and colonial survival was ensured by the increasing precariousness of Paiute individual and community life.

Indian Bureau census records of Paiutes themselves read as speculative estimates of population by gender, age group, and willingness to work for wages, alongside estimates of commodities, which list items by kind, dimensions, and number. Though colonizers obsessed over census making in order to collect, organize and deploy "facts" toward extending and maintaining colonial rule, these records are based less on empirical fact than on conjecture. The availability of commodities at certain prices, at specific times, mirrors conjectures about the size and makeup of Paiute communities, fixing them in time and place, and indicating their receptiveness to Capital. Interest in wage labor and "industriousness" were key forms of information recorded on these census forms.[37] The political economy of the Nevada settler colonial rumor has shaped the historiography of the region, producing empiricist history based on rumors masquerading as facts. This is especially the case when it comes to seeming knowledge and expertise about Native peoples.

Recapitulating rumors as facts, historians and their audiences assume membership in the rumor community, breathing new life into the rumor of counter-sovereignty with each variation, with each retelling. What historical actors saw clearly as nakedly political claims, as stories of justification after the fact, subsequent readers take for facts, for the whole story. It is in this small way that rumors of Chinese and Paiute interactions filed in the archives of nineteenth-century Nevada might take on a broader significance. These particular rumors expose the broader workings of the settler colonial archive, of the political claim trumpeted by the faceless reporters, territorial legislators, journalists, and corporate leaders who compiled these records in the heat of the moment, or with the ruminative remove of some months or years. This is the claim of counter-sovereignty. In these rumored interactions between Paiutes and Chinese people, the function of the colonial archive, and the historiography that proceeds from it, is the prose of counter-sovereignty.

In its form of address, its mode of authorship and transmission, and its content, the prose of counter-sovereignty orients itself toward delegitimizing indigenous control and solidifying a settler sovereignty unmoored from it. Its genres are well known: indigenous disappearance, social evolution, and the inevitability of the bourgeois political economic order. It works seductively, enticing listeners to participate in its founding fictions, to seek redress in the rights and recognition that it delegates, rights and recognition that, as they are based on a foundation of rumor, can be swiftly and capriciously revoked or amended once they are granted.

It is this prose of counter-sovereignty that is visible in the archival appearances of interactions between Paiutes and Chinese people in nineteenth-century Nevada Territory. It is the record of these groups embalmed in the pages of history, named as disappearing natives on the one hand, and threatening aliens on the other, that delineates the space in between: the rumor community of counter-sovereignty, the settlers who naturalize their history and presence on the land. In the rumors that register interactions across these communities, this legitimacy, this presence that refuses to provide an explanation for itself, that scoffs at any request for an explanation, frays and unravels, underscoring the institutions and ideas of Nevada and the United States as not native, but alien; not natural, but reproduced through colonialism.

The rumor that began this essay, Charles Crocker reporting that Paiute stories dissuaded Chinese desires to work on the Central Pacific Railroad in Paiute territory, appears at a junction in the tracks of corporate and immigration policy, in questions of access to and control over racially marked land and labor. The Central Pacific Railroad embodied the large-scale processes that brought Paiutes and Chinese migrants into contact with each other. The western leg of the transcontinental railroad, it held a charter from the state of California and was fueled by congressional land grants and railroad rights-of-way. Passing through the southern edge of the Pyramid Lake reservation, for example, the Central Pacific augured a controversy over reservation boundaries that remained unresolved for over a decade.[38] Central Pacific directors struck an agreement (they referred to it as a "treaty") with Paiutes that allowed them to ride atop trains and flatbed railcars, free of charge.[39] Paiutes adapted railroad mobility to meet their own needs, riding trains to places important to them, to seek wage labor, and to meet in social gatherings.[40] Significantly, this travel appears in the Indian Bureau archives, in instances where agents attempted to control the movements of starving Paiutes and Shoshones seeking food in towns along the railroad line, or blocking the movement of people from the Walker River Reservation after a smallpox outbreak, in order to halt the spread of the disease to nearby towns.[41]

As the Central Pacific moved incrementally through the Sierra Nevada Mountains, Chinese workers composed the majority of its workforce. The use of Chinese migrant labor was integral to the business plans of the Central Pacific directors. This is consistently clear in the speculative plans that the directors laid for railroad production, in their ongoing efforts to recruit Chinese migrants in California and in southern China, and especially in their responses to the Chinese workers' strike of July 1867. For their part, Chinese migrants' railroad work brought them far from the established centers of the California Chinese community in San Francisco, Stockton, and Marysville. Chinese merchants followed workers, selling provisions and contracting and managing Chinese work gangs.[42]

What to make of Crocker's story? The story shifts attention from the abuses of the Central Pacific Railroad, which led Chinese workers to strike in the first place. Moreover, it provides a convenient shift of attention away, a clearing of the conscience, from the brutal means of breaking the strike, when the Central Pacific managers colluded with Chinese merchants who supplied food to the work camps, to prevent food from going to the camps until the workers could be starved into submission. The Central Pacific would likely have been reluctant to hire Chinese workers in the same numbers after they struck once, and especially after the most grueling part of construction, the summit tunnel, was completed. Crocker provided this improbable explanation less than a year after he and his managers broke the strike. Did he invoke this story rather than explain the construction managers' distaste for Chinese labor, now a liability after the most difficult terrain was traversed, after the cost of their labor increased? The bilious irony is that construction proceeded much more quickly and easily, with less loss of life and exposure to harsh winter conditions, once the summit tunnel was complete. Knowledge of these rumors drew its community into relations of insiderdom and control, carefully managed and concentrated, of the railroad production process.

Paiutes may have had their own reasons for circulating these stories among Chinese workers, as a calculated attempt to delay railroad construction through their territory, or perhaps in an attempt to open space for their own employment. They were, by this time, involved in the mining economy of the region as wage laborers. If this was the case, they may have improvised stories to the moment. Perhaps Paiutes fed these stories to Chinese workers in an effort to derail the smooth progress of railroad construction through their land. It is interesting to note that after the Donner Party passed through their land, Paiutes associated whites with cannibalism.[43]

The Chinese workers may have had their own reasons for telling such stories. Why fear giant cannibals elsewhere, when Chinese migrants were already caught in the ravenous maws of the Central Pacific Railroad Company? Perhaps they concocted this story in order to leave difficult work conditions by subterfuge, after direct confrontation failed to succeed.[44] Facing the devastation of a broken strike, they may simply not have had the collective morale to continue working such abusive and risky conditions. A reluctance to move further away from the Pacific Coast and its community institutions, and more direct connections to their home communities in Guangdong, might have provided another motive. Significantly, one of their strike demands was the right to leave work when they wished, and telling these stories, explaining or feigning the depth of their fears, might have been a way to wrest this right from their managers, even after their strike was broken.

Ultimately, an empirical, settled explanation of this story is impossible for the historian. Employing these stories, the historian is drawn into the rumor community, which naturalizes the racialized importation and exploitation of Chinese labor, and the industrial colonization of Paiute life and territory. As such, this record operates as the prose of counter-sovereignty. For an anticolonial historiography, this rumor is significant, not for revealing limits to the power of railroad capitalists, or those capitalists' ability to shift the blame for firing Chinese workers. Rather, this rumor underscores the ongoing process of displacing anxieties about the unfinished and incomplete colonial project that underlay the functioning of racial capitalism. Crocker invoked a rumor that Paiutes may have passed through Chinese work camps near the Sierra Nevada summit tunnel in the spring and summer of 1867, and the two groups of people communicated with each other in language and idioms they both understood, to answer questions about railroad production and railroad profits.

In a second case, archaeologists have excavated what they identify as Chinese medicinal vials from a late nineteenth-century Paiute campsite in the Mono Basin.[45] This particular finding, so material and concrete in itself, raises questions about the objects, their use and meaning, and their distribution. Holding such a tangible object in hand, the scholar can only ask intelligent questions, and answer them with intangible, speculative answers. The historiography of settler colonialism follows the methodological boundary lines of archaeology in this instance.[46] These questions and answers, the meaning we ascribe to these objects, are the prose of counter-sovereignty.

This prose works by presenting presumptions as certainties, arriving at plausible stories that exclude other perspectives, other possible trajectories of power and authority, and flatter the coherence of a trajectory of counter-sovereignty. If the Mono Basin was not *terra nullius*, then it was perhaps a place without history. The spatial bias of archaeologists resonates in sympathy with the temporal bias of national (colonial) historians, scribes of counter-sovereignty who situate objects within cause and effect chains foreordained to end in the plenary power doctrine.[47] It is a short step from here to what Ranajit Guha has exposed as "geography by history."[48]

Unable to tell a story, these vials raise a host of questions that cannot be answered. These unanswered questions animate the prose of counter-sovereignty. Paiutes interacted with Chinese workers whose work camps passed through their lands, and with Chinese workers and merchants in the towns and cities that were built throughout their region. Some Paiutes, for example, bought opium from Chinese merchants to seek temporary relief from hard labor.[49] Glass collectors and archaeologists have narrowed down the particular qualities and identifying characteristics of the glass bottles typically used to store Chinese medicines, as a way to access the history of Chinese people in Virginia City.[50] However, we have no certainty that Paiutes received these bottles directly from Chinese people, what was kept inside the bottles, and what those materials were used for.[51]

What does this hint of interaction between these two communities, one bearing the full brunt of a virulent, violent process of colonization, the other existing at the edges of racialized labor importation, control, and surveillance, tell us about the prose of counter-sovereignty, about the invention and justification of counter-sovereignty from the echoing fragments of a shabby melody? Can these objects help us understand the maintenance of that fiction standing as prose through the shifting consolidation of colonial control in the region from the late nineteenth century to the present?

These are unanswered questions, and the answers proffered draw their speakers and audience into the rumor community of counter-sovereignty. The unanswerability of these questions is itself a product of colonialism, and of the evasions that colonized and racialized communities necessarily made in order to sustain themselves. Indian Bureau authorities took a particularly strong stand against Paiute medical practices and practitioners and attempted to supplant them with white nurses and doctors, a policy that only intensified in the early twentieth century.[52] Paiutes, themselves, turned to their own medicinal knowledge to treat smallpox, and other new diseases introduced by colonists.[53] Where the settler ear turns toward objects and boundary lines that rationalize its claims to control, these medicinal vials are objects that speak other languages, intone other histories. The rumor community of counter-sovereignty is unable to hear these histories clearly. The colored glass of the vials refracts and distorts a history that looks clear at first glance.

Pointing neither to a pristine prehistory before the arrival of Europeans on Paiute land, nor to an unvarnished modernity organized under the gears of State and Market, these medicinal vials instead point to other possibilities, of material and cultural exchange that emerged out of histories of colonialism and capitalism, but that developed independently of it. Can settlers acknowledge themselves as peripheral in their own stories, in their own rumors?   •

Another rumor of Paiute interactions with Chinese people on their lands finds its general location in cemeteries. These stories circulated, most often, through that exemplary genre of the rumor community, the settler memoir. It is striking that in these memoirs, Paiutes and Chinese are held aside from other social groups and social markings, organized under their own chapter headings, ethnographic asides from the telos of the main story. The two groups converge, most often in these memoirs, in cemetery scenes, which might constitute a stock pattern in the rumor of counter-sovereignty, so concerned with establishing its preeminence over what it has displaced, so anxious about what might displace it. In these cemeteries, spirits of the past and portents of the future haunt the prose of counter-sovereignty.

These stories are most often set in Chinese cemeteries. They begin with a break from the general narrative, often a coming-of-age story, or a narrative of migration and settlement, to provide some ethnographic details on Chinese burial practices and customs, which also describe the outline and hierarchies within the Chinese communities in the area. These are some of the only places in these memoirs where Chinese people appear independent of their connections to whites.

It is when the portrayals turn to food, in conjunction with burials, that Paiutes enter the narrative, tricking superstitious Chinese mourners by feasting on the food left at graves.[54] The white narrator, and implicitly, the white audience, is here privy to the entire exchange from a position of amused detachment.[55] Insulated from the ravages of hunger caused by their colonial presence, on solid ground in their ability to command a hegemony of burial practices, of ways of relating to the dead, the rumor community establishes itself, in part, by looking at other people's dead, at other people's activities at cemeteries.[56] Portraying these interactions between Chinese mourners and Paiutes through comic vignettes, the rumor community also dismisses other possibilities that could arise, of the recovery or production of a common sense of humanity through funerary ceremonies, of the sort that Vincent Brown described among black mourners in Jamaican slave society.[57] Northern Paiute histories cut against these comic stories, with memories of white people robbing Paiute graves.[58]

Chinese people are playing dead here, continuing to be foreign even after their death. The rice left on their graves, which Paiutes spit away in disgust, exemplifies their alienness to the landscape. Paiutes, on the other hand, figuratively eat the dead. Holdovers, relics from a time that predates the rumor community, theirs is a prehistory that continues only at the margins of life and death.

At the same time, both Paiutes and Chinese people exemplify grounding anxieties of the replacers being themselves replaced in the rumor community in these anecdotes. Chinese people, buried in the ground and building their own cemeteries, might supersede here the claims of whites, who populated the hills and valleys with their own dead as part of their process of staking a claim of control and ownership. In this way, the Chinese dead haunted white racial control of settler colonial space, for example, in regulations that restricted Chinese miners to specific places.[59] The structure of the rumor—its nervous repetition, its focus on comic details and displacement, its suggestion of the dispassionate observer—itself records an anxiety about the sanctity of the settler order.

Kalpana Sheshadri-Crooks has written that "all comic stories about natives carry within them the anxious joke of Whiteness." In her argument, comedy functions in colonial contexts to veil anxieties and ambivalences of colonial whiteness.[60] This is apparent with the focus on Chinese spirits, whose graves are stark reminders of nightmare future possibilities of racial invasion and supplantation. Moreover, Paiute people continued to survive and maintain themselves against the violence of colonization. Unassimilated into the ceremonial mores of Christianity or the prerogatives of bourgeois rationality, they refused to be controlled by others. As Paiutes endured the advent of colonialism, they laid claim and control to the dead among the settlers who were buried in their land. There is an anxiety about the coherence of the prose of counter-sovereignty in the face of these basic realities.

One more instance of Paiute and Chinese interactions recorded in the settler colonial archive outlines the possibility of a political encounter, the participation of Paiute men and women in anti-Chinese rallies in Nevada Territory during the 1870s and 1880s. Paiute and Chinese conflicts over the bottom rungs of the racial division of labor spilled into fuller archival view, providing some context to the larger political economy of Nevada society during this period, and the positions of Paiutes and Chinese people within it. Those Paiutes who marched in these rallies carried placards that repeated the slogans of anti-Chinese whites in the area, slogans charging that Chinese workers drove down the wages of working men and degraded the status and position of (working) women. Paiutes took up the banners and strategies of white nativist politics. They decried Chinese workers for driving down wages and siphoning money to China, and they joined in white protests that culminated in physical violence and threats of massacre.[61] Despite the appearance of repetition and engagement, these charges and accusations, as uttered by Paiutes, carried somewhat different meanings than those uttered by white townspeople and city dwellers.

Most of the Paiute conflicts with Chinese men were over access to resources and to waged labor. For example, a group of former Chinese railroad workers was allowed to live in the vicinity of Winnemucca Lake, sustaining themselves by fishing, until they started selling the fish to local whites, thereby undercutting the Paiute fish trade.[62] Paiute men competed with Chinese men during this period of Nevada history in two primary forms of waged work. The first was teamstering. Men from both communities vied to transport goods via wagon and mules. For Paiute men, this often involved working for an Indian agent.[63] The second was competition over lumber, specifically, the stumps of trees that had been felled by earlier rounds of settlement. The earlier lumber was used for both construction material and heating fuel. After this round of development, the hills had been largely stripped clean of trees.[64] Indian agents saw lumber as a key commodity, not only as a possible source of wage labor for Paiute men, but also as a necessary resource in building the physical plant of Paiute reservations: agency buildings and homes for reservation residents. This dovetailed neatly with the interests of Nevada settlers in economic development, using federal appropriations to Paiutes as a subsidy for colonial development. In 1863, James Nye, governor and superintendent of Indian affairs in Nevada, reported to the secretary of the interior on plans to use annuities to establish a sawmill and begin lumber production on the Truckee River Reserve, which would be available for colonists to use.[65]

As one of the largest corporations working in the area, the Central Pacific Railroad attempted to claim control of vital timber resources on Paiute land. The Central Pacific subcontracted with local concerns to provide wood for the railroad. For example, the company contracted with J. B. Chinn, a Nevada settler, for 150 cords of pinewood bolts in 1869.[66] It is unclear who cut and processed the wood, but this was the kind of wage-labor, short-term piecework contracts for unskilled, strenuous labor that Paiute men turned to for survival during these years. Once the railroad was built, groups of Paiutes established encampments near the tracks, and significant numbers of Paiute men found employment with the railroad company.[67]

Claims on Paiute lumber were important to Central Pacific Railroad Company business strategies. As E. B. Crocker, elder brother of Charles, wrote to Collis Huntington, another Central Pacific director, "As to that Indian Reservation [Pyramid Lake], the reserve ought to be removed and have it returned to the public land."[68] According to the surveyed line of the track, the Central Pacific would pass through the southern part of the reservation, which held most of the valuable timber and agricultural land within its boundaries. Railroad claims to Paiute timber were also part of Indian policy. As T. T. Dwight, superintendent of Indian affairs, explained to the commissioner of Indian affairs, "The rapid construction of the Pacific Railroad running as it will directly through these reservations, will necessarily consume the greater portion of the timber as well as scatter the Indians from their present locations."[69] In 1868, the commissioner of Indian affairs notified the secretary of the interior of his support in opening the timber reserve on the Truckee River to Central Pacific grants.[70]

The railroad company and the Pyramid Lake Paiutes entered a long-standing dispute on whose claim took legal precedence. The Central Pacific claimed lands on the Truckee River reservation that gave access to productive fisheries that were lucrative in the 1870s.[71] These claims seamlessly blended with control over Chinese labor in the Central Pacific's business plan. E. H. Derby, a booster for the Central Pacific, wrote in 1869, "As respects ties, the line has great resources in the lumber of the Sierra Nevada. It can command Chinese labor and resort to the rolling mills of San Francisco, for the renewal of its rails."[72] In this description, Chinese labor joined Paiute labor as basic prerequisites for railroad construction. Paiutes, themselves, vanished from the company register and the historical record, buried in subcontracting schemes, or simply pushed aside in the bloodless conquest of private property.

Later railroad companies attempted to make their own claims on Paiute lands. Writing in support of the Virginia and Truckee Railroad Company's application for a right-of-way through the Walker River Reservation in 1880, John Kincaid, then governor of Nevada wrote:

> The company desires the right of way through that reservation. I favor it for reasons above set forth and for the further reason that in my judgment, the Walker Lake reservation is productive of no especial benefit to the Indians.
>
> You are aware that in our State the proportion of agricultural land is very limited. The Walker and Pyramid Lake reservations cover a very considerable portion of our available land in that direction. The close proximity of railroads make their reservations simply loafing places for the Indians. They go there when annuities are paid only, the balance of their time is spent in living upon the whites along the lines of railway, of course there are exceptions, a good many of the Piutes prefer to live as the whites do by farming, notably at Big Meadows, Humboldt Co, the proportion of this class to the whole tribe is small. . . . I believe the entire system of Indian matters in this state should undergo a very thorough reformation. . . .
>
> The extension of the V. and T. R.R. south will certainly open up a very important mining region, besides bringing into market the product of Mason and other agricultural valleys contiguous to, and adjoining the Walker Lake Reservation, and I consider that any judicious aid rendered by the Government of our state will be wise policy.[73]

The railroad, according to the governor's argument, enabled the modernization and tilling of Nevada soil for the fertile fruits of Capital. Paiute sovereignty, as recognized by the federal government, stood as an impediment to this process, an impediment for both colonists and Paiutes alike. A few months later, James Spencer, the agent at Pyramid Lake, wrote to the commissioner of Indian affairs on behalf of Walker River Paiutes, inquiring after $750 pledged by the railroad company in a contract made with the community. According to Spencer, "They distinctly understand that they are to have free rides for themselves, their fish, game, &c., and though it is not stated in the contract, being as I understand an after-thought, it was also verbally agreed that all government supplies for the Indians should be transported free over that road."[74] He wrote this during a period of rank destitution and struggle for food and shelter. Spencer had reported, just two months before, "There is now a great scarcity of food among these Indians and a greater scarcity yet to come."[75]

For adult Paiutes, wage labor was an important means of ensuring the survival and maintenance of their communities. For Paiute men, digging up the roots of the old, massive trees, and cutting and stacking them into bundles of firewood, was an important source of income, especially because it was grueling, backbreaking work that few others were willing to do, except, that is, for Chinese men.[76] For Paiutes, this was partly a question of control over resources, with Chinese workers turning the refuse of colonization, such as the roots of piñons, which had provided a basic food source for Paiutes before colonists tore the trees down in their search for heating fuel, into commodities of some meager value. The conflict did not preclude other kinds of exchange, with Chinese merchants selling alcohol and opium to Paiutes, in an uncanny aftershock of the British opium trade.[77] The exchange drew the attention of local authorities, who attempted to manage and police both communities. In April 1866, H. G. Parker, superintendent of Indian affairs in Nevada, wrote to the commissioner of Indian affairs about a growing trade in gunpowder between Chinese merchants near Nevada towns and Paiutes who sought to head off colonists' violence toward them. This was, again, based in rumor, as was Parker's response. As he reported, "I could not prove the charge against any one or more of them in particular, because they all look so much alike it is almost impossible to tell one from another. I think however, I have succeeded in stopping this trade in future, though I have secured the assistance of detectives in order to apprehend them, and shall punish them severely if possible, in case I find they continue the practice."[78]

Many Paiute women, for their part, sought employment in the forms of domestic work and laundry work, which again, was work that few whites in the area were willing to do.[79] This was feminized work, and white women in these jobs could garner comparatively higher wages than in other places. Paiute women gained reputations for themselves among employers as good workers, appropriate to their employers' own needs and desires of station and status.[80] Chinese men, as a group, were the only men to cross gender lines and compete for this work.[81] They were employed as domestic workers, and as cooks in restaurants.[82] Their washhouses were centralized sites for washing, especially for poorer colonists.[83] Conflicts between male Chinese workers and Paiute men and women over wage labor were profitable, driving down wages and pushing the limits of wage-labor subsistence for both groups.

Paiute men and women marching in anti-Chinese parades were participating in the settler order, but they were not assimilating into whiteness as the fantasies of Indian policy makers of the era would have it. Their adaptations were born out of commitments to the continuity of their communities and desires to stay on their territories, and they worked out strategies that would allow them to do so. Paiute critiques of the role of Chinese workers in making the conditions of life more difficult for them, then, bore a double edge in the context of the white nativist movement, for here, "native" whites' anxieties about the possibility of invasion and supplantation by Chinese people were unmasked as anxieties about the function of whiteness itself, in relationship to Paiute and other Native people in the area. White nativism was exposed as a claim of settler colonial control. In Virginia City, for example, Mary McNair Mathews listed the local secret societies: the Knights of Pythias, the Order of the Red Men, and Anti-Chinamen.[84] As John Higham argued about racial nativism, "The concept that the United States belongs in some special sense to the Anglo-Saxon 'race' offered an interpretation of the source of national greatness."[85] Paiutes' presence in nativist marches belied this interpretation. If Paiutes carried posters charging that "the Chinese Must Go!," then what of the whites they marched with?

In (racial) Capital, the figures of Native and Alien were enfolded into a process that enabled the maintenance of communities and cultures through invasion, occupation, and importation, underscoring unresolved tensions of conquest and slavery that fueled the expansion of industrial capitalism in the nineteenth-century United States. The directors of the Central Pacific Railroad embodied these contradictions: proud abolitionists, who decried violence against indigenous people in Nevada and California, whose own business plans rested on the racial exploitation of Chinese migrant labor, and corporate inroads on Paiute sovereignty.[86]

In this process, interactions between Chinese and Paiutes were reduced to rumors. Instead of the triumphal procession of Capital, pushing back the frontier to strike a path toward the riches of China, here was the labor of China moving eastward, engaging indigenous people whose autonomy survived the enclosure of their land and lives. This rumor was the nightmare of U.S. industrial colonization. It cannot be resolved into fact, leaving loose threads in any attempt to relegate the history of conquest and uneven expansion safely to the past.

The prose of counter-sovereignty, which is the history of the United States as a nation, remains, essentially, an unanswered question. Rumors constantly repeat with subtle variations, only to be answered in increasingly frustrated terms. The historian crafting narrative through the prose of counter-sovereignty dwells on frustrated terrain. For no matter how polished the horn, the tune remains defiantly forlorn. It can find no proper resolution in the prose of counter-sovereignty, only endless deferrals. Emil Billeb, for example, relayed a visit to his San Francisco office by Sam Leon, a Chinese migrant, his Paiute wife, and their children.[87] This kernel only raises more questions. What structural conditions might have drawn a Paiute woman and a Chinese man to seek mutual companionship in this time and place?[88]

How to control and contain the prose of counter-sovereignty, with its countless tongues and countless mouths, its voice of iron? We are on grounds here that Sharon Holland previously traversed: "Memory must be animated so that it can subvert the effects of its manipulation by the nation."[89] Moving from this common frame of history, with its fossilized pretensions to truth grounded in colonial authority, we might imagine histories that are transient, always at play in a field of changing politics, shifting emphasis from evidence to interpretation, from the historian who intones, to an audience that calls up and invokes histories in order to more fully understand their present, and imagine their future.

NOTES

The generous and critical engagement of Antoinette Burton, Alyosha Goldstein, Kristin Hoganson, Frederick Hoxie, and David Roediger helped shape the arguments in this chapter.

1. Charles Crocker to Collis Huntington, June 15, 1868, *Collis Huntington Papers*.
2. Ford, *Settler Sovereignty*, 2.
3. Ford, *Settler Sovereignty*, 12.
4. J. P. Usher to William Fessenden, February 11, 1865. *Letters Sent by the Land and Railroad Division of the Office of the Secretary of the Interior, 1849–1904*, National Archives Microfilm Publication, M 620 Roll 8.
5. L. Scott, *Karnee*, 34.
6. Guha, "The Prose of Counter-Insurgency," 69.
7. White, *Speaking with Vampires*, 210.
8. White, *Speaking with Vampires*, 5–6, 10.
9. White, *Speaking with Vampires*, 70–86.
10. For example, see DuBois, *A Colony of Citizens*, 88–92, 105.
11. Colonialism was a significant factor in the history of rumors in imperial epicenters, as well. Farge and Revel, *The Vanishing Children of Paris*, 30–33, 95.
12. Guha, "The Prose of Counter-Insurgency," 69.

13. Guha, "The Prose of Counter-Insurgency," 48.
14. Coward, *The Newspaper Indian*, 45–62.
15. Knopf, *Rumors, Race and Riots*, 81–82.
16. Knopf, *Rumors, Race and Riots*, 161.
17. Knopf, *Rumors, Race and Riots*, 164.
18. Shibutani, *Improvised News*, 13–14.
19. Guha, "The Prose of Counter-Insurgency," 61.
20. Fine and Turner, *Whispers on the Color Line*, 57.
21. Rosnow and Fine, *Rumor and Gossip*, 4.
22. Shibutani, *Improvised News*, 17.
23. Knopf, *Rumors, Race and Riots*, 108.
24. Knopf, *Rumors, Race and Riots*, 8.
25. Rosnow and Fine, *Rumor and Gossip*, 24–29.
26. Knopf, *Rumors, Race and Riots*, 159–60.
27. Shibutani, *Improvised News*, 21–22.
28. On rumor and standards of evidence, see Knopf, *Rumors, Race and Riots*, 2–3.
29. Guha, "The Prose of Counter-Insurgency," 51.
30. Rosnow and Fine, *Rumor and Gossip*, 11.
31. Shibutani, *Improvised News*, 73.
32. Rosnow and Fine, *Rumor and Gossip*, 77–78. On the role of rumor in the rapid development of extractive economies, see Tsing, *Friction*.
33. Knack and Stewart, *As Long as the River Shall Run*, 45.
34. Knack and Stewart, *As Long as the River Shall Run*, 46.
35. Knack and Stewart, *As Long as the River Shall Run*, 46–47.
36. Kelly, *Southern Paiute Ethnography*, 22, 43.
37. *Records of the Nevada Superintendency of Indian Affairs*, 1869–70, National Archives Microfilm Publication, M 837 Roll 1.
38. Knack and Stewart, *As Long as the River Shall Run*, 90.
39. On these types of agreements, and their questionable legality, see Deloria and DeMallie, *Documents of American Indian Diplomacy*, 514–17.
40. Knack and Stewart, *As Long as the River Shall Run*, 103; Inter-Tribal Council of Nevada, *Numa*, 70.
41. C. A. Bateman, to F. A. Walker, Wadsworth, Nevada. February 17, 1872, March 28, 1872. *Letters Received by the Office of Indian Affairs*, 1824–80, National Archives Microfilm Publication, M 234 Roll 540C.
42. The best published work of scholarship on Chinese Central Pacific workers remains Saxton, "The Army of Canton in the High Sierra." See also Chew, *Nameless Builders of the Transcontinental Railroad*.
43. In her book, Winnemucca also recorded a story of a conflict between Paiutes and a neighboring tribe of cannibals, in distant memory. Hopkins, *Life among the Piutes*, 12, 73–75; Downs, *Two Worlds of the Washo*, 42.
44. These types of rumors may have arisen from a familiar cultural repertoire. Barend Ter Haar analyzed rumors and prophecies that circulated in nineteenth-century southern China that described cannibalism. Ter Haar, *Telling Stories*, 92–93, 157.
45. Arkush, *The Archaeology of CA-Mno-2122*, 41.
46. Givens, *The Archaeology of the Colonized*.
47. Wobst, "Power to the (Indigenous) Past and Present!," 18–23.

48. Guha, *History at the Limits of World-History*, 12.

49. Inter-Tribal Council of Nevada, *Numa*, 54. See also Johnson, *Walker River Paiutes*, 89–93. Johnson discussed interactions between Walker River Paiutes and Chinese merchants who followed the Carson and Colorado Railroad, who sold opium and alcohol.

50. Ferraro and Ferraro, *The Past in Glass*, 71.

51. On Chinese medicine in the United States, see Culin, "The Chinese Drug Stores in America." On Paiute medicine, see Beat Whiting, *Paiute Sorcery*, 27.

52. Knack and Stewart, *As Long as the River Shall Run*, 101–2.

53. Inter-Tribal Council of Nevada, *Numa*, 52.

54. Mathews, *Ten Years in Nevada or Life on the Pacific Coast*, 291.

55. Waldorf, *A Kid on the Comstock*, 37.

56. Lalla Scott provides an account of this type of story, from the perspective of a Paiute girl, who joins a group of white children in eating food from a Chinese gravesite. In her telling, this episode highlights examples of racial differences between the Paiute girl and her white companions. Scott, *Karnee*, 48–50.

57. Brown, *The Reaper's Garden*, 59, 69–70.

58. Inter-Tribal Council of Nevada, *Numa*, 41.

59. De Quille, *The Big Bonanza*, 11, 40.

60. Sheshadri-Crooks, *Desiring Whiteness*, 101–2.

61. Maghnaghi, "Virginia City's Chinese Community," 142.

62. Inter-Tribal Council of Nevada, *Numa*, 69.

63. For example, see John How, R. E Trowbridge, Western Shoshone Agency, Elko, Nevada, May 26, 1880. *Letters Received by the Office of Indian Affairs, 1824–1880*, M 234 Roll 545.

64. Waldorf, *A Kid on the Comstock*, 35.

65. James Nye, to J. P. Usher, Carson City, Territory of Nevada, August 22, 1863. *Selected Classes of Letters Received by the Indian Division of the Office of the Secretary of the Interior, 1849–1880*, National Archives Microfilm Publication, M 825 Roll 21.

66. Amos Dallam, letter to Hopkins, December 14, 1869. *Mark Hopkins Papers*.

67. Billeb, *Mining Camp Days*, 128; De Quille, *The Big Bonanza*, 179, 196.

68. E. B. Crocker to Collis Huntington, March 20, 1868, *Collis Huntington Papers*.

69. T. T. Dwight to S. F. Bogy, Carson City, Nevada, January 9, 1866. *Letters Received by the Office of Indian Affairs 1824–1880*, M 234 Roll 538.

70. Joseph Wilson to N. G. Taylor, June 16, 1868. *Letters Received by the Office of Indian Affairs 1824–1880*, M 234 Roll 538.

71. U.S. Indian Inspector Report to Commissioner of Indian Affairs, San Francisco, June 11, 1875. *Letters Received by the Office of Indian Affairs*, 1824–80, M 234 Roll 541.

72. Derby, *The Overland Route to the Pacific*, 74.

73. John Kincaid to Carl Schurz, February 2, 1880. *Letters Received by the Office of Indian Affairs*, 1824–80, M 234 Roll 545.

74. James Spencer to R. E. Trowbridge, Nevada Agency, Pyramid Lake Reservation, July 13, 1880. *Letters Received by the Office of Indian Affairs*, 1824–80, M 234 Roll 545.

75. James Spencer to R. E. Trowbridge, Nevada Agency, Pyramid Lake Reservation,

May 26, 1880. *Letters Received by the Office of Indian Affairs, 1824–80,* M 234 Roll 545.

76. De Quille, *The Big Bonanza,* 291; Waldorf, *A Kid on the Comstock,* 22; Mathews, *Ten Years in Nevada or Life on the Pacific Coast,* 224–25.

77. Billeb, *Mining Camp Days,* 119–20, 131.

78. H. G. Parker to D. W. Cooley, Carson City, Nevada, April 10, 1866, *Letters Received by the Office of Indian Affairs 1824–1880,* M 234 Roll 538.

79. Knack and Stewart, *As Long as the River Shall Run,* 47.

80. Mathews, *Ten Years in Nevada or Life on the Pacific Coast,* 287.

81. De Quille, *The Big Bonanza,* 291.

82. Emil Billeb relays the story of one Chinese cook who fed himself and his "Indian friends" the steaks, roasts, and varieties of meats sent to the boarding house where he worked, and fed the boarders stews supplemented with chipmunk meat. Billeb, *Mining Camp Days,* 123. Mary Mathews complained of the "filthy China cooks" in most restaurants in Virginia City. Mathews, *Ten Years in Nevada or Life on the Pacific Coast,* 171, 251.

83. Mathews, *Ten Years in Nevada or Life on the Pacific Coast,* 54, 252–55.

84. Mathews, *Ten Years in Nevada or Life on the Pacific Coast,* 180.

85. Higham, *Strangers in the Land,* 9.

86. See Collis Huntington Papers, Series 4.

87. Billeb, *Mining Camp Days,* 205–6.

88. This was suggested by Danika Medak-Saltzman.

89. Holland, *Raising the Dead,* 74.

A Sorry State

Apology Politics and Legal Fictions
in the Court of the Conqueror

A "sorry state" marks both the sorry state of Hawaiian affairs and the 1993 Apology Resolution passed by Congress to "Native Hawaiians," when the U.S. government said it was a sorry state for the 1893 overthrow of the Hawaiian Kingdom. The sorry state of Hawaiian affairs includes the constant barrage of assaults against Kanaka Maoli (indigenous Hawaiians) such as the ongoing siege of high incarceration rates; short life expectancy; ill mental and physical health, including depression, drug and alcohol addiction, and colonial health problems like diabetes, heart disease, and hypertension; high mortality rates; everyday forms of racism; the desecration of sacred sites, including the unearthing of ancestral burials to make way for the rampant development of exclusive homes and hotels; displacements of land speculation; homelessness; environmental devastation; expanding military encroachment—the list goes on. This bombardment is exemplified by the Supreme Court of the United States (scotus) case of *State of Hawaii v. Office of Hawaiian Affairs et al.*, which presented a legal question over whether or not the executive branch of Hawai'i's state government has the right to sell 1.2 million acres of land, the Hawaiian Kingdom Crown and Government Lands (originally totaling 1.8 million acres).[1] This case is one particular instantiation of an extended history of U.S. colonialism, one that reinscribes the colonial prerogatives established in the "court of the conqueror." It also reveals the logic of the neoliberal juridical state and the degraded social conditions that are allowed to flourish under its legalistic authority.

The case was first brought about in 1994 by Native Hawaiian scholar Jonathan Kamakawiwoʻole Osorio, who initiated the suit against the executive branch of the state when the Housing and Community Development Corporation of Hawaiʻi was set to sell some of these lands. Three other Kanaka Maoli individuals—Pia Thomas Aluli, Charles Kaaiai, and Keoki Maka Kamaka Kiili—along with Office of Hawaiian Affairs (itself a state agency) joined Osorio in the case against the state, which started out as *Office of Hawaiian Affairs, et al v. Housing and Community Development Corporation of Hawaiʻi (HCDCH), et al.* The plaintiffs claimed that the state does not have the right to sell these lands, especially in light of the Apology Resolution, which acknowledges, "The indigenous Hawaiian people never directly relinquished their claims to their inherent sovereignty as a people or over their national lands to the United States, either through their monarchy or through a plebiscite or referendum." The plaintiffs asserted that the state had an obligation to hold onto the land until Native Hawaiian claims are settled. The U.S. government claimed the lands at the center of this lawsuit when it unilaterally annexed the Hawaiian Islands through a joint resolution by the U.S. Congress in 1898,[2] after they had been "ceded" (stolen) by the Republic of Hawaiʻi, which was formed by the white American men who stole the lands in the 1893 overthrow.

From 1843, when the United States, the United Kingdom, and France first acknowledged the monarchy, to 1893, all major global powers recognized the Hawaiian Kingdom as an independent state. Of the treaties between the kingdom and the many European nations, as well as some Pacific nations, Japan, and even the United States, none of these were treaties of cession—they specified relations of peace and friendship, commerce, and navigation (not any cession of sovereignty or territory). However, through the nineteenth century, the number of elite foreigners residing in Hawaiʻi eventually grew to the point where they threatened the autonomy of the kingdom.[3] In 1887, a white militia associated with the U.S. military, the Honolulu Rifles, seized strategic points in the city and mounted armed patrols forced the ruling monarch at the time—King Kalākaua—to sign what became known as the "Bayonet Constitution." This document stripped him of his most important executive powers and diminished the Kanaka Maoli voice in government.[4] After the king's death, his sister Liliʻuokalani took position as monarch, and it was her attempt to promulgate a new constitution to replace the Bayonet Constitution that prompted the U.S.-backed overthrow.

On January 17, 1893, U.S. Minister of Foreign Affairs John L. Stevens coordinated the coup with the support of a dozen white settlers and U.S. Marines. Confident that President Benjamin Harrison would endeavor to undo their actions, the queen yielded her authority under protest. But given the timing of the overthrow and the change in U.S. administration, the Queen was not reinstalled, and those who overthrew the kingdom established the provisional government. Eventually, after sending an investigator on the matter, the next president, Grover Cleveland, declared the action under Stevens an "act of war" and acknowledged it as unlawful (Silva 2004). He signed an executive agreement with the queen but never moved to restore formal recognition because of political obstacles he faced during his term. As this struggle for control was taking place, the provisional government established the Republic of Hawaii, on July 4, 1894, with Sanford Ballard Dole as president (Trask 1993; Silva 2004). Besides asserting jurisdiction over the entire Island archipelago, this group seized roughly 1.8 million acres of lands—Hawaiian Kingdom Crown and Government Lands—and declared them free and clear from any trust or claim. This de facto government ceded these same lands in 1898, when the U.S. government annexed the archipelago through its own internal domestic law—the Newlands Resolution.[5]

The Hawaii Admission Act of 1959 transferred the "ceded lands" from federal to state control, where they became managed as "public lands." At the time of Hawai'i (U.S.) statehood, legally problematic in and of itself, section 5f of the Admissions Act outlined how these lands were to be used.[6] Section 5(f) of the Hawaii State Admissions Act details five purposes for the income and proceeds derived from the leases of these lands. These purposes include support of public education, the development of farm and home ownership, public improvements, provision of lands for public use, and "the betterment of the conditions of native Hawaiians" as defined in the Hawaiian Homes Commission Act, by a 50 percent blood quantum rule.[7] The Hawaii State Constitution provides that lands shall be "held by the State as a public trust for native Hawaiians and the general public" (Article VII, § 4).

This chapter critically analyzes the legal case of *Office of Hawaiian Affairs, et al v. State of Hawai'i* and the way the Apology was taken as law in the state supreme court ruling, then subsequently dismissed by the SCOTUS when it unanimously ruled to remand the case back to the state on March 31, 2009, with the stipulation that the Apology not be used as a basis for prohibiting land sales by the state because it is merely "symbolic." In a 2008 unanimous opinion authored by Chief Justice Ronald Moon, the Hawai'i Supreme Court placed a moratorium on the sale of the public trust lands until Native Hawaiian claims to the land were resolved. In *Office of Hawaiian Affairs, et al. v. Housing and Community Development Corporation of Hawai'i et al.*, the court reasoned that the Apology Resolution and select state laws gave rise to the state's fiduciary duty to preserve the trust lands until a resolution of Native Hawaiian claims. Although the court declined to rule on the ultimate claims of Native Hawaiians, it sought to protect the trust lands until a political resolution could be achieved. As Justice C. J. Moon wrote in the opinion of the court: "In our view, the Apology Resolution acknowledges only that unrelinquished claims exist and plainly contemplates future reconciliation with the United States and the State with regard to those claims. . . . Clearly, the Apology Resolution is not per se a settlement of claims, but serves as the foundation (or starting point) for reconciliation, including the future settlement of the plaintiffs' unrelinquished claims."[8] However, the state administration sought SCOTUS review. According to the high court, the Apology Resolution was merely conciliatory; its findings had no operative effect, and so do not substantively alter the state's obligations. I focus on the politics of the case and the role of the state of Hawai'i and the U.S. government's theft of these lands and how the court ruling serves to underwrite continuous land dispossession and the theft of the Hawaiian Kingdom.

What is an apology anyhow? What difference does it or could it make? An apology is something offered in explanation or defense and usually applies to an expression of regret for a mistake or wrong with implied admission of guilt or fault and with or without reference to mitigating or extenuating circumstances.[9] At its best, an apology can be an admission of error or discourtesy accompanied by an expression of regret (especially in the form of a public apology). But it can also simply serve as a formal justification, defense, or excuse—that is, as a poor substitute. While tropes of reconciliation and state apologies such as the U.S. apology to the Hawaiian people can be seen as instantiations of liberal tolerance, in terms of actual resolution regarding the original damage, it is clear that this particular apology is nothing but an empty gesture that served a limited political goal to recognize the one hundredth anniversary of the U.S.-backed unlawful overthrow of the Hawaiian Kingdom. As is clear from the outcome of the court case, the U.S. government views the resolution as a "no fault" apology.[10]

APOLOGY POLITICS

What do we make of state apologies? In her book, *The Politics of Official Apologies*, Melissa Nobles suggests that state apologies are linked to interest in past injustices that lie at the center of contemporary world politics and can be understood as emerging from truth commissions, trials, and other related decisions, following political transitions. She examines the political uses of official apologies in Australia, Canada, New Zealand, and the United States to explore why specific groups (including racial minorities, veterans, and indigenous peoples) demand such apologies and why governments do or do not offer them. She argues that apologies can help to alter the terms and meanings of national membership, where minority groups demand apologies in order to focus attention on historical injustices. Similarly, as she suggests, state actors support apologies for ideological and moral reasons, driven by their support of group rights, responsiveness to group demands, and belief that acknowledgment is due. Nobles argues that apologies serve as indicators of moral codes and illuminate what is considered "right" and "wrong" in the social order.[11] She suggests that "apologies are desired, offered, and given in order to change the terms and meanings of membership in a political community."[12] Furthermore, they "help bring history into conversation, providing justification for political and policy changes and reforms."[13] The historical injustices that created the grievance are central to the addressing of a contemporary grievance.

In an *American Historical Review* forum on Truth and Reconciliation in History, James Campbell described the United States as "a nation notoriously reluctant to confront the darker chapters of its own past (even as it demands that other nations confront theirs)." Campbell argues that "in recent years the US has become, almost despite itself, a bellwether in the global reconciliation movement."[14] In trying to explain this development he suggests that, "to some extent, the proliferation of initiatives is simply a function of the number of authoritarian regimes that collapsed in the post–Cold War era, and of the unfinished business that such states inevitably leave behind."[15] He notes that in the United States, "criticism has come chiefly from conservatives, who decry the endless rehashing of past injuries as yet more evidence of the fraying of America, the triumph of group identity and self-victimization over national pride and self-reliance."[16] He also mentions criticism from the left: "For historian John Torpey, for example, the current enthusiasm for 'making whole what has been smashed' reflects not only the subsumption of the political into the therapeutic but also a widespread progressive paralysis brought about by the collapse of socialist and social democratic movements around the world."[17]

Campbell takes up the U.S. Apology Resolution to Native Hawaiians but misconstrues its passage. He suggests, "Bill Clinton offered two presidential apologies during his tenure: one of Health deliberately withheld treatment from African Americans infected with syphilis in order to study the unchecked disease, and the other to indigenous Hawaiian for the U.S. government's role in the destruction of Hawaiian sovereignty."[18] First, it should be noted very clearly that the apology was not offered by Clinton; he signed it into U.S. public law as a joint congressional resolution passed as legislation by both the House and Senate. Second, the resolution was not an apology for the U.S. government's role in any "destruction of Hawaiian sovereignty." Indeed, the apology affirms the endurance of that sovereignty and addresses the role the U.S. military played in backing the unlawful overthrow of the Hawaiian Kingdom—the government, not the sovereignty itself.

Nobles cites the U.S. apology to Hawaiians as an example of an apology "resulting from the shared political goals of an organized constituency and members of the political elite."[19] Individuals in the Hawaiian sovereignty movement as well as Hawai'i's U.S. senators pursued the resolution as a corrective to an official report that denied that the United States was responsible for the overthrow of the Hawaiian Kingdom. Prior to its passage, a government report that was a result of a study issued in 1983 by the Native Hawaiians Study Commission established by Congress in 1980 (Reagan appointees) asserted that the U.S. government bore no responsibility for the overthrow. Several members dissented from this historical interpretation advanced in the final report and outlined their own in a separate volume.[20] Within a decade, the United States issued the apology, acknowledging its role in the overthrow, but only after four unsuccessful attempts in three congresses of Senator Akaka to remove the statements about a trust relationship and instead focus on Hawaiian history and reconciliation (90). Finally, when presenting the bill to the session in which it passed, Senator Akaka asserted:

> If we are to continue to tout our Nation as a model to the world community on freedom, justice, and democracy, then it is incumbent on us as leaders to reflect on America's own history and recognize past wrongs committed against all of its native peoples. The purpose of Senate Joint Resolution 19, Mr. President, is to educate my colleagues, as I mentioned earlier, and the American public on events surrounding the overthrow. It would also provide for reconciliation between the United States and the native Hawaiian people.[21]

But his assertion was not accepted without heated debate.

Among supporters of the resolution, many downplayed the effect it would have. For example, Bill Richardson (D-NM) assured opponents:

The purpose of Senate Joint Resolution 19 is to spell out the events which led to the overthrow of the government of Hawaii, annexation, and finally to statehood in 1959. It is foremost an educational document. It is also meant to finally apologize to the people of Hawaii for the improper actions taken by a representative of this government . . . [but] *does not infer any new rights to native Hawaiians.* It is an apology that is long overdue and I urge my colleagues to support it."[22] (emphasis added)

Senator Slade Gorton (R-WA) was perhaps the most vocal opponent in the hearing on the bill, in raising the threat of land claims that could arise from it: "That combination of ethnic politics and claims to particular pieces of land is literally lethal across stretches of Eastern Europe, throughout much of Africa, and in many nations in Asia. *It is an evil which we as Americans have largely avoided.* And with all of the respect that I can possibly muster for my two friends and colleagues from Hawai'i and for all of the evident goodwill in the world which they show, *this resolution is a signpost pointing toward that dark and bitter road.*"[23] Here Gorton collapses nationalist strife in Europe with violent intolerance of postindependence nations in Africa and Asia in his attempt to introduce the specter of ethnic violence for the Hawai'i case. He makes no distinctions between racism, injustice, or tolerable reparations for the history of the U.S. imperialist annexation and subsequent colonial policies in Hawai'i. He further warned that the apology would be disruptive because at the heart of it lies the question of citizenship and nationhood: "It divides the citizens of the State of Hawaii who are of course citizens of the United States into two distinct groups, Native Hawaiians and all other citizens."[24] Here, he notes that the outcome of the apology would be a distinction between citizens of the United States and Native Hawaiians—one that might be appreciated by Hawaiian nationalists. However, he does so not to concede Hawaiian sovereignty; his point is that there should be no distinction made at all, no acknowledgment. He also expressed his worry that that "the logical consequences of this resolution would be independence."[25]

In considering how the apology to the Hawaiian people specifically differs in its potential for reparations from the legislative passed by the U.S. Congress to apologize to Japanese Americans for the internment during World War II that violated their civil rights, Gorton argued:

Mr. President, these demands for compensation differ profoundly from those offered to Japanese-Americans by this body in a bill of which this Senator believes that he was a sponsor not many years ago. Those reparations were given to individuals who were greatly wronged by their Government, who were *deprived of their homes and of their livelihoods solely by reason of their race and ethnic origin, and who were alive to receive reparations granted to them* by Members of this body and the other body almost all of whom were alive when that terrible injustice to individuals took place. *This coup took place more than 100 years ago. No one is alive who played any role in it. No one is alive,* [sic] perhaps there are a couple of centenarians who may have been there when this took place. This is a different time and a different generation."[26] (emphasis added)

There are several issues that arise in his contrast between the question of reparations for the Japanese Americans and the apology for the overthrow. For one, Gorton notes that the internment was based on racial and ethnic discrimination, and not nationality—even though the rationale at the time was precisely that the U.S. government questioned their national loyalty.[27] Second, he hinges his support for *that* legislation on the fact that there were still individuals living who had directly undergone the experience of internment, where on the other hand he suggests that, since few if any who directly endured the U.S.-backed overthrow of the kingdom were living at the time of the legislative proposal, "this is a different time, a different generation." In other words, it happened too long ago for it to be an issue now. Here what is missing is any recognition about the fact that a government's sovereignty does not expire simply because of the passage of time unless the people of that government have acquiesced to the rule of another governing body. Moreover, Gorton suggests that the ramifications of the overthrow had no meaning to or negative impact on those descendants whose forebears where alive at the time—namely, the Native Hawaiian people, along with others of nonindigenous origin who were also subjects of the kingdom. Also, the racial comparison to Japanese Americans seems to be crucial to the "sorry state," in which the comparison becomes effective in making Hawaiian sovereignty claims the antithesis to racial justice, as an "antijustice" movement driven only by group economic interests. To discount the Hawaiian position this way—including the specific history and legal claims—entails a twisted reinterpretation of the meaning of sovereignty as morally problematic.

Next Gorton asked a question that now reads as ominous since he wonders aloud whether the resolution can be given effect without the aid of legislation or if it actually underwrites claims that could be raised after its passage.

> Is this a purely self-executing resolution which has no meaning other than its own passage, or is this, in their minds, some form of claim, some form of different or distinct treatment for those who can trace a single ancestor back to 1778 in Hawaii which is now to be provided for this group of citizens, separating them from other citizens of the State of Hawaii or the United States? At the very least, before we vote on their resolution, we ought to understand what the two Senators from Hawaii mean those ramifications and consequences to be.[28]

Notice here how the claim based on ancestry is trivialized as providing "some form of different or distinct treatment for those who can trace a single ancestor back to 1778" in a way presumed to be separatist. While the Apology Resolution defined "native Hawaiian" as those with ancestry to the Hawaiian people dating back to 1778 (the common threshold date to mark "precontact" given that it is the year Cook first arrived in Hawai'i), and the Apology was eventually issued only to "native Hawaiians," the kingdom that was overthrown with support by the U.S. military did not limit its citizenship to indigenous Hawaiians. In any case, the questioning of supposedly "different or distinct treatment" based on ancestry is framed here as akin to something absurd.

Other U.S. senators who opposed the legislation did so on different grounds altogether. For example, George Hanks Brown (R-CO) was bothered by mention of traditional Hawaiian society having communal land tenure. "Included in the whereases that precede this is a recitation that at that time it involved communal land tenure. That, as my friend knows, has been replaced by a concept of private property. Surely, we do not mean to suggest that we apologize for bringing the concept of private property to replace the concept of a communal land tenure system."[29] What is curious about his comment is that the whereas clause that mentions communal land tenure simply acknowledges that as the system prior to Cook's arrival in the Hawaiian Islands in 1778. It is the first whereas clause of the legislation: "*Whereas*, prior to the arrival of the first Europeans in 1778, the Native Hawaiian people lived in a highly organized, self-sufficient, subsistent social system based on communal land tenure with a sophisticated language, culture, and religion"[30] (emphasis in original). In Brown's delineation of his concern for whether the apology is "for bringing the concept of private property to replace the concept of a communal land tenure system,"[31] he seems ignorant of the fact that land in Hawai'i was privatized in 1848 during the reign of King Kamehameha III. Moreover, the two whereas clauses that raise the point of the U.S. government's culpability with regard to land is the one that describes them as *national lands*. The first one refers to them as lands ceded to the U.S. government by the Republic of Hawaii, which was the governmental entity formed in 1894, a year after the overthrow by those who deposed the queen: "*Whereas*, the Republic of Hawaii also ceded 1,800,000 acres of crown, government and public lands of the Kingdom of Hawaii, without the consent of or compensation to the Native Hawaiian people of Hawaii or their sovereign government"[32] (emphasis in original). The second place this is mentioned is in the clause already mentioned above: "*Whereas*, the indigenous Hawaiian people never directly relinquished their claims to their inherent sovereignty as a people or over their national lands to the United States, either through their monarchy or through a plebiscite or referendum"[33] (emphasis in original). Note that this clause does not have anything to do with communal lands or private property per se, but with the national lands of the Hawaiian Kingdom: the Crown and Government Lands. Still, Brown's deliberate oppositions between good private/bad public with regard to property are illuminating for the ways in which he works to justify U.S. imperialism and colonial domination, where communal property is pinned on the monarchy, without mention of the fact that the king authorized the privatization of land) in contrast to private land being linked to U.S. democracy. Nonetheless, it is precisely the kingdom that Brown takes issue with. He makes a point of discussing the monarchical form of government that existed prior to the overthrow and the subsequent annexation by the U.S. government.

> The whereases also note a unified monarchical government. As everyone knows, that has been replaced by a representative democracy. Surely, we do not intend—and *I do not mean to imply that anyone intends that we apologize for having replaced a monarchy or a form of monarchy with a representative democracy.* My guess is, [sic] Hawaiians take great pride in our representative democracy, just as every American does. I notice in the first section, it ends with these words, referring to the "event which resulted in suppression of the inherent sovereignty of the Native Hawaiian people." Mr. President, it seems to me, *we ought to be clear that we are not here apologizing for democracy or the concept of private property.* We do indeed and should apologize for a violent, forceful overthrow of the government.[34] (emphasis added)

Here, note that while Brown concedes that it is appropriate for the U.S. government to apologize for "a violent forceful overthrow," he makes a point of saying that the United States has nothing to be sorry for in replacing the Hawaiian monarchy with "a representative democracy."[35] Despite the fact that two other whereas clauses delineate just that those in charge of the overthrow representing themselves as a white minority, with their own interests in mind, and not any form of democracy, Brown assumes that this was a democracy project despite its illegality:

> *Whereas*, on the afternoon of January 17, 1893, a Committee of Safety that represented the American and European sugar planters, descendants of missionaries, and financiers deposed the Hawaiian monarchy and proclaimed the establishment of a Provisional Government;[36]

> *Whereas*, the United States Minister thereupon extended diplomatic recognition to the Provisional Government that was formed by the conspirators without the consent of the Native Hawaiian people or the lawful Government of Hawaii and in violation of treaties between the two nations and of international law.[37]

That Brown could assert that the overthrow constituted an installment of a representative democracy when the conspirators did not have the consent of the Native Hawaiian people is preposterous.

As Stephen Kinzer documents, the United States has deployed its power to gain access to natural resources, stifle dissent, and control the nationalism of newly independent states and political movements. He argues that the case of Hawai'i served as the model for subsequent U.S.-backed regime changes given how the elite white minority worked in collaboration with the U.S. Navy, the White House, and Washington's local representative to conspire to remove Queen Lili'uokalani from the throne in order to protect the continental U.S. sugar market.[38] Furthermore, the overthrow was timed to prevent the queen from promulgating a new constitution that would have reenfranchised Native Hawaiians, peoples of Asian descent, and others who had been cut out by the 1887 "Bayonet Constitution" forced on King Kalākaua by a white militia, the Honolulu Rifles, who forced him sign it or be deposed.

U.S. senator Daniel Inouye calmed all of these concerns with his own assertion of American patriotism. He also undermined Hawaiian independence claims while at it. "Mr. President, I indicated that we submitted this resolution because of our love for our country. It is that simple. Because we believe that our country is big enough and great enough to recognize wrong and admit it. It is simple. . . . No, no, this is not seceding or independence. We fought for statehood long enough and we cherish it and we want to stay there. I can assure you, I do not wish to leave this place."[39] Here patriotism is deployed by Inouye as a significant trope to effect American claims to territorial legitimacy. As a high-ranking senator who is well known for his consistently promilitary stance, the assertion that "we want to stay there" evokes regimes of safety and defense advanced by the extensive military presence and the ongoing expansion—most notably through the U.S. Pacific Command based in Honolulu. In response, Slade Gorton (R-WA) asked him: "What are the appropriate consequences of passing this resolution? Are they any form of special status under which persons of Native Hawaiian descent will be given rights or privileges or reparations or land or money communally that are unavailable to other citizens of Hawaii?"[40] Inouye replied: "Are Native Hawaiians Native Americans? This resolution has nothing to do with that. . . . It is a simple apology."[41]

The final stated purpose of the apology was: "To acknowledge the 100th anniversary of the January 17, 1893, overthrow of the Kingdom of Hawaii, and to offer an apology to Native Hawaiians on behalf of the United States for the overthrow of the Kingdom of Hawaii."[42] Importantly it admitted that "the Republic of Hawaii also ceded 1,800,000 acres of crown, government and public lands of the Kingdom of Hawaii, without the consent of or compensation to the Native Hawaiian people of Hawaii or their sovereign government."[43] And, as stated earlier with regard to the lawsuit analyzed herein, the Apology Resolution acknowledges: "The indigenous Hawaiian people never directly relinquished their claims to their inherent sovereignty as a people or over their national lands to the United States, either through their monarchy or through a plebiscite or referendum."[44] The actual "sorry" was spelled out this way:

> The Congress . . . apologizes to Native Hawaiians on behalf of the people of the United States for the overthrow of the Kingdom of Hawaii on January 17, 1893 with the participation of agents and citizens of the United States, and the deprivation of the rights of Native Hawaiians to self-determination; . . . expresses its commitment to acknowledge the ramifications of the overthrow of the Kingdom of Hawaii, in order to provide a proper foundation for reconciliation between the United States and the Native Hawaiian people; and . . . urges the President of the United States to also acknowledge the ramifications of the over-

throw of the Kingdom of Hawaii and to support reconciliation efforts between the United States and the Native Hawaiian people.[45]

And while it also included a disclaimer (section 3) stating, "Nothing in this Joint Resolution is intended to serve as a settlement of any claims against the United States,"[46] the whereas clauses are still congressional findings of fact.

After the resolution passed, the entire Hawaiian sovereignty movement seemed to shift, as this official admission cleared a space for a new generation of independence activism. However, the state government rapidly attempted to co-opt this groundswell by trying to contain the movement with governor-appointed commissions and promises of settlements over land claims. Those engaged in reactionary opposition to assertions of Hawaiian sovereignty employ the twisted rhetoric of "civil rights" to assault and dispossess Kanaka Maoli who have legally challenged the meager U.S. federal funds allotted to Native Hawaiians for health, housing, and education (for example, *Rice v. Cayetano*, the *Arakaki* cases, and *Doe v. Kamehameha*).[47]

THE "NO-FAULT" APOLOGY

It is now obvious now that the U.S. government views the resolution as a "no fault" apology. This was made abundantly clear in the scotus case of *State of Hawaii v. Office of Hawaiian Affairs, et al.* On March 31, 2009, the scotus issued its ruling in the case, where the state of Hawai'i asked the high court whether or not the state has the authority to sell, exchange, or transfer 1.2 million acres of land formerly held by the Hawaiian monarchy as Crown and Government Lands.[48] Prior to the state's appeal to the scotus, the state supreme court unanimously ruled that the state should keep the land trust intact until Hawaiian claims to these lands are settled, and prohibited the state from selling or otherwise disposing of the properties to private parties; it did so based on the 1993 Apology Resolution issued by Congress to the Hawaiian people.

The scotus unanimously ruled to reverse the judgment of the state supreme court and remanded the case for further proceedings with the stipulation that the outcome not be inconsistent with the scotus opinion that the Apology is merely symbolic and that it does not cloud the state's title to these lands. At issue was the acknowledgment I mentioned earlier— the whereas stating that "the indigenous Hawaiian people never directly relinquished their claims to their inherent sovereignty as a people or over their national lands to the United States, either through their monarchy or through a plebiscite or referendum." The Court claims that pursuant to the 1898 Newlands Resolution, the Republic of Hawaii "ceded absolutely and without reserve to the United States of America all rights of sovereignty of whatsoever kind" and provided that all "property and rights" in the so-called ceded lands are "vested in the United States of America." This is a legal fiction to cover up the fact that the U.S. government accepted the stolen lands from the Republic of Hawaii government that confiscated these lands after the overthrow of the Hawaiian Kingdom. The Republic of Hawaii could not have ceded these lands in "absolute fee" to the United States because they were stolen. The U.S. government accepted the stolen goods and cannot prove title because they were stolen without Hawaiian people's consent and without compensation.

The scotus ruled as it did to legitimize this theft. The ruling serves to shore up the government's rampant criminality in an attempt to tie up all loose threads that could implicate the United States in an international case if the geopolitical dynamics of the world were to ever shift to enable such a case. In other words, I view the ruling, as well as the Akaka bill, not only as efforts to reify U.S. state power, but also as preemptive moves to foreclose the possibility of restoring the Hawaiian nation under international law.[49] The Court insists that the Apology does not change the legal landscape or restructure the rights and obligations of the state. Written by Justice Alito, the ruling states that the Apology would "raise grave constitutional concerns if it purported to 'cloud' Hawaii's title to its sovereign lands more than three decades after the State's admission to the union."[50] The Court further opined that "Congress cannot, after statehood, reserve or convey submerged lands that have already been bestowed upon a State."[51]

If the Apology Resolution has no teeth in the court of the conqueror, then how is it that the Newlands Resolution that unilaterally annexed Hawai'i does? The Court could not dismiss the Apology on grounds that it was a joint resolution of Congress (rather than an act of Congress, for example) because it would have to declare the Newlands Resolution impotent. Instead, the judges did some grammatical backflips and focused instead on six verbs in the thirty-seven preambular whereas clauses,[52] which they found have no legal bite: *acknowledges, recognizes, commends, expresses, urges,* and even *apologizes!* According to the Court, these verbs used by Congress do not have the force of a demand under the law that must be obeyed. According to the Court, such terms are "not the kind that Congress uses to create substantive rights."[53] The opinion notes that the Hawai'i Supreme Court's reading of the Apology Resolution would effectively repeal the Admission Act, which ceded the lands at issue to the state, and that the "whereas" clauses contain no plain statement of such an intent. Of course, the Court also cited the disclaimer at the end of the resolution carefully crafted in order to preclude restitution of the Hawaiian nation and appropriate reparations after recognizing Hawai'i's full sovereignty.

When the U.S. Supreme Court issued its ruling, Osorio published a "Response to the 'Ceded' Lands Settlement: An Open Letter to the Lāhui May 23rd, 2009." Note here that this is an open letter to the Lāhui, the Hawaiian Nation. In it, he wrote:

> Finally, America's insistence that it has legally taken our sovereignty has consequences for the fate of the Crown and Government lands. Whenever the US or state governments can assert an unchallenged claim to these lands, we as a nation are a step closer to losing them. Thus far, both governments have been able to assume ownership merely by possessing and controlling these lands and by virtue of US declarations in the Newlands Resolution, the 1900 Organic Act and the 1959 Statehood Act. The Hawai'i Supreme Court's 2008 injunction against the sale of Ceded Lands because of our "un-relinquished claims" was a significant protection of our lands and claims which would afford us the time and the political support that our movement has only rarely received.

> When the US Supreme Court's opinion remanded the case back to Hawai'i, I concluded that we needed to fight this case again, arguing even more strenuously than ever that the Crown and Government lands are the property of the Hawaiian Nation and that the US permanent control over it is unlawful. OHA and the other plaintiffs chose to dismiss the suit in exchange for state legislation which, in my opinion, simply emphasizes the State's possession of these lands and maintains the fiction that our national claim is limited or unobtainable. It is my belief that we should attempt to secure this injunction once more in the Hawai'i courts and require the United States to call forth or create the law that dispossesses us. That, at least, would clarify our relationship with America and bring forth the patriots who will lead us home.[54]

Here Osorio is clearly critical of any federal or state claim to have title to the lands of the Hawaiian Kingdom. He rightly points out that the Lāhui is vulnerable to losing the land in a way unknown before, since, although the U.S. government and its subsidiaries have already claimed them in terms of possession and control, overall they have not been privatized; this makes the project of reclamation less unfeasible in some ways, since while having lands sold off bit by bit does not mean the land title of the buyers is legitimate, it would make buyers one step further removed. Hence, Osorio insists on the need to draw attention to the illegitimacy of the state's claim and to call for an injunction against the sale of these lands. But that if the state was to move ahead, those committed to the Hawaiian Nation would at least know where we stand. Although Osorio refers to the committed patriots of the Lāhui, unfortunately the trustees of the Office of Hawaiian Affairs trustees, and the other three original plaintiffs in the case, showed themselves ultimately in cahoots with the executive branch of the state. Here we must remember that OHA is not only a state agency; the trustees no longer represent the Native Hawaiian people, since the 2000 U.S. Supreme Court ruling in *Rice v. Cayetano*, as they are all now elected by Hawaii state residents, not Native Hawaiians in Hawai'i alone.[55]

BACK AT THE RANCH

It is important to recall what remains invisible in the name of the case, *State of Hawaii v. Office of Hawaiian Affairs et al.*, since the "et al." (et alia, meaning "and others") includes Osorio and three individual Kānaka Maoli. Prior to when the case was heard before the SCOTUS, Osorio noted how his stake in the case was always vastly different from the interests of the OHA. Had the four individuals not been party to the lawsuit, one could have more easily surmised that this case involved collusion between the executive branch of the state government and its state agency, which draws revenues from these lands.[56] Indeed, in the oral arguments before the SCOTUS, the attorney chosen by the Office of Hawaiian Affairs (Kannon Shanmugam), like the state attorney general (Mark Bennett), argued that the state of Hawai'i has "perfect title" to the Hawaiian lands. Osorio's argument, however, was and remains clearly very different, as he told me: "the United States has absolutely no title over these lands . . . they have no legal foundation."[57]

In response to the Court's ruling that remanded the case back to Hawai'i, Osorio concluded that the Hawaiian people need to fight this case again, arguing even more strenuously than ever that the Crown and Government Lands are the property of the Hawaiian nation and that the United States permanent control over them is unlawful. However, following the SCOTUS decision, the Hawaii state legislature passed SB1677 (SD HD CD), which was signed into law as Act 176 of 2009. The OHA and the three other individual plaintiffs chose to dismiss the suit in exchange for state legislation this act that simply emphasizes the state's possession of these lands and maintains the fiction that the Hawaiian national claim is limited or unobtainable. But OHA and the other three individual Kanaka plaintiffs could not follow through with the settlement so long as Osorio was the last standing plaintiff in the case, or so it seemed. On July 15, 2009, the State of Hawai'i filed a motion to dismiss the claims of Osorio by contending his claims "are not justiciable" because he lacks standing to pursue the case because he does not meet the 50 percent blood quantum rule that currently defines "native Hawaiian" in the Hawaii State Admissions Act in relation to the "public lands," because the case is "no longer ripe for adjudication," and because he was seeking "an impermissible advisory opinion."[58]

OHA trustee Melody MacKenzie explained: "After the U.S. Supreme Court decision, most of the plaintiffs settled with the State, agreeing to dismiss the lawsuit without prejudice." She rationalized this move by noting that:

> The 2009 Legislature passed Act 176 implementing the settlement by requiring a super-majority legislative approval for the sale or gift of trust lands. Ironically, land exchanges, which require only a two-thirds disapproval of either house or disapproval by a majority of the entire legislature, have often been a method to dispose of trust lands. Moreover, in the 2010 legislative session, only six months after Act 176 became effective, an effort [although it failed] was made to bypass the super-majority requirement and sell trust lands.[59]

Similarly, OHA trustee Rowena Akana was defensive about the deal OHA and the other plaintiffs struck with the State in a piece titled, "Setting the Record Straight about the Sale of Ceded Lands." In it she also clarified how OHA and the State diverged in their grounds for opposing Osorio's continuance of the case.

> While OHA simply asked that the case be dismissed without prejudice, the State, represented by Attorney General (AG) Mark Bennett, filed a Motion to Dismiss that went much further. AG Bennett argued that Professor Osorio does not have standing because he is not a Native Hawaiian as defined by the term is used in § 5(f) of the Admission Act and Art. XII, § 4 of the Hawaii Constitution. OHA does not agree with this and explained to the AG that this type of argument should not be made. However, the AG did not change his position. The danger with

making this argument in this case is that even if the Hawaii Supreme Court does not dismiss Professor Osorio's claim on standing grounds, other people may use these statements against OHA and the State in other cases. OHA also does not agree with the assertions made by AG Bennett that the "Newlands Resolution" gave all of our lands to the United States.[60]

While Akaka insists that OHA does not agree with the stand of the state attorney general in the motion to dismiss, it was obviously no "deal breaker" for the state agency and the other three individuals who went ahead with requesting that the case be dismissed.

Osorio subsequently filed a Memorandum in Opposition to the Defendants-Appellees' Motion to Dismiss. In it he and his attorneys point out that the act fails to preserve the trust pending resolution of the claims of Native Hawaiians since it permits transfers of ceded land to third parties with a two-thirds approval of both houses or an exchange of ceded lands that would be preventable only with a majority disapproval in both houses or a two-thirds vote of disapproval in either house of the legislature. Hence, the memo asserted that the OHA "has breached its fiduciary duty to beneficiaries by abandoning the lawsuit." Moreover, they argue that there would be "irreparable harm to Kanaka Maoli if these lands were transferred to a third party prior to any reconciliation with the Native Hawaiian community" (3, August 5, 2009, Plaintiff-Appellant Jonathan Kamakawiwoʻole Osorio's Memorandum in Opposition to the Defendants-Appellees' Motion to Dismiss). Akana contested Osorio's memo alongside her critique of the position take by Bennett as attorney general. "The State and Osorio have made very negative statements against each other in the media. OHA has not been involved in the 'name-calling' other than refuting Osorio's accusation that OHA breached its fiduciary duty. OHA's continuing position is to dismiss the case without prejudice."[61] The Hawaiʻi State Supreme Court ruled on this matter on October 27, 2009. Judge Moon issued the opinion for the unanimous court: "Based on the discussion below, we hold that (1) Osorio has standing in this case, but (2) his asserted claims are not ripe for adjudication. Thus, we vacate the circuit court's January 31, 2003 judgment and remand the case for entry of a judgment dismissing Osorio's claims against the State without prejudice."[62] Thus, although the court recognized Osorio standing, it claimed that a case was not ripe for adjudication since it was contingent future events that may not occur as anticipated, or may not occur at all. So, what we have here is a genealogy of legal maneuvering in the court(s) of the conqueror in the United States and state quest to preempt assertions of Hawaiian national sovereignty.

It should be noted in relation to the question of "ripeness" that the threat to the lands loomed as soon as just eight weeks later with several bills introduced in the Hawaii legislature proposing to begin sales in piecemeal fashion.[63] Osorio critically assessed this move on behalf of the legislature by linking the push to sell these lands to the economic crisis that has hit Hawai'i especially hard.

> In February of 2010, the House finance committee actually considered a bill that would set a minimum price of three quarters of a billion dollars for the sale of several properties controlled by the State. These specific properties are part of the Ceded Lands—Hawaiian Kingdom and Crown Lands—whose ownership has been contested politically and in court by the Hawaiian sovereignty movement, and the sale of which this very same Legislature had agreed to impede in legislation a mere two months before. The State seems to believe that it is easier to sell these lands off to meet this year's budget deficit through one big yard sale, than to do the hard work of really managing these lands.[64]

Here he points to the always pressing issue of private real estate speculation in the context of Hawai'i's contemporary colonial economy of "development."

Fortunately, to date (at the time of this writing), none of those bills passed because of the progressives in the Democratic caucus who organized with some Republicans to oppose them. However, even with a new administration in the state since the November 2010 election, time will tell in the "sorry state."

Regardless of political party, the court ruling has consistently been misrepresented as somehow equitable for all Hawai'i residents, while the federal recognition legislation continues to be framed as a form of reconciliation that is beneficial to both Native Hawaiians and Hawai'i state residents at large, despite the fact that its passage would pave the way for the state and federal government aim to settle Hawaiian land claims once and for all. The ruling in the court case shows there is absolutely no guarantee that if the bill passes the Native Hawaiian Governing Entity would have any land at all. Federal recognition would allow for nothing more than a Hawaiian nation as a domestic and dependent entity under the full and exclusive plenary power of the federal government, and even that parity with tribal nations is questionable given the myriad of revisions to the bill to make it more palatable to conservatives. For example, recent revised versions of the bill prohibit having land held into trust and even say the Native Hawaiian Governing Entity would be subject to both state civil and criminal jurisdiction. If there is no territory and no jurisdiction, there is not even a modicum of domestic self-governance within the tribal model. Most immediately, federal recognition would set up a process for the termination of Hawaiian land claims in exchange for that recognition. Thus, there is a radical political division between Native Hawaiians seeking internal self-determination within U.S. federal policy and those who are striving for full self-determination under international law with the option of independence from the United States.[65]

CONCLUSION

The colonial dynamics of occupation in Hawai'i entail particular elements of property regimes, militarization, and the imperial construction of law that enable an understanding of present-day formations of U.S. colonialism. On the one hand, Hawai'i was recognized as an independent state, yet because Kanaka Maoli are an indigenous minority, the fact that Hawai'i is regarded by the United States as the fiftieth state of the Union means that in many respects, the Native Hawaiian case parallels that social status of American Indians. However, unlike federally recognized tribes in the lower forty-eight states, there is no Native Hawaiian governing entity. And, given the ways in which Hawai'i was handed over to the United States by the people who overthrew the Hawaiian Kingdom and subsequently organized their own government—the Republic of Hawaii—the case of Native Hawaiians also has parallels to the case of Native Alaskans who were annexed by the U.S. government through a treaty with Russia. And yet, because the U.S. government organized the Hawaiian Islands into a colonial territory, after the unilateral annexation of 1898, through the Hawaii Organic Act of 1900, Hawai'i also has a comparable history with other unincorporated U.S. territories during that period until statehood in 1959—including the Philippines (until 1946), and Guam, Puerto Rico, American Samoa, and the U.S. Virgin Islands (from 1917)—through its inclusion in insular case law.

The crimes against the Hawaiian nation in 1893 and their ramifications, which continue to this day, deserve careful scrutiny by an international court, not the court of the conqueror. Indeed, many Kanaka Maoli and other kingdom heirs insist that the U.S. government submit its legal position to the Permanent Court of Arbitration for a fair and just resolution.[66] In the absence of that option at this time, besides planning for the fall of the hegemon, the ongoing work of demilitarization and environmental restoration of these lands (at the very least) is essential—not only to life in the islands, but indeed the entire world. This is no exaggeration given that Hawai'i is home to the U.S. Pacific Command, whose "Area of Responsibility . . . encompasses about half the earth's surface, stretching from the waters off the west coast of the US to the western border of India, and from Antarctica to the North Pole." [67] This area also includes thirty-six nations that are collectively home to more than 50 percent of the world's population, and three thousand different languages. Needless to say, the destiny of Hawaiian sovereignty is inextricably tied to the fate of U.S. domination. A sorry state, indeed.

NOTES

1. "Crown lands" were lands specifically for the Hawaiian monarch, whereas the "Government" lands were for the Hawaiian Kingdom.
2. "Newlands Resolution, to Provide for Annexing the Hawaiian Islands to the United States," Resolution No. 55, 2nd Session, 55th Congress, July 7, 1898; 30 Sta. at L. 750; 2 Supp. R.S. 895.
3. Osorio, *Dismembering Lāhui.*
4. Osorio, *Dismembering Lāhui.*
5. This legislation passed in 1898 despite massive indigenous opposition well documented by Noenoe K. Silva in *Aloha Betrayed.* Kanaka Maoli organized into two key nationalist groups—Hui Aloha 'Āina and Hui Kalai 'Āina—each of which submitted petitions representing the vast majority of the indigenous people; the combined signatures amounted to over thirty-eight thousand. Because only one of the two petitions has been recovered, it is unclear how many individuals signed both petitions. However, it should be noted that only forty thousand Kanaka Maoli resided in Hawai'i at the time (Silva 1998; 2004). In the two petitions, Kanaka Maoli clearly stated their opposition to becoming part of the United States "in any shape or form." In 1897, the U.S. Senate accepted these petitions and in the face of such resistance found it impossible to secure the two-thirds majority vote needed for a treaty. Regardless, under President McKinley the following year, proannexationists proposed a joint senate resolution, which could pass with only a simple majority in both houses of Congress.
6. Like many other colonial territories, in 1946 Hawai'i was inscribed onto the United Nations List of Non-Self-Governing Territories. As such, Hawai'i was eligible for decolonization under international law. However, the U.S. government predetermined statehood as the status for Hawai'i. The 1959 ballot in which the people of Hawai'i voted to become a state of the Union included only two options: incorporation and remaining a U.S. colonial territory (Trask, "The Politics of Oppression," 68–87). By UN criteria established just months later in 1960 through the decolonization protocols for colonies on the List of Non-Self-Governing Territories, a ballot would have included both free association and independence

as choices. In addition—among those who were allowed to take part in the vote that eventually marked Hawai'i's supposed transition from colonial status— Hawaiians were outnumbered by settlers as well as military personnel.

7. Congressional Record. U.S. House of Representatives. State Admissions Act of March 18, 1959. 73 Stat. 4. For a critical account of the passage of the Hawaiian Homes Commission Act and the creation of the 50 percent blood quantum rule, see Kauanui, *Hawaiian Blood*.

8. Justice C. J. Moon, "Opinion of the Court." *Office of Hawaiian Affairs et al. v. Housing and Community Development Corporation of Hawaii et al.* Supreme Court of the State of Hawai'i. Case No. 25570. January 31, 2008. Accessed March 2, 2011. http://www.state.hi.us/jud/opinions/sct/2008/25570.htm.

9. Apol·o·gy (noun)—etymology: Middle French or Late Latin (1533); Middle French apologie, from Late Latin apologia, from Greek, from apo- + logos speech. Ap·o·lo·gia (noun)—etymology: Late Latin (1784): a defense especially of one's opinions, position, or actions. *Merriam-Webster Online Dictionary.* http://www2 .merriam-webster.com/.

10. Thanks to Cynthia Walker for helping to coin this term, forged through Facebook dialogue regarding the decision of the Supreme Court.

11. Nobles, *Politics of Official Apologies*, x.

12. Nobles, *Politics of Official Apologies*, x.

13. Nobles, *Politics of Official Apologies*, x–xi.

14. Campbell, "Settling Accounts?," 964.

15. Campbell, "Settling Accounts?," 965.

16. Campbell, "Settling Accounts?," 966.

17. Campbell, "Settling Accounts?," 966; Torpey, *Making Whole What Has Been Smashed*.

18. Campbell, "Settling Accounts?," 969.

19. Nobles, *Politics of Official Apologies*, 79.

20. Nobles, *Politics of Official Apologies*, 90.

21. Congressional Record—Senate. October 27, 1993. 103rd Cong. 1st Sess. 139. S26424.

22. Congressional Record—House. November 15, 1993. 103rd Cong. 1st Sess. 139. H9627.

23. Congressional Record—Senate. October 27, 1993. 103rd Cong. 1st Sess. 139. S26424.

24. Congressional Record—Senate. October 27, 1993. 103rd Cong. 1st Sess. 139. S26424.

25. Congressional Record—Senate. October 27, 1993. 103rd Cong. 1st Sess. 139. S26425.

26. Congressional Record—Senate. October 27, 1993. 103rd Cong. 1st Sess. 139. S26425.

27. Interestingly, at the turn of the twentieth century, when Hawai'i was a U.S. territory, political representatives contrasted Native Hawaiians with Japanese when it came to U.S. national loyalty. While Hawaiians were seen as nationalistic, they were not perceived as a threat quite like the Japanese. Most Hawaiians still acknowledged the leadership of Queen Lili'uokalani. Perhaps because of this, the army viewed the largely Hawaiian National Guard with suspicion (Linn, "The Long Twilight of the Frontier Army"). But the presence of a Japanese civilian

majority, with strong political and cultural ties to its homeland, was seen as more dangerous (Linn, "The Long Twilight of the Frontier Army," 155).

28. Congressional Record—Senate. October 27, 1993. 103rd Cong. 1st Sess. 139. S26425.

29. Congressional Record—Senate. October 27, 1993. 103rd Cong. 1st Sess. 139. S26427.

30. Congressional Record—Senate. October 27, 1993. 103rd Cong. 1st Sess. 139. S26427.

31. Congressional Record—Senate. October 27, 1993. 103rd Cong. 1st Sess. 139. S26427.

32. Congressional Record—Senate. October 27, 1993. 103rd Cong. 1st Sess. 139. S26429.

33. Congressional Record—Senate. October 27, 1993. 103rd Cong. 1st Sess. 139. S26429.

34. Congressional Record—Senate. October 27, 1993. 103rd Cong. 1st Sess. 139. S26425.

35. Congressional Record—Senate. October 27, 1993. 103rd Cong. 1st Sess. 139. S26427.

36. Congressional Record—Senate. October 27, 1993. 103rd Cong. 1st Sess. 139. S26426.

37. Congressional Record—Senate. October 27, 1993. 103rd Cong. 1st Sess. 139. S26429.

38. Kinzer, *Overthrow*. Yet although he argues that the Hawai'i case set the paradigm, Kinzer remains an apologist for the Hawaiian case by setting it apart from the other case studies by claiming that there was no resistance here because Native Hawaiians gained so much by becoming fully incorporated within the United States. He further suggests that Native Hawaiians are pleased with statehood, and that when the U.S. government assumes responsibility for the territories it seizes, "it can lead toward stability and happiness." His book was published in 2006 after Noenoe Silva's *Aloha Betrayed*, which documents massive Native Hawaiian resistance during this same period. Importantly it was also Native Hawaiian resistance that brought about the Apology Resolution in the first place.

39. Congressional Record—Senate. October 27, 1993. 103rd Cong. 1st Sess. 139. S26427.

40. Congressional Record—Senate. October 27, 1993. 103rd Cong. 1st Sess. 139. S26428.

41. Congressional Record—Senate. October 27, 1993. 103rd Cong. 1st Sess. 139. S26428.

42. "To acknowledge the 100th anniversary of the January 17, 1893, overthrow of the Kingdom of Hawaii, and to offer an apology to Native Hawaiians on behalf of the United States for the overthrow of the Kingdom of Hawaii. Resolution No. 19, known as the 'Apology Resolution.'" 103rd Congress. November 23, 1993. U.S. Public Law 103–150. 107 Stat. 1510.

43. 103rd Congress. November 23, 1993. U.S. Public Law 103–150. 107 Stat. 1512.

44. 103rd Congress. November 23, 1993. U.S. Public Law 103–150. 107 Stat. 1512.

45. 103rd Congress. November 23, 1993. U.S. Public Law 103–150. 107 Stat. 1513.

46. 103rd Congress. November 23, 1993. U.S. Public Law 103–150. 107 Stat. 1514.

47. For example, in *Rice v. Cayetano* (2000) the U.S. Supreme Court struck down

Native Hawaiian–only voting for trustees elections for the Office of Hawaiian Affairs. The case was brought by a white American, Harold F. Rice, who claimed the voting structure was a violation of his Fourteenth and Fifteenth Amendment rights under the U.S. Constitution. The court ruled only on the question of the Fifteenth.

In *Arakaki v. Lingle* (formerly *Arakaki v. Cayetano 2002*) plaintiffs challenged the constitutionality of the Office of Hawaiian Affairs and the Hawaiian Homes Commission Act, as well as both state and federal Native Hawaiian–focused programs on grounds that the use of general state and federal income tax revenues was a misuse that violated the equal protection clause of the Fourteenth Amendment of the U.S. Constitution. This case has gone up to the Ninth Circuit Court of Appeals in a decision over whether the plaintiffs had standing as state taxpayers. The judge removed the Hawaiian Homes Commission Act from the case and declared that element of the complaint a political question. In February 2007, the federal appeals court stopped short of dismissing the 2002 lawsuit but overturned its own earlier decision by finding the plaintiffs lacked legal standing. The court sent the case back to U.S. District Court in Honolulu to determine if any of the plaintiffs are eligible "in any other capacity," and the case was unsuccessful. See Kauanui, *Hawaiian Blood*.

In *Doe v. Kamehameha*, the Kamehameha Schools came under fire in the federal courts for its admissions policy that had come to exclusively privilege Native Hawaiians. On behalf of John Doe (who was not named as plaintiff because of his status as a minor), the non-Hawaiian boy's parents charged Kamehameha Schools with violating his civil rights because he was not admitted to the school, which is a private K–12 institution supported by the charitable trust for the education of orphaned and indigent children giving preference to Hawaiians. In August 2005, a panel of the Ninth Circuit Court of Appeals ruled that the racial preferences for Hawaiians that serve as an "absolute bar" against non-Hawaiians violates the Civil Rights Act of 1991. However, in February 2006, the Ninth Circuit granted an en banc review of the case and vacated the August 2005 decision. By December 2006, in an 8–7 ruling, the full judiciary panel upheld the legality of Kamehameha Schools' admissions policy based on the educational imbalances faced by Native Hawaiians that the policy seeks to address. The attorneys representing the plaintiff were set to appeal the case to the U.S. Supreme Court, but the trustees of the Kamehameha Schools were finally able to settle the case out of court. See Kauanui, *Hawaiian Blood*.

48. Supreme Court of the United States. *Hawaii v. Office of Hawaiian Affairs.* 556 U.S. 163 (2009). No. 07-1372. Accessed March 2, 2011. http://www.supremecourt.gov/opinions/08pdf/07-1372.pdf.

49. The U.S. government knows it does not have any legitimate title to these stolen lands. Hence, the only way the United States will ever be able to secure its claim is by constituting a Native Hawaiian governing entity to give up the claim to them in exchange for some sort of cash settlement. It is telling that Robin Puanani Danner, CEO and president of the Council for Native Hawaiian Advancement and Native Hawaiian Economic Alliance—a major driving force for passage of the Akaka bill—issued a statement right after the March SCOTUS ruling and mentioned how the case relates to their proposal for a land claims settlement. Settlement is a sellout, and the Akaka bill provides the legislative framework for that resolution.

50. Supreme Court of the United States. *Hawaii v. Office of Hawaiian Affairs.* 556 U.S. 163 (2009), 11.

51. Supreme Court of the United States. *Hawaii v. Office of Hawaiian Affairs.* 556 U.S. 163 (2009), 11.

52. A preliminary statement is usually something in an introduction to a formal document that serves to explain its purpose. For the slip opinion (syllabus), see Supreme Court of the United States. *Hawaii v. Office of Hawaiian Affairs.* 556 U.S. 163 (2009), 11.

53. Supreme Court of the United States. *Hawaii v. Office of Hawaiian Affairs.* 556 U.S. 163 (2009), 2.

54. Osorio, "Jon Osorio's Response to the 'Ceded' Lands Settlement: An Open Letter to the Lāhui."

55. Kauanui, *Hawaiian Blood*; Kauanui, "The Politics of Blood and Sovereignty in *Rice v. Cayetano.*"

56. Osorio conveyed this to me when I interviewed him for my public affairs radio program, *Indigenous Politics: From Native New England and Beyond*, which aired on February 17, 2009. Accessed July 2012. http://www.indigenouspolitics.org/audiofiles/2009/2–17%20Hawaiian%20Case%20USSC.mp3.

57. For the full transcript of the oral arguments, see http://www.supremecourt.gov/oral_arguments/argument_transcripts/07-1372.pdf. I attended the Court hearings and was able to hear this particular part of the session firsthand.

58. Justice C. J. Moon, "Opinion of the Court."

59. MacKenzie, "The Value of Hawaii."

60. Akana, "Setting the Record Straight about the Sale of Ceded Lands."

61. Akana, "Setting the Record Straight about the Sale of Ceded Lands."

62. Moon, "Opinion of the Court."

63. See HB 2737.

64. Osorio, "The Value of Hawaii."

65. It should be noted that the Hawaiian case for national sovereignty exceeds indigenous claims because the Hawaiian Kingdom had provisions for citizens who were non-Hawaiian.

66. It should be noted, though, that in the Hawaiian land case we see how juridical support early on in the state supreme court ruling and juridical denial by the SCOTUS, and subsequently by the state supreme court, were both methods of controlling the sovereignty movement—how the sorry state uses the law in particular as the locus of the state's meaning. Hence, even recourse to an international court of law—while perhaps practical and strategic for the movement—would not necessarily free the case and its politics from the vise-grip of interpellation by the sorry state and its deployment of morality in matters of colonial and imperial history and dispossession. Thanks to one of the reviewers of this chapter for offering this critical point.

67. United States Pacific Command, "USPACOM Facts." Accessed March 2, 2011. http://www.pacom.mil/about-uspacom/facts.shtml.

PART II   COLONIAL ENTANGLEMENTS

BARBARA KRAUTHAMER

Missionaries, Slaves, and Indians
Fragmented Colonial Exchanges in the Early American South

In the summer of 1818, church officials of the Boston-based American Board
of Commissioners for Foreign Missions (ABCFM) dispatched missionaries
Cyrus Kingsbury, Loring Williams, and Matilda Loomis Williams to the
Choctaw Indians' territory in Mississippi.[1] Having received the backing of
the federal government and the approbation of Choctaw officials, the group
set out for Indian country, eager to bestow on Choctaws the "distinguished
blessing" of Christianity.[2] Not long after Kingsbury and the Williamses
arrived in Mississippi and established the Elliot mission, Reverend Kingsbury held his first public worship service. In his journal he noted that "the
half-breed natives, two white men, and fifteen or twenty blacks" had come
to hear him preach.[3] The list of the initial attendees is noteworthy for a
number of reasons. The reference to "half-breed natives" signals a familiar historical preoccupation with Native Americans' racial composition and
classification that was shared by many white Americans, especially those
who were interested in converting and "civilizing" Indians. But it is Kingsbury's mention of the black attendees that is the primary focus of my attention in this chapter. The black women and men who attended the initial
prayer meeting at Elliot and who soon joined the mission churches were
slaves owned by Choctaws. By the early years of the nineteenth century a
small contingent of prominent Choctaws, mostly but not exclusively men,
owned black people as property and exploited their labor and reproduction
for profit and personal gain. Choctaw slaveholders, like their Chickasaw,
Cherokee, and Creek peers, bought, rented, and sold black men, women,

and children as property, conducting transactions with each other and also with white slaveholders and traders from the states. As in the United States, slavery in the Indian nations rested on a racial ideology of black inferiority that equated blackness with innate degradation and lifelong, inherited servitude and that defined black people as chattel.

As suggested by Reverend Kingsbury's description of his first church service at the Elliot mission, enslaved people's presence and participation in the mission churches was known at the time and is well documented in the historical record. Missionaries were keen observers and reporters. Their correspondence, journals, and newsletters create a detailed, composite image of black people's religious practices and social relationships, and their efforts to blunt or undercut their masters' power. Despite the availability of such documentation, scholars have paid scant attention to the interactions that took shape among missionaries, black slaves, and Indian slaveholders during the early nineteenth century. Many black people had embraced Christianity before their arrival in Choctaw country and thus before the missionaries arrived with the aim of converting and "civilizing" Indians. These conditions raise a number of questions that are key to understanding the complicated ways missionaries interacted with both Indian slaveholders and enslaved African Americans. How did black people's shared faith with the missionaries shape or change their relationships with their Indian masters once missionaries settled in Choctaw communities? Where did slavery and enslaved people of African descent, both Christians and nonbelievers, fit in both missionaries' plans to "civilize" Indians and U.S. colonial expansion of which missionization was a key component?

The history of missionary projects among Native peoples in the United States is part of a larger and longer history of Euro-Americans' colonial expansion and subjugation of indigenous peoples. In the early nineteenth century, U.S. policy makers held that the new republic's territorial expansion was vital, if not inevitable, and also that Indians were not yet "civilized" enough to remain within the United States. Yet, white Americans also contended that with the proper training, including religious conversion, Indians might eventually become "civilized" and would then relinquish their land, cultures, and governance to American domination. Pioneering Native American studies scholar Vine Deloria argues forcefully that Christian conversion went "hand in hand" with colonial land appropriation. Similarly, George Tinker (Osage) describes missionization and conversion as weapons of "cultural genocide." [4]

Other scholars, by contrast, have taken a different approach when considering the early nineteenth-century interactions between missionaries and Indians in the southern United States. Without minimizing the fundamental connections between missionization and federal efforts to seize Indian lands and subjugate Indian peoples, many historians have called attention to the ways that Indians not only wielded influence over missionaries but also selectively, strategically, and also sincerely adopted Christianity. In his analysis of Cherokee Christian David Brown's 1823, ABCFM-sponsored lecture tour, for example, Joel Martin finds that Brown used his lectures as a platform to persuade missionaries and other white reformers of the righteousness of defending Cherokee sovereignty against U.S. aggression. Historian Tiya Miles, likewise, writes of Cherokees' early nineteenth-century interest in one mission school, "the Cherokees living near [James] Vann's place wanted one thing from the missionaries: an English school where Cherokee children could learn needed skills."[5] Historian Clara Sue Kidwell, likewise, argues that many Choctaw leaders supported the mission schools and churches because these men desired an American education to acquire the knowledge and skills necessary to defend their people and territory against U.S. encroachments.[6]

This increased scholarly attention to the sincerity, pragmatism, and complexity of Native people's embrace of Christianity and their sustained relationships with missionaries points to some of the ways Native peoples adapted and survived in the face of colonial aggression, often using their "civilized" knowledge to lay bare the hypocrisies and cruelties of colonial policies and ideologies. It also allows us to see that the U.S. colonial stance toward Indians was rife with contradictions, inconsistencies, and fissures. United States policy makers anticipated that the "civilization" campaigns waged by missionaries would pave the way for federal measures that eroded tribal sovereignty and appropriated Indian land. Many missionaries, however, steadfastly opposed the seizure of Indian land and the emergent plans to relocate Indian peoples even while they believed fervently in the need to "civilize" Indians through conversion and assimilation. The policy makers who designed U.S. colonial policies toward Indians and the missionaries who carried out those policies never held identical views and goals. As anthropologist Ann Stoler cautions, scholars should be mindful not to conflate the "makers of metropole policy" with "its local practitioners."[7] It is along this line that scholars such as Martin and Kidwell have pushed for more detailed and contextualized understandings of the early nineteenth-century interactions between missionaries and Indians.

Interestingly, the place of enslaved Africans and African Americans in both the complicated relationships between missionaries and Indians and also in the larger story of U.S. efforts to subjugate the indigenous peoples in the Deep South remains largely unexamined. A better understanding of slavery and the relationships between missionaries, slaves, and slaveholders in the Native nations in the southern United States enhances our understandings of what Bill Ashcroft describes as the rhizomic nature of colonial power. Ashcroft explains that the metaphor of the *rhizome,* an elaborate root system that extends horizontally rather than vertically and expands "in a fragmented, discontinuous, multidirectional way," allows for a more nuanced conception of the "ambivalent, fluid, chaotic relationships within the colonial exchanges."[8]

A closer investigation of black people's interactions with missionaries reveals the complexities of missionaries' roles as proxies of U.S. colonial domination. Missionaries, for example, condemned Indians' ownership of slaves, claiming it reflected both their indolence and cruelty. At the same time, however, missionaries and Choctaws shared an understanding of black racial inferiority and viewed black people as beasts of burden best suited for arduous physical labor. Yet, missionaries were heartened by black people's religiosity and frequently deemed them more "civilized" than Indian nonbelievers. Focusing more closely on black people's lives in the Choctaw allows us to consider the various ways they engaged Christianity, individual missionaries, and the colonial project of missionization.

In 1816, Cyrus Kingsbury, a Congregational minister from Massachusetts, wrote to Secretary of War William H. Crawford to express his interest in establishing a mission school among the Cherokees. Kingsbury and his fellow missionaries believed that their work was more than a "duty enjoined by the Gospel" but also an "act of justice" toward Indians.[9] Members of the American Board of Commissioners for Foreign Missions concerned themselves not only with converting Indians but also pressuring Congress and federal officials to treat Indian peoples justly. The ABCFM was comprised of many prominent reformers and politicians who were especially concerned about what they perceived as the inhumane greed at the core of the federal government's efforts to usurp Indian land and press Indian peoples to move west of the Mississippi River. By the end of 1816, the Choctaws, Chickasaws, and Creeks had already ceded millions of acres of their Mississippi and Alabama lands to the United States.[10]

In the early nineteenth century, federal policy makers pursued an Indian policy that set forth two interrelated goals: peaceful land acquisition through treaties and programs to "civilize" Indians. American policy makers contended that Indian nations claimed an excess of land that they failed to use appropriately, devoting too much time and space to hunting and not enough to farming. United States Indian policy, consequently, aimed to secure land cessions from Indians by pushing them to adopt the social and economic practices of American yeomen farmers. Policy makers anticipated that seemingly benevolent "civilization" programs would have a domino effect, drastically altering Indian cultural, social, and economic practices in ways that would eventually result in their ceding both their land and governance to the United States.[11] Those officials who favored the less overtly violent tack of "civilization" espoused the view that "our laws and manners ought to supersede [Indians'] present savage manners and customs."[12] To achieve this end, Congress approved the Indian Civilization Fund Act (1819), authorizing the appropriation of funds to support "capable persons of good moral character" who would instill in Indians "the habits and arts of civilization."[13] The Civilization Fund Act did not directly address the issue of Christianity and conversion, but by the time of its passage missionaries had already established schools for Indian students, and thus they continued and expanded their work with assistance of federal funds.

The men and women associated with the ABCFM bristled at federal efforts to winnow Indian landholdings and feared that forcing Indians off their land was an affront to the laws of man and God. In the 1820s and 1830s, prominent members of the ABCFM openly challenged the federal government's efforts to drive Indian peoples, most notably the Cherokees, from their Georgia territory. Yet through the early decades of the century, missionaries and the ABCFM leadership never assumed a singular stance regarding the dispossession of Choctaws' land, nor did their heterogeneous opinions on this issue remain constant over time. In 1825, for example, Cyrus Kingsbury decided that plans for removing southern Indians to the trans-Mississippi West were for the best as Indians would not become "civilized" and assimilated quickly enough to suit the demands of white Americans. Only a few years later, however, another missionary to the Choctaws rejected the idea of removal, writing, "What account will our people render to God, if, through their neglect, this people, now ripe for the gospel, should be forced into the boundless wilds beyond the Mississippi, in their present state of ignorance?"[14] When an 1829 prayer meeting closed with a number of Choctaw men discussing the possibility of losing their country to white Americans, Loring Williams deflected their concerns by instructing them to concentrate on the afterlife and God's judgment.[15]

Missionaries were no more unified among themselves than they were with the federal lawmakers who planned for the acquisition of Indians' land. Missionaries and federal officials had divergent perspectives on the question of U.S. territorial expansion, but they shared the view that Indians needed training that would instill in them the dominant social, economic, and Christian tenets of American society. Whether missionaries acknowledged their role in advancing American political and territorial domination of Indian peoples, they certainly understood themselves as morally and culturally superior to Indians, whose personal and tribal longevity required the benevolent intercession of white, Christian reformers. The missionary archive reflects these multiple interests. Letters, ledgers, and annual reports provide conflicting and sometimes contradictory accounts of specific events and people. The sources do not present a stable and straightforward narrative of colonial domination enacted by missionaries but rather suggest the negotiations, compromises, uncertainties, and concessions enacted in missionaries' daily encounters with both Indian slaveholders and black slaves in the Indian nations.

The ABCFM concentrated its efforts on the Choctaws, but it also established missions in the Cherokee nation, and circuit riders and other missionary societies picked up the slack in Chickasaw country. A year and a half after Kingsbury and the Williamses established the Elliot mission in 1818, they counted sixty Choctaw students in its school and had the support of prominent Choctaw leaders, including David Folsom, Mushulatubbee, and Pushmataha.[16] In subsequent years, they recorded Choctaw men's and women's increased interest in attending prayer meetings and formally joining church congregations. Certainly, there were more than a few Choctaws who were wary of the missionaries, regarding them as surrogates of the federal government who would advance its land-hungry, assimilationist agenda and profit from Indians' losses.[17] At the same time, however, many leading Choctaws facilitated the missionaries' presence in their towns by providing land, money, and students to ensure the smooth running of mission schools. In fact, missionaries depended heavily on the funding and resources provided by their Choctaw hosts because the federal government routinely allocated far smaller sums than the missionaries had requested. Choctaw leaders courted, funded, and patronized mission schools for pragmatic reasons, as historian Clara Sue Kidwell explains. They hoped to obtain the linguistic and cultural fluency necessary to interact with but not submit to the demands of their white neighbors and federal and state officials.[18] Choctaws and missionaries thus had overlapping but not identical expectations of missionization. Where missionaries sought to rescue Indians from heathenism and prepare them for eventual inclusion in American society, Choctaws hoped to acquire the resources to safeguard their difference and distance from American cultural and political domination.

The Choctaws who supported and attended mission churches and schools did not clash with missionaries over religious doctrine but were routinely at odds with them over the issue of slavery. Ironically, this central point of dispute among Choctaws and missionaries was a cornerstone social and economic institution in the United States. Human bondage, whether in the states or Indian country, did not fit easily in missionaries' vision of a Christian society. As missionaries saw it, Indians' ownership of slaves and reliance on their labor to generate food and commodity crops did not signal their deliberate adoption of American practices of private property and market-oriented production. Instead, missionaries drew on prevailing racial categories and traits, arguing that slave ownership highlighted Indian's laziness and cruelty. Unwilling to work for themselves, missionaries charged, indolent Indians subsisted on the labor of their slaves. Certainly, antislavery clergy directed similar critiques toward white slaveholders, but they did not classify white slaveholders' dependency or brutality as both the sign and symptom of racial identity and inferiority.

Slavery, Kingsbury wrote, was "one of the greatest obstacles to the progress of the Gospel [and] civilization" in the Indian nations. In subsequent correspondence Kingsbury elaborated on the subject of Indians as slaveholders, writing, "The indolent slave of an indolent, ignorant Indian . . . is an unfortunate being. . . . Negroes raised in the states & especially those raised under the Gospel are much more intelligent & industrious than those raised among the Indians."[19] The harsh criticism Kingsbury and his colleagues directed toward Indian slaveholders certainly reflects their disdain for slavery but also indicates their paternalist ideas about Indians as a racially backward and uncivilized people.

Despite their antislavery sympathies, missionaries had a number of strategic and spiritual reasons for their tolerating Indian slaveholders as congregants. Missionaries did not want to alienate slaveholding Indians as potential converts and received them in the church with the hope of enlightening them through discussion and prayer. One missionary to the Cherokees explained that because their "opportunities for knowledge" about the wickedness of slavery had "not been as great as white people's," Indians should not be held fully accountable for their participation in the sinful institution.[20] Moreover, missionaries could not afford to estrange the slaveholding Indian leaders who committed funds from their nations' annuities to help cover the costs of running the missions. The simultaneous toleration, condemnation, and exculpation of Indian slaveholders point to the complicated and often contradictory nature of Euro-Americans' early nineteenth-century racial thinking.

In the early decades of the nineteenth century, Euro-American intellectuals, statesmen, and reformers routinely compared and contrasted Indians and black people in terms of their racial traits. Thomas Jefferson's 1785 *Notes on the State of Virginia* endures as one of the most familiar works to set forth such a comparison. In this work, Jefferson contrasts Africans' absolute lack of beauty, intellect, and imagination with Indians' potential for mental and moral development. Jefferson was not alone in comparing the racial fitness of black people and Indians or in determining that neither could be incorporated into the American social and political mainstream on equal footing with white people.[21] Yet, other leading lawmakers and reformers came to different conclusions about the fixity of black people's racial inferiority. In contrast to Jefferson's views, proponents of African colonization—removing freeborn blacks and manumitted slaves to Africa—anticipated that once they were removed from the United States black people would achieve their potential to flourish and build a glorious society. The ABCFM leadership and missionaries included a number of men who supported African colonization as a benevolent measure that would cultivate black people's intellectual and moral capacities.

Like virtually all white American intellectuals of the early nineteenth century, missionaries did not advocate racial egalitarianism. But they did not take up the emergent, hard-line biblical and biological arguments for the immutability and permanence of black and Indian racial inferiority. Rather, they posited that habitual behavior rather than innate traits informed the differences between black, Indian, and white people. The notion that black people, specifically those steeped in Christianity, were intellectually and morally sounder than non-Christian Indians, especially those without Euro-American ancestry, prevailed among the missionaries.[22] Consequently, in their efforts to uplift both the slave and slaveholder in Indian country, missionaries welcomed enslaved people into their flock. Missionaries anticipated that black slaves would assist in spreading the word of the Gospel and thus promoting civilization among the Indians.

A great deal of what is known about the lives of the early generations of black slaves in the Choctaw Nation comes from the records of northern missionaries, those evangelical men and women who saw themselves as benevolent reformers who might "civilize" Indians through the spread of

Christianity. Missionaries did not intend to preserve individual life stories or compile a collective history of enslaved people. They dutifully recorded their efforts to run the mission stations. In the course of writing personal reflections and generating official correspondence about their schools and churches, they penned both general and detailed images of the enslaved people who worked, prayed, and studied at the missions.

My reading of these documents as part of a U.S. colonial archive heeds anthropologist Ann Stoler's admonition to read "along the grain" and to consider the ways that "colonial categories reappear in the analytic vocabulary of historians."[23] With notable exceptions, scholars interested in the history of slavery in the southern Indian nations have used missionary records primarily to confirm the presence of black slaves. Given the paucity of sources regarding slavery and the lives of enslaved people in the Indian nations, missionary records appear to offer a wealth of "facts" about black people's lives. While scholars of Native American history have approached these sources cautiously and critically, these sources have not been subjected to similar scrutiny in discussions of the history of slavery and the enslaved. Missionary records have not been read as a colonial archive of slavery and the enslaved.

In personal letters, mission ledgers, and church reports, accounts of black people's lives in Indian country often appeared as key elements in broader narratives about race, gender, religion, and "civilization." Missionaries narrated black people's lives in an effort to demonstrate their own success at converting and "civilizing" Indians and also thwarting the expansion of chattel slavery. Black people's intellectual vigor and political acumen, for example, is either ignored or dismissed in the sources. Similarly, black people's community dynamics and emotional lives are not readily visible on the pages of the missionary archive. This does not render missionary documents worthless for discerning black people's lives, including the ways they saw themselves. It does mean, however, that scholars must use care not to reinscribe the missionary archive in our own writings.

Enslaved people in the Choctaw Nation had many reasons for seeking out missionaries and joining mission churches. Across the south, the organized, collective expression of religious faith was an important component of many enslaved people's lives.[24] For those enslaved people who had been sold from masters in the states to Choctaw slaveholders, joining religious communities in the Indian nations sustained spiritual ties to the kin and communities that had been left behind. Establishing close relations with mission churches also allowed enslaved people to locate critical resources and opportunities that undermined their master's authority and served to ameliorate their bondage. Missionaries generally attributed black people's participation in church services to the success of the missionary venture, praising themselves and Indian converts for showing black people the road to Christian conversion. Yet, in most instances, black people's participation in mission churches derived from their religious history and political aspirations.

Among the slaves Choctaws purchased from Georgia masters were a number of African and African American women and men who had previously been members of black Baptist and Methodist churches in and around Savannah. In the earliest years of the nineteenth century, free and enslaved African Americans in and around Savannah had formed their own Baptist congregations, sometimes joining the white congregations that were open to them and participating in the region's denominational associations.[25] The first cohort of enslaved evangelicals that gravitated toward the mission churches in the Choctaw Nation in the early 1820s included a number of people who had previously been enslaved in Georgia, where black Christianity thrived. Thirty-year-old Rosa, owned by the Leflores, was originally from Georgia, "where she became Baptist." Another elderly enslaved woman had also been a "church member in Georgia" before she was purchased by a Choctaw master. One African-born man at the mission indicated that he, too, had found salvation in Georgia. The black evangelical community in the Choctaw Nation included at least one man who had previously belonged to the black Baptist church in Savannah under the leadership of the prominent black minister, Reverend George Sweet.[26] Enslaved people gravitated toward the missions in part because joining that religious community resonated with their earlier church experiences. Coming from communities saturated with churches and religious organizations, enslaved converts from Georgia were not only devoted churchgoers but often also skilled preachers and adept leaders.

The missionaries who received them, however, believed that enslaved Baptists needed close supervision and instruction to ensure they did not backslide into sinful or heathenish ways. In his early correspondence with the leadership of the ABCFM, missionary Cyrus Kingsbury credited himself with bringing education and salvation to both Indians and enslaved African Americans. He scarcely acknowledged the religious education, practices, and institutions that enslaved Baptists had already developed on their own. In the winter of 1820, Kingsbury noted in his journal that he had preached to a number of black people who "appeared very thankful for the instruction." That spring, he concluded that the number of black attendees at Sabbath services was on the rise because "they have an opportunity to learn to read in the morning."[27] Missionaries, like so many other white Americans, could not perceive the extent and vibrancy of black people's spiritual and intellectual lives. Even as missionaries witnessed black people's literacy and intellectual engagement with theology, they recorded the events in terms that rendered black people unthinking and unintelligent.

Kingsbury and his colleagues were certainly not exclusively responsible for spreading literacy among the enslaved in the Choctaw and Chickasaw nations. A number of enslaved people already knew how to read. Teaching enslaved people to read was a fairly common component of early nineteenth-century efforts to spread the Gospel in slave quarters in the southern states, explains historian Janet Duitsman Cornelius. Numerous Baptist and Methodist ministers and missionaries in the southern states, many of whom supported slavery, taught enslaved people to read the Bible but generally did not teach people how to write. In the hands of southern clergymen and slaveholders, biblical instruction served the social and economic interests of slavery. The religious schooling provided to slaves in the Choctaw Nation, therefore, does not necessarily distinguish missionaries and Choctaw slaveholders as kinder or more lenient than their counterparts in other parts of the South. Kingsbury and other missionaries positioned themselves as champions of the enslaved, but they nonetheless adhered to a racial hierarchy of white superiority. They taught reading as a means of instilling in black people virtues such as humility and obedience to white people and also preparing them to assist in the campaigns to Christianize and civilize Indians.[28]

A number of enslaved men and women did assume the role of intermediary between missionaries and Indians, serving mainly as interpreters. Records covering the early missionary presence in the Chickasaw Nation, which was socially and politically connected with the Choctaw Nation in the early nineteenth century, provide valuable examples and insights. During his 1799 tour of the Chickasaw nation, the Presbyterian missionary Reverend Joseph Bullen engaged the services of a black interpreter in Big Town, a Chickasaw village known to its residents as Chaguiliso. Also in the Chickasaw nation, an enslaved woman named Dinah worked as an interpreter to the Reverend Stuart. Dinah had been born in the Chickasaw nation but was fluent in both English and the Chickasaw language. Earthquakes in 1811 and 1812 had prompted her concern about the afterlife, and she attended prayer meetings at Monroe mission, where she learned to read and write. Because of her linguistic skills and professions of faith, Stuart relied on Dinah for many years to translate his sermons. In the Choctaw Nation, by contrast, Cyrus Kingsbury bemoaned the shortage of interpreters, which precluded him from devoting as much time as he would have liked to teaching religion.[29] But because many Choctaw and Chickasaw slaveholders already spoke English, enslaved converts did not necessarily face language barriers when they spoke to their masters about religion.

It is hard to know what enslaved people thought about the roles as proselytizers they either chose or into which they were cast by missionaries. We must remain mindful that enslaved translators and preachers worked for missionaries as their subordinates. Missionaries hired slaves from Indian masters and at times purchased slaves, albeit with the intention of manumitting them. Dinah, for example, ultimately purchased her freedom through her work as Stuart's interpreter. Certainly, by calling on slaves to assist with the religious education of Indians, the missionaries drew them into the assimilationist project and directed them to act in ways that would have been unthinkable in the southern states.[30] In the Indian nations, enslaved people participated in the education of the ruling class, assuming positions of intellectual and moral authority over free people and slaveholders. What did these moments of elevation mean to enslaved translators and interpreters? Did they and other enslaved converts pray for their masters because they saw them as sinners, as slaveholders, or as "savages"?

Well into the twentieth century, former slaves spoke of their Indian masters in the racial lexicon of the day, identifying Indians as "full blood" and "mixed blood" and often associating specific personality traits, such as kindness, cruelty, and avarice, with these classifications. For example, Choctaw freedman Edmond Flint said of Indian slaveholders, "There were humane and inhumane masters [and] . . . as a rule the slaveowning Indians were of mixed blood."[31] The ex-slave narratives of the 1930s tell us a great deal about how later generations of enslaved people thought and spoke about Indians in their interviews. These assessments, however, cannot easily be projected back one hundred years to the 1830s. Indeed, as historian Laura Lovett demonstrated in her assessment of the 1930s narratives, black people's discussion of their Indian ancestry and supposed racial traits can be best understood as an effort to blunt the force of early twentieth-century antiblack racism and violence.[32]

In the early antebellum period, enslaved believers seem to have given little thought to whether their masters were "civilized" by the standards of white Americans and focused instead on whether they were saved in the eyes of God. After hearing Reverend Bullen preach in 1799, one elderly woman owned by Chickasaw William Colbert proclaimed her joy at hearing the Gospel after having lived "long in heathen land."[33] Missionary Loring Williams reported, "Negroes are praying for their masters." But sometimes when enslaved people called loudly and openly for their masters to repent and seek salvation, the meanings of their prayers could be ambiguous, cloaking visions of deliverance from bondage in the evangelical language of faithful devotion to the Lord. At an 1822 prayer meeting, for example, one older woman testified, "Long time have I prayed for this wicked people. I first used to pray that Judgements of afflictions might bring them to repentance."[34] Echoing Old Testament calls for repentance, this woman's testimonial hints at the anticipation of the judgment that awaited slaveholders at the end of time. Not surprisingly, missionaries seized on these sentiments and utterances. From missionaries' vantage, slaves' prayers for their Indian masters appeared to demonstrate the power of conversion and offer proof of missionaries' expansive efforts to gain Indian converts.

Many enslaved Africans and African Americans arrived in Indian country conversant in the precepts of evangelical Christianity. They did not necessarily turn to missionaries as much for religious training. Rather, enslaved believers recognized that connections with missionaries afforded them resources and opportunities that might undercut the reach of their masters' control. No matter how grateful the enslaved were for the chance to learn and pray at the missions, they were never wholly reliant on the missionaries for religious and secular instruction. It is evident in mission records that generations of enslaved men and women organized their own spiritual gatherings, apart from the direction and supervision of both missionaries and masters.[35] In the summer of 1822, enslaved people in the Choctaw Nation's Western District attended services at Newell, a newly established mission in the area, but "nearly every evening the blacks in different places meet for prayer among themselves." Among the enslaved people in that area, a man named Peter, the son of a black Baptist preacher from the states, distinguished himself in their "social meetings [as] the principal leader." Despite their inability to read, Peter's group was able to "exhort with much feeling & propriety and sing several hymns very well." Another enslaved man named Solomon, whose literacy predated the missionaries' arrival, also preached and sang to gatherings of his fellow slaves. Perhaps drawing on earlier experiences of autonomy in black churches in Savannah and other urban settings, enslaved men and women developed and sustained their own religious institutions even as they formed close relationships with missionaries.[36]

Establishing ties with the local missions may very well have provided enslaved men and women with precisely the opportunities they desired to evade and resist their masters' control. In the 1820s more enslaved people than Indian slaveholders attended mission services. In the spring of 1822, "an unusual number of people, chiefly blacks" gathered for prayer meetings at Newell mission, and that summer Loring Williams found that enslaved people were far more serious about prayer and salvation than either the Indian children or women in the area.[37] Though some slaveholders joined the church, there is little indication that Choctaw slaveholders relied on proslavery interpretations of the Bible when directing and disciplining their slaves. Slaveholders, as missionaries complained, invested little energy in propagating the Gospel in slave quarters.[38] Given masters' general lack of interest in their slaves' religiosity, enslaved people had the opportunity to organize their own meetings without arousing their masters' suspicion or intrusion in ways that mirrored the practices of enslaved people in coastal South Carolina and Georgia.[39] Joining mission churches in Indian country likely provided enslaved people with the cover they needed to gather on their own for religious and secular reasons.

In addition to holding their own prayer meetings, individual enslaved men and women also seized the time and space to pray spontaneously and privately. One elderly woman, for example, testified at a mission meeting that when she felt the power of the Holy Spirit move her, she would "go in de bush" near her master's farm and pray. It should be noted that this woman felt "so heavy burden wid sin" when she was working in her master's fields. "I pray & pray and pray all de time when I go work in de field," she said. Stealing away to pray at such moments relieved her of the weight of a hoe or plow, along with the load of her sin. Other women and men, too, spoke of receiving spiritual inspiration and praying fervently in secluded spots away from their masters' homes and fields.[40] Large gatherings in each other's cabins and individual prayer sessions in brush arbors are best understood in the context of what Stephanie Camp terms a "rival geography," the ways enslaved people used and moved through time and space on their masters' plantations to serve their own needs and interests. In the Choctaw and Chickasaw nations, as in other parts of the Deep South, bondspeople's rival geography created opportunities for private reflection, communal exchanges, and respite from work but did not secure enslaved people's unmitigated autonomy or threaten to destroy the institution of slavery.[41]

The religious gatherings and prayerful moments orchestrated by enslaved men and women in the Choctaw and Chickasaw nations afforded them distance but not independence from either their masters or missionaries. Enslaved people connected to the mission stations effectively lived and labored under the surveillance of two masters—their Indian owners and the missionaries. Missionaries kept a close watch on enslaved worshippers, determined to stamp out the last vestiges of heathenism among black worshippers. Believing that the path to salvation lay in opening one's heart and soul to the workings of the Holy Spirit, missionaries watched slaves closely for the outward signs of their inner conversion. Missionaries were also on the lookout for insincerity, scrutinizing enslaved people's words and actions in religious settings to determine if they were sufficiently serious and pious. When an enslaved woman named Kate felt called to testify to other slaves about her religious rebirth, it was noted in a mission journal, "She has always been considered a very ignorant woman."[42] Missionaries in the Choctaw Nation had few kind words for the enslaved man Solomon who preached to other slaves. Though he regularly attended services at the Bethel mission, the missionaries objected to his insistence on preaching and reading the Bible to his fellow slaves because he lacked the "self-abasement and lowliness of mind" that the missionaries preferred among enslaved congregants.[43] Missionaries were pleased to welcome enslaved people into their prayer meetings and congregations, but they were less gratified to see the enslaved organizing their own gatherings and nominating teachers and preachers from within their ranks.

Choctaw slaveholders may have found themselves at odds with missionaries over the notion of Indian savagery and desirability of extending American "civilization" into Indian country, but they shared a firm belief in the need to monitor and contain black mobility and autonomy, especially when it came to visiting and praying at the missions. Contrary to the widespread antebellum sentiment, which continues to appear in current scholarship, Choctaws and other Indians were not lenient or benevolent masters by virtue of their Indian-ness. Though slaves often received permission to attend church meetings at the missions, they did not have free rein to travel and worship at will. In the early 1820s few enslaved people in the Choctaw Nation went to the church at the recently established Bethel mission because many masters looked askance at "any private attempt to instruct or converse with them," convinced that religious education, including learning to read the Bible, would "spoil" slaves.[44] When Harry, an enslaved man, professed his faith, he was "treated poorly and whipped without cause" by his mistress. A Choctaw slaveholding woman forbade her slave Hannah from attending services at Elliot mission in the winter of 1822.[45]

Such characterizations of *Indian* violence, of course, call to mind prevailing nineteenth-century racist stereotypes of Indian savagery; and these depictions of brutal *slaveholders* echo abolitionist writings in the states. At the same time, however, missionary accounts of slaveholders' domination and violence are substantiated by a variety of other sources, including sources authored by both slaveholders and former slaves. Rather than focus on missionaries' articulations of their perceptions of Indians or Indians' perceptions of their slaves, scholars would do well to consider the dynamics of power and control that arose as Indians, slaves, and missionaries encountered each other.

Choctaws' opposition to U.S. colonial intrusions played out in part through their resistance to the missionization project. It is a bitter irony of Native American and African American history that in the antebellum period Choctaws defended their autonomy against the United States in part by defending the institution of chattel slavery and Indians' ownership of black people as property. Choctaw slaveholders harbored a persistent distrust of the missionaries in large measure because of their antislavery stance. In public venues and private exchanges, the refrain was the same: Indian slaveholders suspected missionaries of working to destabilize their nation by disrupting if not destroying slavery.[46]

Choctaw slaveholders and lawmakers paid close attention to the issues of time, mobility, and independence that arose when enslaved people traveled to and from mission stations and interacted with missionaries. Eventually, Choctaw slaveholders' determination to limit slaves' contact with missionaries and thus exert greater control over enslaved people's time and movement found clear expression in the legal code. In 1836, shortly after the Choctaws had been removed from Mississippi and relocated in Indian Territory, Choctaw lawmakers, governing both the Choctaw and Chickasaw nations, prohibited teaching slaves "to read, to write, or to sing in meeting-houses or schools or in any open place" without their master's permission. Subsequent laws restricted enslaved people's possession of horses in an effort to hinder them from attending mission church services.[47]

Suspicious of northern missionaries' colonial agenda toward Indians, including their antislavery leanings, Choctaw slaveholders struck a double blow when they prevented enslaved people from attending the mission churches. The ban on church attendance aimed to disrupt the missions' viability and strengthen masters' control over their slaves' mobility and social relations. By prohibiting their slaves from worshipping at the missions, slaveholders used them to strike back against the religious branch of the larger federal project of cultural assimilation and land appropriation. When leading Choctaws tired of the missionaries' condescending attitudes or questioned their pedagogical approach toward both Indian pupils and African American worshippers, they withdrew their children and slaves, as well as their financial support, from mission schools and churches. In 1824, for example, Louis Leflore objected to the course of education and discipline imposed on his son and other Indian boys at the Bethel mission school, and he withdrew eight Indian children from the school; he also barred his fifty slaves from attending prayer services at the mission.[48] Withdrawing students, as well as funds, rendered the federal government's and missionaries' investments of time and resources in the schools and churches virtually worthless. In the wake of Leflore's removal of the Indian pupils and black congregants from Bethel, missionary Loring Williams lamented, "The vast expense incurred—for what?"[49]

In the early nineteenth century, U.S. colonial projects directed toward Native peoples took shape as complex, contradictory, and often uncertain endeavors. The so-called civilization programs crafted by missionaries, reformers, and federal policy makers did not aim to exterminate Indian peoples but rather sought to remake the fabric of Indians' social, economic, and political life. A growing number of scholars, especially Clara Sue Kidwell, Joel Martin, and Tiya Miles, have produced powerful and compelling works that illuminate the ways Native peoples adopted, adapted, and repurposed the tenets of American "civilization" campaigns.[50] Without minimizing the catastrophic effects of disease, war, dispossession, and forced removal, recent scholarship has illuminated the multifaceted nature of colonial projects and the ways colonial subjects influenced and even dictated the terms of engagement with colonial authorities. Bringing slavery and the enslaved to the foreground offers a previously neglected vantage from which to consider the ways local conditions and actors shaped the lines of authority and relations of power in the colonial setting of missionary settlements in the Native South.

The missionary record, like any other archive, requires careful and critical attention. Too often, missionaries rendered black men and women as unthinking actors, following the directives of either their masters, their missionary teachers, or even the supposed impulses of their racial traits. Even as missionaries recorded events, actions, and conversations that openly or more subtly challenged their authority, they attributed disruptive behavior and discordant speech to black people's racial inferiority—their lack of intelligence, morality, and self-control. The missionary archive in effect creates "slave" subjects and situates them in a colonial history of missionaries' efforts to "civilize" Indians. Scholars must therefore read these sources critically but must also bring a critical eye to the historiography and current scholarship that too often replicates colonial, racist categories and hierarchies by minimizing black people's social, emotional, political, and intellectual engagement with the world around them.

The relationships between missionaries, black slaves, and Indian slaveholders demonstrate the difficulty of drawing a single and clear line of distinction between "colonizer" and "colonized." As proxies of a colonial government, missionaries embraced some elements of U.S. efforts to subjugate Indian peoples more than others. Many missionaries, for example, objected vehemently to dispossession and removal. Missionaries found common cause with Christian slaves, deeming them more advanced or "civilized" than Indian slaveholders, but missionaries also shared Indians' perspective that black people should be contained and controlled. As outsiders, missionaries were intermittently or partially reliant on enslaved people's knowledge, skills, and cooperation. Enslaved people were never empowered as colonial agents, but they were positioned and situated themselves as important intermediaries. They recognized the potential for turning their shared Christian fellowship with missionaries to their own advantage. They pushed against the weight of both slaveholders and missionaries to fragment and redirect the lines of power.

NOTES

1. The most comprehensive history of the ABCFM missions to the Choctaws is Kidwell, *Choctaws and Missionaries in Mississippi*.
2. Cyrus Kingsbury wrote of the "distinguished blessing" of Christianity in an 1816 letter to Secretary of War William H. Crawford. Quoted in Kidwell, *Choctaws and Missionaries in Mississippi*, 25.
3. Cyrus Kingsbury's list of attendees quoted in Kidwell, *Choctaws and Missionaries in Mississippi*, 29.
4. V. Deloria, *Custer Died for Your Sins*, 102; Tinker, *Missionary Conquest*.
5. Miles, *The House on Diamond Hill*, 68.
6. Martin, "Crisscrossing Projects of Sovereignty and Conversion"; Kidwell, *Choctaws and Missionaries in Mississippi*.
7. Stoler, *Carnal Knowledge and Imperial Power*, 23.
8. Ashcroft, *Post-Colonial Transformation*, 50.
9. Portnoy, *Their Right to Speak*, 23–25; Cyrus Kingsbury quoted in Kidwell, *Choctaws and Missionaries*, 25.
10. Kidwell, *Choctaws and Missionaries*, 35; Atkinson, *Splendid Land*, 218.

11. Horsman, "The Indian Policy of an 'Empire for Liberty'"; Rothman, *Slave Country*. Secretary of War to William Cocke, March 19, 1816, in *The Territorial Papers of the United States*, ed. Clarence Edwin Carter, 669.

12. John C. Calhoun, December 5, 1818, in *Documents of United States Indian Policy*, ed. Francis Paul Prucha, 3rd ed. (Lincoln: University of Nebraska Press, 1975; 2000), 32.

13. 3 U.S. Stat. L., 85, Act on March 3, 1819.

14. Cyrus Kingsbury to Jeremiah Evarts, August 8, 1825, vol. 3, folder 12 ABCFM 18.3.4; *Christian Advocate and Journal and Zion's Herald*, April 3, 1829, 122.

15. *Missionary Herald* 25 (August 1829): 251; *Missionary Herald* 26 (March 1830): 82–84.

16. Kidwell, *Choctaws and Missionaries*, 29, 41.

17. Cyrus Kingsbury to Jeremiah Evarts, August 8, 1825, vol. 3, folder 12 ABCFM 18.3.4; Kidwell, *Choctaws and Missionaries*, 37, 41.

18. Kidwell, *Choctaws and Missionaries*, 38, 56, 68.

19. Cyrus Kingsbury to Rev. David Greene, December 25, 1844, vol. 8, folder 7; Cyrus Kingsbury to Rev. David Greene, May 31, 1845, vol. 8, folder 13, ABCFM 18.3.4.

20. Quoted in Miles, *Ties that Bind*, 93.

21. Thomas Jefferson, *Notes on the State of Virginia*; Miles, "'His Kingdom for a Kiss'"; Guyatt, "'The Outskirts of Our Happiness'"; Portnoy, *Their Right to Speak*, chaps. 3 and 4.

22. "The Prejudice against Color," in *Colored American*, June 3, 1837; Portnoy, *Their Right to Speak*, chaps. 3 and 4.

23. Stoler, *Along the Archival Grain*, 50.

24. Raboteau, *Slave Religion*, chap. 5.

25. Sobel, *Trabelin On*, 202, 214–15.

26. Loring Williams to Jeremiah Evarts, June 1823, vol. 2, folder 173, ABCFM 18.3.4; Loring Williams to Jeremiah Evarts, June 18, 1822, vol. 2, folder 169, ABCFM 18.3.4; Journal of the Mission at Elliot, January 7, 1821, vol. 1, folder 12–24, ABCFM 18.3.4; Journal of the Mission at Elliot, September 31, 1819, printed in *Missionary Herald*, vol. 16, no. 7, July 1820, 319.

27. Cyrus Kingbury journal, February 27, 1820, reprinted in *Missionary Herald*, vol. 16, no. 8, August, 1820, 366; Journal of the Mission at Elliot, March 1820, reprinted in *Missionary Herald*, vol. 16, no. 8, August, 1820, 364; Journal of the Mission at Elliot, February 18, 1821, vol. 1, fol. 12–24, ABCFM 18.3.4.

28. Loring Williams to Jeremiah Evarts, June 1823, vol. 2, folder 173, 18.3.4. Cyrus Kingsbury to Reverend C. B. Treat, February 1, 1854, vol. 8, folder 102, ABCFM 18.3.4. Cornelius, *When I Can Read My Title Clear*.

29. Phelps, "Excerpts from the Journal of the Reverend Joseph Bullen, 1799 and 1800," 262; Littlefield, *The Chickasaw Freedmen*, 8; Cyrus Kingsbury to Thomas McKenny, May 5, 1826, vol. 4, folder 278, ABCFM 18.3.4. For descriptions of Chickasaw towns, see Atkinson, *Splendid Land*, 186.

30. See Littlefield, *The Chickasaw Freedmen*, 5–10 for discussion of black people's roles in the assimilation project.

31. Edmond Flint in Rawick, *The American Slave*, vol. 12, 128–29.

32. My argument here is not that the sources are unreliable but that they reflect the thoughts of a much later generation of enslaved people, most of whom were children during their enslavement in Indian Territory not Mississippi. And the

interviews also reflect the conditions of both the interview process and the Depression. For studies that have used the WPA narratives to study Black/Indian history, see Naylor, *African Cherokees in Indian Territory*, and Lovett, "African and Cherokee by Choice"; Bay, *The White Image in the Black Mind*. For discussions of the possibilities and limitations of the sources, see Blassingame, "Using the Testimony of Ex-Slaves"; Shaw, "Using the WPA Ex-Slave Narratives."

33. Phelps, "Excerpts from the Journal of the Reverend Joseph Bullen 1799 and 1800," 271.

34. Loring Williams to Jeremiah Evarts, June 18, 1822, vol. 2, folder 169, ABCFM 18.3.4.

35. For references to secret religious gatherings in "brush arbors" see the narratives of Kiziah Love and Polly Colbert in Baker and Baker, *The WPA Oklahoma Slave Narratives*, 89, 260.

36. Creel, *A Peculiar People*, 149.

37. *Missionary Herald*, vol. 18, no. 9, September 1822, 290; Loring Williams to Jeremiah Evarts, June 18, 1822, vol. 2, folder 169, ABCFM 18.3.4.

38. Israel Folsom to Peter Pitchlynn, August 22, 1842, box 1, folder 81, Pitchlynn papers, Western History Collection, University of Oklahoma, Kidwell, *Choctaws and Missionaries*, 73–76.

39. Creel, *A Peculiar People*, 180–85.

40. Loring Williams to Jeremiah Evarts, June 18, 1822, vol. 2, folder 169, ABCFM 18.3.4; Raboteau, *Slave Religion*, chap. 5.

41. Camp, *Closer to Freedom*, 7.

42. Bethel Journal, 116, reprinted in *Missionary Herald*, April 1823, vol. 19, no. 4.

43. Loring Williams to Jeremiah Evarts, June 1823, vol. 2, folder 173, ABCFM 18.3.4.

44. Loring Williams to Jeremiah Evarts, June 1823, vol. 2, folder 173, ABCFM 18.3.4.

45. Journal of Elliot Mission, 1822, vol. 1, folder 31–37, ABCFM 18.3.4; Loring Williams to Jeremiah Evarts, June 1823, vol. 2, folder 173, ABCFM 18.3.4.

46. Krauthamer, *Black Slaves, Indian Masters*, chap. 2.

47. *The Constitution and Laws of the Choctaw Nation*, 21–22; Cyrus Kingsbury to Rev. David Greene, May 31, 1845, vol. 8, folder 13, ABCFM 18.3.4; Littlefield, *The Chickasaw Freedmen*, 13.

48. Loring Williams to Jeremiah Evarts, February 14, 1824, vol. 2, folder 174, ABCFM 18.3.4; Kidwell, *Choctaws and Missionaries*, 96. Missionaries were rarely surprised when Choctaws and Chickasaws took exception to their methods of education and correction and looked elsewhere for teachers and schools. Cyrus Kingsbury wrote to the Office of Indian Affairs in the spring of 1826, "The system of labour adopted and [pursued?] in our schools has been the principal ground of objection on the part of the natives, and was I believe the primary reason for them wishing to have a school in Kentucky." Cyrus Kingsbury to the War Department, Office of Indian Affairs, May 5, 1826, vol. 4, folder 278, ABCFM 18.3.4.

49. Loring Williams quoted in Kidwell, *Choctaws and Missionaries*, 96.

50. Kidwell, *Choctaws and Missionaries*; Martin, *Native Americans and Christianity*; Miles, *The House on Diamond Hill*.

6 AUGUSTO ESPIRITU

American Empire, Hispanism, and the Nationalist Visions of Albizu, Recto, and Grau

"For us, race has nothing to do with biology. . . . Race is the perpetuation of virtues and characteristic institutions. We distinguish ourselves by our culture, by our courage, by our nobility, by our Catholic sense of civilization."

—Pedro Albizu Campos

Between 1930 and 1960, Pedro Albizu Campos (1893–1965), head of the Nationalist Party of Puerto Rico, Claro Mayo Recto (1890–1960), Naciona-lista Party stalwart of the Philippines, and Ramón Grau San Martín (1887–1969), founder of the Partido Revolucionario de Cuba, Auténtico (Authentic Cuban Revolutionary Party) became household names in their respective countries. Whether it was because they inspired militant nationalist move-ments or aroused fear in the U.S. government and their local allies for their uncompromising anti-imperial positions, each figure would loom large in the histories of the Caribbean and Asia. During an era of American domi-nation, when it was unpopular to criticize the United States, Albizu, Recto, and Grau risked their reputations and their lives to expose the machina-tions of U.S. (neo)colonialism. In turn, their vocal anticolonial resistance helped to empower local nationalist movements. Perhaps testifying to the power of their criticisms was the epithet hurled at them in the American press, that of "anti-American." But unlike various left-leaning, working-class critics of America, these three intellectuals were in fact among the elite, Western-educated, and professionally accomplished intellectuals of their time, a fact that likely made their words more appealing to a more mainstream audience.

In this chapter, I will explore the anti-imperial nationalist politics of Recto, Albizu, and Grau, in the general context of American empire and its unique imperial relations with Puerto Rico, the Philippines, and Cuba. Alyosha Goldstein's statement in the introduction that "analyzing U.S. colonialism demands understanding U.S. empire and the imperial nation-state as itself a comparative project and mode of power" is especially germane here, as the imperial transfer from Spain to the United States creates different conditions of hegemony and counterhegemonic maneuver in each national setting. I attempt as well to map the complex nationalist politics of Recto, Albizu, and Grau, whose goal was to deconstruct and dismantle empire's economic, political, and legal assumptions. Certainly, what lends an intensity to their appraisals of the United States and its colonial policies is their frequent contact with or experiences of living in the U.S. metropole, as much as their experience with (neo)colonialism at home. As a kind of "strategic essentialism," they sought to deploy elements of hispanismo as the basis for nationalist identity and resistance to the extremes of Americanization. As the epigraph of Albizu shows, hispanismo was imbued with deep emotional resonance and involved a conception of *raza* that drew from what he says is "our culture," "our courage," "our nobility," and "our Catholic sense of civilization," the very same congeries of values from which Recto and Grau, in differing registers, would draw on. Still, as we shall see, hispanismo, despite its powerful rhetoric, was, like its cousin *négritude*, not without its blind spots.[1]

In the (neo)colonial context, hispanismo belongs to what the Venezuelan cultural critic Magdalena López has labeled "transculturation discourses,"[2] those hybrid cultural languages developed in response to American imperial cultural hegemony. The label draws in part from Fernando Ortiz's famous delineation of "transculturation" in terms of overlapping ethno-racial influences on contemporary Cuban culture. Transculturation discourses would be critical to the rearticulation of "Americanization" in the U.S. insular empire in the Caribbean and the Pacific and shaped as well the political discourses of the three intellectual figures under examination here. For López, as for Dominican intellectual historian Silvio Torres-Saillant, "conceptions such as 'transculturation,' *negritude*, Hispanism, cultural *mestizaje* share the realization that Caribbean and/or Latin American entities responded in lesser or greater measure to the 'imperial instigation of the West.'"[3] Two are of particular significance for this study—"Hispanism," or hispanismo, as the valorization of Spain and the "Latin" cultural and civilizational legacy, as against the "Saxon," Anglophone, American civilization; and "mestizaje," the national valorization of various forms of interracial mixing in response to the ideology of American racism.

In what follows, I begin with an account of American empire's development with respect to its Caribbean and Pacific colonies. I then discuss the irruption of Recto, Albizu, and Grau in the American national imaginary and the grounds for their criticism of America. My goal in this section is to highlight the importance of these figures in reexamining American empire during the first half of the twentieth century, especially from the combined viewpoints of the Philippines and the Caribbean. In this sense, they join the anti-imperial, anticolonial intellectuals of their time, especially from Latin America, whose voices challenged the unmitigated expansion of the American behemoth. In the second part of the essay, I explore the cultural dimensions of Americanization of relevance to these U.S. dependencies and, in response to these challenges, explore the politico-cultural contexts that provided the foundations for the unique cultural politics of Recto, Albizu, and Grau. My concern in this section is to highlight the survival and rearticulation of the often dismissed Spanish cultural legacy, which is of long duration and deeply imprinted in the psyches of its former colonial subjects.

THE AMERICAN IMPERIAL BACKGROUND

First, the years in which Albizu, Recto, and Grau lived marked American empire's transition from a long period of "continental" imperialism to a brief period of "insular" imperialism and toward a much longer era of "informal empire."[4] As many of the essays in this volume can attest, U.S. empire building began in the eighteenth century, not in the twentieth century. Its east-west trajectory was shaped by the hunger for land among European settlers and the ongoing conflicts with European imperial powers and American Indian tribes and nations. In the nineteenth century, as is extensively discussed in Alyosha Goldstein's introduction to this book, America's national boundaries and continental dimensions would emerge from the varied deployment of legal precedents and landmark treaties, for the purposes of U.S. expansionism, such as the Louisiana Purchase, the Treaty of Guadalupe-Hidalgo, and the Alaska Purchase, the creation of a colonial system of reservations, the extension of slavery, and the reinforcement of racial discrimination. Along with these territorial acquisitions, various social dynamics of this period would profoundly shape future U.S. imperial enterprises, especially the racial ideologies of Anglo-Saxonism ("Manifest Destiny"), nativism, and white supremacy.[5]

Thus, the Spanish-American and Philippine American Wars as well as the Treaty of Paris of 1898, by which the Philippines, Puerto Rico, Guam, and Cuba became U.S. dependencies, could hardly be said to be departures from the history of territorial expansion, the foreign affairs, and the legal evolution of the United States as an empire. The United States embraced the acquisition of Spain's former colonies of Puerto Rico, the Philippines, and Cuba, and the suppression of their aspirations for autonomy or independence. United States military occupation followed and along with it the spread of racial ideologies that justified both American projects of reform *and* racial discrimination in these islands as well as a two-tier legal system in which the colonies were regarded as unincorporated territories, decidedly of an inferior nature to American states, whose fates were to be left to Congress and the executive branch of the government.[6] The Philippines, Puerto Rico, and Guam became colonies, while Cuba was granted nominal independence, though much circumscribed by the Platt Amendment, which provided the United States with the legal cover for repeated military interventions. However, there was one essential feature that was new in the United States' imperial legal arsenal, what Goldstein describes in his introduction as "unincorporation." American imperial policy makers, wary of bitter anti-imperialist sentiment and nativism at home, soon realized the political unsustainability of direct colonial rule and would respond in various ways to deflect those challenges. Thus, under the Platt, Cuba became a protectorate. In the meantime, responding from popular pressures from below as well as the complaints of American sugar producers and labor leaders, the Congress set a timetable for Philippine "independence" while acting to establish "commonwealth" status for Puerto Rico.[7] Yet, while Americans were dismantling most of the trappings of *formal* empire, they were at the same time replacing them with the instruments of *informal* empire. These included official pronouncements of policies such as the "Open Door," "Dollar Diplomacy," and the "Good Neighbor," which aggressively promoted free trade, the use of economic pressures for leverage, and the acknowledgment of the right of nations to self-determination in a world of relative equals.[8] Indeed, this "free trade imperialism" was not anything new, as Robinson and Gallagher have argued—European powers in the nineteenth century had already been moving toward such a subtle innovation emphasizing trade and mutual benefit and recognizing their effectiveness, as opposed to direct, military methods of conquest. Such pronouncements accompanied more severe U.S. practices in its dependencies, including the limitation of power to landowning, pro-American elites or authoritarian strongmen, the preservation of economic dependency on U.S. markets, and the establishment of U.S. military bases for the preservation of American interests after the scaling back or formal withdrawal of U.S. occupation.[9] Such practices would survive past World War II and into the Cold War as the United States granted the Philippines independence in 1946, allowed Puerto Rico "associated free state" status in 1948, and supported the Batista dictatorship in Cuba from 1952 to 1959. The various forms of formal and informal empire would become the very target of the anticolonial, anti-imperial criticisms of Albizu, Recto, and Grau.

The second transition of this era, especially germane to Albizu, Recto, and Grau, involved the accompanying cultural transformation of the colonies, from a long process of "Hispanization" (Spain's sovereignty over Puerto Rico, the Philippines and Cuba, as opposed to the other Latin American ex-colonies, lasted several decades longer) to a fairly rapid "Americanization" (of half a century) that resulted in Caribbean and Pacific intellectuals exchanging a European orientation for a North American one. Albizu, Recto, and Grau all directly experienced the tail end of the Spanish colonial period, as children or adolescents, and they would spend formative years of their education during the early part of U.S. (neo)colonial rule when Hispanic influences remained strong. The social atmosphere prevailing during their time combined the rising expectations of patriotic and Hispanicized elites and masses (made up of natives, mestizos, blacks, Chinese, and white creoles) whose sentiments had been aroused by long nineteenth-century struggles for assimilation, autonomy, or separation from Spain, or, as in the case of Cuba, for annexation to the United States. At the same time, with the United States' sudden victory over Spain and its suppression of movements for independence or local autonomy, frustrations lingered among the veterans of these national struggles, giving rise to feelings of an "unfinished revolution" or "stolen independence."[10] The brief hiatus between the collapse of Spanish rule and the advent of U.S. occupation, which allowed for invaluable experiences of self-rule, tended to reinforce their love for the Spanish motherland, Spanish monuments in the colonies, the Spanish language, Spanish Catholicism, and Spanish honor and manhood.

By contrast, "Americanization" irrupted into the lives of the colonized through its constellation of ideologies, arising out of U.S. needs for "pacification." Both the War of 1898 and the Philippine-American War impressed colonized intellectuals like Albizu, Recto, and Grau as displays of

Anglo-Saxon racial supremacy and disdain for brown, black, yellow, and mixed-race peoples. This violent side, however, was only one aspect of Americanization. Reflecting its origins in the era of Progressivism, Americanization was also about bringing the benefits of Anglo-Saxon government, expressed in various projects of improvement, education, and reform, to colonized peoples who were deemed capable of being civilized. Notable among these benevolent reforms was the attempt to make English either an official language or the language of instruction in the public schools. Apropos of Vicente Rafael's observation in this volume that linguistic diversity has historically accompanied the insistence that the United States "has always been, was meant to be, and must forever remain a monolingual nation," Spanish and, in the case of the Philippines, other vernaculars were tolerated by the U.S. colonial administration, although the campaign for English clearly sought to *replace* the existing languages, not supplement them. Consequently, while public education and English-language instruction provided opportunities for social mobility for masses of people previously excluded from politics, administration, and the economy, attempts to impose English as an official language or as a language of instruction resulted in some cases in a reaction against Americanization efforts.[11] In line with these developments, U.S. imperialism mobilized the "Black Legend," an old stereotype prevalent in Europe and the United States, of the exceptional savagery of the Spanish Conquest and the "decadence" of the Spanish Empire, which was expressed especially during the Wars of 1898 and the Philippines in cartoons that depicted "Spanish misrule" over its colonies, Spanish "butchery," and a lack of chivalry toward colonized women.[12] Such views, of course, which Americans felt the need to utilize, served conveniently to distract attention from American empire's own violent methods of conquest and to reinforce Protestant, Anglo-American claims to civilizational superiority over Latin Spain.

Ironically, while the Black Legend held some purchase among Philippine and Latin American intellectuals in the late nineteenth century, America's victory over Spain and its own conquest of Cuba, Puerto Rico, Guam, and the Philippines served to "desatanize Spain" and to "satanize the United States" among Latin American and Filipino intellectuals.[13] In Puerto Rico, the U.S. attempt to impose English in the schools met with fierce resistance among nationalist leaders as well as a broad segment of the population for whom Spanish was the mother tongue. Nationalist leaders like José de Diego, Salvador Brau, and Luis Muñoz Rivera provided the inspiration for the rise of cultural nationalism among intellectuals (women as well as men) in the 1920s and 1930s, centered around the search for Puerto Rico's unique insular culture, the affirmation of its unique racial elements, and its strong connections to Spanish culture.[14] This constellation of cultural nationalist elements has had a powerful impact down to present times as a result of its impact on Puerto Rican nationalist political parties, inspiring both the Nationalist Party and the Popular Democratic Party alike. The former believed in political confrontation with the United States while the latter—which has become the hegemonic institution of modern-day Puerto Rico through the leadership of Luis Muñoz Marín—in political accommodation.

In the Philippines, nationalist leaders unified in demanding that Spanish, not English, as the Americans decreed, should be the national language, claiming that English-language requirements would remove the country's best leaders from office.[15] While this initial resistance would end in defeat, the demand for Spanish would make it the language of elite society, law, and government for some time, while political leaders would preserve its use well into the era of increasing English-language dominance in the 1930s and 1940s.[16] Until the Japanese occupation in the 1940s, the small minority of Spaniards in the Philippines, many of them sympathetic to the fascists and General Franco's Falange Party, also played a disproportionately important role in Philippine politics. Indeed, despite the U.S. propaganda coup of English-language success in the Philippines in one generation, the foundations of that view have been coming under increasing scrutiny and suggest that Spanish might have remained more widespread among Filipinos than previously thought.[17] Of course, Hispanic cultural influences, the legacies of centuries of Hispanization, have been undeniable.

And in Cuba, where the United States mandated English and also relied on civil society institutions like the Protestant missionaries and American corporations to "assimilate" the Cubans, Spanish-language use and Hispanism remained strong. The predominance of Spaniards in the economy, the continuation of pre-1898 policies favoring white Spanish immigration to offset the fear of a black, ex-slave majority, and the strength of Spanish provincial associations led to widespread efforts at maintaining Spanish language and culture through newspapers, journals, travel to Spain, and various local activities well into the 1930s, when the sugar trade declined precipitously in the worldwide depression and drastically cut Spanish immigration.[18] Nonetheless, there was one group of Spanish migrants—the Republican refugees of the Spanish Civil War—that would have a widespread influence in both Cuba and Puerto Rico, and, much less so, in the Philippines. As leading academics, writers, journalists, poets, and artists, these Spaniards would come to occupy important positions in the society of both countries until their return to Spain or migration elsewhere.[19]

It was precisely at the cusp of both empires that Albizu, Recto, and Grau would emerge, as their beneficiaries and their most strident, nationalist critics. In this section, I examine the anti-imperial politics for which they were known. In the subsequent section, I explore the cultural dimensions of their thinking, especially its Hispanist foundations, which have often been obscured in standard considerations of their nationalist politics.

U.S. EMPIRE AND ITS ANTI-IMPERIAL OTHERS

Albizu irrupted into the consciousness of Americans during the 1930s because of his leadership of the Nationalist Party. After a dismal showing in the 1932 elections, Albizu shifted to militant actions that challenged American authority and exposed U.S. imperialism. Harold Ickes, for one, painted the Harvard-trained lawyer as "a very dangerous person" because "he [was] opposed to United States sovereignty."[20] He became a target of U.S. repression, and for his alleged role in the disturbances in Ponce in 1937, he was sent to Atlanta federal penitentiary for six years. Albizu believed that U.S. rule over Puerto Rico was illegal because the Treaty of Paris had excluded an already self-governing Puerto Rican nation from the negotiations. Moreover, he charged that American economic policies toward Puerto Rico favoring free trade, sugar dependency, and land concentration were impoverishing Puerto Ricans. And he not only rejected compromise with the United States but also thought that Luis Muñoz Marín's proposal for a "free associated state" was a selling out of the nation. Albizu's later life was like a revolving door, with brief moments of freedom alternating with long stretches in prison. Whether rightly or not, he was blamed for the spectacular terroristic actions of his followers, and he would die in 1965 without having seen an independent Puerto Rico.

Like Albizu, Claro M. Recto opposed American imperialism, especially during the Cold War era.[21] As a young lawyer and politician who visited the United States to lobby for Philippine independence, Recto caught the attention of American officials as a promising leader of an independent Philippines, which it was to become in 1946. It was after independence that Senator Recto would become a thorn in the side of Americans. United States officials and the largely pro-American Philippine political elite branded him as an "anti-American" for his nationalist economic policies, his questioning of U.S. Cold War strategy in East Asia, and his opposition to the renewal of U.S. military bases in the country. The U.S. government was apparently so worried that Recto would be elected president in the 1957 elections that it had the CIA plant stories that he was "a Communist Chinese agent" and even made plans to assassinate him, abandoning the idea only for "'pragmatic considerations rather than moral scruples.'"[22] While Recto failed to gain the nomination of his party, he continued to be influential because of the "Filipino First" policies of the Carlos P. Garcia administration, which shared Recto's nationalist philosophy. Recto's life, however, would be cut short. While on a cultural goodwill tour of Europe and Latin America, he died of a heart attack in Rome in 1960.

Similar to Albizu and Recto, Ramón Grau San Martín was a popular nationalist figure in Cuba.[23] While a medical doctor with a flourishing practice in Havana, Dr. Grau became involved in the opposition to the U.S.-backed Machado dictatorship. In the Revolution of 1933 that forced Machado into exile, Grau was chosen president by the provisional government. He called on the United States to exercise its "spirit of fair play" and support his program,[24] which included progressive social legislation and the abrogation of the Platt Amendment. He was beset, however, by the Roosevelt administration's refusal to recognize his government and Ambassador Sumner Welles's behind-the-scenes maneuvers to depose him. At Welles's prompting, military strongman Fulgencio Batista, who promptly berated the Grau government's "Communist and Socialist tactics,"[25] led a military coup that sent Grau to Miami. After several years of exile, Grau returned to Cuba and ran successfully for the presidency in 1944. As president, Grau was not an easy partner for the United States, despite the mellowing of his nationalist politics and the corruption in his government. He negotiated for a greater share of the American market for Cuban sugar, called for the removal of American air bases from Cuban soil, and consistently sided with labor in its conflicts with American capital. After his stint in public office, the venerable Grau would oppose the Batista dictatorship, and subsequently, Fidel Castro's Communist regime. Unlike many Cubans of his social class, Grau chose to remain in Havana, where he died in 1968.

THE TRANSCULTURATION DISCOURSES
OF THE ANTI-IMPERIALISTS

It is thus in the cultural contexts provided by the American colonial discourse of civilization and the ideology and practice of Americanization, most intensely in terms of its policy of English-language nationalism or Anglophone imperialism, that we can understand the *other*, cultural dimensions of anticolonialism and its hybrid constructions, what López describes as the congeries of "transculturation discourses." Along the Caribbean-Pacific axis, those of "Hispanism" and "mestizaje," in particular, had particularly important influences. And while Hispanism has traditionally referred to the imperial Spanish colonial project and later the Creole elite's nationalist project of enlisting Spanish culture in the service of anticolonial nationalist unification and subsequent domination of indigenous cultures in Latin America, it becomes the basis for an alternative cultural form to Anglo-Saxon culture.[26]

Indeed, alongside of and just as crucial to Albizu's philosophical and political critique of American empire and uncompromising demand for Puerto Rico's independence was an equally powerful Hispanism. While Pedro was considered a mulatto and an illegitimate child, his father was Spanish, of Basque origins, a fact that seems to have been significant for the young Albizu's embrace of Spain. Conceivably, Albizu could have embraced more forcefully his African descent, especially because his mother was black and because he had been born and had grown up in Ponce, Puerto Rico's second largest city, its most prosperous because it had been the center of sugar production, and the center of African culture because of the large number of Afro–Puerto Ricans there. Albizu, however, chose a different path culturally, embracing Spain's royal heritage, Spanish language, and Catholicism. In this perhaps, he was most influenced by his long years of expatriation in the United States during the Progressive Era, especially his education at Harvard University, where he met Indian nationalists like Subash Chandra Bose and the Nobel Prize winner Rabindranath Tagore. He also volunteered for the U.S. Army when war broke out—that is, before U.S. citizenship for Puerto Ricans was granted in the 1917 Jones Act—and experienced the blatant segregation and racism that characterized the U.S. military during this time. Similar to José Martí in the late nineteenth century, Albizu's American experiences had led not only to respect for America's power but also to profound knowledge of and anger at its flaws—racism, labor exploitation, and imperialism to name a few. These, in turn, sharpened his sense of difference, that is, the belief that he as a Puerto Rican *was not, nor could ever be*, an "American." Unbeknownst to, or perhaps denied by, many in Puerto Rico during his time, "America" was a *racial* and not a *political* community, and Americans could never accept equality for Puerto Ricans because of their dark skins, a fact that Albizu was to use as an argument again and again against those advocating U.S. statehood for Puerto Rico.

It would seem that Albizu's outlook while in America focused on two directions; one was toward the very Catholic Irish nationalist resistance to the British Empire, and the other was toward the writings of Latin Americans, for whom the expansion of American empire and cultural imperialism had necessitated that a *cultural* response be deployed. With respect to the former, Stephens Arroyo has written of Albizu's meeting with Eamon de Valera and the influence of militant Irish nationalism on his views of nationalist organizing in Puerto Rico. Both de Valera and Albizu shared a common influence in the Catalan cleric and philosopher Jaime Balmés, who sought to rearticulate Spanish Catholicism into a militant tradition, one that would nonetheless adapt itself to the needs of modernity. At the same time, Albizu seemed to have read widely of Latin American nationalist writers who increasingly argued for a cultural, Hispanist response to North American racism and Anglo-American cultural influences. He had been exposed to the writings of José Enrique Rodo (Uruguay), Pedro Henriquez Ureña (Dominican Republic), and José Vasconcelos (of Mexico).

At the core of Albizu's Hispanism was his defense of Puerto Rico's heritage of Spanish language, Catholicism, imperial administration, and independent landholding gained from several centuries of apprenticeship under Spain. He rejected English and American values, the values of the *yanqui* of soulless materialism, which he counterposed to Puerto Rico's soul.[27] At times, Albizu's Hispanism was so absolute that even during a public celebration for the liberal victory over the reactionary monarchy in Spain in the early 1930s, he extolled the virtues of the Spanish monarchs who had established such order and virtue in their empire.[28]

But lest we be thrown off into an exclusive focus on his spiritualist attack on America and embrace of Spain, we need to recall that Albizu's Hispanism had a pragmatic international political dimension as well, as evidenced by Albizu's trip to Latin America during the late 1920s and early 1930s, sponsored by the Nationalist Party, as well as his or the party's attendance at various pan-American conferences from the 1930s to the 1950s. Hispanism in this instance provided the cultural basis for an attempt to make the Latin world aware of Puerto Rico's plight under American imperialism, to unmask its hemispheric role as America's "show window," and to announce the significance of Puerto Rico's nationalist struggle against U.S. imperialism for the rest of the Western Hemisphere.[29]

It has been and will perhaps continue to be debated whether Albizu's Hispanism was farsighted or retrogressive, indispensable or inimical to the cause of Puerto Ricanness and independence for which he fought and for which many have continued to struggle. Arcadio Díaz Quiñones has noted the profound contradictions in Albizu—he was biracial and fully bilingual but an ardent Hispanist (not minding Catholic Spain's troubling whiteness and racism), he believed in a military solution to colonialism that most Puerto Ricans had rejected, and though a firebrand for national liberty, he believed in the segregation of the sexes in the schools.[30] The more so, I would argue, that to exclude or occlude these striking cultural aspects from his political philosophy and social impact would be to disfigure his legacy.

Similarly, a purely political rendering of Recto would leave out the profound sense of "cultural" nationalism that infused his political philosophy and social life, one that simultaneously involved a romantic Hispanism. Recto was the son of a Spanish army officer and a mother who was descended from a British officer who had fought in the 1762 British invasion of Manila. He grew up in the prosperous and very Hispanic town of Lipa, Batangas, in the late nineteenth century. Lipa's elite, as Glenn May writes, became prosperous as a result of the rising prices of coffee and sugar, as the Philippines became more and more integrated in the world market. The town's *principalía*, however, were not satisfied with global economic integration but also sought to display their wealth and power through conspicuous consumption, which for them meant the building of Spanish-style architecture (churches and homes), the collection of commodities and luxury items from Europe, and the acquisition of the elements of cultural capital, which under the Spanish colonial dispensation meant education in the colonial capital of Manila, mastery of the Spanish language, and similar to the *ilustrados* described by Schumacher, the sending of their youth overseas to study in Europe's universities. According to Batangueño intellectual Teodoro M. Kalaw, this high society was Hispanized:

> Its language was Spanish; Spanish were its customs, manners, and
> social forms; Spanish were its dances, its music. The social atmo-
> sphere was an importation from Spain and included its peculiar faults
> and vices. Money was splurged on clothes, interior decoration, and
> pictures; on rare crystals and china ordered from Europe; on curtains
> of the finest silk, on stuffed chairs from Vienna, on exquisite table
> wines and foods. Lipa society sought to equal the halls and banquets
> of Spain herself, the Metropolis, the Guiding Star, the Ideal.[31]

While he came of age during the U.S. colonial period, Recto's education was entirely in the Jesuit-run, Spanish-language instruction of the Ateneo de Manila and Universidad de Santo Tomás. As a budding poet and writer in

Spanish, Recto was critical early in his career of what he labeled the "violent Saxonization" of Philippine culture—grounded in materialism and individualism—and advocated greater balance between the conflicting Hispanic and the Anglo-Saxon forces among Filipinos.[32] For writing poems and a play embodying such ideals, he was unjustly pilloried in the press, forcing a switch of career, from literature to politics. In order to do so, he abandoned literary writing in Spanish and soon mastered the new occupier's language, English.[33]

Hispanism was not an occasional tendency in Recto but a *world*, though but *one* world, in the Philippines' complex, multilingual, and multicultural society, providing both a sense of aesthetic pleasure and moral foundation as well as subterranean roots for his criticisms of Americanism. He had much to draw from, from José Rizal to Apolinario Mabini to Isabelo de los Reyes, all of whom wrote vigorous literary works, academic treatises, or political tracts in Spanish and experienced firsthand the racism and arrogance of the new American empire.[34] Recto never gave up being in some way involved with the promotion of Spanish in the Philippines, either as a judge of literary contests, or through acquaintance with the Spanish government in the Philippines, which was, under General Francisco Franco's diplomatic offensive, eager to promote Hispanism and gain international support from its former colonies. Recto seems to have refrained from any criticism of the Franco dictatorship, a troubling silence for someone who saw himself as a defender of freedom. Under its auspices, Recto was to finally make this connection to Hispanism a reality by touring Spain and Latin America, places he had never visited, in 1960. Prior to this journey, he had traveled several times to the United States during various independence missions, and, in his capacity as Philippine foreign minister during the wartime collaboration government, he had traveled to Japan. For his long-awaited visit to Spain, he had prepared seven speeches in Spanish on the cultural connections between Spain and the Philippines. The speeches included a group of five that establish the poetical, political, aesthetic, moral, and linguistic legacies of Spain in the Philippines: "Cecilio Apóstol (El Poeta—cumbre de Filipinos)," "Manuel Luis Quezon, primer presidente del Commonwealth de Filipinas (conferencia)," "La mujer española," "La cruzada por el Español en Filipinas," and "Por los fueros de una herencia." A second group of two speeches, "Los convenios sobre bases militares entre España y Estados Unidos y entre Filipinas y Estados Unidos (Un paralelo)" and "El Pacto del Atlántico y el Pacto del Pacífico (un paralelo)," includes comparison of U.S. military agreements signed with Spain and with the Philippines and an indictment of the disparities in U.S.

security concerns for its Atlantic allies as opposed to its Pacific allies.[35] Like Rizal before him, whose voyage to Cuba was curbed by his arrest in Barcelona and execution in the Philippines, Recto likewise failed to reach Spain and Latin America. He died in Italy before he could complete his journey.[36]

Finally, even for such a secular political figure such as Ramón Grau San Martín of Cuba, cultural questions need to be explored to get a fuller sense of his anti-Americanism. While Grau differs from Recto and Albizu in not having a strident literary connection to Hispanism, one might profitably inquire into various kinds of cultural influences on his political views. It is amazing that for such an important historical figure in U.S.-Cuban relations, there remains no biographical study of Grau in the English language. And even in Spanish, only two works on Grau might properly be termed biographical, neither of them placing Grau within the larger *cultural* developments out of which he emerged or within the fertile period of cultural, philosophical, and political reflection in Cuban intellectual circles during the 1920s. Hence, given the paucity of studies on Grau's cultural milieu, what follows relies as much on what we know about Grau and attempts to answer certain questions arising out of it with some historical speculation.

First, it is important to note Grau's thoroughly Spanish background and upbringing in western Cuba. Grau's father and mother were both recent Spanish immigrants of the late nineteenth century, from Catalonia and Asturias, to the western sugar growing province of Pinar del Río.[37] They came at a time in which Spain was encouraging white immigration to offset the island's large black population, recently emancipated in 1886, while simultaneously discouraging the white Creole landlords from espousing revolutionary sentiments by feeding on their racial fears of a vengeful, empowered black community, symbolized by the *mambises*.[38] Grau's grandfather, the patriarch of the plantation family that Grau's father married into, was, moreover, deeply pro-Spanish in sentiments, if we are to believe the image painted by Grau biographer Rodriguez Morejón of his nostalgic patriotism upon seeing El Morro, the Spanish castle walls of La Habana and the bulwark of Spanish colonialism in Latin America for several hundred years.

> La vista de la severa silueta del castillo de 'El Morro,' excita el orgullo patrio de don Antolín, quien, no pudiendo resistir el entusiasmo que como buen español le produce la contemplación de la arcaica fortaleza, comienza a darle al jovencito observador [Ramón Grau], una vehemente y apasionada conferencia sobre la inexpugnabilidad de ese baluarte de la Corona de España. (The view of El Morro's severe silhouette

excited Don Antolín's patriotic pride. Unable to resist the enthusiasm that the contemplation of such an ancient fortress naturally produces in a Spaniard, he began to give the youth observing [the fortress from the arriving boat] a vehement and impassioned lecture on the inexpungibility of that bastion of the Spanish Crown.)[39]

Something of Don Antolín's passion for Spain probably rubbed off as well on Grau's brother, Francisco, who, as mentioned earlier, became a columnist for Spanish newspapers before his suicide. Grau's parents, who were prominent in the elite social circles of Las Palmas, sent Grau away from his home in Pinar del Río for fear of General Antonio Maceo's war on the hacendados of the region, and soon enough, Maceo did invade and wreak havoc in Las Palmas. Upon their deaths, Grau's parents left him and his brother a rich inheritance,[40] which Ramón Grau used to pursue medical studies by traveling to Italy, France, and Spain before returning to Cuba, working as a physician, and then becoming professor of physiology at the University of Havana.

Hence, for Grau, entry into Cuba's white elite circles would have been something quite natural. As cited in Alfonso Schweyer's work as well as that of Hugh Thomas, Spanish immigrants made up by far the largest source of immigration into Cuba during the first three decades of the twentieth century, even larger than all the other migrants from the Caribbean combined. But not only were their numbers important, the Spanish community was extremely active and influential. Since before the War of 1898, social clubs of provincial origin, most notably El Casino Gallego, had been founded, playing a largely conservative role in being stalwarts for the continuation of Spanish colonial rule in Cuba. In the War of 1898, the United States, while militarily defeating Spanish army and naval forces, did not, as in the case of Santiago, divest them of their ability to remain influential in Cuba's politics, and even more so, in Cuba's economic life, where they had been among the largest and most prosperous landowners. With Spain's defeat, as Schweyer acutely observed, the Spanish community in Cuba set about the task of revising Cuban historical memory, especially through its influential and long-lasting newspaper, *Diario de la Marina*, by downplaying Cuban nationalism and Spanish colonialism, and instead creating an exclusively favorable view of Spain's contributions to Cuban society while promoting continued cultural and economic attachments to the "mother country."

Moreover, as Lillian Guerra has so ably argued, this Hispanist dimension did not remain in the sidelines but was embraced by Cuba's first president,

Tomás Estrada Palma, and the Republican Party around him. As Guerra notes, Estrada unabashedly accepted the Asturias Prize, a symbol of the largesse of the Spanish royal family, and likewise of its white, Catholic, and absolutist dimensions, without blinking an eyelash for the sensitivities of so many veterans of the Cuban Liberation Army who had so recently fought against Spain or for the countless Cubans who had died in that war. Moreover, the aggressive, pro-Spanish political elite led by Estrada practiced racial discrimination in government appointments, especially in his cabinet appointments, which were exclusively white, a stance that was consistent with the segregation and widespread racism that afflicted American life during the Progressivist period, say from the ruling legalizing discrimination in *Plessy v. Ferguson* (1896) to the severely antiblack film by D. W. Griffith, *The Birth of a Nation* (1915). As Guerra goes on to suggest, in an argument much more involved than can be fully explored here, these racial exclusions of Afro-Cubans helped provide the basis for the continuation of Afro-Cuban struggles against racism and state discrimination, which started during the Revolution against Spain, found expression in the failed 1912 veterans' revolt, and continued throughout much of the twentieth century.

This economic and political backdrop of "Hispanism," into which Grau was probably welcomed, provides the bases for the articulations of Hispanism in the intellectual community, especially through the passionately pro-Spanish writings of Ramiro Guerra and Jorge Mañach. According to Magdalena López, the two authors articulated a view of Cuban culture as being founded on its Hispanic roots, similar to their precursors in Latin America, the Uruguayan Enrique Rodó, the Nicaraguan Ruben Darío, the Dominican Pedro Henriquez Ureña, and the Mexican José Vasconcelos, who argued for the predominance of Latin, Mediterranean, Catholic (spiritual), and Hispanophone values among Latin Americans as opposed to the cultural onslaught of Anglo-Saxonism and its northern European, Protestant, materialistic, and anti-Catholic cultural perspectives. This Hispanist discourse of the 1920s would similarly provide a basis for the rise of Puerto Rican cultural nationalism in the 1930s and beyond through key intellectual figures, like Antonio Pedreira and Margot Arce Vazquez, whose literary and critical works would greatly influence both Albizu Campos and the Nationalists and likewise the trend toward populism embodied by Albizu's archrival, Luis Muñoz Marín.

The question in Cuba, however, is why, despite the powerful appeal of this Ibero-American Hispanism, Grau did not embrace this discourse. Instead, during his presidency and subsequent administration, he shunned

Hispanism and instead espoused a kind of anti-imperialist, working-class, profeminist, and problack Cuban nationalism that was sensitive to Afro-Cuban concerns. Here is where U.S. imperialism and Americanization comes in, for during the 1920s, the limitations of both were exposed in Cuban intellectual discourse. Among Cuban intellectuals, the depradations made possible by the Platt Amendment, by way of the repeated U.S. invasions of Cuba, included hegemony of sugar and American sugar interests in Cuban society; the dominance of what was considered foreign Spanish and American ownership of Cuban sugar industries and their disproportionately large share of the national wealth; and perhaps the practice of racial discrimination and the underside of black rebellions—all of these were coming to a boil in the fertile political ground of Cuban politics, for indeed, not only had large-scale Spanish immigration brought a conservative political tendency in Cuban politics; it had also transported numerous Spanish anarchists, socialists, anticolonialists, and labor unionists for the working class, veterans of various working-class struggles in Catalonia and throughout Europe. By the 1920s, the Communist Party of Cuba had been founded, with an increasingly powerful base of voters and members among blacks, working people, and women. Moreover, the bankruptcy of antiblack racism and the racial Anglo-Saxonism emanating from Americanization was also becoming apparent in the pervasive influence of American English, mass advertising, film, literature, and popular music, as well as American folklore in Cuban society.

Given the challenges of U.S. empire, Americanization, and the political entrée of a large, broad base of militant working-class, Afro-Cuban, and women voters and activists playing a powerful role in Cuban politics, especially through the CPC, the ideology of Hispanism promoted by Guerra and Mañach would have seemed increasingly irrelevant and in the service of the oppressive status quo. It was increasingly being superseded, Magdalena López writes, by a new cultural synthesis of mestizaje, or racial intermixture and cultural fusion, that spoke to the diversity of these mass popular actors. Perhaps the quintessential and influential work of that period was Fernando Ortíz's *Contrapunteo cubano del tabaco y el azúcar*, published in 1940, but its ideas had circulated as early as the 1920s. Through the metaphors of tobacco and sugar, Ortiz's essays combined the racial, economic, and cultural influences so prevalent in Cuban life, which Ortiz brought together through the connective notion of "counterpoint." More precisely, he coined the new concept of "transculturation," the historicized description of the phases of conquest (slavery), compromise, adjustment, self-assertion, and integration that characterized the Hispanic and African cultural encounters seminal to the formation of Cuban national culture.

Thus, by the time of Grau's ascendancy in 1933, the question of which cultural tendency in Cuban society would become predominant—Anglo-Saxonism, Hispanism, or mestizaje—had been settled, and even more interestingly, rapidly subsumed, becoming part of the common sense of Cuban politics. The rapid dissemination, popularization, and absorption of this new cultural tendency is perhaps the reason why Cuban nationalism of the late 1920s and early 1930s, especially as outlined by Luis Aguilar in his influential book on the Cuban Revolution of 1933, seems devoid of cultural content and concentrates exclusively on a critique of economic imperialism and the demoralizing impact of the Platt Amendment,[41] while at the same time sprouting forth new articulations of a wide array of politico-economic positions—nationalism (including fascism), gangsterism, American Progressivist–inspired reformism, Marxism, anarchism (including political terrorism), and others. Such a cultural transformation, as occurred with the articulation of mestizaje, would provide the backdrop for a number of politically diverse formations, from the fascist leaning ABC to the Directorio Estudiantil Universitario (the Student Directory) to Grau's Authentic Cuban Revolutionary Party to Fulgencio Batista's comrades-in-arms in the Cuban armed forces.

This would probably also partly explain the sense of tremendous expectation that the Cuban masses had for Grau's Provisional Government in 1933, when he first became president, and in 1944, when he became president for a second time. In the first instance, Grau and his student revolutionary comrades passed a series of popular prolabor, prowomen, and antiracist laws, as well as nationalist laws that curbed excessive foreign ownership of Cuban natural resources and companies and gave Cuban workers preference over foreign workers, these despite the opposition of the United States and various interests of both the Left and the Right inside of Cuba. While these hopes were dashed by the military coup sponsored by the United States, which forced Grau into exile and installed Batista as kingmaker of Cuban politics, the momentary institutionalization of these progressive laws lingered long in the minds of the Cuban masses, indeed finding partial satisfaction in Fulgencio Batista's presidency, New Deal–type of reforms, and embrace of the Communist Party.

Similar to the first instance, Grau's second coming as president in 1944 produced a high level of popular expectation, especially given Cuba's economic problems and Grau's long years in exile. But these hopes were soon dashed by the corruption that permeated his administration, especially during a period of rising wartime sugar prices and the vast market for sugar in the United States that he successfully negotiated. But, as Alejandro de la Fuente has also noted, Grau's racial perspectives became increasingly irrelevant, if not, at times, inane. He had lost not only the productive energies of the earlier movements of the 1920s but, even more so, had acquired the spirit of anti-Communism imposed on Cuba by the United States' Cold War strategy, which in Cuba, as perhaps in the United States of the 1930s, meant the persecution not only of the militant workers in the Cuban Communist Party, but likewise the persecution of *black* workers who made up the majority of the Cuban working class as a whole. To these concerns, Grau had become decidedly unconcerned, as he moved forward with a rival program of prolabor legislation under the auspices of his Authentic Party.[42] Indeed, members of his cabinet had begun the witch hunt of Communists that would spread in the subsequent Prío regime.[43] Perhaps, in regards to Grau, Marx's inimitable saying holds true, that "all great world-historic facts and personages appear, so to speak, twice: the first time as tragedy, the second time as farce."

CONCLUSION

In this chapter, we have seen how three intellectual figures in Spain's ex-colonies and the new colonies of the United States—Pedro Albizu Campos, Claro M. Recto, and Ramón Grau San Martín—sought to deal not only with the economic and political challenges posed by U.S. empire building but also with the cultural onslaught of "Americanization." Albizu, Recto, and Grau were the sharpest critics of U.S. colonial or neocolonial rule of their respective countries of Puerto Rico, the Philippines, and Cuba, and through the venue of electoral politics, legislation, or the bully pulpit that political struggles provide, they articulated their indictments of American machinations that were serving to impoverish, weaken, and then provide the basis of what they perceived as the takeover of their countries. None of the three were Communists, but left-leaning liberal nationalists who were in fact anti-Communist in varying degrees. None preached the overthrow of capitalism and the creation of an entirely new economic structure, but all preached the removal of U.S. imperialism and the end of its meddling in local affairs (not the end of all relationships with the United States), as well as criticized those among the local elites who buttressed America's demands. Nonetheless, all three were deemed as "anti-Americans" and were vilified in the North

American press. And all three were feared by the U.S. government and their local allies, and as a result all three came under the surveillance of the State Department, the CIA, or the FBI for their supposedly subversive activities or the threat they posed if they ever came into power. And all three were imprisoned in some way related to their opposition to American policies. For these similarities alone, these three figures deserve extensive comparative study and reflection in the literatures of U.S. foreign relations, Caribbean studies, and Southeast Asian histories, a fact that has eluded them.

But besides these political dimensions of their nationalism, Albizu, Recto, and Grau share deeper cultural similarities that I have sought to highlight, for they all shared in various ways a deep Hispanism. All were profoundly influenced by Catholic thought, temperament, and religious values, perhaps none more so than the convert to Catholicism, Albizu. Albizu and Recto had a deep admiration for imperial Spain and to a certain extent saw the Spanish colonial period as a kind of golden age, certainly as against the rapacious imperialism, materialism, and absence of spiritual foundations and traditions of the U.S. empire. Meanwhile, for Grau, who was the most biologically Spanish of the three, there was very little need to perform his obvious Hispanism—from his birth to wealthy Spanish parents, to the elite, landed Hispanic social circles of La Palma in Pinar del Río, his rich inheritance, his education in Europe, and his successful medical and professorial career in Havana—inasmuch as the privileges of whiteness need not be ostentatiously displayed. These were simply *known*. Hispanism provided reservoirs of resistance and potential visions for the future for Albizu and Recto, whereas for Grau, Hispanism had to be modulated in changing times, as in the Cuban cultural climate of the 1930s, which called for a valorization of a new racial perspective beyond the corrupt, pro-Hispanist elite politics of the first twenty years of the twentieth century, that of mestizaje. The unique articulations of Hispanism in these three different intellectuals says much about Spain, the United States, and the unique national and transnational responses of Puerto Ricans, Filipinos, and Cubans to the challenges of Americanization and the legacies of Spanish rule. Albizu articulated a Hispanist legacy that remains widespread and vital in today's Puerto Rico. As was the career of Hispanism in the Philippines, Recto's profound Hispanism was aborted by his premature death in Italy and his inability to reach the terra firma of the former mother country, Spain, and her fellow offspring among the Latin American countries. And Grau's Hispanism, or the attractions of Hispanism for most Cubans, was dimmed by its association with a discredited, corrupt, pro-American regime (of the Platt era) and the need to respond culturally to the emergence and militancy of a new mixed-race or Afro-Cuban working-class majority.

Whether politically or culturally, I have only limned the surface of this deep reservoir of comparative knowledge, which demands more extensive treatment elsewhere. My goal here has been straightforward, to suggest the imbrication between political discourses on the one hand and cultural discourses on the other hand, which have largely been ignored or deemphasized in the appraisals of these nationalist figures. These leaders cannot be fully understood solely with reference to their public political offices, their avowed stances in politics, nor the machinations in which they were involved. They were also cultural personas, part of larger cultural trends, especially of racial, class, and national transformations, for which the ideologies of hispanismo and mestizaje provide a larger window.

NOTES

1. I have in mind here the incisive criticisms of *negritude* as racial essentialism or simply a strategy of reversal that Frantz Fanon, Tyler Stovall, and Brent Edwards have unpacked. See, for instance, Edwards, *The Practice of Diaspora*.
2. See López, "El otro de Nuestra América," 8, and 260–62, for cultural rearticulations that made possible the Auténtico position, alongside of the Communists and Batista, in a way similar to those in Puerto Rico's Generation of 1930 that enabled the divergent political parties embodied by Albizu and Muñoz Marín.
3. "Concepciones como 'trasculturación,' *negritude*, hispanismo, mestizaje cultural partieron del reconocimiento de que las entidades culturales caribeñas y/o latinoamericanas respondieron en menor o mayor medida a la 'instigación imperial de occidente' (Torres-Saillant 23)" (cited in López, "El otro de Nuestra América," 8).
4. Sparrow, *The "Insular Cases" and the Emergence of American Empire*, 230–35; W. A. Williams, *The Tragedy of American Diplomacy*, 47–48.
5. Horsman, *Race and Manifest Destiny*.
6. See Go and Foster, *The American Colonial State in the Philippines*, 3–8.
7. Merk, *Manifest Destiny and Mission in American History*, 257–59; Sparrow, "Insular Cases," 230–31, 240–46.
8. W. A. Williams, *Tragedy of American Diplomacy*, 37–38; Rosenberg, *Financial Missionaries to the World*, 2–3, 41.
9. Sparrow, "Insular Cases," 232–33.
10. Go, *American Empire and the Politics of Meaning*, 57–59; Cano, "Filipino Press between Two Empires," 412–19; Guerra, *The Myth of José Martí*, 89–91.
11. A. Gonzalez, *Language and Nationalism*, 28–29, 30–31; Morales Carrión, *Puerto Rico*, 237–38; Pérez, *On Becoming Cuban*, 148–57.

12. Retamar, "Against the Black Legend," 58, 68; Guzmán, *Spain's Long Shadow*, 175–85; Hoganson, *Fighting for American Manhood*, 51–55.

13. Fuentes, Introduction, 16.

14. Duany, *The Puerto Rican Nation on the Move*, 37.

15. Cano, "Filipino Press between Two Empires: *El Renacimiento*," *Southeast Asian Studies* (Kyoto) 49, no. 3 (2011–12): 414–15.

16. Gonzalez, *Language and Nationalism*, 30–31.

17. Rodao, "Spanish Falange in the Philippines, 1936–1945," 5–6.

18. Motes, *Nación e inmigración*, 145–51; Gott, *Cuba*, 118–20.

19. Naranjo Orovio and Puig-Samper, "Los lazos de la cultura se convierten en lazos de solidaridad," 309–19, and González Lamela, *El exilio artístico español en el Caribe*.

20. "Albizu Dangerous, Says Ickes," *New York Times*, March 6, 1936, 12.

21. For Recto's biography, I rely on Yuvienco Arcellana, *Recto*, 1–27; Medina and Feliciano "Biographical Notes," in *The Complete Works of Claro M. Recto*, xvii–xx.

22. Blum, *Killing Hope*, 44.

23. For biographical information on Grau, see Whitney, *State and Revolution in Cuba*, 2; Commission on Cuban Affairs, *Problems of the New Cuba*, 14; Perez, *Cuba and the United States*, 194–201, 206, 233.

24. "Cuban President Asks Americans to Help New Regime by Not Hindering Program," *New York Times*, September 11, 1933, 3.

25. "Mendieta Is Made President of Cuba; Grau Resigns, Hevia Rules Only One Day," *Clewiston News*, March 2, 1934, 2.

26. See Mabel Moraña's introduction to *Ideologies of Hispanism*, x–xi, and Faber's useful discussion of the problems in the concept of Hispanism, "'La hora ha llegado,'" 62–68; and Grandin, "Your Americanism and Mine," 1048–49.

27. Albizu Campos, *La conciencia nacional puertorriqueña*, 19–21; for a perceptive discussion about this culturalist challenge from the "South" to nationalist discourse from the "North," a reading of Chatterjee's *Nationalist Discourse in the Colonial World* as applied to Puerto Rican politics, see Rodríguez Vázquez, *El sueño que no cesa*, 164–83.

28. Angel Ferrao, *Pedro Albizu Campos y el nacionalismo puertorriqueño*, 66–70. Ferrao provides a critical account of Albizu's speech to the Spanish Republican Association of Puerto Rico, which was celebrating the abdication of King Alfonso XIII and the installation of the Second Republic on June 14, 1931, in the Municipal Theater of San Juan.

29. Carmen Gautier Mayoral, "El nacionalismo y la descolonización internacional hemisférica en la posguerra," 97.

30. Díaz Quiñones, "La Pasión, según Albizu," 92–94.

31. Kalaw, *Aide-de-Camp to Freedom*, 1–2, quoted in May, *The Battle for Batangas*, 9–10.

32. See the introduction to his early play, *Solo entre las sombras*, in *The Complete Works of Claro M. Recto*, 1: 291.

33. Yuvienco Arcellana, *Recto: Nationalist*, 4.

34. "Historical Essays: Literature in Spanish," 93–95.

35. The speeches drafted beforehand and never delivered are in Medina and Feliciano, *The Complete Works of Claro M. Recto*, 9: 683–760.

36. B. Anderson, *Under Three Flags*, 154–56.

37. Rodriguez Morejón, *Grau San Martín*, 11–20.
38. Gott, *Cuba*, 118–20.
39. Rodriguez Morejón, *Grau San Martín*, 23.
40. Grau, Alsina, and Ridderhoff, *Cuba desde 1930*, 30.
41. Wright, "Cuba, Sugar and the United States," 22; Aguilar, *Cuba 1933*, 28–47.
42. Fuente, *Nation for All*.
43. See Helg, *Our Rightful Share*, and Ferrer, *Insurgent Cuba*.

Becoming Indo-Hispano

Reies López Tijerina and the New Mexican
Land Grant Movement

In August 1962, Reies López Tijerina decided to write an open letter to Spanish-speaking New Mexicans. Wisdom dictated keeping a low profile at least until an Arizona warrant for his arrest expired the following year. But this former Pentecostal preacher was eager to broadcast his new crusade: he sought "to resurrect . . . the Treaty of Guadalupe-Hidalgo." Resurrection was the right word. The treaty that had ended the U.S.-Mexico War more than a hundred years before was hardy breaking news in New Mexico or anywhere else during the early 1960s. More people were concerned about the African American civil rights movement and ongoing tensions with the Soviet Union. According to Tijerina, however, the United States had not merely forgotten the treaty but killed it through repeated violations. "The federal government has never wanted to comply with the treaty's stipulations," he asserted, and thus it has "robbed us of everything," including "all our land." Reassuring members of his *nuevomexicano* audience that they were not alone in being treating liked "despised insects" by those who had conquered them, Tijerina wrote: "We declare that the treatment that the Anglo-Saxon has given us over the past 120 years, is the same as the treatment he has given to the poor and humble peoples of Africa, and Asia, as well as of Latin America."[1]

The singular Anglo-Saxon that Tijerina invoked deliberately melded British imperial history with the history of the American empire. Just as European nations had colonized areas of the globe, he contended, the United

States had operated and continued to operate as a colonial power in New Mexico. Six months later, Tijerina formally founded the Alianza Federal de Mercedes (the Federal Alliance of Land Grants), whose members sought to regain land that the Spanish and Mexican governments had deeded to their ancestors but that after 1848 had become the property of others through means more often foul than fair.[2] Over the decades, nuevomexicanos had fought to retain or regain this land, but mostly through the courts and usually one land grant claim at a time. In contrast, Tijerina reenvisioned the land grant movement as an anticolonial effort, one aimed at securing territory and economic independence if not complete political sovereignty.

The movement that Tijerina led was unique within the history of American expansion and possibly within the history of settler colonialism itself. That was because Tijerina operated in a "double settler colonization context," which Laura Gómez describes as a condition under which those colonized "were forced to navigate two different racial regimes simultaneously" and competed for standing in a decidedly uneven multiracial order, as well as struggled to make claims to land and recognition across sometimes incommensurable legal regimes.[3] While the United States became the official colonizer of New Mexico in 1848, the Spanish empire had launched its colonial endeavor in the region two and a half centuries before. Like Tijerina himself, however, scholars have tended to see the United States as the prime example of a white settler nation while considering the Latin American experience outside the settler colonial mold. Among academics, this distinction traditionally hinges on the fate of the indigenous population. Thus, Jürgen Osterhammel, in his classic text *Colonialism*, spoke repeatedly of a "New England–type" colony, which Osterhammel defined as predicated on the ruthless removal of a "demographically weak" and "economically superfluous" indigenous population.[4] Indigenous populations throughout the Spanish empire, including in New Mexico, suffered an enormous loss of life though war, disease, slavery, and the erosion of their land base. At the same time, the Spanish empire promoted intermarriage between Spanish colonists and indigenous peoples and included mixed offspring, whether issuing from a marriage or not, within its terms of political membership. In fact, María Josefina Saldaña-Portillo suggested that the "success of *mestizaje* as a racial ideology"—with its simultaneously celebration and displacement of indigenous peoples—might account for the relative absence of Latin America within the literature on settler colonialism.[5] Proving her point, Patrick Wolfe, in his seminal essay that equated settler colonialism across the globe with "the elimination of the native," invoked the experience of the

Cherokees and the Trail of Tears several times but mentioned the Spanish empire just once. Europeans, whether British, Dutch, Spanish, or French, Wolfe argued, inevitably traced their right to dominion based on the original "discovery" of the lands in question.[6]

Wolfe's single mention regarding discovery, however, neatly captured New Mexico's origins as settler colony. Claiming the region for crown and Christ, conquistadors first passed through the region in the 1540s. Official Spanish-speaking settlement began on April 30, 1598, when the *adelantado* Don Juan de Oñate arrived on the south bank of the Rio Grande near present-day El Paso. There, in the name of the Spanish king, he declared possession of all the lands drained by that great river, and possession of all the Indian natives who lived on those lands too, that is, possession of everything and everyone "without exception or any limitation" from "the leaf of the mountain to the sands and rock of the river" and back again.[7] New Mexico's future within the Spanish empire never matched these sweeping inaugural proclamations. Without mineral wealth and far from Mexico proper, it remained a backwater colony. Nevertheless, for the next several centuries a small population of Spanish-speakers lived clustered along the upper Rio Grande and its tributaries, that is, they lived in the new colonial capital of Santa Fe and regions north. They called themselves *pobladores*, from the Spanish word *pueblo* or village, precisely because they sought to carve out new settlements along a frontier dominated by Native Americans.[8]

The Spanish borderlands paralleled the British settler colonial experience in North America in another way. Both empires gave way to new nations that continued to aggressively appropriate native land. In the U.S. context, the Northwest Ordinance of 1787 institutionalized westward expansion by providing for the establishment of territories as a prelude to statehood and the full incorporation of new lands and new settlers into the Union. Although the ordinance called for peace and friendship with Native Americans already there, it also expected that their land claims would eventually be "extinguished."[9] For its part, the Mexican government not only continued to dispense land grants along its northern frontier between 1821 and 1848 but also did so in New Mexico with greater enthusiasm than the Spanish empire ever had.[10]

Thus, in leading an anticolonial movement, Tijerina was forced to navigate a complex history in which Alianza members objected to the consequences of a colonization begun in 1848, while seeking to secure the benefits of another begun in 1598. Flatly rejecting any implication that the land grant cause was illegitimate, Tijerina instead exploited this unique constellation of historical circumstances to forge a usable past in ways un-available to other victims of U.S. colonialism. Unlike Native Americans in the United States whose claims to sovereignty had to contend with the legal fiction of dependent domestic nation status, Tijerina attempted to envelop the land grant cause within the full national sovereignty of an independent Mexico. As he never tired of saying, both the United States and Mexico had signed the Treaty of Guadalupe-Hidalgo, and both nations were responsible for the enforcement of its provisions.[11] And unlike Filipinos and Puerto Ricans whose quests for independence had begun as anti-Spanish efforts and then transitioned into opposition to U.S. rule after 1898, Tijerina looked favorably on the days of the Spanish empire. In his estimation, centuries of Spanish rule had brought Native Americans and Mexican Americans closer together culturally and biologically. In contrast, Tijerina condemned the American empire. As a result of U.S. westward expansion, the two groups were closer together than ever before, he argued. But that was because both populations shared a similar colonial relationship to the United States.

Two innovative strategies resulted from his uniquely configured anticolonial perspective. First, Tijerina spent the years from 1959 to 1964 courting Mexico to take an interest in her "orphaned children."[12] Long before statehood in 1912, Spanish-speaking New Mexicans had hung their attempts to secure property rights, and civil rights in general, on their status as American citizens.[13] Yet to Tijerina, the "law of nature" dictated a transnational approach to politics. As he once argued, "You will never see a stepmother treating a step-child the same as she treats a legitimate child of her own."[14] Second, Tijerina vigorously pursued alliances with Native Americans within New Mexico and across the United States. Again, this tactic ran counter to political tradition in New Mexico whereby nuevomexicanos had distanced themselves from their Native American neighbors—and their own indigenous heritage—by adopting the ethnic label "Spanish American" and insisting they were "white."[15] Not even numerous unresolved land disputes between Pueblo Indians and Spanish-speaking New Mexicans stopped Tijerina from lobbying for solidarity. To those critics who charged that Spanish-speaking New Mexicans seeking land had stolen it in the first place, Tijerina countered that a shared history since 1848 was far more important. Native Americans on reservations and nuevomexicanos dependent on welfare were equally victims of American conquest, he insisted: "Here is the root of our misery and poverty."[16] Offering this formulation during the height of the Cold War when, domestically, consensus politics were at a premium, Tijerina presented a direct challenge not only to how Americans saw their role within the world but also to how Mexican Americans saw their role within the United States.

For good reason, Tijerina is best known as a man of action versus a man of ideas. On June 6, 1967, Tijerina secured his reputation as a militant when he led an armed raid on the Río Arriba County Courthouse in the tiny town of Tierra Amarilla, New Mexico. Although the dramatic protest brought unprecedented national attention to the land grant cause, by then Tijerina had been pondering land grant matters for more than twenty years. The Texas-born Tijerina was first introduced to the topic in 1945 when he passed through northern New Mexico while traveling from Michigan to Texas on his way back from a summer spent working in the fields to an Assemblies of God Bible school that he attended outside of San Antonio.[17] Intrigued by the topic, Tijerina nonetheless followed his calling at the time: to become a preacher. After finishing school, subsequent pastoral trips through northern New Mexico became occasions to learn more about what he later called the "long, sad, and violent" history of land dispossession.[18] Finally, in 1957, after experiencing a powerful dream that he took as a prophetic vision telling him to move to New Mexico, he decided to devote himself full-time to the land grant cause.[19]

Once he did so, Tijerina recalled nuevomexicanos in Tierra Amarilla bitterly complaining that, "for more than 100 years we have asked Washington and heaven [for aid] but no one does us justice."[20] Indeed, a turning point in the dispute over the Tierra Amarilla land grant dated to 1860 when the U.S. Congress recognized Francisco Martínez as the sole owner of 594,515 acres of land in what was then the Territory of New Mexico. In contrast, in the original 1832 grant the Mexican government had protected the pasture and other resources of the grant for common use by deeding the land to Francisco's father, Manuel, and to his sons, including Francisco, as well as to the settlers who accompanied him. Further complicating matters, in 1861 Francisco Martínez started handing out *hijuelas*, or specific kind of deeds that reaffirmed the rights of settlers to use the land grant communally. In other words, while Congress declared the land private property, the designated new owner continued to honor an older Mexican and, before that, Spanish tradition of communal land use. To the dismay of Spanish-speakers throughout New Mexico, U.S. courts sided with Congress. Not only in 1874 did the U.S. Supreme Court declare that congressional decisions in the case of the land grants could not be revisited, but in general the U.S. judicial system consistently valorized the "chain of title" of private owners while largely refusing to recognize common property claims.[21] Although the details of dispossession differed from grant to grant, this judicial context ensured that the story of land loss across New Mexico remained much the same. While some nuevomexicanos sold their property, many found it sold out from under them and then could not find redress in the courts. One estimate is that by the time that New Mexico became a state in 1912, property owned by former Mexican citizens there had shrunk by 80 percent.[22]

Similar land loss occurred throughout the new American Southwest, but the particular circumstances of New Mexico explain why Tijerina found a receptive audience for his anticolonial analysis more than one hundred years after conquest. The focus of Spanish colonization efforts along the northern frontier since 1598, pobladores pushing north along the Rio Grande and its tributaries braved severe isolation, a beautiful but unforgiving desert climate, and constant Indian attack. Indigenous populations had lived in the region for millennia. Although the sedentary and agricultural Pueblo Indians posed no significant threat to Spanish rule after the 1690s, roving bands of Comanches, Utes, Apaches, and Navajos did. No doubt the enduring collective memory of establishing villages despite such obstacles contributed to a stubborn conviction among many nuevomexicanos after 1848 that the land belonged to them and they to the land, adverse court rulings or legal transfers of property to the contrary notwithstanding. Demographics buttressed the collective memory. At the time of the American takeover, the vast majority of Mexican citizens in the ceded territory called New Mexico home: estimates are that some sixty-thousand Mexican citizens lived there (not counting Pueblo Indians) as compared to roughly seventy-five hundred Mexicans each in California and Texas and fewer than one thousand in Arizona.[23] Then, after 1848, a paucity of natural resources protected the numerical majority of Spanish-speakers in the state for decades. As relatively few Anglo Americans moved to New Mexico, not until the 1940s did nuevomexicanos become a minority within the state. Even then, they retained their overwhelming majority in northern counties (as they still do today).[24] Thus, in New Mexico a larger population of Spanish-speakers had lived in the area for a longer time than anywhere else in the U.S. Southwest. In comparison to *californios* who during the Gold Rush were quickly overrun and ousted, nuevomexicanos fought to maintain their strong connection to the land. Between 1940 and 1960, Tierra Amarilla grant claimants, for example, pursued five different court cases in an effort to establish their legal right to use the land. They lost all five cases.[25] While a less determined population might admit defeat at this point, nuevomexicanos around Tierra Amarilla, and beyond it too, instead lent an ear to Tijerina's anticolonial analysis.

Fortunately for Tijerina, New Mexico also provided a convenient enemy: the U.S. Forest Service. Founded in 1905, the U.S. Forest Service eventually became the largest landholder in northern New Mexico. Through its management of Carson and Santa Fe National Forests alone, it controlled close to three million acres.[26] These acres included sizeable portions of former land grant land that had either first passed through private hands before ending up under federal control or that had been ruled the property of the U.S. government by the courts.[27] No matter the method of acquisition, charged with protecting natural resources nationally, the U.S. Forest Service operated as an agent of colonial administration locally. Through the issuance of licenses, the Forest Service determined who could hunt, graze, and harvest wood, and to what extent, on government-held land that many nuevomexicanos still considered their own. As Lisbeth Haas once suggested, conquest is a process.[28] Similarly, Patrick Wolfe insisted that settler colonialism must be understood as the establishment of a structure not a singular event.[29] In New Mexico, ongoing tensions between Spanish-speakers and forest rangers testified to the truth of both statements. To be sure, nuevomexicanos opposed plenty of private owners too. As leader of the Alianza, however, Tijerina avoided entering countless legal disputes with individual property owners by targeting a single colonial opponent, the federal government, which held all land in the public domain.

Trips to Mexico spurred Tijerina's anticolonial analysis. Mexico appealed for several reasons. Growing up in the border region, Tijerina had always retained a strong sense of his Mexican identity. As a preacher, in addition to crisscrossing the United States, he had visited Mexico for months at a time. Family members recalled that he was always loath to leave.[30] In addition, although thoroughly bilingual, Tijerina spoke English with a heavy accent. Mexico offered the luxury of presenting himself and his goals in Spanish. In 1956, he spent three months there, meeting with people in Mexico City and navigating the massive Archivo General de la Nación.[31] It was the first of many visits.

During this initial trip, Tijerina pondered two key documents that informed his understanding of land grant rights from then on: the 1848 Treaty of Guadalupe-Hidalgo, which had figured so prominently in his 1962 letter, and the multivolume *Recopilación de las Leyes de las Indias*, which compiled nearly two centuries of Spanish colonial law. Already familiar with the Treaty of Guadalupe-Hidalgo from his jaunts through New Mexico, he was glad to be able to purchase a personal copy at the outdoor market.[32] Today, the treaty figures prominently within the field of Chicana/o history. In the mid-1950s, however, few scholars had studied the treaty, and none saw it as a foundational text to understand the contemporary plight of Mexican Americans in the United States.[33] Motivated to understand the origins of land loss, Tijerina connected the dots in a new way. As he often pointed out, Article 8 of the treaty promised that the property of former Mexican citizens was to be "inviolably respected." Similarly, Article 9 stated that the conquered population was to "be maintained and protected in the free enjoyment of their liberty and property."[34] As far as Tijerina was concerned, if only the United States had kept these promises as outlined in the treaty, then the land grants would still be in the hands of the descendants of the original grantees. Tijerina in the archives also poured over the more than sixty-five hundred laws contained within the *Recopilación*. These laws had governed the Indies for more than three hundred years, and consequently, he later wrote, they "gave form and character to the Mexicans."[35] Demonstrating what Rudy V. Busto termed an "obsession with text-based authority," Tijerina read both the treaty and the Laws of the Indies with the same intensity with which he had once read the Bible.[36] Tijerina concluded that the United States had robbed nuevomexicanos not only of their land but also of their precious cultural inheritance as Mexicans.

The future land grant leader was eager to share the results of his research with others. He moved permanently to New Mexico in 1957, a fugitive from the law in Arizona, where he had skipped town to avoid facing trial on charges of breaking his brother out of jail. Tijerina quietly started attending countless land grant meetings to learn all he could. The task literally gave him an education in hard knocks. At one meeting of the Corporation of Abiquiú, the latest entity pursuing Tierra Amarilla land claims, one member, not trusting this outsider, cracked Tijerina's head open with a wooden club.[37] Eventually, however, Tijerina's interloper status diminished. In the fall of 1958, he returned to Mexico and stayed an entire year, during which time he worked as the official representative of the corporation.[38]

Taking full advantage of the greater freedom that Mexico provided him while he was a wanted man within the United States, Tijerina worked as diligently outside the archives as he did within them to build support for the land grant cause. One early contact was Benjamin Laureano Luna, one of Mexico's leading human rights activists and the founder of a group called the Frente International de Derechos Humanos (International Human Rights Front). Known in high government circles, Luna agreed to lobby on behalf of the land grant movement within Mexico and evidently helped Tijerina secure an audience with the Mexican foreign minister.[39] (In return, the Alianza stationery for years proudly stated its membership in the Frente.) In 1959, Tijerina also forged a close friendship with Augustín Cue Cánovas, a historian particularly interested in the fate of "forgotten Mexico," as the scholar dubbed the Mexican-origin population within the United States. During subsequent visits, Tijerina met with prominent left-wing politicians and unionists including the former president of Mexico, Lorenzo Cárdenas, who had enacted major land redistribution during his tenure, and Vicente Lombardo Toledano, a dedicated Marxist who helped found a national labor union in 1936.[40] He also met with Jacinto López, another unionist who had gained fame during the late 1950s for occupying land held by the American-held Cananea Cattle Company in the Mexican state of Sonora.[41] Most intriguing was Tijerina's association with more obscure and fringe groups. These included the Movimiento por la Reintegración Teritorial and an organization known as the Comité de Anahuak, Anahuac being an Aztec name for an ancient indigenous empire that once ruled Mexico.[42] While the archives reveal little about these organizations, their names suggest that members looked on the U.S. Southwest as a Mexican Sudetenland.

A 1959 press release revealed how even his earliest conversations and investigations pushed Tijerina's thinking toward anti-American, anti-imperialist directions. Although unsigned, the press release clearly exhibited the former preacher's distinctive voice. It appealed to all of Latin America to hear the cry of the "oppressed Mexican population" in the states of New Mexico, Colorado, California, Texas, Arizona, Utah, and Nevada. While he contended that the central crime of the "Anglo-Saxon" was to have "broken and dishonored his own word" by failing to fulfill the Treaty of Guadalupe-Hidalgo, Tijerina roamed far and wide in his condemnations of American society and empire. "The Saxon," he maintained, used American public schools "to brainwash the minds of our children and erase the historical deeds that reveal his savage and black crimes." He also vigorously condemned U.S. actions on the world stage. Writing less than three weeks after Fidel Castro had deposed of the U.S.-backed dictator in Cuba, Tijerina celebrated the Cuban Revolution as a form of inspiration to the dispossessed people in New Mexico. "We congratulate the valiant Cubans. . . . Blessed is the man who broke the yoke upon Cuba and happy are his faithful followers who have reached . . . liberty," he gushed. In a related fashion, Tijerina took the opportunity to condemn the United States for its decision to use the atomic bomb against Japan years before. Preoccupied by the end times since his preacher days, he had frequently linked the use of the atomic bomb with the end of the world. In this document, however, he drew a parallel between what he saw as U.S. failure to honor the Treaty of Guadalupe-Hidalgo and the country's decision to bomb Japan with a weapon of mass destruction: both demonstrated the propensity of the United States to commit crimes against humanity.[43]

Most important, within this early document, Tijerina clearly identified the land grant struggle with Mexico and defined land grant activists as Mexicans. After 1848, those above the river were "sold to the enemy," he lamented, leaving "the life of a Mexican valued and respected south of the Río Grande only." Having suffered "110 years of opprobrium" and "110 years of servitude," Tijerina asked, "how can we ever say that we are contented [as] Mexicans?" In what was to become a familiar metaphor, the text labeled Mexico "mother," while the United States was a "stepmother," and an evil one to boot. Describing nuevomexicanos lives as filled with anguish and pain, Tijerina implored his fellow Mexicans to pursue justice on behalf of their "blood brothers" to the north perhaps through some sort of international tribunal. "Is there no one in all of the land who will come to our aid?" he asked.[44]

With each visit to Mexico, Tijerina sharpened his list of grievances. In an April 1962 press release, Tijerina explained that he needed help from beyond the borders of the United States because "the forgotten people" had never received justice in American courts. As far as he was concerned, U.S. courts were not a viable solution to land grant disputes but instead part of the problem. He pointed out that recent court decisions continued to kick Spanish-speakers off the land, as did American holders of property, although in each case the land in question originally had been part of a recognized land grant. Tijerina mentioned one notorious incident. In November 1961, John Taylor and two of his workers discovered three Spanish-speakers on land that Taylor had purchased the year before. The land fell within the boundaries of the Sangre de Cristo land grant. Since the days of the Mexican Republic, Spanish-speakers had collected wood and grazed animals there. Determined to stop those practices, Taylor and his two ranch hands rounded up the three men, beat them, and then drove them to the local sheriff so that he could arrest them.[45] Claiming to speak on behalf of millions of Mexican Americans across the Southwest, Tijerina appealed to Mexico to help stop such vigilantism. He even mentioned the possibility of taking the matter of land grant justice to the United Nations.[46]

Tijerina's turn toward Mexico fundamentally shifted the conventional frame for understanding land grant protest. A series of disparate legal battles over disputed property had become a broader struggle for independence and justice on the part of an oppressed minority. While New Mexico was always ground zero for land grant conflict, Tijerina saw himself as representing the interests of all Mexican Americans precisely because his understanding of the problem began with a wider war of conquest. Tijerina also connected past and present by insisting that land loss had fostered a debilitating form of dependency. Such a connection was easy to make in New Mexico, where local county welfare rates in the north approached 50 percent. As Tijerina explained in another 1962 document, because the United States had committed this "vile robbery," a people who had once grazed their own cattle without restriction now received federal food subsidies in the form of "LECHE DE POLVO," that is, powdered milk. The capitalized letters in the original screamed the injustice.[47] The land grant movement was a fight not only for land but also to secure economic and cultural independence for a conquered people. Here was the real significance of the turn toward Mexico: if nuevomexicanos were really Mexicans, then they were not Americans. Foregrounding a war of conquest and a legacy of dispossession, Tijerina suggested instead that they constituted a subjugated, colonized population within the United States.

Tijerina's analysis was radical for its time. With only a third-grade education and some Bible school training to his name, he made fundamental connections between conquest, land loss, and the current socioeconomic conditions confronting nuevomexicanos long before historians had coined the term "the legacy of conquest."[48] By reviling the United States and looking toward Mexico as a natural ally, Tijerina's colonial analysis also stood outside the Mexican American political mainstream. Since before World War II, ethnic group leaders had pursued first-class citizenship by emphasizing Mexican Americans' overwhelming loyalty and patriotism toward the United States. Key organizations in this regard were the League of United Latin American Citizens and the American GI Forum, both founded in Texas but with chapters throughout the Southwest by the 1960s. Alfonso Sanchez, the district attorney of Río Arriba County and Tijerina's nemesis at the time of the courthouse raid, for example, was a proud member of the GI Forum.[49] An organization mostly of veterans, the GI Forum had pressed for equal treatment by upholding the admirable service record of many Mexican American vets. But what was a point of pride for many Mexican Americans represented another instance of abuse to Tijerina. "We have gained nothing from sacrificing so many thousands of our fathers and brothers in the many wars this nation has fought," he emphasized. Boldly asserting that nuevo-mexicanos comprised a "landless and refugee" population within their own homeland, Tijerina was never particularly interested in civil rights per se.[50] He wanted land. If only the U.S. government returned the land, he argued, then justice would ensue.

Tijerina's anticolonial message resonated with some of the poorest and most marginalized members of New Mexican society. Officially incorporated on February 2, 1963, the 125th anniversary of the Treaty of Guadalupe-Hidalgo, the Alianza Federal de Mercedes grew quickly as Tijerina turned his energy toward recruiting members. Via a regular newspaper column, a radio program, and countless face-to-face talks with people he called land grant heirs, Tijerina continued to blame a long-ago war and all-but-forgotten peace treaty for present-day poverty. But he also railed against a sense of cultural inferiority that widespread poverty aggravated. A few months after the Alianza's founding, he spoke of the day "when we will no longer look like refugees in our own land, needing to depend on Public Welfare and to suffer the shame of wearing used clothing that our oppressor and dispossessor has thrown away."[51] Once that day arrived, he insisted, "every race will feel proud of itself and no one will feel embarrassed to be who he [or she] is." Tijerina's early statements looked forward to this day of judgment: "The day is coming when all of the black crimes committed against the impoverished heirs of these royal land grants are going to come to the light . . . and the wicked guilty ones will have to be punished," he wrote in early 1964.[52] Tapping into the simmering resentments of many nuevomexicanos, Tijerina witnessed the rapid expansion of the organization. Within three years, the Alianza boasted a membership that numbered in the thousands and represented at least 152 different land grants.[53]

Both Tijerina's faith in text-based authority and his orientation toward Mexico shaped the Alianza's early strategy. In January 1964, Tijerina sent Mexican president Adolfo López Mateo a five-page memorandum delineating the Alianza's case. As a child, Tijerina had been called by his elder brother an "abogado sin libros," literally, a lawyer without books. The nickname paid tribute to both his combative personality and his sharp mind despite his lack of formal education. Fittingly, Tijerina constructed a highly legalistic argument in defense of land grant rights based on his understanding of several important texts. In addition to pointing out the significance of Articles 8 and 9 of the Treaty of Guadalupe-Hidalgo, Tijerina also insisted that the Treaty of Guadalupe-Hidalgo was uncontestable within the borders of the United States because Article VI of the U.S. Constitution ensured that all treaties made by the federal government "shall be the supreme Law of the Land." Tijerina's memo to the Mexican president also referred to sections of the U.S. Constitution, the state constitution of New Mexico, and the Laws of the Indies, all of which he believed confirmed the fundamental land rights of New Mexicans. Aware that Mexico was powerless to enforce U.S. laws, Tijerina nonetheless hoped that with the weight of the evidence he had, Mexico would help expose the existence of such blatant injustices. He pleaded with the Mexican president to demand "satisfaction" from the United States. In closing, Tijerina noted that the Alianza later that year planned to stage a grand automobile caravan of members who hoped to bring their concerns directly to the president.[54]

Unfortunately for Tijerina, the caravan never transpired. Planning all through the summer, Tijerina expected that more than two hundred cars would participate in the caravan. Still never having heard directly from the Mexican president, in August 1964, Tijerina traveled to Mexico City to finalize the logistics. To his great surprise, police officials rounded him up at the home he was staying at in Mexico City and deported him before he could even put on a shirt.[55] Tijerina's nostalgia for the mother country aside, Mexico was more concerned about antagonizing its neighbor to the north than about investigating the fate of land seceded long ago. But Tijerina was not one to give up. Instead, he continued to revisit the past, turning to the days of the Spanish empire to strengthen his criticism of the current American one.

In the spring of 1966, ten years after his first extended research trip to Mexico, Tijerina spent a month in Spain, mostly exploring the holdings of Seville's Archivo General de las Indias, which constituted the major depository of centuries of paperwork that had accompanied Iberian expansion across the Atlantic. In these archives, Tijerina hoped to find information about colonial laws that might help the land grant cause. Out of the archives, he also hoped to meet a lawyer or two whose expertise he might tap. As he later explained, the trip sprang from his conviction that the land laws governing New Mexico had all originated in Spain; the country was "the mother" of nuevomexicano civilization.[56] Temporarily placing his Mexican identity on the back burner for the moment, Tijerina highlighted this cultural connection in an interview with Seville's daily newspaper during his stay. As he told the newspaper reporter at the time, "Our culture is Spanish. We want to speak Spanish. But the Anglos press [us] so that this cultural legacy is lost." A champion of self-determination for an entire people, Tijerina looked forward to the day when a people he increasingly called "Indo-Hispanos," would control their own language, their own education, and their own land. Impressed, the newspaper reporter anointed him a Martin Luther King Jr. for all Hispanics.[57] The comparison was an awkward one to the extent that King sought full inclusion within the United States for African Americans while Tijerina favored a form of separation for a conquered population. It also failed to emphasize the connection that Tijerina drew between Hispanos and indigenous peoples.

After suffering Mexico's rejection, moreover, Tijerina deliberately turned to Spain for the advantages it might offer toward advancing this goal. He discovered four. First, Tijerina, already familiar with the Laws of the Indies, was pleased to discover an earlier set of medieval laws called the *Siete Partidas*, which upheld communal use and ownership of village or pueblo land.[58] Second, after several years of living in the state, Tijerina was familiar enough with New Mexican history and its racial politics to realize the enormous pride that many nuevomexicanos took in their long presence in the region. Invoking the Spanish colonial era thus became a way of appealing to this population. Third, Tijerina was always looking for ways to focus media attention on the land grant cause. As he was well aware, seemingly outlandish associations to a long-ago monarchy helped secure publicity for an upstart organization. Fourth and most important, however, the Alianza leader celebrated the Spanish colonial past in an attempt to prevent the land grant organization from appearing fatally Spanish-centric. Specifically Tijerina revisited the days of the Spanish empire to foster his outreach efforts to Native Americans by underscoring a dual genealogy that provided *nuevomexicanos* with a distinctly combined claim to the land.

Counterintuitive, this strategy was also easy to miss amid the glorification of all things Spanish. While references to a conquistador heritage arose frequently enough in New Mexico, within his early radio addresses and newspaper columns Tijerina went a step further by linking impoverished nuevomexicanos directly to nobility. In one typical radio address, for example, he insisted that the "royal crown of Spain" had by its "royal seal" and "royal law" established "royal land grants."[59] Along the same lines, Tijerina liked to mention *Ordenanza 99*, one of those Laws of the Indies. Issued in 1543, this one promised that all settlers in the Americas would automatically be granted hidalgo status, that is, the rank of minor noblemen.[60] Even in Spain at the time, the privileges were restricted: hidalgos mostly enjoyed the right to be addressed as "don" and exemption from taxation.[61] In New Mexico, when weighed against the hardscrabble quality of life on the frontier, these privileges no aristocracy made.[62] In Tijerina's repeated telling, however, Americans had robbed nuevomexicanos of not just their land but also of their royal inheritance. A 1966 booklet that the Alianza published directly after Tijerina's return from Spain likewise advanced that argument. "The Spanish Land Grant Question Examined" declared that nuevomexicanos were a "noble people" who were determined "to recover and preserve their birthright and cultural heritage." Expounding on this theme, the booklet asserted that nuevomexicanos: "remember that they are the descendents of the Conquistadores," continuing, "They remember the glory of the Spanish Monarchy, that was a world power for more than three hundred years (twice the length of time of the existence of the United States of America)."[63] Broadcasting a powerful "we were here first" message to Anglo America, these royal references no doubt also appealed to the mostly rural folks in humble circumstances who made up the core of the Alianza's membership.

The culmination of Tijerina's Spanish strategy occurred a few months after he returned from Spain when *aliancistas* forcibly took over a portion of Kit Carson National Forest. Even more so than the courthouse raid, the Alianza's reclamation of this territory, which fell within the borders of the San Joaquín del Río de Chama grant, directly challenged the U.S. occupation of New Mexico. At the same time, fanciful references to a once magnificent empire swaddled the entire effort. An advance notice of the takeover that the Alianza sent to law enforcement, for instance, transformed the original land grant into an independent "pueblo" established by no less an esteemed figure than "Don Carlos IVth, King of the Eastern and Western Indies and Mainlands of the Ocean-Sea Continent and of the Spains."[64] Several letters that Alianza staff members sent to President Lyndon Johnson adopted the same flowery tone. An area resident and land grant activist named Victoriano Chavez signed each in his capacity as a "Hidalgo and *Caballero* (gentleman) *de las Indias*, [and] Governor of the Pueblo Republic San Joaquín del Río de Chama, a sovereign city-state."[65] Such grandiose statements pertained more to the realm of historical fiction than fact: the Spanish empire encouraged settlement not settler independence. At the same time, the entire episode precisely because it seemed surreal also proved impossible to ignore.

Yet also capturing attention was Tijerina's invention of a new ethnic label. Initially in his written work and speeches, Tijerina most often referred to nuevomexicanos as the "forgotten people" or "*herederos* (heirs)" or simply "Mexicans." During his archival research, however, Tijerina had discovered that even before the conquest of Mexico the Spanish crown had ruled that intermarriages between Spaniards and Indians should occur without impediment. As far as he was concerned, the exact date of this law, October 19, 1514, marked the birthday of a new people, born in the Americas, who were the mixture of both Indian and Spanish blood, that is, who were Indo-Hispanos.[66] In 1967, in one of his earliest uses of the term, he noted that consequently Indo-Hispanos were a relatively young group: "we have just hit the stage. . . . We now know that the continent has . . . brewed a new people, a new breed."[67] Although the term that Tijerina crafted was unique, the idea was not. Within Mexico, an acknowledgement of *mestizaje* had long been part of the national narrative of the country.

In the context of the land grant struggle, however, the name change appeared blatantly self-serving. In one fell swoop, Tijerina neatly extended nuevomexicano land claims back in time even before the arrival of Oñate. Tijerina's statements often fueled such suspicions. In 1968, for instance, Tijerina asserted that Indo-Hispanos "are native children (*hijos*) of the American continent, we are native blood," continuing, "We did not come from Europe. . . . We are not foreigners. This is our land."[68] Forced to choose between his "parents," moreover, Tijerina once stated, "the Indian was our true mother. Our father, the Spaniard, left us. We decided to stay with our mother, the Indian here in New Mexico."[69] Nor could the children be blamed for the sins of the parent. "Sure, Spain made her mistakes and crimes and whatever you want to call them. But it was not the new breed," Tijerina stated in 1967. "Why should we have to pay for the crimes of Spain?"[70] In his telling, all the violence of Spanish conquest belonged to the progenitor and did not carry forward as an inheritance with the birth of this "new breed" of people. From this perspective, Tijerina might stand accused of simply "playing Indian" to advance his particular goals.[71]

More accurately, Tijerina was creating a politicized Indo-Hispano identity. As Philip Deloria noted, whites most often played Indian. During the 1960s, white hippies looking for cultural authenticity and white antiwar activists seeking to critique American empire uncritically borrowed from Native America society and history.[72] Yet Tijerina had no need to search for meaning; he was trying to defend what was in front of him. In his writings, he recognized the villages as reservoirs of tradition and strove to defend them against the repercussions of land loss. Just as important, Tijerina did not consider himself white. The term *Indo-Hispano* broadcast that fact. On the one hand, the critics were right: the new ethnic label was an attempt to legitimize Spanish- and Mexican-era land claims against a complex sweep of history. On the other hand, by inventing the term *Indo-Hispano*, Tijerina publicly promoted a bond between two groups that had been divided and, he stressed, united by conquest. To his credit, especially in a context where Hispano identity was often predicated on the adamant disavowal of any trace of "Indianness" and an unequivocal assertion of Spanish lineage, Tijerina embraced mestizaje as a foundational point of unity within the anticolonial movement he was building.

True to his fundamentalist background, Tijerina looked to the written word to make his case. Just as a royal ordinance had sanctioned intermarriage between Indians and Iberians as early as 1514, the Spanish empire had prohibited indigenous slavery as early as 1542 under a series of "New Laws for the Good Treatment and Preservation of the Indians." As far as Tijerina was concerned, Spanish law proclaimed the legitimacy of nuevomexicanos as a mixed-race people (unlike Anglo Americans who were born, in his idiosyncratic phrasing, "out of lock, out of law").[73] Spanish law also upheld the rights of Native Americans. The enormous gap between such legal pronouncements and the colonial reality thousands of miles away in New Mexico failed to spark Tijerina's concern. What mattered most to him was that Native Americans and Spanish-speaking New Mexicans shared a cultural—and genetic—connection by virtue of shared centuries under Spanish rule. It was this connection that allowed him to praise the Spanish empire even as he condemned the American one. The first empire had united two people through the bonds of family and culture, he insisted, while the second had united them only in suffering.

A 1964 report by a Spanish journalist attending the second Alianza convention captured Tijerina's tendency to accentuate the positive. In this news report, a writer named Manuel Roglán, who clearly relied on Tijerina as his major source of information, portrayed Spanish colonialism as mostly an era of good feelings between the colonizers and the colonized. "The friendship with the Indians, which at the beginning was very difficult," the news report explained, "eventually transformed into a true friendship, even to the point that among the Pueblo Indians that still exist in the state of New Mexico, all but two of the village governors, or chiefs, have a Spanish surname and speak Spanish."[74] That beginning "difficulty," of course, was a near century of brutal treatment that culminated in the Pueblo Revolt of 1680, which violently banished the colonizers from New Mexico for a dozen years. Little wonder that several scholars have suggested that the Alianza leader relied on a selective memory as much as a collective one.[75]

To dwell on the more unsavory aspects of Spanish colonialism like slavery, however, hardly served Tijerina's interests. He was right, moreover, about the extent of racial intermixing in New Mexico. Most nuevomexicanos originated as mixed-race migrants from earlier frontiers. Some were entirely Indian, like the many Tlaxcalans who accompanied Oñate. Nevertheless, throughout the centuries, to be "Spanish" was a way for settlers to distinguish themselves from the defeated Pueblo Indians and from surrounding hostile indigenous nations. The tendency prevailed even in Río Arriba, where many settlers traced their arrival to the establishment of Abiquiú, a *genízaro* settlement. Whether of Navajo, Apache, or Plains Indian descent, genízaros had entered Spanish-speaking society mostly as ransomed captives. Indeed, the entire point of settling on the far frontier was that it offered the chance to escape such lowly and generally despised origins.

Furthermore, Tijerina challenged the politics of whiteness in New Mexico across *successive* conquests. After 1848, the shift in sovereignty introduced U.S. racial prejudices to New Mexico. Given that Spanish-speakers constituted a majority of the population, statehood advocates understood that congressmen nursed doubts as to whether nuevomexicanos could be trusted with the vote. (Already disenfranchised, Pueblo Indians posed no such worry.) A glorious conquistador heritage quickly struck many political elites, Anglo American and Spanish American alike, as a good vehicle for establishing the superior racial credentials of a suspect population. Consequently, poor or not, dark or not, Spanish-speakers in New Mexico enjoyed a certain amount of privilege accorded to those with white skin no matter their actual color. The privilege could be narrow indeed when it stood against continued land loss and subsequent economic marginalization. Nevertheless, as "whites," nuevomexicanos were technically equal. The refusal to acknowledge racial difference thus made acknowledging racial injustice much more difficult.[76] Tijerina bucked tradition by doing both.

Even more revealing, Tijerina's actions matched his words. Thoroughly convinced that nuevomexicanos and Native Americans confronted the same colonial oppressor, Tijerina launched outreach efforts to Native America even before the founding of the Alianza in 1963. In his memoir, he told of meeting with Pueblo Indian governors as early as 1960 and of spending time with *"mis amigos los apaches"* in Dulce, New Mexico, before that, in 1957 and 1958.[77] Outside the state, Tijerina's first successful Native American was Frank Tom-Pee-Saw, executive secretary of the League of Nations-Pan-American Indians, an advocacy organization with a handful of chapters in the United States and Canada. Originally founded in 1935, the Native American group was always small and controversial in part because during the conformist 1950s it engaged in controversial politics, such as petitioning the United Nations for recognition, and in part because many disputed Tom-Pee-Saw's claims of Cherokee descent.[78] Nevertheless, Tijerina hoped he had found a potential ally. "We too are a people which have been deprived of our constitutional rights," Tijerina wrote in his imperfect written English, continuing. "Notwithstanding the Treaty of Guadalupe-Hidalgo, all of our lands were taken away from us, Justice was denied to our forfathers." That parallel was of preeminent importance to Tijerina. "We are trying to find simpathy and support with other people who are in the same cituation," he explained, and then pleaded, "Please, if you think that we should help each other, ansur our letter. We need good and real friends. Ansur us."[79] Tom-Pee-Saw soon did. In fact, he invited the Alianza to join the league as another "Indian group" interested in obtaining lost land.[80]

Despite Tom-Pee-Saw's quick acceptance, the Alianza was far from another "Indian group," as Tijerina was well aware. Despite his best efforts, most early attempts at coalition building fell flat. A letter that Tijerina dashed off to Dennis Lovato of the Santa Clara Pueblo prompted no response.[81] Nor did one that Tijerina wrote to Bob Burnette, leader of the National Congress of American Indians, a pan-Indian organization founded twenty years before and headquartered in Washington, DC. "We are asking for your morale support," Tijerina wrote, apparently with some secretarial help because the writing is much more polished. "If you are interested in our support as we are in yours, let us hear from you."[82] In contrast to Tom-Pee-Saw, Burnette's Native American bona fides were impeccable. He was Lakota Sioux and a member of the Rosebud Reservation. He also apparently had no interest in working with Tijerina. Indeed, beyond Tom-Pee-Saw, the only Native American who expressed solidarity with Tijerina during the early years of the Alianza was a Pueblo Indian who appeared in the Roglán report complaining about the size of the present-day Navajo and Mescalero Apache reservations. Identified by neither name nor village, this man expressed solidarity with nuevomexicanos in opposition to these other Native American groups. Speaking of the post-1848 era, he insisted, "We, the Indians of the Río Grande, the Pueblo Indians, along with the Spaniards and the Mexicans, we are the ones who suffered the loss of land."[83] Given his singular presence (no other news account mentioned Pueblo participants), he was no doubt an outlier in his opinion.

Not until 1966 following the attention-getting Echo Amphitheater protest did Tijerina's efforts to forge alliances with Native Americans yield results. Even then, he encountered this initial success among the Hopi, a Pueblo people based in Arizona who remained outside the reach of the

Spanish empire after 1680. Among the Hopis, Tijerina first found friends in the breakaway village of Hotevilla, which was founded in 1906 after internal divisions had split the ancient pueblo of Oraibi asunder. In one telling, the founders of Hotevilla were cast out of Oraibi because they favored zero cooperation with U.S. authorities, then placing massive pressure on the Hopi to assimilate. Supporting this thesis, Hotevilla refused to send any representative to the tribal council for decades precisely because the body acted as an intermediary between the general Hopi population and the U.S. government.[84] Such adversarial views closely paralleled Tijerina's own negative attitudes toward U.S rule.

In 1966, Tijerina's initial visit to Hopiland prompted a friendly correspondence between Arizona and New Mexico. From Hotevilla, Oswald Fredericks, also known as White Bear, wrote to the Alianza asking for a copy of the Treaty of Guadalupe-Hidalgo, translated into English. "If you do this, I will be the happiest man in Ariz.," he explained.[85] Also requesting a copy of the map of the Mexican Republic circa 1847, Fredericks was apparently interested in exploring to what extent the provisions of the Treaty of Guadalupe-Hidalgo might advance Hopi land claims. Tijerina was only too happy to help, sending a copy of the treaty five days later and, because he could not find a copy of the map, sending explicit directions how to acquire one. In closing, Tijerina approximated a Native American farewell: "Walk in the ways of the Great Spirit, and may he bless you and your people in their work."[86]

Tijerina's closest Hopi ally, however, was Thomas Banyacya, who since 1948 had traveled the country on a mission to share Hopi prophecy. According to Banyacya, that year Hopi elders had charged him with the task of warning the world of the dangers of atomic weaponry. In the mushroom clouds above Hiroshima and Nagasaki, he explained, they had seen the "gourd of ashes" that forecast impending doom according to Hopi cosmology. Tijerina and Banyacya thus shared an interest in the end times and an acceptance of prophetic visions.[87] Most important, the two men were in sync politically: they both viewed the United States as a colonial power in the Southwest. Like Fredericks, Banyacya strongly rejected cooperation with U.S. institutions. During World War II, Banyacya's denial of American sovereignty over Hopiland and over his personal fate had cost him seven years in jail when he had declined to register for the draft. Once an activist, he traveled the globe on a homemade buckskin passport because he refused to carry an American one.[88] Closer to home, just like Tijerina's colonial overlord was the Forest Service, Banyacya's was the Bureau of Indian Affairs (BIA). Like Tijerina, Banyacya also saw strategic value in the Treaty of Guadalupe-Hidalgo. Indeed, he may have learned about the treaty from Tijerina himself.[89] Finally, Banyacya admired Tijerina's move toward direct protest. Even before the takeover of the Echo Amphitheater, Alianza members had staged a march from Albuquerque to Santa Fe. In a letter written to one of Tijerina's associates in December 1966, Banyacya wrote that many elders admired "the courage and truthfulness and sincerity of the President Reies Lopez Tijerina and all those who stood by him during his march to Santa Fe and the takeover of your land grant within the Forest Area controlled by the U.S. Forest Department." Revealing of anticolonial aspirations, Banyacya's stationary carried the letterhead "Hopi Independent Nation."[90] The correspondence between the two culminated the following year when Tijerina invited Banyacya to attend the fifth annual convention of the Alianza in Albuquerque.

Featuring a spectacular cast of characters, the convention underscored that Tijerina now occupied a central position in the swirl of 1960s protest politics. In the wake of the courthouse raid, Tijerina had been invited to countless college campuses and conferences and had widened his circle of political contacts. The convention thus brought together black power activists from California and Chicano militants from Texas, representatives from both groups condemning the "blue-eyed devil." Along with a Hopi elder who sprinkled sacred corn from the podium, Banyacya was there too speaking out against the BIA. The essential political connection between Banyacya and Tijerina passed unnoticed, however, as commentators rushed to cast Banyacya as the exotic "other," describing his hair, long and glossy, his shirt, loud and flowered, and his jewelry, lots of silver and turquoise. For his part, Tijerina, who had asked aliancistas attending the convention to don traditional ethnic costumes, was easy to spot too. He wore a ruffled shirt and brightly colored sash: the invented costume of the Indo-Hispano.[91]

The convention also reflected Tijerina's belief that Indo-Hispanos should ally with African Americans as well as Native Americans. In another manifestation of the politics of whiteness, into the twentieth century many nuevomexicano leaders vigorously distanced themselves from blacks politically. In contrast, Tijerina pursued opportunities to work with black leaders. As early as 1961 while visiting family in Chicago, Tijerina had met with an upstanding Chicago businessman and civic leader, Alton A. Davis. Davis later attended the Alianza's first convention in 1963 in his capacity as executive director of the American Emancipation Centennial.[92] Yet during the same trip, Tijerina had made it a point to visit with Elijah Muhammad of the Nation of Islam to seek his advice.[93] Willing to seek aid wherever he might find it, Tijerina was eager to work with black power *and* black civil rights leaders. Four years later, the story was much the same. Tijerina had met several of the black power representatives who appeared at the Alianza's 1967 convention the month before in Chicago when he had attended the National Conference on New Politics. A special thrill of the trip, however, was bumping into Martin Luther King Jr. in the Chicago airport as King was leaving and Tijerina was heading toward the New Politics conference. Tijerina instantly recognized the advantage of linking his cause to the most well known civil rights leader in the country. He was absolutely ecstatic when King named him the leader of the Southwest Contingent to the Poor People's Campaign to take place the following year.[94] Indeed, in one interview following King's assassination, Tijerina even claimed that the idea of fostering a coalition between black and brown people had originated with him.[95]

Nonetheless, Tijerina's political affinities rested first with Native Americans as his performance at the 1968 Poor People's Campaign revealed. Once in Washington, Tijerina's narrow focus on the land and his considerable ego soon rubbed many people the wrong way. Mocking his eagerness to grab the limelight, young Chicanos from Colorado, for example, gave him the nickname "T.V.-rina."[96] All the more remarkable then was Tijerina's willingness to support Native Americans by stepping back and, when asked, keeping quiet. That is just what Hank Adams, a Native American activist, requested when he invited Tijerina to participate in a demonstration at the U.S. Supreme Court early in the campaign. That May, the U.S. Supreme Court had decided that limiting native fishing rights in the interest of environmental conservation was permissible.[97] Soliciting Tijerina's aid in organizing a large protest against the ruling, Adams also asked that Tijerina help maintain a "central focus on . . . Indian issues" and a "controlled situation on non-Indian speakers."[98] T.V.- rina complied on both counts. The next day about five hundred Mexican Americans joined one hundred Native American activists on the steps of the Supreme Court. Smoking peace pipes and beating on drums, Native Americans and their demands did occupy the center of attention throughout the demonstration. Although Tijerina later joined a delegation that had been invited inside the building, he also had proved willing to subordinate the Alianza cause to the Native American one.[99]

That generosity was a direct outcome of his anticolonial analysis. As Tijerina said during the Poor People's Campaign, "We support our Indian brothers at all times, in all places, and under all conditions, when it is a matter of their treaty rights for their fight and our fight are one and the same."[100]

Tijerina also was concerned about the African American struggle for equality. He even hoped that Indo-Hispanos, as a mixed-race people, might be perfectly positioned to mediate conflict between blacks and whites.[101] But Tijerina did not include African Americans within a colonial framework. As he summarized the political differences years later, "Black people had their objectives, more jobs, more and better education, better public assistance." In contrast, "Native Americans and the Indo-Hispanos had the same grievance and complaint against the government of the United States: namely, the violation of treaties to the detriment of our land and culture."[102] Native Americans and Mexican Americans shared a similar colonial status vis-à-vis the United States. Both groups not only had suffered conquest but also had endured the white colonizer's disdain as racialized subjects: Indo-Hispanos since 1848 and Native Americans since long before that. That is why Tijerina was willing to give them priority in demonstrations.

Even at the height of his popularity, Tijerina was a controversial figure. While many found him profoundly inspirational and charismatic, others dismissed him as naively autodidactic and relentlessly ego driven. Tijerina's reputation has only deteriorated since then. Unfortunately, before the decade of the 1960s was out he had decided that his "new breed" faced persecution by the "oldest breed," which according to his Bible count was the Jews. Warning of a vast Jewish conspiracy for power became his new crusade. More recently, accusations of a deeply troubled family history have also cast doubt on his judgment.[103] Admittedly, recouping Tijerina's political significance means separating it from these other aspects of his distinctly polarizing personality.

To overlook Tijerina's anticolonial analysis as it emerged during the late 1950s and 1960s, however, is to fail to understand the profound appeal of the land grant movement. In developing an anticolonial critique of U.S. history, Tijerina spoke directly to the aspirations and sense of injustice that many Spanish-speaking New Mexicans shared. As he saw it, more than one hundred years after the U.S.-Mexico War and some fifty years after statehood, conquest persisted among nuevomexicanos in the form of continued landlessness, poverty, and cultural marginalization. Although Tijerina was always better at articulating past injustices than outlining future plans, he looked backward to understand better the contemporary conditions afflicting Spanish-speaking New Mexicans and, implicitly, people of Mexican descent across the U.S. Southwest.

It may be that understanding U.S. expansion as colonialism was Tijerina's one good idea. But it was a really good one. By looking at American expansion from the perspective of the conquered versus the conqueror, he could not help but question the story that Americans liked to tell themselves during the Cold War: that in spreading its influence across the continent and then across the globe, the United States had spread freedom, both the free enterprise system and the freedom to vote. Neither capitalism nor democracy had helped New Mexicans maintain their land base or escape the conditions of colonization. Today the term *Indo-Hispano* still has currency among some academics. Scholars of all stripes today also routinely refer to New Mexico as a colony and westward expansion as conquest. Yet none as far as I know credit Tijerina with advancing both these premises so thoroughly. That he did so prior to most black power and brown power internal colonial theorists of the 1960s and in a way that drew thousands to the land grant cause only highlights the need to understand better his contribution in this regard.

NOTES

1. August 3, 1962, Box 1, Folder 1, Reies López Tijerina Papers, Center for Southwest Research, University of New Mexico, Albuquerque, hereafter RLT. The message used the verb *resucitar*, which means both to resurrect and to resuscitate, and the verb *conquistar*, to conquer. I use the term *nuevomexicano* to distinguish those New Mexicans who trace their presence in the region to before the U.S.-Mexican War. Like most identity labels, it is imperfect. In this case, the label excludes Spanish-speakers from New Mexico who traveled north into what is now Colorado and settled there before 1848.
2. Ebright's *Land Grants and Lawsuits in Northern New Mexico* traces eight representative cases.
3. Here I build on Laura E. Gómez's mention of New Mexico's "double colonization context" in her *Manifest Destinies*, 47.
4. Osterhammel, *Colonialism*, 7.
5. Saldaña-Portillo, "'How Many Mexicans Is a Horse Worth?'"
6. Wolfe, "Settler Colonialism and the Elimination of the Native."
7. Text of La Toma can be found at the New Mexico Office of the State Historian website. Accessed August 13, 2013. http://www.newmexicohistory.org/filedetails_docs.php?fileID=305.
8. Swadesh, *Los Primeros Pobladores*.
9. The text of the Northwest Ordinance of 1787 can be found at a National Archives and Records Administration website showcasing "100 milestone documents." Accessed August 7, 2013. http://www.ourdocuments.gov/doc.php?flash=true&doc=8&page=transcript.

10. D. Weber, *The Mexican Frontier*, 190.
11. See, for example, "1964 file," Box 1, Folder 1, and "Para Todo Heredero," Box 2, Folder 1, RLT.
12. Martínez, "Reies López Tijerina's 'The Land-Grant Question,'" 97.
13. Nieto-Phillips, *The Language of Blood*, 73, 83–84.
14. Martínez, "Reies López Tijerina's 'The Land-Grant Question,'" 94.
15. In addition to Nieto-Phillips, see Montgomery, *The Spanish Redemption*.
16. "Nosotros los Herederos antes teníamos riqueza en la tierra . . . ," Box 1, Folder 1, RLT.
17. Handwritten recollection, Box 53, Folder 43, RLT.
18. Tijerina, *Mi Lucha por la Tierra*, 33.
19. Tijerina, *Mi Lucha por la Tierra*, 30–32; Busto, *The Religious Vision of Reies López Tijerina*, 122–23.
20. Tijerina, *Mi Lucha por la Tierra*, 33.
21. Correia, *Properties of Violence*, especially 19, 21, 28–46. Also see Ebright, *The Tierra Amarilla Land Grant*, 21.
22. Dunbar-Ortiz, *Roots of Resistance*, 84.
23. D. Weber, *Foreigners in Their Native Land*, 140.
24. N. Gonzalez, *The Spanish Americans of New Mexico*, ix; according to the 2010 census, Rio Arriba County's population of Hispanic origin was 71.3 percent, and neighboring Mora County's was 81 percent. United States Census Bureau, "State and County Quickfacts." Accessed August 13, 2013. http://quickfacts.census.gov/qfd/states/35/35033.html.
25. Correia's chap. 4 in *Properties of Violence* traces the first four of these cases, 84–119.
26. This figure is based on the U.S. Forest Service's own estimates, "Table 4—Areas by State," February 29, 2008. Accessed August 13, 2013. http://www.fs.fed.us/land/staff/lar/2007/table_4.htm.
27. deBuys, *Enchantment and Exploitation*, 190. The key case here is the 1897 U.S. Supreme Court decision in *U.S. v. Sandoval*.
28. Haas, *Conquests and Historical Identities in California*, 2.
29. Wolfe, "Settler Colonialism and the Elimination of the Native," 388.
30. Author's interviews with Mary Escobar, Reies López Tijerina's first wife, and Rosita Tijerina, his eldest daughter.
31. Tijerina, *Mi Lucha por la Tierra*, 34.
32. Tijerina, *Mi Lucha por la Tierra*, 35.
33. Griswold del Castillo, *The Treaty of Guadalupe-Hidalgo*, especially chap. 7.
34. Griswold del Castillo, *The Treaty of Guadalupe-Hidalgo*, 189–90.
35. Tijerina, *Mi Lucha por la Tierra*, 34.
36. Busto, *The Religious Vision of Reies López Tijerina*, 151.
37. Tijerina, *Mi Lucha por la Tierra*, 46; Gardner, *Grito!*, 95.
38. Letter to the Frente Mexicano Pro Derechos Humanos, dated August 1, 1959, Box 46, Folder 22, RLT.
39. News clipping, "Mexicanos Residentes en Estados Unidos," n.d., Box 59, Folder 80, RLT.
40. Tijerina, *Mi Lucha por la Tierra*, 54, 65, 87. For more on Lombardo, see Coerver, Pasztor, and Buffington, *Mexico*, 110–11.

41. News clipping from August 19, 1964, edition of *Política*, Box 2, Folder 14, RLT. For more on Jacinto López, see Ochoa, *Feeding Mexico*.
42. Slim documentation on these organizations can be found in Box 31, Folder 16, and Box 49, Folders 15–17, RLT.
43. Press release dated January 17, 1959, Box 1, Folder 1, RLT.
44. Press release dated January 17, 1959, Box 1, Folder 1, RLT.
45. "Range Wars Fears Rise in Colorado," *New York Times*, December 3, 1961, 58; Tijerina, *Mi Lucha por la Tierra*, 112.
46. Press release dated 1962, Box 1, Folder 1, RLT.
47. "Agosto 3, 1962," Box 1, Folder 1, RLT.
48. Tijerina viewed his lack of formal education as a point of pride, mentioning it in countless interviews and recollections. See, for example, handwritten sheet with numeral 6 at top, in Box 53, Folder 43, RLT.
49. A short biography of Sanchez that mentions his forum membership is available as part of the Alfonso Sanchez Papers, Center for Southwest Research, University of New Mexico.
50. "Agosto 3, 1962," Box 1, Folder 1, RLT.
51. "November 4, 1963," Box 1, Folder 1, RLT.
52. "Violación del Tratado de Guadalupe-Hidalgo," Box 1, Folder 1, RLT.
53. A petition sent to President Johnson in January 1965 included the signatures of 152 land grant representatives. Box 1, Folder 9, RLT. The organization claimed six thousand members by 1964 ("Heirs to Land Grants Meet This Week to Plan Strategy," *North Valley News*, August 27, 1964), but a more conservative estimate, based on archival membership records, would be three thousand members.
54. "Atento Memorandum," Box 47, Folder 24, RLT.
55. Tijerina, *Mi Lucha por la Tierra*, 108–9.
56. Tijerina, *Mi Lucha por la Tierra*, 118.
57. ABC interview, Box 42, Folder 3, RLT.
58. See especially Partida 3, Title 28, Law 9 in Burns, *Las Siete Partidas*, 822.
59. "Para Todo Heredero," Box 2, Folder 1, RLT.
60. For mention of the Ordenanza, see "April 1966" and "Boletín de Información," both in Box 1, Folder 1, RLT.
61. Simmons, *The Last Conquistador*, 65.
62. D. Weber, *The Spanish Frontier in North America*, 89–91.
63. "The Spanish Land Grant Question Examined," Box 2, Folder 1, RLT.
64. "News-Bulletin," Box 2, Folder 1, RLT.
65. January 3, 1967, letter from Victoriano Chavez to Lyndon Johnson, Box 47, Folder 19, RLT.
66. Tijerina, *Mi Lucha por la Tierra*, 73.
67. See speech reprinted in Gottheimer, *Ripples of Hope*, 306, for "new breed."
68. "Obligación de cada raza o pueblo," dated January 26, 1968, Box 54, Folder 8, RLT.
69. As quoted in Bus, "The Presence of Native Americans in Chicano Literature," 149.
70. Gottheimer, *Ripples of Hope*, 314.
71. P. Deloria, *Playing Indian*.
72. P. Deloria, *Playing Indian*, 159–61, 168–70.
73. Gottheimer, *Ripples of Hope*, 309.

74. "El Pueblo Olvidado," Box 52, Folder 4, RLT.

75. See, for example, Kosek, "Deep Roots and Long Shadows," 352.

76. Montgomery called the result a "trap." Montgomery, "The Trap of Race and Memory."

77. Tijerina, *Mi Lucha por la Tierra*, 70, 77.

78. Crum, "Almost Invisible," 50–53.

79. Letter dated March 25, 1964, Box 47, Folder 4, RLT.

80. Letter dated April 9, 1964, Box 47, Folder 4, RLT.

81. Letter dated August 17, 1963, Box 41, Folder 40, RLT.

82. Letter dated March 25, 1964, Box 47, Folder 4, RLT.

83. "El Pueblo Olvidado," Box 52, Folder 4, RLT.

84. For different views on the division of Oraibi, see Clemmer, *Roads in the Sky*, especially chap. 5, and Whiteley, *Deliberate Acts*.

85. Letter dated December 12, 1966, from White Bear, Box 34, Folder 17, RLT.

86. Tijerina letter to White Bear, Box 34, Folder 17, RLT.

87. For more on Banyacya, see Nagata, "Dan Kochhongva's Message," 76–77; "Banyacya Thomas (1910–1999)" entry in Shearer, *Home Front Heroes*, 48–49; and Banyacya's *New York Times* obituary, which originally appeared on February 19, 1999. Accessed August 12, 2013. http://www.nytimes.com/1999/02/15/us/thomas-banyacya-89-teller-of-hopi-prophecy-to-world.html.

88. Both the jail time and the passport were also mentioned in Banyacya's *New York Times* obituary, which originally appeared on February 19, 1999, and can be found on the newspaper's website.

89. Griswold del Castillo, *The Treaty of Guadalupe-Hidalgo*, 148–49. Also see "Say U.S. Violates Indians Treaty; Asked to Fight White Man's War," news clipping dated November 10, 1966, Box 47, Folder 4, RLT.

90. Letter dated December 12, 1966, Box 34, Folder 17, RLT.

91. Pictures of Tijerina in his ruffled shirt and with other attendees can be seen in the gallery of photos in Nabokov, *Tijerina and the Courthouse Raid*.

92. *Albuquerque News Chieftain*, September 20, 1968, 1.

93. Tijerina, *Mi Lucha por la Tierra*, 80.

94. Blawis, *Tijerina and the Land Grants*, 113–14; Gardner, *Grito!*, 204.

95. See speech reprinted in Rosales, *Testimonio*, 309.

96. Vigil, *The Crusade for Justice*, 56.

97. Wunder, *The Indian Bill of Rights*, 229.

98. May 28, 1968, handwritten letter, Box 47, Folder 4, RLT.

99. Blawis, *Tijerina and the Land Grants*, 126–27; Tijerina, *Mi Lucha por la Tierra*, 210–14; Mantler, *Power to the Poor*, 162.

100. Press release, May 29, 1968, Box 31, Folder 21, RLT.

101. *New York Times*, December 19, 1968, 36.

102. Tijerina, *Mi Lucha por la Tierra*, 208.

103. Author's oral history interviews with Tijerina family members and with Tijerina himself are in the author's possession.

Seeking New Fields of Labor

Football and Colonial Political Economies
in American Samoa

Although American Samoa remains one of a handful of polities on the United Nations' List of Non-Self-Governing Territories, whether it can be properly described as a colony of the United States has been a matter of debate for some time. Its status as an unincorporated, unorganized territory of the United States has afforded a measure of liminality that not only has served to create a condition of subordination but has also provided a buffer from the full application of the U.S. Constitution, viewed locally with some suspicion. Nevertheless, the impact of U.S. dominion over the islands has been significant, transforming all aspects of Samoan life over the past century. The question of territoriality—and the status of unincorporation—is a key dimension of historical transformation in the islands,[1] including routes of movement abroad, because the reality of attenuated sovereignty is materialized in structures of opportunity available to local people.[2]

Drawing on ethnographic and archival research, this chapter examines contemporary Samoan participation in the sport of American football in order to shed light on the ways in which the territory's condition of attenuated sovereignty has shaped ideological, discursive, and material possibilities for Samoans in the local, transnational, and U.S. diasporic contexts. Rooted in U.S. developmentalism of the mid-twentieth century (itself a new elaboration of earlier overseas expansion and ensuing governance policies fundamentally shaped by U.S. racial hierarchies and imperial ambitions), the case of American football is a rich one. It illustrates the evolution of structures of opportunity within which local people have increasingly moved transnationally to the United States as part of new (raced, gendered, classed) labor routes. Football, then, must be understood in relation to the island's history as a territory in the constellation of U.S. empire, as well as the history of U.S.-led development and modernization projects on the island. These two factors have created the conditions of possibility for the phenomenon of Samoan football success we see today by promoting discourses and institutions aimed at inculcating capitalist discipline and producing Samoans as modern subjects.

The transformation of bodies and subjectivities that are part of football participation in Samoa is not only consonant with but serves to support and maintain wider relations of subordination to the United States precisely by masking them, and their histories, with overwrought visions of spectacular success. Yet the people of American Samoa, like others subject to U.S. plenary power, should not be seen as destitute migrants or helpless wards at the whims of U.S. imperial policy. Indeed, as the case of football shows, Samoans have engaged in complex ways with American regimes of tutelage, development, and modernization, thereby revealing structural analyses as necessarily partial. Indigenous epistemologies and cultural sensibilities historically have shaped these capital formations; they also shape contemporary strategies of engagement and the different meanings attached to them.[3] This analysis traces the particular formation of U.S. colonialism in Samoa through the case of American football and also challenges the conventional narrative of U.S. hegemony in Samoa as minimal and benign.

"SUNDAY SAMOANS" AND "FOOTBALL ISLAND"

On January 17, 2010, following the National Football League's conference divisional playoffs, CBS's television program *60 Minutes* broadcast a segment entitled "Football Island." At the start of the segment, correspondent Scott Pelley begins his introduction amid a backdrop that contains a palm tree, what appears to be a beach, and a large football in the center. Says Pelley, "There's a small community that produces more players for the NFL than anyplace else in America. It isn't in Texas, or Florida or Oklahoma. In fact, it's as far from the foundations of football as you can get. Call it "Football Island"—American Samoa, a rock in the distant South Pacific." Estimating that players of Samoan heritage are fifty-six times more likely to play in the NFL than players with any other racial/ethnic background in the United States, the correspondent sets out to document and explain this amazing statistic to the American public. In the course of the segment, Pelley highlights the islands' geographic distance and isolation, Samoan exotic cultural difference, and poverty and underdevelopment as key themes in the story. Ending with a focus on a local quarterback whose father has recently passed away, Pelley speculates that the real reason the islands with a population of sixty-five thousand have so many NFL players: "Turns out it's not the size—it's the heart."

In this representation of island life and football opportunity, we can read important narratives that have been central to U.S. imperial formations in American Samoa. The first centers on the islands' geographic distance and isolation. A key theme in "Football Island" is the nature of the islands—not ones that are akin to Manhattan (often envisioned as a center of cultural, economic, and political power) but rather, islands that are firmly set in the long genealogy of Pacific-island-as-isolated-outpost.[4] Pelley tells us, "American Samoa is a paradise—clear seas and 80 degrees most of the time. It's a land that roared out of the Pacific in a volcanic eruption. Nearly 5,000 miles from California and way past Hawai'i, it's the only inhabited American possession south of the Equator. Of the seven islands in the chain, the largest is just over 19 miles, end to end." To reinforce this cartographic reading, on the screen an arrow slowly stretches across the Pacific Ocean from California to American Samoa, and then a map view of the islands appears. This particular rendering establishes a framework of distance from the colonial metropole (the continental United States), and isolation that reinforces a larger narrative of relative deprivation and serves as a proxy for social distance from the mainstream American public (never mind that Samoans are part of this public).[5]

This social distance is reinforced in the focus on Samoan exotic cultural difference. On the field, while we see footage of Jonathan Fanene, Domata Peko (both of the Cincinnati Bengals), and Troy Polamalu (Pittsburgh Steelers), Pelley notes, "The NFL's 'Sunday Samoans' are hard to miss, with their vowel-laden names and trademark hair." While the players themselves mark their bodies in ways that may highlight their cultural heritage, in the context of sport this exoticized difference often gets coded with positive moral overtones as cultural heritage becomes equated with the kinds of discipline valued in sport.

In the footage of Aiulua Fanene (Jonathan Fanene's younger brother) cutting grass on family property, Pelley notes, "This is a place where kids use machetes to do their chores. Come to think of it, it's a place where kids *do* chores. Seventeen-year-old Aiulua Fanene does a day's work before school, under the direction of his father, David." Something that would be rather unremarkable in everyday life in the islands—young people doing chores, and using the machete for outside work—becomes a point of contrast with mainland U.S. youth. Interestingly, the customary practice of youth performing disciplined domestic labor as illustrated by Aiulua presents a toughness and discipline typically imagined as part of a bygone era of American tradition. The mainland or continental U.S. youth today are implicitly invoked, perhaps imagined here as "soft," indulged, and privileged, embodying middle-class whiteness and parental permissiveness. The Samoan youth also serve as a contrast for the alternative depiction of the wayward and undisciplined behavior of urban youth (usually racialized as nonwhite). These inferred contrasts not only are meant to highlight Samoan cultural difference encoded in a vision of tradition and discipline but also serve the larger narrative that the "old-school" mentality of Samoan society coupled with conditions of underprivilege produce superior players. As Pelley suggests amid close-ups of gravelly fields, beaten-up equipment, and rusted shipping containers that serve as equipment storage, "It seems they do well despite the adversity. But getting cut up on lava rock and playing in sneakers without equipment are the keys to their success. Samoans are born big, but the island makes them tough." The place of the island not only is depicted as central to Samoan football success but underscores the exotic cultural difference of the players.

Documentary stories like "Football Island" trade on the vision of the island as poor, backward, and underresourced—in short, undeveloped. This vision rearticulates the much longer view that Samoa occupies anachronistic space: the Edenic view of the landscape and the continuation of customary cultural practices somehow places it in another time,[6] in the world of the traditional premodern (in standard development-speak). This can be attributed as much to anthropological representations of Samoa as to the discourses and dynamics of geopolitics and capitalism that produce U.S. advancement in relation to ideas of the backwardness of its colonial territories.[7] United States empire has been, and continues to be the sign of the modern, with all its attendant (positive and negative) meanings in Samoa. In light of this, football has become one path to modernity and the American dream of upward mobility.

To be sure, American football has provided important opportunities for Samoan transnational mobility—geographic, social, and economic. On the one hand, football is seen as an unmitigated benefit in many Samoan communities, on and off the islands. It has provided an important opportunity for material and symbolic cultural rewards, touching the lives of countless individuals and shaping the experience of thousands of Samoan families (including my own), not through removed spectatorship but engaged participation. Football, like the U.S. military,[8] is an integral part of American Samoan family histories and experiences; current players and those who support them often draw on longer family histories of participation in the game that may span three generations. Attending games, watching practices, and drawing extended family together to support one's father, uncle, brother, or cousin as they play or coach can be an important element of community life, whether in Samoa, Hawai'i, or the continental United States. American gridiron football has provided visibility and recognition of spectacular success on the national and international stage for Samoan men. One has to think only of the widely televised exploits of the late Junior Seau or Troy Polamalu in the Super Bowl to see that accomplished Samoan players symbolize a successful embodiment of American modernity that is fanatically supported and admired by wide swaths of the American public (and Samoan communities across the globe). Yet this embodiment is highly gendered and implicitly (hetero)sexualized: as football is arguably one of the most hypermasculine and homophobic sports in the United States, access is largely limited to biological males, and achieving success is predicated on performing a dominant masculinity and repressing any indication of nonnormative heterosexuality.[9]

Sporting success in the United States is often portrayed as a symbol of the American dream—riches and recognition rewarding discipline and hard work, irrespective of one's background. Whether rich or poor, local-born or immigrant, white or nonwhite, sport has long been held as an arena where social markers like class, status, or race are superseded by individual physical performance. As such it has been an idealized realm of possibility, even if the reality is much more brutal.[10] In the figures of legendary Samoan sports heroes like Al Lolotai, Mosi Tatupu, Jesse Sapolu, and now Troy Polamalu to name a few (Isaac Sopoaga and Mike Iupati are the most recent Samoan Super Bowl champions), the possible futures of football success are made real and viable for new generations of Samoan youth. In this process football has become a new locus of fantasies of the future that are firmly linked to transnational movement and the mastery of modern institutions of education and sport. In the rendering presented by "Football Island," Jonathan Fanene of the Cincinnati Bengals is cited as one player who has achieved this dream through spectacular football success. Pelley tells us, "While humble, the Fanenes know the rewards of NFL success. Football has been very good to the family—Jonathan built them a spacious home back on the island. From an island where the average income is a little over $4,000 a year, Jonathan Fanene is making more than $1 million in Cincinnati." Here we see footage of a very large, new house—what appears to be a small mansion. Contrasted with other scenes that stand for relative poverty, it becomes clear what the rewards of football success are in monetary terms, and that there are few opportunities locally for generating that kind of wealth.

This view of football as an important path of mobility is confirmed by Troy Polamalu in his interview with Pelley.[11] Pelley asks, "What does football mean for a kid growing up in Samoa?" To which Polamalu answers, "It's our meal ticket, you know. Just like any marginalized ethnic group, you know, if you don't make it to the NFL, what do you have to go back to?" Pelley observes, "A lot of these kids would never go to college, if it wasn't for a scholarship with football." Polamalu agrees and adds, "that's the beautiful thing about football, it's allowed us to get an education." In this exchange Polamalu acknowledges the importance of football in providing educational access for many young Samoan men. But he also articulates a subtle critique which nonetheless does not get taken up in the segment or the longer interview. Here he points to the experience of generations of Samoan youth in the United States as marginalized politically, economically, and socially from mainstream America. In this context, football has become an important route for mobility and a source of status and prestige for families, villages, and Samoan national identity. College and NFL success have been important avenues not only for material rewards, but for recognition on the local and national stage. As Polamalu contends, "it's a voice for our Samoan heritage," and in response to Pelley's prodding he adds, "I hope I represent the fa'asāmoa on the football field."

This particular rendering of the islands and the generative context for Samoan football success in "Football Island" is centered on geographic distance and isolation, exotic cultural difference, and underdevelopment. This narrative dominates contemporary U.S. American understandings of Samoan football participation. What this framing also does is undermine a critical reading of U.S. imperialism and global capitalism in contemporary social, political, and economic conditions in the archipelago. Pelley explains in the opening to the segment, "It was back in 1899 that the U.S. Navy sailed into this harbor and figured that it was perfect for refueling ships. The islands have been American ever since." In so doing he passes over a hundred years of U.S. presence in the islands in a matter of seconds. I argue that the consistent disavowal of empire in the media narratives serves to support assumptions of American superiority, exceptionalism, and historical amnesia (or continued ignorance) on the part of the mainstream United States, with regard to the role of the United States abroad. The elision of the fact that American Samoa is part of the constellation of territories that established the United States as an imperial power, coupled with the focus on Samoan alterity and spectacular sporting success, obfuscates the role of the United States in sustaining asymmetrical global economic relations that compel Samoan movement abroad through sport labor migration. Not only do these narratives obscure the history and present workings of U.S. colonialism in Samoa, they also signal the realization of the purported dream of developmentalism: the successful transition of Samoan communities into the modern era. In so doing, they in turn reinvigorate projects of U.S. empire abroad.

AMERICAN SAMOA IN THE GLOBAL (IMPERIAL) CONTEXT

Enduring anthropological depictions of the past have portrayed Samoan society as isolated and primitive, practicing a holistic culture and preserved in a timeless ethnographic present.[12] These portrayals get reproduced in media stories whose close focus on "cultural" aspects of participation obscure the important historical and political factors. Samoan players have been described as "a swarm of Polynesian warriors . . . strong, fierce men, six to seven feet tall"[13] and "affect-the-tides large,"[14] signaling a particular vision of indigenous Pacific masculinity being produced in and through these kinds of representations.[15] These descriptions focus on size and physical dominance, invoking a ferocity typically associated with "native" warriors, thereby recapitulating a long-standing colonial representation of the "savage."[16] Meanwhile, narratives about the islands as "remote" with diminishing isolation[17] or a "secret museum of oceanic antiquities"[18] depicts them as curio cabinets housing specimens that are frozen in time, only to emerge for combat on the gridiron. More recent stories like "Football Island" engage with this popular trope but maintain a focus on cultural difference that marginalizes history and politics, and the ways Samoans are shaped by and refashion themselves within parameters of specific transnational configurations of power. Understanding the Samoan football phenomenon locally and in the American diaspora requires attention to local, national, and international relations of power that structure possibilities for everyday life.

At the level of formal politics, American Samoa is unique in the constellation of overseas American territories in that it remains an "unincorporated unorganized" territory of the United States. Like other overseas territories that have inhabited the "unincorporated" status that have been so designated by American institutions of power, the island chain remains "foreign, in a domestic sense."[19] This ambiguous legal distinction of unincorporation, in turn, has led to the uneven application of U.S. laws, left obscure the question of jurisdiction, and allowed for considerable freedom in local exercise of sovereignty.[20]

The Samoan islands are now two separate polities, reflecting a division largely imposed by the colonial powers at the end of the nineteenth century through the Berlin Act of 1899. This agreement delineated competing colonial claims between the three imperial powers agitating in Samoa at the end of the nineteenth century and formed the basis of the political arrangement of United States' sovereignty and de facto local rule over the islands. The act placed the western part of the archipelago under German colonial rule and the eastern section under American rule and withdrew Great Britain's claims in the islands. In the post–World War I accord that created the Mandate System under the League of Nations, American Samoa remained a U.S. territory while Western Samoa was designated a New Zealand mandate. An important vision of modernity and development was articulated in the categorization of the Mandate System. Former colonies were separated according to their perceived levels of "development": those "which [were] inhabited by peoples not yet able to stand by themselves under the strenuous conditions of the modern world" were to submit to tutelage "entrusted to advanced nations."[21] In line with the political rhetoric of the time, one of the ways the United States justified the legitimacy of its overseas colonial possessions—including Guam, Puerto Rico, Cuba, and the Philippines—was in terms of its duty to continue its "tutelage" of the native peoples over whom it retained sovereignty.

The political relationship between the United States and what is now known as American Samoa took shape under the U.S. Navy administration of the island until 1951 and was further configured under the leadership of the Department of the Interior from that point forward. Although American entry into Samoa was clearly part of a larger plan to advance the United States' strategic interests on the international stage at the close of the nineteenth century, public support for its continued presence in the islands was linked to discourses of humanitarianism, missionization, and development. "Modernization and development" were key pillars of U.S. colonial policy more broadly, designed to differentiate the American approach from "classic" European empires.

Beginning with the colonial regime in the Philippines, the United States differentiated itself from other imperial powers by taking up the "exceptional" role as a guardian to its native wards.[22] The goal was to achieve Filipino self-governance in the form of American-style liberal democracy, which Michael Adas points out, required "a constellation of institutions, attitudes, and orientations that American leaders were convinced added up to the very essence of modernity."[23] In order to sustain liberal democracy, the islands needed first to be comprehensively "developed," which included a "system of mass education, a capitalist market economy, and an up-to-date public works infrastructure."[24] Casting themselves as the bearers of modernity, U.S. colonial officials stressed their unique systematic and scientific approach. The improvements, in the American view, rivaled anything brought by European powers, and the difference was "a more coherent and ambitious development agenda" in service of the goal of eventual self-governance.[25] A brief look at the history of American Samoa reveals that similar technologies of rule were instituted there (although much later); it also helps to situate this particular case within the wider ambit of U.S. colonialism.

Contrary to the popular depictions of "Football Island," U.S. colonialism in Samoa has a long history and has required a plethora of active policies and projects to expand and sustain American authority there. In Samoa, the first appointed U.S. naval governors were charged with the military objective of securing a naval station in Pago Pago, a coaling site, and access to the best deepwater harbor in the area. These objectives supported the expansion of U.S. trade networks and military influence in the Pacific, part of overseas imperialism that articulates with the closure of the western frontier.[26] Still, the naval governors needed to both pacify the local population and keep public perception at home positive in order to be successful. In this effort, the American authorities pledged to both keep "Samoa for Samoans" and "civilize" their Samoan charges.

On the one hand, cultural preservation and the protection of native communal land tenure practices anchored the U.S. administration's policy of "Samoa for Samoans." Starting in 1900, the island's first naval governor, Commandant Tilley, promulgated a series of regulations that set out the framework of American policy for the island. The early policies addressing cultural practices and native lands began the process of codifying and regulating in the attempt to preserve (but also delimit and control) culture that would later become the cornerstone of U.S. policy in the Samoan Islands. The policy of cultural preservation began with the language of the Deeds of Cession and initial government regulations that explicitly protected Samoan customs that were not considered to violate U.S. laws. Meanwhile, Commandant Tilley's fourth regulation (1900) prohibited the sale of native lands to foreigners from that point forward.[27] The U.S. policy followed the 1899 Treaty of Berlin, which stipulated a prohibition on further land alienation in Samoa in response to frenzied land-grabbing connected to factional warring and colonial contest in the late nineteenth century. Two other historical considerations of the time were first, the aftermath of the 1848 Mahele, which together with a law passed in 1850 that allowed foreigners to own land, instituted sweeping land tenure changes in Hawai'i that would eventually favor planters and other foreign capitalists over native Hawaiians;[28] and second, the process of allotment of Native American tribal lands in the continental United States under the 1887 General Allotment Act (also known as the Dawes Severalty Act). The prohibition on alienation of land to nonnatives marks an important difference in U.S. policy in American Samoa as compared to its other territories and Native American lands.

On the other hand, colonial policy articulated a concern with bringing "native wards" into the modern era.[29] The logic used to construct sovereign Native American nations, rendering them *domestic dependent nations, wards,* and subject to paradigms of *tutelage* animates the approach to what would become American Samoa even if the outcome was not the same: recognizing the authority of local chiefly leaders while working to circumscribe its scope and power, rendering Samoans as subjects of U.S. plenary power in a process that was naturalized and justified in part by the construction of indigenous Samoans as underdeveloped, nonmodern natives.[30] The issue of development and modernization opened up a space in which local leaders would continue to agitate for more power in the lawmaking process, more control over governance, and more access to infrastructure development and various programs on the island in the years to come. Patrick Wolfe's work here is useful in making sense of these divergent forms of U.S. imperial colonialism—American Samoa was not and was never intended to be a settlement.[31] This may help explain why federal law directed at American Samoa as a territory has evolved differently than other areas where the American presence is felt with much more force, such as Guam. Widespread expropriation of land was not the preferred technology of rule in the Samoan Islands as it was in the continental United States and Hawai'i; rather, it became a strategic staging ground for U.S. imperial ambitions, and over time, labor became the most important way Samoans were incorporated into U.S. national projects (in terms of economic, military, and sport production). The development and modernization of Samoan subjects provided the precondition for incorporating their labor into sectors of the U.S. economy and moreover was to support the triumphant legitimacy of American colonial rule abroad.

THE DEVELOPMENT AGENDA IN AMERICAN SAMOA

Developmental frameworks as applied to Samoa have historically turned on a mythical narrative of modernity: the possibility of modern transformation of the island and its inhabitants, and the ensuing access (in some form) to the American dream—education, a high standard of living, consumer products and new technologies, and productive accumulation of wealth. Developmentalism in American Samoa is rooted in visions of progress and modernity that were worked out in the context of colonial politics of the late nineteenth and early twentieth centuries; it was also central to U.S. policy in the islands (and elsewhere) in the post–World War II Cold War era of decolonization. This latter time period is my focus here, and the case of football clearly illustrates the kinds of transformations that have been taking place in the islands in conjunction with movement abroad for the past several decades.

Over the course of the twentieth century, U.S.-led development policies in American Samoa have been focused on capital improvements (institution and infrastructure building); extending the reach of the market economy and promoting capitalist accumulation; and transforming Samoans as modern citizen-subjects of American empire. Taken together, they have stimulated what Lewthwaite, Mainzer, and Holland called a "quiet revolution in rising expectations" that could not be fulfilled within the context of the local economy, thus giving rise to a permanent condition of transnational migration and movement to the United States in search of education, capital, and life experience.[32]

In the 1960s and 1970s development programs on the islands were intended to showcase the United States in a positive light on the international stage, thereby demonstrating its commitment to its colonies and successful global leadership. The new developmentalism of the mid-twentieth century marked a decisive shift, even as it drew on some of the same basic assumptions about the importance of progress and proper forms of the modern. Developmentalism was an important attempt to stabilize the post–World War II world capitalist order of the time.[33] It was both an ideal and institutionalized policy in that while it cast the United States as the pinnacle of industrialized civilization, it held a promise of inclusion for "First World" working classes and colonial and postcolonial populations.[34] United States–based development theories of the 1950s and 1960s supplied an explicitly non-Communist, modern capitalist solution to poverty and underdevelopment that relied on large amounts of capital, technology, and modern social institutions and values to industrialize poor countries.[35] These modernization efforts also worked to undermine the case for decolonization in American Samoa (and in many ways underpin the continued rejection of colonial status).[36]

I contend that football in Samoa must be understood not simply as another instantiation of the growth of sporting labor markets, but as part of a crystallized formation in which local agendas and desires for status and upward mobility intersect with a longer history of U.S. strategies of empire and projects of modernization. The development policies set in place in the 1960s expanded existing migration possibilities, with the sport of football being established as one route to (educational and other) opportunities in the United States. While elsewhere I focus on local engagements with U.S. empire,[37] here I am concerned with the strategies and dynamics of U.S. empire that produce the conditions of possibility that shape the character and effective horizons of those local engagements.

The project of remaking colonial subjects into modern citizen-subjects through a variety of pedagogical projects (religious conversion, educating and civilizing, regimes of training and discipline) is a central feature of colonial formations. Early development and modernization projects in the colonies or the "Third World" were rooted in colonial politics of the late nineteenth and early twentieth century and grounded in visions of progress and modernity. In this process the "modernity" and "civilization" of the Western metropoles were constituted in and through colonial and imperial projects abroad. Within this framework the sociopolitical structures of native cultures in these areas were considered to be antiquated and unsuited to governing in the modern era. The "great modern experiment by which formerly isolated racial and cultural groups [were] being swept into the currents of the world life" required not only the foundation of new administrative systems and knowledgeable specialists, but also that governing entities modernize and develop the places and peoples in question so as to bring them out of "childhood" into proper "adulthood."[38] The United States in American Samoa was no exception. Over the course of the twentieth century, the projects of tutelage focused on labor, politics, and formal education worked to transform American Samoans as modern citizen-subjects of U.S. empire.

While each of these tutelary projects emerged at times independently, all three intersect clearly in the case of football.

The first of the tutelary undertakings, the effort to transform Samoan patterns of labor and agricultural production and induce Samoans to work in "productive" ways according to a capitalist logic,[39] began with the U.S. Naval administration of Tutuila.[40] The success of development and modernization depended on either overcoming or sufficiently adapting Samoan cultural practices—not only in patterns of work, but in orientations toward labor and accumulation.[41] The discourse of the "lazy native" here, as in other places, was part of the inducement to capitalist labor. Over the years, agricultural export, military, and cannery labor have been central to the expanding capitalist economy in American Samoa and the incorporation of its inhabitants into wage work.[42] This pattern is continued in the exportation of sporting labor for American football. As we see in "Football Island," cannery work and military enlistment stand as two conspicuous local occupations. For those who have the right mix of abilities, fortune, and discipline football has become an important alternative because it allows some to transcend the limited opportunities available locally; not to escape the capitalist economy but rather to become better positioned within it.

The second project of tutelage was outlined as explicitly political, with an American-style liberal democracy posited as a goal, and a slow process of political education assumed to be the means by which the nonmodern sociopolitical institution of the *fa'amatai* (the indigenous system of chiefs and titles) would eventually be transformed into a rational system of governance in the form of the modern nation-state.[43] Still, the project of colonial dominance was an ongoing and incomplete one. Almost from the beginning of the tenure of naval governors in the islands, local leaders pressed for infrastructure improvements, health services, nurse training, and educational instruction, as well as greater inclusion in and power over the nascent state administration, accompanied by debates around the promise and potential effects of modernization and the wisdom of adopting particular American forms.[44] In the governors' resistance to Samoan encroachment on the power of the state apparatus, we can see perhaps most clearly what Ann Stoler asserts is the quintessential form of American empire: the enactment of political and economic domination through the creation and flexible maintenance of zones of ambiguity and gradated rights.[45]

In this early period, local self-determination was in a state of deferral, subject to colonial tutelage. Scholars Ann Stoler and Carole McGranahan argue: "As states of deferral, imperial formations manage and produce their own exceptions, which can be easily named: conditions of delayed sovereignty, temporary intervention, conditional tutelage, military takeover in the name of humanitarian intervention, or violent intervention in the name of human rights. Imperial formations thrive on deferred autonomy, meted out to particular populations incrementally, promised to those in whose lives they intervene."[46] In many ways the story of the naval governance of American Samoa in the first half of the twentieth century was not one of "benign neglect" as many have argued, but rather an imposition of attenuated sovereignty and deferred autonomy against which local leaders struggled for greater power, with varying success.[47] Nonstate power was already being exercised by chiefs in the villages, according to the preexisting sociopolitical organization of *matai*, but they were being incorporated into the apparatus of the nascent state in a way that subordinated their authority while legitimating that of the U.S. government. This continued under the Department of the Interior, but local leaders won important political concessions—like the formation of the Fono, or legislature, and a locally elected governor, lieutenant governor, and delegate to the U.S. Congress—that would devolve more political power wielded through the state apparatus to local leaders. Thus there were steps made toward increasing self-determination, without a strong move toward independence in the second half of the twentieth century.

The third project of tutelage was focused on formal educational institutions, but this was somewhat neglected in the early years of U.S. naval governance. While the early naval administration was unwilling to assume the additional expense of public education, the expansion of the educational system would become a central feature of American development and modernization projects on the island beginning in the 1960s. The 1960s and 1970s signal a seismic shift stimulated by capital investment in which intertwined changes in the economy, education, and migration pull the ties to the United States ever tighter. In the second half of the twentieth century the U.S. imperial formation in American Samoa is characterized by expanding avenues of economic, geographic, and social mobility for the people of American Samoa. In the context of previous military-related movement and the mantra of progress and modernization, these changes strengthened the link to the United States, opening new horizons for wider swaths of the population, thereby transforming structural possibilities and dreams and desires for the future. One of the central interventions of the new developmentalism was the expansion of an Americanized educational system which, rather than stemming the rising tide of migration by preparing residents to take positions in the local economy, ended up better positioning them to migrate. Instituted in the local high schools shortly after their expansion, and in the context of widened migration possibilities, the sport of football becomes one route of economic, geographic, and social mobility for Samoans that winds through the educational institutions of the United States. It is to this project that I now turn, focusing on the emergence of football within this expansion and larger project of pedagogy and discipline.

A New Regime: Developmentalism and Football Foundations

Overlapping crises in the 1950s, including an economic recession following the closure of the local naval station, the beginning of widespread and sustained migration out of the islands, and international criticism of U.S. management of its colonies and territories, precipitated a substantial shift in U.S. administration of the islands. As a result, several key development policies instituted beginning in the 1960s shaped the course of local economic growth and routes of transnational movement taken since that time—most notably the expansion of physical, bureaucratic, and educational infrastructure. A technical assistance report produced in 1969 for the U.S. Department of Commerce Economic Development Administration, by Wolf Management Services, a New York firm, noted: "In spite of its isolated location and pronounced cultural differences, American Samoa's economic development is firmly linked to the United States. Although the territory still retains aspects of an emerging area, it is essentially a U.S.-linked economy that, by chance, is set geographically in the underdeveloped world."[48] While the islands' territorial status provided the foundation for this linkage, it is the development and modernization policies of the 1960s and 1970s, which responded to crises stemming from the World War II buildup and later withdrawal from American Samoa, that forge this link in earnest. Increasingly, local residents looked abroad for opportunities for life experience and to earn a living. These journeys to the United States were supported by open migration policies and were later reinforced especially by the expanded educational system that imparted the kinds of skills (especially knowledge of the English language) that made attending college or seeking employment in the United States possible. These shifts also provide the foundation for the growth of football on the islands and Samoan football success in transnational communities in the United States that media segments like "Football Island" highlight.

While some scholars point out that there is a long history of movement in the Samoan islands and the wider Pacific that far predates colonial activity, they nevertheless agree that changes in the direction and volume of movement that began in the nineteenth century intensified in the twentieth.[49] Following World War II, a dramatic shift in migration flow began to take place. One American Samoa Government Annual Report stated: "Thousands of Samoans, finding the natural resources of their islands inadequate, have expressed a desire to go to Hawai'i, Guam, or the mainland, where they believe the existence of a wage economy offers better opportunities than in their overcrowded and underdeveloped home islands. Hundreds have already left, among them many of the more experienced and skilled employees of the government."[50] This kind of framing recapitulates the vision of development and progress, highlighting the "inadequate" and "underdeveloped" "natural resources" of the islands in comparison to "better opportunities" offered by a "wage economy" in Hawai'i, Guam, and the continental United States. Yet residents were no doubt responding to the fact that the local economy had already been transformed by the presence of thousands of people enlisted or commissioned by the U.S. military stationed in Tutuila for the World War II effort. This presence created wage opportunities both within the military and in the secondary economy that emerged to service military personnel. When the naval station was closed in 1951 and the military extended the opportunity for enlisted personnel to be restationed, many seized on it and brought their families with them. In addition to an already transformed economic and social landscape, the lower hourly wages available locally was a big factor in trained and ambitious workers leaving the island for the United States.[51] The reasoning given for higher salaries for off-island workers (usually whites) was that recruiting expertise required attractive compensation. This institutionalized inequality brought a number of American workers (mostly in government, education, and health services) to the island even as it encouraged local residents to try their luck in the United States. By 1972 it appeared that the diasporic Samoan population outstripped the resident population in the islands. The population of American Samoa had increased from nineteen thousand in 1950 to twenty-nine thousand in 1972, with perhaps as many as fifty thousand settled in the United States. [52]

The movement apparently caused the local government some concern and was perceived as a threat to American policy and prestige in the island.[53] With the backdrop of an increasingly alarming (from the administration's perspective) exodus of residents from the islands, and responding to public critiques of failure of the United States to develop and modernize Samoa according to the political rhetoric of development that had been invoked for a number of years prior,[54] the Kennedy administration mobilized a massive amount of capital for local development efforts. In 1961 newly appointed governor Hyrum Rex Lee embarked on a systematic effort to shepherd the "progress" of the islands. Charged with overseeing large infrastructure investments primarily in Tutuila, a variety of capital improvement projects were completed during his six-year tenure, including: harbor, airport, and hotel construction in support of trade and tourism; expansion of medical, educational, and social services; and the opening of a second fish cannery on the island of Tutuila. The development program also included beautification efforts, the construction of a new Fagatogo marketplace, the opening of the territory's first television station, expansion of the water and sewage system, and the paving of new roads. In fiscal year 1967 alone the boom in construction projects generated $4 million in profit for the local government construction department.[55] This path of capital intensification, while not predetermined, has nonetheless been maintained in years since. Federal funds have risen steadily, representing a significant portion of government revenue for more than five decades.

It is important to understand the growth of football as emerging, but distinct from, the economic development efforts, modernization projects, and narratives of progress that preceded it. It can also only be understood in a context of expanding educational infrastructure and transnational movement made possible by the new developmentalism of the 1960s. From 1962 until the end of the decade, public schooling was modeled on the K–12 system in the United States and expanded to include the provision of compulsory free elementary and high school education for American Samoan children with English-language curriculum.[56] The local government contracted many American educators to come teach in the schools, and the school system used the media infrastructure to deliver educational content to the schools through television broadcasts.[57] At the same time that educational infrastructure was being expanded, so was organized sport.

Sports had long been part of the social landscape of Samoa,[58] but concentrated capital investment institutionalized them in formal community recreation programs, some of which would later become part of the schooling infrastructure. In the years that followed, the growth of organized sport continued apace: according to the 1968 American Samoa Government Annual Report, the Office of Parks and Recreation directed thirty-two rugby teams, thirty Little League teams, twenty-four volleyball teams, and thirty softball teams, along with two hundred teenage boys participating in a boxing program.[59] By 1970 a new five-year plan for a parks and recreation program was approved, as was a five-year plan for outdoor recreation. The Office of Parks and Recreation employees organized, directed, and supervised athletic programs for the elementary and secondary schools throughout the territory; they also promoted intervillage cricket competitions.[60] In 1973 and by governor's executive order, community recreation became a task of the Department of Education. The Health, Physical Education and Recreation Division administered the schools' competitive sports program for 1,810 upper elementary and high school students.[61] During the summer of 1974 the first reported football clinic was held with off-island coaches, and the next year Faga'alu Beach Park, Tafuna tennis courts, and a running track in Utulei were designed.[62]

The expansion of football was consonant with a larger effort to establish sports and recreation activities for local residents, but linked specifically to the expanding educational infrastructure. While the World War II era (if not an earlier one) brought early exposure to the game of football on the island of Tutuila, later American expatriate teachers, coaches, and administrators were instrumental to initial efforts at establishing the game locally.[63] Some of these administrators had contacts at football programs in the continental United States and the NFL and solicited not only equipment in support of the new local sport, but also tapes of NFL games that would later be included in the evening program broadcast on the new educational television system. These films became important teaching tools for young Samoan men (some of whom became players), their families, and men in the community who would become coaches. In this way educational media technology facilitated sport pedagogy even while the expanded infrastructure would come to house the sport itself.

It was more than learning a new game. A culture of migration related to military movements was already well entrenched.[64] At this time, not only was the educational system expanding opportunities to move abroad; there was also an active sports landscape administered by the Office of Parks and Recreation, and the media coverage of sport represented a new set of possibilities for young Samoan men. This new institutionalization of sport also generated tensions. Previously, sporting competitions were often part of church and village functions. The new bureaucratization signaled a shift because in inducing students to participate, the sport administrators and coaches were making a claim on the players' time and energy that may not have been supported by the players' families.

By 1968 five of the high schools built were organized into an athletic league.[65] The first island-wide championship game was known as the "Kava Bowl" played at the new field at Pago Park. In it, the undefeated Samoana Sharks played an all-star team of players from three other schools. One player from the United States whose parents were in the islands on contract described the time to me:

> The practice field conditions were horrible, rocks all over the place, little or no grass. We had to cut the fields ourselves, and yardage markers where nothing more than a large rock or biscuit can [cracker tin]. We would practice rain or shine. [Concerning] transportation for the players after school, [it] was pretty much left up to them to find a ride home. We also had the Samoan cultural customs to overcome. The families of the players didn't see why their sons wouldn't be home to accomplish their chores and such. So coaches had to walk a fine balance of practice with customs.

Football, in its institutionalization within the formal education system (rather than being incorporated primarily as a village or family leisure activity) was part of the new developments that were transforming the rhythm of everyday life, and the patterns of activity and labor. As I found in my interviews with former players, families were slow to relent but eventually did because football was emerging as a new professional opportunity, and one that was directly linked to educational access. By the late 1970s, the first few players from American Samoa made their way to two-year and small four-year American colleges; in the years that followed, football became another avenue of development through which local people could pursue new opportunities for recognition, travel, formal education, and migration. The trend of former college and professional players returning to coach and work in sport administration on the island also continued and has sustained the growth of football and its expansion as a path of (trans)migration and mobility over the past three decades.[66]

A central factor in the growth of football on the island was the rise of collegiate and professional football in the United States in the 1970s, which created new possibilities for Samoan immigrants in the United States. In the expansion of football as an industry, new pipelines of talent recruitment were created, one of them being the so-called Polynesian Pipeline, which drew Pacific Islanders (initially from Hawai'i and then from Guam, American Samoa, and Tonga via transnational communal and institutional networks) into all parts of the United States to play the game. This player pipeline has a long history, but the mid-1970s mark a watershed in its consolidation.[67] A new class of Samoan players at the college and professional level (mostly from Hawai'i and the West Coast of the United States, but some also from American Samoa) created new paths that others would follow. Into the 1980s on-island recruiting occurred largely by word of mouth and through personal contacts—networks forged at stateside programs were used by former players who had moved back to the island and were involved in growing the sport locally in their capacities as coaches and program administrators. At the same time, transnational media flows made American football (both college and professional) a household staple on the island. Inspired in part by the success of Samoan players in the United States and the return migration of former players, American Samoa slowly became a node in the transnational football industry.

SEEKING NEW FIELDS OF LABOR

Today football in the territory is inextricably linked to the educational system. The schools are largely designed on the American model, with adoption of American curriculum, and teacher training through American institutions. As socializing institutions, the schools are designed to ideally funnel students to the local two-year college or to off-island colleges to earn bachelors and advanced degrees; they may also be prepared for vocational occupations. While in many cases the schools have Samoan aesthetics or forms of sociality that inform instruction, the curriculum is drawn from the continental United States, and the schools remain subject to federal education laws like the Elementary and Secondary Education Act (the reauthorization is also known as "No Child Left Behind"). Now, as in the mid-1900s, the goal is to develop students as members of a local and globalized economy. In this process, the school as a civilizing institution is central, not only in imparting particular kinds of knowledge but also in inculcating certain kinds of dispositions.[68]

In many ways the local educational system is oriented for export: rather than stem the tide of migration, it actually supports the labor migration of young adults to the United States. Still, the working of U.S. empire in projects of development and the growth of sport is not just a story about the educational system; it is about structural and subjective transformations and the strangled field of possibility that Samoan youth come to see clearly as they come of age. For many boys football is held up as a way to avoid a future in the canneries, symbolizing instead a golden ticket toward a future of abundance. What were once considered a shining symbol of development—

the tuna canneries—are now used to warn students of the importance of education. Whatever else its effects, in its insistence on a strong work ethic cultivated in the service of meritorious success, football is also a site in which young Samoan bodies and minds are trained in accommodation to an Americanized capitalist economy.

It follows, then, that football participation is more than mere pastime, constituting an important form of highly prestigious labor in Samoan communities and in the wider United States. Football labor can be situated in larger Samoan histories of labor that include agricultural production for export, military enlistment, and cannery and other kinds of industrial work. These forms all depend on a particular relationship to the metropole and the larger global economy and entail the extraction of raw resources for sale. (This is, in fact, how many players from the Samoan islands are described by American coaches: "raw.") In this way, player-exports power the American football–industrial complex. In a more destructive way, football success not only obscures the failure of development paradigms and projects in the islands more generally but may also become a substitute for them in the form of sport labor for export. In this sport labor may be one end in itself (NFL dreams) or a means to various ends (a college degree, various kinds of mobility, family prestige, and expanding family access to resources).

In stories like "Football Island" we are reminded that spectacular material success (like the Fanenes' house) is possible only through migration abroad and taking advantage of opportunities provided by the United States. Football becomes a site for achieving and demonstrating development in the sense of developing young boys into men and into player prospects, but also in signaling the successful transition of Samoan communities into the modern era. Football is part of the historical discourses of American colonialism in the continental United States and overseas—remaking the indigenous subject through a variety of disciplinary practices, drawing them into the orbit of U.S. empire, winning loyalty, and extending sovereign power over them. In this we can see clear connections to other indigenous peoples under the American flag and the ways in which investment in practices and institutions like sport (or education, or the military) foster deep attachments to the nation even for those who are positioned at the margins. Still, the dynamics of empire are suffused with tensions,[69] and the case of sport is no exception. Although football can be understood as symbolizing American modernity, its appeal abroad and in the U.S. territories cannot be dismissed as a simple case of cultural imperialism.[70] Football is not merely a technology of assimilation or acculturation (as was the goal with many early uses of sport in the colonial context)[71] but serves as a site in which a variety of interests, values, and investments are articulated.[72]

While the narrative of colonial development and decolonization holds that the "wards" will eventually be sufficiently modernized to take full responsibility for the nation's future and achieve independence, this possibility in American Samoa is seen by many as neither inevitable nor desirable. Today, the alliance with the United States is no longer phrased as contingent or temporary but rather has taken on a more permanent character as a result of changes in patterns of work and consumption, and of ideas of success and what constitutes "the good life." These transformations owe much to imperial pedagogies but also take account of individual and collective projects shaped by cultural sensibilities. For this reason, the case of American Samoa begs us to question what constitutes meaningful self-determination and what the legacy of decolonization is for many territories and former territories of the United States.

Thinking about the particular formation of U.S. colonialism in American Samoa, I have argued that its key has been its nonsettler character, even though the dynamics of empire, in terms of the imposition of gradated sovereignty, have been intertwined with the histories and dynamics of settler colonialism in the continental United States and Hawai'i. It is not a settler colony; it is not a fortified military outpost; it is not a site of American capitalist agricultural production for export, nor is it a tourist mecca. In the absence of occupation or systematic land expropriation (as can be seen clearly in the case of Guam, Hawai'i, and the continental United States) it can be difficult to recognize this sociopolitical formation as colonial or imperial. But that is precisely its resilience, because the filaments of empire are woven in and through other kinds of social practices. In the case of football, local and imperial interests intersect, and the multivalent nature of participation incorporates at once love of the game, projects of status and prestige, and loyalties, as well as capitalist discourses and practices. In it we see processes of articulation, syncretization, and indigenization of discourses of development, projects of modernity, and American capitalism connected to a global American sporting-industrial complex. American football constitutes an important conduit for movement between educational institutions, draws Samoans into its orbit, and bridges or articulates what are often understood as separate or mutually exclusive social worlds. Depictions of player success in stories like "Football Island" show Samoan culture and the "modern" sport of football fused together in new ways: as a way of claiming the modern, mastering but also performing and representing culture, thereby enacting complex engagements with a U.S. modernity. While the consequences of these enactments are varied, one of them is reinforcing American global dominance and U.S. sovereignty in Tutuila and Manu'a.

NOTES

I am grateful to Vernadette Gonzalez, Hokulani Aikau, and Jonna Eagle, as well as to the two anonymous reviewers, for generous comments on earlier drafts.

1. The polity of American Samoa is constituted by five volcanic islands (Tutuila, the largest and most populous; the Manu'a group comprises Ofu, Olosega, and Ta'u islands; and Swains Island) and two coral atolls (Aunu'u and Rose Atoll). In this chapter, *island* in the singular always refers to Tutuila.
2. On American Samoa's (and other U.S. territories) unincorporated territorial status and attenuated sovereignty, see Uperesa and Garriga-Lopez, "Contested Sovereignty."
3. Lilomaiava-Doktor, "Beyond 'Migration': Samoan Population Movement (*Malaga*) and the Geography of Social Space (*Vā*)"; Linnekin, "Structural History and Political Economy"; Sahlins, "Cosmologies of Capitalism"; Salesa, "'Travel Happy' Samoa."
4. See P. Lyons, *American Pacificism*; B. Smith, "Constructing 'Pacific' Peoples."
5. See Hau'ofa, "Our Sea of Islands," for an important critique of development frameworks and the significance of rendering of Pacific Islands as small and isolated.
6. Fabian, *Time and the Other*.
7. Keesing, *Modern Samoa*; Mead, *Coming of Age in Samoa*; Shore, *Sala'ilua*.
8. It is noteworthy that the two manuscript-length histories of American Samoa are both of the naval station (Darden, *Historical Sketch of the Naval Administration of the Government of American Samoa*; Gray, *Amerika Samoa*). See also Fa'aleava, "Fitafita," and Rachel Kahn Taylor's short film *Warriors Born: American Samoans in the U.S. Military* (2010).
9. See, for example, Messner, *Power at Play*; Burstyn, *The Rites of Men*; Diaz, "Tackling Pacific Hegemonic Formations on the American Gridiron"; or the autobiography of former NFL player Esera Tuaolo, *Alone in the Trenches*. Although recently more current players have spoken out against homophobia, the online scandal involving Manti Te'o exposed the ways one's career chances can be jeopardized by any implication of nonheteronormative sexuality.
10. See, for example, James, *Beyond a Boundary* for a compelling discussion of the way sport is held as a separate social arena, a potential pure space of competition and opportunity, yet shot through with all the inequalities and prejudice of a colonial society of which it is a part. See also Farred, "A Nation in White," and the accompanying articles in the special volume "The Politics of Sport" in *Social Text*.
11. "Web Extra: Troy Polamalu Interview with Scott Pelley." CBS, *60 Minutes*. Accessed April 22, 2014. http://www.cbsnews.com/video/watch/?id=6107259n.
12. See for example Mead, *Coming of Age*.

13. Johnston, "Shake 'Em Out of the Coconut Trees."

14. Syken, "Football in Paradise."

15. See Diaz, "'Fight Boys, 'Til the Last . . . '"; Hokowhitu, "Tackling Maori Masculinity"; Tengan and Markham, "Performing Polynesian Masculinities in American Football."

16. See C. R. King, *Unsettling America*, for useful analyses of the appropriation of Native American culture in the service of U.S. sports.

17. Syken, "Football in Paradise."

18. Johnston, "Shake 'Em Out of the Coconut Trees."

19. Burnett and Marshall, *Foreign in a Domestic Sense.*

20. See, for example, D. Hall, "Curfews, Culture, and Custom in American Samoa"; Thompson, "The Imperial Republic"; and Uperesa and Garriga-Lopez, "Contested Sovereignty"; as well as Burnett and Marshall, *Foreign in a Domestic Sense.*

21. Article 22 of the covenant of the League of Nations (June 28, 1919). See Anghie, "Colonialism and the Birth of International Institutions"; Anghie, "Development as Governance."

22. For more on U.S. colonialism in the Philippines, see J. Go, *American Empire and the Politics of Meaning*; V. Gonzales, *Securing Paradise*; Rafael, *White Love and Other Events in Filipino History*; Shaw and Francia, *Vestiges of War*; Tadiar, *Things Fall Away.*

23. Adas, "Improving on the Civilizing Mission?," 50.

24. Adas, "Improving on the Civilizing Mission?," 51.

25. Adas, "Improving on the Civilizing Mission?," 51.

26. W. L. Williams, "United States Indian Policy and the Debate over Philippine Annexation"; W. A. Williams, *Empire as a Way of Life.*

27. Noble, "Codification of the Regulations and Orders for the Government of American Samoa," 54.

28. Hasager and Kelly, "Public Policy of Land and Homesteading in Hawai'i"; Kame'eleihiwa, *Native Land and Foreign Desires.*

29. See Keesing, *Modern Samoa*, for an analysis of the challenges facing U.S. administration of the territory and "modernizing" Samoa.

30. These distinct but overlapping and intersecting histories show the affinity between various constructions of indigenous peoples under U.S. law, and the ways in which those constructions undergirded the exertion of U.S. dominion. See Barker, "For Whom Sovereignty Matters," and Barker, *Native Acts*. See also Bruyneel, *The Third Space of Sovereignty*; Kauanui, *Hawaiian Blood*; N. Silva, *Aloha Betrayed*; and Burnett and Marshall, *Foreign in a Domestic Sense.*

31. Wolfe, "Land, Labor, and Difference."

32. Lewthwaite, Mainzer, and Holland, "From Polynesia to California."

33. McMichael, "Globalization," 220.

34. McMichael, "Globalization," 221.

35. Roberts and Hite, *The Globalization and Development Reader*, 8.

36. The Declaration on the Granting of Independence to Colonial Countries and Peoples issued in 1960 affirmed colonial peoples' right to self-determination and sovereignty. Western Samoa was the first of the colonies in the Pacific to achieve independence in 1962, yet American Samoa never achieved formal independence, in large measure because of development and modernization programs instituted during this time period.

37. Uperesa, "Fabled Futures" (2010).

38. McClintock, *Imperial Leather*; Stoler, *Carnal Knowledge and Imperial Power*; and Keesing, *Modern Samoa*, 13.

39. Moses, "The Solf Regime in Western Samoa: Ideal and Reality"; and Meleisea, *The Making of Modern Samoa*.

40. Tutuila is the largest and most populous island of the American Samoa archipelago; it was also the site of the Naval Station, Tutuila outpost.

41. As Pitt, *Tradition and Economic Progress in Samoa; a Case Study of the Role of Traditional Social Institutions in Economic Development* (Oxford: Clarendon Press, 1970), points out, there was already a strong work ethic present when the U.S. and German colonial officials arrived in Samoa, but it was organized according to different rhythms and logics that were centered on village and family agendas and exchanges rather than on capitalist accumulation.

42. Robert W. Franco, *Samoan Perceptions of Work*.

43. For example, Regulation No. 5 put forth by Governor Tilley in 1900 set out a form of government for American Samoa that superimposed a new political organization (including the partition of districts, the appointment of district governors and county chiefs, the establishment of a framework of judicial administration with village courts and a high court, and a department of public health, a department of public works, and a secretary of native affairs), on an existing one (the decentralized network of matai).

44. Uperesa and Garriga-Lopez, "Contested Sovereignty"; Uperesa, "Fabled Futures" (2010); Sunia, *The Story of the Legislature of American Samoa*.

45. Stoler, "On Degrees of Imperial Sovereignty"; Stoler and McGranahan, "Refiguring Imperial Terrains."

46. Stoler and McGranahan, "Introduction," 9.

47. These histories of American "benign neglect" (like Gray, *Amerika Samoa*) often ignore the Mau movement, a local movement that opposed the autocratic character of naval governance in the islands; see Field, *Mau*, or Chappell, "The Forgotten *Mau*."

48. Wolf Management Services, "Economic Development for American Samoa," Technical Assistance Project, Economic Development Administration, U.S. Department of Commerce 1969, 3.

49. See for example Salesa, "'Travel Happy' Samoa," which argues that circuits of movement were "re-wired" in the nineteenth and twentieth centuries by colonial agendas in the Pacific and the rise of borders and the international system of regulated migration.

50. American Samoa Governor, *American Samoa Government Annual Report: Report to the Secretary of the Interior* (Washington, DC: Government Printing Office), 1952, 2.

51. Lewthwaite, Mainzer, and Holland, "From Polynesia to California."

52. Lewthwaite, Mainzer, and Holland, "From Polynesia to California," 133.

53. Lewthwaite, Mainzer, and Holland, "From Polynesia to California," 144.

54. See, for example, Hall, "Samoa."

55. Wolf Management Services, "Economic Development," 8.

56. Wolf Management Services, "Economic Development," 5–6.

57. Schramm, Nelson, and Betham, *Bold Experiment*.

58. See, for example, Churchill, "Sports of the Samoans."

59. American Samoa Governor, *American Samoa Government Annual Report* (1968).

60. American Samoa Governor, *American Samoa Government Annual Report* (1970), 43.

61. American Samoa Governor, *American Samoa Government Annual Report* (1973), 44.

62. American Samoa Governor, *American Samoa Government Annual Report* (1975).

63. While Samoan football participation certainly precedes this date (Bob Apisa was a collegiate standout at Michigan State in the 1960s, and Al Lolotai played professionally in the 1940s, later joining the local administration in the 1970s), it appears that the early efforts to institutionalize the sport on the island were spearheaded by white American school personnel who were hired by the local government or the Church of Jesus Christ of Latter-Day Saints. See Uperesa, "Fabled Futures" (2010), and Markham, "An Evolving Geography of Sport."

64. The phrase "culture of migration" is drawn from Choy, *Empire of Care*.

65. Johnston, "Shake 'Em."

66. My father was one of these returnees, and from the early 1980s to the early 1990s, I witnessed this growth. See Uperesa, "Fabled Futures" (2014).

67. Still, it is not a well-documented one. See Franks, *Crossing Sidelines, Crossing Cultures*, and "Pacific Islanders and American Football"; see also Markham, "An Evolving Geography," and Uperesa, "Fabled Futures" (2014).

68. Bourdieu, *Distinction*.

69. Cooper and Stoler, *Tensions of Empire*.

70. See Gems, *The Athletic Crusade*.

71. See, for example, Mangan, *Pleasure, Profit, Proselytism*; Vamplew, *Sport and Colonialism in 19th Century Australasia*; Hokowhitu, "'Physical Beings'"; Eisen and Wiggins, *Ethnicity and Sport in North American History and Culture*; Bloom, *To Show What an Indian Can Do*.

72. See Uperesa, "Fabled Futures" (2014). This is a different argument about affect and attachment than offered by Ganguly, "Of Totems and Taboos," which focuses on the commodification of consciousness through totemic Indian mascot worship under late capitalist conditions.

9   DEAN ITSUJI SARANILLIO

The Kēpaniwai (Damming of the Water) Heritage Gardens
Alternative Futures beyond the Settler State

Located in ʻĪao Valley on the island of Maui, the Kēpaniwai Park Heritage Gardens is a popular tourist attraction that narrates modern Hawaiʻi as a liberal multicultural democracy with seeming racial harmony. Its construction begun in 1968, the Kēpaniwai Heritage Gardens (as it is more commonly known) was eventually comprised of eight diverse architectural structures among six gardens that are culturally representative of different groups in Hawaiʻi—a Japanese tea house, Filipino nipa hut, Chinese pavilion with moon gate, New England saltbox house (missionary house), Portuguese home with cement oven, Puerto Rican monument, and Korean pavilion replete with pots for kimchi, and different Kanaka ʻŌiwi structures. One Kanaka ʻŌiwi structure was built on January 16, 2013, the anniversary of the U.S. military–backed overthrow of Hawaiʻi, importantly disrupting the overall narrative of the park, and will be addressed below. Spread across six acres and intended as a material expression of "modern Hawaiʻi," one that presumably repudiates a plantation era dominated by white racist exclusion, the diverse architectural structures and gardens together represent a new multicultural order based on liberal equality, a kind of cultural diversity with global implications as a model for world peace. Reminiscent of earlier U.S. world's fairs, with its domestically (settler colonial) and global (imperialist) reach, the impressive natural beauty of the valley serves as a backdrop that lends itself to legitimizing the politics of scientific display and nation narration, educating tourists about the supposedly pluralist harmony in

9.1. Kēpaniwai Japanese Tea Garden.

the Hawaiian Islands—a presumed historical outcome of the U.S. control of Hawai'i.

When the area for the Kēpaniwai Heritage Gardens was first being cleared, a Kanaka 'Ōiwi (Native Hawaiian) bulldozer operator came across a giant *pōhaku* (boulder) that he was unable to move. Believing the boulder could not be moved because it had *mana* (spiritual or divine power), he asked a Kanaka 'Ōiwi family living in the valley about the boulder. The family is said to have told him that the boulder's name was Kapiliokaka'e, the companion of Kaka'e who governed Maui in the fifteenth century. The next day the man approached the boulder and prayed to it. He called it by name and asked it to move to safety or others would use dynamite. Only then was he able to use the bulldozer to move the pōhaku into the middle of Kapela Stream. Soon after this, however, a flashflood destroyed the park grounds and washed out Kinihāpai Bridge, and the boulder is said to have disappeared.[1] Today, only a few residents know its location. That such instances of the "supernatural," for lack of a better word, are commonly linked to this valley is well known to most Maui residents.

Where a boulder having the agency to leave on its own terms may be dismissed as exotic folklore, such "inconceivable" moments might also have the potential to trouble certain commonsense logics that gatekeep the thinkable. Avery Gordon has notably argued that such manifestations are capable of unsettling pristine zones of knowledge and space, forcing us to confront the haunting presence of past injustices and future possibilities:

9.2. Kēpaniwai Chinese pavilion.

"It gives notice not only to itself but also to what it represents. What it represents is usually a loss, sometimes of life, sometimes of a path not taken. From a certain vantage point . . . [it] also simultaneously represents a future possibility, a hope. We are in relation to it and it has designs on us such that we must reckon with it graciously, attempting to offer it a hospitable memory *out of a concern for justice*."[2] Just as Kapiliokakaʻe refused to move for the construction of the multicultural park, not to mention its very ability to withstand the bulldozer (and there are other boulders in Hawaiʻi who have similarly refused to move), the pōhaku places ʻĪao Valley within a broader history, forcing us to consider another way of knowing.[3] Representative of a "path not taken," perhaps the "loss" or disruption of an indigenous way of life, the pōhaku opens the Kēpaniwai Heritage Gardens to a wider range of interpretation set by different epistemological possibilities and historical contexts.

Besides the heritage gardens, ʻĪao Valley is perhaps more noted for its Wailuku Stream, one of four that run through separate valleys and are together referred to as Nā Wai ʻEhā (the Four Great Waters). "Kaulana Nā Wai ʻEhā" (Famous are the Four Great Waters) is made up of four streams—Waikapū (water of the conch), Wailuku (water of destruction), Waiʻehu (water spray), and Waiheʻe (squid liquid)—that irrigated the largest continuous area of *loʻi kalo* (taro farm) in all of Hawaiʻi, considered the pinnacle of Hawaiian agriculture. Loʻi kalo is a renewable and sustainable mode of Hawaiian farming that makes use of intricate *ʻauwai* (irrigation canals) to irrigate a diversity of *kalo* (taro) and an array of other plants and animals but then returns this water back to the stream or river. This fresh water, rich with nutrients having traveled through the *loʻi*, then flows to the shoreline mixing with salt water to create brackish water essential to the health of fisheries and reefs. Centuries of creative practices have shaped knowledge of the specific environmental features of Nā Wai ʻEhā holding positive implications for the overall ecology of the island from mountain to ocean. For more than ten centuries the vast cultivation of different varieties of taro—the food staple and genealogical ancestor of Kanaka ʻŌiwi—nourished one of the largest and densest populations on the island.[4]

In the latter half of the nineteenth and early twentieth centuries, however, sugar planters claimed ownership of these rivers. White settler planters, seeking infrastructure for a burgeoning sugar and water industry, diverted water away from Kanaka ʻŌiwi communities to arid areas of the island in order to expand the industrial production of sugar sold on the U.S. market.[5] No longer able to access the required amount of water necessary for loʻi kalo, these water diversions had devastating genocidal effects for Kānaka ʻŌiwi who were divorced from the means of production necessary for indigenous food ways to continue. Yet, this original sin of primitive accumulation, the historical robbing of a way of life via water diversion and the enclosure of the *ahupuaʻa* system did not succeed in eliminating local residents' continued knowledge and memory of another way of organizing Nā Wai ʻEhā. In 2004, taro farmers calling themselves the Hui ʻo Nā Wai ʻEhā and environmentalists of Maui Tomorrow, both supported by a nonprofit public interest environmental law firm Earth Justice, petitioned for the restoration of these four streams to counter environmental degradation, to recharge rapidly depleting groundwater sources, and to support nonindustrial local agriculture in the area.

The Kēpaniwai Heritage Gardens is a cultural production that sits at the crossroads of U.S. empire, where settler state formation and U.S. imperialism convene. Within this context, one is able to examine the role liberal multiculturalism plays as a moral regime that facilitates settler colonialism and global imperial structures, highlighting an economy based around settler accumulation by Native dispossession.[6] I thus begin this chapter by offering a history of the Kēpaniwai Heritage Gardens, examining the ways in which the planning, construction, and cultural politics of the gardens is characteristic of multicultural forms of settler colonialism. This form of settler colonialism is underpinned by a moral economy of multiculturalism that sets the conditions for the desecration of sacred Native spaces. I then contextualize liberal multiculturalism within global imperial politics, examining the industries—tourism and militarism—that utilized Hawai'i's racial diversity to their ideological advantage. This essay ends by taking seriously those forms of subjugated Indigenous knowledge and economies often construed as logically impossible to our present moment. Although the diversions of water away from Nā Wai 'Ehā and the Kēpaniwai Heritage Gardens seem to have nothing to do with each other, I show how the heritage gardens facilitates the diversion of water by representing Kanaka 'Ōiwi knowledges, ways of life and economies as dead in the past. In this way, the gardens go beyond providing an alibi for settler and imperial violence; it forecloses alternative futures to the settler state. In other words, the work of restoring Kanaka 'Ōiwi economies, as opposed to the Kēpaniwai Heritage Garden representing Hawaiian ways of life as dead in the past, instead offer land-based economies as viable futures for Hawai'i. I thus highlight grassroots interest in sustaining memory and commitment to another way of life and knowing. Much like Kapiliokaka'e, those fighting for the complete return of water to Nā Wai 'Ehā trouble the commonsense logics of an unsustainable, increasingly war-obsessed, capitalist system.

MULTICULTURAL SETTLER COLONIALISM AND THE KĒPANIWAI HERITAGE GARDENS

The Kēpaniwai Heritage Gardens is cultural evidence of hegemony in its changing and transformational process, a transition from a form of settler colonialism organized around whiteness to one organized around multiculturalism.[7] Although I offer a critique of liberal multiculturalism, exposing its relation to Kanaka 'Ōiwi dispossession and its maintenance of imperial formations, this liberalism was formed through constant political struggle against white racist political and economic subordination. Primarily, however, I contend with the asymmetrical power relations between these groups, the complex ways in which enunciations of Kanaka 'Ōiwi histories are interrupted or rearranged by another marginalized liberal Asian American historical narration. Examining their projects and aims in complex unity helps us to be mindful of the different ways these variegated groups relate differently to settler state formation and projects of empire without losing sight of the ideological collisions, moments of accountability, and/or work at solidarity. In fact, it was a moment of solidarity that kept Kēpaniwai from being turned into a real estate development in the prewar period.

An attempt in 1940 by developer John Duarte to divide Kēpaniwai into subdivisions for luxury homes including "small Hawaiian style cottages for weekenders" led to community protest. The Maui Hawaiian Women's Club opposed Duarte's real estate development, advocating instead to turn the valley into a public park. The Maui Hawaiian Women's Club wrote letters to other community groups asking for support to designate Kēpaniwai a public park.[8] Converting sites into public parks was a common tactic used to block the encroachment of real estate development. The opposition to Duarte's real estate scheme grew to include the Maui Rotary Club and Chamber of Commerce, Young Buddhists Association, Junior Chamber of Commerce, and Maui Lions Club, who together through a dime campaign raised nearly $2,000. Petitions opposing the subdivisions received thousands of signatures, and through a combination of property exchanges and county lands sold, Kēpaniwai was eventually turned into a public park owned by Maui County.[9]

A different historical moment, however, shaped by new arrangements of race and capitalism turned Kēpaniwai into a tourist destination. The emergence of various labor movements in the prewar and postwar period by plantation and dockworkers, the changing demographics and its impact on voting, and the disenfranchisement of rights through martial law during World War II dramatically altered Hawai'i's political landscape.[10] Indeed, different Asian groups had historical reason to agitate. Prior to the 1900 Organic Act, when Hawai'i adopted the immigration and naturalization laws of the United States, the 1887 Bayonet Constitution prohibited Asian groups from naturalization or voting. Designed to give white settlers electoral advantages, the Bayonet Constitution was signed by King David Kalākaua under threat of force and dramatically limited his political influence while disenfranchising a majority of Hawaiians from vote through income, property, and literacy requirements. Labeled "ineligible to citizenship" with the passing of racist U.S. federal laws, the first generation of immigrants would have to wait for their children to come of voting age to gain political representation. In 1936, Romanzo Adams, University of Hawai'i sociologist and proponent of the "immigration assimilation model," predicted that by 1944 two-thirds of Hawai'i's Asian population would be able to vote, consequently increasing the strength of the "non-caucasian majority" and leading to a redistribution of power.[11]

Realizing that a previously closed window of political opportunity was potentially ready to open, many Asian Americans helped form the Democratic Party to challenge the Republican Party's control over the legislature. Historian of Asian Americans Ronald Takaki was the first to argue that

Asian Americans are settlers. Perhaps unaware of its colonial implications, he used the term to challenge the notion that Asian Americans have no claim to the United States since they were imagined as sojourners who did not immigrate to the United States to stay. Takaki writes that Japanese American struggles against the *haole* (white) oligarchy reflected a new consciousness, "a transformation from sojourners to settlers, from Japanese to Japanese Americans."[12] By 1952, Congress passed the Walter-McCarren Act, making it possible for the first generation of Japanese to naturalize and vote; by 1954 Japanese Americans were the largest voting bloc in the territory and the Democratic Party, with the support of the ILWU (International Longshore and Warehouse Union), dislodged the Republican plantation oligarchy from the legislature in what has been termed in Hawai'i as the "Democratic Revolution."

This so-called revolution transformed the racial makeup of the legislature, but its primary aim was economic and political ascendancy. Hawai'i historian Tom Coffman explains that this "revolution" was not a political uprising but mostly "centrist and moderate in nature."[13] Indeed, Matsuo Takabuki, 442nd Regimental Combat Team veteran and major player in land development in the postwar period, explains that prior to the "Democratic Revolution" Japanese Americans and Chinese Americans participated in creating a "financial revolution."[14] After the attack on Pearl Harbor, many white businessmen left Hawai'i fearing further military attack and martial law.[15] This consequently led to an economic vacuum, enabling many Japanese American and Chinese American entrepreneurs to capitalize on abandoned businesses and wide-open markets. Takabuki writes:

> The Fukunagas of Servco started a small garage in Haleiwa, which grew into a large conglomerate of auto and durable goods dealerships, discount stores, and financial institutions. . . . The Teruyas' small restaurant and market in the 1950s and 1960s eventually became Times Supermarket. Chinn Ho started Capital Investment. K. J. Luke and Clarence Ching created Loyalty Enterprises, while Aloha Airlines began with Ruddy Tongg. As the number of local professionals, lawyers, and doctors grew in postwar Hawai'i, the economic, professional, and political landscape also changed rapidly.[16]

Through a web of economic relations coupled with the passing of statehood in 1959 and the arrival of jet planes increasing tourist travel, tourism eventually displaced industrial agriculture as the new lucrative monocrop for Hawai'i.[17] On Maui, Alexander & Baldwin together with Amfac, two of the

Big Five who dominated Hawai'i economically, began converting sugarcane and pineapple fields into large-scale resorts. In *Land and Power in Hawai'i: The Democratic Years* George Cooper and Gavan Daws explain that after the "Democratic Revolution," Japanese Americans and Chinese Americans in the Democratic Party gained political power but had no land and limited amounts of capital, while the Big Five had large tracts of land and capital but were limited politically. These groups thus created numerous partnerships, or *huis*, in Hawai'i. Individuals publicly imagined on opposite ends of the political spectrum collaborated on a variety of tourism development projects, and a substantial portion of these partnerships targeted Maui for profit. This new historical bloc worked with the county, state, and federal governments to build large-scale infrastructure to support the new and lucrative (for some) tourism industry, much of which included the creation of tourist attractions to both lure tourists and get them to stay longer.

By the 1960s, Maui's notoriety as a tourist destination increased. Although overall travel to the neighbor islands (islands other than O'ahu) decreased by 8 percent, overall travel to Maui rose 16 percent by 1961.[18] Rudy Tongg, mentioned above, was an entrepreneur who helped found Aloha Airlines, increasing interisland air travel to the neighbor islands by competing with the Hawaiian Airlines monopoly.[19] Significantly, Rudy Tongg is the brother of Richard Tongg, an award-winning landscape architect who was responsible for designing the Kēpaniwai Heritage Gardens. Through such familial and economic relations, Richard Tongg designed the heritage gardens with an eye toward increasing travel to Maui while supplying "international cultural interest to entice tourists to spend an extra day on the Valley Isle, adding to Maui's economy."[20] During the creation of the heritage gardens, Aloha Airlines added a third jet plane to its fleet. Heritage and tourism, indeed, are interconnected industries. As Barbara Kirshenblatt-Gimblett notes, the heritage industry lures tourists by creating exhibits that are capable of transforming places into tourist destinations, which in turn increase the profit potential of the overall tourism industry.[21]

Transforming Kēpaniwai into a tourist destination required producing the uniqueness that makes this site visually appealing to tourists. With its local and global reach, and linear notions of progress and history, the Kēpaniwai Heritage Gardens is also instructive of the kinds of temporal and racial logics that organize U.S. state formation and settler colonial power. Built with federal, state, and county funding, the Kēpaniwai Heritage Gardens' exotic diversity of non-European settlers coupled with the death of the indigenous that shrouds Kēpaniwai makes the gardens unique. Richard

Tongg determined that ʻĪao Valley was "vast enough to compare with Yosemite in California," a site worthy enough to memorialize the "large number of immigrants who came to Hawaii starting in 1852."[22] The heritage gardens uses the "vast" valley as a backdrop to tell a story not just of white settlement but of Asian settlement. It describes Hawaiʻi as a place where Asians helped to bring a primitive territory in the middle of the Pacific Ocean into modernity—a place where the cultures of the East and West merged to create an American melting pot of the Pacific. Yet, it does all of this at a site of memorial for Kanaka ʻŌiwi dead.

Placing the valley within a broader Indigenous temporal scope, many Kanaka ʻŌiwi view the valley as itself a storied landscape rooted in deep historical significance and spiritual meaning as opposed to a triumphant multicultural landscape narrative. ʻĪao Valley has long been revered as a sacred site where twenty-four generations of *Aliʻi* (royalty) were buried alongside those deemed to possess mana.[23] Kapiliokakaʻe, the previously mentioned boulder who refused to move for the bulldozer, was a part of the preparation for those entombed in ʻĪao Valley. Through interviews in the ʻĪao area in 1924, anthropologist J. F. G. Stokes writes: "Flesh was stripped from the bones, burned to ashes which were placed in a deep pool in the upper stream. The pool was called Kapela. The bones were dried on a large rock called Kapili-o-Kakae, and then wrapped in tapa and encased with braid."[24] The bones were then placed in burial caves that remain hidden in ʻĪao.

Furthermore, the Kēpaniwai Heritage Gardens was built on the exact site of a 1790 battle between Kamehameha and Kalanikupule during which Kamehameha, from the island of Hawaiʻi and armed with canons and muskets, slaughtered Maui warriors, who in previous battles had outmatched the Hawaiʻi island forces. Named after this battle, Kēpaniwai translates as the "damming of the waters," caused by the bodies of the thousands who died in the stream. At a site of Kanaka ʻŌiwi death, now lies a heritage garden teeming with settler life. It is here that one can identify a moment where settler subjects are attempting to work through "their anxieties and obsessions in textual form."[25] By placing the heritage gardens at Kēpaniwai, a site of Kanaka ʻŌiwi death, settlers can not only settle Kēpaniwai, but they can do it with an outwardly clear conscience for producing a garden espousing liberal multicultural tolerance and preserving indigenous culture through the Kanaka ʻŌiwi exhibit.

It is for some of these reasons that in 1960, the Central Maui Hawaiian Civic Club opposed the construction of a Japanese Tea Garden, arguing that it would be more appropriate for a Kanaka ʻŌiwi garden to exist there. In letters to the newspaper, the Hawaiian Civic Club explained that, "back in the 1400's Iao Valley was designated as the burial place of kings," further stating that the name ʻĪao means "of the dawn" and that the interpretation of the word was closely associated with Kanaka ʻŌiwi sacred beliefs. Inez Ashdown, member of the Hawaiian Civic Club, points out that "everything in the valley and all of the names are sacred to the people who know its history."[26] The Central Maui Hawaiian Civic Club wrote in the *Maui News* appealing to the general public to reconsider the building of the Japanese Tea Garden: "We were amazed to learn that the reclamation of forestland now in progress is to build a Japanese Tea Garden. We appreciate Japanese art, and are glad to assemble the art of the entire world BUT . . . the tombs of the greatest Aliʻi (royalty) are still hidden in Sacred ʻIao Valley. It is a sacred valley hallowed by deification ceremonies and burial of Hawaiian Kings. . . . We do not feel that anything but a Hawaiian Garden would be appropriate in a Hawaiian Temple of the Dead!" Given the burials in the valley and other sacred sites, the group argued that it would be more appropriate to create a Kanaka ʻŌiwi garden to project cultural and spiritual meanings into the future, as opposed to building over them. Maintaining Kanaka ʻŌiwi historical and cultural continuity with this valley was denied, however, as these aims collided with the county's ostensible celebration of the heritage of all groups.

After the park's construction, Ashdown wrote in the *Honolulu Star-Bulletin* that while the park serves as a "playground" for tourists, to many Kānaka ʻŌiwi it remains "the Sacred Valley of Worthy Kings whose consecrated bones are hidden in the Burial Caves of ʻIao."[27] In April of 1966, as plans for the Japanese Tea Garden were finalized, a member of the Central Maui Hawaiian Civic Club, Hymie Meyer, stated to the group, "Nalu wale nua mea pau loa" (Everything is lost, or gone). Meyer added, "Let them have it! We shall join our aoʻao [family gods/ancestors] soon. It is all right."[28] In July of 1967, an announcement in the *Maui News* read, "Hawaiian Group Meets Tuesday on Garden Plan," and it explained that "suggestions for the Hawaiian garden and pavilion of the Kēpaniwai Heritage Gardens in Iao Valley will be *so heated* at a meeting scheduled Tuesday night in the Iao School cafetorium."[29]

Arguments for the construction of a Kanaka ʻŌiwi garden, as opposed to a Japanese Tea Garden, which laid the precedent for the construction heritage gardens, were made in a moment when liberal multiculturalism framed the rules of discourse for civil society. A "moral sensibility" demanded that good citizen subjects commit to multicultural diversity that was often defined in binary opposition to "monocultural" demands in the form of white racist assimilation or Kanaka ʻŌiwi seemingly anachronistic cultural and political claims.[30] The limits of this commitment to a liberal moral sensibility are exposed when the question of economic profit versus maintaining the cultural integrity of indigenous cultural and spiritual sites are posed. Jodi Melamed argues that liberal multiculturalism is a marker of legitimate privilege and universality possessing an uncanny ability to define those whom it dispossesses as "monocultural," a cultural stigma that can be used to justify different forms of violence.[31] Japanese American and Chinese American political ascendancy in the postwar period, coupled with a need for more tourist destinations, added up, in complicated ways, to the relegation of Kanaka ʻŌiwi to anachronistic ideological spaces, even as the tourism industry promulgated a popular image that embraced certain constrained formulations of Kanaka ʻŌiwi. Liberal multicultural forms of settler colonialism, however, had global implications in its articulation with U.S. imperialist ambitions for global hegemony during the Cold War. Selected narrations of Hawaiʻi as a racially harmonious fiftieth state aided the projection of an image of the United States as distinct from the "monoculturalism" of other Western powers. This set Hawaiʻi's racial narrations to public memory through global circulation and publicity, while Kanaka ʻŌiwi political and cultural associations with Hawaiʻi were designated for misrepresentation, containment, or omission.

LIBERAL MULTICULTURALISM AT THE CROSSROADS
OF SETTLER COLONIALISM AND U.S. IMPERIALISM

With the admission of Hawaiʻi as a U.S. state, the number of tourists to Hawaiʻi increased by an average of 20 percent per year.[32] Statehood made it possible for Hawaiʻi's tourism industry to grow exponentially. As long as Hawaiʻi was not a U.S. state, large banks and insurance companies were prohibited by their corporate accords from issuing large loans or insurance policies since, as a U.S. territory and one that had previously been under martial law, Hawaiʻi was deemed an offshore investment. Malcolm MacNaughton, former president of both Castle & Cooke and the Chamber of Commerce of Honolulu, reflected on statehood in 1986: "We couldn't get this money. And air travel was increasing. Tourism was coming. . . . We needed this money. Statehood would get it for us."[33]

In order to admit Hawaiʻi as a U.S. state, statehood proponents needed to defeat a notion that Hawaiʻi was unqualified for statehood because it was considered a largely "Asiatic" territory. In order to make statehood more attractive in the eyes of Congress, proponents of statehood used Hawaiʻi's alterity to their favor. By the 1950s and 1960s, Cold Warriors were aware that the admission of Hawaiʻi as a U.S. state had ideological value for gaining the allegiance of newly decolonized nations. In 1950, Edward L. Bernays, called by some the "father of public relations," was a visiting professor at the University of Hawaiʻi. Bernays had been widely known for his corporate and government opinion campaigns, most notably for his public relations work for the United Fruit Company in the 1950s that led directly to the CIA overthrow of the democratically elected government of Guatemala in 1954.[34] While in Hawaiʻi, Bernays argued for Hawaiʻi statehood, stating that Hawaiʻi's citizenry—theorized as racially diverse but culturally American— should be showcased above all other American achievements for the world to see what only American democracy could accomplish. Bernays believed that Hawaiʻi statehood would be beneficial both nationally and internationally to "dramatize" to Americans on the continent that diverse racial groups could in fact "live together in harmony," while supporting American interests in the "Orient" by disproving communist accusations that "imperialism and racism are our national policy."[35] As Christina Klein cogently argues in *Cold War Orientalism*, Hawaiʻi statehood had the ability to rearticulate U.S. imperialism as the spreading of democracy, which created a misleading distinction between European colonial powers and the United States.[36] Hawaiʻi's majority Asian American and Pacific Islander population could thus represent a militarily powerful and economically dominant United States— one that would ideologically assist the maintenance and establishment of U.S. military bases and secure access to resources and markets throughout Asia and the Pacific.

An outcropping rock profile of Cold War president John F. Kennedy was dedicated in 1970 and is a popular tourist attraction located just above the Kēpaniwai Heritage Gardens.[37] This rock profile, however, was previously hailed as that of a *kahuna* (priest) named Kaukaʻiwai, who lived in the fifteenth century and is said to protect the Aliʻi burials in the valley. In June of 1963, Kennedy spoke from Hawaiʻi viewing the Islands as an appropriate "intra-racial backdrop" for his civil rights message challenging Alabama governor George Wallace's refusal to desegregate the University of Alabama.[38] Given only two days before his national presidential address calling for civil rights legislation, Kennedy's speech addressed "Negro-white relations" at a national conference in Honolulu, calling on mayors of cities and county leaders to consider the economic value of racial harmony. Kennedy often made mention of Hawaiʻi's racial diversity, going so far as to state that "Hawaiʻi is

9.3. Kēpaniwai JFK outcropping rock profile. Long determined to be the outcrop rock profile of Kaukaʻiwai, in 1970 it became known as the profile of John F. Kennedy. Currently, it is listed as "Changing Profile Rock."

what the United States is striving to be."[39] His New Frontier administration, a phrasing that also has both settler colonial and imperial implications, maintained a similar pronouncement for global diversity wherein Kennedy argued that the goal of liberalism was to "help make the world safe for diversity."[40] With transnational support from foreign dignitaries including Imelda Marcos and Prince and Princess Hitachi of Japan, the Japanese Tea House was constructed in Kyoto, Japan, and the Chinese Pavilion was assembled in Taiwan before being shipped to Maui. Indeed, Kennedy is present in the heritage gardens, not only through the literal and figurative resignifying of sacred sites such as the profile of Kaukaʻiwai, but through the fact that the heritage gardens can be read simultaneously as a mosaic of races, a domestic expression of liberal multiculturalism via a nation of immigrants narration, and a mosaic of nations, an international garden framed by U.S. global hegemony.[41]

Kennedy's pronouncement about future U.S. race relations using Hawai'i as a model constructs Hawai'i as both a "primitive" space against which to define U.S. modernity and also an alternative modernity toward which the United States was attempting to strive. Such conflicting views of Hawai'i speak not to different, but rather concomitant representational strategies of settler colonialism and empire formation. That is to say, modern Hawai'i is no longer temporally behind the U.S. continent, but instead made into a glorious future model for the United States *only after* liberal multicultural settler state formation. For instance, in the book *Maui Remembers* the authors write: "As in ancient times, Wailuku retains much of its status as a population and government center and upholds its reputation as a combat site. The only difference is that, today, legal battles in Wailuku's courthouse replace the bloodshed of old."[42] The "peaceful multiculturalism" represented in the heritage gardens is thus defined against a portrayal of presettler Hawai'i as savage, reducing Kanaka 'Ōiwi to a caricatured people who solved their differences through bloodshed. As such, Kanaka 'Ōiwi are seen to lack, unlike the United States, the capacity to cause harmonious and peaceful relations to occur. In this way, settler colonialism and American exceptionalism are made evident in the heritage garden's location, where once was war and now exists peace, and the "bloodshed of old" is replaced by a seemingly nonviolent approach to resolving conflict through mutual understanding. Hawai'i becomes an object of knowledge that serves as evidence of the United States' ability to foster the cultural diversity of non-Europeans that previous colonial projects sought to extinguish. The United States is thus poised with the seeming democratic power and intelligence to arrange this multiplicity in peaceful harmony globally.

While such liberal Cold War representations portray U.S. expansion as merely the spreading of democracy, U.S. influence in this region is structured instead by imperial domination and war, often made ideologically invisible by Cold War epistemes. Penny Von Eschen has argued that U.S. cultural hegemony is accompanied by a coercive force, specifically through a violent geopolitics of U.S. military power; "the view that culture was decisive in winning the Cold War assumes an illusory separation of the categories 'culture' and 'militarism.'"[43] The East-West Center on the campus of the University of Hawai'i, for instance, was seen as part of a "Pacific Rim strategy" to champion U.S. corporate and military culture into the development of newly decolonized Asian and Pacific nations by training thousands of Asian and Pacific Islander students to continue to espouse an identification with the values and aspirations of U.S. capitalism after achieving key posts in their nations. Yet, this was not simply a nonviolent exchange of ideas to promote "cultural harmony, interchange, and understanding." The East-West Center is known, among other things, for having coordinated sixty-five grants for Indonesian military officials in 1962 and 1965 to receive "small-arms training," just prior to the military coup that targeted the Indonesian Communist Party, leaving half a million dead.[44]

While both the Kēpaniwai Heritage Gardens and the Kennedy rock profile narrate an ability for the United States to create a peaceful world based on reciprocal exchange and interdependence, this liberal multiculturalism is in fact a part of a developmentalist discourse propagated by liberal proponents who were belligerent in asserting their military prowess for the purposes of achieving U.S. global hegemony in the postwar period. With roots in the American progressive tradition, modernization theory was a social science discourse foundational to Cold War liberalism that sought to transport American ideas and institutions to "primitive" societies who needed guidance in development. The aim to espouse global liberalism was two-fold: first, to integrate recently decolonized nation-states into capitalist market relations, and second, to prevent nations targeted for development from becoming communists.[45] Kennedy's "making diversity safe for the world" was palatable so long as notions of diversity did not extend into diverse culture-based economies outside of U.S. capitalism. In other words, anything disobedient to U.S. global capitalism was perceived as a threat that justified an ultimatum, what Ngugi Wa Thiong'o succinctly formulates as "accept theft, or death."[46]

Arguing that the Cold War is more than a historical event but also a knowledge project that determined the possibilities and impossibilities for "telling, querying and knowing," Jodi Kim further shows that the logics of the Cold War obfuscated the extreme violence of U.S. global hegemony. Using an Asian American critique as an "unsettling hermeneutic," a transnational analytic productive of both exposing the atrocities of the Cold War and locating Asian Americans within this violent genealogy of U.S. imperialism, this critical edge can be used to think "against the grain of American exceptionalism and nationalist ontology": "while the master narratives of Asian migration to the United States chart a putatively desirable and desired teleology troped as the American Dream—an escape from an unstable, economically devastated, and politically repressive homeland to safe haven in an America full of freedom and opportunity—the home that one leaves often needs to be left precisely because of the havoc wreaked by U.S. imperialist intervention there."[47] Framing Asian American cultural politics as a site for "staging, imagining, and remembering differently" offers a key critical lens through which to examine how the Kēpaniwai Heritage Garden is shaped not by peace, but by a global landscape torn by U.S. militarism. In other words, by reading the heritage gardens against the grain, each national/ethnic structure also represents imperial relations established through the military violence of U.S. empire. The Filipino nipa hut represents where upward of two million Filipinos died as a result of a genocidal U.S. military campaign for occupation of the Philippines that beginning in 1899 made Filipinos U.S. nationals of a war-torn country available as exploitable labor for Hawai'i's sugar plantations.[48] The Japanese Tea Garden highlights the forced opening of Japan in 1854 by U.S. Commodore Matthew Perry, which set in motion the Meiji restoration that displaced many Japanese to Hawai'i. And one cannot forget the firebombing of major cities and the atomic bombs that targeted Japanese civilians in World War II. Indeed, the Korean pavilion is reminiscent of the Korean War, often referred to as "The Forgotten War," which resulted in over three million Korean civilian casualties, two million missing or wounded, and almost ten million Koreans separated from friends and relatives with fewer than ten thousand subsequently reunited.[49] The most recent addition to the heritage gardens, however, speaks directly to an alternative way of viewing the heritage gardens. On January 16, 2013, the eve of the anniversary of the 1893 U.S. military–backed overthrow of the Hawaiian Kingdom, a group called Pu'uhonua 'o Iao created an altar in the Kēpaniwai Heritage Gardens using an uncut stone that was strategically placed to represent the Kū'ē petitions. These petitions, signed in 1897, include over 90 percent of the eligible Native population who opposed U.S. citizenship throughout the islands. The newest addition to the heritage gardens offers an unsettling hermeneutic from which to uncover a critical history of settler colonialism and U.S. military occupation.

While the heritage gardens represents a U.S. presence in Hawai'i as bringing peace to both Hawai'i and the world, in opposition to Hawaiians' "bloodshed of old," many of Maui's multicultural residents have lost their lives in the service of the United States. The War Memorial Stadium and Gym, with the names of the hundreds of Maui residents who died in World War I, World War II, the Korean War, Vietnam, and the Gulf War, currently stands on the road leading to the gardens. The names of soldiers who have been killed in the recent wars in the Middle East have yet to be engraved. Down the road from this memorial, at the Ka'ahumanu Shopping Center in the "Plantation Section," exists the recruitment stations for the army, marines, navy, and air force. What is more, the recruitment stations are in aesthetic continuity with the heritage gardens, completed with *totan* roof and plantation-style design.

Not only have Maui residents lost their lives in U.S. wars, the U.S. military presence in the islands made it a target by other imperialist nations. Although Pearl Harbor is defined in U.S. national public memory as the only site in Hawai'i attacked by the Japanese military on December 7, the fact that Maui was the site of three attacks by the Japanese military is all but forgotten. On December 15, 1941, and again on December 31, Japanese military submarines fired torpedoes onto the island, missing their primary targets, one of which was the town of Pu'unene. In 1942, however, a Japanese submarine successfully sank an army transport, killing twenty-four men. Such attacks were cause to occupy the island with more than 200,000 soldiers from the marines, navy, army, and air force. With more than fifty military training sites on the island, Maui residents were eventually outnumbered four-to-one by military personnel. In preparation for fighting in the sugar fields of Saipan and Tinian, Maui plantation workers were used to teach marines how to maneuver through dense and sharp sugarcane as well as how to set cane fires. The key training site, however, was at the nearby island of Kaho'olawe. Controlled by the navy, Kaho'olawe was used for live fire training exercises through which seamen rehearsed taking over islands in the Pacific from the Japanese. In fact, marines in the Fourth Division who fought in Iwo Jima named the first street rebuilt after U.S. occupation "Maui Boulevard."[50] Kaho'olawe continued, after World War II, to be used for live fire training exercises until Kanaka 'Ōiwi activists in the Protect Kaho'olawe 'Ohana (PKO) occupied the island to stop the bombing and filed a successful lawsuit, putting a halt on the use of the island as a weapons range in 1990.

"THE DAMMING OF THE WATER": KĒPANIWAI AND NĀ WAI 'EHĀ

Kaho'olawe is an island only eight miles to the south of Maui, and the hydrology of the two islands are interdependent. In the last half of the nineteenth century, the island of Kaho'olawe was used as a sheep pasture. By World War II, the island was used by the U.S. armed forces as a training ground and missile range. Each contributed to the elimination of once-dense forests on both islands.[51] In 1909, an unnamed Kanaka 'Ōiwi woman from 'Ulupalakua on Maui explained that forests on the island of Kaho'olawe previously attracted clouds to the island in the morning. By the afternoon, these clouds, laden with moisture, would travel across the channel to rain over ʻUlupalakua, an area on the leeward slopes of Maui. When both ranchers and the U.S. military eliminated the forests on Kahoʻolawe, the clouds no longer gathered over Kahoʻolawe, and the ecology at South Maui also went from wet to dry. These factors, combined with earlier deforestation of sandalwood, contributed to the rapid deforestation such that only 5 percent of the Native forests in South Maui remain.[52]

In a master plan drafted in 1959 for the economic development of Maui, lack of water sources in South Maui was considered an obstacle toward development. Planners stated that, "the expansion of the water system for the Kīhei, Makena, and Wailea areas must be considered," because the region was "served by a water system unable to take care of any material expansion of residential or agricultural activity."[53] Mansel G. Blackford explains in *Fragile Paradise: The Impact of Tourism on Maui, 1959–2000* that as South Maui was targeted for the development of luxury resorts, the demand for water increased but no adequate water sources could be found. In 1975, development companies building large-scale resorts struck a deal with Maui County's Board of Water Supply. Four companies—the Wailea Development Company; Seibu, a Japanese development company; and two Big Five corporations owned by C. Brewer and by Alexander & Baldwin—were permitted to jointly finance a multimillion-dollar project drilling new wells into the ʻĪao aquifer, twenty-five miles away from South Maui. The ʻĪao aquifer was intended to support a renewable withdrawal of thirty-six million gallons per day (mgd) and consequently the county of Maui offered to construct the infrastructure necessary to transport 19 mgd of water away from Nā Wai ʻEhā to South Maui luxury resorts. The estimate of 36 mgd, however, was much higher than the actual 20 mgd that the aquifer could sustainably yield. This did not sway further development, however, and as tourism slumped, future developments were deemed necessary. Water extraction from the ʻĪao aquifer rose to 20.5 mgd, and by 1985 salinity levels increased, and the state water commission threatened to seize control of the aquifer from the county by designating it a water management area. Determining that the water resources were in jeopardy in 2008, the state of Hawaiʻi designated the ʻĪao aquifer a water management area, taking control away from the county.

The diversion of water away from indigenous communities to arid areas for the purposes of development has a long role in settler state formation dating back to the expansion of the American West. The doctrine of prior appropriation, a frontier logic that developed in the mining camps there, not only discounted a Native American presence on and relationship to land

and resources prior to settler encroachment but also deemed Native peoples without rights as part of the wildlife itself. Donald Worster explains that the doctrine of prior appropriation meant a vested right to the water as a form of property: "Under the doctrine, it mattered not at all how far from the river he lived or how far he diverted the water from its natural course, mattered not at all if he drained the river bone-dry. There was only one rule in that appropriation: *'Qui prior est in tempore, potior est in jure'*—he who is first in time is first in right."[54] The control of rivers for economic development was a colonial obsession that signified a mastering of nature and an assertion that settlers were more deserving of disputed space. Aiming to make the desert bloom, water diversion claimed that allowing rivers to travel their natural path to the sea was wasteful. President Theodore Roosevelt argued: "If we could save the waters running now to waste, the western part of the country could sustain a population greater than even the legendary Major Powell dreamed."[55] Yet, Vandana Shiva points out that Major Wesley Powell, director of the U.S. Geological Survey between 1881 and 1899, whom Roosevelt mentions, believed that development in areas without adequate water sources set a dangerous precedent: "It would be almost a criminal act to go on as we are doing now and allow thousands and hundreds of thousands of people to establish homes where they cannot maintain themselves."[56]

While the doctrine of prior appropriation has never been instituted as law in Hawai'i, settler practices have enacted its logics. Unlike water diversion projects on the U.S. continent, however, private groups funded the transportation of water to arid areas for the purposes of agriculture, not the government. By 1866, only four years after the Wailuku Sugar Company was established, the production of taro in Nā Wai 'Ehā had been radically limited and the landscape drastically alterred. Ty Kāwika Tengan, in his cultural report on these changes, notes an article in the Nūpepa Kū'oko'a written in 1866: "DESPAIR! WAILUKU IS BEING DESTROYED BY THE SUGAR PLANTATION—A letter by S. D. Hakuole, of Kula, Maui arrived at our office, he was declaring that the land of Wailuku is being lost due to the cultivation of sugarcane. Furthermore, he states the current condition of once cultivated taro patches being dried up by the foreigners, where they are now planting sugarcane."[57] Sugarcane is considered a water-thristy crop, and one pound of sugar requires four thousand pounds of water, roughly five hundred gallons.[58]

At the turn of the twentieth century, water was seen as a vital new industry with plantations employing gravel miners from California to mine 'Iao Valley for further groundwater sources.[59] Carol Wilcox notes that by 1920,

9.4. An empty Wailuku Stream in Paukukalo near the shoreline.

the sugar industry was utilizing 1,200 mgd of surface and groundwater compared to the entire city of Boston, which used 80 mgd in 1929.[60] Kapuʻala Sproat, attorney for Earth Justice, a nonprofit law firm that has fought steadily for the acknowledgement of water as a public trust asset, states that after statehood in 1959 judges were appointed who understood Hawaiian custom and tradition. In the landmark 1973 *McBryde Sugar Company v. Robinson* case, Chief Justice Kazuhisa Abe wrote the majority decision that although both sugar companies could gain access to water, this did not translate into ownership of the water.[61] Instead, the state of Hawaiʻi held these waters as a public trust asset for the benefit of the entire community. In 1978, the Hawaiʻi Constitutional Convention created amendments that protected Hawaiʻi's natural resources, including water. In 1987, the state legislature enacted Hawaiʻi's Water Code, establishing a framework for water resource management based on protection and reasonable use.[62] Vanadana Shiva argues that water should be viewed as a commons, since all life is dependent on it and its existence relies on the cooperation, not competition, of those who use it.[63]

Indeed, the seemingly pristine Wailuku Stream that flows through ʻĪao Valley does not actually continue out of the valley. Huge grates that extend the width of the river divert this water to irrigate sugarcane, golf courses, resorts, and new real estate subdivisions. Tourists who visit ʻĪao will most likely marvel at the natural beauty of both the valley and Wailuku Stream. At the opposite end of Wailuku Stream, however, they would find a river filled in with concrete, where life cannot exist and not a drop of water reaches the ocean. Kaleikoa Kaʻeo, interviewed in the guerilla documentary *Noho Hewa: The Wrongful Occupation of Hawaiʻi*, calls this an "environmental crime." "Life actually comes from that mix of that fresh and salt water. And you have of course the production of seaweed. And from the small seaweed of course then you have smaller fish that's eaten by the big fish that's eaten by the Kanaka. . . . ʻHaihai no ka ua i ka ululaʻau.' Rain follows the trees. If the trees are gone, that mean the rain is gone. If you got no rain in the uplands then you got no rain in the lowlands. And having no rain in the lowlands of course has a direct effect of the amount of life that's being produced." Of the thirty-four streams and rivers on the island of Maui, currently only four make its natural path to the sea.[64] Many of the fish, shrimp, and snails in Maui's streams and rivers are diadromous, which means they use both fresh and salt water in their life cycles but often die because they are unable to make their way back upstream. After storms hit, however, Skippy Hau, a member of the Hui ʻo Nā Wai ʻEhā, scoops these otherwise doomed species and drives them five miles upstream to release them into the fresh water.

Many residents of Nā Wai ʻEhā have long been at the forefront of contentious debates over the political and ecological transformations and limits of the island. The original sin of water expropriation and competing claims for water tied to opposing modes of production continue to haunt Maui's present. Hawaiian Commercial and Sugar Company (HC&S) and Wailuku Water Distribution Company (formerly Wailuku Sugar Company), the two companies responsible for the original water diversions from Nā Wai ʻEhā, argued that without continued access of up to 70 million gallons of water a day their already declining industry would be in jeopardy and eight hundred HC&S workers would be at risk of losing their jobs. Workers at HC&S thus organized themselves into a group called Hui ʻo Ka ʻIke, arguing desperately, "Our jobs are at stake, our very livelihood and the ability to support our families."[65] In June of 2010, the water commission ruled to return only a third of the stream flow for which the groups petitioned, and to only two of the four streams—Waiheʻe and Waiehu. Hōkūao Pellegrino, whose family loʻi (taro farm) sits along Waikapū Stream, which did not receive any of the petitioned water, responded: "I may not be able to employ 800 people, but I can feed 800 people—if I was able to grow on all of my land."[66] Pellegrino's statement illuminates how the diversion of water alienates Kanaka from the productivity of their land, maintaining a capitalist necessity of having wage laborers—who are both dependent on and exploited by capitalism—buy their food at the market.

Hōkūao Pellegrino's response forces one to consider a preceding moment in time, a different arrangement of land, resources, and a way of life that predates the settler state. Although not relying on wages to support one's family is inconceivable within the limits of liberal multicultural tolerance framed by U.S. capitalism, Pellegrino's response and community work show that loʻi kalo in Nā Wai ʻEhā are viable foundations for Maui's future. Such knowledges are, in fact, grounded in both centuries-old knowledges and ongoing creative practices. Not so much a process of "going back," this work is an articulation of Maui's present environmental, social, and economic problems in conjunction with ongoing indigenous technologies and knowledges, particularly a deep and historical knowledge of the specific environmental features and making of Nā Wai ʻEhā. In *The Seeds We Planted: Portrait of a Native Hawaiian Charter School*, Noelani Goodyear-Kaʻōpua illustrates just how Indigenous knowledge and economies can materially transform the structures of settler colonialism: "The marginalization and suppression of Indigenous knowledges has gone hand in hand with the transformation and degradation of Indigenous economic systems and the ecosystems that nourish us. Conversely, settler-colonial relations might be transformed by rebuilding, in new ways, the Indigenous structures that have historically sustained our societies."[67] Land-based economies have the possibility of creating new noncapitalist and noncolonial ways of relating to each other. Goodyear-Kaʻōpua sets the conditions for cultivating mutual respect between different groups by challenging both the "fragmenting and harmful forces of racism and settler colonialism."[68] Kanaka ʻŌiwi ways of life illuminate other paths that are distinct from an overreliance on imported food—85–90 percent—and an economy sustainable only through militarism and environmental degradation. Viewing Indigenous knowledges as irrelevant to present problems replicates the initial logics of colonialism that subjugated these knowledges by deeming Kanaka ʻŌiwi culture a giant "wasteland of non-achievement."[69] The Hui ʻo Nā Wai ʻEhā and Maui Tomorrow have since appealed the water commission's ruling to the Hawaiʻi Supreme Court.

Together Hōkūao Pellegrino and his father, Victor Pellegrino, reopened their taro farm on their property. Despite the fact that it had lain dormant since the 1930s, the original stones of the loʻi were still in place. With the help from community and from Charlie and Paul Reppun, farmer activists from the island of Oʻahu who are well known for gaining water rights through an earlier case at Waiāhole, the loʻi was functioning within two days. Through research, Hōkūao Pellegrino learned that the loʻi was named Nohoʻana, which translates as "a way of life." The two have used the farm since 2004 as a community resource to teach traditional subsistence and organic and sustainable farming techniques to students from preschool to the university level. Although it has twelve terraced patches that are up to 450 years old, Nohoʻana was able to restore and maintain only three with the amount of water the plantation allows to flow into the stream. Victor Pellegrino has since written of the restoration of the loʻi in a children's book called *Uncle Kawaiola's Dream*. He writes that restoring the loʻi on Maui "is a dream shared by a small but growing number of passionate, dedicated, and hard-working people." Because *ʻāina* (land) translates as that which feeds, Pellegrino's aim is to "return the ʻāina for its intended use—agriculture."[70]

Unlike the Pellegrino's Nohoʻana Farm, a living community resource that feeds and educates the public about a possible "history of the future," the Kēpaniwai Heritage Gardens educates the public toward a way of seeing Kanaka ʻŌiwi ways of life as dead and in the past. Barbara Kirshenblatt-Gimblett makes the important point that heritage "depends on display to give dying economies and dead sites a second life as exhibition of themselves."[71] Celebrating the people of Hawaiʻi through *heritage* commemorates these ways of life as forever in the past, as archives of discredited and disregarded modes of production. Like in earlier world's fairs, the ethnological structures comprising the heritage gardens are animated by a body of knowledge that categorizes primitives, orientals, and the civilized through a contrived unity of global harmony while simultaneously deploying cultural difference as a means to reinforce a pyramidal view of the world. In the planning of the heritage gardens, the exhibits were imagined as showing groups' "manner of farming and transportation and a natural landscape."[72] As such, the heritage garden exhibits, not unlike ethnographic museums, use material culture to signify ways of life as objects that can be juxtaposed in hierarchical relation.

Indeed, the heritage garden exhibits are more than simply signifiers of racialized bodies. To borrow Denise Ferreira da Silva's phrasing, these "signifier[s] of the mind" and the cultural politics of the heritage gardens not only aim to reflect an authentic example of these cultures but, further, also exhibit the power relationship between those who are subjected as objects of study and those who are the producers of knowledge.[73] For instance, the New

England saltbox house, complete with a white picket fence and American flag, represents the first American Calvinist missionaries who traveled from Boston to proselytize in the islands in 1820. The missionaries, vis-à-vis the house, are celebrated in the following ethnological description on a plaque in front: "Within fifteen years of their arrival, the ABCFM [American Board of Commissioners for Foreign Missions] missionaries had put the Hawaiian language into writing, established hundreds of schools, trained native Hawaiian teachers in Western ways, and printed textbooks, newspapers and government documents in Hawaiian." The purposeful juxtaposition of the New England missionary house with the Kanaka 'Ōiwi house in the background combined with the description of missionaries as responsible for progress portrays Kanaka 'Ōiwi as an affectable race, subject to the superior intellect of the more enlightened missionaries.[74]

The embodied presence of visitors is made to walk through the different sections to be affected by the pedagogy of their surroundings. Part museum, garden, and park that traverse Asia and the Pacific, this gives the impression of having been transported to these various sites, fitting neatly into the "having the world at your fingertips" mentality that is a hallmark of U.S. Cold War ideology. Although the park offers visitors a totalizing view of global sites within a six-acre stretch on the one hand, the park also obscures the visitor's view of the largest water diversion from 'Īao Valley, on the other. Materially and symbolically, the visitor is limited from viewing the park's obstruction of a Hawaiian *way of life*, one that has historically and currently been hindered by the expropriation of water from 'Īao. The Kēpaniwai Heritage Gardens, much like landscape paintings and other "poetics of primitive accumulation," ideologically and materially facilitate the enclosure of a water and land commons.[75] By portraying Kanaka 'Ōiwi ways of life as dead, while foreclosing the ability for visitors to see the environmental and social impact of liberal multiculturalism via tourism and militarism, the Kēpaniwai Heritage Gardens exhibits the same ways of life that it itself makes impossible.

Public signs in the parking lot at the 'Īao State Park warn tourists not to leave their valuables in their rental cars or risk having them stolen as they venture into the park. One such sign, however, was defaced by adding "LOCALS WILL," boldly stating just *who* will remove their valuables. While the sign's defacement reveals, in a teasing manner, the underlying animosity that many in Hawai'i feel toward tourists, the sign's very location in 'Īao Valley also reveals an inconsistency in just what kinds of thefts are crim-

9.5. State sign at the ʻĪao State Park parking lot.

inalized and which are otherwise normalized as a natural part of history. Property crimes against tourists are often taken most seriously; as one reporter stated, they tarnish "Hawaiʻi's reputation as a place with gentle people where tourists can relax and unwind."[76] Yet, historical and ongoing crimes in this same valley, such as the desecration of sacred burials, the continued enclosure of land and water commons leading to the death of rivers, or the theft of an entire nation and consequently a way of life, are normalized forms of violence indexed only outside of official histories.

Although aims to return water to Nā Wai ʻEhā and to implement Hawaiian food ways are disqualified as irrelevant to the present, such alternatives to the settler state might just put a halt on the systemic death of the conditions that sustain life. The colonial trope of an island, as a place untouched by time and replete with abundant resources, where life is easy, elides the fact that the Hawaiian Islands possess delicate ecosystems. On Maui, global warming has contributed to an increasing amount of brush fires, floods, and droughts, as well as landslides on the neighboring island of Lānaʻi. Dipesh Chakrabarty argues that the distinction between human and nature is no longer tenable as humans become geological agents capable of enormous environmental change—"Humans now wield a geological force."[77] Histories that not only construct nature as the passive backdrop for human narratives but consider the environment's changes slow and subsequently inconsequential now need to contend with the human populations' potentially catastrophic impact on the environment. Since centuries of violent moments of contact with settlers have led to dramatic environmental shifts in their societies, such environmental transformations are nothing new to most indigenous peoples.

By taking subjugated indigenous knowledges seriously, expanding on a concern with the governance of human bodies to include bodies of land and water, delicate ecosystems, and other life forms necessary to the conditions that sustain life, the project of returning water back to streams and rivers poses the very real threat of possibility that these farmers will be able to create a mode of production in dialectical tension with or perhaps outside of capitalism. Such possibilities serve as the foundation for the materialization of an alternative way of life to the settler state that would radically challenge the current system. As is often noted, water in the Hawaiian language is *wai*, and wealth in Hawaiian translates as *waiwai*. In a period when water wells on the island of Maui are drying up at the same time that need for water residential areas is increasing, this shift in thinking tells us that nature, not profit, needs to determine the conditions of possibility for Maui.

NOTES

1. "Ghost Picture Excites Japanese," *Maui News*, April 18, 1919; "Work Starts on Picnic Grounds in Iao Valley," *Maui News*, November 3, 1951; Inez Ashdown, "The Valley Worthy of Kings," *Sunday Star-Bulletin*, July 24, 1960.
2. Gordon, *Ghostly Matters*, 63–64.
3. At the Bishop Museum, Kāneikokala is the name of a kiʻi pōhaku who decided not to leave Hawaiʻi Hall when decisions were made to move the pōhaku outside. It currently remains in Hawaiʻi Hall at the Bishop Museum. Or take for instance the quote from Abraham Piianaia about his grandfather: "Kalākaua sent him to England, and still he always said something nice to rocks" (Meyer, *Hoʻoulu*, 141).
4. Handy and Handy, *Native Planters in Old Hawaii*, 272.
5. "Tunneling for Water: A New and Important Industry Being Developed on Maui," *Maui News*, February 2, 1901.
6. Harvey, *The New Imperialism*, 137–82.
7. R. Williams, *Marxism and Literature*, 113–14.
8. "Drive to Establish Park in Iao Valley Opens Here," *Maui News*, November 23, 1940.
9. "Thousands Sign Park Petitions: Purchase of Iao Valley Site Sought," *Maui News*, November 27, 1940; "Iao Valley Park Drive Nears Goal," *Maui News*, November 30, 1940; "Shortage of Funds Halts Iao Project: Final Decision Is Up to Legislature and County," *Maui News*, January 8, 1941; "Land Change on Iao Park Project Okayed by Board: Deal to Raise $6,000," *Maui News*, January 18, 1941; "County to Sell Main-Market St. Lot at Auction," *Maui News*, February 5, 1941; "Main-Market

Street Lot to be Auctioned Today," *Maui News*, March 29, 1941; "T. Ikeoka Buys County Lot at Main-Market St. Corner with $7,350 Bid," *Maui News*, April 2, 1941; "County Gets Park Site: Kēpaniwai Property Is Conveyed for Public Park," *Maui News*, April 30, 1941; "Kēpaniwai Park Is Dedicated: New County Playground in Iao Valley Now Open to Public," *Maui News*, July 19, 1952.

10. Anthony, *Hawaii under Army Rule.*
11. Adams, *The Peoples of Hawaii.*
12. Takaki, *Strangers from a Different Shore*, 171.
13. Coffman, *The Island Edge of America*, 152.
14. Takabuki, *An Unlikely Revolutionary*, 79.
15. Takabuki, *An Unlikely Revolutionary*, 65.
16. Takabuki, *An Unlikely Revolutionary*, 65.
17. Saranillio, "Colliding Histories."
18. Blackford, *Fragile Paradise*, 20.
19. Hawaiian Airlines had previously refused to hire Asian Americans but changed their policy in 1946 after Tongg established his Trans-Pacific Airlines, which would be renamed Aloha Airlines. See Cooper and Daws, *Land and Power in Hawaii*, 151.
20. "International Gardens in Kēpaniwai Park Scheme," *Maui News*, April 11, 1964.
21. Kirshenblatt-Gimblett, *Destination Culture*, 151.
22. Johnson, "Cultural Heritage Park Proposed for Iao Valley," *Honolulu Advertiser*, March 13, 1967.
23. Kamakau, *Hawaiian Annual.*
24. A special thank you to Ty Kāwika Tengan for sharing with me his research. Tengan, Perry, and Armstrong, *Report on the Archival, Historical and Archaeological Resources of Nā Wai ʻEhā, Wailuku District, Island of Maui*, 12.
25. Johnston and Lawson, "Settler Colonies," 364.
26. "Development of Iao Is Aim of Civic Club," *Maui News*, July 9, 1960.
27. Ashdown, "The Valley of Worthy Kings," *Sunday Star-Bulletin*, July 24, 1960.
28. Ashdown, Ashdown Papers, Bailey House Museum, H919.68.
29. "Hawaiian Group Meets Tuesday on Garden Plan," *Maui News*, July 7, 1967.
30. For more on a "moral sensibility" in relation to multicultural forms of settler colonialism, see Povinelli, *The Cunning of Recognition*, 9.
31. Melamed, "The Spirit of Neoliberalism," 16.
32. Blackford, *Fragile Paradise*, 19.
33. McNaughton, *Perspectives on Hawaiʻi's Statehood*, 52–53.
34. See Tye, *The Father of Spin*, 23–50, 155–84.
35. Bernays, "HAWAII—The Almost Perfect State?," *New Leader*, November 20, 1950.
36. Klein, *Cold War Orientalism*, 250–51.
37. One Maui county councilman attempted to turn this rock profile into a national monument for John F. Kennedy. Signage of this profile was changed back to Kaukaʻiwai. "Monument for JFK Profile in Iao Valley," *Maui News*, July 22, 1970; "Kennedy Studying Iao Memorial to Brother," *Maui News*, August 19, 1971.
38. Frankel, "Isles Called Appropriate for Kennedy Rights Talk," *Honolulu Star-Bulletin*, June 6, 1963; "Text of Kennedy's Speech to Mayors," *Honolulu Star-Bulletin*, June 10, 1963.
39. As cited in Coffman, *The Island Edge of America*, 2.
40. Fisher, "'A World Made Safe for Diversity,'" 218.

41. Kennedy's posthumously released book, *A Nation of Immigrants*, popularized the term in the national lexicon. Kennedy, *A Nation of Immigrants*.

42. Batholomew and Bailey, *Maui Remembers*, 128.

43. Von Eschen, *Satchmo Blows Up the World*, 254.

44. Witeck, "The East-West Center: An Intercult of Colonialism," *Hawaii Pono Journal*, May 1971, 3; Kent, *Hawaii*, 145–46.

45. Nashel, "The Road to Vietnam," 132–54.

46. Thiong'o, *Decolonising the Mind*, 3.

47. Kim, *Ends of Empire*, 12.

48. Rodriguez, *Suspended Apocalypse*.

49. Kim, *Ends of Empire*, 276.

50. Batholomew and Bailey, *Maui Remembers*, 146–47.

51. Spriggs, "'Preceded by Forest.'"

52. "1909 Article Tells Why Ulupalakua Dried Up," *Maui News*, November 9, 1977; *Noho Hewa: The Wrongful Occupation of Hawai'i*, dir. Anne Keala Kelly, A Kuleana Works Production, 2009.

53. Blackford, *Fragile Paradise*, 122.

54. Worster, *Rivers of Empire*, 88.

55. Shiva, *Water Wars*, 54.

56. Shiva, *Water Wars*, 54–55.

57. Tengan, Perry, and Armstrong, *Report on the Archival*, 16.

58. Wilcox, *Sugar Water*, 5.

59. "Tunneling for Water: A New and Important Industry Being Developed on Maui," *Maui News*, February 2, 1901.

60. Wilcox, *Sugar Water*, 1–11, 16.

61. *McBryde Sugar Company Ltd. v. Robinson* 517 P.2d 26 (1973), 175.

62. Sproat, "Water."

63. Shiva, *Water Wars*, 24–36.

64. *Noho Hewa: The Wrongful Occupation of Hawai'i*, dir. Anne Keala Kelly, A Kuleana Works Production, 2009; Hamilton, "Streams Flow Again—along with Controversy and Conflict," *Maui News*, August 10, 2010.

65. Hamilton, "Na Wai Eha: HC&S Speaks Jobs, Fields at Risk in Stream Water Dispute," *Maui News*, October 9, 2009.

66. Hamilton, "Na Wai Eha: Decision in but Dispute Lingers," *Maui News*, June 13, 2010.

67. Goodyear-Ka'ōpua, *The Seeds We Planted*, 127.

68. Goodyear-Ka'ōpua, *The Seeds We Planted*.

69. Thiong'o, *Decolonising the Mind*, 3.

70. Pellegrino, *Uncle Kawaiola's Dream*, 4.

71. Kirshenblatt-Gimblett, *Destination Culture*, 7.

72. "'Heritage Pavilion' in Kēpaniwai Park Plans," *Maui News*, May 17, 1967; Johnson, "Cultural Heritage Park Proposed for Iao Valley," *Honolulu Advertiser*, March 13, 1967.

73. Lidchi, "The Poetics and the Politics of Exhibiting Other Cultures," 191.

74. Such moves to define Western modernity against indigenous primitivism are characteristic of social scientific colonial discourse but as contemporary Kanaka 'Ōiwi scholars armed with language and cultural knowledge have pointed out, Kanaka 'Ōiwi asserted a long and commanding intellectual tradition throughout

the nineteenth century (and beyond). Utilizing newspapers to express anticolonial sentiments, many Kanaka ʻŌiwi responded to the 1893 U.S. military–backed overthrow, led by descendants of missionaries, in the Hawaiian language as a means to, as Noenoe Silva has asserted, "make it harder for the oppressor to decipher." N. Silva, *Aloha Betrayed*, 5; N. Silva, "Nā Hulu Kupuna," 43.

75. Linebaugh, *The Magna Carta Manifesto*; Halperns, *The Poetics of Primitive Accumulation*; Bermingham, *Landscape and Ideology*.
76. Yamanouchi, "When Tourists Become Victims," *Honolulu Advertiser*, November 30, 2003.
77. Chakrabarty, "The Climate of History," 206.

PART III POLITICS OF TRANSPOSITION

Our Stories Are Maps Larger Than Can Be Held

Self-Determination and the Normative Force of Law
at the Periphery of American Expansionism

This chapter is about the multidimensional struggle of colonized and indigenous peoples to wrestle into their real lives the promise of international law, specifically the international legal norm of self-determination, which is singularly responsible for the liberation of some 750 million people across the planet from alien, colonial, and racist domination and subjugation. Although self-determination enjoys more liberatory muscle than any other norm of international law, for these groups, whose subjugator states wield inordinate power in the current topography of global power and bring it to bear in discussions about any hoped-for alterations in the power-imbalanced relationship, even the phrase self-determination falls flat. Even more problematic is the invocation and application by the subjugating state of its own dubiously designed domestic law to first frame the question of their disposition as more or less open and then quickly close the question by resolving it in its favor. In the courts of the United States, perhaps more than any other country, such legal innovations abound and are responsible for the continued subjugation of two specific sets of peoples within (or outside) the American political family: Peoples living in the U.S. insular areas or overseas colonial possessions, which U.S. courts term "unincorporated territories," on the one hand, and native peoples living within the fifty states of the Union and organized into collectivities termed "federally recognized Indian tribes," on the other hand.

This essay summarily explores the legal innovations first articulated at the turn of the twentieth century by the U.S. Supreme Court (and fully developed by it over the course of the same) in order to legitimize the acquisition and governance of the newly acquired overseas possessions of Guam, Puerto Rico, and the Philippines, but withhold from them the promise of eventual statehood or incorporation into the Union as integral parts thereof. As will be shown, these innovations created a kind of constitutional nether-zone whereby the apparatuses of U.S. federal power have been legally enabled to rule these and subsequently acquired possessions as colonies in perpetuity. This essay also briefly explores the equally (if not more) dubious legal innovations fashioned by the Court for Indian tribes. Like the territorial incorporation doctrine in the case of the unincorporated territories pursuant to which even the most basic rights may be withheld, the doctrine of discovery followed later by the congressional plenary power doctrine work a similar legal sanction of subjugation in the case of the tribes, denominated as "domestic dependent nations" and surreptitiously seen as only "quasi" sovereign.

The aim of this essay, however, is not to finely map the contours of either corpus, that is, federal-territorial law or federal Indian law, which has already been ably done,[1] but rather to illustrate why these bodies of law should hardly be called law in the first instance, or, more rightly, to show how law has been historically called on to play a conspiratorial role in what was ultimately a political project of American expansionism. This essay does not suggest that an attempt by a state to cloak its subjugation of certain groups with domestic legal cover is anything new. Rather, this essay suggests only that, when faced with state mischief of this degree and kind, these groups ought invoke international law despite its deficiencies on the theory that it may prove useful, if only normatively, to those seeking to flee the mischievous legal fictions their colonizers have cooked up in the kitchens of history to sanction their subjugation. Toward that end, this essay's principal aim is to the aid those so fleeing first by setting out with precision the contours of the international law on self-determination and second by reminding them, gently, that on their journey they will need a lot more than law. This is so because while it is true that colonized and indigenous peoples have been able to appropriate and redeploy international legal norms in service of liberation struggle, it remains equally true that those norms are nevertheless indelibly marked by some form of fundamental allegiance to the imperial powers and as such are always already insufficient.[2]

This essay is divided into four subsequent parts. Part II addresses how international law separately frames the rights of colonized and indigenous peoples on the one hand, and states' corresponding duties on the other. Specifically, this part sets out the conceptual evolution of self-determination from a principle to a right to an exalted normative domain of international law. Part III addresses the case of colonized peoples and the applicable decolonization regime as developed within the United Nations system. Part IV addresses the case of indigenous peoples and the applicable indigenous rights regime recently bolstered by the passage in 2007 of the Declaration on the Rights of Indigenous Peoples. This part also explains the declaration's status in the universe of international law. Part V addresses the issue of how subjugated peoples such as non-self-governing and indigenous peoples can tap into international law's normative power to fuel political change. Using the case of the indigenous Chamoru people of the American colony of Guam as an example, this part endeavors to connect a number of seemingly unconnected points about what it looks like (and how it feels) to be a people under particular siege at this time, wielding as a weapon the promise of rights. To do this, a Sherman Alexie poem is invoked to facilitate a deeper meditation on law, power, maps, imagination, and love.

SELF-DETERMINATION

Upon the founding of the United Nations at the end of World War II and continuing thereafter, the international community increasingly recognized that the plight of colonized peoples, and later of indigenous peoples, must be terminated and their self-determination assured. The UN Charter itself, being both a political compact and an organic document, made but cursory references to this norm. Its Article 1 called for the development of "friendly relations among nations based on respect for the principle of equal rights and self-determination of peoples."[3] Article 55 then states that the United Nations shall promote, among other values, "universal respect for, and observance of, human rights and fundamental freedoms for all."[4] Article 73, which addresses the rights of peoples in non-self-governing territories who have not yet attained a full measure of self-government, commands states administering them to "recognize the principle that the interests of the inhabitants of these territories are paramount."[5] These "Administering Powers" accept as a "sacred trust" the obligation to develop self-government in the territories, taking due account of the political aspirations of the people.[6] Toward this end, subsection (e) of Article 73 commands Administering Powers to submit annual reports to the United Nations on the steps they have taken and the progress they have made to move the territories toward self-government.[7] Note that Article 73 references "self-government" and not "independence."[8] The ambiguous first term was used originally to avoid the unambiguous second term, which European colonial powers, especially Winston Churchill's U.K., rejected.[9] Such tactics were employed by the imperial powers at the time to avoid conflict by stipulating the terms under which they would divvy up the colonial spoils.

The interpretation of these charter articles has been set out in major declarations adopted by the General Assembly (GA). While declarations are not legally binding,[10] they do set out and interpret the obligations of UN member nations. The 1960 Declaration on the Granting of Independence to Colonial Countries and Peoples, or Resolution 1514, states that "the subjection of peoples to alien subjugation, domination, and exploitation constitutes a denial of fundamental human rights, is contrary to the Charter of the United Nations and is an impediment to the promotion of world peace and co-operation."[11]

Major international conventions have lent further meaning and growth to the concept of self-determination. Both the International Covenant on Civil and Political Rights,[12] and the International Covenant on Economic, Social and Cultural Rights[13] (known collectively as the 1966 Human Rights Covenants), enshrine self-determination as a right. Approved by the UN General Assembly in 1966, and legally binding as of 1976, these treaties bind countries that ratify them. The first article in each covenant, identically worded, indicates the fundamental importance of the right of self-determination in international law and sets out its classic wording: "All peoples have the right of self-determination. By virtue of that right they freely determine their political status and freely pursue their economic, social and cultural development."[14]

Finally, the 1970 Declaration on Principles of International Law concerning Friendly Relations and Cooperation among States, also known as Resolution 2625 (XXV), provides: "By virtue of the principle of equal rights and self-determination of peoples enshrined in the Charter of the United Nations, all peoples have the right freely to determine, without external interference, their political status and to pursue their economic, social and cultural development, and every State has the duty to respect this right in accordance with the provisions of the Charter."[15] Unlike the 1966 Human Rights Covenants, which bind only those states that ratify them, Resolution 2625 has become a "datum of customary international law" as its drafting and adoption "re-involved all states in the debate over the *who*, the *what*, and the *how* of self-determination generated by Resolutions 1514 and 1541, which also constitute manifestations of customary law."[16]

The above instruments collectively enshrine the norm of the self-determination of "peoples." However, the meaning of the term "peoples" in this context remains contentious in international law. This was demonstrated by the indigenous-state debate over two and a half decades long at the United Nations regarding its meaning as the 2007 Declaration on the Rights of Indigenous Peoples was being hammered out.[17] On one side, many states feared that a broad definition of "peoples" would encourage secessionist movements, threatening state territorial integrity.[18] On the other side, indigenous representatives supported the broadest possible reach for the term "peoples," as a narrow definition would, in their view, impair the prospects of all indigenous peoples in their negotiations with states. It would also frustrate desires for outright independence of a smaller number, particularly in the Pacific region, such as Kanaks, West Papuans, Maohi, Kanaka Maoli, and Chamoru.

Today, the right to self-determination is generally accepted as a *jus cogens* or peremptory norm from which no deviation is allowed. That is to say the self-determination right is, in theory, unbreachable.[19] That said, a number of commentators, likely desirous of limiting the right of self-determination so as to preserve the current distribution of power in the world, have argued that the right of self-determination has two dimensions—internal and external—with differing mandates yet fail to produce a single instrument of international law to date that sets out this bifurcation. These commentators depict internal self-determination as the right of a people within a state to authentic self-government in its community affairs.[20] They identify external self-determination, in contrast, as a people's right to reject alien subjugation in totality, usually in the contexts of colonization or foreign military occupation.[21] While this jesuitical framing of self-determination has been challenged in the academic literature, the debate in any event has no bearing on the noncontroversial proposition that the exercise of the self-determination right, at least in certain contexts such as the decolonization of a non-self-governing territory, necessarily includes, indeed highlights, the external element. That is, a colonized people is entitled to the full, unequivocal, and, one might add, immaculate opportunity to throw off colonialism via a plebiscite that offers the full range of political status choices, from forms of incorporation, through forms of free association, to full independence. It must be noted here that the conflation by these commentators of the international norm of self-determination with interim arrangements of self-governance dangerously misrepresents the existing international law parameters of self-determination, particularly those on decolonization—

dangerous because the colonizer is all too happy with the confusion that allows self-governance, a lid, to be mistakenly acquiesced to when the colonized have all along been entitled even to outright independence. The meaning of the "self" in self-determination, however, remains contentious. That is, who constitutes a people for purposes of self-determination? Let's turn first to the case of colonized peoples and the applicable decolonization regime.

COLONIZED PEOPLES

While self-determination has been declared a right, decolonization is not a right per se but a remedy that restores the right. Specifically, decolonization is a remedy for the wrongful and illegal abrogation of a people's right to self-determination, which includes the right to form an independent sovereign state of one's own.[22] With the adoption of the UN Charter in 1945, the world community took its first step toward establishing decolonization as a legal remedy with an attendant processual regime to enable subjugated peoples to exercise their self-determination and to recover what was at first termed full self-government, and later independence, if they so wished. The charter, however, did not provide a universal regime of decolonization. Instead, it recognized two categories of subjugated peoples to whom two different regimes applied.[23] The first category, dealt with under Chapter XI, was denominated "non-self-governing territories" and included the colonial possessions of Western states.[24] At base, Chapter XI requires colonial rulers, or Administering Powers, to assume a "sacred trust" obligation to promote the welfare of the peoples they administered.[25] The second category was denominated "trust territories" and was dealt with under Chapters XII and XIII.[26] Trust territories referred to peoples and places previously subjugated by the defeated Axis Powers, and they alone were explicitly expected to evolve, under an administering state selected by the United Nations, toward independence.[27]

The 1960 Declaration on the Granting of Independence to Colonial Countries and Peoples, also known as Resolution 1514, had the effect of amalgamating the two regimes in a fundamental way. First, it proclaimed self-determination to be more than a principle. It declared it a right: "All peoples have the right to self-determination."[28] Although Resolution 1514 itself avoided defining "peoples," the adoption on the following day of Resolution 1541 acted to "fill in some of what Resolution 1514 left unsaid."[29] This latter Resolution 1541 primarily sets out the reporting duty of the administering states that retained control of the non-self-governing territories under the charter. The charter itself only cryptically requires the states to report to the secretary-general on the status of these territories until such time as they had reached full self-government, a term also left undefined. Resolution 1541 further explains that a prima facie duty to report exists with respect to any territory that is "geographically separate and is distinct ethnically and/or culturally from the country administering it."[30] From this language emerged a legal interpretation favored by Third World states known as the "blue water" or "salt water" thesis, which posited that the 1960 Declaration on the Granting of Independence applied only to peoples "separated by a sea from their subjugators,"[31] thereby rendering self-determination applicable only to overseas territories. Seeking to thwart their overseas possessions so singled out for independence, Western powers took their interpretive cue instead from the earlier Resolution 1514, which identified the holders of the right to self-determination in the decolonization context as those who existed, without more, under "alien subjugation, domination and exploitation."[32] This second theory, known as the "Belgian thesis," thus holds that all peoples subject to alien domination, including those living in independent states, are entitled to the remedy of decolonization.[33] Guam would qualify for decolonization under both theses.

To oversee the implementation of the Declaration on the Granting of Independence to Colonial Countries and Peoples, and to make recommendations for improvement, the General Assembly established the Special Committee on Decolonization.[34] The committee, confusingly known as the Committee of 24 because of the number of its state-members, reviews the situation in each of the remaining colonies and prepares annual reports for the GA reflecting their findings. In 1990, the General Assembly proclaimed 1990 to 2000 as the International Decade for the Eradication of Colonialism.[35] Toward this end, the GA adopted a detailed Plan of Action to expedite the unqualified end of all forms of colonialism.[36] In 2001, citing a wholesale lack of progress during the first decade, the GA proclaimed a second decade to effect the same goal. The second decade having come and gone with only Timor-Leste, or East Timor, managing to attain independence from Indonesia in 2002,[37] the GA pronounced a third decade in 2010. Indeed, the situation is so outrageous that commentators have decried the current policy of the Committee of 24 as one of "colonial accommodation."[38]

As for the trust territories—those territories spread across Africa and the Pacific that were explicitly entitled to evolve toward independence after World War II pursuant to Chapters XII and XIII of the UN Charter—all eleven have either become independent or have entered into some form of voluntary association with other countries.[39] Palau (Belau) was the last of these to achieve independence in 1994.[40] Although the trusteeship system set up by Chapters XII and XIII effectively ended in 1994 with Belau's independence, ambiguity remains. The political status of the Commonwealth of the Northern Mariana Islands (CNMI), for example, remains steeped in controversy. Although some commentators maintain that the agreement the CNMI concluded with the United States should have left it a sovereign state in free association with the United States,[41] the United States counters that the CNMI is still nothing more than a U.S. territory properly subject to the unilateral prerogatives of the U.S. government.[42] The United States made this abundantly clear when it unilaterally altered the U.S.–CNMI relationship without regard for prior assurances of mutual consent.[43] Not surprisingly, there is now talk among people in the CNMI about devising a legal strategy to revisit the political agreement concluded with the United States, on the theory that the agreement worked an unlawful subversion of international law requirements for decolonization. However devised, that strategy will doubtless entail a redeployment of the norm of self-determination in what will be a critical retelling of the record respecting the decolonization of the trust territories.

Let's turn now to indigenous peoples and the indigenous rights regime.

INDIGENOUS PEOPLES AND THE INDIGENOUS RIGHTS REGIME

The most frequently invoked and widely accepted definition of "indigenous peoples" is that provided in 1986 by UN Special Rapporteur Jose Martinez Cobo,[44] who conducted the first comprehensive UN study on the situation of indigenous peoples globally. Cobo developed the following description of indigenous peoples:

> Indigenous communities, peoples and nations are those which, having a historical continuity with pre-invasion and pre-colonial societies that developed on their territories, consider themselves distinct from other sectors of the societies now prevailing in those territories or parts of them. They form at present non-dominant sectors of society and are determined to preserve, develop and transmit to future generations their ancestral territories, and their ethnic identity, as the basis of their continued existence as peoples, in accordance with their own cultural patterns, social institutions and legal systems.[45]

This definition of indigenous peoples is in accordance with what some consider part of the core of indigenous-state relations: unresolved historic injustice.[46] Citing and discussing the noted Mexican anthropologist Rodolpho Stavenhagen, Maivân Lâm submits that "it is a type of unjust social relationship, and not some abstraction, that creates the 'indigenousness' that many now seek to protect via an international regime."[47] Thus, while tensions may accompany attempts to precisely define indigenous peoples under international law, it is "generally agreed"[48] that indigenous peoples share plights "not of their own making but follow from the actions that others took, and continue to take, in the earlier colonial and now global phases of the industrial capitalist economy."[49] UN Special Rapporteur on the Situation of Human Rights and Fundamental Freedoms of Indigenous Peoples, James Anaya, likewise asserts that indigenous peoples are identified, and identify ourselves, "by reference to identities that predate historical encroachments by other groups and the ensuing histories that have wrought, and continue to bring, oppression against their cultural survival and self-determination as distinct peoples."[50]

On September 13, 2007, in the General Assembly, 144 countries adopted the Declaration on the Rights of Indigenous Peoples, an international human rights instrument that for the first time in history formally and unequivocally recognized the world's indigenous peoples as "peoples" under international law, with the same human rights and freedoms as other "peoples."[51] The declaration was the fruit of more than twenty years of negotiations between indigenous representatives, nation-states, and independent experts in Geneva and, briefly, New York. It embodies new norms governing indigenous-state relations.

The declaration's preamble places its lineage in the comprehensive body of human rights norms that protect and promote human dignity, diversity, nondiscrimination, equality, self-determination, environmental integrity, and nonmilitarization.[52] The declaration makes explicit the application to indigenous persons of all human rights and fundamental freedoms previously enshrined in individual human rights law.[53] Most importantly, it makes explicit the applicability of the right of self-determination to indigenous peoples, which is not an individual human right, but rather a collective political right.[54] The declaration protects indigenous peoples against ethnocide, genocide, forcible relocation, and assimilation.[55] It ensures our right to practice and transmit our culture, which is a concept conceived broadly and progressively.[56] It safeguards our access to nondiscriminatory employment as well as to education and to media that honor our culture and language.[57]

It establishes our right to participate fully in decision-making processes that affect us,[58] to determine our own development,[59] to be secure in the enjoyment of our own means of subsistence,[60] and to access institutions of the state.[61] It recognizes our comprehensive control over our traditional lands, territories, and resources,[62] including the right that countries obtain our "free and informed consent" prior to undertaking any project affecting these rights.[63] It also recognizes our entitlement to the recognition and enforcement of treaties we have concluded with states,[64] and to have access to just and fair procedures for the resolution of conflicts with states.[65] The declaration further requires nation-states to give it full effect[66] and the UN system to follow up on its efficacy.[67] Finally, the rights contained within the declaration constitute the "minimum standards for the survival, dignity and well-being of the indigenous peoples of the world."[68]

For all its virtue, however, the declaration also harbors certain state betrayals of indigenous peoples. For instance, while earlier negotiations in Geneva between states and indigenous peoples gave rise to a high degree of consensus around key provisions of the declaration, this consultative process did not carry through to New York in the final days of negotiations in September 2007.[69] There, powerful states went to work in the eleventh hour to ensure that the final document would cloud the nature and scope of the self-determination right extended to indigenous peoples. In its fourth article, the declaration states that, "indigenous peoples, in exercising their right to self-determination, have the right to autonomy or self-government in matters relating to their internal and local affairs."[70] This provision is troubling for two reasons. First, self-serving states will argue that its placement immediately after the article extending the right to self-determination to indigenous peoples has the effect of qualifying or limiting the self-determination right, as opposed to being merely illustrative of the right. To bolster that argument, these states will point out that in the 1994 draft version of the declaration, the above-quoted provision was placed lower in the text. Second, though the 1994 draft version linked self-determination to autonomy, it did not equate the first with the second.[71] To date, the instrument that has received the widest and most enthusiastic approval of the world's indigenous peoples was the 1994 draft version.[72]

Keen to this political backdrop, the American Indian Law Alliance (AILA), which closely followed and indeed contributed to the declaration's genesis, proposes that indigenous peoples adopt a selective approach to the declaration. According to Lâm, who for many years served as an advisor to AILA, such an approach is justified on at least three grounds. First, indigenous peoples are only morally bound by the negotiated agreements of the five hundred peoples' representatives who assiduously attended the Geneva sessions for over two decades.[73] States later made significant changes in New York with the participation of, at best, only 5 percent of this contingent, who were allowed to be consultants but not negotiators.[74] Second, the worldwide indigenous peoples' enthusiasm for the Geneva version contrasted starkly with their muted acceptance of the New York instrument, a disparity that must be honored.[75] Finally, inasmuch as the instrument adopted on September 13, 2007, "muddied indigenous peoples' rights in, among others, the key areas of demilitarization and self-determination,"[76] indigenous activists must be careful not to establish a record of acquiescence to the muddied waters.

THE STATUS OF THE DECLARATION IN INTERNATIONAL LAW

Although the general rule is that declarations and resolutions of the UN General Assembly are not in themselves binding,[77] to the extent that they illuminate and record the position of the international community on any given subject, they may be, and are frequently invoked as, evidence of the practice of states, which is a source of customary international law.[78] According to international law scholar Ian Brownlie, where General Assembly resolutions concern general norms of international law, their acceptance by a majority vote both "constitutes *evidence* of the opinions of governments" on any given subject and provides a "basis for the progressive development of the law and the speedy consolidation of customary rules."[79] The International Court of Justice (ICJ), in its 1975 advisory opinion in the *Western Sahara* case,[80] adopted this perspective when it "relied heavily on General Assembly resolutions to establish basic legal principles concerning the right of peoples to self-determination."[81] The General Assembly itself has recommended that the ICJ heed its declarations and resolutions as instruments in which "the development of international law may be reflected."[82] International law scholar Mark Janis asserts that "the soundest way to account for the legal effect [of General Assembly declarations and resolutions] is to note that [they] are particularly useful evidence of the simultaneous attitudes of a number of states with respect to a specific legal issue or topic."[83] As such, the vote of a state on any given matter before the assembly is itself an act of that state, and moreover, the balloting of many states on a specific question may effectively illustrate the emerging consensus regarding a rule of customary international law.[84] In this light, the dramatic September 13, 2007, vote in which the UN General Assembly adopted the declaration by an overwhelming majority of 144 to 4 powerfully launched the norms contained in the declaration on their way to becoming rules of customary international law.

The declaration, as is typical with all human rights declarations adopted by the General Assembly, is a normative instrument that exhorts states to behave in accordance with the principles it sets out. Because of the declaration's normative, as opposed to strictly legal, nature, indigenous peoples continue to enjoy a measure of latitude and indeed creativity regarding their reading and application of its provisions. That is, indigenous peoples should unhesitatingly endorse most of the document's provisions but simultaneously lodge serious reservations regarding other key provisions that were formulated or modified in the eleventh hour in New York by states acting in the absence of the broad-based indigenous input and assent that had marked the prior twenty years of the declaration's creation in Geneva. To be precise, only when the declaration's provisions are formalized in a convention or are so consistently obeyed by states out of a sense of legal obligation that they "harden" into rules of customary international law may they be considered legally binding. For the declaration's provisions to transmute into rules of customary international law, state practice regarding its norms need neither be unanimous nor ancient.[85] As the ICJ held in 1969 in the *North Sea Continental Shelf* case,[86] a "passage of only a short period of time is not necessarily, or of itself, a bar to the formation of a new rule of customary international law," so long as state practice is "extensive and virtually uniform" and occurs in "such a way as to show a general recognition that a rule of law or legal obligation is involved."[87] What is key, then, is whether states adhere to a given rule out of a sense of legal obligation, as opposed to mere courtesy. This aspect of compulsion versus volition is known in international law as *opinio juris*.

Recent legal responses to the declaration suggest that the rights it enshrines may eventually be transmuted into binding rules of customary international law. In October 2007, the Supreme Court of Belize invoked legal norms contained in the declaration to recognize the property rights of two groups of indigenous Maya peoples in southern Belize.[88] While initially remarking that the declaration is technically nonbinding, the judge in *Aurelio Cal v. Attorney General of Belize* determined that principles of general international law contained in the declaration are not to be disregarded, taking special notice that an overwhelming number of countries adopted it, thus reflecting the "growing consensus and the general principles of international law on indigenous peoples and their lands and resources."[89] The Belize case is most important for its reasoning, not its holding. The judge, without stating he was doing so, conceptualized and imported norms contained in the declaration as rules of customary international law. Indeed, "much of the work of discerning and developing customary international law is done by judges in the process of preparing and rendering judicial decisions and by scholars in researching and writing legal doctrine."[90]

In addition, recent practice of at least one human rights treaty body, the Committee on the Elimination of Racial Discrimination (CERD), strengthens the position that the declaration embodies rules of customary international law. The CERD, or the body created by the International Convention on the Elimination of All Forms of Racial Discrimination to oversee its implementation, deals with the international norm of non-discrimination.[91] In a recent report to the United States, the CERD instructed the United States to use the Declaration on the Rights of Indigenous Peoples to interpret its obligations under the convention on racial discrimination, as they relate to indigenous peoples.[92] Significantly, the CERD made this recommendation after the United States asserted it was not bound by the declaration.

Of note also, in 2007 Bolivia affirmed the importance of the declaration by incorporating it in its entirety into domestic law.[93] Hopefully, several more states will follow suit. In any event, the declaration's transmutation into customary law will result from a range of state practice and requires time. It should be noted that the absence of state denunciations of the 2007 declaration, which would be politically costly to them, is itself a datum of transmutation. Once transmuted, the declaration would theoretically be binding in U.S. courts pursuant to the 1900 U.S. Supreme Court decision in the *Paquete Habana* case.[94]

It must be noted, however, that certain states, upon signing the declaration, engaged in an unfortunate but classic constructionist sleight of hand, placing on the instrument such limiting constructions so as to effectively withhold endorsement for its key provisions. To take but one example, though the United States signed the declaration, it went to great lengths to clarify that it was not supporting self-determination per se, but rather only "self-determination specific to indigenous peoples."[95] In other words, the United States would not support according to indigenous peoples within its borders the right of self-determination as it is understood in the expansive context of international law, but rather only as it is understood in the atrophied context of its own domestic law through which it governs Indian tribes, that is, federal Indian law.[96]

JUST HOW SLIGHTING THE SLEIGHT OF HAND IS:
A MEDITATION ON MAPS AND MORE

In tracing the contours of the self-determination right as it applies in the separate albeit at times overlapping contexts of colonized and indigenous peoples, one realizes that any analysis that could be up for the challenge would have to borrow the energies of poetry, literature, art, and music. The truth is that the law, which relentlessly seeks to maximize order and pre-dictability even at the sake of smashing squares into circles, cannot accom-modate certain stories such as those of colonized and indigenous peoples.

In "The Lover of Maps," Sherman Alexie, the gifted Spokane/Coeur d'Alene Indian poet, writes:

> She unfolds and folds me
> directs me
> to an exact place
> on the reservation
>
> where nothing is ever written down.
> She tells me
> our stories are maps
> told on a scale
>
> larger than can be held
> by our clumsy hands.[97]

There is a softness about Alexie's words that to me more precisely cap-tures what it *feels* like to be in the business of arguing oneself into exis-tence. In my own experience as an international law scholar and practitioner working to advance the cause of a people at once colonized and indigenous, against increasingly enormous odds, this touch of the tender rings true. There is also a deep awareness that clothes the poem; a sense that what is, is not what always was, or what ought to be. The only way I know how to put it is that this awareness has more to do with love than anything else.

This likening of stories to maps is interesting. What are maps but flat-surface representations of any given set of known points? By their very nature, maps tell only of chartered territory, of the known world, mutilated at that. But what of unchartered territory, of the unknown world? What of worlds once known but now lost, forgotten, muted? Alexie's maps are, of course, of this unknown world. *Maps told on a scale larger than can be held by our clumsy hands.* There it is. And so—to borrow from Neruda, another gifted poet—"the verse falls to the soul like dew to the pasture"[98]: *Maps that cannot be held are stories that cannot be accommodated by law.*

So beyond the question of whether or not the declaration is technically binding is a richer inquiry about whether and how colonized and indigenous communities like the Chamoru people of Guam can tap normative power, legal and prelegal, to fuel political change on their own terms. As stated earlier, the declaration's normative force is already challenging and perhaps also changing the power equation between indigenous peoples and states. Until now, states could cloak, as needed, their oppression of subjugated peoples (and exploitation of their resources) with domestic legal justification. The U.S. Supreme Court *Cherokee Cases* are but one example.[99] The legal theory constructed by these cases have been used for more than a hundred years to keep American Indians in "pupilage,"[100] or bondage, to the United States. Their societies, American courts continue, are "domestic dependent nations" vis-à-vis the United States.[101] In the United States today, there are some 565 federally recognized Indian tribes.[102] All remain governed by the anachronistic jurisprudence first laid out by the U.S. Supreme Court in the nineteenth century and then later mutated over the course of the twentieth with maddeningly contradictory fits and starts. The general terrain of this body of law, rickety as it might be, is as follows. The United States sees itself as standing in a special political relationship with the tribes, which it sees as quasi-sovereign and denominates "domestic dependent nations" inasmuch as the latter are understood as being in a relationship to the United States akin to that of a ward to its guardian. Pursuant to the Commerce Clause of the U.S. Constitution, Congress is deemed to have "plenary power" over these tribes and may unilaterally enact legislation on their behalf. Underpinning this entire structure is the legal fiction that American Indian nations were not "civilized" (read "European") nations at the time of European contact and thus were not amenable to political recognition on the same level as internationally recognized nation-states for purposes of the law of conquest. Instead, the dubious doctrine of discovery applied to lands occupied by indigenous peoples, pursuant to which they had the only the right of occupancy but not legal title to their lands. While the United States had to respect the native peoples' right of occupancy, it enjoyed a unilateral right to terminate it by purchase or conquest.

Today the more salient contemporary aspect of federal Indian law is that at any given moment a federally recognized Indian tribe's very existence can be extinguished by congressional whim. As the U.S. Supreme Court itself unambiguously put it, "The sovereignty that the Indian tribes retain is of a unique and limited character. It exists only at the sufferance of Congress and is subject to complete defeasance."[103] As demonstrated in the 1950s by a series of federal statutes extinguishing recognition of selected Indian tribes, aptly called "termination legislation," Congress unilaterally terminated its political relationship, such as it was, with more than one hundred tribes and bands that it had once recognized.[104] The ruinous effects of termination on these groups are well documented and the lesson is clear: What Congress giveth, it can taketh away.[105]

Law's inability to accommodate the stories of subjugated peoples is also evident in the case of U.S. federal territorial law, whose origins trace back to the 1901 *Insular Cases* and whose record is similarly haunted.[106] Here the rub is that the United States, through its judicial branch, still cannot come up with a satisfactory legal justification for maintaining modern colonies— territories deemed not to be a part of the United States, but instead merely possessions of the United States.[107] Compounding the interpretive violence done to the text of the U.S. Constitution in the name of the colonial enter- prise is the psychic violence inflicted on folks who must find our way in a country that neither wants us nor wants to let us go. The general terrain of this body of law, however legally and morally indefensible it might now be, is as follows. At the close of the Spanish American War, with little to no guidance offered by the plain language of the Constitution itself, the Court struggled, as did the country as a whole, over the political and legal questions of whether the United States should or could maintain overseas colonial possessions it did not intend to later fold into the Union. Although at the time the well-settled assumption was that every contiguous terri- tory acquired by the United States would eventually become an integral part, that is, a state, of the Union upon fulfillment of certain conditions,[108] that assumption was thrown on the trash heap with respect to the newly acquired noncontiguous (overseas) possessions of Guam, Puerto Rico, and the Philippines. The idea at the root of the turn-of-the-century desire to govern these possessions without admitting them into the Union was that the Anglo-Saxon race was superior to the "alien races" inhabiting the newly acquired territories, who, it was argued, lacked the requisite sensibilities for law and order to be admitted to the American polity as integral parts thereof.[109] Beginning in 1901 in a series of decisions that would come to be called the *Insular Cases*, the Court went to work legitimizing, on a case-by- case basis, European-style colonial governance. Such is the jurisprudential framework that continues to govern the relationship between the U.S. federal government and its so-called unincorporated territories, which today include Guam, the Commonwealth of the Northern Mariana Islands, American Samoa, the Commonwealth of Puerto Rico, and the U.S. Virgin Islands. Although each of these territories has its own distinct relationship to the United States, they have several features in common: "Congress governs them pursuant to its power under the Territorial Clause of the U.S. Constitution; none is a sovereign independent country or a state of the Union; people born in the territories are U.S. citizens, or, in the case of American Samoa, U.S. 'nationals'; all are affected by federal legislation at the sole discretion of Congress; none has representation at the federal level."[110]

Translation? Congress is free to discriminate against U.S. citizens living in the territories so long as that discrimination is supported by any conceivable rational basis.[111] This has meant, among others, the exclusion of the territories from the federal Supplemental Security Income (SSI) program;[112] a territories-only cap on what was the Aid to Families with Dependent Children (AFDC) and is now the Temporary Assistance to Needy Families (TANF) welfare benefit program;[113] and the discrimination against the territories with respect to both the Medicaid and Medicare programs, resulting in a situation where, for example, the Medicaid per capita spending even in the poorer states has been some twelve times the amount received by the territories.[114]

Today, the features of this federal-territorial relationship are threatening to wreak singular havoc on at least one territory: Guam.

The United States first announced plans to increase its military presence in Guam in 2005, reportedly as part of a larger design for the Asia-Pacific region, the centerpiece of which was a self-styled "hedge" policy aimed at "containing" China's rise as a global power. Its military strategists having apparently determined it of the "utmost importance . . . to ensure China's integration into U.S. dominated global systems through engagement and, as necessary, containment,"[115] the United States ominously pronounced that the United States is a "Pacific nation . . . in every regard" and that the United States would do whatever it took to seize the opportunities of the twenty-first century.[116] Though the military's plans for the island have repeatedly changed since the 2009 release of its environmental impact statement, as nevertheless formally proposed, the military buildup of Guam was to include three major proposed actions, including: (1) the construction of permanent facilities and infrastructure to support the full spectrum of warfare training for the relocated marines, which would have meant, among other things, the clearing of whole limestone forests, the desecration of burial sites roughly two thousand years old, the elimination of hundreds of acres of jungle rich in plants necessary for indigenous medicinal practice, and the wholesale denial of access to places of worship and traditional fishing grounds; (2) the construction of a new deep-draft wharf in the island's only harbor to provide for the passage of nuclear-powered aircraft carriers, which would have entailed the destruction of some seventy acres of healthy coral reef; and (3) the construction of an Army Missile Defense Task Force for the practice of intercepting intercontinental ballistic missiles.

If executed according to plan, the buildup would arguably also imperil the long-standing struggle of the colonized people of Guam to exercise self-determination in accordance with decolonization requirements. Specifically, there is growing concern that the dramatic demographic changes incident to the buildup might impede any future political status referendum. To illustrate, by 2009, the U.S. military's plans for Guam included the transfer of some eighty thousand new residents to the island to include more than eight thousand U.S. Marines and their nine thousand dependents, seven thousand so-called transient U.S. Navy personnel, six hundred to a thousand U.S. Army personnel, and some twenty thousand foreign workers on military construction contracts.[117] This "human tsunami," as it was called, would have represented a roughly 40 percent increase in the island's population in a roughly four- to six-year window.

Brewing anxieties over the uncertain future of Guam's political status came to a boil in November 2011, when retired U.S. Air Force officer Arnold "Dave" Davis sued the government of Guam in federal court in hopes of overturning the Guam law limiting the electorate in any future self-determination plebiscite to those falling within the statutory definition of a "native inhabitant of Guam," or those persons who became U.S. citizens by virtue of the passage in Congress of the 1950 Organic Act of Guam (and descendants of those persons).[118] Davis, represented by the Center for Individual Rights, a right-wing outfit based in Washington, DC, argued that the Guam statute was unconstitutional race-based discrimination prohibited under, among others, the Voting Rights Act of 1965 and the Equal Protection and Due Process Clauses of the U.S. Constitution.[119] Put another way, Davis and his lawyers—engaging in a fiction all their own by the eliding of the legally significant difference between a *state* and a *colony* of the Union—were in effect attempting to extend the already problematic holding of *Rice v. Cayetano*.[120] If successful, they would have done by day in Guam what was done by night in Hawai'i.[121] Ultimately, however, the district court agreed with amicus that the case was not ripe for adjudication and dismissed it, without prejudice, noting that Davis would be allowed to file suit if and when he is able to demonstrate that the plebiscite will occur for certain in the future. At the time of this writing (August 2013), Davis' appeal is before the Ninth Circuit.

This case represents the height of cynicism. The charge that limiting the international law remedy of decolonization to the colonized is unconstitutional vis-à-vis the colonizer's constitution so prominently displays the failure, so prevalent in the United States, to reach for international law to help solve a problem that is clearly international in nature. Beyond the cynicism inherent in the call to conform a project of potentially separating from the United States to U.S. law, the failure marks a chilling conceptual inability in the American legal imagination to see the world in any light other than what the establishment has shone. This is particularly true in light of the fact that self-determination's legal parameters, as explained above, are already well demarcated in international legal instruments, by international jurists, and, albeit to a less consistent extent, through the practice of states. No matter how hard a state may beat the "race" drum, self-determination is not, and has never been, principally a race-based issue. Indeed, self-determination is not a *purely* political, as opposed to legal, construct such that the power of the day can bend its meaning to its every political machination.

All this to say that while it should not surprise us that law has been called on by states to provide domestic legal cover for their subjugation of chosen peoples within their polities, it is not enough to throw up our hands with the mere pronouncement of that truth. Rather, it is imperative that groups living under/within such states as the United States, which not only invokes these anachronistic legal innovations but also fails to lower its head in contemporary shame when it does so,[122] reach for international law, at least to the extent that the latter may have something to say on the subject—and in certain cases, such as the case of collective human liberation, quite a profound something. So long as international law registers as a powerful normative domain for perpetual struggle, as opposed to a progressive realization of universal justice, its strategic deployment can only help. After all, to get to where some of us need to go, there is no map on offer. We have to think on our feet. This is true right now, for my own people, in a spectacular sense. Although I would not presume to pronounce the course, I am at least convinced that in the beginning there must be a tearing to pieces of all the colonial maps, all the stories that speak only of death, the stories that curtail the possible, constrict the imagination, obstruct the light.

NOTES

An earlier version of this chapter appeared as "On Loving the Maps Our Hands Cannot Hold: Self-Determination of Colonized and Indigenous Peoples in International Law," UCLA *Asian Pacific American Law Journal* 16 (2012): 47, 52–73.

1. See generally, for example, Torruella, "The Insular Cases"; Burnett and Marshall, *Foreign in a Domestic Sense*; see also generally Ball, "Constitution, Court, Indian Tribes"; Williams, "The Algebra of Federal Indian Law."
2. That international law has been historically bound up in Western imperialism is the subject of much scholarship and needs no further elaboration here. See Anghie, *Imperialism, Sovereignty and the Making of International Law.*
3. UN Charter, art. 1, para. 2.
4. UN Charter, art. 55, para. c.
5. UN Charter, art. 73.
6. UN Charter, art. 73.
7. UN Charter, art. 73, para. e.
8. UN Charter, art. 73, para. b.
9. See Cassese, *Self-Determination of Peoples*, 42.
10. Brownlie, *Principles of Public International Law*, 15.
11. Declaration on the Granting of Independence to Colonial Countries and Peoples, GA Res. 1514 (XV), at 67, UN Doc. A/4684 (December 14, 1960).
12. International Covenant on Civil and Political Rights, art. 1, March 23, 1976, 999 U.N.T.S. 171.
13. International Covenant on Economic, Social, and Cultural Rights, art. 1, January 3, 1976, 993 U.N.T.S. 3.
14. International Covenant on Economic, Social, and Cultural Rights, art. 1, January 3, 1976, 993 U.N.T.S. 3.
15. Declaration on Principles of International Law concerning Friendly Relations and Co-operation among States in Accordance with the Charter of the United Nations, GA Res. 2625 (XXV), at 123, UN Doc. A/8082 (October 24, 1970).
16. Lâm, *At the Edge of the State*, 124; see also Cassese, *International Law*, 47.
17. UN Declaration on the Rights of Indigenous Peoples, GA RES/61/295, UN Doc. A/RES/61/295 (October 2, 2007) (hereinafter, Declaration on the Rights of Indigenous Peoples).
18. Various commentators conclude that most indigenous peoples do not seek secession in the first place. See, for example, Anaya, *Indigenous Peoples in International Law*, 191, 219; see also Morris, "International Law and Politics," 78.
19. See Brownlie, *Principles of Public International Law*, 510–11; see also Cassese, *International Law*, 133–40.
20. See Cassese, *International Law*, 101–40.
21. Cassese, *International Law*, 71–100.
22. Cassese, *International Law*, 75.
23. Lâm, *At the Edge of the State*, 96.
24. Lâm, *At the Edge of the State*, 96.
25. UN Charter, art. 73.
26. Lâm, *At the Edge of the State*, 97.
27. Lâm, *At the Edge of the State*, 96.

28. Declaration on the Granting of Independence to Colonial Countries and Peoples, GA RES 1514 (XV), UN Doc. A/4684 (December 14, 1960).
29. Lâm, *At the Edge of the State*, 115–16.
30. Principles Which Should Guide Members in Determining Whether or not an Obligation Exists To Transmit the Information Called for Under Article 73e of the Charter, GA RES 1541 (XV), UN Doc. A/4684 (December 15, 1960).
31. Lâm, *At the Edge of the State*, 116.
32. Declaration on the Granting of Independence, *supra* note.
33. Lâm, *At the Edge of the State*, 116–17.
34. GA RES 1810, at 72, UN GAOR, 17th Sess., Supp. No. 17, UN Doc. A/5217 (1962).
35. GA RES 43/47, UN GAOR, 43d Sess., Supp. No. 49, at 49, UN Doc. A/43/49 (November 22, 1988).
36. GA RES 55/146, at 96, UN GAOR, 55th Sess., Supp. No. 49, UN Doc. A/55/49 (December 8, 2000).
37. Press Release, General Assembly, General Assembly Decides to Remove East Timor from List of Non-Self-Governing Territories upon Independence, Set for 20 May, UN Doc GA/10014 (May 1, 2002).
38. Mililani Trask, Int'l Human Rights Attorney, Address at the United Permanent Forum on Indigenous Issues, Seventh Sess., New York (April 23, 2008) (on file with author).
39. Hinck, "The Republic of Palau and the United States."
40. Palau's status as a trust territory was terminated by Security Council Resolution 956, and the Republic of Palau became a UN member state under Security Council Resolution 963. SC RES 963, at 130, UN SCOR, 49th Sess., 3469th Mtg. UN Doc. S/RES/963 (November 29, 1994); SC RES 956, at 128, UN SCOR, 49th Sess., 3455th Mtg. UN Doc. s/RES/956 (November 10, 1994).
41. See Lâm, *At the Edge of the State*, 117n330; see also, generally, Leibowitz, *Defining Status*, 519–90.
42. See, for example, Commonwealth of the Northern Mariana Islands v. Atalig, 723 F.2d 682, 688–91 (9th Cir. 1984).
43. Pursuant to the "Covenant to Establish a Commonwealth of the Northern Mariana Islands in Political Union with the United States of America," 48 U.S.C. § 1801 (1976) et seq., the CNMI was to be exempt from specific federal laws including minimum wage laws. See art. V, § 503(b); see also Kirschensheiter, "Resolving the Hostility," 245n46. However, beginning in 2007, the United States reversed course, essentially engaging in a federal takeover of CNMI immigration and minimum wage laws.
44. Any definition of indigenous peoples purporting to encompass the more than 370 million indigenous peoples worldwide is, more accurately, a description. See Lâm, *At the Edge of the State*, 7.
45. Working Group on Indigenous Populations Report, ¶ 379, UN Doc. E/CN.4/Sub.2/1986/7/Add.4. http://www.cwis.org/fwdp/International/96-12980.txt.
46. Lâm, *At the Edge of the State*, 2–4.
47. Lâm, *At the Edge of the State*, 3.
48. Lâm, *At the Edge of the State*, 13.
49. Lâm, *At the Edge of the State*.
50. Anaya, *Indigenous Peoples in International Law*, 5.

51. For purposes of determining who holds the right of self-determination in international law, "peoples" are those groups understood to be under alien, colonial, and racist domination and subjugation. Historically, this has largely meant that only those in the classic colonial setting were "peoples" entitled to the right of self-determination and the attendant remedy of decolonization. Conversely, through much of the twentieth century, international law had little to say one way or the other on the issue of the right of self-determination of indigenous peoples qua indigenous peoples. The latter were, when attended to at all, typically conflated with minority groups enclosed within states. Though colonized and indigenous peoples are not one and the same, in certain cases, such as in Guam and New Caledonia, the colonized population at the onset of colonization also features, today, as the relevant colony's indigenous people. In such cases, it would seem evident that the latter's right to self-determination is weighted with a double gravitas inasmuch as redress means the recovery of independence as well as of indigeneity, as spelled out in the 2007 declaration.

52. See generally Declaration on the Rights of Indigenous Peoples, *supra* note 17, pmbl.

53. Declaration on the Rights of Indigenous Peoples, art. 1.

54. For an insightful discussion on how special emphasis was placed on the collective nature of indigenous rights throughout years of advocacy in international forums, see Williams, *supra* note 51, at 685–88.

55. Declaration on the Rights of Indigenous Peoples, *supra* note 17, arts. 7–8.

56. Declaration on the Rights of Indigenous Peoples, arts. 11–13.

57. Declaration on the Rights of Indigenous Peoples, arts. 14–17.

58. Declaration on the Rights of Indigenous Peoples, arts. 18–19.

59. Declaration on the Rights of Indigenous Peoples, arts. 23, 32.

60. Declaration on the Rights of Indigenous Peoples, art. 20.

61. Declaration on the Rights of Indigenous Peoples, arts. 24, 39, 40.

62. Declaration on the Rights of Indigenous Peoples, art. 26.

63. Declaration on the Rights of Indigenous Peoples, art. 32.

64. Declaration on the Rights of Indigenous Peoples, art. 37.

65. Declaration on the Rights of Indigenous Peoples, art. 40.

66. Declaration on the Rights of Indigenous Peoples, art. 38.

67. Declaration on the Rights of Indigenous Peoples, art. 42.

68. Declaration on the Rights of Indigenous Peoples, art. 43.

69. Telephone interview with Maivân Lâm, International Law Advisor, American Indian Law Alliance, and Professor of International Law, Ralph Bunche Inst. for Int'l Studies, Graduate Center, City University of New York (December 4, 2008).

70. Declaration on the Rights of Indigenous Peoples, *supra* note 17, art. 4. For further reading on this issue, see Aguon, "Other Arms," 115n24.

71. See Declaration on the Rights of Indigenous Peoples, *supra* note 17, art. 4.

72. E-mail from Maivân Clech Lâm to Julian Aguon (November 24, 2008, 20:52 HST) (on file with author).

73. Telephone interview with Maivân Clech Lâm (February 25, 2010).

74. Telephone interview with Maivân Clech Lâm (February 25, 2010).

75. Telephone interview with Maivân Clech Lâm (February 25, 2010).

76. Lâm, e-mail.

77. Brownlie, *Principles of Public International Law*, 15.

78. Brownlie, *Principles of Public International Law*, 15.
79. Brownlie, *Principles of Public International Law*, 15.
80. Western Sahara, Advisory Opinion, 1975 I.C.J. 12 (October 16).
81. Janis, *An Introduction to International Law*, 43–44 (citing Western Sahara, 1975 I.C.J. at 31–37).
82. Janis, *An Introduction to International Law*, 44 (citing Preamble, GAOR Res. 3232 [XXIX], November 12, 1974).
83. Janis, *An Introduction to International Law*, 44 (citing Preamble, GAOR Res. 3232 [XXIX], November 12, 1974).
84. Janis, *An Introduction to International Law*, 44 (citing Preamble, GAOR Res. 3232 [XXIX], November 12, 1974).
85. Janis, *An Introduction to International Law*, 40.
86. North Sea Continental Shelf (F.R.G. v. Den. & F.R.G. v. Neth.), 1969 I.C.J. 4 (February 20).
87. North Sea Continental Shelf (F.R.G. v. Den. & F.R.G. v. Neth.), 1969 I.C.J. 4 (February 20), 74, at 43.
88. See Aurelio Cal v. Att'y Gen. of Belize, 2007, Claim No. 171 and 172 (Belize).
89. Aurelio Cal v. Att'y Gen. of Belize, 2007, Claim No. 171 and 172 (Belize), ¶ 131.
90. Janis, *An Introduction to International Law*, 44.
91. 660 U.N.T.S. 195 (entered into force January 4, 1969).
92. UN Comm. on the Elimination of Racial Discrimination [CERD], Consideration of Reports Submitted by States Parties Under Article 9 of the Convention: Concluding Observations of the Committee on the Elimination of Racial Discrimination 10, ¶ 20, UN Doc. CERD/C/USA/CO/6 (February 18–March 7, 2008).
93. Rick Kearns, "UN Declaration Becomes Law of the Land in Bolivia," *Indian Country Today*, December 10, 2007. http://www.globalexchange.org/countries/americas/bolivia/5234.html.
94. 175 U.S. 677, 700 (1900).
95. U.S. Department of State, "Announcement of U.S. Support for the United Nations Declaration on the Rights of Indigenous Peoples. http://www.state.gov/documents/organization/153223.pdf.
96. U.S. Department of State, "Announcement of U.S. Support for the United Nations Declaration on the Rights of Indigenous Peoples. http://www.state.gov/documents/organization/153223.pdf.
97. Alexie, *The Summer of Black Widows*, 63.
98. Neruda, "Tonight I Can Write," 57.
99. Cherokee Nation v. State of Ga., 30 U.S. 1 (1831); Worcester v. State of Ga., 31 U.S. 515 (1832).
100. Cherokee Nation, 30 U.S. at 17.
101. Cherokee Nation, 30 U.S. at 17.
102. U.S. Government Accountability Office, GAO–12–348, *Indian Issues: Federal Funding for Non-Federally Recognized Tribes* 6 (2012). http://www.gao.gov/assets/600/590102.pdf.
103. United States v. Wheeler, 435 U.S. 313, 323 (1978).
104. See Wilkinson and Biggs, "The Evolution of Termination Policy," 151–54 (listing terminated tribes and discussing effects of termination legislation).
105. Wilkinson and Biggs, "The Evolution of Termination Policy," 151–54.
106. See U.S. Department of the Navy, *Guam CNMI Military Relocation, Draft Envi-*

ronmental Impact Statement, vol. 2 (2009). http://www.guambuildupeis.us/draft_documents.

107. See generally Burnett and Marshall, *Foreign in a Domestic Sense*, 1.
108. Northwest Ordinance of 1787, reprinted in 1 U.S.C. at LV–LVII (Office of the Law Revision Counsel of the House of Representatives, ed.) (2006).
109. See, for example, Torruella, "The Insular Cases," 289.
110. Burnett and Marshall, *Foreign in a Domestic Sense*, 1–2.
111. See, for example, Harris v. Rosario, 446 U.S. 651 (1980).
112. Califano v. Torres, 435 U.S. 1 (1978).
113. Harris v. Rosario, 446 U.S. 651 (1980).
114. General Accountability Office, *U.S. Insular Areas: Multiple Factors Affect Federal Health Care Funding*, Report to Congressional Requesters. GAO-06-75 (October 2005). http://www.gao.gov/new.items/d0675.pdf.
115. Joseph Gerson, Director, Peace and Economic Security Program, American Friends Service Committee, Keynote Address: Why? Washington's Continued Pursuit of Empire in the 21st Century (March 22, 2011) (quoting former assistant secretary of defense for International Security Affairs).
116. Joseph Gerson, Director, Peace and Economic Security Program, American Friends Service Committee, Keynote Address: Why? Washington's Continued Pursuit of Empire in the 21st Century (March 22, 2011) (quoting former assistant secretary of defense for International Security Affairs).
117. See U.S. Department of the Navy, *Draft Environmental Impact Statement: Guam CNMI Military Relocation*.
118. Davis v. Guam, No. 11-00035 (D. Guam). http://www.cir-usa.org/legal_docs/davis_v_guam_mtd_opp.pdf.
119. Davis v. Guam, No. 11-00035 (D. Guam). http://www.cir-usa.org/legal_docs/davis_v_guam_mtd_opp.pdf.
120. 528 U.S. 495 (2000).
121. See generally Aguon, "The Commerce of Recognition (Buy One Ethos, Get One Free)" (explaining the major international law claims normatively available for curing the harm occasioned by the United States' international wrongful acts in the Hawaiian Islands in 1893 and thereafter); see generally also Kauanui, "Precarious Positions" (criticizing the Akaka bill as wholly insufficient redress for international wrongful acts committed by the United States in the Hawaiian Islands).
122. Some jurists have squarely and forcefully challenged the continuing validity of the *Insular Cases*. See, for example, Torruella, "The Insular Cases."

Governmentality and Cartographies
of Colonial Spaces
The "Progressive Military Map of Puerto Rico," 1908–1914

In 1908, the recently formed "Porto Rico Regiment of Infantry" assigned three officers to produce a topographical, tactical map of Puerto Rico, which scarcely ten years prior had become a possession of the United States. One of these officers, Lieutenant William Henry Armstrong, created a number of detailed field books in which he documented his topographical work and, in addition, provided descriptions, including sketches, postcards, and photographs of towns and villages, the countryside, and the transportation networks that linked them. The Army War College printed the topographical map of Puerto Rico in twelve quadrants in 1914, but it has only recently been rediscovered.[1] By means of a close examination of these cartographic materials, this chapter will examine the intersecting processes of imposing sovereignty, establishing disciplinary institutions, and exercising governmental rationality in the colony of Puerto Rico. First, I will show how the military map traced the division of coercive power between military and police forces. Second, I will consider the spatial dispersal of disciplinary institutions—the military service, the police force, and the public schools— in Puerto Rico. Finally, I will examine the cartography of appropriation, reconfiguration, and modification of economic spaces and transportation networks that linked them. With military cartography as our point of departure, the intent of this chapter is to shed light on the deployment of techniques of power as a means of creating colonial spaces. This chapter will show how cartography divided and distributed sovereign functions over the territory, how it visualized the dispersal of disciplinary institutions, and how it represented the population and its political economy. In short, this chapter seeks to discover the ways in which the U.S. imperial state created, normalized, and documented variegated colonial spaces.

IMPERIAL FORMATIONS, GOVERNMENTALITIES, AND CARTOGRAPHIES OF COLONIAL SPACES

Much of Michel Foucault's work focused on different techniques of power and their effects on subjects. His concept of "governmentality" defined the objects, forms of power, mechanisms, and historical expansion of the rationality associated with the rise of modern states. First, the objects of governmental rationality are populations, which are understood in the terms of political economy and the demography of civil society. Biopolitics, which seeks to manage and foster "life" and well-being, is an essential technique. Second, governmental rationality differs from, but is articulated with, the rationalities of sovereignty and discipline. "Sovereignty" refers to the exercise of authority over political subjects by means of laws, decrees, and coercive apparatuses. "Discipline" refers to the techniques of regulating and normalizing bodies, their forces and capacities, in the context of institutions such as schools, prisons, military barracks, factories, monasteries, and so forth. One might summarize the different rationalities—governmental, sovereign, and disciplinary—in terms of their objects of observation, judgment, and normalization: populations, political subjects, and bodies, respectively. Third, governmental rationality deploys techniques and apparatuses, such as the census, that produce knowledge about the population in order to effectively promote that conduct conducive to prosperity and well-being. In this way, it provides for state security just as much as the coercive apparatuses such as armies, police forces, and surveillance agencies. Finally, the history of the modern state may be theorized as the "governmentalization of the state," a process through which the governmental rationality gradually reinscribes, recodes, and predominates over the rationalities of sovereignty and discipline.[2] In this sense, "governmentality," in the broad sense of the term, refers to the configuration of three intersecting elements of power: governmental rationality, discipline, and sovereignty.

Foucault's theorization was oriented, above all, toward liberal European states. What, then, of colonial states? The question at hand is whether governmentality takes on a particular configuration in the colonies.[3] Mitchell Dean has argued that the liberal state regularly divides the population into those who qualify as political subjects and those who do not possess the attributes necessary for the full rights of citizenship. Indeed, liberal democracies often discriminate against internal populations by means of ethnic or racial criteria, as this volume amply demonstrates. Likewise, they commonly establish nonliberal, or authoritarian, governments in their colonies.[4] Dean concluded that "authoritarian governmentality" differs from liberalism in that it delimits subject populations (whether internal or colonial), denies their capacities and rights as citizens, and expects unquestioned obedience. Authoritarian governmentality deploys more intensive and general "sovereign instruments of repression" in order to neutralize or eliminate any opposition to the dominant state formation. In this context, racism becomes a way of consolidating "national" populations, ensuring their welfare, and protecting them from the perceived contamination of internal or external "others."[5]

One possible reading of this theorization is that colonial governmentality is simply an instance of authoritarian governmentality. While not incorrect, this interpretation seems too simplistic. Stephen Legg argued that sovereignty, discipline, and governmental rationality intersect in unique and multiple configurations in the colonies and urged us to carefully consider the specificities of colonial governmentalities, which may vary considerably over time and place. In his contribution to the debate over the "colonial difference," Legg concluded that the colonial state deployed more violence (techniques of sovereignty), invested less in disciplinary institutions, and used governmental rationalities to exclude, racialize, and pathologize subject populations. Furthermore, the state favored economic enterprises that were less modern and more extractive and exploitative. In addition, in his thorough study of urban development in Delhi, India, he found that the organization and representation of space was a central mechanism of exclusion and control.[6] James Duncan reached similar conclusions regarding nineteenth-century Ceylon, where the colonial state focused on practices of surveillance, coercion, and corporal punishment to ensure the extraction of agricultural wealth. He concluded that the colonial state, for the most part, "rejected governmentality in favour of authoritarian biopower."[7]

Similarly, Achille Mbembe noted that Foucault's concept of biopolitics did not adequately explain the "practical conditions in which the sovereign claims the right to kill, to allow to live, or to expose to death." He coined the term "necropolitics" to refer to the sovereign right to decide who may live and who should die. He argued that governmental rationality in the colonies was directed less toward biopolitics (the promotion of the life of populations) and discipline (the institutional control of bodies), and more toward necropolitics (the separation of the population into those who should live and the massacre of those who should die). According to Mbembe, two additional principles of sovereignty, the state of exception and the state of siege, formed the basis of necropolitics. The state of exception defined the colony as outside the norms of the modern state while the state of siege treated some segments of the populations as the enemy.[8] First, the "right" of the state was absolute and, consequently, "rights" were absent for subjects, who were not treated as viable citizens. Second, the sovereignty of the colony rested on violence: the founding violence that imposed control over a territory and its inhabitants; the authorizing violence that was self-legitimizing; and the repeated violence that reproduced its dominion.[9] In sum, the notion of necropolitics helped clarify some of the particular manifestations of what other authors have called the authoritarian governmental rationality in the colonies.

Paul Kramer's history of the "race war" in the Philippines suggests that necropolitics was also deployed within some areas of the U.S. overseas empire. The use of guerilla warfare tactics by Filipino revolutionaries led to their characterization as savages, and the U.S. Army quickly adopted strategies aimed at entire populations in insurgent areas. Specifically, the practice of "reconcentration," previously condemned as a Spanish atrocity, relocated rural inhabitants and confined them to garrisoned towns. This was combined with "scorched earth" tactics of burning evacuated villages, destroying crops and livestock, and torturing or killing anyone outside of the pacified areas and towns. Starvation and epidemics quickly ensued in many municipalities in several provinces. These tactics expressed clearly the principles of necropolitics: the assertion of a state of exception let the colonial regime declare war, kill, and starve entire segments of the native population. After most areas were pacified, the deployment of techniques of power changed; the race war in the Philippines was soon supplanted by the collaborative racial state, which, as we shall see, continued to use coercive techniques.[10]

A serious limitation of many interpretations of governmentality is that they are circumscribed by the boundaries of uniform states, whether modern sovereign states or colonies. The "liberal governmentality" of the national state is conceptually distinct from the "authoritarian governmentality" in the colonies. Recent historical research on the U.S. "imperial state" has expanded the notion of the state beyond the narrow confines of the national bureaucratic apparatus to include complex and transnational processes that articulate both national and colonial state formations, national and colonial elites, and a myriad of empire builders, both public and private, that circulated widely among empires and their colonies.[11] The introduction to this volume suggests further that the United States, like all imperial powers, has never been a uniform political entity but rather a "variable and uneven constellation" of states, territories, districts, and all kinds of sovereign relations over distinct populations.

The research discussed above suggests that the modern imperial state was created through the synergetic interaction of three processes. First, colonial states were hybrid forms created from shifting national institutions and principles, including internal colonialism and settlement as well as overseas expansion and colonial state making. Second, the establishment of colonial states provided for the expansion and dispersal of various techniques of state power in the colonies and stimulated bold governmental experimentation, especially in areas of policing, drug prohibition, education, public health, environmental organization, warfare, and military organization. Finally, many of these governmental innovations in the colonies were repatriated back to the national sphere and dispersed to other colonies. The work of Alfred McCoy regarding the "surveillance state" in the Philippines is a convincing illustration of the value of this perspective. He showed how the U.S. colonial regime in the Philippines, built on the centralized and authoritarian Spanish police system, expanded its use of information technology and surveillance in order to both crush the revolutionary movement and control local politicians. The surveillance techniques were later repatriated to the United States and used by the FBI and also applied in counterinsurgency practices in other neocolonies.[12]

A recent book by Julian Go further broadens the scope of analysis and proposes a theoretical definition that facilitates systematic comparisons of systems of colonial governance. He conceptualizes "imperial formations" as hierarchical relations in which a state establishes subordinate territories, subject peoples, and dominated societies by means of "multiple tactics, policies, practices, and modalities of power."[13] In his comparative study of U.S. and British empires he focuses on the exercise of political power (formal or informal), the legal status of colonial subjects, the characteristics of dominant groups (religious, racial, or class), and various tactics of control (outright aggression, covert operations, protectorates, economic aid, and so forth). Go's work is explicitly directed at refuting the claims of U.S. exceptionalism, and he adopts a long-term, cyclical model of comparison that shows how social, economic, and political conditions in the colonies were determinate in the establishment of different modalities of governance.

This allows him to show that, contrary to the theory of U.S. exceptionalism, the British and U.S. empires responded in similar ways to the variegated conditions in their respective colonies. Nevertheless, his broad comparative perspective must necessarily leave out finely grained analysis of processes of creation of subjects, populations, and spaces. Except for the political systems of governance, he does not examine other techniques of power, namely, the particular apparatuses of security, discipline, and governmental rationality that constituted the mechanics of imperial power and knowledge.

These two concepts, "imperial state" and "imperial formation," suggest the possibility of a wider and more integrated application of the notion of governmentality than Foucault originally conceptualized within the confines of European nation-states. First, the concept of the imperial state emphasizes the circulation and dispersion of techniques of power. As yet, however, these techniques have not been carefully conceptualized. Second, the concept of imperial formation stresses the importance of comparative analysis. As yet, however, we lack careful studies that compare and contrast the diverse mechanisms that produce power and knowledge in different colonial contexts. Furthermore, absent in both of these concepts is the careful consideration of the creation of colonial spaces as an element in the deployment of different techniques of power dispersed throughout territories and institutions.

If Foucault was entirely negligent when it came to the analysis of empires and their colonies, he was much less so regarding the relationships between space and power. His work on disciplinary institutions is filled with observations regarding the design and use of architectural spaces, such as the Panopticon, even though he does not address geography as such, except for his idea of the "spaces of dispersion" of disciplinary techniques. His later conversation with a group of French geographers associated with the journal *Hérodote* is one of the founding texts of critical geography, although his conclusions were at best tentative. Much of Foucault's discussion of governmentality also refers to geographic dimensions, but without much explicit theorization.[14] The techniques of governmental rationality imply the delimitation and administration of space. Foucault writes:

> The things with which in this sense government is to be concerned are in fact men, but men in their relations, their links, their imbrication with those other things which are wealth, resources, means of subsistence, the territory with its specific qualities, climate, irrigation, fertility, etc.; men in their relation to that other kind of things,

customs, habits, ways of acting and thinking, etc.; lastly, men in their relation to that other kind of things, accidents and misfortunes such as famines, epidemics, death, etc.[15]

The first part of this definition stresses geography, namely, the relationship of the population ("men"), the spatial distribution of material resources ("things"), and the characteristics of the territory. Like governmental rationality (relative to the management of populations), sovereignty (relative to the control of political subjects) is also delimited geographically, at least in part. Cartography has served as a central technique of both. In contrast, disciplinary institutions organize and manage internal spaces, as we shall see later in the instance of the graded public school. Even so, the spatial distribution of such institutions throughout a territory can also be mapped. Cartography demarcates and defines territories and their administrative units; it delineates populations and describes their distribution in space; it provides inventories of demographic, economic, and natural resources. Maps also provide the basic grid for other techniques of knowledge production such as the national census and industrial surveys. In addition to the demarcation of national territories, cartography has been central in the division of the globe into colonies and the establishment of imperial control.

Yet, the paradox of imperial mapping is that its cartographical methods are virtually indistinguishable from those deployed in the governing of national territories. Matthew Edney has argued that the difference between national and imperial mapping resides in the deployment of similar techniques for diverse ends; namely, nation building versus empire building. In the first instance, maps became a symbol of the nation just as the geographical and demographic information created a certain administrative unity. In the second instance, maps were but another method to claim territory and produce information allowing imperial administrators to subjugate colonial subjects. In the first instance, there existed a certain unity of knowledge between the national subjects and maps of themselves while in the second instance there was a disjunction between the colonial subjects and the administrators who mapped them. The "imperial map," then, is not a "distinct cartographical category." However, this does not mean that imperial maps were neutral with respect to colonial power; to the contrary, cartographers were agents of the imperial state, and they produced knowledge that delimited, defined, and controlled colonial spaces.[16] Indeed, we might generalize: there can be no colony without a map, even though a map does not always designate a colony.

Therefore, by fusing these notions of imperial state, imperial formation, and governmentality we propose that the dispersal of techniques of governmental rationality, discipline, and sovereignty extend geographically throughout the whole of the empire and even among different imperial formations. Furthermore, national and colonial state formations constitute uneven and unequal fields of dispersion of power and should express different configurations of governmentality. This idea of a wide, but variegated, dispersal of techniques thus suggests the necessity of comparative analysis. The continental United States and its imperial archipelago did not institute a single, uniform pattern of government for colonial rule.[17] Consequently, different sites should also exhibit different configurations of governmentality. Indeed, many of the above generalizations regarding colonial governmentality do not neatly coincide with the history of early twentieth-century Puerto Rico. What particular configuration of governmentality did the United States deploy? The following is a working hypothesis based on a reading of the secondary literature.

First, the use of governmental techniques, such as public health and hygiene, urban ordering, military cartography, and the census, were well known in the Spanish colonial regime even though their extensive deployment often lacked sufficient material support. The new regime in Puerto Rico simply broadened and deepened already established practices during the nineteenth century. Biopolitics, rather than necropolitics, were prominent.[18] Second, the new regime also adapted many of the Spanish techniques of coercion that included the modern prison, rural and municipal police, centralized command structure, and virtually unchecked executive power. In Puerto Rico, however, the deployment of sovereign techniques seems to have been less intense than in the Philippines, largely because of the lack of armed revolutionary resistance.[19] Third, the new regime financed the development of the most modern forms of road and railway construction and promoted the expansion of advanced sugar production and refining: the highly mechanized sugar mill (central).[20] Finally, as we shall see below, a key attribute of governmentality in Puerto Rico was the establishment and wide distribution of disciplinary institutions, principally the graded public school. In addition, nursing schools, a normal school, and an officers' school were also created in the first few years of colonial rule. Even the integration of Puerto Ricans into the state apparatus also took on disciplinary aspects of political tutelage.[21]

The dynamic of resistance and collaboration took place within the particular context of Puerto Rico, one of the oldest European colonial settlements.

Unlike many colonial and settlement contexts, the "governance of prior" did not mean intractable conflicts and violence.[22] In 1898, Puerto Rico was already a modern, settler colony, albeit Spanish, and its inhabitants aspired to democratic rule and economic development; indeed, there was a general acceptance of advanced strategies of modernization of the United States. The Puerto Rican elite shared considerable values with the officials of the new regime, and one could argue that there was a meeting of the minds regarding the political and economic modernization of the country. The elite, however, expected that "autonomy" would be politics as usual on the island and their exercise of patronage, at least at the municipal level, would be held intact or even expanded. Recently granted an autonomous government by Spain, they hoped for a U.S.-style territorial government with even more political power. Instead, they were disappointed when the new colonial administrators established firm central control over the government and regularly admonished or removed municipal leaders for corruption, inefficiency, and party politics. Conflicts and resistance to the new regime arose frequently over the meanings, practices, and extent of autonomy and democratic participation. In addition, the domination of the economic interests of the United States, and the expansion of capital-intensive forms of wage exploitation, met with resistance by the displaced commercial and agricultural owners and class struggle among the working classes.[23]

The following sections will detail the configuration of sovereign, disciplinary, and governmental rationalities as exhibited by the *Progressive Military Map of the United States, Eastern Division: Porto Rico*. Cartography will be understood as part of the process of appropriation (by a colonial state), reconfiguration (under a new sovereign), and modification of colonial spaces (the Americanization of transportation, political economy, and education).[24] Let us turn first to the Regiment of Infantry, which produced the map, and its relationship with other security apparatuses.

PORTO RICO REGIMENT OF INFANTRY AND THE INSULAR POLICE: THE INTERSECTION OF SOVEREIGN POWER AND DISCIPLINE

As soon as the U.S. troops disembarked in July 1898, army officers, with the cooperation of the local elite, organized the Porto Rican Scouts, to assist with reconnaissance and military maneuvers against the Spanish troops, and the Porto Rican Guards, to help maintain law and order in the areas under U.S. control. When the war with Spain concluded the following August, the United States faced an even greater challenge than the Spanish Army:

unrest and violence in the countryside. Seeking provisions, money, and vengeance against the propertied classes, groups of armed men throughout the interior attacked the stores and haciendas of Spanish and Puerto Rican property owners and merchants. The U.S. Army established rural patrols, provided guards for rural property, and tracked down the perpetrators of violence. Again, the cooperation of the Puerto Ricans was essential for surveillance, reconnaissance, and troop movement.[25]

By 1899, most of the unrest in the countryside had been put down, and the United States began to organize and recruit its first overseas colonial regiment, with the plan of separating police and military functions. The result was the creation, in 1899, of the Porto Rico Battalion. Composed of American officers and Puerto Rican enlisted men, it was conceptualized both as defensive force against foreign threats and a backup reserve for the Insular Police, created that same year to patrol the rural areas. The following year, an additional mounted battalion was created. In 1901, Congress combined the two battalions and created the Provisional Porto Rican Regiment of Infantry, with headquarters in the capitol, San Juan, and barracks in the central mountain town of Cayey. The provisional regiment was initially comprised of Puerto Rican enlisted men and U.S. officers. In 1902, qualifying exams were offered to Americans who aspired to a commission in the regiment. Two years later Puerto Ricans were also permitted to receive commissions as officers, and several passed the exams and were commissioned as second lieutenants. Puerto Rican officers were subordinate to higher-ranking American officers. In 1908, the provisional regiment became a regular unit of the U.S. Army: the Porto Rico Regiment of Infantry. [26]

From the very beginning, the regiment had strictly defensive military objectives; it did not have police functions, except to serve as backup for the Insular Police. The organization of a colonial regiment in distinct units from the Insular Police meant that American soldiers were not required to intervene directly in the maintenance of law and order among the local population. The army itself was not envisioned as the principal means of internal control, and only San Juan and Cayey were garrisoned. Given the absence of armed rebellion against the colonial state, regular and volunteer troops of the U.S. Army were retired from Puerto Rico, and many went on to serve in the Philippines. The Insular Police was organized precisely in order to reduce the necessity of military occupation. At first, the previously existing municipal guards remained active in the urban areas; later they would be disbanded, and the Insular Police would cover both rural and urban areas. The Insular Police had a parallel structure with a military chain of command: American police officials occupied the highest ranks while Puerto Ricans made up the subordinate officers and the rank and file. In this way, the police force could exercise control and vigilance of the population, while at the same time policemen, detectives, and subordinate officers were subject to the hierarchical discipline of their superior U.S. officers.[27] Under the centralized command of high-ranking U.S. police officials, the Insular Police, composed of local policemen, was responsible for keeping order in the towns and the countryside.

This model was a variant of the Spanish system of municipal and rural guards, which was adapted with great success by the United States in Cuba, the Philippines, and Puerto Rico. [28] The hallmarks of the Spanish system were centralized, intrusive law enforcement and the modern prison. These two attributes were carried over to the new regime in Puerto Rico with minor adjustments. In contrast, in the Philippines the new regime quickly created a much larger and more complex security apparatus in order to wage war against the Filipino revolutionary army, to implement overt and covert counterinsurgency techniques against guerrilla forces, and to deploy secret police forces to demoralize and discredit nationalist leaders. The civilian government, established in 1901, created a complex security system for policing the provincial municipalities (lightly armed police), the capital city (Manila Metropolitan Police), and the countryside (the Philippine Constabulary). In addition, an infantry unit composed of Filipino soldiers and U.S. officers (the Philippine Scouts) were integrated with the U.S. Army. In addition, three of these security organizations, Manila Metropolitan Police, Philippine Constabulary, and U.S. Army, had covert surveillance units: the Secret Service Bureau, the Information Division, and the Military Information Division, respectively.[29] Since there was no armed, nationalist challenge to the colonial state in Puerto Rico, the security apparatus was far simpler and much reduced, although admittedly very little historical research in this area has been done.

Indeed, perhaps as important as its coercive function, the regiment in Puerto Rico was a disciplinary regime dedicated to the training of hearts, minds, and bodies. Writing in 1905, Governor Winthrop justified the Porto Rico Provisional Regiment of Infantry, not on military grounds, rather for its positive effect on the soldiers and officers, many who later entered civilian life. He wrote:

> It is true that the maintenance of this regiment is unnecessary in
> so far as it affects the peace of the island, but the same may be said

of the regiments stationed in posts throughout the United States. The continuance of the regiment is of great moment to the people of Porto Rico, affording, as it does, a school for the mental and physical development of many of the natives of the island. It is a noticeable fact that after service with the regiment, owing to the regular life, nutritious food, and daily exercise, the men improve considerably in size and physique. Of the 800 men who have been discharged from this regiment, many have been enabled through their knowledge of the English language, secured in the regiment, to pass civil-service examinations for entrance to the Federal service. In others, the habits acquired of discipline and steady attention to duty have caused them to be sought after by the plantation owners and merchants to fill responsible places. The existence of the regiment, composed of native Porto Ricans, is a source of great satisfaction and pride to these people, and does much to inspire an impressive respect for the American flag.[30]

The governor's description suggests that more than merely a coercive function, the regiment was a "school of mental and physical development," a disciplinary regime that trained subjects for both military service and civilian life. In effect, the report portrayed the regiment as an instrument of Americanization: the men learned English and were trained for civil service positions and jobs in the expanding plantations and commercial concerns. They both learned and inspired in others a respect for and loyalty to the colonial state. Their military capacity was of secondary importance.

Similar to the regiment, the Insular Police was also a coercive apparatus that functioned simultaneously as disciplinary regime. The Insular Police was organized along military lines, with a centralized chain of command, under the direction of an American officer. The governor considered the police an "impartial, model, and well-disciplined force." Discipline was achieved through various techniques, including constant evaluation and one-year, renewable appointments. Other disciplinary techniques were the drill, the concentration, and the police academy. The governor wrote:

The concentrating of the police force for drill and instructions is of the greatest importance. A great deal has been accomplished toward bringing the force to a high degree of efficiency by concentrating the men four or five days, teaching them their duties and maintaining their discipline. These concentrations should take place at least twice a year, and each time in a different section of the island, so that those guardsmen who take part in the first concentration would not have to called upon to take part in the second, thereby making them less expensive.[31]

The Insular Police, then, was a disciplinary institution similar to the army. Both attempted to train subjects, whether policemen or enlisted men, and submit them to the hierarchy of a centralized system under the control of U.S. officers in the colonial government. Officers and guardsmen worked long hours and were assigned a wide variety of tasks, including supervising elections and strikebreaking. In general, the Insular Police functioned to control the "dangerous classes" and to manage the "popular illegalities" related to their survival in and resistance to the new economic regime. In addition, the Insular Police sought to circumscribe mob violence in the political sphere and to contain collective actions by workers that threatened agriculture and industry.[32] To date, scholars have produced little evidence of widespread use of surveillance as a method of military pacification and political control in Puerto Rico during this period. The concerted methods of surveillance that have been documented in the Philippines are not evident.

THE PROGRESSIVE MILITARY MAP, THE FIELD BOOKS, AND THE MILITARY GAZE

When the U.S. military forces first arrived in the Puerto Rico, they updated existing Spanish maps, including transportation, agriculture lands, and communications, and quickly mapped the changes underway in the first decade of the twentieth century. The extensive cartography of Puerto Rico was also a primary concern during the first civilian administrations.[33] In May of 1908, the U.S. Army ordered Lieutenant William Armstrong and two officers of the Porto Rico Regiment of Infantry to produce a "progressive military map" of the island.[34] This topographic map was a part of the progressive military map of the United States, a large-scale project of the U.S. Army that attempted to produce "progressively" a collection of tactical maps of strategic areas of the states and territories.[35] In this context, "progressively" meant gradually or piecemeal. Cartographic field books, including detailed road itineraries and town descriptions, were an essential part of the standard methods of the army for making military maps. However, Armstrong's field books, which will be the primary sources for the following analysis, were unique in style, materials, and presentation. He collected postcards, took photographs, and sketched towns, and then he meticulously annotated, arranged, cross-referenced, and bound all of these materials. Among other innovations, he included annotated panoramic photographs of the countryside and created urban panoramic sequences with photographs. The ten existing field books cover about thirty towns, their agricultural environs, and the transportation infrastructure that linked them.

In this section we are interested in the military "gaze," a way of seeing objects and of speaking about them; a field of visibility and a mode of enunciation. The gaze was a part of a social apparatus, a *dispositif,* which created knowledge, established relationships of power, and defined subjects.[36] The principal objects of the cartographer's gaze were the territory, its resources, and population; the enunciations described the military value of the towns, the strategic topography, and the lines of troop movement. In Puerto Rico, the map was a function of the division between the reduced responsibilities of the army and the increased centralization of the Insular Police. First, it provided the means of mobilization of troops or of additional police in the case that the local police forces required additional forces to control unrest or in the case that foreign invaders threatened the island. For this reason, it paid attention to the elements essential to troop movement: roads and trails, bridges and culverts, railroads and trolleys, and sea ports. Second, the field books provided information on provisioning and quartering: campsites, food and water, fuel, pasturage, medicines, hospitals, and sanitary conditions. Within the field books, detailed town maps outlined urban spatial organization, prominent buildings, and the spatial distribution of commerce and class. Third, the map provided tactical information regarding topography and troop deployment.

Thus, the map used techniques of governmental rationality—the description of populations and territories—but was an exercise of sovereign power in that it consolidated military control and prepared for possible threats, both internal and external. Indeed, the military cartographers' presence in the field embodied and exemplified the dominion of the army over the entire island: Armstrong and his two assistants moved freely for several years with without impediment or threat at any time. The completion of the map further enabled the army's quick deployment if, when, and wherever necessary. This cartography was concerned, not so much with the delimitation of a sovereign territory, but rather with the careful description of an already demarcated space: the colony of Puerto Rico. The map reiterated and deepened colonial spaces, but it was a primarily a work of governmental rationality: the description of a population, its territory, and resources.[37]

Thus, the principal function of the map and the field books was military, but the technique was governmental. For example, the field books defined subject populations but did not interpolate individual subjects. In his notations, Armstrong expressed concern over the military character of the population and its loyalty to the colonial state. He continuously posed the following questions: Is the town pro-American? Are they willing to fight for the United States? How many local men can effectively bear arms? Is the police force reliable? Again, the technique was one of governmental rationality (the description of a population), but the issue was one of sovereignty, that is, the loyalty of political subjects to the sovereign power. Armstrong's work was one of reconnaissance rather than of surveillance; he sought to survey the topography and resources of a territory, not to keep a close watch over individuals, whether criminals or subversives. The element of surveillance, that is, the collection of information regarding individual political subjects, was entirely absent.

In general, Armstrong was not optimistic about the capacity of the local police forces or the towns' population to defend of the island from foreign invasion. He found them to be neither disciplined militarily nor loyal to the United States. In these discussions about loyalty and military character, Armstrong identified the perceived opponents of the regime: the Spanish, the Catholic clergy, and the local native politicians. The following description of a small town, Añasco, on the west coast (see figure 11.1) captures the tone and the content of the field books regarding military character and the adversaries of the colonial regime.

As most of the business men are Spaniards and the greater part of the rest of the male population the peon class, it is doubtful if more than 200 would be of any use with arms. Of these, 25–30 might make good shots under most favorable conditions. As defenders of the American flag I have but very little confidence in them. The picture [see figure 11.1] shows exactly what the people are. *Mostly* bare footed illiterate negros or half breeds. Of course there are many people of a better class. There are six or seven Americans in the town all engaged in missionary or in school work. There are few if any of other nationalities than Spanish or American. The people are indifferent toward Americans but it is safe to believe that their love for Americans is limited. The greater part of feeling toward Americans is encouraged by the town priest who has pronounced all Americans as 'demonios' and the public school as the 'casa de demonios' (devils and houses of devils). Nearly

11.1. "The Public Market at Añasco." Courtesy of the Biblioteca Digital Puertorriqueña de la Universidad de Puerto Rico.

all the trouble throughout the island is caused by the half educated native priests and the cheap politicians. Romanism leaves its black trail in all parts of the island.[38]

Armstrong's language deployed elements of class, race, and national origin, not as systematic, discrete categories, rather as the components of complex descriptions shaped by the military gaze. Except for the distinction between the agricultural "peon" and the urban laborer, he was oblivious to distinctions among the working classes; he dismissed them all as poor, illiterate, and barefoot and often referred to them pejoratively as negro, black, nigger, mulatto, or half-breed. He found very few men capable of bearing arms, and even fewer were able to shoot well. He found that working classes were neither ready nor willing to fight for any cause. Likewise, among the educated and propertied classes he also found poor military character and very little loyalty. He often distinguished between Spanish and Puerto Rican. This national distinction often delineated class differences: he stressed that the wealthy merchants were "Spanish" as distinguished from the Puerto Ricans who composed the working classes. This class and nationality division was described for practically every town. Armstrong identified the Spanish and native priests as opponents of the American regime and one of its central institutions, the public school. Yet, there is no evidence that Armstrong considered the Spanish Catholics to be a military threat, instead the issue was one of loyalty to the new regime and its institutions. Nevertheless, some larger towns had wealthy, educated Puerto Ricans, who constituted the local elite, and their loyalty to the political regime was shaped by the transition to capital-intensive, export-driven sugar production.

Loyalty was not entirely a question of religion or nationality. A close reading of his evaluations of the various towns suggests that it was, in part, related to recent economic turns of fortune: the depressed coffee areas were sometimes "anti-American" but at the same time desperate for government assistance and schools. In his travels through the coffee regions, he found much opposition to the change of colonial regime and the subsequent collapse of the coffee market. He stopped at several coffee plantations in the interior and found the owners to be "very anti-American" even though they were usually "very friendly." He found little open hostility to his presence; instead, he usually found the population in the coffee regions friendly and courteous.

In contrast, the inhabitants of the booming sugar areas were somewhat positive with respect to the American political economy, but at best indifferent toward the colonial government. The expansive sugar production had made many wealthy men, but paradoxically many of them now desired more political autonomy or independence. He noted that local politicians were both courteous to him and fond of stirring speeches against the colonial regime. He considered them to be misguided but not a military threat. At no time did he suggest that there was any armed resistance; indeed, he found very few men even capable of handling firearms.[39] In general, the population was described as passive, both unable and unwilling to fight for any cause, except for the Spanish inhabitants who were seen as impediments to the colonial regime. In contrast, the Spanish population was seen as an intractable obstacle to the American regime, both opposed to the public school and in conflict with the Protestant denominations. Instead of a military threat, however, opposition was directed at the new disciplinary institutions that increasingly occupied central spaces both in the towns and the countryside, as we shall see later.

Armstrong was not only a military agent; he was also a witness to the transformation of the landscapes and cityscapes of Puerto Rico under the new colonial government. His field books documented the material expansion and improvement of transportation, urban services, and agricultural production. First, the field books captured the processes of improving old trails and roads and creating new macadam roads. Armstrong commented that his map would soon be obsolete since the government was building

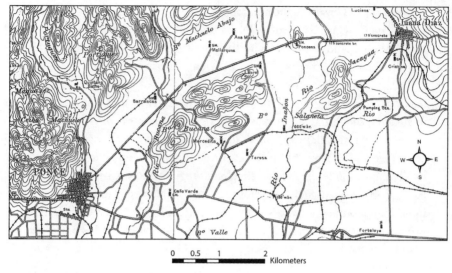

11.2. Detail of Progressive Military Map of the United States Eastern Division: Porto Rico.

"good macadam roads in all sections of the island and before many years trails now found on the map will be roads."[40] Second, the field books documented the improvement of urban services, in particular water works and electrification, in various towns throughout the island, but especially in the sugar regions. In addition, he recorded the establishment of hospitals, clinics, anemia stations, and, of course, public schools. Third, the decline of coffee and the advent of sugar were evidenced in the reconfiguration of the landscape: the panoramic views and the topographical map illustrate the geographic distribution of cultivation, the location of coffee haciendas, old sugar mills, and modern *centrales*. The map is both littered with ruins of old mills and filled with the expansive new mills. Armstrong's cartographic work left impressive documentation of the first phase of expansion of the sugar industry in Puerto Rico, and his panoramic landscapes appear as if it were natural spaces for capital investment in sugar.[41]

The segment of the topographical map (see figure 11.2) shows the modern sugar mill, Mercedita (left of center). It was located just east of the major city of Ponce and west of the small town Juana Díaz (upper right corner). It is a thoroughly modern mill, surrounded by a network of good roads, with internal railways to bring sugar in from the fields for grinding, and with a pumping station for irrigation. All around are the remnants of old mills, identified as O.M., whose lands have been absorbed by Mercedita to supply sugar cane to the mill. Although the map segment did not indicate

Guanica Sugar Mills
Harbor looking S.E. From Hill X.
Cocos road to Yauco.
Town of Guanica.
Guanica light.
ocean channel
Residence of the Manager
ocean
Mary E. Barrett
Guanica Bay
Ensenada.

11.3. "Guánica Sugar Mills." Courtesy of the Biblioteca Digital Puertorriqueña de la Universidad de Puerto Rico.

cultivation, it is clear that all of the flat lands shown were dedicated to the cultivation of sugar cane. Armstrong also documented this process of expansion of the modern mills by means of photography. One photograph (see figure 11.3) is a panoramic view of the Guánica sugar mill, at the time the largest sugar mill in the world. It transported sugar cane by railroad from all around Puerto Rico and shipped in sugar cane from the neighboring Dominican Republic to be processed by the most capital intensive, advanced technology of the period.

In sum, Armstrong participated in and documented the creation of colonial spaces by means of cartographic techniques. First, the military map applied a military gaze in order to produce strategic knowledge about the topography, the infrastructure, and the population. The field books provided detailed information essential to troop movement, provisioning, and the military character of the men. Second, the material process of "Americanization" may be seen in the landscapes and cityscapes: new roads and sugar mills. In many respects, they captured the changes of fortune of the elites due to the decline of coffee and the rise of sugar. The field books also commented on the impediments to the U.S. regime, namely the local politicians, the Spanish upper class, and the Catholic priests and nuns. Although Armstrong witnessed the material transformation of the landscape, he was not convinced that roads and sugar mills would transform the hearts and minds of population. That task, perhaps, would be left to other colonial spaces, those circumscribed by that archetypical disciplinary institution, the public school.

Before Armstrong entered military service, he had worked for two years (1900–1902) as a district supervisor in the public school system in San Juan. In this capacity, he was charged with supervising teachers and students and establishing the first "graded schools" in Puerto Rico. The graded schools had clear curricular sequences based on the organization of progressive levels or grades. The graded school was central to a new disciplinary regime that sought to manage both students and teachers. The effective use of pedagogical and supervisory techniques associated with the new school system required the centralization of authority in the Department of Education. Several kinds of struggles arose over the new disciplinary structure of the department: between teachers and students; between supervisors and teachers; and between the centralized department and municipal control. In addition, conflicts arose over the specific content of the teaching, specifically instruction in English. Armstrong had been an active participant in these conflicts, and his topographical work demonstrated close attention to the widespread distribution of public schools throughout the towns, villages, and countryside. In the larger towns he took photographs of the new concrete graded schools, and in the countryside he mapped the locations of rural and agricultural schools. His work evidenced the wide dispersal of these disciplinary institutions; however, in order to identify the particular mechanisms of control of students and teachers, we must consult the reports of the first two commissioners of the Department of Education, Martin Brumbaugh (1900–1901) and Samuel Lindsay (1902–4). These two men had been Armstrong's immediate superiors when he was district supervisor.

When Brumbaugh took office he found that there were no virtually no public school buildings. This meant the department had to rent facilities for that purpose. His report enumerated the difficulties of vacating the rented buildings, their deplorable sanitary conditions, the time and cost for their renovation, and the resistance of the current residents or owners. The Department of Education responded quickly to this situation by implementing a program of constructing new schools. During its first years of operation, the department built scores of one-room rural schools, vocational schools (agricultural or industrial), modern graded schools (including primary and secondary), and a normal school for the training of local teachers.[42] These new schools were widely dispersed through the towns and the countryside and Armstrong's military map included many details of their geographic

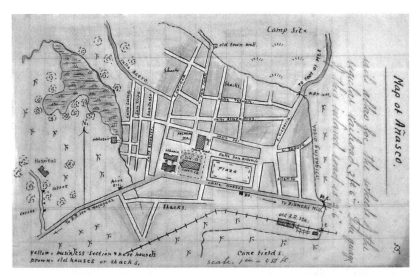

11.4. Map of Añasco. Courtesy of the Biblioteca Digital Puertorriqueña de la Universidad de Puerto Rico.

reach in the towns and countryside. In the field books he included descriptions and photographs of the new urban structures and located them on his sketch maps of the towns. One sketch map (see figure 11.4) details the town of Añasco, which we have discussed earlier. The map shows the spatial location of the central disciplinary institution, the graded school. It is worthy of note that in this town the two new graded schools, one of four rooms (two hundred students) and the other of six rooms (three hundred students), were built directly behind the Catholic church. It is no coincidence that the schools, symbols of the new regime, were centrally located, and at least one of the schools was partially visible from the central square (see figure 11.1). The Catholic clergy, as we have seen in Armstrong's field book (quoted above), was opposed to secular education and referred to these new schools as *"casas de demonios"* or houses of devils. The grouping of boys and girls in the same classroom was also a novel idea that was initially questioned by the clergy and parents. Two other wooden school buildings were built just outside of town, near the railway station, but were not indicated on the sketch map. Armstrong also included in his map the anemia station, the police headquarters, and the town hall, which included the jail, telephone, and telegraph station.

Closely related to the inadequate school buildings, the lack of discipline in the early classrooms was a problem in the first years of the new regime. In 1902, Lindsay complained that when he took office "there was no uniform course of study; no attempt at rules, regulations, or order; no thought of the rights of the child; no endeavor to apply pedagogical principles nor to furnish teachers with adequate equipment for their work."[43] Lindsay's strategy focused on textbooks and desks. The introduction of textbooks, whether in English or Spanish, outlined a course of study by year and grade. The department purchased thousands of school desks, which were to replace the existing benches and tables "at which the children were formerly huddled together without any possibility of maintaining good order and without any regard for health and comfort." Lindsay explained: "New individual desks create a change in discipline of the school and in the spirit of pride and degree of efficiency with which both teacher and pupil carry on the work." The textbooks and individual desks were articulated with the architecture of the new school buildings; the construction of modern multiroom, graded school houses provided for the spatial separation of grades corresponding to the curriculum outlined in the textbooks.[44] Thus, the construction of the graded school, the installation of individual desks, and the use of textbooks assured the repartition of bodies, the temporal control of activities, and the division of sequential tasks in which students were watched, evaluated, and sanctioned as individualized subjects.[45]

In addition to the discipline of students, conflicts arose over the supervision of the teachers. Brumbaugh described the conflicts between the district supervisors, who were most often American, and the local teachers: "The difficulty attending their work is due to the friction of races and languages. The teachers who speak no English, and who are not wholly willing to accept the new order of things, look upon these supervisors as official meddlers. This has led to a few unpleasant and unfortunate experiences. But in general the teachers welcome this supervision, and now appreciate its value to them and to the schools."[46] It is not clear exactly what Brumbaugh meant when he referred to the conflict of "races," but the context of the comment suggests that the races in question were American supervisors and Puerto Rican teachers. Likewise, Lindsay identified the "English supervisors" as the main agents of disciplinary management of teachers. "Those who willfully neglect their work, close their schools before the regular hour for closing, neglect to open them at the proper time, sham sickness, and in general do as little work as possible when the supervisor is not in sight are dealt with severely when they are found out. We have had the risk of closing some schools altogether, by suspending within the last three months about twenty-five teachers for serious cause." Since teachers were also to be model citizens, they could be suspended for lack of morals in private life: "We must not place the care and training of innocent children in the hands of any teacher whose life is not clean, wholesome, and earnest, no matter what other qualifications he may have."[47]

The early commissioners of education recounted several conflicts and difficulties that arose from the establishment of a new disciplinary regime, or in Brumbaugh's words, the "new order of things." Both commissioners emphasized the clashes between supervisors and teachers. These conflicts centered on the issues of the use of the English language, teacher preparation, and the authority of the Department of Education to hire, evaluate, and dismiss teachers. In addition to direct supervision, another instrument in the disciplining of Puerto Rican teachers was the establishment, in 1903, of the normal school, which trained persons to teach in graded schools as well as the rural, agricultural, and industrial schools. The idea was to convert subjects into students of the disciplinary regime, and only then would they become proper teachers. The financing and construction of graded schools, as well as the supervision and training of teachers, required a centralized administration. The official reports indicated that the department was structured in a way to remove the power from the local school boards and the municipalities. The local school boards were often politically subservient to the mayor while at the same time without a budget. The Department of Education was centrally structured and financed in order to establish a clear chain of command from the commissioner through the supervisors to the teachers. The local boards were weakened, but not eliminated.

The discursive themes in the official reports centered on conflicts arising from student discipline and teacher supervision. The first two official reports of the Department of Education provided evidence of the establishment of a new disciplinary discursive social formation in the public school system in Puerto Rico. Several changes in the school system were at the center of the department's disciplinary regime. The techniques of discipline, broadly speaking, related to the distribution of bodies within institutional spaces, the control of activities, the division of tasks, and establishment of a chain of command: the graded school, the supervision of teachers, and the centralization of the Department of Education. Although Puerto Rico was without armed resistance to the colonial state, Lindsay used a bellicose metaphor; he wrote that the colonization of Puerto Rico was to be "carried forward by the armies of peace, whose outposts and garrisons are the public schools of the advancing nation."[48] Apparently, Armstrong took this metaphor to heart: in his military map he was careful to include all of these disciplinary "outposts and garrisons." These schools were the signs of the new order and had an important spatial presence as well as a demographic impact.

Despite these initial conflicts, many parents and students, teachers and trainees soon took advantage of the opportunities provided by primary, secondary, and postsecondary education. Basic literacy increased in the population, and enrollment increased rapidly. In addition, the Department of Education provided employment, advancement, and even social mobility for men and, importantly, women in Puerto Rico. In 1911, teachers formed a union to promote their class interests and influence pedagogical policy. Teachers were able to negotiate their differences arising from the imposition of English as the language of instruction and the colonial assimilationist content ("Americanization"). For the most part, resistance to the new pedagogy was expressed within the confines of the educational system. For example, instead of emphasizing the "colonial form of nationalism," teachers adopted strategies to develop a modern, national, Puerto Rican identity.[49] Whether English should be a language of instruction or taught as a second language was more controversial and generated both open political conflicts and frequent policy changes.

I have argued that colonial spaces are created through the deployment of techniques of sovereignty, discipline, and governmental rationality. In the U.S. imperial formation, these techniques were widely, yet unevenly, dispersed throughout the colonies. In Puerto Rico, sovereign techniques of repression and surveillance were not as prevalent as the wide spatial dispersal of disciplinary institutions that sought to train the hearts, minds, and bodies of the newly colonized subjects. Likewise, governmental techniques of collecting information about populations and political economy were equally important. Using the *Progressive Military Map of the United States, Eastern Division: Porto Rico* as a point of departure, I have shown how cartography was an instrument of appropriation, reconfiguration, and modification, not only of landscapes, but also of colonial subjects and populations. First, it mapped the space of sovereignty and made possible the functionality of its scant security forces. It helped make possible the division between policing the local population, undertaken by the Insular Police, and the defense of the island from foreign attack or internal disturbance, responsibilities of the Regiment of Infantry. Both institutions were simultaneously disciplinary institutions, in that they sought to shape the bodies and minds of their members, and security apparatuses that used, or threatened, coercion to maintain internal order and external defense. Sovereign techniques were minimal because of the relative political and military stability of Puerto Rico, especially when compared with the Philippines. Second, it mapped spaces of discipline and their distribution. In particular, the small, internal spaces of disciplinary institutions of the public school house were shown to have a wide geographical dispersal throughout the cities, towns, and countryside. Third, the map documented the recent transformation of scale and extension of sugar production and the intricate transportation networks that facilitated the export-based economy. The map traced the increasingly dense networks of transportation and their connections to the changing landscape of agricultural production. These were the colonial spaces created, normalized, and documented by the progressive military map of Puerto Rico: spaces of sovereignty and their functionality; spaces of discipline and their dispersal; spaces of economic production and their connection. The colonial difference of Puerto Rico may be characterized by a particular configuration of governmental rationality: the limited, but effective, uses of coercive techniques; the wide dispersal of disciplinary institutions; and the expansive, modern capitalist transformations of the political economy along with the management of populations through biopolitics.

NOTES

1. The topographical map is located in the Map Collection of the Library of Congress; *Progressive Military Map of the United States Eastern Division: Porto Rico*, William H. Armstrong, 1st Lieut., P.R.R.I. Authority for Topography and Teofilo Marxuach, 1st Lieut., P.R.R.I. Authority for Topography; F. B. Essex, draftsman; surveyed 1908; drawn 1914; scale 1:62,500. Used with permission. María Dolores Luque, María Mercedes Carrión, Aurora Lauzardo, and I are currently preparing a bilingual facsimile edition of the field books to be published by Ediciones Puerto. Some field books may be consulted online: Colección Manuscritos, William Armstrong, Biblioteca Digital Puertorriqueña, Universidad de Puerto Rico, Río Piedras. I will use the abbreviation F B, followed by the original enumeration and page number, to reference quotes from the field books.
2. Foucault's principal text is "Governmentality." I have followed Dean, *Governmentality*. See also Lemke, *Biopolitics*.
3. This question was originally posed by David Scott in his study of Ceylon. However, he did not distinguish precisely the colonial difference in the deployment of governmental rationality. Rather, he sought to refocus the analysis away from attitudes of the colonizer and the forms of exclusion of colonial subjects and toward the analysis of the objects and techniques that define the political ratio-

nality of the colonial state. I take a similar theoretical position although I hope to distinguish better the techniques of governmentality in the context of the colonial state of Puerto Rico. See D. Scott, "Colonial Governmentality."

4. Dean, *Governmentality*, 133–35.
5. Dean, *Governmentality*, chap. 7.
6. Legg, *Spaces of Colonialism*. He summarized the pattern of colonial governmentality in India as a mixture, on the one hand, of excesses in the realms of violence, ceremony, segregation, incarceration, exploitation, the ethos of Western civilization, social experimentation, and hyper-regulation and, on the other hand, of neglect in the realms of civil rights, direct rule, broad social integration, free markets, social welfare ethos, and the recognition of individuality.
7. Duncan, *In the Shadows of the Tropics*, 190.
8. Mbembe, "Necropolitics."
9. Mbembe, *On the Postcolony*, 25–35. He referred to these two fundamental principles of sovereignty in the colonies as *commandement*.
10. Kramer, *The Blood of Government*, chap. 2.
11. McCoy, Scarano, and Johnson, "On the Tropic of Cancer: Transitions and Transformations in the U.S. Imperial States," 13–14, 24–25, 33. See also Tomes, "Crucibles, Capillaries, and Pentimenti." Mbembe noted the multiple origins and circulation of necropolitics in a wide range of historical and geographical contexts spread across Europe and its colonies; see Mbembe, "Necropolitics."
12. McCoy, *Policing America's Empire*.
13. Go, *Patterns of Empire*, 12.
14. Foucault's principle text on disciplinary institutions is *Discipline and Punish*. Foucault's interview is translated, commented, and analyzed in Crampton and Elden, *Space, Knowledge and Power*. See also Crampton and Krygier, "An Introduction to Critical Cartography."
15. Foucault, "Governmentality," 93.
16. Edney, "The Irony of Imperial Mapping." On the use of maps of the Philippines in U.S. mass media and in the army, see Brody, "Mapping Empire." Compare Appadurai, who argues that the modern census has a different effect in Britain than in India, even though the same basic techniques were used; see Appadurai, "Number in the Colonial Imagination."
17. Thompson, *Imperial Archipelago*.
18. On public health and hygiene, see Duprey, *Bioislas*. On urban ordering, see Cortés Zavala, "Los Bandos de Policía y Buen Gobierno en Puerto Rico." On social hygiene and eugenics, see Carmen Baerga, "Transgresiones corporales." On the census, see Scarano, "Censuses in the Transition to Modern Colonialism." On cartography, see Sepúlveda Rivera, *Puerto Rico urbano*.
19. On the transition from Spanish to U.S. prisons in Puerto Rico, see Santiago-Valles, "American Penal Reforms and Colonial Spanish Custodial-Regulatory Practices in Fin de Siècle Puerto Rico."
20. García Muñiz, *Sugar and Power in the Caribbean*.
21. For a comparative study of the disciplinary aspects of political tutelage, see Go, *American Empire and the Politics of Meaning*.
22. Povinelli conceptualized the "governance of the prior" in the context of encounters of settler colonies with local indigenous populations (the prior); see Povinelli, "The Governance of the Prior."

23. Cabán, *Constructing a Colonial People*; García, "I Am the Other"; Go, *American Empire and the Politics of Meaning*.

24. Edney, "The Irony of Imperial Mapping," 19.

25. Negrón Portillo, *Cuadrillas anexionistas y revueltas campesinas*; Picó, *1898*.

26. Marín Román, *¡Llegó la gringada!*, 208–16.

27. Marín Román, *¡Llegó la gringada!*, 208–16.

28. Cabán, *Constructing a Colonial People*; Santiago-Valles, *"Subject Peoples" and Colonial Discourses*; McCoy, *Policing America's Empire*.

29. McCoy, *Policing America's Empire*.

30. Winthrop, *Fifth Annual Report of the Governor of Porto Rico*, 33–34.

31. Winthrop, *Fifth Annual Report of the Governor of Porto Rico*, 145.

32. Santiago-Valles, *"Subject Peoples" and Colonial Discourses*, 77–110.

33. The most comprehensive history of cartography in Puerto Rico is Sepúlveda Rivera, *Puerto Rico urbano*.

34. First Lieutenant William H. Armstrong, First Lieutenant Teófilo Marxuach, and Second Lieutenant Louis Emmanuelli were ordered to complete a progressive military map of Puerto Rico. Of the twelve quadrants that made up the final map, Armstrong signed as topographer on ten and Marxuach on two. Apparently, Emmanuelli worked as an assistant to Marxuach. Efficiency report of 1st Lt. Wm. H. Armstrong, P.R.R.I., for the period from July 1, 1908, to June 30, 1909. Record Group 94, National Archives and Records Administration, Washington, DC.

35. A detailed background and description of the process of producing a map, as well as field notes, is provided by Roy Robert Lyon, "Field Work on the Progressive Military Map of the United States," thesis for advanced degree in civil engineering, Michigan Agricultural College, 1914. A general description is also found in Ehrenberg, "Up in the Air in More Ways Than One," 220–22.

36. The notion of the "gaze" is found in Foucault's early work on the clinic. I have extended the scope of the concept by following Deleuze, "What Is a Dispositif?," 159–61.

37. McCoy refers to this as "mute and blind information" because it did not contain information on specific individuals that might be used as a means of political control. His emphasis on surveillance techniques leads him to overlook the interaction of sovereign and governmental rationalities in the colonial state. See McCoy, *Policing America's Empire*, 21.

38. FB 8, 42–44.

39. For description of the coffee areas, see FB 10. The sugar areas are described, above all, in FB 8 and 11.

40. FB 1, n.p.

41. García Muñiz, *Sugar and Power*.

42. Brumbaugh, *Report of the Commissioner of Education for Porto Rico*, 757.

43. Lindsay, "Report of the Commissioner of Education," 230. For a discussion of Lindsay's policies, see Negrón de Montilla, *La americanización*, 77–108.

44. Lindsay, "Report of the Commissioner of Education," 236.

45. I follow closely Foucault, *Discipline and Punish*.

46. Brumbaugh, *Report of the Commissioner of Education for Porto Rico*, 749.

47. Lindsay, "Report of the Commissioner of Education," 248.

48. Lindsay, "Report of the Commissioner of Education," 257.

49. del Moral, *Negotiating Empire*; Bobonis and Toro, "Modern Colonization and Its Consequences."

"I'm Not Running on My Gender"

The 2010 Navajo Nation Presidential Race, Gender,
and the Politics of Tradition

On November 2, 2010, I traveled to my home community of Tohatchi, on
the eastern side of the Navajo Nation, to vote in the Navajo presidential
and council election. This particular election garnered international and
national American attention because it seemed very possible that for the
first time a woman could be president of the Navajo Nation. Interest in
New Mexico senator Lynda Lovejoy's candidacy was pronounced because
she had survived the primary elections, making her the first serious woman
contender for the Navajo presidency. In the months following her win in
the primary and on the campaign trail, Lovejoy, as had other Navajo women
who sought elected leadership positions in the Navajo government, faced
criticism from many Navajos who believed that women should not be leaders in the public sphere, a belief said to be grounded in creation narratives.
Throughout her presidential campaign, Senator Lovejoy repeatedly insisted
that she "was not running based upon her gender."[1] The senator raised the
specter of tribal officials who had run amuck with the tribal coffers where
even her opposition, Vice President Ben Shelly, was being charged with
corruption and fraud.[2] Rather, Lovejoy declared, if she were to be elected,
her administration would be devoted to raising the standard of living for
all Navajo families and to reconsidering Navajo energy policies around its
natural resources. Her selection of longtime Navajo environmental activist
Earl Tulley as her running mate certainly spoke to her aspirations to shift
Navajo Nation policies around energy and development.[3]

In the months and days before the election, journalists called me to get a perspective from a Diné woman and scholar on the question of whether Diné tradition prohibited women from holding the highest leadership position on the Navajo Nation. Four years earlier, Lynda Lovejoy had run against Joe Shirley Jr., and just as I had participated in the conversations around the meaning and significance of a woman being elected president of the Navajo Nation, I again heard similar questions and debates about Diné tradition and gender. Did traditional Navajo teachings practice gender discrimination? If a woman were elected president, would she bring much-needed feminine qualities to the Navajo leadership? If, traditionally, Navajo women exercised a significant measure of authority in a still matrilineal Navajo society, then why were women being criticized for running for the highest office in the Navajo Nation? If a woman is elected president, does this mean that Navajos have finally embraced Western democratic notions about gender equality and civil liberties? Or does the election of a Navajo woman to the presidency indicate a return to traditional principles where women have always been acknowledged as leaders?

In the aftermath of her loss to president-elect Ben Shelly, Lovejoy admitted that strong feelings against upsetting traditional gender balances had contributed to her loss at the polls. Several days after Shelly's successful bid for the Navajo presidency, Lovejoy interviewed with reporter John McBreem and declared that as a gay man, vice president–elect Rex Lee Jim did not face the kind of gender discrimination she had endured. Although Navajos appeared to remain silent to Lovejoy's charges, *Navajo Times* correspondent Bill Donovan castigated Lovejoy and called her out as homophobic. Donovan's declaration that homophobia was so intense on the Navajo Nation that to call one a homosexual "was a slur of the worst sort" and anyone accused faced horrors beyond imagination. The reporter then wrote of the senator, "Who was she to comment on anyone else's sexuality?" His final remarks included Jim's response about his sexuality: "he emphatically denied being homosexual." Given that the Navajo Nation is a hotbed of homophobia, charged Donovan, the vice president would be forced to "deal with the fallout of Lovejoy's statement."[4] The public comments about Navajo lesbian, gay, and transgender issues, although seemingly secondary to presidential and tribal council elections, raised consciousness of Navajo heterosexuality as the national norm and questions about the bifurcation of gender as normative.

Also, the public discussions were presented as taking place in the private domain, even though international and national news media were commenting on the phenomenon and interviewing Navajos on the topic. As

Navajo reporter Erny Zah declared about supposed Navajos' reluctance to discuss whether gender discrimination was sanctioned by tradition, "No one so far is willing to be the public face of this view, but in casual conversation and on the Internet, it is there."[5] Indeed the Navajo Nation's passage of the Diné Marriage Act in 2005 indicates that the discussions about gender, sexuality, and belonging to the nation are very public forums. This supposed reluctance to speak publicly about troubling gender relations marks the ways in which gendered space has been bifurcated by Western conventions, where domestic matters should remain relegated to the intimate spaces.

This chapter aims to open up space to consider how the formations of tribal nations are founded on Western democratic frameworks and therefore have inherited structures that reproduce patriarchy to perpetuate gender inequality, sexism, and homophobia. Further, this essay is interested in how discursive practices of invoking tradition are used to legitimate tribal nation building as a patriarchal enterprise. Certainly, most studies of tribal nation building ignore the intersections of nation building and gender.[6] Finally, rather than seeking some sort of corrective or directive about what is the "right" thing to think about tribal nations, gender, and tradition, this examination takes decolonization as an engagement with the ongoing consequences of settler colonialism for tribal nations and their citizens. The term *settler colonialism* helps us to understand the ongoing occupation by non-Indian settlers of Native territories and lands and how this appropriation is supported through cultural, legal, and religious structures. A theory of settler colonialism illuminates how the colonial project seeks to eliminate Native peoples either through genocide or disavowal.[7] The ongoing consequences of settler colonialism are evident with Native peoples' concerns about the state of Indian country and how to create better tribal communities. Raising questions about how the imposition of Western democratic ideals about nation and sovereignty on tribal nations have transformed our relationships to each other is an act of decolonization, for then we have space to reflect on the present state of our respective nations and a future where our citizens live according to our traditional principles. In a recent conversation, Diné scholar Hannabah Blue and I both remarked that when we talk about our nation, tradition, gender, and sexuality, although we both have been cautioned in various ways to refrain from talking about these issues, it is critical and necessary to have these conversations, otherwise, we may never be able to create a nation that treats all of its citizens justly.

Theories of settler nations, tribal nation building, and decolonization have been addressed in Native studies; and yet, the intersection of tribal nations and gender continues to be explored separately, thereby making it difficult to make connections between nation and gender violence. Although national and tribal national attention is now aimed at the epidemic of violence toward Native women—thanks to the issuance of two Amnesty International reports that castigated Canada and the United States for their failure to check epidemic gender violence and the Violence against Women Act (VAWA)—it remains critical to scrutinize how patriarchy as a hierarchal structure perpetuates gender violence in the tribal national political arena.[8] Further, articulating what is "traditional" within a modern institution such as tribal governments requires historicizing its establishment and how the language of tradition and cultural events are used to legitimate and sanction heteropatriarchy. As indigenous scholar Isabel Altamirano-Jiménez observes, violence and gender discrimination against indigenous women are often constructed as cultural problems, rather than the result of multiple social markers and power relations that structure social, economic, and political systems.[9] This requires an examination of how Navajo women and the question of leadership and tradition expose the construction of dichotomies that remove women from the political arena by inscribing the boundaries of the "domestic" along Western democratic notions.

Seeking to denaturalize tribal nations as heteropatriarchies, this study draws on a number of theoretical streams—including Indigenous feminisms, women of color critiques, Queer Native/Indigenous studies, and critiques of development and progress—in order to recast the 2010 Navajo presidential election and raise questions around nation, "tradition," and gender.[10] The Dakota historian Waziyatawin defines decolonization as "the intelligent, calculated, and active resistance to the forces of colonialism that perpetuate the subjugation and/or exploitation of our minds, bodies, and lands, and it is engaged for the ultimate purpose of overturning the colonial structure and realizing Indigenous liberation." She elaborates, "An analysis of colonialism allows us to make sense of our current condition, strategically develop more effective means of resistance, recover the pre-colonial traditions that strengthen us as Indigenous Peoples and connect with the struggles of colonized peoples throughout the world to transform the world."[11] Both Mohawk scholar Taiaiake Alfred and Navajo legal scholar Raymond Austin challenge us to critique how Euro-American notions of sovereignty have replaced Indigenous forms of governance, sovereignty, and leadership.[12] Austin provides a specific Navajo study of nation and sovereignty and articulates a vision: "Empowerment through customary ways ensures longevity of Indian nation sovereignty, fosters nation building, and preserves, transmits, and perpetuates culture, language, spirituality, and identity."[13]

Extending these visions of tribal nations re-created on traditional principles, Native feminist Joanne Barker interrogates the ways in which tribal nations engage with the categories of "tradition" and "authenticity" as tribal leaders determine who belongs as citizens. As Barker shows, these terms have been deployed in ways that undermine the status of women and Native queers. Given that Native cultures and traditions have been vastly transformed as a result of settler colonialism, it is not necessarily the objective to return precolonial traditions, for such aspirations put us in impossible situations of seeking ideals that have been determined by the U.S. federal government and those anthropologists and other intellectuals whose scholarship shaped federal Indian policy.[14] Rather, it is crucial to recognize the ways in which the federal government acknowledges Indian nations and citizenship to reinforce U.S. domination over Native peoples. Importantly, tribal governments have internalized these non-Indian ideals and standards, thereby advancing racist, sexist, homophobic, and extreme perspectives that uphold U.S. nationalist narratives.[15]

In this essay, I scrutinize the incorporation of the Diné into American multicultural narratives about U.S.-Indigenous relationships, which are intended to reinscribe colonial U.S.-Navajo relationships of hierarchy and dominance. Such discursive practices naturalize the nation as a family predicated on a nuclear unit where a husband is considered the head and the wife his subordinate. As feminist scholars have pointed out, such articulations that describe nation in the language of family veils patriarchy and relationships of dominance and subordination. In the case of the Diné, different meanings have been assigned to what nation building looks like, as well as against the casting of the Navajo Nation as a "domestic dependent" of the United States, and critiques and evaluations of what it means to be a truly sovereign nation are ongoing. For an example, on the one hand, Raymond Austin points out how the Navajo Nation has exercised its sovereign powers by applying traditional philosophy to judicial decisions, mostly in the domestic and civil arena, while Dana Powell and Dáilan Long argue that the formation of the modern Navajo Nation is so linked to the development of Navajo natural resources, that it is difficult for leaders to envision a present and future without Western concepts of development and progress.[16] Further, meanings of tribal sovereignty are moving from articulating sovereignty "as an ontological ground of power and order, expressed in law or in enduring ideas of legitimate rule, in favor of a view of sovereignty as a tentative and always emergent form of authority grounded in violence that is performed and designed to generate loyalty, fear, and legitimacy from the neighborhood to the summit of the state."[17] This shift in articulations of tribal sovereignty illuminates the deployment of tribal authority as violence and acknowledges gender as a legitimate tool of analysis that challenges male authority.

Native feminist analyses, which are informed by feminists of color and Native queer theories, are tied to the project of reclaiming tribal sovereignty. As law professor Rebecca Tsosie reaffirms, Native women's leadership is tied to "notions of land and community and cultural views of relationship and responsibility."[18] The last two decades of studies on Native/Indigenous feminisms have yielded great promise as scholars move beyond recovery projects to investigate how the structures of inequality and violence have shaped tribal nations in ways where gender inequality and violence are entrenched.[19] Feminist scholar Zillah Eisenstein defines feminism as what identifies women politically and brings the patriarchal and misogynist structures of power into view to break the silence of male privilege by denaturalizing and denormalizing it. She notes that "because power and oppression are never static, but rather dynamic, feminisms are always changing to address these historical and newly formed systems."[20] In conversation with critiques such as Eisenstein's, Native feminisms allow for the possibility of seeing theoretically how women's oppression has newly formed sites and, significantly, which are tied historically to the experiences of Native under cycles of colonial invasions. Feminist of color scholarship intersects with indigenous feminisms by revealing how gender violence is integral to colonization and that Native peoples needed to learn the value of hierarchy and how physical abuse maintains that hierarchy where women must be submissive to their men.[21] A Diné perspective on gender relations raises questions about the intersections of traditional gender roles and formations of tribal nations and accounts for the realities of living with modern institutions where the effects of settler colonialism has meant the naturalization of patriarchy, including the loss of knowledge about multiple genders.[22] As Chris Finley asserts, "Native nations' use of heteronormative citizenship standards also disallows nonheteronormative identity formations from belonging in Native nations."[23] Feminist Native scholars and their allies call for a reenvisioning of nationalist struggles that move beyond a heteronormative nation-state framework to realize justice for all of our citizens.

Four years after Lynda Lovejoy's first run at the presidency and on the day after the 2010 primary elections, the media reported that intense monsoon storms had resulted in flooding in several areas and a tornado had touched down in Many Farms, Arizona. Three people also died from storm-related causes that week, two by lightning strikes.[24] The unusual weather added fuel to the discussions about traditional gender sanctions. The message from the natural world reflected the Navajo deities' warnings that Navajo society would be in chaos if genders became unbalanced.[25] Given that Navajo society is traditionally matrilineal where women's roles are acknowledged as crucial to the perpetuation of the people and the contemporary warnings against women holding the presidency of the Navajo Nation, how do we reconcile these seemingly contradictory positionings? And what is at stake if we do not acknowledge formerly high statuses of Navajo women and the present where they experience high levels of violence?[26] This section examines popular media depictions of the 2010 Navajo presidential election and then moves to the uses of traditional Navajo narratives about gender roles to offer interpretations about a perceived crisis in tribal leadership.

Local, regional, and national news sources used Navajo interpretations about the natural disaster as a springboard to heighten national interest in questions about the nature of "traditional" Navajo society and the intersection of nation and gender. Their stories exoticized the possibility of a woman becoming the top leader of the Navajo Nation by suggesting that if Navajos elected a woman, they were finally realizing the benefits of liberal mainstream American values. In these scenarios, the intersections of Navajo and non-Indian understandings of gender constructions are conflated and in doing so, they make it difficult to think through the relationships between questions about traditional sanctions against women as leaders in the political sphere and how domestic space is conceptualized in Navajo thought. Interviews with Navajo voters were used to suggest that if a woman were elected, she might possibly bring much-needed nurturing and mothering qualities to the presidency. These concerns about how the feminine qualities of women might bring needed changes to tribal leadership are part of the standard scholarship on women and leadership that perpetuates assumptions about the natural qualities of the feminine or the masculine and does not examine the structures of oppression and violence in which leadership operates.[27]

Al-Jazeera's Rob Reynolds brought international attention to the 2010

Navajo presidential election when he reported Senator Lovejoy's campaign stop in Kayenta, Arizona. Reynolds reported that Lovejoy faced traditionalists and men who refused to vote for a woman. "Nontraditionalists" who supported Lovejoy thought that as president she might address critical issues such as the epidemic of violence toward Navajo women.[28] The coverage noted some traditionalists' fears that if Lovejoy were elected, the natural world would show its disapproval with natural disasters. At the same time, as the title of the news sources suggested, the election of a woman to the presidency would most presumably bring resolution to epidemic domestic violence that Navajo women faced. Associated Press reporter Felicia Fonseca also followed the story of Lovejoy's campaign and noted, "No woman has served as Navajo president, although the matriarchal society has strong reverence for women as caretakers and heirs to everything from homesite leases to sheep. When introducing themselves, Navajos start with their mother's clan name."[29]

In several news stories, Phil Bluehouse and Anthony Lee, who are members of the Navajo Medicine Men's Association, shared their views on the prospects of a woman becoming Navajo Nation president. Bluehouse asserted that there are distinctive leadership differences between a man and a woman. "A woman is nurturing," said Bluehouse, adding, "Women aren't as ambitious as men." Bluehouse's criticism of the tribal administration echoed the sentiments of other Navajo citizens, including those by Maynard Becenti of Window Rock, Arizona, who said: "I just wanted to see a change. I wanted to see what a woman could do," and "I don't have any gripes with a woman leading."[30] However, Anthony Lee declared that, traditionally, Navajo men and women were separated by job duties. Women were expected to be leaders in domesticity: household chores, cooking, cleaning, caring for children, and butchering. Men were separated as leaders in hunting, livestock labor, and politics. The president of the Navajo Medicine Men's Association, Lee offered that a woman in the race "is yet another sign that Navajo people aren't following tradition established by Navajo deities in which men are public leaders and women are the backbone of the matriarchal society."[31] Based on egalitarianism, women's rightful place was in the domestic sphere, and just as custom limits women's roles in traditional ceremonies, so too should women follow proscriptions about domestic and public spheres. Lee noted that based on traditional precepts, the association, which is made up of Navajo medicine men and women, had collectively endorsed Ben Shelly, Lovejoy's opposition. Days after the Tuesday election, when it was certain that Ben Shelly had won the presidency, a flyer came to me via e-mail, one that no doubt had been circulating in the weeks before the general election. The flyer warned about the chaos that would ensue if Lynda Lovejoy were elected president of the Navajo Nation. Contact information included a phone number for Anthony Lee. In the aftermath of the election, with Ben Shelly garnering 52 percent of the votes, Erny Zah described how many Navajos positioned the issue of gender in the tribal elections, "Many voters expressed it not as gender inferiority, but rather the different roles that Navajo culture has traditionally assigned men and women." Alberta Bunny, forty-two, helped to elect Ben Shelly to the Navajo presidency because of her mother's advice, saying, "I voted for [Ben] Shelly. . . . [Men's] words tend to be more [important than] women's." "That's what my mom says," she said.[32] What exactly the difference across gender will bring to the Navajo presidency, however, is never developed, and the disavowal that women should not be leaders in the Navajo Nation government suggests that Western conceptualizations of gender and difference mark how many Navajos are understanding Navajo concepts of gender difference. Traditional gender roles, then, are always also a matter of how and why they are understood in particular ways in a present shaped by the experience of colonialism.

The ways in which national media have structured attention on the question of tradition and gender discrimination is mostly understood within American gender politics where gender equality remains central. Such understandings have also shaped the refusal of feminism by women of color, including many Native women. For example, declarations by Navajo women such as poet Laura Tohe exemplify Native peoples' rejection of feminisms because it's said that Navajo and Native women are already enmeshed in communities where traditional values assign them a significant amount of authority and autonomy.[33] Unfortunately, such positioning, while laudatory about the traditional roles of Navajo women, fails to engage with the ongoing consequences of colonialism, which have been devastating for Navajo women.

Navajo voters' remarks, intended as criticism at the current tribal administration, whose members faced charges of fraud and various ethics violations, reflect contemporary tribal national news and feminist scholarship that sought to address sustained criticism levied at some of the first Native women to become chair or president of their tribal nations, including Wilma Mankiller. As the history of the establishment of modern tribal governments indicates, women were not seen as agents in the political realm because the foundation of U.S. federal Indian policies was premised on patriarchy. Certainly the earliest studies of Navajo government and leadership made scant notice of women's political influence or leadership.[34] Given that tribal governments and their leadership were almost exclusively male dominated, the appearance of women who sought to be chairwomen and presidents of their nations brought about discussions about what feminine qualities would bring to leadership. In focusing on these topics, discussions have emphasized how gender is most often addressed in American and Native American scholarship, where that attainment of gender equality is seen as a marker of a superior civilization and progress. For example, Denise Lajimodiere interviewed nine Native women about their experiences in leadership and asked them to speak about the components that allowed them to be successful. Lajimodiere noted that all of the women had faced race and gender discrimination at different times. Overall, this study's objective was to make visible Native women leaders and to offer advice about success to the next generation of Native women aspiring to be leaders in their nations and communities.[35] Thus, questions around Native women and tribal leadership emphasize essentialized gender qualities and the need to achieve gender equality and have been the basis for a rejection of white feminisms.[36]

Perspectives that essentialize gender qualities and question the benefits of women's leadership because of their femininity highlight the failure to scrutinize the links between tribal nations and the status of Native women, because as feminist scholars Anne McClintock and Veena Das point out, analysis of the transformations of women's roles within the structure of modern nations are still emerging. Das's argument illuminates how the construction of nation assigns men to the political community and women to the domestic so that naming certain practices of home as violent are difficult.[37] McClintock points out not only that women are implicated in nation building, for they are producers—biologically, culturally, and symbolically—but importantly, that the language of nation is often conflated with Western concepts of family so that the ways in which the modern nations are constituted have been naturalized where gender relations are hierarchical. Nations are "frequently figured through the iconography of familial and domestic space" so that the family offers a "'natural' figure for sanctioning social hierarchy within a putative organic unity of interest" and offers a "'natural' trope for figuring historical time." McClintock goes on to note the effects of naturalizing the shape of nation through the language of family: "The metaphoric depiction of social hierarchy as natural and familial—the 'national' family, the global 'family of nations,' the colony as a 'family of black children ruled over by a white father'—thus depended on the prior naturalizing of the social subordination of women and children within the domestic sphere." The nation and the family appear as reservoirs of inherent meaning that must be honored and obeyed.

McClintock's analysis of the social and political subordination of women and children within the domestic sphere of nation building through language and the processes of culture can be applied to Navajo nation building. Such configurations obscure the specific ways that gender operates in nation building and that "tradition" is remade through particular discursive practices, making it difficult to address the structures that keep intact oppression, violence, and inequalities.[38] For example, Raymond Austin's examination of how the Navajo Nation has worked to return to traditional principles as part of government reform illuminates how gender relationships are shaped by the language of nation and family. In *Navajo Courts and Navajo Common Law*, he explicates the Navajo government's historical efforts to resist the imposition of foreign American concepts of justice and leadership by showing how fundamental principles of Navajo philosophy have been applied by Navajo justices in the domestic and civil courts. Through a discussion of specific Navajo concepts such as *K'é*, concepts of relationships, and their application to Navajo social organization, Austin makes strong arguments for the use of Navajo principles as a method to return to a society based on traditional precepts. Although Austin's efforts in this regard are commendable, it is also necessary to note troubling questions around nation and gender. In his treatment, Austin acknowledges historically that women had political presence, but the Anglo form of power, hierarchical and coercive, has resulted in the silence of women in governance. He notes that traditionally, when the people returned from their forced removal to a concentration camp at Fort Sumner, New Mexico, to their homelands, "the primary task of rebuilding—or, more appropriately, nation rebuilding—fell to the traditional Navajo leaders and other men and women who came to prominence in the later 1880s and early 1890s."[39] Traditional leaders consulted respected elders, *hastói* (elder men) and *sáanii* (elder women), on behalf of their bands, the form of political units that Navajos practiced before American contact.[40] However, because Austin's study is focused on domestic and civil courts, gender is examined only within the realm of domestic issues, including questions of legitimate Navajo identity, the validity of traditional Navajo marriages and divorces, domestic violence, and other matters related to the domestic sphere. Austin argues, "The home could also be said to be the source of Navajo Nation sovereignty and Navajo nation building, because Navajo culture, knowledge, language, spirituality, identity, and all things that compose the Navajo Nation flow outwards from inside the Hogan."[41]

Of marriages, the jurist declares that marriage has always been between one man and one woman: "Using a traditional analysis, the assertion that a Navajo man can be married to two women simultaneously is inaccurate because by custom a man could not marry another woman in a traditional wedding ceremony while he was married to his present wife." However, prior to this statement, Austin acknowledges that traditionally, although not prevalently, men had "more than one wife."[42] Discussions around Navajo nation building and the conflation of nation with the "natural" order of family, where men are placed in hierarchy to women, which Austin does not examine, deserve to be scrutinized and need to be historicized, especially because the modern nation as a structure is relatively new and the United States, in particular, is less than 250 years old. Thus, the idea of nation and the nuclear family are relatively recent ideas. Further, anthropologist Elizabeth Povinelli argues that settler nations, including the United States, embraced indigenous cultural values and practices only when they did not violate Western sensibilities and only if traditional practices could be incorporated into the multicultural narrative of diversity and belonging.[43] This one-sided approach to accommodation makes Navajo traditional practices appear comprehensible to and commensurate with Western understandings while actually making differences that have not been incorporated increasingly difficult to address.

TRADITIONAL NARRATIVES AND NAVAJO LEADERSHIP

As the presidential candidates crisscrossed Navajoland, they included appearances at the regional fairs. At the Tuba City fair in October, as Senator Lovejoy waved at the throngs of Diné who lined the parade route, she heard a woman yell, "Women belong in the kitchen!" Journalist Daniel Kraker's report included part of an interview with *hataalii* (healer) Eunice Manson. According to Kraker, as he stood among the throng of parade-goers at the Tuba City fair to interview Navajo citizens about their views of a woman possibly becoming president, Eunice Manson sent another Navajo woman over to him to interpret for her. Manson sought to share her perspectives on the matter in a national forum. Although Manson's interview with Kraker was extensive and layered with multiple meanings, neither the interpreter nor the reporter was able to provide a meaningful context for mainstream consumption. Neither was Kraker able to provide any sort of understanding about traditional perspectives on gender in Navajo society.

Through an interpreter, Eunice Manson introduced herself, saying that she was from Dził Hajiin (Black Mesa), and named her clans. As a *hataalii*, Eunice performed the Blessingway and several other ceremonies, including the Emergence Way. She had learned the ceremonies from her uncle, who had also given her the story of a time when a woman had declared herself to be a *naat'áanii*—the leader. Manson shared a version of the "Separation of the Sexes," in which during the time of creation, a woman, who was the wife of a *naa'táanii*, had declared herself to be a *naa'táanii*—a leader. She was lying to her husband and going to the river to have sex with another man. Suspicious, her husband followed her to the river, where he saw his wife with the other man. Incensed, he argued with his wife, whereupon she complained to her mother. The mother-in-law grew angry with her son-in-law and declared that men were not necessary to making life. Her declarations led to the men moving away from the women. As a result of their separation from the men, the women indulged in all sorts of sinful sexual acts, which led to their giving birth to monsters. In strong words, Manson predicted that if a woman became a naa'táanii, the Diné women would once again give "birth to monsters." She cautioned that traditional proscriptions must be followed especially in light of the American wars in the Middle East. Manson urged that a woman not be elected a leader of the Navajo Nation because "our children are fighting a war" and we would be overcome by the enemy if we did not heed traditional warnings. Manson's connections between traditional proscriptions about proper gender roles and the American imperial war in the Middle East highlights the ways in which Navajos, regardless of positions in their society, are not immune to U.S. narratives about itself as exceptional or its claims to moral authority in the world. After Manson delivered her lengthy interview, she acknowledged that other medicine people did not fully agree with her prophecy about the dire consequences of electing a woman as president and that her children often asked her to desist. Nevertheless, Manson declared, she was obligated to deliver her warnings based on what she has been taught about traditional narratives and proper gender roles.

The cultural context for the warnings from the natural world about proper gender roles and relationships pivoted around cultural constructions where much of the Navajo world is presented as feminine and masculine. For example, this duality is noted with the earth symbolized as feminine and reflected in the roles of mothers as the creators of life and nurturers. The sky is symbolized as masculine and reflected in the roles of men as the protectors, warriors, and the natural leaders in the public sphere. Further, the hogan (Navajo for "home") is also feminine and masculine space but considered the domain of women. The body itself is also represented as having the duality of masculine and feminine, for as human beings, we are birthed as a result of the sexual mingling of men and women. Thus, the left side of our bodies represents the masculine and the right side represents the feminine. This duality, then, reflects Navajo ideals about what gender relationships should be: the feminine and the masculine are both crucial to the survival of the people and the perpetuation of traditional values and practice.

However, it must also be noted that the ways in which space is configured as domestic and public have been shaped by Western democratic notions, which may not align with Navajo concepts of gender and space. The earliest American observers of Navajo gender relations expressed confusion, dismay, and alarm that Navajo men did not appear to know how to control their women and suggested that they had been effectively emasculated by their failure to assert themselves as a patriarchy.[44] For the most part, non-Indian attention to Navajo gender politics focused on gender equality as a democratic ideal. Attention to the presidential election and the question of gender should also be seen as engagements with the consequences of colonialism as Navajos grappled with the epidemic violence toward women and how traditional values might bring about harmony and balance.

As Navajo studies scholars point out, because Navajo society is matrilineal, identity begins with women, and all relationships revolve around matrilineal clans. Women, then, are positioned to speak and act on matters that often are not seen as part of the domestic sphere. For example, matrilineal clans, headed by elder women, make decisions about land use and tenure, and women owned hogans and planting fields and have authority over children.[45] Historically, women as weavers and livestock owners were directly involved in economic commerce that supported their families.[46] Women also were esteemed for the ceremonial and sacred knowledge they held, which is most evident in their roles as weavers. Further, as Dana Powell and Dáilan Long argue, because Navajo women have authority over the domestic, which includes Mother Earth, women have formed the backbone of the leadership that has challenged U.S. colonial policies around the ongoing appropriation of Navajo natural resources. Powell and Long, in particular, show that gender binaries in Navajo society do not necessarily mirror those of American society.[47] Women's places in Navajo society, then, expanded beyond Western assumptions about what constitutes the domestic sphere.

Creation narratives not only delineate proper gender roles but also indicate what can happen if the rules are not followed. The story of the separation of the sexes, which is the one most referenced during the course of the 2010 presidential election, suggests that if men and women do not follow the traditional directives about proper gender roles, there will be chaos and confusion in the world. Rather, both should work together to ensure the survival of the people and maintain harmony. Although there are different versions, the narrative of the separation of the sexes is about a time during the creation when men and women disputed over the superiority of their sex. After a length of time, and after each side engaged in prohibited activities, the men and women were reconciled and agreed to work with each other. Notably, in some versions, when the men left after the disagreement between First Man and First Woman, the hermaphrodite, the *Ná'dleehí*, left with the men to perform the domestic duties such as cooking. In some versions, the *Ná'dleehí* also took care of the men's sexual desires. The *Ná'dleehí* is attributed with the duty of bringing about reconciliation between men and women. The narrative also indicates the presence of third or multiple genders that Navajos acknowledged, although this aspect of the story was not discussed in the debates surrounding the allegations that Rex Lee Jim is gay. As a reporter related, many Navajos cited the narrative to support the belief that women should not run for the presidency of the Navajo Nation. For example, Navajo voter James Henderson avowed that traditionalists were against having a woman as president of the nation and related a version of the separation of the sexes to support his claim: "in the distant past when Navajo women went to live on the other side of a river. There they tried to make a go of it but in the end the women had no place to go so they had to ask for help from men"; he continued, "At that time, the women promised that they would never try to go ahead of the men again." Henderson stressed, "People are listening to the medicine men and the traditionalists."[48] But the separation of the sexes has too many versions and interpretations to be invoked definitively in this manner. The role of the *Ná'dleehí*, for instance, suggests that normative Western gender roles may not be as self-evident in the narrative as certain tellings assume.

Eunice Manson's reiteration of the separation is not adequately contextualized for Kraker, and once again, non-Navajo constructions of gender relations are reinscribed. The Navajo woman who agreed to translate Manson's story informed Kraker, "There is a lot in the story." The tenor of her voice suggests that she is at a loss as to how to proceed, not because she does not understand the story, or that she cannot adequately translate, but more likely because providing the non-Navajo reporter with a cultural context would take considerable time. Perhaps as is true of other instances where creation narratives are invoked to make statements about the present, the retelling of the story became an opportunity to comment on the status of the Navajo Nation and its leaders; it is significant that the debates indicate the vibrancy of oral tradition and suggest that the retelling of these traditional narratives are linked to contemporary concerns. As the Cree historian Winona Wheeler notes about oral traditions, many times these stories may seem to lack specific teachings, but those who have an understanding of the stories and their nuances will draw lessons from them, for these stories offer moments to reflect on the state of the world.[49] For many Diné, the question of whether a woman should be president offered moments to comment on a perceived crisis in Navajo leadership, the state of the Navajo Nation, gender relationships, and the status of women. Further, Navajo citizens followed and built on earlier efforts to find solutions to the crisis in their government in traditional narratives about gender relations and leadership.

In an earlier study on the development of the modern Navajo nation, I argued that the Navajo embracing of American national ideals of democracy and independence occurred at time when people of color were being subjected to the normative imperatives of Western democracy.[50] Throughout the world, as empires like the United States expanded their reach in order to extract resources from "underdeveloped" regions, inhabitants were expected to embrace Euro-American values. As male leaders of "underdeveloped" nations emerged, who were often installed by colonialist foreign governments, they actively led reforms where women's bodies were under surveillance and their entry into the capitalist labor force and politics was restricted in much the same way that white women's access to all aspects of the public sphere were controlled and denied.[51] In much the same way, Navajo male leaders who were installed by the U.S. federal government took on the role of their colonial oppressors by legislating women's bodies and restricting women's access to the Navajo Nation's resources and to the decision-making body. Scrutiny of the relationships between traditional narratives and the evocation of ideals about gender relationships, how history has transformed those relationships, and how traditional teachings are applied to gender relations within a modern Navajo Nation is important to illuminating the present status of Navajo women and the questions about whether or not tradition sanctions gender discrimination. How are traditional teachings utilized to legitimize the subordination of women within the Navajo Nation? What happens to gender relations at the intersections of nation, gender, and tradition? As Scott Morgensen argues, settler nations like the United States engage in forms of violence against Indigenous peoples in order to bring them under state control and especially included the surveillance of Indigenous bodies—identities, sexualities—so that by the mid-twentieth century, minorities in the United States had formed on normatively white and national terms.[52] In much the same way, a similar phenomenon is evident in the historical formation of the modern Navajo political structure as male leaders legislated proper gender roles and excluded other genders as nonnormative.

The status of Navajo women has severely diminished as evidenced by the number of stories about violence toward them, which indicates that the Navajo Nation is in a crisis.[53] Moreover, a recent comment by a fellow Diné when I brought up gender during a discussion about the troubles of the government—"Gender is not an issue"—indicates that few have yet to seriously consider how tribal nations are gendered. Lynda Lovejoy and the 2010 Navajo presidential campaign provide one opening through which to begin such a consideration. As the Diné woman translating Eunice Manson's interview intimated, too often what might appear to be self-evident to non-Navajo publics about the gendered dimensions of tradition is far more complicated or contentious than such apparent legibility allows.

NOTES

1. Daniel Kraker, "Navajo Nation Could Elect First Female President," National Public Radio. October 30, 2010. Accessed April 16, 2014. http//:www.npr.org/templates/story/story.php?storyId=13091332.
2. Marley Shebala, "vp's Charges Dropped, Deal for Prez in Works," *Navajo Times*, January 13, 2011, A-1, A-4; Marley Shebala, "Heft Bill Due for Travel Advances, Delegates Cry 'Foul,'" *Navajo Times*, December 22, 2010, A-1, A-3; Bill Donovan, "High court rejects dismissal motion in slush fund case," *Navajo Times*, March 3, 2011, A-1, A-3.
3. Bill Donovan, "Lovejoy Picks Activist, Administrator," *Navajo Times*, August 12, 2013. Accessed April 16, 2014. http://www.navajotimes.com/politics/election2010/081210lovejoy.php.
4. Bill Donovan, "Gay Remark Taps Wrong Emotions," *Navajo Times*, November 18, 2010, A-6.
5. Erny Zah, "Lovejoy Candidacy Prompts Review of Role of Diné Women," *Navajo Times*, September 4, 2010. Accessed February 25, 2011. http://www.navajotimes.com/opinions/2010/0910/090510notebook.php.
6. See, for example, Wilkinson, *Blood Struggle*; Jorgensen, *Rebuilding Native Nations*; and Harvard Project on American Indian Economic Development, *The State of*

Native Nations, among others. It is still the case that indigenous feminisms and tribal nation building are showcased in Native women and gender studies. See for example, Suzack et al., *Indigenous Women and Feminism*.

7. Wolfe, "Settler Colonialism and the Elimination of the Native."

8. Amnesty International, *Stolen Sisters* and *Maze of Injustice*.

9. Altamirano-Jiménez, "Neoliberalism, Racialised Gender and Indigeneity."

10. See, for example, Denetdale, "Securing the Navajo National Boundaries"; Denetdale, "Carving Navajo National Boundaries"; Denetdale, "Chairmen, Presidents, and Princesses"; Taylor, *Me Sexy*; Driskill, Finley, Gilley, and Morgensen, *Queer Indigenous Studies*.

11. Waziyatawin, "Colonialism on the Ground," n.d. http://waziyatawin.net/commentary/wp-content/themes/waziyatawin/colonialism.pdf.

12. Alfred, *Peace, Power, Righteousness*, 141.

13. Austin, *Navajo Courts and Navajo Common Law*, xx.

14. Barker, *Native Acts*.

15. Barker, *Native Acts*, 5–7. See also Rifkin, *When Did Indians Become Straight?*

16. Powell and Long, "Landscapes of Power."

17. Das, "Violence, Gender, and Subjectivity," 284.

18. Tsosie, "Native Women and Leadership."

19. A. Smith, *Conquest*.

20. Eisenstein, *Against Empire*, 82.

21. A. Smith, *Conquest*.

22. See, for example, Morgensen, "Settler Homonationalism."

23. Finley, "Decolonizing the Queer Native Body (and Recovering the Native Bull-Dyke)," 39.

24. Associated Press, "Navajo VP, NM Senator Seek Tribal Presidency," November 10, 2010. Accessed November 10, 2010. http://northernarizonanews.com/blog/2010/11/02/navajo-vp-nm-senator-seek-tribal-presidency/.

25. The Holy People are the Navajo people's deities and include both feminine and masculine holy beings. In the Navajo language, they are called Diyiin Diné, or Sacred Beings.

26. Mary J. Rivers, "Navajo Women and Abuse," 83–89, and McEachern, Van Winkle, and Steiner, "Domestic Violence among the Navajo."

27. One of the first writings to bring attention to Native women in tribal leadership roles was Wilma Mankiller's autobiography. Mankiller described Cherokee male leadership's responses to her becoming principal chief. See Mankiller, *Mankiller*. See Carrillo, *Readings in American Indian Law*, for a treatment of tribal governance and Native women.

28. Rob Reynolds, "Navajo Pushes for Female Rights," Carbonated.tv on u-tube. Aljazeera. Accessed April 16, 2014. http://www.carbonated.tv/news/navajo-pushes-for.

29. Felicia Fonseca, "Lynda Lovejoy Fights to be the Navajo's First Female President," October 17, 2010. Accessed October 17, 2010. http://www.stateman.com/news/nation/lynda-lovejoy-fights-to-be-the-navajos-first-97736.html.

30. Paige Buffington, "Navajo Nation Not Ready for Female President," *IAIA Chronicle*, December 7, 2010. Accessed February 25, 2011. http://iaiachronicle.com/2010/12/navajo-nation-not-ready-for-female-president/.

31. Associated Press, "Navajo VP, NM Senator Seek Tribal Presidency," November 2,

2010. Accessed April 16, 2014. http://northernarizonanews.com/blog/2010/11/02/navajo-vp-nm-senator-seek-tribal-presidency/.

32. Erny Zah, "Tradition Edges Out Change in Northern Agency," *Navajo Times*, November 3, 2010. Accessed April 16, 2014. http://www.navajotimes.com/politics/election2010/110310northern.php.
33. Tohe, "There Is No Word for Feminism."
34. See, for examples, Shepardson, *Navajo Ways in Government*; A. Williams, *Navajo Political Process*; and Link, *Navajo*.
35. Lajimodiere, "Ogimah Ikwe."
36. Jaimes and Halsey, "American Indian Women."
37. Das, "Violence, Gender, and Subjectivity."
38. Kuokkanen, "Globalization as Racialized, Sexualized Violence."
39. Austin, *Navajo Courts and Navajo Common Law*, 8, 9.
40. Austin, *Navajo Courts and Navajo Common Law*, 10.
41. Austin, *Navajo Courts and Navajo Common Law*, 159.
42. Austin, *Navajo Courts and Navajo Common Law*, 160, 161.
43. Povinelli, *The Cunning of Recognition*.
44. In my earliest studies of how Navajo women have been represented, I discovered that Navajo women's roles were difficult for non-Indians to understand because Navajo women did not behave in ways that aligned with Western notions of the feminine. See Denetdale, "Representing Changing Woman."
45. Weisiger, *Dreaming of Sheep in Navajo Country*.
46. M'Closkey, *Swept under the Rug*.
47. Powell and Long, "Landscapes of Power."
48. Bill Donovan, "Lovejoy Landslide Fails to Appear," *Navajo Times*, November 3, 2010. Accessed April 16, 2014. http://navajotimes.com/news/2010/1110/110310wrap.php.
49. Wheeler, "Indigenous Oral History in the Academy." I was fortunate to be able to attend several lectures by Winona Wheeler. Her lectures on the vitality of Native oral history were affirming and useful to my own research.
50. Denetdale, "Chairmen, Presidents, and Princesses."
51. Mohanty, "Cartographies of Struggle."
52. Morgensen, "Settler Homonationalism."
53. As a member of the Navajo Nation Human Rights Commission, during my first year on the commission, in 2011, I was gratified to have the commission, under the direction of executive director Leonard Gorman and chair of the commission Duane Chili Yazzie, host a public hearing to determine the amount and nature of violence toward Navajo women. It was a day where many came to share their testimonies. The narratives and reports indicated that the violence is epidemic.

13 VICENTE L. RAFAEL

Translation, American English, and the National Insecurities of Empire

The United States as an imperial power shares with its European prede-cessors a set of common ideas. Among other things, these include the insistent association of empire with a civilizing order (broadly conceived) directed at quelling the barbarism of native societies (crudely put), hence of conquest and exploitation with salvation (both in its religious and secu-lar senses), and of colonial occupation sustained by military interventions with the evangelical-like spread of universal truths.[1] As with previous em-pires, the United States has relied on an extensive state apparatus, includ-ing an ever growing military machine whose maintenance requires vast sums of money to govern and exploit its colonial holdings. Bureaucracies and militaries, however, have never been sufficient to hold on to occupied territories or to influence nominally sovereign ones from a distance. The use of force always has had to be supplemented, indeed rationalized, by securing the consent of the occupied. Thus has it always been necessary not only to subjugate territories and peoples; it has also been imperative to co-opt and appropriate the very way of life of their inhabitants: their language, their beliefs, their desires. Such an appropriation has entailed a double process: on the one hand, conversion from below, that is, transform-ing the colonized culture in ways that make it receptive to and dependent on a power at once above and beyond them; on the other hand, conversion from above, that is, translating imperial power from a foreign into a famil-iar, everyday, but no less awesome, even transcendent force in the lives of the colonized.[2] How has this double conversion, which we can think of as a kind of translation, taken place?

Modern empires come equipped with complex infrastructures and technologies designed to expropriate not only the bodies of colonized subjects but also their souls, not just their lives but also their afterlives. In churches or schoolhouses, in printed catechisms or Hollywood movies, through the spread of Christianity or elections or capitalist markets or human rights, imperial regimes have historically sought to enforce among subject peoples the sense that their interests lie with the interests of empire, that their desires are legitimate and normal only so long as these coincide with the desires of those above them. Among the mechanisms for extracting consent and establishing hegemony, translation has come to play an extremely important role. How exactly is translation related to empire?

The United States for its part has relied on various media of communication to reach colonized populations and turn them on, in all senses of that phrase, to the imperatives of imperial control. But communication could work only if it were in a language or languages that could be understood by both colonizer and colonized. Communication in an imperial context is thus inseparable from translation insofar as each moment of encounter between and among occupiers and occupied entails the mediation of signs, intentions, and meanings from one language into another. Put differently, imperialism brings into startling and often violent contact different languages and the various life worlds they imply. Responding to the sudden and recurring emergence of cultural and linguistic differences, translation seeks to parry the shock of strange signs and unintelligible speech. It attempts to render the foreign into the familiar even as it tries to make the familiar available to the foreign. It therefore assumes the power of mediation vital to the commerce between and among rulers and ruled. To the extent that translation is conscripted to play an enabling role in consolidating empire, its practice grows out of specific ideas about language and what it means to communicate, what it means to mean, and who gets to decide when something is meaningful or not. In a word, translation in colonial contexts (but no doubt in all other social situations) is predicated on dominant signifying conventions at home that are believed to extend abroad. It is in this sense that we can think of translation as a mediating power that bears an ideological form. That is to say, the workings of translation are shaped by ideas regarding the nature of language and its role in conveying the structures of social power. However, to say that translation is ideological is also to see it is as irreducibly political, which is to say, at odds with its ideological moorings. What do I mean by this, that translation is simultaneously ideological and political?

Translation is political to the extent that it betrays its ideological context in both senses of that word. As a practical act that arises from the contingent and fluid encounter with different languages and their speakers, the work of translation tends to exceed, if not undercut, dominant assumptions about the proper exchange of meanings and the transport of intentions. As we all know, there can never be such a thing as a perfect translation that establishes exact equivalents between and within languages. In its very imperfection and errancy, translation can take on a political significance. Its shortcomings and excesses vis-à-vis the original potentially puts in crisis the interpretation and circulation of meaning as well as the authority of the original and its author. But translation also remains tied to the ideological. To the extent that translation can be marshaled to reproduce conventions of signification that tend to domesticate the otherness of the other, it sutures rather than dwells on differences. It reduces—for this is a common synonym for translation—the foreign into the familiar, establishing the rule of the original over its copies, of the singular Word of those above over the varied, multiple words of those below. Translation hence is Janus-faced. It is divided not only between the irreconcilable demands between a faithful and free rendition of the original, but also between the tendency to reproduce as much as to resist the dominant conventions of meaning and signification. Nowhere is this tension between the ideology and the politics of translation more apparent than in the history of empire. In what follows, I argue that in the context of the U.S. empire, translation has been harnessed as an instrument for reproducing and safeguarding the signifying conventions of empire even as it simultaneously works to dislodge such notions, producing instead unanticipated effects.

TRANSLATION AND EMPIRE

Addressing a gathering of university presidents attending a conference at the State Department on January 5, 2006, then president George W. Bush spoke of the country's dire need for translators to shore up national security. He promised to spend $114 million to expand the teaching of so-called critical languages such as Arabic, Farsi, Chinese, and so forth at the university as well as K–12 levels as part of a new federal program called the National Security Language Initiative. The president then illustrated the importance of learning such languages in the following way: "In order to convince people we care about them, we've got to understand their culture and show them we care about their culture. You know, when somebody comes to me and speaks Texan, I know they appreciate Texas culture. When somebody takes time to figure out how to speak Arabic, it means they're interested in somebody else's culture. . . . We need intelligence officers who when somebody says something in Arabic or Farsi or Urdu, know what they're talking about."[3]

Bush's view on the learning of foreign languages, however crudely phrased, reflects certain ideas about translation and empire that have a long history. Since the Spanish conquest and religious conversion of the native peoples of the New World and the Pacific, various projects of translation have enabled as much as they have disabled the spread of European empires. Spanish missionaries, for example, labored to Christianize native peoples in the Americas and the Pacific by preaching in the local languages while retaining Latin and Castilian as languages of ritual and rule. British philologists codified Indian languages to spread and consolidate imperial power and, in a similar vein, French and Belgian missionaries and colonial administrators seized on Swahili as an instrument for establishing knowledge of and control over Central Africa in the late nineteenth and early twentieth century.[4]

In this chapter, I want to focus on the United States to show not so much its similarities with and differences from earlier empires—though such comparisons are implicit throughout—but to delineate the historical specificity of a nationalist idea of translation in the making of an American empire. Can thinking about translation contribute to understanding the history of the United States in relation to the spread of its power overseas? In particular, what role does American English as the national language of rule and allegiance have in shaping American ideas about the translation and, by extension, assimilation of foreign languages and their speakers? What are the limits of this American notion of translation as assimilation? At what point does such a connection fail? And what are the consequences of such a failure for thinking about America's imperial presence in the world?

To address these questions, let me return briefly to Bush's remarks above. In referring to his language as "Texan," Bush in fact indexes the centrality of English in mapping America's place in the world. Perhaps said half in jest, his reference to "Texan" as his native idiom, nonetheless, makes it seem as if it is also a kind of alien tongue analogous to Arabic, Farsi, and Chinese. Like them, it would call for translation. But if Arabic, Urdu, and Chinese are functionally equivalent to Texan, they could also be construed merely as dialectical variations of the universal lingua franca, which no doubt is imagined by Bush to be English. By placing these languages in a series so that they all appear equally foreign, the president reduces their singularity. Setting aside their incommensurability, he sees them all terminating in English. He thereby evacuates foreign languages of their foreignness. From this perspective, learning one language is no different from learning another in that they are all meant to refer to English. In this way, all speech comes to be assimilated into a linguistic hierarchy, subsumed within the hegemony of an imperial lingua franca. The strangeness of "Arabic," "Farsi," etc., like that of "Texan," can be made to yield to a domesticating power that would render these languages wholly comprehensible to English speakers and available for conveying American meanings and intentions. As supplements to English, so-called critical languages are thought to be transparent and transportable instruments for the insinuation and imposition of America's will to power.[5]

The systematic instrumentalization of foreign languages to serve nationalist ends runs far and deep in American thinking. It is evident, for example, in the discourse of the Department of Defense. Recent documents such as the *Defense Language Transformation Roadmap* describe knowledge of foreign languages as "an emerging core competency of our twenty-first century Total Force." The ability to translate is deemed "an essential war-fighting skill," part of the "vital force capabilities for mission accomplishment." In this regard, critical languages, or what are sometimes referred to as "Global War on Terrorism languages," can only exist as part of a "critical weapons system." As a "war-fighting skill," translation is thus weaponized for the sake of projecting American power abroad while insuring security at home. Such sentiments circulate as common sense in official circles regardless of political affiliations. Hence it is not surprising that Senator Daniel Akaka, a liberal Democrat and chair of the oversight committee on Homeland Security, should state in a recent congressional hearing, "We know that proficiency in other languages is critical to ensuring our national security. The inability of law enforcement officers [and] intelligent officers . . . to intercept information from [foreign] sources . . . presents a threat to their mission and the well-being of our Nation."[6]

The current preoccupation with foreign-language proficiency has its roots in the Cold War. In 1958, Congress passed the National Defense Education Act (NDEA) in response to what it called an "educational emergency." In the midst of widespread anxieties about the threat posed by Soviet scientific advances such as the launching of the Sputnik satellite, the NDEA provided funding for the development of what Congress referred to as "those skills essential to national defense." Such skills included knowledge of what even then were already referred to as "critical languages." These were to be taught in area studies programs newly established in various universities and colleges. From the point of view of the state, the teaching of foreign languages was not about eroding the primacy of English. It was rather the reverse. Programs for the study of "critical languages" tended to be limited to graduate students and a smaller number of undergraduates. They were designed to create area studies experts whose knowledge of other cultures would help to shore up "our way of life," where, naturally, English held unchallenged supremacy.[7] We might paraphrase the logic of the law this way: By fostering the ability to translate, "we" make use of the foreigner's language in order to keep their native speakers in their proper place. In learning their language, "we" therefore do not wish to be any less "Americans," but in fact to be more so. For "we" do not speak a foreign language in order to be like them, that is, to assimilate into the culture of their native speakers. Instead, we do so because "we" want to protect ourselves from them and to insure that they remain safely within our reach whether inside or outside our borders.

From this brief historical sketch, we can glean the rough outlines of the state's interest in foreign languages—interests which, I hasten to add, did not always coincide with those of individual area studies scholars. To begin with, a nationalist imperative linked to an imperial project not surprisingly has governed the programmatic teaching of foreign languages. Translation can be useful to the extent that it responds to this imperative. It is possible then to begin to see an American notion of translation, at least as it is articulated from above and ratified, though unevenly, from below. Such a notion turns on at least four assumptions. First, there is the belief that language as such is merely an instrument of communication subservient to human control. It is thus considered to be no more than a malleable media for conveying human ideas and intentions, as if ideas and intentions could exist outside their material constitution in writing and speech. Second is the belief that languages are inherently unequal in their ability to communicate, and as such, they can be arranged into a hierarchy, for example, "critical" over "less critical" languages, depending on their utility and reach. In the U.S. context, American English as I mentioned earlier (and which I will return to later) has been deemed exceptionally suited above all other languages for conveying all things exceptionally American to the citizens of the country and to the rest of the world. Third, there is the belief that given the exceptional qualities of American English as a kind of universal lingua franca, all other languages ought to be reducible to its terms and thereby assimilable into the national linguistic hierarchy. And fourth, this process of reduction is believed to be precisely the task of translation. In times of emergency, translation is pressed to mobilize foreign languages as parts of a "complex weapons system" with which to secure America's borders even as it globalizes the nation's influence.

The U.S. state thus sees the relative value of foreign languages in relation to their usefulness in the defense of the nation. Their translation is meant to inoculate American citizens from foreign threats. Through translation, foreign languages furnish the tools with which to understand and domesticate what is alien and unfamiliar. In this way, they are charged with the job of keeping America at home in the world. In the official, and arguably popular imaginary, the foreign can be recognized only when it is subordinate to the domestic. It follows that the apprehension of alien tongues can amount only to their conversion into appendages of a common national speech, English.

AMERICANIZING ENGLISH

The relationship between the task of translation and the privileged place of English in the United States has a complex history. From its beginnings, the United States had always been a polyglot country.[8] While the majority of European settlers were English speaking, there had always been sizeable communities of non-Anglophones. By the late eighteenth century, over one-fourth of the white population spoke a language other than English. In Pennsylvania alone, there were sufficiently large numbers of German speakers that Benjamin Franklin thought of publishing his first newspaper in that language, the *Philadelphische Zeitung* (1732), and another founding father, Benjamin Rush, even put forth the idea of establishing German-language colleges. Additionally, Dutch and French were spoken in various parts of the early Republic and so, too, were hundreds of Native American languages both in and outside the Union. There is also ample evidence to show that enslaved Africans in resisting their abject condition continued to speak their native languages well into the nineteenth century, or in the case of Muslim Africans, knew Arabic, even as Americanized Africans developed a creolized version of English.[9] Continental expansion by way of purchase and war throughout the nineteenth century incorporated large numbers of non-Anglophone groups into the Union, such as French and Spanish speakers in the Northeast, South, and Southwest, while the Treaty of Guadalupe-Hidalgo in 1848 was interpreted to mean that Mexicans who had chosen to stay in the newly annexed areas of the California and New Mexico territories retained the right to use Spanish in the public sphere. In the wake of the wars of 1898, the colonization of Puerto Rico in the Caribbean; of Hawai'i, Guam, and other islands in the Pacific; and of the Philippines in Southeast Asia, where as many as eighty languages are spoken, along with Spanish added to the linguistic complexity of the United States. In addition, waves of immigration from East, South, and Southeast Asia, Eastern and southern Europe, Scandinavia, Africa, the Caribbean, and the Middle East through the last 250 years have further intensified the nation's linguistic mix. Indeed, one can wander around large metropolitan areas like New York, Los Angeles, Chicago, or Seattle today without having to hear or speak English. As the Canadian scholar Marc Shell once remarked, "if ever there were a polyglot place on the globe, other than Babel's spire, the US is it."[10]

It is important to note, however, that this history of linguistic diversity has unfolded alongside a history of insisting that the United States has always been, was meant to be, and must forever remain a monolingual nation. John Jay, for example, writes in *The Federalist Papers*, "Providence has been pleased to give this one connected country to one united people, a people descended from the same ancestors, speaking the same language, professing the same religion."[11] Conceived as Anglophone by Divine dispensation, "America" is understood here to be a unitary formation, where language, religion, and kinship are seamlessly woven into each other. Still, in the aftermath of the American Revolution, the fact remained that "English" was the language of the British colonizer. It could not become the language of the new Republic without first being transformed, or better yet, translated, into a distinctly American idiom. Postcolonial figures such as John Adams, Noah Webster, and Benjamin Franklin felt that British English bore all the hallmarks of the decadence of its native speakers. Unlike the English of Milton, Locke, and Shakespeare, the British English of the 1780s, Americans thought, was in a state of serious decline. "Taste is corrupted by luxury," Webster intoned, "utility is a forgotten pleasure; genius is buried in dissipation or prostituted to exalt and to damn contending factions."[12] For postcolonial Americans then, there was a pressing need to "improve and perfect" English, to remake it into something wholly American. At stake was nothing less than the very survival and progress of the nation.

John Adams, for example, wrote optimistically about the prospects of this new American language. It would be destined to become, like Latin, "the language of the world," furnishing "universal connection and correspondence with all nations."[13] Once Americanized, English would serve as the medium for imparting the exemplary nature of the nation abroad. It would also serve as the means for cultivating a democratic citizenry. According to Adams, the "refinement" and "improvement" of the English language was essential in a democracy where "eloquence will become the instrument for recommending men to their fellow-men, and the principle means of advancement through various ranks and offices."[14] In a society where aristocratic filiations no longer mattered, "eloquence," or a certain facility with the national language, would be an important way of making and remaking reputations and delineating social distinctions.

Early American concerns with the transformation of English echoed in some ways long-standing European attempts at reforming vernacular languages in the wake of the hegemony of Latin. As early as the momentous year of 1492, for example, the Spanish humanist Antonio de Nebrija, in the preface of his grammar of the Castilian language, wrote that "language is the perfect instrument of empire." Looking back at Antiquity, Nebrija concluded that "language was always the companion of empire; therefore, it follows that together they begin, grow, and flourish and together they fall." Securing Castilian hegemony in the Iberian Peninsula and spreading it overseas would thus require the codification of the Castilian language.[15]

In eighteenth-century England, political, commercial, and imperial expansion led to calls for linguistic reform with the view of establishing a "systematized doctrine of correctness."[16] Various attempts were made to standardize spelling and punctuation along with the codification of grammar in order to lend to English the uniformity necessary for governing all spheres of life. In part, this search for linguistic regularity grew out of a widespread anxiety among English writers that their language had been on the decline from the standards of Latin and earlier English writing. Jonathan Swift complained in 1712, "From the civil war to this present time I am apt to doubt whether the corruptions in our language have not at least equaled the refinements to it." And John Dryden remarked that the inadequacies of English in his time forced him to first think in Latin as way of arriving at the proper English expression. John Locke, in *An Essay Concerning Human Understanding*, warned that one of the dangers to forging contracts was the "doubtful and uncertain use of Words, or (which is the same) indetermined Ideas, which they are made to stand for." Thus, the need to "purify" English and guard against its "degeneration" from arbitrary foreign borrowings and idiomatic "barbarisms" was inseparable from securing the social contract on the basis of a commonly understood language of consent. So did Samuel Johnson regard his task in writing his dictionary as one of "refin[ing] our language to grammatical purity [and] clear[ing] it from colloquial barbarisms, licentious idioms, and irregular combinations." The "purification" of English would allow the English themselves to "ascertain" and "perfect" its use. Such would lead, Joseph Priestly wrote, to the spread of "their powers and influence abroad, and their arts, sciences and liberty at home."[17] These projects of linguistic reform tied to the imperatives of both domestic order and imperial expansion clearly influenced American postcolonials such as Noah Webster in their efforts to, as he saw it, "redeem" English from the "degradations" of empire.[18]

For Noah Webster, the Revolution that overthrew British imperial authority should also continue with the overthrow of its linguistic standards. "As an independent nation," he wrote in 1789, "our honor requires us to have a system of our own, in language as well as in government. Great Britain whose children we are, and whose language we speak, should no longer be our standard, for the taste of her writers is already corrupted and her language on the decline."[19] Ridding "ourselves" of a corrupt state necessitated purifying its "corrupt" speech. Hence, while "we" have abandoned the mother, we can retain the mother tongue only if it can be reformed and turned into "our" national language. The emergence of this revitalized American English, Webster speculated, would prove to be momentous. In the face of its inevitable advance "all other languages [spoken in the country] will waste away—and within a century and a half, North America will be peopled with hundreds of millions of men all speaking the same language. . . . [T]he consequence of this uniformity [of language] will be an intimacy of social intercourse hitherto unknown, and a boundless diffusion of knowledge."[20]

Webster thus envisions the national language to be poised between overcoming its origins in the "corrupt" language of empire while laying the foundation for a kind of new empire over all other languages in the Republic. Once established, this "common tongue" promised to subsume linguistic differences into what Webster calls a "uniformity." At the same time, and for the same reason, American English would foster an "intimacy of social intercourse hitherto unknown." Its telecommunicative force, that is, its capacity to bring distances up close, would conjure a perfect Union. But it would be one where polylingual realities would have to give way to a monolingual hegemony.

In his attempts to wean English from its British origins, Webster not surprisingly laid great stress in reforming by simplifying spelling in order to standardize a distinctly American pronunciation. His spellers and his dictionary (after meeting with initial resistance and ridicule) came to be widely used in schools and by the American public. Addressing the readers of his *Dictionary* as "my fellow citizens," Webster viewed his linguistic work to be part of "the common treasure of patriotic exertions." The United States emerges here as the rejection of a certain Europe, one "grown old in folly, corruption and tyranny . . . where literature is declining and human nature debased." By developing a "purity of language," this "infant Empire," as Webster calls it, would come to "promote virtue and patriotism."[21] In a similar vein, he was also concerned with correcting what he regarded as the "barbarisms" and "gross violations" that local idioms committed against English as is evident in the "vicious pronunciation which had prevailed extensively among the common people of this country."[22] He urged Americans to "unite in destroying provincial and local distinctions, in resisting the stream of corruptions that is ever flowing from ignorance and pride, and in establishing one uniform standard of elegant pronunciation." It is in the interest of protecting the language from "disfigurement" that Webster put forth his orthographic reforms in what would become his remarkably popular spelling book.[23] "Nothing but the establishment of schools and some uniformity in the use of books can annihilate differences in speaking and preserve the purity of the American tongue," Webster wrote.[24]

Like Adams's interest in the popular acquisition of eloquence, Webster's fixation on elocution and "a sameness in pronunciation" grew out of a larger political concern: that local variants of English would inevitably, no matter how small "excite ridicule—[for] a habit of laughing at the singularities of strangers is followed by disrespect; and without respect, friendship is a name, and social intercourse a mere ceremony. . . . Small causes such as a nickname or a vulgar tone in speaking have actually created a dissocial spirit between the inhabitants of a different state." Left to themselves, linguistic differences would proliferate and inflame "pride and prejudice," leading Webster to worry that without "uniformity" in speech, "our political harmony" would be at serious risk.[25]

It is possible to see in Webster's linguistic reforms a practice of translation working *within* the same language, or what some scholars have called intralingual translation.[26] We can think, for example, of such locutions as "in other words," "put differently," "that is to say," "for example," and so forth as speech acts that indicate the working of translation within the same language. In Webster, intralingual translation is two-fold. The translation of the more mannered British speech into the more straightforward American idiom occurs alongside the attempt to contain or "annihilate," as Webster puts it, dialectical variants of American English. The national language thus emerges from a kind of double translation. On the one hand, the original language is altered, its spellings "simplified" and "purified." On the other hand, what Webster referred to as the "shameful mutilations" wrought by local idioms are corrected and superseded.[27] American English as the language of "political harmony" and democratic civility requires as its condition of possibility the violent reworking of differences into sameness. The original in all its "corrupt," which is to stay stylistic, profusion, is to be sublated, while local variants, which is to say all other competing translations, are to be suppressed. Out of this prescribed supersession and suppression, a "uniformity" of speech is thought to arise, one that would underwrite the national security of the Republic. Translation within the same language thereby brings about the promise of a lingua franca connecting citizens across geographical and social divides, allowing them mobility and advancement. But it also requires the "annihilation" of differences, effecting the systematic annexation of the mother tongue and her wayward children into the governing home of a single national speech.

I want to hypothesize that the Americanization, which is to say, translation, of English into a national language popularized by Webster in his spelling books and dictionary served as an important model for dealing with foreign languages in the years to come. In the following section, I argue that the early postcolonial history of vernacularizing English offered a way to assimilate non-Anglophone languages into a linguistic hierarchy, thereby containing polylingualism within the borders of national monolingualism.

THE BABEL OF MONOLINGUALISM

In the wake of Noah Webster's reforms, it is not difficult to detect in both liberal and conservative writers a recurring insistence on the unassailable link between American English and American nationality conceived as synonymous with American democracy. One is seen to be inconceivable without the other. A common language ruling over all others is held to be the prerequisite for achieving a common life steeped in an egalitarian ethos. Non-Anglophones have long been expected by the nation and by the state— at least since the later nineteenth and twentieth century—to exchange their mother tongues for the national language in order to become full citizens.[28] Equality under the law implied—though it did not legally mandate—the inequality of languages. Non–English speakers marked as foreigners are expected to publicly set aside their first language in acknowledgement of the ever-present demand to speak the lingua franca. The priority of the latter lay in the fact that it is the language of laws and rights. In this regard, it is useful to note that American English has never been declared the official language of the United States, though a number of states have written such a provision into their own constitutions.[29] Rather, its hegemony is based precisely on the fact that it seemed to arise as a handmaiden of democracy, the lingua franca with which to claim equal protection under the law. Viewed as *the* obligatory common language, English is thus invested with an uncommon power that no other idiom has been able to match.

The systematic privileging of American English not surprisingly sustains a pattern of marginalizing the mother tongues of native peoples and non-Anglophone immigrants alike. At the best of times and places, such marginalization might give rise to a liberal tolerance for bilingualism, whereby the first language is seen as a way of bridging the speaker's transition to English. Within the context of this liberal view, the retention of the mother tongue is a means with which to soften the shocks of assimilation. Rather than as an alternative, the native language is regarded like any other foreign language: as an instrument for consolidating the dominant place of English.[30] In times of crisis and war, however, the marginalization of non-Anglophone languages tend to give rise to urgent calls for either the rapid assimilation or expulsion of their speakers. For instance, we read in the annual report of the federal commissioner of Indian affairs in 1887 a great animosity toward native languages commonly held by whites. In the interest of crushing Indian resistance and producing among them a "sameness of sentiment and thought," the commissioner urged that "their barbarous dialects should be blotted out and the English language substituted." It was only through English that Native Americans, rendered irredeemably foreign in the eyes of white settlers, could be converted into real Americans, "acquir[ing] a knowledge of the Constitution and their rights and duties there under." For unlike Indian languages, which were regarded as "utterly useless," English was seen as "the language of the greatest and most powerful enterprising nationality beneath the sun [sic] . . . which approaches nearer than any other nationality to the perfect protection of its people."[31] In the name of maintaining this "perfect protection," translation would not only substitute the first for a second language but obliterate the former and presumably the very cultures that it sustained.

In a similar vein, Theodore Roosevelt wrote in 1917 about the danger of harboring immigrants who, by virtue of speaking a foreign language, were most likely "paying allegiance to a foreign power." Riding the wave of anti-immigrant hysteria directed particularly at German speakers that swept the country amid the First World War, Roosevelt explicitly links the question of language to national security: "We have room for but one language here, and that is the English language. . . . It would be not merely a misfortune but a crime to perpetuate differences of language in this country." For Roosevelt, the "crime" of allowing linguistic diversity to prosper would result in opening up the country to foreign agents who in their comings and goings would transform America into a "huge polyglot boarding-house." Doing so would subvert the very idea of America as a "crucible [that] must melt all who are cast in it . . . into one American mould." As "children of the crucible," Americans were the products of "the melting pot of life in this free land," where "all the men and women of all nations who come hither emerge as Americans and nothing else. . . . Any force which attempts to retard that assimilative process is a force hostile to the highest interest of the country."[32] English of course would be the measure and means of assimilation. Being "American and nothing else" meant speaking English and nothing else. Roosevelt thus situates the monolingual citizen on the side of national identity and security. But in doing so, he also places him or her in relation to the menacing presence of his or her shadowy other: the polyglot foreigner whose uncertain allegiance and rootless existence make it into a dangerous enemy.

In the context of this militant monolingualism, we sense how the work of translation was geared to go in only one direction: toward the transformation of the foreign into an aspect of the domestic, and thus of the plurality of native tongues into the imperious singularity of a national one. The imperative of assimilation underlay the substitution of languages so that translation was ordered not only toward the subordination of the original but to its outright abandonment. But there is something more. Roosevelt and those who follow in his wake—for example, the "100 percent American" nativists of the early twentieth century, the advocates of the official English constitutional amendment of the 1980s, the proponents of English-only laws in the 1990s, all the way up to a broad range of Americans today who, anxious about "terrorists" and "immigrants," and often conflating the two, indignantly ask why they should have to be told by phone answering services and ATM machines to "press '1' for English" and "oprima dos por Espanol"[33]—all of them in their mania for monolingualism see translation as a kind of labor that only non-Anglophones should have to do. Since it is "they" who must assimilate, it is therefore "they," not "us," who must translate their native tongues into English. The reverse would be unthinkable. For as citizens of this country, aren't we already fully assimilated? Haven't we already successfully forgotten our polylingual origins? As such, aren't we entitled to think that we have arrived at a condition of complete monolingualism?

Indeed, because it is brought about by a process of translation—of repressing one's first language in favor of a second—monolingual citizenship is assumed to be a kind of achievement rather than a limitation. Among other things, this achievement brings with it a certain freedom, which is nothing less than the emancipation from the labor of translation. It is not surprising then that the recurrent of signs of linguistic difference are experienced by those who think of themselves as assimilated, or perhaps on their way to being so, either as an occasion for racially tinged humor, or as a kind of "cultural assault." In either case, evidence of an enduring polylingualism appear to English-only speakers as an unsettling return of what should have been repressed. The sight of Chinese or Hindi writing on billboards or the sound of Tagalog or Russian can only infringe on the latter's freedom from translation and the enjoyment that accrues to monolingual entitlement.

The popular appeal of American English from this perspective lies precisely in its capacity to grant American citizens the powerful illusion of freedom not only from their origins. Monolingualism as the successful substitution of one's first language for a second also affords the semblance of release from the demands of repressing one language in favor of another. Only those still dwelling in "polyglot boarding-houses" of the nation are expected to toil in the fields and factories of translation. By contrast, fluency in English as the privileged proof of full citizenship—certainly in a cultural though not necessarily in a legal sense—means simply this: no further translation is necessary. The end of translation, assimilation, thus marks an end to translation. It is the cure to the curse of linguistic difference bedeviling humans since Babel's destruction.

Or is it?

The historical wishfulness for and of monolingual citizenship grows in part out of the remarkable tenacity of the myth of America as exceptional and exemplary in its capacity to melt differences into sameness.[34] This exceptionalist faith with its Christian genealogy arguably lies at the basis of American nationalism. It is worth noting, however, that the fable of the melting pot is often accompanied by its opposite image, the fragmentation and confusion of Babel. To cite just one example, the historian Arthur Schlesinger, in response to the post–civil rights emergence of multicultural and multilingual polities, wrote: "The national ideal had once been *e pluribus unum*. Are we now to belittle *unum* and glorify *pluribus*? Will the center not hold? Or will the melting pot yield to the Tower of Babel?"[35] The linguist and one-time senator from California S. I. Hayakawa used to put it more bluntly in his campaign mailers for a constitutional amendment to make English the official language: "Melting pot, yes. Tower of Babel, no."[36] "Babel" here is another version of Roosevelt's "polyglot boarding-house," a country besieged by Webster's "dissocial spirit." It is the dystopic counterpoint to the monolingual melting pot where the confusion of tongues augurs national collapse.

It is perhaps worth recalling the story of Babel in the book of Genesis. Coming after the Great Flood, it relates the fate of the descendents of yet another Noah who sought to build a tower that would reach up to the heavens. It is instructive to note in this regard that the word *babel* has two meanings: one, the more common, from the Hebrew *balal*, means "to confuse." But the other, seen in the word's Akkadian root *babilu*, means "gateway of God." "Babel" thus harbors two mutually opposed meanings: a state of confusion and a passage to unification. The very word encapsulates the allegory of exile from the state of perfect unity between words and things, between signs and their referents, thereby making translation into an unending task. Men's attempts to build a tower that would have led to the heavens was a way of saying that they did not need a messiah, or what in the New Testament would be pronounced as the Word of God; rather, it said that they themselves could save themselves since they already spoke one language. Seeking to punish their hubris, God decides to "confound their language" and scatter them about the face of the earth. Folk retellings and pictorial depictions of this story show the tower itself laid to waste by God's wrath.[37]

In the American invocations of Babel, its double meaning is usually forgotten. Only its divine dispersion into a state of linguistic confusion is recalled, not its linguistic unity prior to God's punishment. It is the fallen Babel with its wild profusion of languages that is made to stand in stark contrast to the idealized linguistic order of the United States. As Babel redeemed, the United States is precisely where *unum* comes to rule over *pluribus*. Yet, the structural proximity of "Babel" to "America" suggests that the latter does not simply negate the former but in fact retraces its fate. "Babel" is the specter that haunts American English. It informs, in the strong sense of that word, the hierarchy of languages on which monolingual citizenship rests. For as we saw, the hegemony of English is an *effect* of translation, both intralingual, within English, and interlingual, between English and other languages. In this way, national monolingualism is itself divided, requiring even as it disavows the labor of translation. The universality of the lingua franca is thus radically contingent on the endurance and mutation of regional dialects and creole speech: Spanglish, Taglish, Hawai'ian pidgin, black English, and rural and regional dialects of all sorts, to name only a few. Similarly, American monolingualism is never quite free from the polylingualism of its non-Anglophone citizenry: native peoples of the continent and the islands, first-generation immigrants from all over the world, Spanish speakers from Puerto Rico and Latin America spread out across the country, and so on. Demanding recognition and participation in the public sphere, some push for bilingual education and others for multilingual ballots. Many continue to inhabit mediascapes, from print to TV to radio, in their native languages, and expect to press something other than "1" for English on the phone or the ATM. We can see then how "America" is less the New World repudiation of "Babel" than it is its uncanny double. For Babel is not the catastrophic downfall of the city upon the hill, but in fact its condition of possibility. How so?

Recall that the allegory of Babel connotes the state of unregulated linguistic difference. To dwell in this state requires the constant labor of translation—constant insofar as no single act of translation can ever exhaust, much less reduce, the singularity of any particular language. "Babel" therefore reveals not only the necessity of translation but also its limits. The persistence of difference means that there is something about languages that resists assimilation and therefore translation into a single linguistic hierarchy, into a single tower, as it were, much less into Twin Towers. It is possible, for example, to translate Tagalog or Spanish poetry into English (or vice versa), but not without losing the rhythmic elements and myriad references of the original. To compensate for this loss, the translator must provide explanatory notes, thereby introducing an excess that was not there in the original. Subtracting while adding, translations always come up short even as they exceed the original. Thus the impossibility of definitive translations, given that there is no perfect equivalence of one language with another. Rather, there are only the uneven and imperfect approximations. In this way, each language remains to a significant degree untranslatable even as it calls out for more translation. It is as if in translating your Arabic into my Texan, and my Texan into your Arabic, we find ourselves mutually mistranslating, then trying again, only to add to our earlier mistranslations. And since my Texan and your Arabic are incommensurable, neither of them can be annexed to a single lingua franca. Instead, what we come to understand is that there is something that resists our understanding. What we end up translating is the sense that something in our speech remains untranslatable and yet remains the basis for any future translations.

This Babel of ongoing translation amid what remains untranslatable is the "other" that is set against "America." Imagined as an egalitarian community based on a unifying language that, as Webster wrote, "lays to waste" other idioms, America is usually conceived as the overcoming of Babel. As the "melting pot," it is that which, as we saw, was ordained to put an end to translation and the untranslatability of all originals. But this idealized vision of America requires that there be a Babel to vanquish and overcome, again and again. For without the specter of the untamed profusion of tongues, the New World myth of a monolingual America would make no ideological sense. At the same time, the very nature of Babel guarantees that there will never be such a thing as a perfectly monolingual country. To put it another way, Babel simultaneously makes and unmakes America as myth *and* as the reality that requires such a myth in order to make sense of itself in the world. To translate this further would strain the very limits of translation, but let me try: there is America only if there is Babel. But this also means that there can be no America when there is Babel.

Nowhere is this strange intimacy and impossible possibility of Babel and America more apparent in recent years than in the U.S. occupation of the country of Iraq, where the very site of the biblical Babel lies, or Babylon as it more commonly referred to, along the Euphrates River near present-day Baghdad. It is there where the allegory of Babel is literalized even as the metaphorical towers of American exceptionalism are reerected. In U.S.-occupied Iraq, as I hope to show, translation is dislodged and dislocated from its subservience to assimilation. Rather than render language suppliant to the will of its speakers, translation in this modern day American Babel confounds both the identity and intentions of its users. Yielding neither a stable social nor linguistic order, translation instead brings about the ongoing suspension of both. In the confused conditions of military occupation, the work of translation, as we shall see, is constantly arriving at its limits, overtaken by the return of that which remains untranslatable. How does this happen?

UNTRANSLATABILITY AND WAR

Since the beginning of the American invasion and occupation of Iraq, a number of news accounts have appeared about the role, at once indispensable and troubling, of Arabic-speaking translators in the occupation. I want to set aside for the moment the role of American and Arab American translators and instead concentrate on Iraqi nationals serving as translators for the U.S. military, though I suspect that my remarks about the latter will have some implications for understanding the role of the former.[38]

Translators are also called interpreters, which is why among the U.S. soldiers they are popularly referred to as "terps." Unlike the Americans they work for, interpreters are forced to hide their identities. They often cover their faces with ski masks and sun glasses as they venture outside the military bases and adopt American pseudonyms such as "Eric" or "Sally" so as to protect themselves from being singled out for insurgent attacks. At the same time, their identity within the U.S. military remains unsettled and unsettling inasmuch as their presence generates both relief and suspicion among soldiers. Some interpreters earn the military's trust and gratitude, and a handful of the Iraqi nationals are granted asylum to move to the United States. The small numbers who manage to acquire visas do so usually through the personal intercession of the particular American soldier they worked for rather than through any systematic U.S. policy to resettle them. Once relocated in the United States, they come to depend on the kindness of the soldier who brought them while often avoiding other Iraqis for fear of suffering reprisals.[39] Aliens in their new surroundings, they continue to be alienated from their own countrymen. Other translators who are killed, especially among the very small number of women, are treated with tender regard, often memorialized by U.S. soldiers as "one of us."[40]

Still, doubts linger amid reports of some interpreters sending information to the insurgents. As one U.S. soldier puts it, "These guys [i.e., interpreters] have guts to do what they do. And we'd be nowhere without them. We'd be lost. But you always have this fear that they might be leaking op-sec [operational security] stuff. You want to trust them but you're still reserved."[41] Given the inability of most American soldiers to speak Arabic, interpreters, as one report puts it, provide the "public face of the occupation."[42] Essential in conducting military operations, they nonetheless are thought to threaten them by leaking information. They mediate the vast gulf that separates American soldiers from the Iraqi people, often defusing conflict by being able to decipher, for example, documents that to Americans may look like plans for smuggling weapons but turn out to be in fact no more than sewing patterns.[43] Without them, soldiers "were as good as deaf and dumb on the battlefield," as one marine told a Senate hearing.[44] Yet, despite their essential function in fighting insurgents, they are also feared as potential insurgents themselves. Moving between English and Arabic, translators allow largely monolingual Americans to communicate with Iraqis and for this reason are integrated into the ranks, given uniforms and salaries. But their loyalty is always suspect. Interpreters are the only ones searched within the base, especially after every meal, forbidden to carry cell phones and cameras, send e-mail, play video games, and as of this writing, even swim in the pool.[45] They are subjected to incessant racial insults—"raghead," "jihad," "camel jockey," among others—at the same time that they are forced to go out of base with neither weapons nor armor to protect themselves.[46] Just by being who they are, translators thus find themselves stirring interest and sending out messages beyond what they had originally intended. Without meaning to, they generate meanings outside of their control. In this way, they come across as alien presences that seem to defy assimilation even as they are deemed indispensable to the assimilation of aliens. They are "foreign in a domestic sense," as much as they are domestic in a sense that remains enduringly foreign.[47]

It is precisely because they are of such great value to the U.S. forces that translators are targeted by insurgents and reviled by most Iraqis. They are accused of being mercenaries, collaborating with the United States to kill other Iraqis, so that they face constant threats of being kidnapped and killed themselves. One Iraqi interpreter with the pseudonym "Roger" says, "If you look at our situation, it's really risky and kind of horrible. Outside the wire, everybody looks at us like we are back-stabbers, like we betrayed our country and our religion, and then inside the wire they look at us like we might be terrorists."[48] Interpreters thus come to literalize that old adage: "traduttore—traditore," "translator-traitor," at times with tragic results. Stranded between languages and societies, translators are also exiled from both. Neither native nor foreign, they are both at the same time. Their uncanny identity triggers recurring crisis among all sides. It is as if their capacity for mediation en-dows them with a power to disturb and destabilize far out of proportion to their socially ascribed and officially sanctioned positions. But it is a power that also constitutes their profound vulnerability.

These and many other stories about interpreters give us a sense that within the context of the U.S. occupation of Iraq, translation works only too well. That is, it produces effects and relations that are difficult if not impossible to curb. Faced with the translator, both Americans and Iraqis are gripped with the radical uncertainty about the interpreter's loyalty and identity. Translators come across as simultaneously faithful and unfaithful, or more precisely, faithful to their task by being unfaithful to their origins. Rather than promote understanding and hospitality, the work of translation seems to spawn misgivings and misrecognition. In dealing with an inter-preter, one is addressed in one's own language—Arabic or English—by an other who also has access to an idiom and culture alien because unavailable to one. Faced with the need to depend on such an other, one responds with ever intensifying suspicions. Such suspicions are repeatedly manifested in racial insults, often escalating into violence and, in some cases, murder, thereby stoking even more suspicions. Iraqis see in the translator one of their own used against them, a double agent who bears their native language now loaded like a weapon with alien demands. For the majority of U.S. soldiers whose English only cut them off from rather than connect them with Iraqis, the indispensability of interpreters is also the source of the latter's duplicity, making them potential insurgents. From all sides, "terps" appear as enemies disguised as friends whose linguistic virtuosity masks their real selves and their true intentions.

The task of the translator is thus mired in a series of intractable and irresolvable contradictions. It begins with the fact that translation itself is a highly volatile act. As the displacement, replacement, transfer, and transformation of the original into another language, translation is incapable of fixing meanings across languages. Rather, as with the story of Babel, it consists precisely in the proliferation and confusion of possible meanings and therefore in the impossibility of arriving at a single one. For this reason, it repeatedly brings into crisis the locus of address, the interpretation of signs, the agency of mediation, and the ethics of speech. Hence is it impossible for imperialists as well as those who are opposed to them to fully control much less recuperate its workings. The treachery and treason inherent in translation in a time of war are the insistent counterpoints to the American notion of translation as monolingual assimilation with its promise of democratic communication and the just exchange of meanings. In the body of the interpreter, translation reaches its limits. As we've seen, "terps," as the uncanny doubles of U.S. soldiers and Iraqi insurgents, are productive neither of meaning nor domination, but only the circulation of what remains untranslatable. It would seem then that in the war on terror, translation is at permanent war with itself.

Translation *at* war and *as* war: how do we understand this? I want to conclude with a brief response to this question. If translation is like war, is it possible that war is also like translation? It is possible I think if we consider that the time of war is like the movement of translation. There is a sense that both lead not to the privileging of order and meaning but to emergence of what I've been calling the untranslatable. "Wartime" spreads what Nietzsche called in the wake of the Franco-Prussian war "an all consuming fever" that creates a crisis in historical thinking. So much of the way we think about history, certainly in the Westernized parts of our planet since the Enlightenment, is predicated on a notion of time as the succession of events leading toward increasingly more progressive ends. Wartime decimates that mode of thinking. Instead, it creates mass disorientation at odds with the temporal rhythms of progress and civilization. In this way, wartime is what Samuel Weber refers to as "pure movement." It is a "whirlwind . . . that sweeps everything up in its path and yet goes nowhere. As a movement, the whirlwind of war marks time, as it were, inscribing it in a destructive circularity that is both centripetal and centrifugal, wrenching things and people out of their accustomed places, displacing them and with them, all [sense] of place as well. . . . Wartime thus wrecks havoc with traditional conceptions of space and time and with the order they make possible."[49]

It is precisely the disordering effect of war on our notions of space and time that brings it in association with translation that, as we saw, scatters meaning, displaces origins, and exposes the radical undecidability of references, names, and addressees. Put differently, translation in wartime intensifies the experience of untranslatability and thus defies the demands of imperial assimilation. It is arguably this stark exposure of translation's limits that we see, for example, in the uncanny body of the Iraqi interpreter. Such a body, now ineradicably part of our own national-imperial body politic, generates the sense of severe disorientation, sending back to us a Babel-like scattering of discourses and opinions about the war. Just as civilizational time engenders the permanent possibility of wartime, the time that is out of joint and out of whack, so the time of translation is haunted by untranslatability, the feverish circulation of misrecognition and uncertainty from which we can find neither safety nor security, national or otherwise.

NOTES

1. There is as yet no definitive study comparing U.S. imperial formations with that of Western Europe, but one could get a sense of rich comparative possibilities in the essay by Paul Kramer, "Power and Connection," and Go, *Patterns of Empire*. See also the essays in McCoy and Scarrano, *The Colonial Crucible*. See especially the insightful essays by Fraders, "Reading Imperial Transitions"; McCormick, "From Old Empire to New"; and Kramer, "Race, Empire and Transnational History," as well as several of the other essays in this collection. Also highly instructive are recent books by Elliott, *Empires of the Atlantic World*, and Hamalainen, *The Comanche Empire*. There are of course the classic studies on the U.S. empire, which, however, tend to insulate it from those of Europe, such as LaFeber, *The New Empire*, and W. A. Williams, *Empire as a Way of Life*.

2. For a more sustained exposition of these ideas, see Rafael, *Contracting Colonialism* and *The Promise of the Foreign*.

3. Michael Janofsky, "Bush Proposes Broader Language Training," *New York Times*, January 6, 2006. For more details on the National Security Language Initiative, see United States, Department of Defense, Defense Language Transformation Roadmap, http://www.defense.gov/news/mar2005/d20050330roadmap.pdf. It is unclear, however, as to how much of the funding for this program has actually been released as of the date of this writing. I am grateful to Mary Pratt for referring me to this story on Bush's language initiative.

4. For the Spanish empire, see, for example, MacCormack, *Religion in the Andes*; Rafael, *Contracting Colonialism*. For the British empire, see Cohn, *An Anthropologist among Historians and Other Essays*; and for Central Africa, see Fabian, *Language and Colonial Power*.

5. The logocentrism that frames this American notion of translation predicated on the reorganization of foreign languages into a hierarchical relationship to American speech is comparable to that of sixteenth-century Spanish missionary ideas about translation that regarded all languages as gifts from God. They were thus available for the conversion of their native speakers, a process that among other things entailed the translation of native speech into vessels for carrying and conveying Christ, the Word of God. All words at all times and all places were then mere derivatives of the divine lingua franca. For an extended discussion of this Spanish history of colonial translation, see Rafael, *Contracting Colonialism*, especially chap. 1.

6. U.S. Senate, Committee on Homeland Security and Governmental Affairs. *Lost in Translation*, 2.

7. For the text of the National Defense Education Act, see the appendix in Clowse, *Brain Power for the Cold War*, 162–65. See also Bigelow and Legters, NDEA. For critical examinations of area studies in the wake of the Cold War, see Miyoshi and Harootunian, *Learning Places*; Rafael, "The Culture of Area Studies in the United States."

8. See Shell, "Babel in America," *American Babel*. Lepore, *A Is For American*, 27–29; Dodd, *Historical Statistics of the States of the United States*; Heath, "Why No Official Tongue?"; Sagarin and Kelly, "Polylingualism in the United States of America"; Fishman, *Language Loyalty in the United States*.

9. See Gomez, *Exchanging Our Country Marks*, 170–84; Lepore, *A Is for American*, 120–21; Dillard, *Black English*.

10. Shell, *American Babel*, 105. The contemporary hegemony of English notwithstanding, the persistence of linguistic diversity in the United States remains impressive. See, for example, the Modern Language Association Language Map, http://www.mla.org/map_main.

11. In Hamilton, Madison, and Jay, *The Federalist Papers*, 6.

12. Webster, *Dissertation on the English Language*, 178.

13. Adams, cited in Crawford, *Language Loyalties*, 26–27, 32.

14. Crawford, *Language Loyalties*, 32.

15. Nebrija, *Gramatica de la lengua castellana*.

16. Howe, *Language and Political Meaning and Revolutionary America*, 15.

17. For an insightful discussion of eighteenth-century projects for reforming English, see Howe, *Language and Political Meaning and Revolutionary America*, 13–27. The quotations above are taken from these pages.

18. Webster, "Author's Preface," xiii.

19. Webster, *Dissertation on the English Language*, 21.

20. Webster, *Dissertation on the English Language*, 21. See also Webster, *An American Dictionary of the English Language*, xiii.

21. Webster, *An American Dictionary of the English Language*, xiv; Webster, *A Grammatical Institute of the English Language*, 14–15.

22. Webster, *An American Dictionary of the English Language*, xi.

23. Webster, *Grammatical Institute*, 6–7. First published in 1783, Webster's blue-backed spellers sold close to ten million copies by 1823 and was the most commonly used book for teaching American children how to read through the latter nineteenth century. Frederick Douglass credits Webster's spellers with helping him to gain fluency in the national language. Indeed, sales of the books experienced one of its most dramatic spikes shortly after the Civil War, when freedmen sought it out in order to acquire the literacy that had been forbidden to them as slaves. See Lepore, *A Is for American*, 6, 125–26.

24. Webster, *Dissertation on the English Language*, 19.

25. Webster, *Dissertation on the English Language*, 20.

26. See, for example, Derrida, *Monolingualism of the Other* and "What Is Relevant Translation?" See also Emad, "Thinking More Deeply into the Question of Translation." Indeed, much of Heidegger's writings exemplify the inescapable task of translating within the same language. For a brilliant ethnographic study of the poetics and politics of intralingual translation in the context of Javanese, see Siegel, *Solo in the New Order*.

27. Webster, *Dissertation on the English Language*, 103–22.

28. Heath, "Why No Official Tongue?"; Sagarin and Kelly, "Polylingualism in the United States."

29. For the texts of various "official English" amendments to state constitutions, see "State Official Language Statutes and Constitutional Amendments," in Crawford, *Language Loyalties*, 132–35.

30. Sagarin and Kelly, "Polylingualism in the United States," 42; Solarz, "Official English: A Concession to Nativism," 124–27; Solarz, "The English Plus Alternative," 151–53; Solarz, "Native American Language Act," 155–57. Indeed, the Native American Language Act of 1990, which provides official encouragement, though not funding, for the learning and preservation of Native languages, including Hawai'ian, designates these languages as "foreign," so that studying them allows students to fulfill credits toward the satisfaction of a foreign-language requirement.

31. Atkins, *Report of the Secretary of the Interior*, 2: 18–19. For the vicissitudes of Indian language policies under the U.S. government, see Reyhner, "Policies toward American Indian Languages," 41–46.

32. Roosevelt, "Children of the Crucible," 45–46; a shorter version appears in Crawford, *Language Loyalties*, 84–85. See also "The Children of the Crucible," *Outlook*, September 19, 1917, 80.

33. See for example Ryan Lizze, "The Return of the Nativist," 48. For accounts of nativist insistence on English as a touchstone of assimilation, see Higham, *Strangers in the Land*; Kellor, *Straight America*.

34. For a genealogy of American "exceptionalism," see Rodgers, "Exceptionalism." See also Elliott, *Empires of the Atlantic World*, 184–218.

35. Cited in Shell, "Babel in America," *American Babel*, 104.

36. Cited in Crawford, *Language Loyalties*, 100.

37. Samuel Weber has discussed in detail the complications of the word *Babel* in his essay "A Touch of Translation: On Walter Benjamin's 'Task of the Translator.'" For an important explication of Babel, see Derrida, "Des Tours des Babel."

38. See for example the case of Captain James Yee, who had converted to Islam and, fluent in Arabic, was assigned to serve as a chaplain to detainees in Guantanamo. In 2003, he was arrested on charges of espionage, though he was convicted of much lesser charges a few years later. Yee's example is discussed in M. Pratt, "Harm's Way."

39. Deborah Amos, "Iraqi Interpreters Grateful for US Troops' Support"; Joseph B. Frazier, "Oregon Guardsman Returns the Favor for his Iraqi Interpreter"; Michael Breen, "The Debt We Owe Iraqi Interpreters."

40. John Koopman, "Interpreter's Death Rattles Troops"; Moni Basu, "Iraqi Interpreters Risk Their Lives to Aid GI's"; Howard LaFranci, "Remembering Allan: A Tribute to Jim Carroll's Interpreter."

41. Charles Levinson, "Iraq's 'Terps' Face Suspicions on Both Sides," *Christian Science Monitor*, April 17, 2006. Accessed April 30, 2014. http://www.csmonitor.com/2006/0417/p01s01-woiq.html; Nick Wadhams, "Iraqi Interpreters Face Death Threats from Countrymen, Alienation from U.S. Troops," *Associated Press*, January 23, 2006."

42. Levinson, "Iraq's 'Terps" Face Suspicions on Both Sides." See also Ann Scott Tyson, "Always in Hiding, an Iraqi Interpreter's Anguished Life," *Christian Science Monitor*, September 15, 2004.

43. John M. Glionna and Ashraf Khalil, "'Combat Linguists' Battle on Two Fronts," *Los Angeles Times*, June 5, 2005; Matthew D. LaPlante, "Speaking the Language; A Vital Skill; Interpreters in High Demand in Iraq," *Salt Lake Tribune*, October 13, 2005; C. Mark Brinkley, "Translators' Fears Disrupt Vital Lines of Communication," *Army Times*, December 8, 2004.

44. Amos, "Iraqi Interpreters Grateful for US Troops' Support."

45. Amos, "Iraqi Interpreters Grateful for US Troops' Support."

46. David Washburn, "Dangerous Work of Contractors in Iraq," *San Diego Union-Tribune*, November 22, 2006.

47. The term "foreign [to the United States] in a domestic sense" comes of course from the concurring opinion of Supreme Court Justice Edward Douglas White describing the "unincorporated territories" held by the United States in the wake of the wars of 1898—the Philippines, Puerto Rico, and Guam—in *Downes v. Bidwell*, one in a series of decisions collectively known as the *Insular Cases* of 1901. See Burnett and Marshall, *Foreign in a Domestic Sense*, especially 1–17. For a sustained inquiry into this notion of foreignness that at once conjures and troubles the domestic, see Kaplan, *The Anarchy of Empire in the Making of U.S. Culture*. My own attempt to specify foreignness as the recurrence of untranslatability amid the imperative to translate can be found in Rafael, *The Promise of the Foreign*.

48. Levinson, "Iraq's 'Terps' Face Suspicions on Both Sides."

49. Samuel Weber, "Wartime," 92.

BIBLIOGRAPHY

"1909 Article Tells Why Ulupalakua Dried Up." *Maui News*, November 9, 1977.
Abert, James W., and William G. Peck. *Map of the Territory of New Mexico, made by order of Brig. Gen. S. W. Kearny, under Instructions from Lieut. W. H. Emory, U.S.T.E. by Lieut's J. W. Abert and W. G. Peck. U.S.T.E. 1846–47*. Washington, DC: United States Government Printing Office, 1847.
Abu El-Haj, Nadia. *Facts on the Ground: Archaeological Practice and Territorial Self-Fashioning in Israeli Society*. Chicago: University of Chicago Press, 2001.
Adams, Romanzo C. *The Peoples of Hawaii*. Honolulu: American Council, Institute of Pacific Relations, 1935.
Adas, Michael. "Improving on the Civilizing Mission? Assumptions of United States Exceptionalism in the Colonisation of the Philippines." *Itinerario* 22 (1998): 44–66.
Aguilar, Luis E. *Cuba 1933: Prologue to Revolution*. Ithaca, NY: Cornell University Press, 1972.
Aguon, Julian. "The Commerce of Recognition (Buy One Ethos, Get One Free): Toward Curing the Harm of the United States' International Wrongful Acts in the Hawaiian Islands." *OHIA* (April 2013).
Aguon, Julian. "Other Arms: The Power of a Dual Rights Legal Strategy for the Chamoru People of Guam Using the Declaration on the Rights of Indigenous Peoples in U.S. Courts." *University of Hawai'i Law Review* 31, no. 1 (winter 2008): 113–54.
Akana, Rowena. "Setting the Record Straight about the Sale of Ceded Lands." *Ka Wai Ola* (November 2009). http://www.rowenaakana.org/2009/11/setting-the-record-straight-about-the-sale-of-ceded-lands/.
Albizu Campos, Pedro. "Concepto de la raza." *Pedro Albizu Campos: Escritos*, edited by Laura Albizu-Campos Meneses and Fr. Mario A. Rodríguez León, O. P., 27. Hato Rey. Puerto Rico: Publicaciones Puertorriqueñas, 2007.
Albizu Campos, Pedro. *La conciencia nacional puertorriqueña*. Edited by Manuel Maldonado-Denís. 2nd ed. Mexico City: Siglo Veintiuno Editores, S.A., 1974.
"Albizu Dangerous, Says Ickes." *New York Times*, March 6, 1936.
Alexie, Sherman. *The Summer of Black Widows*. Brooklyn, NY: Hanging Loose Press, 1996.
Alfred, Taiaiake. *Peace, Power, Righteousness: An Indigenous Manifesto*. New York: Oxford University Press, 1999.
Altamiran-Jiménez, Isabel. "Neoliberalism, Racialised Gender and Indigeneity." In *Indigenous Identity and Resistance: Researching the Diversity of Knowledge*, edited by Brendan Hokowhitu, Nathalie Kermoal, Chris Andersen, and Michael Reilly, 193–206. Dunedin, New Zealand: Otago University Press, 2010.

American Indian Policy Review Commission Final Report to Congress, vols. 2 and 3, issued May 17, 1977. Education Resources Information Center. Accessed April 2010. http://www.eric.ed.gov.

American Samoa Governor. *American Samoa Government Annual Report: Report to the Secretary of the Interior.* Washington, DC: Government Printing Office, 1968.

American Samoa Governor. *American Samoa Government Annual Report: Report to the Secretary of the Interior.* Washington, DC: Government Printing Office, 1970.

American Samoa Governor. *American Samoa Government Annual Report: Report to the Secretary of the Interior.* Washington, DC: Government Printing Office, 1973.

American Samoa Governor. *American Samoa Government Annual Report: Report to the Secretary of the Interior.* Washington, DC: Government Printing Office, 1975.

Amnesty International. *Maze of Injustice: The Failure to Protect Indigenous Women from Sexual Violence in the USA.* New York: Amnesty International USA, 2007.

Amnesty International. *Stolen Sisters: A Human Rights Response to Discrimination and Violence against Indigenous Women in Canada.* New York: Amnesty International USA, 2007.

Amos, Deborah. "Iraqi Interpreters Grateful for US Troops' Support." National Public Radio. October 17, 2007. Accessed May 1, 2014. http://www.npr.org/templates/story/story.php?storyId=15347832.

Anaya, S. James. *Indigenous Peoples in International Law.* 2nd ed. New York: Oxford University Press, 2004.

Anaya, S. James. *International Human Rights and Indigenous Peoples.* New York: Aspen, 2009.

Anderson, Benedict. *Under Three Flags: Anarchism and the Anti-Colonial Imagination.* New York: Verso, 2005.

Anderson, Kevin B. *Marx on the Margins: On Nationalism, Ethnicity, and Non-Western Societies.* Chicago: University of Chicago Press, 2010.

Anderson, Kim. *A Recognition of Being: Reconstructing Native Womanhood.* Toronto: Sumuch Press, 2001.

Angel Ferrao, Luis. *Pedro Albizu Campos y el nacionalismo puertorriqueño.* Harrisonburg, VA: Banta, 1990.

Anghie, Antony. "Colonialism and the Birth of International Institutions: Sovereignty, Economy, and the Mandate System of the League of Nations." *New York University Journal of International Law and Politics* 34, no. 3 (2002): 513–633.

Anghie, Antony. "Development as Governance: Sovereignty and the Mandate System of the League of Nations." Paper presented at the Annual Meeting of the Law and Society Association. Las Vegas, 2009.

Anghie, Antony. *Imperialism, Sovereignty and the Making of International Law.* Cambridge: Cambridge University Press, 2004.

Anthony, J. Garner. *Hawaii under Army Rule.* Palo Alto, CA: Stanford University Press, 1955.

Appadurai, Arjun. "Number in the Colonial Imagination." In *Modernity at Large: Cultural Dimensions of Globalization,* 114–38. Minneapolis: University of Minnesota Press, 1996.

Arkush, Brooke S. *The Archaeology of CA-Mno-2122: A Study of Pre-Contact and Post-Contact Lifeways Among the Mono Basin Paiute.* Berkeley: University of California Press, 1995.

Arrighi, Giovanni. *Adam Smith in Beijing: Lineages of the Twenty-First Century.* London: Verso, 2007.

Ashcroft, Bill. *Post-Colonial Transformation.* New York: Routledge, 2001.

Ashdown, Inez. Ashdown Papers, Bailey House Museum, Wailuku, Hawai'i.

Ashdown, Inez. "The Valley of Worthy Kings." *Sunday Star-Bulletin,* July 24, 1960.

Associated Press, "Navajo VP, NM Senator Seek Tribal Presidency," November 2, 1010. Accessed April 16, 2014. http://northernarizonanews.com/blog/2010/11/02/navajo-vp-nm-senator-seek-tribal-presidency/.

Atkinson, James. *Splendid Land, Splendid People: The Chickasaw Indians to Removal.* Tuscaloosa: University of Alabama Press, 2004.

Atkins, J. D. *Report of the Secretary of the Interior.* U.S. Congress. House. 50th Session. 5 vols. Washington, DC: Government Printing Office, 1887.

Austin, Raymond D. *Navajo Courts and Navajo Common Law: A Tradition of Tribal Self-Governance.* Minneapolis: University of Minnesota Press, 2009.

Baker, T. Lindsay, and Julie P. Baker, eds. *The WPA Oklahoma Slave Narratives.* Norman: University of Oklahoma Press, 1996.

Ball, Milner S. "Constitution, Court, Indian Tribes." *American Bar Foundation Research Journal* 12, no. 1 (winter 1987): 1–140.

"Banyacya Thomas (1910–1999)." In *Home Front Heroes: A Biographical Dictionary of Americans During Wartime,* edited by Benjamin Shearer, 48–49. Westport, CT: Greenwood Press, 2006.

Barker, Joanne. "For Whom Sovereignty Matters." In *Sovereignty Matters: Locations of Contestation and Possibility in Indigenous Struggles for Self-Determination,* edited by Joanne Barker, 1–32. Lincoln: University of Nebraska Press, 2005.

Barker, Joanne. *Native Acts: Law, Recognition, and Cultural Authenticity.* Durham, NC: Duke University Press, 2011.

Basso, Keith H. *Wisdom Sits in Places: Landscape and Language among the Western Apache.* Albuquerque: University of New Mexico Press, 1996.

Basu, Moni. "Iraqi Interpreters Risk Their Lives to Aid GI's." *Cox News Services,* November 2, 2005.

Batholomew, Gail, and Bren Bailey. *Maui Remembers: A Local History.* Taiwan: Mutual Publishing, 1994.

Bay, Mia. *The White Image in the Black Mind: African-American Ideas about White People, 1830–1925.* New York: Oxford University Press, 2000.

Beach, W. W. *The Indian Miscellany: Containing Papers on the History, Antiquities, Arts, Languages, Religions, Traditions and Superstitions of the American Aborigines; with Descriptions of Their Domestic Life, Manners, Customs, Traits, Amusements and Exploits; Travels and Adventures in the Indian Country; Incidents of Border Warfare; Missionary Relations; etc.* Albany, NY: J. Munsell, 1877.

Benjamin, Walter. *The Arcades Project.* Translated by Howard Eiland and Kevin McLaughlin. Cambridge, MA: Harvard University Press, 1999.

Bermingham, Ann. *Landscape and Ideology: The English Rustic Tradition, 1740–1860.* Berkeley: University of California Press, 1986.

Bernays, Edward L. "Hawaii—The Almost Perfect State?" *New Leader,* November 20, 1950.

Bieder, Robert E. "The Grand Order of the Iroquois: Influences on Lewis Henry Morgan's Ethnology." *Ethnohistory* 27, no. 4 (1980): 349–61.

Bierhorst, John. "The Delaware Creation Story." In *Algonquian Spirit: Contempo-*

rary Translations of the Algonquian Literatures of North America, edited by Brian Swann, 62–71. Lincoln: University of Nebraska Press, 2005.

Bigelow, Donald, and Lyman Legters. NDEA: *Language and Area Center. A Report on the First Five Years*. Washington, DC: Government Printing Office, 1964.

Billeb, Emil W. *Mining Camp Days*. Berkeley, CA: Howell North, 1968.

"Biographical Notes." In *The Complete Works of Claro M. Recto*. Vol. 1. Edited by Isagani R. Medina and Myrna S. Feliciano, xvii–xx. Centennial Edition. Pasay City, The Philippines: Claro M. Recto Memorial Foundation, 1990.

Blackford, Mansel G. *Fragile Paradise: The Impact of Tourism on Maui, 1959–2000*. Lawrence: University Press of Kansas, 2001.

Blackhawk, Ned. *Violence over the Land: Indians and Empires in the Early American West*. Cambridge, MA: Harvard University Press, 2006.

Blassingame, John. "Using the Testimony of Ex-Slaves: Approaches and Problems." *Journal of Southern History* 41 (November 1975): 473–92.

Blawis, Patricia Bell. *Tijerina and the Land Grants*. New York: International Publishers, 1971.

Blom Hansen, Thomas, and Finn Stepputat. "Sovereignty Revisited." *Annual Review of Anthropology* 35 (2006): 295–315.

Blomley, Nicholas. "Law, Property, and the Geography of Violence: The Frontier, the Survey, and the Grid." *Annals, Association of American Geographers* 93, no. 1 (2003): 121–41.

Bloom, John. *To Show What an Indian Can Do: Sports at Native American Boarding Schools*. Minneapolis: University of Minnesota Press, 2000.

Blum, William. *Killing Hope: U.S. Military and CIA Interventions since World War II*. Monroe, ME: Common Courage Press, 2008.

Bobonis, Gustavo, and Harold Toro. "Modern Colonization and Its Consequences: The Effects of U.S. Educational Policy on Puerto Rico's Educational Stratification, 1899–1910." *Caribbean Studies* 35, no. 2 (2007): 31–76.

Bosque-Pérez, Ramón, and José Javier Colón Morera, eds. *Puerto Rico under Colonial Rule: Political Persecution and the Quest for Human Rights*. Albany: State University of New York Press, 2006.

Bourdieu, Pierre. *Distinction: A Social Critique of the Judgment of Taste*. Cambridge, MA: Harvard University Press, 1984.

Breen, Michael. "The Debt We Owe Iraqi Interpreters." *Christian Science Monitor*, December 8, 2008.

Brinkley, C. Mark. "Translators' Fears Disrupt Vital Lines of Communication." *Army Times*, December 8, 2004.

Brinton, Daniel G. *The Lenape and Their Legends, with the Complete Text and Symbols of the Walam Olum, A New Translation, and an Inquiry into the Authenticity*. Memphis: General Books, [1885] 2010.

Brody, David. "Mapping Empire: Cartography and American Imperialism in the Philippines." In *Visualizing American Empire: Orientalism and Imperialism in the Philippines*. Chicago: University of Chicago Press, 2010.

Brown, James W., and Rita T. Kohn. *Long Journey Home: Oral Histories of Contemporary Delaware Indians*. Bloomington: Indiana University Press, 2008.

Brown, Vincent. *The Reaper's Garden: Death and Power in the World of Atlantic Slavery*. Cambridge, MA: Harvard University Press, 2008.

Brownlie, Ian. *Principles of Public International Law.* 7th ed. New York: Oxford University Press, 2008.

Brugge, David M. *A History of the Chaco Navajos.* Reports of the Chaco Center 4. Albuquerque: National Park Service, 1980.

Brumbaugh, Martin. *Report of the Commissioner of Education for Porto Rico.* In *Report of the Secretary of the Interior,* 56th Congress, 2nd Session, House Document 5, 757.

Bruyneel, Kevin. *The Third Space of Sovereignty: The Postcolonial Politics of U.S.-Indigenous Relations.* Minneapolis: University of Minnesota Press, 2007.

Buffington, Paige. "Navajo Nation Not Ready for Female President." *IAIA Chronicle,* December 7, 2010. Accessed May 1, 2014. http://iaiachronicle.com/2010/12/navajo-nation-not-ready-for-female-president/.

Burnett, Christina Duffy. "*Untied* States: American Expansion and Territorial Deannexation." *University of Chicago Law Review* 72, no. 3 (summer 2005): 797–879.

Burnett, Christina Duffy, and Burke Marshall. "Between the Foreign and the Domestic: The Doctrine of Territorial Incorporation, Invented and Reinvented." In *Foreign in a Domestic Sense: Puerto Rico, American Expansion, and the Constitution,* edited by Christina Duffy Burnett and Burke Marshall, 1–36. Durham, NC: Duke University Press, 2001.

Burnett, Christina Duffy, and Burke Marshall, eds. *Foreign in a Domestic Sense: Puerto Rico, American Expansion, and the Constitution.* Durham, NC: Duke University Press, 2001.

Burns, Robert Ignatius, ed. *Las Siete Partidas.* Translated by Samuel Parsons Scott. Philadelphia: University of Pennsylvania Press, 2000.

Burstyn, Varda. *The Rites of Men: Manhood, Politics, and the Culture of Sport.* Toronto: University of Toronto Press, 1999.

Bus, Heiner. "The Presence of Native Americans in Chicano Literature." In *International Studies in Honor of Tomás Rivera,* edited by Julián Olivares, 148–62. Houston, TX: Arte Público Press, 1986.

Busto, Rudy V. *The Religious Vision of Reies López Tijerina.* Albuquerque: University of New Mexico Press, 2005.

Byrd, Jodi A. *The Transit of Empire: Indigenous Critiques of Colonialism.* Minneapolis: University of Minnesota Press, 2011.

Cabán, Pedro. *Constructing a Colonial People: Puerto Rico and the United States, 1898–1932.* Boulder, CO: Westview Press, 1999.

Calhoun, Craig, Frederick Cooper, and Kevin W. Moore, eds. *Lessons of Empire: Imperial Histories and American Power.* New York: New Press, 2006.

Camp, Stephanie M. H. *Closer to Freedom: Enslaved Women and Everyday Resistance in the Plantation South.* Chapel Hill: University of North Carolina Press, 2004.

Campbell, James T. "Settling Accounts? An Americanist Perspective on Historical Reconciliation." *American Historical Review* 114, no. 4 (2009): 963–77.

Cano, Gloria. "Filipino Press between Two Empires: *El Renacimiento,* a Newspaper with Too Much *Alma Filipina.*" *Southeast Asian Studies* (Kyoto) 49, no. 3 (December 2011): 395–430.

Carmen Baerga, María del. "Transgresiones corporales: El mejoramiento de la raza y los discursos eugenésicos en el Puerto Rico de finales del siglo XIX y principios del XX." *OP. CIT. Revista del Centro de Investigaciones Históricas* 19 (2009–10): 79–106.

Carrillo, Jo, ed. *Readings in American Indian Law: Recalling the Rhythm of Survival.* Philadelphia: Temple University Press, 1998.

Carroll, Ahnawake. "Cherokee Nation Tribal Profile." *Tribal Law Journal* 3, no. 1 (2002/2003). http://tlj.unm.edu/tribal-law-journal/articles/volume_3/carroll/index.php.

Carter, Clarence Edwin, ed. *The Territory of Mississippi, 1809–1817.* Vol. 6 of *The Territorial Papers of the United States.* Washington, DC: Government Printing Office, 1938.

Cassese, Antonio. *International Law.* 2nd ed. New York: Oxford University Press, 2005.

Cassese, Antonio. *Self-Determination of Peoples: A Legal Reappraisal.* Cambridge: Cambridge University Press, 1995.

Chaco Culture National Historical Park Management Plan. Santa Fe, NM: National Park Service, 1968.

Chakrabarty, Dipesh. "The Climate of History: Four Theses." *Critical Inquiry* 35 (winter 2009): 197–222.

Chappell, David. "The Forgotten *Mau*: Anti-Navy Protest in American Samoa, 1920–1935." *Pacific Historical Review* 69 (2000): 217–60.

Chatterjee, Partha. *Nationalist Discourse in the Colonial World.* Minneapolis: University of Minnesota Press, 1993.

Chatterjee, Partha. *The Politics of the Governed: Reflections on Popular Politics in Most of the World.* New York: Columbia University Press, 2004.

Chew, William F. *Nameless Builders of the Transcontinental Railroad: The Chinese Workers of the Central Pacific Railroad.* Bloomington, IN: Trafford, 2004.

Chow, Rey. *The Age of the World Target: Self-Referentiality in War, Theory, and Comparative Work.* Durham, NC: Duke University Press, 2006.

Choy, Catherine Ceniza. *Empire of Care: Nursing and Migration in Filipino American History.* Durham, NC: Duke University Press, 2003.

Churchill, Llewella Pierce. "Sports of the Samoans." *Outing* 33 (March 1899): 562–68.

Clemmer, Robert O. *Roads in the Sky: The Hopi Indians in a Century of Change.* Boulder, CO: Westview Press, 1995.

Clowse, Barbara Barksdale. *Brain Power for the Cold War: The Sputnik Crisis and the National Defense Education Act of 1958.* Westport, CT: Greenwood Press, 1981.

Cobb, Daniel M. *Native Activism in Cold War America: The Struggle for Sovereignty.* Lawrence: University Press of Kansas, 2008.

Coerver, Don M., Suzanne B. Pasztor, and Robert Buffington. *Mexico: An Encyclopedia of Culture and History.* Santa Barbara, CA: ABC-CLIO, 2004.

Coffman, Tom. *The Island Edge of America: A Political History of Hawai'i.* Honolulu: University of Hawai'i Press, 2003.

Cohn, Bernard S. *An Anthropologist among Historians and Other Essays.* New York: Oxford University Press, 1987.

Commission on Cuban Affairs. *Problems of the New Cuba.* New York: Foreign Policy Association, 1935.

Connolly, William E. "Tocqueville, Territory and Violence." In *Challenging Boundaries: Global Flows, Territorial Identities,* edited by Michael J. Shapiro and Hayward R. Alker, 141–64. Minneapolis: University of Minnesota Press, 1996.

The Constitution and Laws of the Choctaw Nation. Park Hill, Cherokee Nation: Mission Press, 1847. Reprint, Wilmington, DE: Scholarly Resources, 1975.

Cooper, Frederick. *Colonialism in Question: Theory, Knowledge, History*. Berkeley: University of California Press, 2005.

Cooper, Frederick, and Ann Laura Stoler, eds. *Tensions of Empire: Colonial Cultures in a Bourgeois World*. Berkeley: University of California Press, 1997.

Cooper, George, and Gavan Daws. *Land and Power in Hawaii: The Democratic Years*. Honolulu: University of Hawai'i Press, 1990.

Cornelius, Janet Duitsman. *When I Can Read My Title Clear: Literacy, Slavery, and Religion in the Antebellum South*. Columbia: University of South Carolina Press, 1991.

Corntassel, Jeff. "Toward Sustainable Self-Determination: Rethinking the Contemporary Indigenous-Rights Discourse." *Alternatives* 33, no. 1 (January 2008): 105–32.

Correia, David. *Properties of Violence: Law and Land Grant Struggle in Northern New Mexico*. Athens: University of Georgia Press, 2013.

Cortés Zavala, María. "Los Bandos de Policía y Buen Gobierno en Puerto Rico: El ordenamiento urbano y la protección de la salud y la higiene en el siglo XIX." *OP.CIT. Revista del Centro de Investigaciones Históricas* 19 (2009–10): 107–42.

Coulthard, Glen. "Place against Empire: Understanding Indigenous Anti-Colonialism." *Affinities: A Journal of Radical Theory, Culture, and Action* 4, no. 2 (fall 2010): 79–83.

"County Gets Park Site: Kēpaniwai Property Is Conveyed for Public Park." *Maui News*, April 30, 1941.

"County to Sell Main-Market St. Lot at Auction." *Maui News*, February 5, 1941.

Coward, John M. *The Newspaper Indian: Native American Identity in the Press, 1820–90*. Urbana: University of Illinois Press, 1999.

Crampton, Jeremy, and Stuart Elden, eds. *Space, Knowledge and Power: Foucault and Geography*. Aldershot, UK: Ashgate, 2007.

Crampton, Jeremy, and John Krygier. "An Introduction to Critical Cartography." *ACME: An International E-Journal for Critical Geographies*, no. 1 (2006). http://www.acme-journal.org/vo14/jwcjk.pdf.

Crawford, James. *Language Loyalties: A Source Book on the Official English Controversy*. Chicago: University of Chicago Press, 1992.

Creel, Margaret Washington. *A Peculiar People: Slave Religion and Community Culture among the Gullahs*. New York: New York University Press, 1988.

Crum, Steven. "Almost Invisible: The Brotherhood of North American Indians and the League of North American Indians." *Wicazo Sa Review* 21 (spring 2006): 50–53.

"Cuban President Asks Americans to Help New Regime by Not Hindering Program." *New York Times*, September 11, 1933.

Culin, Stewart. "The Chinese Drug Stores in America." *American Journal of Pharmacy* 59, no. 12 (December 1887): 593–98.

Cuvier, George. *The Animal Kingdom Arranged According to Its Organization*. 1817. Whitefish, MT: Kessinger, 2010.

Darden, Thomas F. *Historical Sketch of the Naval Administration of the Government of American Samoa, April 17, 1900–July 1, 1951*. Washington, DC: Government Printing Office, 1952.

Darwin, Charles. *The Descent of Man*. 1871. New York: Penguin, 2004.

Darwin, Charles. *On the Origin of Species*. 1859. New York: Oxford University Press, 2008.

Das, Veena. "Violence, Gender, and Subjectivity." *Annual Review of Anthropology* 37 (2008): 283–99.

Dawdy, Shannon Lee. *Building the Devil's Empire: French Colonial New Orleans.* Chicago: University of Chicago Press, 2009.

Dean, Mitchell. *Governmentality: Power and Rule in Modern Society.* 2nd ed. London: Sage, 2010.

deBuys, William. *Enchantment and Exploitation: The Life and Hard Times of a New Mexico Mountain Range.* Albuquerque: University of New Mexico Press, 1985.

Deer, Sarah, et al., eds. *Sharing Our Stories of Survival: Native Women Surviving Violence.* Lanham, MD: Alta Mira, 2008.

Deleuze, Gilles. "What Is a Dispositif?" In *Michel Foucault: Philosopher,* edited by T. J. Armstrong, 159–61. Oxford: Routledge, 1991.

del Moral, Solsirée. *Negotiating Empire: The Cultural Politics of Schools in Puerto Rico, 1898–1950.* Madison: University of Wisconsin Press, 2013.

Deloria, Philip J. *Playing Indian.* New Haven, CT: Yale University Press, 1998.

Deloria, Vine, Jr. *Custer Died for Your Sins: An Indian Manifesto.* 1969. Norman: University of Oklahoma Press, 1988.

Deloria, Vine, Jr., and Raymond J. DeMallie. *Documents of American Indian Diplomacy: Treaties, Agreements, and Conventions, 1775–1979.* Vol. 1. Norman: University of Oklahoma Press, 1999.

Deloria, Vine, Jr., and David E. Wilkins. *Tribes, Treaties, and Constitutional Tribulations.* Austin: University of Texas Press, 1999.

Denetdale, Jennifer Nez. "Carving Navajo National Boundaries: Patriotism, Tradition, and the Diné Marriage Act of 2005." *American Quarterly* 60, no. 2 (June 2008): 289–94.

Denetdale, Jennifer Nez. "Chairmen, Presidents, and Princesses: The Navajo Nation, Gender, and the Politics of Tradition." *Wicazo Sa Review* 21, no. 1 (spring 2006): 9–44.

Denetdale, Jennifer Nez. "Representing Changing Woman: A Review Essay on Navajo Women." *American Indian Culture and Research Journal* 25, no. 3 (2001): 1–26.

Denetdale, Jennifer Nez. "Securing the Navajo National Boundaries: War, Patriotism, Tradition, and the Diné Marriage Act of 2005." *Wicazo Sa Review* 24, no. 2 (fall 2009): 221–41.

Dennison, Jean. *Colonial Entanglement: Constituting a Twenty-First-Century Osage Nation.* Chapel Hill: University of North Carolina Press, 2012.

Derby, E. H. *The Overland Route to the Pacific: A Report on the Condition, Capacity and Resources of the Union Pacific and Central Pacific Railways.* Boston: Lee and Shepard, 1869.

De Quille, Dan. *The Big Bonanza: An Authentic Account of the Discovery, History, and Working of the World-Renowned Comstock Lode of Nevada.* New York: Thomas Crowell, 1947.

Derrida, Jacques. "Des Tours des Babel." In *Acts of Religion,* edited by Gil Anidjar, translated by Joseph Graham, 102–34. New York: Routledge, 2002.

Derrida, Jacques. *Monolingualism of the Other, or, the Prosthesis of Origin.* Translated by Patrick Mensah. Palo Alto, CA: Stanford University Press, 1997.

Derrida, Jacques. *Rogues: Two Essays on Reason.* Translated by Pascale-Anne Brault and Michael Naas. Palo Alto, CA: Stanford University Press, 2005.

Derrida, Jacques. *Specters of Marx: The State of the Debt, the Work of Mourning, and the New International.* Translated by Peggy Kamuf. New York: Routledge, 1994.

Derrida, Jacques. "What Is Relevant Translation?" *Critical Inquiry* 27 (winter 2001): 174–200.

"Development of Iao Is Aim of Civic Club." *Maui News,* July 9, 1960.

Diaz, Vicente M. "'Fight Boys, 'Til the Last . . . ': Islandstyle Football and the Remasculinization of Indigeneity in the Militarized American Pacific Islands." In *Pacific Diaspora: Island Peoples in the United States and across the Pacific,* edited by Paul Spickard, Joanne L. Rondilla, and Debbie Hippolite Wright. Honolulu: University of Hawai'i Press, 2002.

Diaz, Vicente M. *Repositioning the Missionary: Rewriting the Histories of Colonialism, Native Catholicism, and Indigeneity in Guam.* Honolulu: University of Hawai'i Press, 2010.

Diaz, Vicente M. "Tackling Pacific Hegemonic Formations on the American Gridiron." *Amerasia* 37, no. 3 (2011): 2–25.

Díaz Quiñones, Arcadio. "La Pasión, según Albizu." *El arte de bregar, ensayos.* San Juan, PR: Ediciones Callejón, 2000.

Dillard, J. L. *Black English: Its History and Usages in the United States.* New York: Vintage, 1973.

Dirks, Nicholas B., ed. *Colonialism and Culture.* Ann Arbor: University of Michigan Press, 1992.

Dodd, Don. *Historical Statistics of the States of the United States: Two Centuries of the Census, 1790–1990.* Westport, CT: Greenwood Press, 1993.

Donovan, Bill. "'Gay' Remark Taps Wrong Emotions." *Navajo Times,* November 18, 2010.

Donovan, Bill. "High Court Rejects Dismissal Motion in Slush Fund Case." *Navajo Times,* March 3, 2011.

Donovan, Bill. "Lovejoy Landslide Fails to Appear: Shelly Reverses Primary Elections Positions to Win Presidency." *Navajo Times,* November 3, 2010.

Donovan, Bill. "Lovejoy Picks Activist, Administrator." *Navajo Times,* August 12, 2013.

Drinnon, Richard. *Facing West: The Metaphysics of Indian-Hating and Empire-Building.* Minneapolis: University of Minnesota Press, 1980.

Driskill, Qwo-Li, Chris Finley, Brian Joseph Gilley, and Scott Laurie Morgensen, eds. *Queer Indigenous Studies: Critical Interventions in Theory, Politics, and Literature.* Tucson: University of Arizona, 2011.

"Drive to Establish Park in Iao Valley Opens Here." *Maui News,* November 23, 1940.

Duany, Jorge. *The Puerto Rican Nation on the Move: Identities on the Island and in the United States.* Chapel Hill: University of North Carolina Press, 2002.

DuBois, Laurent. *A Colony of Citizens: Revolution and Slave Emancipation in the French Caribbean, 1787–1804.* Chapel Hill: University of North Carolina Press, 2004.

Dulles, John Foster. "International Unity." *Department of State Bulletin,* June 21, 1954, 936.

Dumont, Clayton W., Jr. *The Promise of Poststructuralist Sociology: Marginalized Peoples and the Problem of Knowledge.* Albany: State University of New York Press, 2008.

Dunbar-Ortiz, Roxanne. *Roots of Resistance: Land Tenure in New Mexico, 1680–1980*. Chicano Studies Research Center Publications, University of California, Los Angeles, 1980.

Duncan, James. *In the Shadows of the Tropics: Climate, Race and Biopower in Nineteenth Century Ceylon*. Aldershot, UK: Ashgate, 2007.

Duprey, Marlene. *Bioislas: Ensayos sobre la biopolítica y gubernamentalidad en Puerto Rico*. San Juan, PR: Ediciones Callejón, 2010.

Eblen, Jack Ericson. *The First and Second United States Empires: Governors and Territorial Government, 1784–1912*. Pittsburgh: University of Pittsburgh Press, 1968.

Ebright, Malcolm. *Land Grants and Lawsuits in Northern New Mexico*. Albuquerque: University of New Mexico Press, 1994.

Ebright, Malcolm. *The Tierra Amarilla Land Grant: A History of Chicanery*. Santa Fe, NM: Center for Land Grant Studies, 1980.

Edney, Matthew. "The Ideologies and Practices of Mapping and Imperialism." In *Mapping an Empire: The Geographical Construction of British India, 1765–1843*, 1–38. Chicago: University of Chicago Press, 1990.

Edney, Matthew. *Mapping an Empire: The Geographical Construction of British India, 1765–1843*. Chicago: University of Chicago Press, 1999.

Edney, Matthew. "The Irony of Imperial Mapping." In *The Imperial Map: Cartography and the Mastery of Empire*, edited by James Akerman, 11–45. Chicago: University of Chicago Press, 2009.

Edwards, Brent Hayes. *The Practice of Diaspora: Literature, Translation, and the Rise of Black Internationalism*. Cambridge, MA: Harvard University Press, 2003.

Ehrenberg, Ralph. "Up in the Air in More Ways Than One: The Emergence of Aeronautical Charts in the United States." In *Cartographies of Travel and Navigation*, edited by James Akerman, 220–22. Chicago: University of Chicago Press, 2006.

Eisen, George, and David K. Wiggins, eds. *Ethnicity and Sport in North American History and Culture*. Westport, CT: Greenwood Press, 1994.

Eisenstein, Zillah. *Against Empire: Feminisms, Racism, and the West*. New York: Zed Books, 2004.

Elden, Stuart. *The Birth of Territory*. Chicago: University of Chicago Press, 2013.

Elliott, J. H. *Empires of the Atlantic World: Britain and Spain, 1492–1830*. New Haven, CT: Yale University Press, 2006.

Emad, Parvis. "Thinking More Deeply into the Question of Translation." In *Reading Heidegger: Commemoration*, edited by John Sallis, 323–40. Bloomington: Indiana University Press, 1993.

Emory, William Hemsley. *Military Reconnaissance of the Arkansas Rio Del Norte and Rio Gila By W. H. Emory, Lieut. Top. Engrs. Assisted . . . by J. W. Abert and W. G. Peck, and . . . by W. H. Warner and Mr. Norman Bestor, made in 1846–7, with the advance guard of the "Army of the West." Under Command of Brig. Gen. Stephn. W. Kearny. Constructed under the orders of Col. J. J. Abert . . . 1847."* Drawn by Joseph Welch. Engraved on stone by E. Weber & Co. Baltimore, 1848.

Espejo, Pauline Ochoa. *The Time of Popular Sovereignty: Process and the Democratic State*. University Park: Pennsylvania State University Press, 2011.

Fa'aleava, Toeutu. "*Fitafita*: Samoan Landsmen in the United States Navy, 1900–1951." PhD diss., University of California, Berkeley, 2003.

Faber, Sebastian. "'La hora ha llegado': Hispanism, Pan-Americanism, and the

Hope of Spanish/American Glory (1938–1948)." In *Ideologies of Hispanism*, edited by Mabel Moraña, 62–68. Nashville: Vanderbilt University Press, 2005.

Fabian, Johannes. *Language and Colonial Power: The Appropriation of Swahili in the Former Belgian Congo, 1880–1938*. Berkeley: University of California Press, 1986.

Fabian, Johannes. *Time and the Other: How Anthropology Makes Its Object*. New York: Columbia University Press, 1983.

Farge, Arlette, and Jacques Revel. *The Vanishing Children of Paris: Rumor and Politics before the French Revolution*. Translated by Claudie Miéville. Cambridge, MA: Harvard University Press, 1991.

Farrand, Max. *The Legislation of Congress for the Government of the Organized Territories of the United States, 1789–1895*. Newark, NJ: William A. Baker, 1896.

Farred, Grant. "A Nation in White: Cricket in Post-Apartheid South Africa." *Social Text* 50 (1997): 9–32.

Felski, Rita, and Susan Stanford Friedman, eds. *Comparison: Theories, Approaches, Uses*. Baltimore: Johns Hopkins University Press, 2013.

Ferguson, T. J. *A Zuni Atlas*. Norman: University of Oklahoma Press, 1990.

Ferraro, Pat, and Bob Ferraro, *The Past in Glass*. n.p., 1965.

Ferrer, Ada. *Insurgent Cuba: Race, Nation, and Revolution, 1868–1898*. Chapel Hill: University of North Carolina Press, 1999.

Field, Michael J. *Mau: Samoa's Struggle against New Zealand Oppression*. Wellington, New Zealand: A. H. and A. W. Reed, 1984.

Fine, Gary, and Patricia Turner. *Whispers on the Color Line: Rumor and Race in America*. Berkeley: University of California Press, 2001.

Finley, Chris. "Decolonizing the Queer Native Body (and Recovering the Native Bull-Dyke): Bringing 'Sexy Back' and Out of Native Studies' Closet." In *Queer Indigenous Studies: Critical Interventions in Theory, Politics, and Literature*, edited by Qo-Li Driskill, Chris Finley, Brian Joseph Gilley, and Scott Lauria Morgensen, 13–43. Tucson: University of Arizona Press, 2011.

Fisher, James T. "'A World Made Safe for Diversity': The Vietnam Lobby and the Politics of Pluralism, 1945–1963." In *Cold War Constructions: The Political Culture of United States Imperialism, 1945–1966*, edited by Christain G. Appy, 217–37. Amherst: University of Massachusetts, 2000.

Fishman, Joshua. *Language Loyalty in the United States: The Maintenance and Perpetuation of Non-English Mother Tongues by American Ethnic and Religious Groups*. The Hague, Netherlands: Mouton, 1966.

Fletcher, Matthew L. M. "Tribal Consent." *Stanford Journal of Civil Rights and Civil Liberties* 8, no. 1 (April 2012): 45–121.

Ford, Lisa. *Settler Sovereignty: Jurisdiction and Indigenous People in America and Australia, 1788–1836*. Cambridge, MA: Harvard University Press, 2010.

Foucault, Michel. *Discipline and Punish: The Birth of the Prison*. Translated by Alan Sheridan. New York: Vintage, 1979.

Foucault, Michel. "Governmentality." In *The Foucault Effect: Studies in Governmentality*, edited by Graham Burchell, Colin Gordon, and Peter Miller, 87–104. Chicago: University of Chicago Press, 1991.

Foucault, Michel. "Nietzsche, Genealogy, History." In *Language, Counter-Memory, Practice: Selected Essays and Interviews*, edited by Daniel F. Bouchard, translated by Daniel F. Bouchard and Sherry Simon, 139–64. Ithaca, NY: Cornell University Press, 1977.

Foucault, Michel. *Power/Knowledge: Selected Interviews and Other Writings.* New York: Pantheon, 1972.

Foucault, Michel. *Security, Territory, Population: Lectures at the Collège de France, 1977–1978.* Edited by Michel Senellart. Translated by Graham Burchell. New York: Palgrave Macmillan, 2007.

Franco, Robert W. *Samoan Perceptions of Work: Moving Up and Moving Around.* New York: AMS Press, 1991.

Frank, Jason. *Constituent Moments: Enacting the People in Postrevolutionary America.* Durham, NC: Duke University Press, 2010.

Frankel, Chuck. "Isles Called Appropriate for Kennedy Rights Talk." *Honolulu Star Bulletin,* June 6, 1963.

Franks, Joel. *Crossing Sidelines, Crossing Cultures: Sport and Asian Pacific American Cultural Citizenship.* Lanham, MD: University Press of America, 2000.

Franks, Joel. "Pacific Islanders and American Football: Hula Hula Honeys, Throwin' Samoans, and the Rock." *International Journal of the History of Sport* 16 (2009): 2397–411.

Frazier, Joseph B. "Oregon Guardsman Returns the Favor for his Iraqi Interpreter." *Seattle Post-Intelligencer,* December 24, 2007.

Fuente, Alejandro de la. *A Nation for All: Race, Inequality, and Politics in Twentieth-Century Cuba.* Chapel Hill: University of North Carolina Press, 2001.

Fuentes, Carlos. Introduction to *Ariel,* by José Enrique Rodó. Translated by Margaret Sayers Peden. Austin: University of Texas Press, 1988.

Gallagher, John, and Ronald Robinson, "The Imperialism of Free Trade." *Economic History Review* 6, no. 1 (August 1953): 1–15.

Ganguly, Keya. "Of Totems and Taboos: An Indian's Guide to Indian Chiefs and Other Objects of Fan Fascination." *South Atlantic Quarterly* 105, no. 2 (2006): 373–90.

García, Gervasio. "I Am the Other: Puerto Rico in the Eyes of North Americans, 1898." *Journal of American History* 87, no. 1 (2000): 39–64.

García Muñiz, Humberto. *Sugar and Power in the Caribbean: The South Porto Rico Sugar Company in Puerto Rico and the Dominican Republic.* San Juan: Editorial de la Universidad de Puerto Rico, 2010.

Gardner, Richard. *Grito! Reies Tijerina and the New Mexico Land Grant War of 1967.* New York: Harper and Row, 1971.

Gems, Gerald R. *The Athletic Crusade: Sport and American Cultural Imperialism.* Lincoln: University of Nebraska Press, 2006.

"Ghost Picture Excites Japanese." *Maui News,* April 18, 1919.

Givens, Michael. *The Archaeology of the Colonized.* London: Routledge, 2004.

Glionna, John M., and Ashraf Khalil. "'Combat Linguists' Battle on Two Fronts." *Los Angeles Times,* June 5, 2005.

Go, Julian. *American Empire and the Politics of Meaning: Elite Political Cultures in the Philippines and Puerto Rico during U.S. Colonialism.* Durham, NC: Duke University Press, 2008.

Go, Julian. *Patterns of Empire: The British and American Empires, 1688 to the Present.* Cambridge: Cambridge University Press, 2011.

Go, Julian, and Anne L. Foster, eds. *The American Colonial State in the Philippines: Global Perspectives.* Durham, NC: Duke University Press, 2003.

Godlewska, Anne. "Map, Text, and Image: The Mentality of Enlightened Conquerors: A New Look at the Description de l'Egypte." *Transactions of the Institute of British Geographers* 20 (1995): 5–28.

Goeman, Mishuana. *Mark My Words: Native Women Mapping Our Nations*. Minneapolis: University of Minnesota Press, 2013.

Goetzmann, William. *Exploration and Empire: The Explorer and the Scientist in the Winning of the American West*. New York: Alfred A. Knopf, 1966.

Goldstein, Alyosha. *Poverty in Common: The Politics of Community Action during the American Century*. Durham, NC: Duke University Press, 2012.

Goldstein, Alyosha. "Where the Nation Takes Place: Proprietary Regimes, Antistatism, and U.S. Settler Colonialism." *South Atlantic Quarterly* 107, no. 4 (fall 2008): 833–61.

Gómez, Laura E. *Manifest Destinies: The Making of the Mexican American Race*. New York: New York University Press, 2007.

Gomez, Michael A. *Exchanging Our Country Marks: The Transformation of African Identities in the Colonial and Antebellum South*. Chapel Hill: University of North Carolina Press, 1998.

Gonzalez, Andrew B. *Language and Nationalism: The Philippine Experience Thus Far*. Quezon City: Ateneo de Manila University Press, 1980.

Gonzalez, Nancie L. *The Spanish Americans of New Mexico*. Albuquerque: University of New Mexico Press, 1967.

Gonzalez, Vernadette Vicuña. *Securing Paradise: Tourism and Militarism in Hawai'i and the Philippines*. Durham, NC: Duke University Press, 2013.

González Lamela, María del Pilar. *El exilio artístico español en el Caribe: Cuba, Santo Domingo y Puerto Rico, 1936–1960*. A Coruña, Spain: Edicios do Castro, 1999.

Goodman, James M. *The Navajo Atlas: Environments, Resources, Peoples, and History of Dine Bikeyah*. Norman: University of Oklahoma Press, 1982.

Goodyear-Kā'opua, Noelani. *The Seeds We Planted: Portraits of a Native Hawaiian Charter School*. Minneapolis: University of Minnesota Press, 2013.

Gordon, Avery F. *Ghostly Matters: Haunting and the Sociological Imagination*. Minneapolis: University of Minnesota Press, 2008.

Gott, Richard. *Cuba: A New History*. New Haven, CT: Yale University Press, 2004.

Gottheimer, Josh, ed. *Ripples of Hope: Great American Civil Rights Speeches*. New York: Basic Civitas Books, 2004.

Grandin, Greg. "Your Americanism and Mine." *American Historical Review* 111, no. 4 (October 2006): 1042–66.

Grau Alsina, Ramon "Mongo," and Valerie Ridderhoff. *Cuba desde 1930*. Madrid: Agualarga Editores, S. L., 1997.

Gray, J. A. C. *Amerika Samoa: A History of American Samoa and Its United States Naval Administration*. Annapolis, MD: United States Naval Institute, 1960.

Great Buildings Collection. "U.S. Custom House." Architecture Week website. Accessed September 25, 2011. http://www.greatbuildings.com/buildings/U.S._Custom_House.html.

Green, Joyce, ed. *Making Space for Indigenous Feminism*. New York: Zed Books, 2007.

Green, Rayna. "The Tribe Called Wannabee: Playing Indian in America and Europe." *Folklore* 99, no. 1 (1988): 30–55.

Greene, Julie. *The Canal Builders: Making America's Empire at the Panama Canal*. New York: Penguin, 2009.

Greeson, Jennifer Rae. *Our South: Geographic Fantasy and the Rise of National Literature*. Cambridge, MA: Harvard University Press, 2010.

Gregory, Derek. *The Colonial Present: Afghanistan, Palestine, and Iraq*. Malden, MA: Blackwell, 2004.

Griswold del Castillo, Richard. *The Treaty of Guadalupe-Hidalgo: A Legacy of Conflict*. Norman: University of Oklahoma Press, 1990.

Guerra, Lillian. *The Myth of José Martí: Conflicting Nationalisms in Early Twentieth-Century Cuba*. Chapel Hill: University of North Carolina Press, 2005.

Guha, Ranajit. "The Prose of Counter-Insurgency." In *Selected Subaltern Studies*, edited by Ranajit Guha and Gayatri Chakravorty Spivak, 45–88. New York: Oxford University Press, 1988.

Guidotti-Hernández, Nicole M. *Unspeakable Violence: Remapping U.S. and Mexican National Imaginaries*. Durham, NC: Duke University Press, 2011.

Guyatt, Nicholas. "'The Outskirts of Our Happiness': Race and the Lure of Colonization in the Early Republic." *Journal of American History* 95 (March 2009): 986–1011.

Guzmán, María de. *Spain's Long Shadow: The Black Legend, Off-Whiteness, and Anglo-American Empire*. Minneapolis: University of Minnesota Press, 2005.

Haas, Lisbeth. *Conquests and Historical Identities in California, 1769–1936*. Berkeley: University of California Press, 1995.

Hall, Clarence. "Samoa: America's Shame in the South Seas." *Reader's Digest*, July 1961: 111–16.

Hall, Daniel E. "Curfews, Culture, and Custom in American Samoa: An Analytical Map for Applying the U.S. Constitution to U.S. Territories." *Asian-Pacific Law and Policy Journal* 2, no. 1 (winter 2001): 69–106.

Hall, Gwendolyn Midlo. *Africans in Colonial Louisiana: The Development of Afro-Creole Culture in the Eighteenth Century*. Baton Rouge: Louisiana State University Press, 1995.

Halperns, Richard. *The Poetics of Primitive Accumulation: English Renaissance Culture and the Genealogy of Capital*. Ithaca, NY: Cornell University Press, 1991.

Hämäläinen, Pekka. *The Comanche Empire*. New Haven, CT: Yale University Press, 2008.

Hämäläinen, Pekka, and Samuel Truett, "On Borderlands." *Journal of American History* 98, no. 2 (September 2011): 338–61.

Hamilton, Alexander, James Madison, John Jay. *The Federalist Papers: A Collection of Essays Written in Support of the Constitution of the United States*, edited by Roy P. Fairfield. Garden City, NY: Anchor Press, 1966.

Hamilton, Chris. "Na Wai Eha: Decision In but Dispute Lingers." *Maui News*, June 13, 2010.

Hamilton, Chris. "Na Wai Eha: HC&S Speaks Jobs, Fields at Risk in Stream Water Dispute." *Maui News*, October 9, 2009.

Hamilton, Chris. "Streams Flow Again—Along with Controversy and Conflict." *Maui News*, August 10, 2010.

Handy, E. S. C., and E. G. Handy. *Native Planters in Old Hawaii: Their Life, Lore, and Environment*. Honolulu: Bishop Museum Press, 1972.

Harley, Brian. "Maps, Knowledge, and Power." In *The New Nature of Maps: Essays in the History of Cartography*, edited by Paul Laxton, 51–82. Baltimore: Johns Hopkins University Press, 2001.

Harrington, Mark R. *Dickon among the Lenape: Indians of New Jersey*. New York: Holt, Rinehart, and Winston, 1938.

Hart, Albert Bushnell. *Actual Government as Applied under American Conditions.* New York: Longmans, Green, 1903.

Hart, Albert Bushnell. "Brother Jonathan's Colonies: A Historical Account." *Harper's* 98 (January 1899): 319–20, 326.

Harvard Project on American Indian Economic Development, ed. *The State of Native Nations: Conditions under U.S. Policies of Self-Determination.* New York: Oxford University Press, 2007.

Harvey, David. *The New Imperialism*. New York: Oxford University Press, 2003.

Hasager, Ulla, and Marion Kelly. "Public Policy of Land and Homesteading in Hawai'i." In *Social Process in Hawai'i: A Reader*, 3rd ed., edited by Peter Manicas, 190–232. New York: McGraw-Hill, 2001.

Hau'ofa, Epeli. "Our Sea of Islands." In *A New Oceania: Rediscovering Our Sea of Islands*, edited by E. Waddel and Epeli Hau'ofa, 2–16. Suva, Fiji: University of the South Pacific, 1993.

"Hawaiian Group Meets Tuesday on Garden Plan." *Maui News*, July 7, 1967.

Heath, Shirley Brice. "Why No Official Tongue?" In *Language Loyalties: A Source Book on the Official English Controversy*, edited by James Crawford, 20–30. Chicago: University of Chicago Press, 1992.

Helg, Aline. *Our Rightful Share: The Afro-Cuban Struggle for Equality, 1886–1912.* Chapel Hill: University of North Carolina Press, 1995.

"'Heritage Pavilion' in Kēpaniwai Park Plans." *Maui News*, May 17, 1967.

Higham, John. *Strangers in the Land: Patterns of American Nativism, 1860–1925.* New Brunswick, NJ: Rutgers University Press, 1955.

Hilferding, Rudolf. *Finance Capital: A Study of the Latest Phase of Capitalist Development*, edited with an introduction by Tom Bottomore. Translated by Morris Watnick and Sam Gordon. 1910. London: Routledge and Kegan Paul, 1981.

Hinck, Jon. "The Republic of Palau and the United States: Self-Determination Becomes the Price of Free Association." *California Law Review* 78, no. 4 (1990): 915–71.

"Historical Essays: Literature in Spanish." In *Cultural Center of the Philippines Encyclopedia*, 9: 93–95. Manila: Cultural Center of the Philippines, 1994.

Hobson, John A. *Imperialism: A Study*. 1902. London: G. Allen and Unwin, 1938.

Hoffman, Virginia. *Navajo Biographies*. Vol. 1. Phoenix: Navajo Curriculum Center Press, 1974.

Hoganson, Kristin L. *Fighting for American Manhood: How Gender Politics Provoked the Spanish-American and Philippine-American Wars*. New Haven, CT: Yale University Press, 1998.

Hokowhitu, Brendan. "'Physical Beings': Stereotypes, Sport and the 'Physical Education' of New Zealand Maori." *Culture, Sport, Society* 6, nos. 2–3 (2003): 192–218.

Hokowhitu, Brendan. "Tackling Maori Masculinity: A Colonial Genealogy of Savagery and Sport." *Contemporary Pacific* 16, no. 2 (2004): 259–84.

Holland, Sharon. *Raising the Dead: Readings of Death and (Black) Subjectivity.* Durham, NC: Duke University Press, 2000.

Hong, Grace Kyungwon, and Roderick A. Ferguson, eds. *Strange Affinities: The*

Gender and Sexual Politics of Comparative Racialization. Durham, NC: Duke University Press, 2011.

Honig, Bonnie. "Declarations of Independence: Arendt and Derrida on the Problem of Founding a Republic." *American Political Science Review* 85, no. 1 (March 1991): 97–113.

Hopkins, Sarah Winnemucca. *Life among the Piutes: Their Wrongs and Claims.* New York: Putnam, 1883.

Horsman, Reginald. *Expansion and American Indian Policy, 1783–1812.* East Lansing: Michigan State University Press, 1967.

Horsman, Reginald. "The Indian Policy of an 'Empire for Liberty.'" In *Native Americans and the Early Republic,* edited by Frederick E. Hoxie, Ronald Hoffman, and Peter J. Albert. Charlottesville: University of Virginia Press, 1999.

Horsman, Reginald. *Race and Manifest Destiny: The Origins of American Racial Anglo-Saxonism.* Cambridge, MA: Harvard University Press, 1981.

Howe, John. *Language and Political Meaning and Revolutionary America.* Amherst: University of Massachusetts Press, 2004.

Hsueh, Vicki. *Hybrid Constitutions: Challenging Legacies of Law, Privilege, and Culture in Colonial America.* Durham, NC: Duke University Press, 2010.

"Iao Valley Park Drive Nears Goal." *Maui News,* November 30, 1940.

"In Congress, July 4, 1776. A Declaration By the Representatives of the United States of America, in General Congress Assembled." In *The Declaration of Independence: A Global History,* edited by David Armitage, 165–72. Cambridge, MA: Harvard University Press, 2007.

"International Gardens in Kēpaniwai Park Scheme." *Maui News,* April 11, 1964.

Inter-Tribal Council of Nevada. *Numa: A Northern Paiute History.* Reno, NV: Inter-Tribal Council of Nevada, 1976.

Jackson, Shona N. *Creole Indigeneity: Between Myth and Nation in the Caribbean.* Minneapolis: University of Minnesota Press, 2012.

Jackson, William H. "Report on the Ancient Ruins Examined in 1875 and 1877." In *Tenth Annual Report of the United States Geological and Geographical Survey of the Territories, embracing Colorado and parts of adjacent Territories, being a Report of Progress of the Exploration for the Year 1876,* edited by F. V. Hayden, 409–50. Washington, DC: Government Printing Office, 1878.

Jacob, Christian. "Toward a Cultural History of Cartography." *Imago Mundi* 48 (1996): 191–98.

Jaimes, M. Annette, with Theresa Halsey. "American Indian Women: At the Center of Indigenous Resistance in North America." In *The State of Native America: Genocide, Colonization, and Resistance,* edited by M. Annette Jaimes, 311–44. Boston: South End Press, 1992.

James, C. L. R. *Beyond a Boundary.* New York: Pantheon Books, 1983.

Jameson, Fredric. "Marx's Purloined Letter." In *Ghostly Demarcations: A Symposium on Jacques Derrida's Specters of Marx,* edited by Michael Sprinker, 26–67. New York: Verso, 1999.

Janis, Mark W. *An Introduction to International Law.* 3rd ed. New York: Aspen, 1999.

Janofsky, Michael. "Bush Proposes Broader Language Training." *New York Times,* January 6, 2006.

Jefferson, Thomas. *Notes on the State of Virginia.* Edited by William Peden. 1954.

Chapel Hill: Published for the Institute of Early American History and Culture at Williamsburg, Virginia, by the University of North Carolina Press, 1982.

Johnson, Edward C. *Walker River Paiutes: A Tribal History*. Schurz, NV: Walker River Paiute Tribe, 1975.

Johnson, Natasha Kaye. "Tears Shed for Chaco: Former Canyon Residents Recall Legacy of Forced Removal." *Gallup Independent*, August 31, 2007.

Johnson, Robert. "Cultural Heritage Park Proposed for Iao Valley." *Honolulu Advertiser*, March 13, 1967.

Johnson, Susan Lee. *Roaring Camp: The Social World of the California Gold Rush*. New York: W. W. Norton, 2000.

Johnson, Walter. *River of Dark Dreams: Slavery and Empire in the Cotton Kingdom*. Cambridge, MA: Harvard University Press, 2013.

Johnston, Anna, and Alan Lawson. "Settler Colonies." In *A Companion to Postcolonial Studies*, edited by Henry Schwarz and Sangeeta Ray, 360–76. Malden, MA: Blackwell Publishing, 2005.

Johnston, Richard W. "Shake 'Em Out of the Coconut Trees." *Sports Illustrated*, August 16, 1976. Accessed on January 17, 2014. http://si.com/vault/article/magazine/MAG1091426/index.htm

Jones, Dorothy V. *License for Empire: Colonialism by Treaty in Early America*. Chicago: University of Chicago Press, 1982.

Jorgensen, Miriam, ed. *Rebuilding Native Nations: Strategies for Governance and Development*. Tucson: University of Arizona Press, 2007.

Jung, Moon-Kie. "Constituting the U.S. Empire-State and White Supremacy: The Early Years." In *State of White Supremacy: Racism, Governance, and the United States*, edited by Moon-Kie Jung, João H. Costa Vargas, and Eduardo Bonilla-Silva, 1–26. Palo Alto, CA: Stanford University Press, 2011.

Jung, Moon-Ho. *Coolies and Cane: Race, Labor, and Sugar in the Age of Emancipation*. Baltimore: Johns Hopkins University Press, 2008.

Kalaw, Teodoro M. *Aide-de-Camp to Freedom*. Translated by Maria Kalaw Katigbak. Manila: Teodoro M. Kalaw Society, 1965.

Kamakau, Samuel. *Hawaiian Annual*. Honolulu: Thomas G. Thrum, 1932.

Kameʻeleihiwa, Lilikalā. *Native Land and Foreign Desires*. Honolulu: Bishop Museum Press, 1992.

Kaplan, Amy. *The Anarchy of Empire in the Making of U.S. Culture*. Cambridge, MA: Harvard University Press, 2002.

Kaplan, Amy. "'Left Alone with America': The Absence of Empire in the Study of American Culture." In *Cultures of United States Imperialism*, edited by Amy Kaplan and Donald E. Pease. Durham, NC: Duke University Press, 1993.

Kauanui, J. Kēhaulani. "Colonialism in Equality: Hawaiian Sovereignty and the Question of US Civil Rights." *South Atlantic Quarterly* 107, no. 4 (fall 2008): 635–50.

Kauanui, J. Kēhaulani. *Hawaiian Blood: Colonialism and the Politics of Sovereignty and Indigeneity*. Durham, NC: Duke University Press, 2008.

Kauanui, J. Kēhaulani. "The Multiplicity of Hawaiian Sovereignty Claims and the Struggle for Meaningful Autonomy." *Comparative American Studies* 3, no. 3 (2005): 283–99.

Kauanui, J. Kēhaulani. "The Politics of Blood and Sovereignty in *Rice v. Cayetano*." *Political and Legal Anthropology Review* 25, no. 1 (2002): 100–128.

Kauanui, J. Kēhaulani. "Precarious Positions: Native Hawaiians and US Federal Recognition." *Contemporary Pacific* 17, no. 1 (2005): 1–27.

Kazanjian, David. "Colonial." In *Keywords for American Cultural Studies*, edited by Bruce Burgett and Glenn Hendler, 52–57. New York: New York University Press, 2007.

Kearns, Rick. "U.N. Declaration Becomes Law of the Land in Bolivia." *Indian Country Today*, December 10, 2007. Accessed April 29, 2014. http://indiancountrytodaymedianetwork.com/2007/12/10/un-declaration-becomes-law-land-bolivia-91875.

Keesing, Felix Maxwell. *Modern Samoa: Its Government and Changing Life*. London: G. Allen and Unwin, 1934.

Kelley, Klara, and Harris Francis. "Traditional Navajo Maps and Wayfinding," *American Indian Culture and Research Journal* 29, no. 2 (2005): 85–111.

Kelley, Klara Bonsack, and Harris Francis. *Navajo Sacred Places*. Bloomington: Indiana University Press, 1994.

Kellor, Frances A. *Straight America: A Call to National Service*. New York: Macmillan, 1916.

Kelly, Anne Keala, dir. *Noho Hewa: The Wrongful Occupation of Hawai'i*. A Kuleana Works Production, 2009.

Kelly, Isabel T. *Southern Paiute Ethnography*. Anthropological Papers, no. 69. Glen Canyon Series no. 21. Salt Lake City: Department of Anthropology, University of Utah, May 1964.

Kelly, John D., and Martha Kaplan, "Legal Fictions after Empire." In *The State of Sovereignty: Territories, Laws, Populations*, edited by Douglas Howland and Luise White, 169–95. Bloomington: Indiana University Press, 2009.

Kennedy, John F. *A Nation of Immigrants*. 1964. New York: Harper Perennial, 2008.

"Kennedy Studying Iao Memorial to Brother." *Maui News*, August 19, 1971.

Kent, Noel. *Hawaii: Islands under the Influence*. Honolulu: University of Hawai'i Press, 1993.

"Kēpaniwai Park Is Dedicated: New County Playground in Iao Valley Now Open to Public." *Maui News*, July 19, 1952.

Kern, Edward. *Map of the Route pursued in 1849 by the US Troops, under the command of Bvt. Lieut. Col. Jno. M. Washington, Governor of New Mexico, in an expedition against the Navajos Indians*. Philadelphia: P. S. Duval's Steam Press, 1850.

Khalili, Laleh. *Time in the Shadows: Confinement in Counterinsurgencies*. Palo Alto, CA: Stanford University Press, 2012.

Kidwell, Clara Sue. *Choctaws and Missionaries in Mississippi, 1818–1918*. Norman: University of Oklahoma Press, 1995.

Kim, Jodi. *Ends of Empire: Asian American Critique and the Cold War*. Minneapolis: University of Minnesota Press, 2010.

King, C. Richard. *Unsettling America: The Uses of Indianness in the 21st Century*. Lanham, MD: Rowman and Littlefield, 2013.

King, Thomas. *The Truth about Stories: A Native Narrative*. Minneapolis: University of Minnesota Press, 2003.

Kinzer, Stephen. *Overthrow: America's Century of Regime Change from Hawaii to Iraq*. New York: Times Books, 2006.

Kirsch, Scott. "John Wesley Powell and the Mapping of the Colorado Plateau, 1869–

1879: Survey Science, Geographical Solutions, and the Economy of Environmental Values." *Annals of the Association of American Geographers* 92 (2002): 548–72.

Kirschensheiter, Gretchen. "Resolving the Hostility: Which Laws Apply to the Commonwealth of the Northern Mariana Islands Where Federal and Local Laws Conflict." *University of Hawai'i Law Review* 21, no. 1 (summer 1999): 237–72.

Kirshenblatt-Gimblett, Barbara. *Destination Culture: Tourism, Museums, and Heritage*. Berkeley: University of California Press, 1998.

Klein, Christina. *Cold War Orientalism: Asia in the Middlebrow Imagination, 1944–1961*. Berkeley: University of California Press, 2003.

Knack, Martha C., and Omer C. Stewart. *As Long as the River Shall Run: An Ethnohistory of Pyramid Lake Indian Reservation*. Berkeley: University of California Press, 1984.

Knopf, Terry Ann. *Rumors, Race and Riots*. New Brunswick, NJ: Transaction Books, 1975.

Koopman, John. "Interpreter's Death Rattles Troops." *San Francisco Chronicle*, August 1, 2004.

Kosek, Jake. "Deep Roots and Long Shadows: The Cultural Politics of Memory and Longing in New Mexico." *Environment and Planning D: Society and Space* 22 (2004): 329–54.

Kraker, Daniel. "Navajo Nation Could Elect First Female President." National Public Radio, October 30, 2010. Accessed May 1, 2014. http://www.npr.org/templates/story/story.php?storyId=130913322.

Kramer, Paul A. *The Blood of Government: Race, Empire, the United States, and the Philippines*. Chapel Hill: University of North Carolina Press, 2006.

Kramer, Paul A. "Power and Connection: Imperial Histories of the United States in the World," *American Historical Review* 116, no. 6 (December 2011): 1348–91.

Krauthamer, Barbara. *Black Slaves, Indian Masters: Slavery, Emancipation, and Citizenship in the Native American South*. Chapel Hill: University of North Carolina Press, 2013.

Kuokkanen, Rauna. "Globalization as Racialized, Sexualized Violence: The Case of Indigenous Women." *International Feminist Journal of Politics* 10, no. 2 (June 2008): 216–33.

LaDuke, Winona, with Sean Aaron Cruz. *The Militarization of Indian Country*. East Lansing, MI: Makwa Enewed, 2013.

LaFeber, Walter. *The New Empire: An Interpretation of American Expansion, 1860–1898*. Ithaca, NY: Cornell University Press, 1963.

LaFranci, Howard. "Remembering Allan: A Tribute to Jim Carroll's Interpreter." *Christian Science Monitor*, March 6, 2006.

Lajimodiere, Denise. "Ogimah Ikwe: Native Women and Their Path to Leadership." *Wicazo Sa Review* 26, no. 2 (fall 2011): 57–82.

Lâm, Maivân C. *At The Edge of the State: Indigenous Peoples and Self-Determination*. Ardsley, NY: Transnational Publishers, 2000.

"Land Change on Iao Park Project Okayed by Board: Deal to Raise $6,000." *Maui News*, January 18, 1941.

LaPlante, Matthew D. "Speaking the Language; A Vital Skill; Interpreters in High Demand in Iraq." *Salt Lake Tribune*, October 13, 2005.

Latour, Bruno. *We Have Never Been Modern*. Cambridge, MA: Harvard University Press, 1993.

Lawson, Gary, and Guy Seidman. *The Constitution of Empire: Territorial Expansion and American Legal History*. New Haven, CT: Yale University Press, 2004.

Lawson, Gary, and Guy Seidman. "The First 'Incorporation' Debate." In *The Louisiana Purchase and American Expansion, 1803–1898*, edited by Sanford Levinson and Bartholomew H. Sparrow, 19–40. Lanham, MD: Rowman and Littlefield, 2005.

Lee, Christopher J., ed. *Making a World after Empire: The Bandung Moment and Its Political Afterlives*. Athens: Ohio University Press, 2010.

Lee, Erika. *At America's Gates: Chinese Immigration during the Exclusion Era, 1882–1943*. Chapel Hill: University of North Carolina Press, 2003.

Legg, Stephen. *Spaces of Colonialism: Delhi's Urban Governmentalities*. Oxford: Blackwell, 2007.

Leibowitz, Arnold H. *Defining Status: A Comprehensive Analysis of United States Territorial Relations*. Norwell, MA: Kluwer Academic, 1989.

Lemke, Thomas. *Biopolitics: An Advanced Introduction*. New York: New York University Press, 2011.

Lenin, V. I. "Imperialism, the Highest Stage of Capitalism" (1916). In *Essential Works of Lenin*, edited by Henry M. Christman, 177–270. New York: Dover, 1987.

Lepore, Jill. *A Is for American: Letters and Other Characters in the Newly United States*. New York: Alfred A. Knopf, 2002.

Levinson, Charles. "Iraq's 'Terps' Face Suspicions on Both Sides." *Christian Science Monitor*, April 17, 2006.

Levinson, Sanford, and Bartholomew H. Sparrow. Introduction to *The Louisiana Purchase and American Expansion, 1803–1898*, edited by Sanford Levinson and Bartholomew H. Sparrow, 1–18. Lanham, MD: Rowman and Littlefield, 2005.

Lewis, Tom. "The Politics of 'Hauntology' in Derrida's *Spectres of Marx*." In *Ghostly Demarcations: A Symposium on Jacques Derrida's Specters of Marx*, edited by Michael Sprinker, 134–67. New York: Verso, 1999.

Lewthwaite, Gordon R., Christine Mainzer, and Patrick J. Holland. "From Polynesia to California: Samoan Migration and Its Sequel." *Journal of Pacific History* 8, no. 1 (1973): 133–57.

Lidchi, Henrietta. "The Poetics and the Politics of Exhibiting Other Cultures." In *Representation: Cultural Representations and Signifying Practices*, edited by Stuart Hall, 151–222. Thousand Oaks: Sage, 1997.

Lilly, C. F. Eli, Ermine Voegelin, Paul Weer et al. *Walam Olum, or Red Score: The Migration Legend of the Lenni Lenape or Delaware Indians, a New Translation*. Indianapolis: Indiana Historical Society, 1954.

Lilomaiava-Doktor, Sa'iliemanu. "Beyond 'Migration': Samoan Population Movement (Malaga) and the Geography of Social Space (Vā)." *Contemporary Pacific* 21, no. 1 (2009): 1–32.

Limerick, Patricia Nelson. *The Legacy of Conquest: The Unbroken Past of the American West*. New York: Norton, 1987.

Lindsay, Samuel. "Report of the Commissioner of Education." In *Second Annual Report of the Governor of Porto Rico*, by William Hunt, 228–84. Washington, DC: Government Printing Office, 1902.

Linebaugh, Peter. *The Magna Carta Manifesto: Liberties and Commons for All*. Berkeley: University of California Press, 2008.

Link, Martin A. *Navajo: A Century of Progress, 1868–1968*. Window Rock, AZ: Navajo Tribe, 1968.

Linn, Brian McAllister. "The Long Twilight of the Frontier Army." *Western Historical Quarterly* 27 (1996): 141–67.

Linnekin, Jocelyn. "Structural History and Political Economy: The Contact Encounter in Hawai'i and Samoa." *History and Anthropology* 5 (1991): 205–32.

Lizze, Ryan. "The Return of the Nativist." *New Yorker*, December 17, 2007, 46–51.

Lofgren, Charles A. *A Legal-Historical Interpretation of the Plessy Case*. New York: Oxford University Press, 1987.

Loftus, Bethan. "Dominant Culture Interrupted: Recognition, Resentment and the Politics of Change in an English Police Force." *British Journal of Criminology* 48, no. 6 (2008): 756–77.

Loomba, Ania. *Colonialism/Postcolonialism*. 2nd ed. New York: Routledge, 2005.

López, Magdalena. "El otro de Nuestra América: Imaginarios nacionales frente a Estados Unidos en la República Dominicana y Cuba." PhD diss., University of Pittsburgh, 2008.

Louis, William Roger, and Ronald Robinson. "The Imperialism of Decolonization." In *Ends of British Imperialism: The Scramble for Empire, Suez, and Decolonization*, 451–502. London: I. B. Tauris, 2006.

Lovett, Laura L. "African and Cherokee by Choice: Race and Resistance under Legalized Segregation." In *Confounding the Color Line: The Indian-Black Experience in North America*, edited by James F. Brooks, 192–222. Lincoln: University of Nebraska Press, 2002.

Lowell, A. Lawrence. "The Colonial Expansion of the United States," *Atlantic Monthly* 83 (February 1899): 145–54.

Lutz, Catherine. *The Bases of Empire: The Global Struggle against U.S. Military Posts*. New York: New York University Press, 2009.

Lyon, Roy Robert. "Field Work on the Progressive Military Map of the United States." Thesis for advanced degree in civil engineering, Michigan Agricultural College [East Lansing, MI], 1914.

Lyons, Paul. *American Pacificism: Oceania in the U.S. Imagination*. London: Routledge, 2006.

Lyons, Scott Richard. *X-Marks: Native Signatures of Assent*. Minneapolis: University of Minnesota Press, 2010.

MacCormack, Sabine. *Religion in the Andes: Vision and Imagination in Early Colonial Peru*. Princeton, NJ: Princeton University Press, 1991.

MacKenzie, Melody K. "The Value of Hawaii: Law and the Courts." *Honolulu Civil Beat*. September 13, 2010. Accessed January 20, 2011. http://www.civilbeat.com/articles/2010/09/13/4440-the-value-of-hawaii-law-and-the-courts-by-melody-kapilialoha-mackenzie/

Maghnaghi, Russell M. "Virginia City's Chinese Community, 1860–1880." In *Chinese on the American Frontier*, ed. Arif Dirlik. Lanham, MD: Rowman and Littlefield, 2001.

"Main-Market Street Lot to Be Auctioned Today." *Maui News*, March 29, 1941.

Malavet, Pedro A. *America's Colony: The Political and Cultural Conflict between the United States and Puerto Rico*. New York: New York University Press, 2004.

Mangan, J. A. *Pleasure, Profit, Proselytism: British Culture and Sport at Home and Abroad, 1700–1914*. London: Frank Cass, 1987.

Mankiller, Wilma, with Michael Wallis. *Mankiller: A Chief and Her People*. New York: St. Martin's, 1999.

Mantler, Gordon K. *Power to the Poor: Black-Brown Coalition and the Fight for Economic Justice*. Chapel Hill: University of North Carolina Press, 2013.

Marín Román, Héctor. *¡Llegó la gringada! El contexto socio-militar estadounidense en Puerto Rico y otro lugares del Caribe hasta 1919*. San Juan, PR: Academia Puertorriqueña de la Historia, 2009.

Markham, Jesse Makani. "An Evolving Geography of Sport: The Recruitment and Mobility of Samoan College Football Players 1998–2008." Master's thesis, University of Hawaiʻi, 2008.

Martin, Joel W. "Crisscrossing Projects of Sovereignty and Conversion: Cherokee Christians and New England Missionaries during the 1820s." In *Native Americans, Christianity, and the Reshaping of the American Religious Landscape*, edited by Joel W. Martin and Mark A. Nicholas, 67–89. Chapel Hill: University of North Carolina Press, 2010.

Martínez, Ruby Ann. "Reies López Tijerina's 'The Land-Grant Question': A Rhetorical Analysis of Metaphors and Motifs." Master's thesis, University of New Mexico, 1991.

Mason, Matthew. *Slavery and Politics in the Early American Republic*. Chapel Hill: University of North Carolina Press, 2006.

Mathews, Mary McNair. *Ten Years in Nevada or Life on the Pacific Coast*. 1880. Lincoln: University of Nebraska Press, 1985.

May, Glenn Anthony. *The Battle for Batangas: A Philippine Province at War*. New Haven, CT: Yale University Press, 1991.

Mayoral, Carmen Gautier. "El nacionalismo y la descolonización internacional hemisférica en la posguerra." In *La Nación puertorriqueña: ensayos en torno a Pedro Albizu Campos*, edited by Juan Manuel Carrión, Teresa C. Gracia Ruiz, Carlos Rodríguez-Fraticelli, 97–121. San Juan: Editorial de la Universidad de Puerto Rico, 1993.

Mbembe, Achille. "Necropolitics." *Public Culture* 15, no. 1 (2003): 11–40.

Mbembe, Achille. *On the Postcolony*. Berkeley: University of California Press, 2001.

McClintock, Anne. *Imperial Leather: Race, Gender, and Sexuality in the Colonial Conquest*. New York: Routledge, 1995.

McClintock, Anne, Aamir Mufti, and Ella Shohat, eds. *Dangerous Liaisons: Gender, Nation, and Postcolonial Perspectives*. Minneapolis: University of Minnesota Press, 1997.

McCoy, Alfred. *Policing America's Empire: The United States, the Philippines, and the Rise of the Surveillance State*. Madison: University of Wisconsin Press, 2009.

McCoy, Alfred W., and Francisco A. Scarano, eds. *Colonial Crucible: Empire in the Making of the Modern American State*. Madison: University of Wisconsin Press, 2009.

McCoy, Alfred, Francisco Scarano, and Courtney Johnson. "On the Tropic of Cancer: Transitions and Transformations in the U.S. Imperial States." In *Colonial Crucible: Empire in the Making of the Modern American State*, edited by Alfred McCoy and Francisco Scarano, 3–33. Madison: University of Wisconsin Press, 2009.

McCutchen, David. *The Red Record: The Wallam Olum; The Oldest Native North American History*. Garden City Park, NY: Avery, 1993.

McEachern, Diane, Marlene Van Winkle, and Sue Steiner. "Domestic Violence among the Navajo: A Legacy of Colonization." *Journal of Poverty* 2, no. 4 (1998): 31–46.

McGuinness, Aims. *Path of Empire: Panama and the California Gold Rush*. Ithaca, NY: Cornell University Press, 2008.

M'Closkey, Kathy. *Swept under the Rug: A Hidden History of Navajo Weaving*. Albuquerque: University of New Mexico Press, 2008.

McMichael, Philip. "Globalization: Myths and Realities" In *The Globalization and Development Reader: Perspectives on Development and Global Change*, edited by J. T. Roberts and A. Hite, 216–32. Malden, MA: Blackwell Publishers, 2007.

McNaughton, Malcolm. In Oral History Project, Social Science Research Institute, University of Hawai'i at Mānoa. *Perspectives on Hawai'i's Statehood*, 47–68. Honolulu: Social Science Research Institute, June 1986.

McNitt, Frank, ed. *The Navaho Expedition: Journal of a Military Reconnaissance from Santa Fe, New Mexico, to the Navajo Country, Made in 1849 by Lieutenant James H. Simpson*. Norman: University of Oklahoma Press, 1964.

Mead, Margaret. *Coming of Age in Samoa: A Psychological Study of Primitive Youth for Western Civilisation*. 1928. New York: HarperCollins, 2001.

Melamed, Jodi. *Represent and Destroy: Rationalizing Violence in the New Racial Capitalism*. Minneapolis: University of Minnesota Press, 2011.

Melamed, Jodi. "The Spirit of Neoliberalism: From Racial Liberalism to Neoliberal Multiculturalism." *Social Text* 89 (winter 2006): 1–24.

Meleisea, Malama. *The Making of Modern Samoa: Traditional Authority and Colonial Administration in the History of Western Samoa*. Suva, Fiji: Institute of Pacific Studies of the University of the South Pacific, 1987.

"Mendieta Is Made President of Cuba; Grau Resigns, Hevia Rules Only One Day." *Clewiston News*, March 2, 1934.

Merk, Frederick. *Manifest Destiny and Mission in American History: A Reinterpretation*. New York: Vintage, 1963.

Messner, Michael A. *Power at Play: Sports and the Problem of Masculinity, Men and Masculinity*. Boston: Beacon Press, 1992.

Meyer, Manulani Aluli. *Ho'oulu: Our Time of Becoming*. Honolulu: 'Ai Pōhaku Press, 2003.

Miles, Tiya. "'His Kingdom for a Kiss': Indians and Intimacy in the Narrative of John Marrant." In *Haunted by Empire: Geographies of Intimacy in North American History*, edited by Ann Laura Stoler, 163–88. Durham, NC: Duke University Press, 2006.

Miles, Tiya. *The House on Diamond Hill: A Cherokee Plantation Story*. Chapel Hill: University of North Carolina Press, 2010.

Miles, Tiya. *Ties that Bind: The Story of an Afro-Cherokee Family in Slavery and Freedom*. Berkeley: University of California Press, 2005.

Miller, Mark Edwin. *Forgotten Tribes: Unrecognized Indians in the Federal Acknowledgment Process*. Lincoln: University of Nebraska Press, 2004.

Miller, Toby, ed. "The Politics of Sport." Special issue. *Social Text* 50 (spring 1997).

Miyoshi, Masao, and Harry Harootunian, eds. *Learning Places: The "Afterlives" of Area Studies*, Durham, NC: Duke University Press, 2002.

Mohanty, Chandra Talpade. "Cartographies of Struggle: Third World Women and the Politics of Feminism." In *Third World Women and the Politics of Feminism*, edited by C. Mohanty, A. Russo, and L. Torres, 1–47. Bloomington: Indiana University Press, 1991.

Montgomery, Charles. *The Spanish Redemption: Heritage, Power, and Loss on New Mexico's Upper Río Grande.* Berkeley: University of California Press, 2002.

Montgomery, Charles. "The Trap of Race and Memory: The Language of Spanish Civility on the Upper Rio Grande." *American Quarterly* 52 (September 2000): 478–513.

"Monument for JFK Profile in Iao Valley." *Maui News*, July 22, 1970.

Morales Carrión, Arturo. *Puerto Rico: A Political and Cultural History.* New York: W. W. Norton, 1983.

Moraña, Mabel. "Introduction: Mapping Hispanism." In *Ideologies of Hispanism*, edited by Mabel Moraña, x–xi. Nashville: Vanderbilt University Press, 2005.

Morgan, Lewis H. *Ancient Society.* 1877. http://www.marxists.org/reference/archive/morgan-lewis/ancient-society/.

Morgensen, Scott Lauria. "Settler Homonationalism: Theorizing Settler Colonialism within Queer Modernities." In "Sexuality, Nationality, Indigeneity," edited by Daniel Heath Justice, Mark Rifkin, and Bethany Schneider. Special issue, GLQ: *A Journal of Lesbian and Gay Studies* 6, nos. 1–2 (2010): 105–31.

Morgensen, Scott Lauria. *Spaces between Us: Queer Settler Colonialism and Indigenous Decolonization.* Minneapolis: University of Minnesota Press, 2011.

Morris, Glenn T. "International Law and Politics: Toward a Right to Self-Determination for Indigenous Peoples." In *The State of Native America: Genocide, Colonization, and Resistance*, edited by M. Annette Jaimes, 55–86. Boston: South End Press, 1992.

Morrison, James D., ed. "Notes from *The Northern Standard*, 1842–1849." *Chronicles of Oklahoma* 19, no. 1 (March 1941): 83–84.

Morrison, Michael A. *Slavery and the American West: The Eclipse of Manifest Destiny and the Coming of the Civil War.* Chapel Hill: University of North Carolina Press, 1997.

Moses, John A. "The Solf Regime in Western Samoa: Ideal and Reality." *New Zealand Journal of History* 6, no. 1 (1972): 42–56.

Motes, Jordi Maluquer de. *Nación e inmigración: Los españoles en Cuba, siglos xix y xx.* Barcelona: Ediciones Jucar, 1992.

Nabokov, Peter. *Tijerina and the Courthouse Raid.* Berkeley, CA: Ramparts Press, 1969.

Nagata, Suichi. "Dan Kochhongva's Message: Myth, Ideology and Political Action among the Contemporary Hopi." *Yearbook of Symbolic Anthropology* 1 (1978): 73–87.

Naranjo Orovio, Consuelo, and Miguel Ángel Puig-Samper. "Los lazos de la cultura se convierten en lazos de solidaridad: Los inicios del exilio español." In *Los lazos de la cultura: El Centro de Estudios Históricos de Madrid y la Universidad de Puerto Rico, 1916–1939*, edited by Consuelo Naranjo et al., 309–19. Río Piedras: Centro de Investigaciones Históricas de la Universidad de Puerto Rico, 2002.

Nashel, Jonathan. "The Road to Vietnam: Modernization Theory in Fact and Fiction." In *Cold War Constructions: The Political Culture of United States Imperialism, 1945–1966*, edited by Christian G. Appy, 132–54. Amherst: University of Massachusetts, 2000.

Naylor, Celia. *African Cherokees in Indian Territory: From Chattel to Citizens.* Chapel Hill: University of North Carolina Press, 2008.

Nebrija, Antonio de. *Gramatica de la lengua castellana*. Edited and with an introduction by Ig. Gonzalez-Llubera. London: Oxford University Press, 1926.

Negrón de Montilla, Aida. *La americanización en Puerto Rico y el sistema de instrucción pública, 1900–1930*. Río Piedras: Editorial de la Universidad de Puerto Rico, 1990.

Negrón-Muntaner, Frances. Introduction to *None of the Above: Puerto Ricans in the Global Era*, edited by Frances Negrón-Muntaner, 1–17. New York: Palgrave Macmillan, 2007.

Negrón Portillo, Mariano. *Cuadrillas anexionistas y revueltas campesinas, 1898–1899*. Río Piedras, PR: Centro de Investigaciones Sociales, Universidad de Puerto Rico, 1987.

Neruda, Pablo. "Tonight I Can Write." In *Twenty Love Poems and a Song of Despair*, 51–54. New York: Penguin, 1978.

Newman, Andrew. "The Walam Olum: An Indigenous Apocrypha and Its Readers." *American Literary History* 23, no. 1 (2009): 26–56.

Ngai, Mae. *Impossible Subjects: Illegal Aliens and the Making of Modern America*. Princeton, NJ: Princeton University Press, 2004.

Nguyen, Mimi Thi. *The Gift of Freedom: War, Debt, and Other Refugee Passages*. Durham, NC: Duke University Press, 2012.

Nichols, Robert. "Indigeneity and the Settler Contract Today." *Philosophy and Social Criticism* 39, no. 2 (2013): 165–86.

Nichols, Robert. "Realizing the Social Contract: The Case of Colonialism and Indigenous Peoples." *Contemporary Political Theory* 4, no. 1 (February 2005): 42–62.

Nieto-Phillips, John. *The Language of Blood: The Making of Spanish-American Identity in New Mexico*. Albuquerque: University of New Mexico Press, 2008.

Noble, A. M. *Codification of the Regulations and Orders for the Government of American Samoa*. San Francisco: Phillips and Van Opden, 1921.

Noble, David Grant. *New Light on Chaco Canyon*. Santa Fe, NM: SAR Press, 1984.

Nobles, Melissa. *The Politics of Official Apologies*. Cambridge: Cambridge University Press, 2008.

O'Brien, Jean M. *Firsting and Lasting: Writing Indians Out of Existence in New England*. Minneapolis: University of Minnesota Press, 2010.

Ochoa, Enrique. *Feeding Mexico: The Political Uses of Food*. New York: SR Books, 2001.

Oestreicher, David M. "The Anatomy of the Walam Olum: The Dissection of a 19th Century Hoax." PhD diss., Rutgers University, 1995.

Oestreicher, David M. "The Tale of a Hoax." In *Algonquian Spirit: Contemporary Translations of the Algonquian Literatures of North America*, edited by Brian Swann, 3–31. Lincoln: University of Nebraska Press, 2005.

Oestreicher, David M. "Unmasking the Walam Olum: A 19th Century Hoax." *Bulletin of the Archaeological Society of New Jersey* 49 (1994): 1–44.

O'Meara, John. *Delaware-English/English-Delaware Dictionary*. Toronto: University of Toronto Press, 1996.

Onions, Charles Talbut, ed. *The Oxford Dictionary of English Etymology*. New York: Clarendon Press, 1992.

Onuf, Peter S. *The Origins of the Federal Republic: Jurisdictional Controversies in the United States, 1775–1787*. Philadelphia: University of Pennsylvania Press, 1983.

Onuf, Peter S. *Statehood and Union: History of the Northwest Ordinance*. Bloomington: Indiana University Press, 1992.

Ortiz, Alfonso. *The Tewa World: Space, Time, Being and Becoming in a Pueblo Society.* Chicago: University of Chicago Press, 1969.

Osorio, Jonathan Kamakawiwoʻole. *Dismembering Lāhui: A History of the Hawaiian Nation to 1887.* Honolulu: University of Hawaiʻi Press, 2002.

Osorio, Jonathan Kamakawiwoʻole. "Jon Osorio's Response to the 'Ceded' Lands Settlement: An Open Letter to the Lāhui," May 23, 2009. Accessed January 27, 2011. http://statehoodhawaii.org/wp/2009/05/27/an-open-letter-to-the-lahui/.

Osorio, Jonathan Kamakawiwoʻole. "The Value of Hawaii: Hawaiian Issues by Jon Osorio," *Honolulu Civil Beat,* August 2, 2010. http://www.civilbeat.com/articles/2010/08/02/2902-the-value-of-hawaii-hawaiian-issues-by-jon-osorio/.

Osterhammel, Jürgen. *Colonialism: A Theoretical Overview.* 2nd ed. Translated by Shelley L. Frisch. Princeton, NJ: Markus Wiener, 2005.

Paine, Thomas. "Common Sense." 1776. In *Political Writings,* edited by Bruce Kuklick, 1–45. New York: Cambridge University Press, 2000.

Parker, Kunal M. *Common Law, History, and Democracy in America, 1790–1900.* Cambridge: Cambridge University Press, 2011.

Peckham, Tom. "Sovereignty Now or Sovereignty Later: Federal Recognition Legislation Proposed." *Delaware Indian News* 29, no. 1 (2006): 1, 4–5.

Pelligrino, Victor C. *Uncle Kawaiola's Dream.* Wailuku, HI: Maui arThoughts Company, 2010.

Pérez, Louis A., Jr. *On Becoming Cuban: Identity, Nationality, and Culture.* Chapel Hill: University of North Carolina Press, 1999.

Pérez, Louis A., Jr. *Cuba and the United States: Ties of Singular Intimacy.* 3rd ed. Athens: University of Georgia Press, 2003.

Phelps, Dawson A., ed. "Excerpts from the Journal of the Reverend Joseph Bullen, 1799 and 1800." *Journal of Mississippi History* 17 (October 1955): 254–81.

Pickles, John. *A History of Spaces: Cartographic Reason, Mapping and the Geo-Coded World.* New York: Routledge, 2004.

Picó, Fernando. *1898: La guerra después de la guerra.* Río Piedras, PR: Ediciones Huracán, 1987.

Pitt, David C. *Tradition and Economic Progress in Samoa: A Case Study of the Role of Traditional Social Institutions in Economic Development.* Oxford: Clarendon Press, 1970.

Political Status Education Coordinating Commission. *Kinalamten Pulitikåt: Siñenten I Chamorro. Issues in Guam's Political Development: The Chamorro Perspective.* Agaña, Guam: Political Status Education Coordinating Commission, 1996.

Pomeroy, Earl S. *The Territories and the United States, 1861–1890: Studies in Colonial Administration.* 1947. Seattle: University of Washington Press, 1969.

Portnoy, Alisse. *Their Right to Speak: Women's Activism in the Indian and Slave Debates.* Cambridge, MA: Harvard University Press, 2005.

Povinelli, Elizabeth A. *The Cunning of Recognition: Indigenous Alterities and the Making of Australian Multiculturalism.* Durham, NC: Duke University Press, 2002.

Povinelli, Elizabeth A. *Economies of Abandonment: Social Belonging and Endurance in Late Liberalism.* Durham, NC: Duke University Press, 2011.

Povinelli, Elizabeth A. "The Governance of the Prior." *Interventions: International Journal of Postcolonial Studies* 13, no. 1 (2011): 13–30.

Powell, Dana E., and Dáilan J. Long. "Landscapes of Power: Renewable Energy Activism in Diné Bikéyah." In *Indians and Energy: Exploitation and Opportunity in the American Southwest*, edited by Sherry L. Smith and Brian Frehner, 231–62. Santa Fe, NM: SAR Press, 2010.

Pratt, Julius W. *America's Colonial Experiment: How the United States Acquired, Governed, and in Part Gave Away a Colonial Empire*. New York: Prentice-Hall, 1950.

Pratt, Mary Louise. "Harm's Way: Language and the Contemporary Arts of War." *PMLA* 124, no. 5 (October 2009): 1515–32.

Pratt, Mary Louise. *Imperial Eyes: Travel Writing and Transculturation*. 2nd ed. New York: Routledge, 2007.

Prucha, Francis Paul, ed. *Documents of United States Indian Policy*, 3rd ed. 1975. Lincoln: University of Nebraska Press, 2000.

Prucha, Francis Paul. *The Great Father: The United States Government and the American Indians*. Vol. 1. Lincoln: University of Nebraska Press, 1984.

Pulitano, Elvira, ed. *Indigenous Rights in the Age of the UN Declaration*. New York: Cambridge University Press, 2012.

Pungong, Victor. "The United States and the International Trusteeship System." In *The United States and Decolonization*, edited by David Ryan and Victor Pungong, 85–101. New York: St. Martin's, 2000.

Quinn, William W. "Federal Acknowledgement of American Indian Tribes: The Historical Development of a Legal Concept." *American Journal of Legal History* 34 (October 1990): 331–64.

Raboteau, Albert. *Slave Religion: The "Invisible Institution" in the Antebellum South*. Updated ed. New York; Oxford University Press, 2004.

Rafael, Vicente L. *Contracting Colonialism: Translation and Christian Conversion in Tagalog Society under Early Spanish Rule*. Durham, NC: Duke University Press, 1993.

Rafael, Vicente L. "The Culture of Area Studies in the United States." *Social Text* 41 (1994): 91–112.

Rafael, Vicente L. *The Promise of the Foreign: Nationalism and the Technics of Translation in the Spanish Philippines*. Durham, NC: Duke University Press, 2005.

Rafael, Vicente L. *White Love and Other Events in Filipino History*. Durham, NC: Duke University Press, 2000.

Rafinesque, Constantine Samuel. *The American Nations; Or, Outlines of Their General History, Ancient and Modern*. 1836. Memphis: General Books, 2010.

Raibmon, Paige. *Authentic Indians: Episodes of Encounter from the Late-Nineteenth-Century Northwest Coast*. Durham, NC: Duke University Press, 2006.

Ramos, Efrén Rivera. *American Colonialism in Puerto Rico: The Judicial and Social Legacy*. Princeton, NJ: Markus Wiener, 2007.

"Range Wars Fears Rise in Colorado." *New York Times*, December 3, 1961.

Rauschning, Dietrich, Katja Wiesbrock, and Martin Lailach, eds. *Key Resolutions of the United Nations General Assembly 1946–1996*. New York: Cambridge University Press, 1997.

Rawick, George, comp. *The American Slave: A Composite Autobiography*. Westport, CT: Greenwood Press, 1972.

Recto, Claro M. *The Complete Works of Claro M. Recto*. Vol. 9. Edited by Isagani R. Medina and Myrna S. Feliciano. Centennial Edition. Pasay City, Philippines: Claro M. Recto Memorial Foundation, 1990.

Reddy, Chandan. *Freedom with Violence: Race, Sexuality, and the US State*. Durham, NC: Duke University Press, 2011.

Reinhartz, Dennis, and Gerald D. Saxon, eds. *Mapping and Empire: Soldier-Engineers on the Southwestern Frontier.* Austin: University of Texas Press, 2005.

Rementer, Jim. "The Arrival of the Whites." In *Algonquian Spirit: Contemporary Translations of the Algonquian Literatures of North America,* edited by Brian Swann, 49–61. Lincoln: University of Nebraska Press, 2005.

Retamar, Roberto Fernández. "Against the Black Legend." In *Caliban and Other Essays,* translated by Edward Baker, 56–73. Minneapolis: University of Minnesota Press, 1989.

Reyhner, Jon. "Policies toward American Indian Languages: A Historical Sketch." In *Language Loyalties: A Source Book on the Official English Controversy,* edited by James Crawford, 41–46. Chicago: University of Chicago Press, 1992.

Rifkin, Mark. "Indigenizing Agamben: Rethinking Sovereignty in Light of the 'Peculiar' Status of Native Peoples." *Cultural Critique* 72 (fall 2009): 88–124.

Rifkin, Mark. *Manifesting America: The Imperial Construction of U.S. National Space.* New York: Oxford University Press, 2009.

Rifkin, Mark. *When Did Indians Become Straight? Kinship, the History of Sexuality, and Native Sovereignty.* New York: Oxford University Press, 2011.

Rivers, Mary J. "Navajo Women and Abuse: The Context for Their Troubled Relationships." *Journal of Family Violence* 20, no. 2 (April 2005): 83–89.

Roberts, J. Timmons, and Amy Hite. *The Globalization and Development Reader: Perspectives on Development and Global Change.* Malden, MA: Blackwell Publishers, 2007.

Rockwell, Stephen J. *Indian Affairs and the Administrative State in the Nineteenth Century.* New York: Cambridge University Press, 2010.

Rodao, Florentino. "Spanish Falange in the Philippines, 1936–1945." *Philippine Studies* (Manila, Ateneo de Manila University) 43, no. 1 (1995): 5–6.

Rodgers, Daniel T. "Exceptionalism." In *Imagined Histories: American Historians Interpret the Past,* edited by Anthony Molho and Gordon S. Wood, 21–40. Princeton, NJ: Princeton University Press, 1998.

Rodriguez Morejón, Gerardo. *Grau San Martín.* 2nd ed. Havana: Ediciones Mirador, 1944.

Rodriguez, Dylan. *Suspended Apocalypse: White Supremacy, Genocide, and the Filipino Condition.* Minneapolis: University of Minnesota Press, 2009.

Rodríguez Vázquez, José Juán. *El sueño que no cesa: La nación deseada en el debate intellectual y politico puertorriqueño, 1920–1940.* San Juan, PR: Ediciones Callejón, Fundación para la Libertad, 2004.

Rogin, Michael Paul. *Fathers and Children: Andrew Jackson and the Subjugation of the American Indian.* New York: Knopf, 1975.

Ronda, James P. "'We Have a Country': Race, Geography, and the Invention of Indian Territory." *Journal of the Early Republic* 19, no. 4 (winter 1999): 739–55.

Roosevelt, Theodore. "Children of the Crucible." In *The Works of Theodore Roosevelt,* vol. 21. Edited by Herman Hagedorn, 45–46. New York: Charles Scribner's Sons, 1926.

Roosevelt, Theodore. "The Children of the Crucible." *Outlook,* September 19, 1917, 80.

Rosales, F. Arturo, ed. *Testimonio: A Documentary History of the Mexican American Struggle for Civil Rights.* Houston: Arte Público Press, 2000.

Rosen, Deborah A. *American Indians and State Law: Sovereignty, Race, and Citizenship, 1790–1880.* Lincoln: University of Nebraska Press, 2007.

Rosenberg, Emily S. *Financial Missionaries to the World: The Politics and Culture of Dollar Diplomacy, 1900–1930.* Durham, NC: Duke University Press, 2003.

Rosnow, Ralph, and Gary Fine. *Rumor and Gossip: The Social Psychology of Hearsay.* New York: Elsevier, 1976.

Rothman, Adam. *Slave Country: American Expansion and the Origins of the Deep South.* Cambridge, MA: Harvard University Press, 2005.

Rupke, Nicolas. "Darwin's Choice." In *Biology and Ideology: From Descartes to Dawkins,* edited by Denis R. Alexander and Ronald L. Numbers, 139–64. Chicago: University of Chicago Press, 2010.

Sagarin, Edward, and Robert J. Kelly. "Polylingualism in the United States of America: A Multitude of Tongues amid a Monolingual Majority." In *Language Policy and National Unity,* edited by William R. Beer and James E. Jacob, 20–44. Totowa, NJ: Rowman and Allanheld, 1985.

Sahlins, Marshall. "Cosmologies of Capitalism: The Trans-Pacific Sector of the World System." *Proceedings of the British Academy* 74 (1988): 1–51.

Said, Edward. *Culture and Imperialism.* New York: Knopf, 1993.

Saldaña-Portillo, María Josefina. "'How Many Mexicans Is a Horse Worth?': The League of Latin American Citizens, Desegregation Cases, and Chicano Historiography." *South Atlantic Quarterly* 107, no. 4 (fall 2008): 809–31.

Saldaña-Portillo, María Josefina. *The Revolutionary Imagination in the Americas and the Age of Development.* Durham, NC: Duke University Press, 2003.

Salesa, T. Damon I. "'Travel Happy' Samoa: Colonialism, Samoan Migration, and a 'Brown Pacific.'" *New Zealand Journal of History* 37, no. 2 (2003): 171–88.

Santiago-Valles, Kelvin. "American Penal Reforms and Colonial Spanish Custodial-Regulatory Practices in Fin de Siècle Puerto Rico." In *Colonial Crucible: Empire in the Making of the Modern American State,* edited by Alfred McCoy and Francisco Scarano, 87–94. Madison: University of Wisconsin Press, 2009.

Santiago-Valles, Kelvin. *"Subject Peoples" and Colonial Discourses: Economic Transformation and Social Disorder in Puerto Rico, 1898–1947.* Albany: State University of New York Press, 1994.

Saranillio, Dean Itsuji. "Colliding Histories: Hawai'i Statehood at the Intersection of Asians 'Ineligible to Citizenship' and Hawaiians 'Unfit for Self-Government.'" *Journal of Asian American Studies* 13, no. 3 (October 2010): 283–309.

Saxton, Alexander "The Army of Canton in the High Sierra." *Pacific Historical Review* 35, no. 2 (May 1966): 141–51.

Scarano, Francisco. "Censuses in the Transition to Modern Colonialism: Spain and the United States in Puerto Rico." In *Colonial Crucible: Empire in the Making of the Modern American State,* edited by Alfred McCoy and Francisco Scarano, 210–19. Madison: University of Wisconsin Press, 2009.

Schramm, Wilbur Lang, Lyle M. Nelson, and Mere T. Betham. *Bold Experiment: The Story of Educational Television in American Samoa.* Palo Alto, CA: Stanford University Press, 1981.

Scott, David. "Colonial Governmentality." *Social Text* 43 (1995): 191–220.

Scott, Lalla. *Karnee: A Paiute Narrative.* Reno: University of Nevada Press, 1966.

Sepúlveda Rivera, Aníbal. *Puerto Rico urbano: Atlas histórico de la ciudad puertor-*

riqueña. 4 vols. San Juan, PR: Centro de Investigaciones CARIMAR y Departamento de Transportación y Obras Públicas, 2004.

Shah, Nayan. *Stranger Intimacy: Contesting Race, Sexuality and the Law in the North American West.* Berkeley: University of California Press, 2012.

Shaw, Stephanie J. "Using the WPA Ex-Slave Narratives to Study the Impact of the Great Depression." *Journal of Southern History* 69 (August 2003): 623–58.

Shaw, Angel Velasco, and Luis Francia. *Vestiges of War: The Philippine-American War and the Aftermath of an Imperial Dream, 1899–1999.* New York: New York University Press, 2002.

Shearer, Benjamin F. *Home Front Heroes: A Biographical Dictionary of Americans during Wartime.* Westport, CT: Greenwood, 2007.

Shebala, Marley. "Heft Bill Due for Travel Advances, Delegates Cry 'Foul.'" *Navajo Times,* December 22, 2010.

Shebala, Marley. "VP's Charges Dropped, Deal for Prez in Works." *Navajo Times,* January 13, 2011.

Shell, Marc. *American Babel: Literatures of the United States from Abnaki to Zuni.* Cambridge, MA: Harvard University Press, 2002.

Shepardson, Mary. *Navajo Ways in Government: A Study in Political Process.* Menasha, WI: American Anthropological Association, 1963.

Shesadri-Crooks, Kalpana. *Desiring Whiteness: A Lacanian Analysis of Race.* London: Routledge, 2000.

Shibutani, Tamotsu. *Improvised News: A Sociological Study of Rumor.* Indianapolis: Bobbs-Merrill, 1966.

Shigematsu, Setsu, and Keith L. Camacho, eds. *Militarized Currents: Toward a Decolonized Future in Asia and the Pacific.* Minneapolis: University of Minnesota Press, 2010.

Shiva, Vandana. *Water Wars: Privatization, Pollution, and Profit.* Boston: South End Press, 2002.

Shore, Bradd. *Sala'ilua, a Samoan Mystery.* New York: Columbia University Press, 1982.

"Shortage of Funds Halts Iao Project: Final Decision Is Up to Legislature and County." *Maui News,* January 8, 1941.

Siegel, James T. *Solo in the New Order: Language and Hierarchy in an Indonesian City.* Princeton, NJ: Princeton University Press, 1986.

Silva, Denise Ferreira da. *Toward a Global Idea of Race.* Minneapolis: University of Minnesota Press, 2007.

Silva, Noenoe K. *Aloha Betrayed: Native Hawaiian Resistance to American Colonialism.* Durham, NC: Duke University Press, 2004.

Silva, Noenoe K. "Nā Hulu Kupuna: To Honor Our Intellectual Ancestors." *Biography* 32, no. 1 (winter 2009): 43–53.

Simmons, Marc. *The Last Conquistador.* Norman: University of Oklahoma Press, 1991.

Simpson, Audra. "Settlement's Secret." *Cultural Anthropology* 26, no. 2 (2011): 205–17.

Simpson, James H. *Coronado's March in Search of the Seven Cities of Cibola and the Discussion of Their Probable Location.* 1869. Washington, DC: Smithsonian Institution, 1884.

Simpson, James H. *Journal of a Military Reconnaissance from Santa Fe, New Mexico,* to the Navajo Country, Made with the Troops under Command of Brevet Lieutenant Colonel John M. Washington, Chief of Ninth Military Department, and Governor of New Mexico, in 1849. Philadelphia: Lippincott, Grambo, 1852.

Simpson, James H. Map of the Route Pursued in 1849 by the US Troops, under the Command of Bvt. Lieut. Col. John M. Washington, Governor of New Mexico, in an Expedition against the Navajos Indians. Philadelphia: Duval, 1849.

Simpson, James H. Reports of the Secretary of War. Washington, DC: Senate Ex. Doc. 64, 31st Congress, 1st Session, 1850.

Sivasundaram, Sujit. "Race, Empire, and Biology before Darwinism." In Biology and Ideology: From Descartes to Dawkins, edited by Denis R. Alexander and Ronald L. Numbers, 114–38. Chicago: University of Chicago Press, 2010.

Slotkin, Richard. Regeneration Through Violence: The Mythology of the American Frontier, 1600–1860. Middletown, CT: Wesleyan University Press, 1973.

Smith, Andrea. Conquest: Sexual Violence and American Indian Genocide. Boston: South End Press, 2005.

Smith, Bernard. "Constructing 'Pacific' Peoples." In Remembrance of Pacific Pasts, edited by Robert Borofsky, 152–68. Honolulu: University of Hawai'i Press, 2000.

Smith, Laurajane. Archaeological Theory and the Politics of Cultural Heritage. New York: Routledge, 2004.

Snow, Alpheus H. The Administration of Dependencies: A Study of the Evolution of the Federal Empire, with Special Reference to American Colonial Problems. New York: G. P. Putnam's Sons, 1902.

Sobel, Mechal. Trabelin' On: The Slave Journey to an Afro-Baptist Faith. Princeton, NJ: Princeton University Press, 1988.

Solarz, Stephen J. "The English Plus Alternative." In Language Loyalties: A Source Book on the Official English Controversy, edited by James Crawford, 151–53. Chicago: University of Chicago Press, 1992.

Solarz, Stephen J. "Native American Language Act." In Language Loyalties: A Source Book on the Official English Controversy, edited by James Crawford, 155–57. Chicago: University of Chicago Press, 1992.

Solarz, Stephen J. "Official English: A Concession to Nativism." In Language Loyalties: A Source Book on the Official English Controversy, edited by James Crawford, 124–27. Chicago: University of Chicago Press, 1992.

Sparrow, Bartholomew H. The "Insular Cases" and the Emergence of American Empire. Lawrence: University Press of Kansas, 2006.

Spriggs, Matthew. "'Preceded by Forest': Changing Interpretations of Landscape Change on Kaho'olawe." Asian Perspectives 30, no. 1 (1991): 71–116.

Sproat, D. Kapu'ala. "Water." In The Value of Hawai'i: Knowing the Past, Shaping the Future, edited by Craig Howes and Jonathan Kamakawiwo'ole Osorio, 187–94. Honolulu: University of Hawai'i Press, 2010.

Squier, Ephraim G. "Historical and Mythological Traditions of the Algonquians; with a Translation of the Walam Olum, or Ark Record of the Linni Lenape." American Review: A Whig Journal Devoted to Politics and Literature 14 (1849): 273–93.

Stephanson, Anders. "A Most Interesting Empire." In The New American Empire, edited by Lloyd C. Gardner and Marilyn B. Young, 253–75. New York: New Press, 2005.

Stoffle, Richard, et al., American Indians and Fajada Butte: Ethnographic Overview and Assessment for Fajada Butte and Traditional (Ethnobotanical) Use Study for CCNHP, NM. Final Report, Grant No. CA-7029-1-0009. February 28, 1994.

Stoler, Ann Laura. *Along the Archival Grain: Epistemic Anxieties and Colonial Common Sense.* Princeton, NJ: Princeton University Press, 2009.

Stoler, Ann Laura. *Carnal Knowledge and Imperial Power: Race and the Intimate in Colonial Rule.* Berkeley: University of California Press, 2010.

Stoler, Ann Laura. "On Degrees of Imperial Sovereignty." *Public Culture* 18, no. 1 (2006): 125–46.

Stoler, Ann Laura. "Tense and Tender Ties: The Politics of Comparison in North American History and (Post) Colonial Studies." In *Haunted by Empire: Geographies of Intimacy in North American History,* edited by Ann Laura Stoler, 23–67. Durham, NC: Duke University Press, 2006.

Stoler, Ann Laura, and Carole McGranahan. "Refiguring Imperial Terrains." In *Imperial Formations,* edited by Ann Laura Stoler, Carole McGranahan, and Peter C. Perdue, 3–44. Santa Fe, NM: SAR Press, 2007.

Sunia, Fofo I. F. *The Story of the Legislature of American Samoa.* Pago Pago: Legislature of American Samoa, 1998.

Sutton, Imre. "Sovereign States and the Changing Definition of the Indian Reservation." *Geographical Review* 66, no. 3 (July 1976): 281–95.

Suzack, Cheryl, Shari M. Huhndorf, Jeanne Perreault, and Jean Barman, eds. *Indigenous Women and Feminism: Politics, Activism, and Culture.* Vancouver: University of British Columbia Press, 2013.

Swadesh, Frances. *Los Primeros Pobladores.* Notre Dame, IN: University of Notre Dame Press, 1974.

Swann, Brian. *Algonquian Spirit: Contemporary Translations of the Algonquian Literatures of North America.* Lincoln: University of Nebraska Press, 2005.

Swentzell, Rina. "Pueblo Space, Form and Mythology." In *Pueblo Style and Regional Architecture,* edited by Nicholas Markovich et al., 23–30. New York: Van Nostrand Reinhold, 1990.

Syken, Bill. "Football in Paradise." *Sports Illustrated.* November 3, 2003. Accessed on April 24, 2014. http://cnnsi.com/vault/article/magazine/MAG1030399/3/index.htm.

Tadiar, Neferti Xina M. *Things Fall Away: Philippine Historical Experience and the Makings of Globalization.* Durham, NC: Duke University Press, 2009.

Takabuki, Matsuo. *An Unlikely Revolutionary: Matsuo Takabuki and the Making of Modern Hawai'i,* assisted by Dennis M. Ogawa, Glen Grant, and Wilma Sur. Honolulu: University of Hawai'i Press, 1998.

Takaki, Ronald. *Strangers from a Different Shore.* New York: Back Bay Books, 1998.

Taylor, Drew Hayden. *Me Sexy: An Exploration of Native Sex and Sexuality.* Berkeley, CA: Douglas and McIntyre, 2008.

Taylor, Rachel Kahn, dir. *Warriors Born: American Samoans in the U.S. Military.* 2010. http://vimeo.com/15806815.

Teaiwa, Teresia K. "On Analogies: Rethinking the Pacific in a Global Context." *Contemporary Pacific* 18, no. 1 (spring 2006): 71–87.

Tengan, Ty P. Kāwika, and Jesse Makani Markham. "Performing Polynesian Masculinities in American Football: From 'Rainbows to Warriors.'" *International Journal of the History of Sport* 26, no. 16 (2009): 2412–31.

Tengan, Ty P. Kāwika, with collaboration from J. L. A. Perry and N. Armstrong.

Report on the Archival, Historical and Archaeological Resources of Nā Wai Ehā, Wailuku District, Island of Maui. Honolulu: Office of Hawaiian Affairs, 2007.

Ter Haar, Barend J. *Telling Stories: Witchcraft and Scapegoating in Chinese History.* Leiden: Brill, 2006.

"Text of Kennedy's Speech to Mayors." *Honolulu Star Bulletin,* June 10, 1963.

Thiong'o, Ngugi Wa. *Decolonising the Mind: The Politics of Language in African Literature.* Portsmouth, NH: Heinemann, 1986.

Thomas, Nicholas. *Colonialism's Culture: Anthropology, Travel, Government.* Princeton, NJ: Princeton University Press, 1994.

Thompson, Lanny. *Imperial Archipelago: Representation and Rule in the Insular Territories under US Dominion after 1898.* Honolulu: University of Hawai'i Press, 2010.

Thompson, Lanny. "The Imperial Republic: A Comparison of the Insular Territories under U.S. Dominion after 1898." *Pacific Historical Review* 71 (2002): 535–74.

Thornberry, Patrick. *Indigenous Peoples and Human Rights.* Huntington, NY: Juris Publishing, 2002.

"Thousands Sign Park Petitions: Purchase of Iao Valley Site Sought." *Maui News,* November 27, 1940.

Tijerina, Reies López. *Mi Lucha por la Tierra.* Mexico City: Fondo de Cultura Económica, 1978.

"T. Ikeoka Buys County Lot at Main-Market St. Corner with $7,350 Bid." *Maui News,* April 2, 1941.

Tinker, George. *Missionary Conquest: The Gospel and Native American Cultural Genocide.* Minneapolis: Fortress Press, 1993.

Tohe, Laura. "There is No Word for Feminism in My Language," *Wicazo Sa Review* 15, no. 2 (fall 2000): 103–10.

Tomes, Nancy. "Crucibles, Capillaries, and Pentimenti: Reflections on Imperial Transformations." In *Colonial Crucible: Empire in the Making of the Modern American State,* edited by Alfred McCoy and Francisco Scarano, 532–40. Madison: University of Wisconsin Press, 2009.

Torpey, John. *Making Whole What Has Been Smashed: On Reparations Politics.* Cambridge, MA: Harvard University Press, 2006.

Torruella, Juan R. "The Insular Cases: The Establishment of a Regime of Political Apartheid." *University of Pennsylvania Journal of International Law* 29, no. 2 (2007): 284–320.

Trask, Haunani-Kay. *From a Native Daughter: Colonialism and Sovereignty in Hawai'i.* Monroe, ME: Common Courage Press, 1993.

Trask, Mililani. "The Politics of Oppression." *Hawai'i Return to Nationhood,* edited by Ulla Hasager and Jonathan Friedman, 68–87. IWGIA-Document 75. Copenhagen: IWGIA, 1994.

Trennert, Robert A., Jr. *Alternative to Extinction: Federal Indian Policy and the Beginnings of the Reservation System, 1846–51.* Philadelphia: Temple University Press, 1975.

Tsing, Anna Lowenhaupt. *Friction: An Ethnography of Global Connection.* Princeton, NJ: Princeton University Press, 2004.

Tsosie, Rebecca. "Native Women and Leadership: An Ethics of Culture and Relationship." In *Indigenous Women and Feminism: Politics, Activism, Culture,* edited by

Cheryl Suzack, Shari M. Huhndorf, Jeanne Perreault, and Jean Barman, 29–55. Vancouver: University of British Columbia Press, 2010.

Tuaolo, Esera. *Alone in the Trenches: My Life as a Gay Man in the* NFL. Naperville, IL: Sourcebooks, 2007.

Tully, James. "The Imperialism of Modern Constitutional Democracy." In *The Paradox of Constitutionalism: Constituent Power and Constitutional Form*, edited by Martin Loughlin and Neil Walker, 315–38. New York: Oxford University Press, 2007.

"Tunneling for Water: A New and Important Industry Being Developed on Maui." *Maui News*, February 2, 1901.

Tye, Larry. *The Father of Spin: Edward L. Bernays and the Birth of Public Relations.* New York: Henry Holt, 1998.

Tyson, Ann Scott. "Always in Hiding, an Iraqi Interpreter's Anguished Life." *Christian Science Monitor*, September 15, 2004.

Uperesa, Fa'anofo Lisaclaire. "Fabled Futures: Migration and Mobility for Samoans in American Football." In "Global Sport in the Pacific," edited by Fa'anofo Lisaclaire Uperesa and Thomas Mountjoy. *The Contemporary Pacific* 27, no. 1 (fall 2014).

Uperesa, Fa'anofo Lisaclaire. "Fabled Futures: Development, Gridiron Football, and Transnational Movements in American Samoa." PhD diss., Columbia University, 2010.

Uperesa, Fa'anofo Lisaclaire, and Adriana Garriga-Lopez. "Contested Sovereignty: Puerto Rico and American Samoa." NAIS *Journal* (under review).

U.S. Department of Defense. *Defense Language Transformation Roadmap.* January 2005. http://www.defense.gov/news/Mar2005/d20050330roadmap.pdf.

U.S. Department of the Navy. *Draft Environmental Impact Statement: Guam and* CNMI *Military Relocation: Relocating Marines from Okinawa,Visiting Aircraft Carrier Berthing, and Army Air and Missile Defense Task Force.* Vol. 2, *Marine Corps Relocation—Guam.* Pearl Harbor, HI: Joint Guam Program Office, November 2009. Accessed August 24, 2013. http://www.guambuildupeis.us/draft_documents.

U.S. Government Accountability Office. *Report to Congressional Requesters: U.S. Insular Areas: Multiple Factors Affect Federal Health Care Funding.* GAO-06-75 (October 2005). http://www.gao.gov/new.items/d0675.pdf.

U.S. Government Accountability Office. *Report to Honorable Dan Boren, House of Representatives: Indian Issues: Federal Funding for Non-Federally Recognized Tribes.* GAO-12-348 (April 2012). http://www.gao.gov/assets/600/590102.pdf.

U.S. General Accounting Office. "Indian Issues: Improvements Needed in Tribal Recognition Process." GAO-02-49 (November 2, 2001). http://www.gao.gov/assets/240/232806.pdf.

U.S. National Park Service. *Chaco Culture National Historical Park Management Plan.* Washington, DC: Department of the Interior, National Park Service, 1968.

U.S. Senate. Committee on Homeland Security and Governmental Affairs. *Lost in Translation: A Review of the Federal Government's Efforts to Develop a Foreign Language Strategy: Hearing before the Oversight of Government Management, the Federal Workforce, and the District of Columbia Subcommittee of the Committee on Homeland Security and Governmental Affairs.* 110th Congress, 1st session, January 25, 2007. Washington, DC: Government Printing Office, 2007.

Vamplew, Wray, ed. *Sport and Colonialism in 19th Century Australasia.* Vol. 1, *Australian Society of Sports History Studies in Sports History.* Bedford Park: Australian Society for Sports History, 1986.

Velasco Shaw, Angel, and Luis Francia. *Vestiges of War: The Philippine-American War and the Aftermath of an Imperial Dream, 1899–1999.* New York: New York University Press, 2002.

Veracini, Lorenzo. *Settler Colonialism: A Theoretical Overview.* New York: Palgrave Macmillan, 2010.

Vigil, Ernesto. *The Crusade for Justice: Chicano Militancy and the Government's War on Dissent.* Madison: University of Wisconsin Press, 1999.

Vimalassery, Manu. "The Wealth of the Natives: Toward a Critique of Settler Colonial Political Economy." *Settler Colonial Studies* 3, nos. 3–4 (2013): 295–310.

Von Eschen, Penny. *Satchmo Blows Up the World: Jazz Ambassadors Play the Cold War.* Cambridge, MA: Harvard University Press, 2004.

Wadhams, Nick. "Iraqi Interpreters Face Death Threats from Countrymen, Alienation from U.S. Troops." *Associated Press,* January 23, 2006.

Wainwright, Joel, and Joe Bryan. "Cartography, Territory, Property: Postcolonial Reflections on Indigenous Counter-Mapping in Nicaragua and Belize." *Cultural Anthropologies* 16 (2009): 153–78.

Waldorf, John Taylor. *A Kid on the Comstock.* Berkeley, CA: Friends of the Bancroft Library, 1968.

Washburn, David. "Dangerous Work of Contractors in Iraq." *San Diego Union-Tribune,* November 22, 2006.

Waziyatawin, "Colonialism on the Ground," n.d. http://waziyatawin.net/commentary/wp-content/themes/waziyatawin/colonialism.pdf.

Weber, David J., ed. *Foreigners in Their Native Land.* 2nd ed. Albuquerque: University of New Mexico Press, 2003.

Weber, David J., ed. *The Mexican Frontier, 1821–1846.* Albuquerque: University of New Mexico Press, 1982.

Weber, David J., ed. *The Spanish Frontier in North America.* New Haven, CT: Yale University Press, 1992.

Weber, Samuel. "A Touch of Translation: On Walter Benjamin's 'Task of the Translator.'" In *Nation, Language and the Ethics of Translation,* edited by Sandra Bermann and Michael Wood, 65–78. Princeton, NJ: Princeton University Press, 2005.

Weber, Samuel. "Wartime." In *Violence, Identity, and Self-Determination,* edited by Hent de Vries and Samuel Weber, 80–105. Palo Alto, CA: Stanford University Press, 1997.

Webster, Noah. Author's preface to *An American Dictionary of the English Language.* Revised and enlarged. 1826. Springfield, MA: George and Charles Merriam, 1862.

Webster, Noah. *Dissertation on the English Language.* Boston: Isaiah Thomas, 1789.

Webster, Noah. *A Grammatical Institute of the English Language.* 1783. Menston, UK: Scolar Press, 1968.

Weisiger, Marsha. *Dreaming of Sheep in Navajo Country.* Seattle: University of Washington Press, 2009.

Weizman, Eyal. *Hollow Land: Israel's Architecture of Occupation.* Brooklyn, NY: Verso, 2012.

Weslager, Clinton A. *The Delaware Indians: A History.* Newark, NJ: Rutgers University Press, 1990.

Wheat, Carl I. *Mapping the Trans-Mississippi West, 1540–1861.* Mansfield Centre, CT: Martino Publishing, 2004.

Wheeler, Winona. "Indigenous Oral History in the Academy—A Report on Works in Progress." Lecture given at the Native Historians' College, Scottsdale, Arizona, October 15, 2005.

White, Luise. *Speaking with Vampires: Rumor and History in Colonial Africa.* Berkeley: University of California Press, 2000.

Whiteley, Peter. *Deliberate Acts: Changing Hopi Culture through the Oraibi Split.* Tucson: University of Arizona, 1988.

Whiting, Beatrice Blyth. *Paiute Sorcery.* Viking Fund Publications in Anthropology, No. 15. New York: Viking Fund, 1950.

Whitney, Robert. *State and Revolution in Cuba: Mass Mobilization and Political Change, 1920–1940.* Chapel Hill: University of North Carolina Press, 2001.

Wilcox, Carol. *Sugar Water: Hawaii's Plantation Ditches.* Honolulu: University of Hawai'i Press, 1996.

Wilder, Gary. *The French Imperial Nation-State: Negritude and Colonial Humanism between the Two World Wars.* Chicago: University of Chicago Press, 2005.

Wilkins, David E. *American Indian Politics and the American Political System.* Lanham, MD: Rowman and Littlefield, 2002.

Wilkins, David E., and K. Tsianina Lomawaima. *Uneven Ground: American Indian Sovereignty and Federal Law.* Norman: University of Oklahoma Press, 2001.

Wilkinson, Charles F. *Blood Struggle: The Rise of Modern Indian Nations.* New York: W. W. Norton, 2005.

Wilkinson, Charles F., and Eric R. Biggs. "The Evolution of Termination Policy." *American Indian Law Review* 5 (summer 1977): 139–84.

Williams, Aubrey W., Jr. *Navajo Political Process.* Washington, DC: Smithsonian Institution Press, 1970.

Williams, J. S., T. J. Blackhorse, J. R. Stein, and R. Friedman. "Iikááh: Chaco Sacred Semantics." In *Religion in the Prehispanic Southwest,* edited by Christine S. Vanpool, Todd L. Vanpool, and David A. Phillips Jr., 103–13. Lanham, MD: AltaMira Press, 2006.

Williams, Raymond. *Keywords: A Vocabulary of Culture and Society.* Rev. ed. New York: Oxford University Press, 1983.

Williams, Raymond. *Marxism and Literature.* Oxford: Oxford University Press, 1977.

Williams, Robert A., Jr. "The Algebra of Federal Indian Law: The Hard Trail of Decolonizing and Americanizing the White Man's Indian Jurisprudence." *Wisconsin Law Review,* no. 1 (1986): 219–99.

Williams, Robert A., Jr. "'The People of the States Where They Are Found Are Often Their Deadliest Enemies': The Indian Side of the Story of Indian Rights and Federalism." *Arizona Law Review* 38 (1996): 981–98.

Williams, Walter L. "United States Indian Policy and the Debate over Philippine Annexation: Implications for the Origins of American Imperialism." *Journal of American History* 66, no. 4 (March 1980): 810–31.

Williams, William Appelman. *Empire as a Way of Life: An Essay on the Causes and Character of America's Present Predicament, Along with a Few Thoughts about an Alternative.* New York: Oxford University Press, 1980.

Williams, William Appelman. *The Tragedy of American Diplomacy.* 1959. New York: Dell, 1962.

Willink, Roseanne Sandoval, and Paul G. Zolbrod. *Weaving a World: Textiles and the Navajo Way of Seeing.* Santa Fe: Museum of New Mexico Press, 1996.

Winthrop, Beekman. *Fifth Annual Report of the Governor of Porto Rico Covering the Period from July 1, 1904, to June 30, 1905.* Washington, DC: Government Printing Office, 1905.

Witeck, John. "The East-West Center: An Intercult of Colonialism." *Hawaii Pono Journal,* May 1971.

Witgen, Michael. *An Infinity of Nations: How the Native New World Shaped Early North America.* Philadelphia: University of Pennsylvania Press, 2012.

Wobst, H. Martin. "Power to the (Indigenous) Past and Present! Or: The Theory and Method Behind Archaeological Theory and Method." In *Indigenous Archaeologies: Decolonizing Theory and Practice,* ed. Claire Smith and H. Martin Wobst, 15–29. New York: Routledge, 2005.

Wolfe, Patrick. "Land, Labor, and Difference: Elementary Structures of Race." *American Historical Review* 106, no. 3 (2001): 866–905.

Wolfe, Patrick. "Settler Colonialism and the Elimination of the Native." *Journal of Genocide Research* 8, no. 4 (2006): 387–409.

Wolf Management Services. "Economic Development for American Samoa." Technical Assistance Project, Economic Development Administration. Washington, DC: U.S. Department of Commerce, 1969.

Wood, Denis. *The Power of Maps.* New York: Guilford Press, 1992.

"Work Starts on Picnic Grounds in Iao Valley." *Maui News,* November 3, 1951.

Worster, Donald. *Rivers of Empire: Water, Aridity, and the Growth of the American West.* New York: Oxford University Press, 1985.

Wunder, John R., ed. *The Indian Bill of Rights, 1968.* New York: Routledge, 1996.

Xanthaki, Alexandra. *Indigenous Rights and United Nations Standards: Self-Determination, Culture and Land.* New York: Cambridge University Press, 2010.

Yablon, Nick. *Untimely Ruins: An Archaeology of American Urban Modernity, 1819–1919.* Chicago: University of Chicago Press, 2010.

Yamanouchi, Kelly. "When Tourists Become Victims." *Honolulu Advertiser,* November 30, 2003.

Yirush, Craig. *Settlers, Liberty, and Empire: The Roots of Early American Political Theory, 1675–1775.* New York: Cambridge University Press, 2011.

Yuvienco Arcellana, Emerenciana. *Recto: Nationalist.* Manila: Claro M. Recto Memorial Foundation, 1988.

Zah, Erny. "Lovejoy Candidacy Prompts Review of Role of Diné Women." *Navajo Times,* September 4, 2010.

Zah, Erny. "Tradition Edges Out Change in Northern Agency." *Navajo Times,* November 3, 2010.

Julian Aguon is an attorney-author-activist whose work centers on the rights of non-self-governing and indigenous peoples in international law. He is the author of several collections of political essays focusing on peoples' struggles in Guam and the wider Micronesian region around issues of colonization, neocolonialism, and militarism and numerous articles in U.S. law reviews and journals on the legal nuances and complexities surrounding the international law on the self-determination of peoples and its present-day invocation and application. Licensed to practice law in Guam, Palau, and the Marshall Islands, Aguon runs a Pacific regional law firm (blueoceanlaw.com) from which he provides legal counsel to these and other Pacific peoples and governments on a range of international human rights law and policy issues.

Joanne Barker (Lenape) is a citizen of the Delaware Tribe of Indians and is associate professor of American Indian Studies at San Francisco State University. She is author of *Native Acts: Law, Recognition, and Cultural Authenticity* (Duke University Press, 2011) and editor of *Sovereignty Matters: Locations of Contestation and Possibility in Indigenous Struggles for Self-Determination.*

Berenika Byszewski is a graduate student in American Studies at the University of New Mexico. Her interests include critical cartography, settler colonial studies, and the cultural politics of archaeology. She is also an adjunct professor in the Historic Preservation and Regionalism Program at the University of New Mexico and a practicing archaeologist.

Jennifer Nez Denetdale is a citizen of the Navajo Nation and associate professor of American Studies at the University of New Mexico. Her research interests include settler colonialism and decolonization, tribal nations, sovereignty, gender, and Indigenous feminisms. She is the author of *Reclaiming Diné History: The Legacies of Navajo Chief Manuelito and Juanita; The Long Walk: The Forced Navajo Exile*; and *The Navajo*, as well as numerous articles and book chapters. She is also coeditor of "Native Feminisms: Legacies, Interventions, and Indigenous Sovereignties," a special issue of *Wicazo Sa Review* (2009), and serves as an appointed member of the Navajo Nation Human Rights Commission.

Augusto Espiritu is the head of the Department of Asian American Studies and associate professor of History at the University of Illinois at Urbana-Champaign. He is the author of *Five Faces of Exile: The Nation and Filipino American Intellectuals*. His contribution in this volume is part of a larger study on Hispanismo and the critique of Americanization in the U.S. insular empire, specifically of Cuba, Puerto Rico, and the Philippines, in the first half of the twentieth century.

Alyosha Goldstein is associate professor of American Studies at the University of New Mexico. He is the author of *Poverty in Common: The Politics of Community Action during the American Century* (Duke University Press, 2012), coeditor of "Settler Colonialism," a special issue of *South Atlantic Quarterly* (2008), and is working on a book about U.S. colonialism, genealogies of racial capitalism, and economies of dispossession and conciliation in the historical present.

J. Kēhaulani Kauanui is associate professor of American Studies and Anthropology at Wesleyan University. She is the author of *Hawaiian Blood: Colonialism and the Politics of Sovereignty and Indigeneity* (Duke University Press, 2008) and is currently completing her second book, which is a critical study of Hawaiian nationalism in relation to land, gender, and sexuality. She is one of six cofounders of the Native American and Indigenous Studies Association, established in 2008, and has also worked as producer and host of a public affairs radio program, *Indigenous Politics: From Native New England and Beyond* (2007–13). She also coproduced an anarchist politics radio show, *Horizontal Power Hour* (2010–13), and is currently coproducing another related program, *Anarchy on Air*.

Barbara Krauthamer is associate professor of History at the University of Massachusetts–Amherst. She is the author of *Black Slaves, Indian Masters: Slavery, Emancipation, and Citizenship in the Native American South* and coauthor of *Envisioning Emancipation: Black Americans and the End of Slavery*.

Lorena Oropeza is associate professor of History at the University of California, Davis. She is the author of *¡Raza Sí! ¡Guerra No! Chicano Protest and Patriotism during the Viet Nam War Era* and coeditor of *Enriqueta Vasquez and the Chicano Movement: Writings from El Grito del Norte*. She is completing a book on Reies López Tijerina and the New Mexican land-grant movement of the 1960s.

Vicente L. Rafael is professor of History and Southeast Asian Studies at the University of Washington in Seattle. He is the author of *Contracting Colonialism: Translation and Christian Conversion in Tagalog Society under Early Spanish Rule* (Duke University Press, 1993); *White Love and Other Events in Filipino History* (Duke University Press, 2000); and *The Promise of the Foreign: Nationalism and the Technics of Translation in the Spanish Philippines* (Duke University Press, 2005). He is currently at work on a book on translation and war in the Philippines and the United States.

Dean Itsuji Saranillio is assistant professor of Asian/Pacific/American Studies in the Department of Social and Cultural Analysis at New York University. His work has been published in the *American Quarterly, Journal of Asian American Studies, Settler Colonial Studies*, and several anthologies. He is currently working on a manuscript titled "The Theatricality of the Settler State: Hawai'i Statehood and the Liberal Politics of Empire Building," which situates the admission of Hawai'i as a U.S. state at the crossroads of U.S. empire, where settler state formation in North America and U.S. imperialist expansion into Asia and the Pacific convene.

Lanny Thompson is professor in the Department of Sociology and Anthropology, University of Puerto Rico, Río Piedras. He is the author of *Imperial Archipelago: Representation and Rule in the Insular Territories under US Dominion after 1898* (2010), *Nuestra isla y su gente* (Centro de Investigaciones Sociales, 2007), and the prize-winning article "Imperial Republic" (*Pacific Historical Review*, 2002). His current project, in collaboration with the Center for Historical Research and the Graduate Program in Translation, is a bilingual facsimile edition of the cartographic field books discussed in this volume.

Fa'anofo Lisaclaire Uperesa is assistant professor of Ethnic Studies and Sociology at the University of Hawai'i–Mānoa. Her current book project is entitled "Fabled Futures and Gridiron Dreams: Migration, Mobility, and Football in American Samoa." She is also the coeditor of a special issue of *The Contemporary Pacific* on "Global Sport in the Pacific" (fall 2014).

Manu Vimalassery is term assistant professor of American Studies at Barnard College. He is working on a book manuscript entitled "Empire's Tracks: Plains Indians, Chinese Migrants, and the Transcontinental Railroad" and is a coeditor of *The Sun Never Sets: South Asian Migrants in an Age of U.S. Power*, and has also published in *Counterpunch, J19, SAMAR Magazine*, and *Settler Colonial Studies*.

The Birth of a Nation (film), 172
Bishop Museum, 258n3
Blackford, Mansel G., 250
"Black Legend" stereotype, 162
black power movement, 201
Blomley, Nicholas, 63
blood quantum rule: in Hawaii, 112; tribal termination and, 62
Blue, Hannaba, 318
Bluehouse, Phil, 323
"blue water" doctrine, 13; self-determination and, 271
Boas, Franz, 55n49
body transformation, Samoan participation in American football and, 208
Bolivia, self-determination principles in, 277
Bose, Subash Chandra, 166
Branch of Acknowledgment and Research (BAR), federal policy toward Native Americans and, 46–51
Brau, Salvador, 162
Brewer, C., 250
Brinton, Daniel Garrison, 36–39
British colonialism: in Pacific, 214; settler experience in, 181–82
British English, American criticism of, 342–47
British opium trade, Chinese opium sales to Paiutes and, 104–6
Brown, Christian David, 139
Brown, George Hanks, 118–20
Brown, John Mason, 38, 54n29
Brown, Vincent, 100
Brownlie, Ian, 275
Brumbaugh, Martin, 308–13
Bruyneel, Kevin, 28n67
Bryan, Joe, 80–81
Bullen, Joseph, 147–49
Bunny, Alberta, 324
Bureau of Indian Affairs (BIA), 35; census records of, 94–106; federal policy toward Native Americans and, 46–51; land grant movement and, 199–200
Burnett, Christina Duffy, 15–16, 20
Burnette, Bob, 198
Bush, George W., 337

Byrd, Jodi, 3, 78
Byszewski, Berenika, 22, 57–84

Campbell, James, 114–15
Cananea Cattle Company, 188
Cañon de Chaco, 67–68
Cañon de Chelly, 64, 72–73
capitalism: American Samoan football players in context of, 210–13; Hawaiian indigenous culture and, 243–56; U.S.-led development policies and, 217–26
Cárdenas, Lorenzo, 188
Caribbean: colonialism in, 4–25; transcultural discourses and, 158–77, 165–75
Carravahal (Mexican guide), 66
cartographic field books, 301–7
"cartographic gaze," Chaco Canyon colonization and, 58–63, 84n6
cartography of colonialism: contested cartographies of antiquity, 81–84; governmentality and, 289–13; heteroglossic nature of, 79; imperial formation and, 290–97; military gaze and, 301–7; Native dispossession and, 57–63; self-determination of indigenous peoples and, 278–83; settler-colonial expansion and, 77–81; U.S. imperialism and, 209–13
Casas Grandes ruins, 69
Castle & Cooke, 243
Castro, Fidel, 188
Center for Individual Rights, 282
Central Maui Hawaiian Civic Club, 241–42
Central Pacific Railroad Company, 22, 87–106
Ceylon, colonialism in, 291, 313n3
Chaco Canyon, colonization of, 22, 57–84; antique structures in, 57–63; contested concepts of antiquity and, 82–84; Iikááh ceremony and, 80; ownership conflicts and, 82–84; Spanish colonialism and, 85n20
Chaco Culture National Historical Park, 58–63
Chaguiliso, 147

Americans and, 279–83; territorial powers of Congress, 17–21; Treaty of Guadalupe-Hidalgo and, 191–92

continuity, definitions of, 49

Contrapunteo cubano del tabaco y el azúcar (Ortiz), 173

Cook, James (Captain), 118–19

Cornelius, Janet Duitsman, 147

Coronado, Francisco Vásquez de, 70, 85n28

Corporation of Abiquiú, 187

Coulthard, Glen, 29n61

countermapping, indigenous practice of, 80–81

counter-sovereignty, 87–106

Crawford, William H., 140

creation narratives, in Navajo culture, 329–30

critical languages concept, 339–41

Crocker, Charles, 87–89, 95–96

Crocker, E. B., 102

Cuba: American missionaries in, 163–64; as American protectorate, 15, 160; Grau's activism in, 157–58, 165, 170–77; Machado dictatorship in, 165; nationalism in, 165; race, gender and nationalist discourse in, 23; Spanish Civil War refugees in, 163–64; Spanish immigration in, 171–72; Spanish language dominance in, 163–64; U.S. military system in, 299–301; as U.S. possession, 173–77, 214

Cuban Liberation Army, 162

Cuban Revolution of 1933, 174

Cuban Revolution of 1959, 188

Cue Cánovas, Augustín, 188

cultural appropriation: imperialism and, 335–56; missionary work and, 138, 153–54; monolingualism and, 349–52

cultural difference: American Samoa in framework of, 209–13; Navajo ruins and, 68–71

cultural preservation: in American Samoa, 215–17; in Puerto Rico, 162–63

Cultural Resource Management, indigenous countermapping and, 80–81

Cuvier, George, 40–41

Danner, Robin Puanani, 133n49

Darío, Ruben, 172

Darwin, Charles, 40–41, 55n48, 69

Das, Veena, 325

Davis, Alton A., 200

Davis, Arnold "Dave," 282–83

Dawes Severalty Act. *See* General Allotment Act (1887)

Dean, Mitchell, 290–91

Declaration of Independence, 28n51

Declaration on the Granting of Independence to Colonial Countries or Peoples (UNGA Resolution 1514), 268–70, 270–71

Declaration on the Principles of International Law Concerning Friendly Relations and Cooperation among States, 268–70

Declaration on the Rights of Indigenous Peoples, 269, 273–75; international legal status of, 275–77

decolonization: self-determination and, 270–72; tribal law and culture and, 319–21

Deeds of Cession, 215–17

Deer, Ada, 51

Defense Language Transformation Roadmap, 339–41

Delaware Tribal Business Committee of the Delaware Tribe v. Weeks et al., 35–36, 50

Delaware tribe, 34–35, 59n7; federal termination of, 49–51; records of, 54n21

Deloria, Philip, 195

Deloria, Vine, 138

Democratic Party, Hawaiian multiculturalism and, 238–43

"Democratic Revolution" in Hawaii, 239–43

Denetdale, Jennifer Nez, 24–25, 316–32

Dennison, Jean, 23

Department of the Interior (U.S.), American Samoa and, 214–15, 220–21

Derby, E. H., 102

Derrida, Jacques, 20, 45–46, 52

descent, genealogy of colonialism and concepts of, 5

Morgan, Lewis Henry, 41–45, 55nn49–50
Morgensen, Scott, 332
Morton, Samuel George, 76
Mosaic genealogies, Wallam Olum epic on Lenape origins in, 37
Movimiento por la Reintegración Teritorial, 188
Muhammad, Elijah, 200–201
multiculturalism: colonial violence and, 24; Kēpaniwai Heritage Gardens and, 236–58; settler colonialism and, 237–43; U.S. imperialism and, 243–49
Muñoz Marín, Luis, 163–64, 172
Muñoz Rivera, Luis, 162
Mushulatubbee, 142

Nacionalista Party (Philippines), 157–77
Ná'dleehí (Navajo), 330
Narbona (Navajo Chief), 64, 74, 76
National Congress of American Indians, 198
National Defense Education Act, 339–40
National Football League (NFL), American Samoan players in, 208–13, 224–26
national identity: cartography in Puerto Rico and, 303–7; monolingualism and, 346–52
nationalism: colonialism and, 23; in Cuba, 173–77; foreign language proficiency and, 340–41; in Hawaii, 131n27; Hawaiian colonialism and, 119; Hispanism and, 157–77; mapping expeditions and, 71–77; in Philippines, 157, 168–70
Nationalist Party of Puerto Rico, 157, 163, 164–65, 167–68
national security: politics of translation and, 337–41; translation and, 337–41
National Security Language Initiative, 337–38
nation building, in tribal law and culture, 319–21
Nation of Islam, 200–201
nation-state concepts, 29n67; apology

politics and, 110–30; settler-colonialism and, 88–89; U.S. colonialism and, 2
Native Acts: Law, Recognition, and Cultural Authenticity, 47–51
Native American Language Act, 359n30
Native Americans: Federal Alliance of Land Grants and, 23–24; framework for elimination of, 62–63; Indo-Hispano identity and, 180, 192–203; knowledges and spatialities of, colonial cartography and, 77–81; land grant movement and, 197–203; languages spoken by, 341; Mexican Americans and, 183; migration mythology concerning, 36–37; missionaries and slaves and, 23, 137–54; modernist ideology and theories concerning, 39–45; Northwest Ordinance provisions concerning, 182; power over missionaries of, 139; self-determination rights of, 278–83; slave ownership by, 138–54; Spanish colonialism and rights of, 196–204; tribal land disputes and, 216–17; U.S. colonialism and, 7–25; U.S. treaties with, 18–21; violence against women and, 319–21; westward expansion and marginalization of, 250–51. See also tribal identity; specific tribes and nations
Native Hawaiian Governing Entity, 128–29
Native Hawaiians Study Commission, 115
natural history, racial difference and discourses on, 40–41
naturalization laws, Kēpaniwai Heritage Gardens development and, 238–43
natural resources, Navajo Nation connection with, 320–21
natural selection, racial difference and discourse on, 41
natural world, Navajo connection to, 327–32
nature, nationalist reshaping of, 72–77
Navajo Courts and Navajo Common Law (Austin), 326

social evolution, 55n48; racial difference and, 40–45; in representations of Navajos, 74–77; U.S. developmentalism and, 218–26; Wallam Olum epic and, 37

Sopoaga, Isaac, 211

southwestern U.S.: land grant movement in, 188–92; mapping antiquity in, 22, 57–84

sovereignty: discipline and, 297–301; governmental rationality and, 290–97; of Hawaiian Kingdom, 115–22; land grant movement and interpretations of, 182–83; settler-colonialism and, 88–89; unincorporated status and attenuation of, 207–8, 220–29

Spain, Tijerina's identification with, 192–204

Spanish-American War: Americanization in wake of, 161–62; Cuba and, 171; governmentality in Puerto Rico and, 297–301; territorial acquisitions and, 15, 160, 280–81

Spanish Catholicism: Hispanism and, 164, 167; language and translation and, 357n5; in Puerto Rico, 303–13

Spanish Civil War, refugees in Cuba from, 163–64

Spanish colonialism, 85n20; Americanization and, 161–77; "Black Legend" stereotype concerning, 162; Chaco Canyon and, 70–71; govermentality in, 296–97; in New Mexico, 181–82; in Philippines, 162–77; in Puerto Rico, 166–75, 301–7; Recto and, 168–70; Tijerina's view of, 183, 192–204; translation as tool of, 338–41

Spanish language speakers, history in United States of, 341–42

Sparrow, Bartholomew, 18

spatiality: cartography of colonialism and, 77–81, 290–97; Native concepts of, 77–81; in Navajo culture, 327–32

Specters of Marx (Derrida), 46, 52

spectrality of imperialism, 51–52

Spencer, Herbert, 55n48

Spencer, James, 103–4

sports institutions in American Samoa, U.S. developmentalism and, 218–26, 229n10, 232n63

Sproat, Kapuʻala, 252

Squier, Ephraim George, 36–39

Stabilization Crew (Chaco Canyon), 82–84

state, governmentalization of, 290–97

State of Hawaii v. Office of Hawaiian Affairs et al., 110, 122, 125–29

statistical extermination, blood quantum regime and, 62–63

Stavenhagen, Rodolpho, 273

Stephanson, Anders, 15

Stevens, John L., 111–12

Stoler, Ann Laura, 8, 21, 145, 219–20

sugar industry: American imperialism in Cuba and, 173; colonialism in Cuba and, 163–65; in Hawaii, 236, 239; in Puerto Rico, 305–7; water diversion in Hawaii and, 252–56

Sundagger petroglyph, 81

Supplemental Security Income (ssi) program, exclusion of territories from, 281

Supreme Court (U.S.): Cherokee Cases of, 279; Hawaiian rulings by, 110, 122–25, 132n47, 134n66; Insular Cases of, 280–83; Native American treaty rulings and, 34–35, 50–51; native fishing rights rulings of, 201; rulings on territory by, 15–21; self-determination legal principles and, 265–66, 277

Sweet, George (Rev.), 146

Swetzell, Rina, 79–80

syndyasmian family, 42

Tagore, Rabindranath, 166

Takabuki, Matsuo, 239

Takaki, Ronald, 238–39

Tatupu, Mosi, 211

Taylor, Edward B., 55n48

Taylor, John, 189

temporality, genealogy of colonialism and, 13–21

Temporary Assistance to Needy Fam-

United Nations Charter, 13; decolonization and, 270–72; self-determination principles and, 267–70

United Nations General Assembly: legal status of resolutions of, 275; Resolution 637 (VII), 13; Resolution 1541, 13; self-determination declarations in, 268–70; Special Committee on Decolonization, 271

United States: American Samoa oversight by, 214–17; anti-imperialism and policies of, 164–65; apology politics in, 114–22; collegiate and professional football expansion in, 225–26; colonialist policies in New Mexico of, 181; colonization of Hawaii by, 22–23; Commonwealth of the North Mariana Islands and, 272; Cuba and, 160, 173–77; English language and insecurities of empire in, 335–56; colonialism of, 1–25; governmentality and imperial formation and, 292–97; Hispanism and imperialism of, 157–77; historical background of imperialism in, 159–64; human rights treaties and, 277; imperialist narrative in, 209–13; missionary projects in, 138–54; "peaceful multiculturalism" ideology of, 246–49; self-determination legal principles and, 265–83; self-determination of Native Americans and, 278–83; settler colonialism in, 9–13; territorial acquisitions of, 14–16

United States v. Kagama, 19

unrecognized tribes, federal policy toward Native Americans and, 46–51

Uperesa, Fa'anofo Lisaclaire, 23–25, 207–29

U.S. Corps of Topographical Engineers, 57, 64–65

U.S. Forest Service, land grant movement and, 186, 199–204

U.S.-Mexican War, 64, 76

U.S. Pacific Command, 130

U.S. Virgin Islands, 15; Hawaiian comparisons with, 129–30; self-determination rights in, 281

Ute tribe, 73, 185

Vasconcelos, José, 172

Vazquez, Margot Arce, 172

Vimalassery, Manu, 22, 87–106

violence: territorial acquisition and, 15; toward Native women, 319–21

Violence against Women Act (VAWA), 319

Virginia and Truckee Railroad Company, 103

Vizcarra, José Antonio, 85n20

Von Eschen, Penny, 246–49

voting rights, Bayonet Constitution in Hawaii and, 238–43

Waiāhole water rights case, 255

Wai-ehu (water spray), 235–36

Waiehu stream, 235–36, 253

Waihe'e (squid liquid), 235–36

Waihe'e stream, 253

Waikapū (water of the conch), 235–36

Waikapū (water of the conch) stream, 253

Wailea Development Company, 250

Wailuku Stream (Hawaii), 235–36, 253–56

Wailuku Sugar Company, 251, 253

Wailuku Water Distribution Company, 253

Wainwright, Joel, 80–81

Walker River Reservation, 103

Wallace, Alfred Russel, 55n48

Wallam Olum, 22, 34–53; Delaware tribal identity and, 51; theories and theorists and, 39–45; translators and translation of, 36–39

Walter-McCarren Act, 240

war, translation in, 352–56

War of 1812, 18

War on Terror: analysis of empire in context of, 11; U.S. nationalism and imperialism and, 25

Washington, George, 74

water diversion in Hawaii, impact on indigenous peoples of, 249–56

Waziyatawin, 319–21
weaving, in Navajo culture, 80
Webster, Noah, 342–47, 358n23
We Have Never Been Modern (Latour),
    33–34
Welles, Sumner, 165
westward expansion: as colonialism,
    183–203; institutionalization of, 182
Wheeler, Winona, 331
White, Edward Douglas, 359n47
whiteness, New Mexico and politics of,
    197–203
Wilcox, Carol, 251–52
Williams, Loring, 137, 141–42, 149–50
Williams, Matilda Loomis, 137, 142
Williams, Raymond, 7, 26n17
Williams, Walter L., 12

Wilmot Proviso of 1846, 18
Wilson, Woodrow, 12
Winthrop, Beekman (Gov.), 299–300
Wolfe, Patrick, 9, 62, 181–82, 186,
    216–17
Wolf Management Services, 221–26
women: in Navaho culture and politics,
    316–32; violence against, 319
Worster, Donald, 251

Yazzie, Duane Chili, 334n53
Yee, James, 359n38
Young Buddhists Association, 238

Zah, Erny, 318, 324
The Zuni Atlas, 80–81
Zuni tribe, 77